THE INTRODUCTION OF THE IRONCLAD WARSHIP

LONDON : HUMPHREY MILFORD
OXFORD UNIVERSITY PRESS

Gloire   Provence   Invincible   Couronne   Normandie   Solférino

THE FRENCH IRONCLAD FLEET SALUTING THE EMPEROR

(*Revue Maritime et Coloniale, November, 1865*)

THE INTRODUCTION OF THE IRONCLAD WARSHIP

BY

JAMES PHINNEY BAXTER, 3RD
ASSOCIATE PROFESSOR OF HISTORY IN HARVARD UNIVERSITY

CAMBRIDGE
HARVARD UNIVERSITY PRESS
1933

COPYRIGHT, 1933
BY THE PRESIDENT AND FELLOWS OF HARVARD COLLEGE

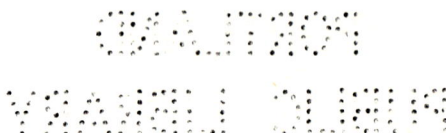

PRINTED AT THE HARVARD UNIVERSITY PRESS
CAMBRIDGE, MASS., U. S. A.

TO

MY WIFE

PREFACE

THE introduction of the ironclad warship has never hitherto been made the subject of a monograph based on the archives of the British Admiralty or of the Navy Department at Washington. Professor R. G. Albion, in his thesis *Forests and Sea Power; the Timber Problem of the English Navy — 1652–1862*, which is based primarily on the Admiralty Papers, devoted a chapter to "The Passing of the Wooden Fleets"; but centered his interest "in the passing of the old order rather than in the coming of the new." Only Dislère, who published his valuable work, *La marine cuirassée*, in 1873, when he was serving as secretary of the *Conseil des Travaux*, seems to have used any considerable portion of the French manuscript records; and Dislère himself left a great deal ungarnered. Commandants de Balincourt and Vincent-Bréchignac have based on official records two brief but excellent articles, "La marine française d'hier: Les cuirassés," published in the *Revue maritime* for May, 1930, and March, 1931.

For documents concerning the period of chief importance in the introduction of ironclads, the British and French naval archives have been open to historians only since the close of the recent World War. It is strange, however, that the manuscripts of the Navy Department in Washington, which have long been accessible, have been so neglected. William Conant Church, the biographer of Ericsson, had at his disposal, in the Ericsson Mss., the letters of Commodore Joseph Smith and Assistant Secretary Fox to the famous inventor. Yet though many of these letters cannot properly be understood without the other half of the correspondence, and though Ericsson kept copies of only a few of his own letters at this period, Church seems not to have used the numerous unpublished letters from Ericsson which are preserved in the Navy Department.

The contemporary newspaper, periodical, and pamphlet material, though often grossly inaccurate, and ill informed as to governmental policies, nevertheless has great value in reflecting public opinion on the subject of ironclads. Some important documents found their way into official publications, especially in Great Britain and the United States. Several of the actors in the great revolution of naval architecture have left helpful accounts, though these were generally written several years after the events described, and with little or no reference to manuscript material. Plans of some of the early ironclads have been published, notably by J. Scott Russell in his *Modern System of Naval Architecture*, and by Vice Admiral Pâris in his *Souvenirs de marine* and in his *L'Art naval*.

The present work is based for the most part on researches in the Admiralty Papers deposited in the Public Record Office in London; in the Archives Nationales, the Archives de la Marine, and the Archives des Constructions Navales in Paris; in the archives of the Navy Department, the Bureau of Construction and Repair, and the Bureau of Yards and Docks in Washington; in the papers of Gideon Welles in the Library of Congress; and in the Ericsson Mss. and Gustavus V. Fox Mss., now in the Library of the New York Historical Society. I wish to acknowledge my indebtedness to the officials of these archives, and especially to M. Georges Bourgin of the Archives Nationales, M. Charles Braibant of the Archives de la Marine, and Captain Dudley W. Knox, U.S.N., of the Navy Department.

The first stages of this study were begun in 1923 under the guidance of the late Professor Edward Channing, whose keen criticism and friendly interest will be remembered with gratitude and affection by a host of students. My colleague Professor Charles K. Webster has read the whole of this manuscript and my friends Captain Dudley W. Knox, Professor Joannès Tramond, and the late Admiral Sir William Hannam Henderson, K.B.E., have read portions of it. To their encouragement and most helpful suggestions I owe more than I can say. Commandant Paul Chack, Chef du Service

Historique de l'État Major de la Marine, greatly facilitated my researches at Paris. General P. Charbonnier, Inspecteur Général de l'Artillerie de la Marine, kindly placed at my disposal his complete file of the *Mémorial de l'artillerie de la marine*, including the rare lithographed volumes, together with an unpublished bibliography of French periodical articles concerning naval ordnance. Dr. Oscar W. Parkes, editor of Jane's *Fighting Ships*, generously furnished from his unrivaled collection four of the photographs illustrating this volume. Colonel Lord Sydenham of Combe, G.C.S.I., F.R.S., R.E.; Admiral Sir Herbert W. Richmond, K.C.B.; Captain Alfred Dewar, O.B.E., R.N.; Commander Carlyon Bellairs, R.N., M.P.; M. Abel Doysié; Colonel James Barnes, President of the Naval History Society; Professor William Hovgaard; L. G. Carr Laughton, Esq.; and the late W. G. Perrin, Esq., O.B.E., Librarian of the Admiralty, have given me many helpful suggestions. My friend Professor Herbert C. Bell most generously communicated to me some of his transcripts of the Russell and Granville papers preserved at the Public Record Office, and kindly permitted me to quote some of them that throw fresh light on British naval policy.

I wish also to express my thanks to the librarians of the Admiralty, the British Museum, and the British Patent Office, in London; the Bibliothèque Nationale, the Conservatoire des Arts et Métiers, the Bibliothèque de la Marine, the École d'Application du Génie Maritime, and the Laboratoire Central de la Marine, in Paris; of the Library of Congress and Navy Department at Washington, and of the New York Public Library, the New York Historical Society, the Boston Public Library, the Bowdoin College Library, the Library of the Massachusetts Institute of Technology, the Library of the Stevens Institute of Technology, and the Library of Harvard University.

Grants from the Bureau of International Research of Harvard University and Radcliffe College have made possible further research in the British and French archives and the employment of research and clerical assistants. Mrs. Violet

Heddon, who has aided me in searching for and copying documents in the Public Record Office, and Miss Marjorie Graves, who helped to prepare this manuscript for the press, have been unfailingly helpful.

Portions of this work formed the basis of seven lectures at the Lowell Institute in Boston in 1931.

JAMES P. BAXTER, 3RD

CAMBRIDGE, MASS.

CONTENTS

I	Introduction	3
II	A Revolution in Naval Ordnance	17
III	Unarmored Iron Warships	33
IV	Ironclad Projects of the Forties	48
V	The Crimean War	69
VI	The First Seagoing Ironclad Fleet	92
VII	Great Britain Enters the Race	116
VIII	The Passing of the Wooden Capital Ship	140
IX	The Origins of the Turret Ship	181
X	Ordnance and Armor in 1861	196
XI	Mallory's Ironclad Policy	211
XII	The North Seeks a Solution	238
XIII	Hampton Roads	285
XIV	The Consequences of Hampton Roads	302

APPENDICES

A	Notes on the Introduction of the Screw Propeller	335
B	The Reintroduction of the Ram	337
C	Project of Napoleon III for Armoring Ships of the Line	342
D	Dupuy de Lôme's Report of April 16, 1858	345
E	Dupuy de Lôme's Report of September 22, 1860	347
F	The Navy Department Plan of 1861	350
G	Ericsson's Proposal of December 23, 1861	358

Bibliography 361
Index 383

ILLUSTRATIONS

The French Ironclad Fleet Saluting the Emperor . . *Frontispiece*
    From the *Revue Maritime et Coloniale*, November, 1865

H.M.S. *Warrior* 158
    From a photograph in the Imperial War Museum

H.M.S. *Achilles* 166
    From a photograph in the Imperial War Museum

H.M.S. *Minotaur* 178
    From a photograph in the Imperial War Museum

Coles's Specification of June 15, 1860 188
    British Patent Office, 1861, no. 1462

C.S.S. *Virginia* 232
    From a sketch by Edward I. Johnston, First Assistant Engineer, C.S.N., in Adm. 1/5819: P.184

H.M.S. *Wivern* 324
    From a photograph in the Imperial War Museum

ABBREVIATIONS

A.C.N. ....Archives du Bureau des Constructions Navales.
Adm. ....Admiralty Papers.
A.M. ....Archives de la Marine.
A.N. ....Archives Nationales.
B.C.R. ....Archives of the Bureau of Construction and Repair.
B.Y.D. ....Old files of the Bureau of Yards and Docks.
G.D. ....Public Record Office, London, Gifts and Deposits.
N.D. ....Navy Department Archives.
N.W.R. ....Office of Naval Records and Library, Navy Department, Washington. Transcripts of the correspondence of the Bureau of Yards and Docks, and of Navy Yard Papers.
O.R. ....*The War of the Rebellion: a Compilation of the Official Records of the Union and Confederate Armies.* 70 vols. Washington, 1880–1901.
O.R.N. ....*Official Records of the Union and Confederate Navies in the War of the Rebellion.* 30 vols. Washington, 1894–1922.
P.R.O. ....Public Record Office, London.

THE INTRODUCTION OF THE IRONCLAD WARSHIP

CHAPTER I

INTRODUCTION

THE Elizabethan seadogs who circled the globe with Drake might have felt at home in the sailing sloop of war *Cumberland*, as she sank with colors flying on the 8th of March, 1862. Of the five great naval revolutions of the nineteenth century — steam, shell guns, the screw propeller, rifled ordnance, and armor — one only had influenced her design or equipment. Nothing but her heavy battery of 9-inch smooth-bore shell guns would have seemed wholly unfamiliar to the conquerors of the Spanish Armada. But the crude *Virginia*, whose iron prow had just dealt the graceful *Cumberland* her deathblow, embodied all five of those revolutionary features.

Attempts to protect ships from fire or shot by increasing the thickness of their bulwarks or covering them with metal may be traced back to antiquity. These early experiments, however, are curious rather than significant. Not until the introduction of shell upset the balance between offence and defence at sea did the need for armored ships become overpowering. And not until the great metallurgical developments of the nineteenth century did a solution really present itself. The Crimean War demonstrated the havoc wrought by shell-fire against wooden ships, and the relative invulnerability of the French armored floating batteries at Kinburn. When rifled ordnance increased the advantages of the offence, the doom of the wooden ship was sealed. By 1861 the great revolution in naval architecture was in full swing: nearly a hundred armored vessels were built or building in Europe.

In 1842 the United States made the first appropriation for an armored steam warship, but this vessel was never completed. Twenty years later the first fight between ironclads took place in Hampton Roads. It was France, however, who really took the lead in the introduction of the ironclad warship. Paixhans introduced the shell gun, which turned the decks of wooden ships into shambles. Napoleon III gave the governmental support necessary to make possible the revolution in naval architecture. Dupuy de Lôme first solved the problem of the seagoing armored warship, and designed the first homogeneous ironclad fleet. When France stopped building wooden ships of the line, produced the *Gloire*, and announced a program of sixteen seagoing and seventeen coast-defence ironclads, built or building, the death knell of the wooden walls had sounded. All the leading maritime powers followed her example. The battle of Hampton Roads demonstrated and emphasized the foresight of the French.

In the accounts of early vessels plated with metal it is difficult to tell whether they were armored against fire and projectiles, or simply sheathed as a protection against the ravages of sea-worms and the accumulation of marine growths. Athenaeus tells us that Hieron, King of Syracuse in the third century B.C., built a huge vessel for the grain trade, plated with lead. Heavy bronze rivets fastened the metal to its backing of tarred sail-cloth and timber. Athenaeus attributed to this ship, which he said was launched by means of a windlass devised by Archimedes, many of the luxuries of a modern transatlantic liner: four-berth cabins, a marble bathroom, a gymnasium, a library, and an aquarium.[1] De Montgéry, one of the first French champions of ironclads in the nineteenth century, who read the classics with the same enthusiasm with which he sought to read the future, mentions this ship and several other early projects for armored vessels.[2] The Northmen, who improvised a protection for their ships of low freeboard by ranging their shields along the sides,

---

[1] The writer is indebted to Professor William Scott Ferguson for information concerning this vessel. See Athenaeus, v, pp. 206 ff., in Ulrich von Wilamovitz-Moellendorf, *Griechisches Lesebuch* (Berlin, 1902, 2 vols.), ii, pp. 265–268. Cf., however, Cecil Torr, *Ancient Ships* (Cambridge, 1894), pp. 27–29, 37.

[2] "Mémoire sur les navires en fer," *Journal des sciences militaires*, i (1825), pp. 488 ff.

strengthened the hulls of some of their craft by a belt of iron or bronze.[1] As a protection against Greek fire, ships in the Middle Ages were sometimes sheathed with raw hides or felt soaked in vinegar.[2] In a war between the Venetians and the Lombards in the fifteenth century the latter used a small vessel called the tortoise, on account of its arched roof covered with iron.[3] Towards the close of the same century Leonardo da Vinci proposed the construction of ships proof against bombs,[4] and suggested that small bomb vessels might be so protected with heavy wooden beams that they might venture to attack large ships.[5]

Early in the sixteenth century the Spaniards began to sheathe the submerged portions of their vessels with lead,[6] and were soon followed in this practice by the French and the English.[7] In 1535 the Knights of St. John contributed to the expedition of Charles V against Tunis a great carrack, the *Santa Anna*, which was plated with lead. This heavily armed vessel, which took part in the capture of the Goletta, "avoit quatre couvertes [decks] hors de l'eau, et deux dans l'eau revestuës de plomb, et les bouchons de bronze qui ne gastoient point le plomb comme le fer, et qui s'appliquoient si pro-

---

1 A. Jal, *Archéologie Navale* (Paris, 1840, 2 vols.), i, pp. 139, 142, 152–153; Charles de la Roncière, *Histoire de la Marine française* (Paris, 1899–1920, 5 vols.), i, p. 97.
2 *Ibid.*, p. 257; *The Mariner's Mirror*, ix, p. 354; x, p. 212.
3 C. Fernandez Duro, *Disquisiciones Náuticas* (Madrid, 1876–1881, 6 vols.) i, pp. 146–147.
4 La Roncière, *Marine française*, ii, p. 500, citing a letter to Ludovico Sforza published in the *Nouvelle Biographie Générale*, xlvi, p. 242, which Charles Ravaisson-Mollien, however, in his *Les Ecrits de Léonard de Vinci* (Paris, 1881), pp. 23–24, 32–35, denies to have been in Leonardo's handwriting.
5 Ravaisson-Mollien, *Les Manuscrits de Léonard de Vinci* (Paris, 1881–1891, 6 vols.), vi, Ms. 2037, in Bibliothèque Nationale, folio 7. Cited in La Roncière, *Marine française*, iii, p. 555, note.
6 See the note by G. de Artiñano in *The Mariner's Mirror*, x, p. 212 (April, 1924); and C. Fernandez Duro, *Armada Española* (Madrid, 1895–1903, 9 vols.), i, p. 121.
7 La Roncière, *Marine française*, ii, p. 473; M. Oppenheim, *A History of the Administration of the Royal Navy* (London and New York, 1896), p. 103. For other instances of early sheathing with metal, beginning with a Roman galley, see Torr, *Ancient Ships*, p. 37, note; La Roncière, *Marine française*, iv, p. 272; John Charnock, *History of Marine Architecture* (London, 1800–1802, 3 vols.), i, pp. 101–102; John Fincham, *A History of Naval Architecture* (London, 1851), pp. 44, 94–100; R. G. Albion, *Forests and Sea Power* (Cambridge, 1926), p. 11; A. L. Cross, "On Coppering Ship's Bottoms," *American Historical Review*, October, 1927, pp. 79–81.

prement que les canons de toute une armée ne l'eussent sçeu mettre à fonds." [1]

When the Japanese invaded Korea in 1592 the Korean admiral Yi-sun designed a "tortoise-ship," with an iron-plated turtle-back deck, impervious to fire, arrows, or bullets, and studded with sharp spikes as a defence against boarders. This craft, with a ram stem and a hull adapted for high speed and quick manoeuvring, led the Korean fleet to several astonishing victories, which demonstrated the havoc a ship of novel design might work when operating on an enemy's lines of communication.[2]

Many attempts were made to render ships proof against shot by increasing the thickness of their wooden sides. Captain Jean de La Salle proposed the construction of shot-proof ships to the King of Navarre in 1557. A few years later a gunboat for river defence, protected by heavy wooden bulwarks, was built at Bayonne.[3] The Dutch fleet which relieved Leyden in 1574 contained the great *Ark of Delft*, which was fitted with shot-proof bulwarks and paddle wheels turned by a crank.[4] At the suggestion of Prince Rupert in 1672, Sir Anthony Deane designed a wooden "bulge" to

---

[1] G. Bosio, *Histoire des Chevaliers de l'Ordre de S. Jean de Jérusalem* (Paris, 1629, 3 vols.), i, p. 332. Cf. Arthur Irving Andrews, *The Campaign of the Emperor Charles V against Tunis and Kheir-ed-Din Barbarossa* (Harvard University thesis, 1905), pp. iii, 96, 181; Colonel C. Field, R.M., "'The Santa Anna'; an early Armour-Clad," in *The Mariner's Mirror*, December, 1923. For doubts as to whether the lead plating was designed to protect her against anything more serious than the teredo shipworm, see *ibid.*, xi, pp. 92, 328. A picture of this vessel is reproduced as the frontispiece of *The Mariner's Mirror* for April, 1924, from plate 35 of G. de Artiñano's *Arquitectura Naval Española* (Madrid, 1920).

[2] Vice Admiral G. A. Ballard, *Influence of the Sea on the Political History of Japan* (London, 1921), pp. 50-72; Homer B. Hulbert, *History of Korea* (Seoul, 1905, 2 vols.), i, pp. 376-400; James Murdoch and Isoh Yamagata, *History of Japan during the Century of Early Foreign Intercourse (1542-1651)* (Kobe, 1903), pp. 335-337. The authors of the last-named work point out in a footnote that Hayashi, in his *Chosen Kinshei-shi*, or *History of Modern Korea*, doubts the use of iron plates on this vessel.

[3] *Archives historiques du département de la Gironde*, i (1859), pp. 120-125; E. Ducéré, *Histoire maritime de Bayonne, Les Corsaires sous l'ancien régime* (Bayonne, 1895), pp. 45-50, 352. Cited in La Roncière, *Marine française*, iii, pp. 554-555.

[4] J. L. Motley, *Rise of the Dutch Republic* (New York, 1856, 3 vols.), ii, p. 567. Cf. the strange craft proposed by Agostino Ramelli in 1588, and the clockwork vessel with sloping roof built by De Son at Rotterdam in 1653, described in La Roncière, *Marine française*, iv, pp. 608-612.

render guardships cannon-proof at the water line, but this project was not carried out.[1]

In the eighteenth century, the Spanish took the lead in projects for armored vessels. Don Juan de Ochoa proposed in 1727 a "barcaza espin," a galley bristling with several iron rams and covered with a sloping roof whose sides, plated with iron, were inclined at an angle of 45° with the horizon.[2] When the Spanish and French besieged Gibraltar in 1780-1782, several projects were presented for gunboats or floating batteries protected either with iron or with heavy wooden bulwarks. Don Antonio Barceló constructed some small gunboats with considerable tumble-home, whose sloping sides and bow were protected by iron plates.[3] Much more ambitious were the ten floating batteries designed for the same siege by a French officer, the Chevalier d'Arçon. As to the exact plans of these vessels, the evidence is conflicting. At least the inclined side of the ship which was designed to face the enemy was composed of heavy timbers about five feet thick, to be protected against hot shot by a constant circulation of water. The ten floating batteries, some with one gundeck, others with two, carried a total of 140 or more guns and over 5000 men. Authorities differ as to whether these vessels had any iron armor or not. D'Arçon's idea was that hot shot could not set fire to the heavy wooden bulwarks if the pumps kept water circulating between the timbers. When these novel craft attacked the fortress on September 13, 1782, he complained that the co-operation of the land forces, gunboats and bomb vessels left much to be desired. The floating batteries themselves, however, showed capital defects: too great draft to permit an approach close enough for breaching; a field of fire much restricted by the great thickness of the bulwarks; and a defective circulation of water. Owing to imperfect caulking, the water leaked so rapidly into the interior

---

[1] A. W. Johns, "Sir Anthony Deane," *Mariner's Mirror*, April, 1925, p. 180.
[2] Duro, *Disquisiciones Náuticas*, i, pp. 147-152. In his *Armada Española*, vi, pp. 317-318, Duro reproduces a drawing of this proposed ironclad.
[3] *Ibid.*, vii, pp. 271 ff., with drawings. Cf. Duro, *Disquisiciones Náuticas*, i, pp. 155, 163-165.

that the circulating pumps had to be stopped. After several hours of fighting, hot shot set fire to some of the batteries, and the rest were abandoned and burned.[1]

The Napoleonic Wars gave rise to some more projects for armored vessels. Congreve is said to have designed in 1805 a floating battery of about 250 tons burden, to carry four large mortars and four 42-pounder carronades, propelled by oars and protected by sloping sides, or by a sloping roof, covered with plates and bars of iron.[2] Don Francisco Lopez and Don Cayetano Escassi proposed to the Spanish Regency in May, 1810, and again in March, 1812, the construction of an armored floating battery.[3] As a defence against Robert Fulton's proposed system of torpedoes and submarine mines, Captain Isaac Chauncey suggested in 1810 that the bows of vessels might be plated with flat bars of iron.[4]

During the War of 1812, while British sea power was giving a practical refutation to the theories of Jefferson and Madison that blockades of large stretches of seacoast were impossible, several Americans proposed floating batteries for coast defence. In June, 1812, Secretaries Eustis and Hamilton reported unfavorably on the project of an inventor named Edward Clark, who had designed a float built of empty casks, supporting a formidable battery.[5] James Marsh of Charleston, South Carolina, submitted in March, 1814, the plan of a guard-ship 200 feet long, 53½ feet wide, and 10 feet draft, with sloping bulwarks formed of 3½ feet of solid timber.[6] At

[1] [D'Arçon], *Mémoire pour servir à l'histoire du Siège de Gibraltar* . . . (Cadiz, 1783); [D'Arçon], *Conseil de guerre privé sur l'évènement de Gibraltar en 1782* . . . (n.p., 1785); E. Heriz, *Memoria sobre los Barcos Acorazados* (Barcelona, 1875), pp. 25–26; Duro, *Armada Española*, vii, pp. 311–328, reproducing a drawing of a cross section of one of the batteries; Duro, *Disquisiciones Náuticas*, i, pp. 154–163. For the floating battery *Spanker*, built in England a few years later, see Charnock, *Marine Architecture*, iii, p. 409, note.
[2] *Naval Chronicle*, xiii (1805), p. 193.
[3] Duro, *Armada Española*, ix, pp. 376–377.
[4] Copy of a letter from Chauncey to Fulton, September 17, 1810, in N.D., Unclassified Mss. On Fulton's system of submarine warfare, see H. W. Dickinson, *Robert Fulton* (London, 1913), pp. 84, 107–108, 182–200, 206–210, 283–288; *American State Papers, Naval Affairs*, i, pp. 211–227, 234–245.
[5] *Ibid.*, i, p. 273.
[6] B.C.R., Plan No. 80-7-15.

some time during the war, John Stevens of Hoboken, New Jersey, whose sons later began the Stevens battery, conceived the idea of a saucer-shaped floating battery plated with iron, to be secured to a swivel, anchored in a river or harbor, and rotated by steam-driven screw propellers so as to bring each gun to bear on the enemy in turn. In 1815 he proposed the construction of several gunboats seventy feet long, plated with iron with heavy wooden backing, each to mount one Columbiad to fire elongated shells, and to be "propelled by men, by means of a spiral water-wheel in the stern." These craft, he suggested, should be carried to the Mediterranean on frigates, and used to destroy the shipping in the harbor of Algiers.[1]

Two American plans for armored vessels with inclined sides, like those so widely adopted during the Civil War, date from this period. Thomas Gregg, of Fayette County, Pennsylvania, patented and submitted to Congress in March, 1814, a project for a shot-proof steam floating battery whose sides sloped at an angle of eighteen degrees.[2] Uriah Brown, an inventor who claimed to have rediscovered the secret of Greek fire, demonstrated his method of attack together with a model of a shot-proof steamboat, before a large crowd at Baltimore, in the summer of 1814. In the following December he submitted to Congress a project for a steamer with inclined sides covered with sheet iron, which he declared would make a speed of five miles an hour, and would project liquid fire against an enemy. Brown's plan, endorsed by a committee of Baltimore citizens headed by Mayor Johnson and Brigadier-General Winder, was favorably recommended to Congress on December 23, 1814, by Benjamin Homans, the Acting Secretary of the Navy. Although Baltimore citizens subscribed funds for the construction of a ship on Brown's plans, and considerable progress towards its completion was

---

[1] A. D. Turnbull, *John Stevens* (New York, 1928), pp. 390–393, 412; R. H. Thurston, *Messrs. Stevens of Hoboken* (Philadelphia, 1874), p. 6.
[2] N.D., *Miscellaneous Letters.* Cf. *Scientific American*, February 7, 1863, and E. S. Maclay, *History of the U. S. Navy* (New York, 1910–1917, 3 vols.), iii, p. 21.

made, the arrival of news of the peace of Ghent put an end to work on this vessel.[1]

The great novelty produced by this war, however, was the *Demologos*, the first steam warship.[2] She was built for the defence of New York at a cost of $320,000 on plans which Robert Fulton submitted to President Madison in November, 1813, and which Captains Decatur, Jones, and Perry strongly recommended. The *Demologos*, whose keels were laid on June 29, 1814, was launched on October 29 and given her first trial on the following first of June. Fulton's untimely death on February 23 had contributed to the delay. He had sought invulnerability by giving his craft twin hulls between which the paddle wheel revolved, and by placing her battery of thirty 32-pounders, for firing red hot shot, behind massive wooden walls four feet ten inches in thickness. She exceeded her guaranteed speed in three trials, averaging five and one-half to six and one-half miles an hour, and she manoeuvered easily; but she never saw active service, for the war ended before she was finished. She lay at the Brooklyn Navy Yard as a receiving ship until her destruction on June 4, 1829, when an accidental explosion killed twenty-five persons and wounded nineteen.[3]

Although destined to revolutionize naval architecture, the introduction of steam in warships made slow progress. Not until 1821 did the British Admiralty purchase the wooden

---

[1] House Report No. 36, 29th Congress, 2d Session, p. 3; *American State Papers, Naval Affairs*, i, pp. 353, 380.

[2] As to Blasco de Garay's steamer tested at Barcelona in 1543 see Duro, *Armada Española*, i, p. 328; La Roncière, *Marine française*, ii, p. 488.

[3] Report of Henry Rutgers, Samuel L. Mitchel, and Thomas Morris, December 28, 1815, printed in Charles B. Stuart, *The Naval and Mail Steamers of the United States* (New York, 1853), pp. 155–159; Dickinson, *Fulton*, pp. 260–266, 326; Frank M. Bennett, *The Steam Navy of the United States* (2d edition, Pittsburgh, 1897, 2 vols.), i, pp. 8–16. The Act of March 9, 1814, appropriating $500,000 for floating batteries passed without a division in the Senate, and by a vote of 82 to 44 in the House of Representatives. *Annals of Congress*, 13th Congress, 2d Session, cols. 627, 631, 633, 1435, 1800–1804; *Statutes at Large*, iii, p. 104. A bill appropriating a second half-million dollars for floating batteries passed the Senate January 9, 1815, only to be postponed indefinitely in the House on February 22, after the news of peace. *Annals of Congress*, 13th Congress, 3d Session, cols. 163, 1062, 1103, 1177.

paddle steamer *Monkey*, of 212 tons and 80 horse power, and order the construction of a similar vessel, H.M.S. *Comet*, of 238 tons, which was launched at Deptford the following year.[1] Prior to 1829 the French navy list contained only five small steamers, although twenty more were added in the next six years, and seven steamers took part in the expedition against Algiers in 1830.[2] The United States, first in the field with the *Demologos*, fell steadily behind.[3] Although both the size and number of the steamers in the European navies steadily increased, their defects were serious. The heavy, clumsy machinery of that day reduced both the space available in the hold, and the weight which might be allotted to the guns and the sail power, while the big paddle boxes encumbered the gun deck and impaired the sailing qualities of the ship. Without producing satisfactory speed, steam increased the risk of fire. Excessive coal consumption limited radius of action; and the vulnerability of their boilers, engines, and paddle boxes confined the steamers for the most part to service as tugs, transports, and despatch vessels. Yet the steamer *Karteria* did good work for the insurgents in the War of Greek Independence under the command of Captain Frank Abney Hastings; and the steamers *Gorgon*, *Vesuvius*, *Stromboli*, and *Phoenix* took part in Admiral Stopford's bombardment of Acre in 1840.[4]

The principal defect of steam warships did not disappear until the introduction of the screw propeller made it possible to place the engines and boilers below the water line. Prior

[1] *Catalogue of the Collections in the Science Museum, South Kensington: Water Transport, III, Steam Ships of War*, compiled by G. L. Overton (London, 1925), pp. 8–13.
[2] *Répertoire alphabétique des bâtiments de tout rang armés par l'état de 1800 à 1828 compris* . . . (Paris, 1830); *ibid.*, for the years 1829 to 1834; Joannès Tramond and André Reussner, *Eléments d'histoire maritime et coloniale contemporaine* (Paris, 1924), p. 53.
[3] Bennett, *Steam Navy*, i, chs. ii, iii; *American State Papers, Naval Affairs*, i, pp. 381, 483, 583, 587, 621, 651, 652, 780, 803, 805, 946, 1015; ii, p. 727; iii, p. 213; iv, pp. 8, 159, 355, 590, 731, 753, 954–956.
[4] Wm. Laird Clowes and others, *The Royal Navy* (London, 1897–1903, 7 vols.), vi, pp. 310–322; William Hovgaard, *Modern History of Warships* (London, 1920), p. 3. As to Captain Hastings, see below, p. 25.

to 1836 at least forty inventors had proposed screw propellers of various types, and several of them had constructed experimental boats which were actually propelled by screws. What influence, if any, these earlier proposals had on later claimants to the invention must remain a matter of conjecture. For the introduction of the screw into general use, however, chief honor is due to Francis Pettit Smith, an English farmer and experimenter, afterwards knighted, and to Captain John Ericsson.[1]

Born July 31, 1803, the son of a Swedish inspector of mines, John Ericsson mastered mechanical drawing and much engineering knowledge while employed as a boy on the Göta Canal. Attaining the rank of captain in the Swedish Army, after six years' service, he resigned in 1826, went to England, and became junior partner in the machine manufacturing firm of Braithwaite and Ericsson. Here he worked on a score or more of inventions, including the use of condensed air for transmitting power, surface condensers, and the steam fire-engine. His steam locomotive, the *Novelty*, competed unsuccessfully with Stephenson's *Rocket* at Rainhill in 1829.[2]

According to an affidavit made by Ericsson in 1845 the problem of stern propellers had absorbed much of his time even before 1833. In 1834 Smith built a model propelled by a submerged screw, which he improved and patented on May 31, 1836, six weeks earlier than Ericsson's patent of July 13. Smith and his friends promptly built a boat of six tons burden and about six horse power, fitted with a wooden screw of two turns, and exhibited it in operation on the Paddington Canal on November 1, 1836. It continued to ply there and on the Thames until the month of September, 1837. In the

---

[1] John Bourne, *A Treatise on the Screw Propeller, with various suggestions of improvement* (London, 1852), chs. i, ii; G. L. Overton, *op. cit.*, pp. 13 ff.; Tramond and Reussner, *Histoire maritime*, pp. 54–56; Xavier Raymond, *Les marines de la France et de l'Angleterre, 1815–1863* (Paris, 1863), pp. 115–120; Frank M. Bennett, *The Monitor and the Navy under Steam* (Boston and New York, 1900), pp. 5–8, 23–25.

[2] This did not prevent Ericsson from asserting, in a manuscript found after his death, that he, not Stephenson, had grasped the subject. William Conant Church, *The Life of John Ericsson* (New York, 1891, 2 vols.), i, p. 58.

latter year Ericsson built the *Francis B. Ogden*, a screw steamer forty or forty-five feet in length, which was launched on the Thames on April 19, and named after his friend and supporter, the American consul at Liverpool. This craft towed the Admiralty barge from Somerset House to Blackwall and back at about ten knots speed. Disappointed in his hopes of converting their Lordships, Ericsson abandoned England for New York, where he landed in November, 1839. It was Smith who triumphed over British official conservatism by constructing, with funds subscribed by a small company, the steamer *Archimedes*, of 237 tons and 80 horse power, fitted with a screw of one convolution. Her successful trials, which began in 1839 and continued several years, led to the purchase by the Admiralty in 1842 of the iron screw steamer *Mermaid*, of 164 tons, renamed the *Dwarf*; and the introduction of Smith's two-bladed screw in the unfinished sailing sloop *Ardent*, of 880 tons, which was launched as H.M.S. *Rattler*, in April, 1843. Her success marked the triumph of the new form of propulsion in Great Britain.[1]

Though Smith's persistent advocacy had greater influence in the conversion of England, Ericsson proved the greatest apostle of the screw in the United States. Before his removal thither he had designed a 50 horse power engine for the iron screw steamer *Robert F. Stockton*, which crossed the Atlantic under sail in 1839 and served for years as a tug boat on the Delaware and Raritan Canal. Ericsson's connection with Stockton soon brought him into touch with the Navy Department.[2]

The U.S.S. *Princeton*, built at Philadelphia during the years 1842 and 1843 under the patronage of Captain Robert

[1] *Dictionary of National Biography*, article on Sir Francis Pettit Smith by W. F. Wallis; G. L. Overton, *op. cit.*, pp. 13–15; Clowes, *Royal Navy*, vi, pp. 196–198; Bourne, *Screw Propeller*, chs. ii, iv, v. References to further material on the introduction of the screw may be found in the Admiralty Digest. P.R.O., Adm. 12/371: 59–1; Adm. 12/375: 97a; Adm. 12/385: 59–1; Adm. 12/388: 97a; Adm. 12/398: 59–1; Adm. 12/402: 91–1; Adm. 12/417: 97a; Adm. 12/445: 59–1. See also Surveyor's Submission Letter Book No. 10, July 26, August 10, October 26, 1841; February 22, March 14, April 4 and 8, July 28 and 30, September 16, 1842.

[2] Bourne, *Screw Propeller*, pp. 89–90; Church, *Ericsson*, i, pp. 90–103.

F. Stockton and the superintendence of Ericsson, embodied a six-bladed propeller, a peculiar type of engine coupled direct to the screw shaft and so constructed as to lie beneath the water line, and several other novelties due to the Swedish genius. She was a full-rigged ship of 954 tons displacement, with auxiliary steam power, a telescopic funnel, boilers designed to burn anthracite coal, and fan blowers for forcing the fires. Her armament included two 12-inch wrought-iron guns. One of these, named the "Oregon," Ericsson had designed, brought from England, and reinforced by two tiers of hoops, each 3½ inches thick, shrunk on the breech of the piece up to the trunnion bands, and arranged to break joints. The second, named the "Peacemaker," Stockton had had forged at Hamersley Forge, and bored and finished under Ericsson's directions. During a trial trip on the Potomac River, February 28, 1844, the "Peacemaker" burst, killing Abel P. Upshur, Secretary of State, Thomas W. Gilmer, Secretary of the Navy, and four other persons, and wounding several more, including Stockton himself. Ericsson's refusal to accept responsibility for this disaster led to a breach with Stockton, thanks to which the inventor failed to receive adequate compensation for his services.[1]

Ericsson's propeller in the *Princeton* was soon replaced by another known as the "Stevens scull." This had shown a superiority over Ericsson's screw of 32 seconds in a mile, or more than one mile in eleven, when the two propellers were tested by time trials in Norfolk harbor in March, 1845.[2] Still unconverted to the superiority of either of these screws, the Navy Department expended considerable sums from

[1] House Report No. 479, 28th Congress, 1st Session; Church, *Ericsson*, i, chs. ix-x; Bennett, *Steam Navy*, i, ch. v; *A Sketch of the Life of Com. Robert F. Stockton* (New York, 1856), ch. vii. Commodore Charles Morris, Chief of the Bureau of Construction, Equipment and Repair, reported on September 4, 1846, in favor of the payment of $2000 to Ericsson for the use of his semicylindrical engine in the *Princeton*. N.D., *Bureau Letters*.
[2] Report of Charles H. Haswell, Engineer-in-Chief, January 30, 1849, N.D., *Bureau Letters*; copies of reports of Captain R. F. Stockton on speed trials of the *Princeton*, March 4 and 22, 1845, in *Ericsson Mss.*, i. A. D. Turnbull's *John Stevens* throws some fresh light on the part played by the Stevens family in developing the screw propeller.

1842 to 1849 on unsuccessful experiments with submerged wheels devised by Lieutenant William W. Hunter; and continued for many years the construction of paddle steamers.[1]

Meanwhile Ericsson's screw found ready acceptance in the merchant service at home and abroad, and was adopted by the French government for the frigate *Pomone* and by the British for the frigate *Amphion*.[2] Yet success brought with it many vexatious difficulties. Labrousse, a French naval officer who distinguished himself as the champion of ironclad rams, roundly declared that Ericsson's screw was "identiquement semblable" to that proposed by Delisle, a French captain of engineers, who had published the results of his researches in the *Annales de la Société des Amateurs de Lille* in 1824. He maintained, furthermore, that F. P. Smith's screw was "absolument semblable" to that patented by Frédéric Sauvage in 1832.[3] In weighing such charges, however, one should bear in mind the large number of cases in which inventions have been made two or more times by different inventors, each working without knowledge of the other's research.[4] The multiplicity of claimants for the invention led to prolonged litigation, which resulted in the decision that the invention of the screw propeller could not be protected by patent in the United States.[5] In the course of these legal proceedings, Ericsson made an affidavit one portion of which, omitted by his biographer, indicates that his part in the technical development of the screw propeller was less than is often believed.[6]

---

[1] Bennett, *Steam Navy*, i, pp. 48–54, 102 ff.; House Executive Document No. 65, 33d Congress, 1st Session. See also the report of Charles H. Haswell, Charles W. Copeland, John Faron, Jr., and A. Hebard to Commodore Charles Morris, February 7, 1846, on various propellers. B.C.R., *Engineers and Constructors Letters*, ii.

[2] Admiral P. H. Colomb describes the *Amphion* in his *Memoirs of Admiral Sir Astley Cooper Key* (London, 1898), p. 221, note.

[3] H. Labrousse, "Des propulseurs sous-marins," *Revue générale d'architecture* (1842), pp. 385–458, 500–532, at pp. 386–390.

[4] See William F. Ogburn and Dorothy Thomas, "Are Inventions Inevitable? A Note on Social Evolution," *Political Science Quarterly*, March, 1922. Cf. A. P. Usher, *History of Mechanical Inventions* (New York, 1929), ch. ii.

[5] Church, *Ericsson*, i, pp. 166–174. Cf. Haswell's report of January 30, 1849, cited above, p. 14.

[6] See Appendix A.

While the patent lawyers were fighting their battles, various inventors undertook the improvement of the new method of propulsion. Captain Bourgois and Naval Constructor Molle of the French Navy soon threw further light on the theory of the screw; and Ericsson, Labrousse, Griffiths, and others devised means of hoisting the propeller when it was not in use. This last device seemed all the more important, since steam, in these early warships, was deemed simply the auxiliary of sail power. As larger and more efficient engines were developed, however, there arose during the forties a school of thought which pressed the claims of steam to the first rank as a motive power, with sails reduced to the secondary rôle. These views, voiced by Labrousse in 1844, triumphed a few years later with Dupuy de Lôme's first great masterpiece, *le Napoléon*.[1]

[1] Bourne, *Screw Propeller*, pp. 46-49, 68, 70, 73; Church, *Ericsson*, i, pp. 158 ff.; Xavier Raymond, *Les marines de la France et de l'Angleterre*, pp. 120-121; Tramond and Reussner, *Histoire maritime*, pp. 55-58; *Notice sur les travaux scientifiques et les services du contre-amiral Labrousse* (Paris, 1866); *Notice sur les travaux scientifiques de M. Dupuy de Lôme* (Paris, 1866). See below, p. 97.

Captain Stockton's letter of February 5, 1844, printed in Bennett, *Steam Navy*, i, p. 67, shows that the *Princeton* was designed to use steam simply as an auxiliary.

CHAPTER II

A REVOLUTION IN NAVAL ORDNANCE

THOUGH a single salvo sufficed to sink a modern battle cruiser in 1916, the stout wooden walls of the heavy ships of the line of the eighteenth century, and of their still heavier successors of the first half of the nineteenth, could withstand a terrific hammering from solid shot. It was the introduction of shell guns in naval warfare that upset the balance between offence and defence. From the first introduction of these formidable weapons, some of their leading advocates foresaw the necessity of increased protection, and proposed the adoption of armor. A series of experiments in shell fire against wooden walls showed ordnance experts and naval constructors the havoc the new guns would work on the heaviest ships afloat. A few practical demonstrations of shell fire in minor wars pointed in the same direction. Not until the annihilation of the Turkish fleet at Sinope in 1853, however, did the general public realize the significance of that revolution in naval ordnance, which was largely due to the efforts of one gifted French artillerist, Henri-Joseph Paixhans.

Born at Metz, in 1783, Paixhans had passed through the École Polytechnique, served as an artillery officer during the Napoleonic Wars, and risen to the rank of Chef de bataillon when, in 1822, he published his *Nouvelle force maritime*.[1]

---

[1] The full title is: *Nouvelle force maritime, et application de cette force à quelques parties du service de l'armée de terre; ou Essai sur l'état actuel des moyens de la force maritime; Sur une espèce nouvelle d'artillerie de mer, qui détruirait promptment les vaisseaux de haut-bord; Sur la construction des navires à voile et à vapeur, de grandeur modérée, qui, armés de cette artillerie, donneraient une marine moins couteuse et plus puissante que celles existantes; Et sur la force que le système de bouches-à-feu proposé offrirait à terre, pour les batteries de siège, de places, de côtes et de campagne.* (Paris, 1822. 4to. xv, 458 pp., with 7 plates.) Pages 1–74 are a revision of his *Nouvelle force maritime, ou exposé des moyens d'annuler la force des marines actuelles de haut-bord, et de donner à des navires très-petits, assez de puissance pour détruire les plus grands vaisseaux de guerre.* (Paris, 1821. 8vo. xix, 118, 4 pp.) Citations in the present work are from the edition of 1822.

Expressly disclaiming the title of inventor,[1] Paixhans cited a long series of experiments and opinions by various officers as the basis of his proposals to substitute, for existing naval ordnance, guns of the same weight, bored to larger calibers, to be used for horizontal shell fire.

In land warfare shell fire at high angles from mortars had been practised from an early date in the history of artillery.[2] Owing to the risk of fire on shipboard, however, shells made their appearance in naval warfare at a considerably later date, and at first were generally confined to use in small, specially constructed bomb or mortar vessels.[3] The French fleet which bombarded Algiers in 1682 contained five such craft, which had been designed by a young Basque, Bernard Renau d'Eliçagaray.[4] A few years later Richard Leake, master gunner of England, invented his "cushee-piece," or "coursie piece," intended to be placed on the forecastle of a ship, to fire shells and carcasses (incendiary shells). Two of these heavy nine-foot brass pieces were mounted in the bomb vessel *Firedrake*, and used with such effect in the battle of Bantry Bay in 1689 that they set a French ship on fire and wholly disabled her.[5]

As the ordinary mortar was too heavy for use as a field piece, light mortars were cast, which became known as howitzers. Their successful use by the armies of Frederick the

---

[1] *Nouvelle force maritime*, pp. vi–vii, 139, note, 230, 351, note; *Journal des Sciences Militaires*, ii (1826), pp. 545–555.

[2] For the difficulties in fixing this date exactly, see Louis-Napoléon Bonaparte and Favé, *Etudes sur le passé et l'avenir de l'artillerie* (Paris, 1846–1871, 6 vols.), i, p. 96; ii, pp. 318–319, 344–345; iii, pp. 273–292, 320–322, 335–338; J. A. Dahlgren, *Shells and Shell-Guns* (Philadelphia, 1856), pp. 1–4; Captain H. Garbett, R.N., *Naval Gunnery* (London, 1897), p. 233; Lieut.-Col. Henry W. Hime, *The Origin of Artillery* (London, 1915), pp. 194–197; Paixhans, *Nouvelle force maritime*, pp. 86–88.

[3] See, however, Sir Julian Corbett, *Drake and the Tudor Navy* (London, 1898, 2 vols.), i, p. 396.

[4] La Roncière, *Marine française*, v, pp. 715–721. A French ordinance of April 16, 1689, created two companies of bombardiers, one at Brest, the other at Toulon. *Historique de l'artillerie de la marine* (Paris, 1889), p. 18.

[5] Stephen Martin-Leake, *Life of Sir John Leake*, ed. by Geoffrey Callender (London, 1920, 2 vols.), i, pp. xvi–xvii, 10–12, 22–23; E. W. H. Fyers, "Jottings from Campbell's 'Naval History,'" *Mariner's Mirror*, June, 1923, pp. 187–188.

Great won for them widespread adoption.[1] At the siege of Ostend in 1602 a French engineer named Renaud-Ville had used one to fire shells horizontally; and some eighteenth-century artillerists experimented with ricochet fire of shells.[2] Occasional attempts to fire shells from guns, as distinguished from howitzers and mortars, were made during the seventeenth and eighteenth centuries. During the siege of Gibraltar in 1779, 5.5-inch shells, with short fuses, were fired successfully from 24-pounder guns.[3] A few years later Lieutenant Henry Shrapnel, R.A., conceived the deadly spherical case shot which bears his name.[4] The story of the introduction of horizontal shell fire in naval warfare, however, remains somewhat obscure.

A council of officers held on board H.M.S. *Triumph* at Spithead, July 31, 1701, approved of a proposal by Lieutenant Colonel Browne, master gunner of England, for "shooting grenade shells and fire-shot out of cannons," and concluded that forty or fifty of each should be furnished to every great ship in time of war, "provided they can be well secured from taking fire and doing mischief in our own ships."[5] It was just this difficulty of the fire hazard, however, which made the naval officers of the eighteenth and early nineteenth centuries reluctant to admit shells on shipboard. The great advantages of using shells against wooden warships,

---

[1] Dahlgren, *Shells and Shell-Guns*, pp. 4–5; Favé, *Etudes sur le passé et l'avenir de l'artillerie*, iv, pp. 41–42, 82, 94–96, 98, 102, 104, 114–115, 140–142.

[2] E. Dusaert, *Essai sur les obusiers* (Paris, 1842), p. 16; Dahlgren, *Shells and Shell-Guns*, pp. 6–7; Favé, *op. cit.*, iv, pp. 3, 5, 27, 41–42; Paixhans, *Nouvelle force maritime*, pp. 89–91, 351, 385–387. The inexact but convenient expression "horizontal shell fire," which the writer employs throughout this work in contrast to high-angle fire, was used by Dahlgren, *Shells and Shell-Guns*, pp. 7, 13, and elsewhere.

[3] Paixhans, *Nouvelle force maritime*, pp. 89, 91, 92, 93; Garbett, *Naval Gunnery*, p. 235; Hime, *Origin of Artillery*, pp. 180–181.

[4] *Ibid.*, pp. 182–183; *Dictionary of National Biography*, s.v. Shrapnel.

[5] Oscar Browning, ed., *Journal of Sir George Rooke* (London, 1897), p. 133. L. G. Carr Laughton, Esq., whose generous contributions from his abundant store of information concerning British ordnance have greatly aided the writer, in calling attention to this passage doubted whether any results followed Browne's proposal. Although the French suffered from shells during the action of Velez Malaga in 1704, it seems clear that these were thrown by the mortars of the bomb vessels.

which had been emphasized by Gribeauval in 1770 and 1778,[1] and the greater probabilities of hitting with horizontal, compared with high-angle fire, must have been obvious. General Robert Melville suggested the use of shells and carcasses in carronades during the War of American Independence, and several British ships carried spherical case shot and shells, for use in their carronades, during the long struggle against Revolutionary and Napoleonic France.[2] Even the idea of shell-fire at sea from long guns seems to have been in the air on the eve of the wars of the French Revolution. In fitting out the Russian Black Sea flotilla for service against the Turks in 1788 Brigadier General Sir Samuel Bentham, then a Lieutenant Colonel in the Russian Army, mounted long 36-pounders, 48-pounder howitzers, and even a 13-inch mortar, on his non-recoil principle. In the successful Russian engagements of that year these heavy guns fired shells "either point blank or with very little elevation, never I believe exceeding ten degrees." [3]

The outbreak of the French wars in 1792 gave a great impetus to ordnance experiments. Andréossy, who in the years 1791 to 1793 had successfully practiced ricochet fire of shells from guns, submitted to General Bonaparte in the following year a *Mémoire sur le tir des corps creux, qu'on propose de substituer au tir à boulets rouges dans les combats de mer*. The stest of shell-fire from 18-, 24-, and 36-pounders against a target representing the side of a ship of the line, which Andréossy initiated at Toulon in June, 1795, were repeated on a large scale at Meudon, three years later. Shells burst in the oak target with devastating effect. A similar experiment at Cherbourg in April, 1797, when 24-pounder shells were em-

---

1 Lieutenant General Count Andréossy, "Essai sur le tir des projectiles creux," *Journal des sciences militaires*, ii (1826), pp. 242–261; Paixhans, *Nouvelle force maritime*, p. 353.

2 *Ibid.*, p. 97; Dahlgren, *Shells and Shell-Guns*, pp. 10–13; Hime, *Origin of Artillery* p. 183; J. Scoffern, *Projectile Weapons of War* (4th ed., London, 1859), pp. 134–135.

3 General Sir Samuel Bentham, "Notes on the Naval Encounters of the Russians and Turks in 1788," *United Service Journal* (1829), part ii, pp. 333–339; M. S. Bentham, *Life of Brigadier-General Sir Samuel Bentham* (London, 1862), pp. 84–88.

ployed against a vessel of lighter scantling, indicated that the heaviest line-of-battle ship would sink in less than fifteen minutes if struck at the water line by such a projectile. Choderlos de Laclos, perhaps more widely known as the author of *Liaisons dangereuses* than as a distinguished general of artillery, obtained in 1799 some trials which he had urged in 1786 and 1792. In these successful tests at Vincennes, shells fired from a 24-pounder at 512 yards range demolished an earthwork.[1] Shells and other incendiary projectiles which were issued to French ships in 1795 proved more dangerous to them, from premature explosion, than to the enemy.[2] Two years later the Dutch ships blockaded by Duncan in the Texel, at Wolfe Tone's suggestion successfully fired shells from their guns.[3] After the renewal of the war in 1803, Lariboissière, Scharnhorst, Willantrois, and others pursued experiments with shell-fire. On June 17, 1803, the First Consul gave orders that an *obusier* should be mounted in each pinnace of the Boulogne flotilla. Paixhans began his own investigations in 1809. In that year he shattered a solid cast-iron 24-pounder shot against an armored target.[4]

The advantages of horizontal shell-fire at sea provoked some discussion in England during the Revolutionary and Napoleonic Wars. General Bentham proposed in January, 1798, that 24-pounder carronades, to throw shells and carcasses as well as solid shot, should be mounted in small coasting sloops. During Sir Sydney Smith's defence of Acre, 32- and 68-pounder carronades and a 42-pounder howitzer were mounted on Bentham's non-recoil principle in small vessels, together with a long 24-pounder to throw shells at 50

---

[1] Andréossy, *op. cit.*; Paixhans, *Nouvelle force maritime*, pp. 94, 95, 97, 98–100, 353–354; *Journal des sciences militaires*, ii (1826), p. 551, note.
[2] Garbett, *Naval Gunnery*, pp. 16–17; Jurien de la Gravière, *Guerres maritimes sous la République et l'Empire* (Paris [1883?], 2 vols.), i, pp. 94–96.
[3] Colomb, *Admiral Sir Astley Cooper Key*, p. 13; W. T. W. Tone, ed., *Life of Theobald Wolfe Tone* (Washington, 1826, 2 vols.), ii, p. 427.
[4] Paixhans, *Nouvelle force maritime*, pp. 101–110, and *Force et faiblesse militaires de la France* (Paris, 1830), pp. 435, note, 442–443; E. Desbrière, *Projets et tentatives de débarquement aux îles britanniques, 1793–1805* (Paris, 1900–1902, 4 vols. in 5), iii, p. 85.

degrees elevation.[1] A few years earlier good ranges were obtained with shells thrown from 68-pounder carronades and long 24-pounders.[2] According to the seventh edition of Adye's *Bombardier and Pocket Gunner*, published in 1813, hand grenades might be fired from 6-pounder guns, 4⅖-inch shells from 12-pounders, 5¼-inch shells from 24-pounders, and 8-inch shells from 68-pounder carronades.[3] In July, 1813, however, the Admiralty rejected the plan of one John Jacob Zornlin, Jr., for a shell to be fired from a gun or carronade on shipboard, which the inventor asserted would rake the deck of a ship after passing through her side.[4]

At almost the same time American inventors were at work on the problem of horizontal shell-fire from guns. Tousard, in his *American Artillerist's Companion*, published in 1809, had called attention to some of the earlier French experiments in firing shells from guns.[5] During the War of 1812 Major George Bomford, later Chief of Ordnance, U.S.A., designed a long chambered piece, combining some of the qualities of the gun, howitzer, and mortar, and capable of firing both solid shot and shells. This he named the Columbiad, in honor of Joel Barlow's epic poem. These guns, and the improved models of 1844, 1858, and 1860, were long relied on for

---

[1] Bentham, *Naval Papers* (London, 1828), No. VII, pp. 6–9, 33–37.

[2] Paixhans, *Nouvelle force maritime*, p. 97.

[3] Captain R. W. Adye, R.A., *The Bombardier, and Pocket Gunner* (7th ed., revised and corrected by Captain W. J. Eliot, R.A., London, 1813), p. 337. In July, 1811, and again in January, 1813, a committee of Field Officers of Artillery, headed by Lieutenant General Vaughan Lloyd, approved proposals made by Rear Admiral Sir Richard Keats and Lieutenant T. H. Stevens, R.M.A., for the use of 68-pounder carronades as mortars in gun brigs and other small vessels. Experiments at Sutton showed that ranges of 3500 yards could be thus obtained, which were much superior to the maximum ranges of under 2000 yards attained by the ordinary 8-inch brass mortars, although inferior by nearly three-quarters of a mile to the range of the heavy sea-service mortars. The committee declined to pass on the proposal of Lieutenant Stevens to arm some gunboats with 68-pounder carronades for use as howitzers, on the ground that it was for naval officers to decide that question. Adm. 1/4021.

[4] Adm. 1/5113. For British experiments in firing hollow shot from carronades in 1821 see Adm. Index 4955; Adm. 1/4024, May 7; Adm. 1/2721, June 11; Adm. 1/758, June 22, 1821.

[5] Lieutenant Colonel Louis de Tousard, *American Artillerist's Companion* (Philadelphia, 1809, 2 vols.), ii, pp. 258–259, 261–264.

the defence of the coasts of the United States.[1] In 1814 Colonel John Stevens of Hoboken and his sons, Robert Livingston and Edwin Augustus Stevens, developed an elongated shell whose effect on a target representing the side of a ship of the line led them to predict a revolution in naval architecture. To demonstrate that the iron armor necessary to protect ships from shells would also resist solid shot, they tested a brass 6-pounder against an oak butt faced with iron, and in 1820 fired 32-pounder shot at 70 yards range against targets protected by iron bars 2½ inches long and ½ inch thick. Although some of their shells were ordered by both the Army and Navy, and Colonel Decius Wadsworth, Chief of Ordnance, expressed the opinion that "the elongated shells are calculated to obviate the principal objections against the use of shells on shipboard," the Stevenses for years in vain bombarded the War and Navy Departments and various members of Congress with proposals for shell guns and war steamers.[2]

Paixhans, who believed that spherical projectiles alone were practicable, thought that the Stevenses were on the wrong track.[3] He agreed with them heartily, however, in the view that shell-fire would revolutionize naval architecture. He argued that the ship of the line, which had practically reached its maximum of development with the old guns,[4] was adequately protected by its wooden walls against solid shot but hopelessly vulnerable when attacked by heavy shells, which would tear great holes in its sides and scatter death and

---

[1] *Dictionary of American Biography*, s.v. Bomford; J. G. Benton, *Ordnance and Gunnery* (2d ed., New York, 1862), pp. 190–192; H. W. Halleck, *Elements of Military Art and Science* (New York, 1846), p. 280, note. Cf. Dickinson, *Fulton*, pp. 260–262. Two 50-pounder columbiads on fixed carriages were captured by the British at Fort Washington, June 30, 1814. *American State Papers, Military Affairs*, i, p. 587.

[2] John Stevens to President James Madison, June 25, 1815, N.D. *Miscellaneous Letters*; *American State Papers, Military Affairs*, i, pp. 851–852, and *Naval Affairs*, i, p. 603; Turnbull, *John Stevens*, pp. 386–414. See above, p. 9, and below, pp. 32, 48–52, 54, 211–219.

[3] *Nouvelle force maritime*, p. 137.

[4] Cf. G. Clerc-Rampal, "Les lois générales de la construction navale," Académie de Marine, *Communications et Mémoires*, iii (Paris, 1924), No. 5.

fire between decks. Mortars, whose installation had proved practicable only on vessels of a special type, unsuited to fight in the line of battle, could be used only for high-angle fire. Foretelling the future with remarkable sagacity, Paixhans declared that the horizontal fire of heavy shells from guns would prove practicable on shipboard; would multiply the chances of hitting as compared to mortar fire; and would drive the old wooden ships of the line from the sea.

In at least two of his conclusions, Paixhans was at fault. He opposed the use of elongated projectiles, whose introduction was destined to increase enormously the power of artillery;[1] and he declared that the day of the large and costly ship had passed.[2] On the other hand, with the foresight of genius, he perceived that his proposed armament, installed on steamships, would upset the established balance between defence and offence. If crews were to fight their ships under a hail of shells, some new form of protection must be found. Paixhans, an artillerist, not a naval constructor, argued that iron thick enough to resist heavy shells, if applied to the vast surface of a lofty ship of the line, would destroy her stability, and sink her by its immense weight.[3] On the other hand, small steamers designed to fight end-on, and floating batteries for coast defence, might adequately be protected by iron armor, whose defensive qualities he had tested in 1809.[4]

On broader grounds, Paixhans adduced arguments which proved of great weight in the determination of French naval policy then and later. Dominated, as Tramond well says, "par notre éternel désir de rendre le faible plus fort que le fort,"[5] he pointed out that a revolution in naval architecture would scrap existing *matériel* and sweep away England's superiority. Arguing that the new steam navy would require fewer skilled seamen, and permit the use of soldiers at sea, he declared that in future the naval power of states would be-

---

[1] *Nouvelle force maritime*, pp. 124, 137, 190–192.
[2] *Ibid.*, pp. 84–85, 237, 290–293, 333–335, 343–345.
[3] *Ibid.*, pp. 258–259.
[4] *Ibid.*, pp. 290, 294–300, 337.
[5] *Eléments d'histoire maritime et coloniale contemporaine*, p. 62.

come proportional to their total population, instead of remaining as at that time proportional to the seafaring portions of their population.[1]

Tests of Paixhans' new guns at Brest in January, 1824, met with great success. His shells burst with terrible effect on the old 80-gun ship of the line, *le Pacificateur*, which was used as a target. The sixteenth shell wrought such havoc that it was believed a similar explosion near the water line might have sunk the vessel. The commission of sixteen in charge of the experiments reported unanimously that Paixhans had solved the problem he had raised in a satisfactory manner; that the weapon he had created had terrible effects, and would, after some improvements, be no more difficult to handle than the ordinary guns; and that it would be of incalculable advantage for use in coast batteries, gunboats, bomb vessels, floating batteries, and steam batteries. By a majority of thirteen to three, moreover, the commission reported that Paixhans' shell gun might be adopted even for ships of the line, "mais en petite quantité, et en prenant des précautions qui doivent être l'objet d'une recherche et d'un examen spécial."[2]

Endorsed by the Académie des Sciences in May, 1824, Paixhans' system successfully stood new tests at Brest in the following September and October. The report of the commission in charge of these experiments strongly recommended the adoption of the new weapons for coast defence, floating batteries, gunboats, and steamers, and the introduction of two or four shell guns in heavier ships after further tests and special precautions.[3]

The shell guns which Captain Frank Abney Hastings introduced on the steamer *Karteria* proved effective in the

---

[1] *Nouvelle force maritime*, pp. vii, xiv, 236, 340–342, 345.

[2] *Expériences faites à Brest, en janvier 1824, du nouveau système des forces navales proposé par M. Paixhans; suivies des expériences comparatives des canons de 80 avec ceux de 36 et 24, et caronades de ces deux derniers calibres* (Paris, 1837), p. 13.

[3] *Ibid.*, pp. 15–42; H. J. Paixhans, *Expériences faites par la marine française, sur une arme nouvelle. Changemens qui paraissent devoir en résulter dans le système naval, et examen de quelques questions relatives à la marine, à l'artillerie, à l'attaque et à la défense des côtes et des places* (Paris, 1825), pp. 45–59.

cause of the Greek insurgents in 1827.[1] In the same year Paixhans' guns were first introduced in the French service. Despite some British strictures on details of the proposed system,[2] the Admiralty ordered tests of a ten-inch and a twelve-inch shell gun in 1829,[3] and throughout the following decade pushed numerous experiments leading to the adoption of this powerful type of ordnance.[4] Gradually the new weapons took their place beside the old-style guns in the ships of the principal maritime powers, and nowhere did they meet with warmer approval than in the United States.[5]

In a pamphlet published in 1825, Paixhans declared that nothing less than iron armor seven to eight inches thick could resist the heaviest shot and shell. Neither ordinary ships of the line, frigates, corvettes, or brigs, he asserted, could carry such weight, even if the area protected were much limited. Nevertheless, three-deckers cut down to carry a single battery of six or eight large shell guns, floating batteries, and large steam frigates carrying a few guns and reduced sail area could all support such a heavy cuirass. Combats between such invulnerable craft must be decided by boarding, sword in hand.[6]

Paixhans did not stand alone at this time in his advocacy

---

[1] See Hastings' *Memoir on the Use of Shells* (London, 1828); *Naval and Military Magazine*, December, 1828, pp. cxli–cxlii; *United Service Journal*, June, 1829, pp. 743–746. Professor E. D. Salmon kindly permitted the writer to consult his interesting unpublished essay on "The Naval Phase of the Greek War of Independence."

[2] Adm. 1/3357, Sir R. Williams to J. W. Croker, March 2, 1827; *Foreign Quarterly Review*, June, 1828, pp. 563–591.

[3] Adm. 1/4028, R. Bingham to J. W. Croker, June 10, 1829; Adm. Index 5016.

[4] Adm. Indexes 5031, 5038, 5045, 5053, 5064, 5076; Adm. 12/346; Adm. 1/4030, January 24, 1832, October 23, 1833; Adm. 1/1382, April 23, 1834; Adm. 1/5099, June 5, 1835; Adm. 1/2954, December 8, 1835. Captain Thomas Hastings, commanding the gunnery ship *Excellent*, declared on June 7, 1834, that "in any future war, three or four 8-inch shells fired horizontally and planted and exploded in the water line, would be fully equal to the destruction of the largest ship of war." Adm. 1/1968.

[5] For the general adoption of shell guns see: *On the new wants arising from the introduction of the Paixhans Gun in the Royal Navy* (London, 1838); Dahlgren, *Shells and Shell-Guns*; and two works by Captain T. F. Simmons, R.A., *Ideas as to the effect of Heavy Ordnance* (London, 1837), and *A Discussion on the Present Armament of the Navy* (London, 1839).

[6] *Expériences faites par la marine française*, pp. 23–25, 52, 92–97.

of the armored warship. That gifted French naval officer, de Montgéry, who foresaw something of the rôles destined to be played in modern warfare by mines, torpedoes, and submarines, preached the advantages of iron over wood in shipbuilding, and advocated the use of water-tight bulkheads. He declared that six- or seven-inch iron armor would resist the heaviest ordnance, and that steel plates would be infinitely preferable. To cut down existing ships of the line and plate them with iron would be possible, but uneconomical in the long run, in view of the inferior durability of wood and the high cost of repairs. Ironclads built wholly of iron were much to be preferred.[1]

In June, 1823, Captain Delisle, whose researches on screw propellers have already been mentioned, proposed the conversion of a ship of the line into a screw steamer protected by iron side and deck armor, equipped with a ram, and mounting ten- and twelve-inch shell guns.[2] An anonymous French pamphleteer, the Marquis D. L. F., proposed in 1826 that large iron frigates be built with shot-proof sides. He declared that as soon as the enemy introduced shell guns, wooden vessels would become useless for purposes of war. Three years later, in his *Aperçus sur le matériel et le personnel de la marine*, Admiral Burgues de Missiessy, Vice-President of the *Conseil d'Amirauté*, proposed a reorganization of the French Navy, including the construction of three "prames cuirassées." [3]

When a French inventor named Esquirol proposed in 1831

---

[1] De Montgéry, "Mémoire sur les navires en fer," *Journal des sciences militaires*, i (1825), pp. 488-507. Also printed in *Annales de l'industrie*, xii (1823), pp. 41 ff.; and separately (Paris, 1824). Among his other writings may be noted: *Règles de pointage à bord des vaisseaux . . . suivies de notes sur diverses branches de l'artillerie* (Paris, 1816; 2d ed., 1828); *Mémoire sur les mines flottantes et les pétards flottants, ou machines infernales maritimes* (Paris, 1819); *Traité des fusées de guerre dites fusées à la Congrève* (Paris, 1825); "Notice sur la navigation et la guerre sous-marine," *Journal des sciences militaires*, ii (1826).

[2] See above, p. 15 and Appendices A and B. Delisle's "Considérations sur l'importance et les moyens de l'application des machines à vapeur à la navigation maritime sous le rapport de guerre," dated November 30, 1825, are reproduced in the *Mémorial du génie maritime*, August, 1862, pp. 102-124. His project was first submitted to the Minister of Marine, June 1, 1823. Delisle refers to de Montgéry's proposals.

[3] P. Dislère, *Marine cuirassée* (Paris, 1873), p. 5.

that warships be built of horizontal beams hooped with iron and armed with a solid iron prow, the *Commission consultative des Travaux de la Marine* rejected the proposed method of construction, but observed that if steamers were destined to form a large part of the fleets of the future, iron rams would be worth trying.[1] Three years later the *Conseil des Travaux*, a body composed of line officers, naval constructors, and naval artillerists, which was created in 1831 to pass on all new projects for naval construction,[2] deemed worthy of further study the suggestion of Lieutenant Bertrand that the artillery and machinery of paddle steamers be protected by coal bunkers, inclined bulkheads, and iron armor.[3] The same council, however, declined in October, 1841, to consider a vague proposal to armor ships of the line made by an artillery captain named Grenier, and declared that similar proposals, by no means rare, had always been rejected on account of the enormous weight that would be needed to give adequate protection.[4]

Although some of the early experiments in firing against armor were designed to test the use of iron to protect fortifications, especially for embrasures, most of them were intended to throw light on the possibility of building armored warships.[5] Experiments by Paixhans in 1809 and the Stevenses in 1814 and 1820 already mentioned, had tested projectiles by firing them against iron plates.[6] At the suggestion of Major General Ford, R.E., 24-pounder solid cast-iron shot were tested at Woolwich, September 26, 1827, against a granite wall cased with a horizontal layer of wrought-iron bars each one inch square, covered by a second vertical layer of bars each 1½ inches square. Since nineteen or twenty shot, striking the target at a range of 634 yards, broke nineteen bars of the top layer and five of the inner layer, the com-

---

1 A.M., BB⁸ 1109, February 3, 1831.
2 *Annales maritimes et coloniales*, 1831, part i, pp. 151–154.
3 A.M., BB⁸ 1110, July 19, 1834.
4 A.M., BB⁸ 1116, October 21, 1841; Dislère, *Marine cuirassée*, p. 6.
5 For some early proposals to use iron in fortifications see Baron Emil Glanz von Aïcha, *Geschichtliche Darstellung der Panzerungen und Eisen-Constructionen* (Vienna, 1873), pp. 5–7.
6 See above, pp. 21, 23.

mittee in charge deemed such armor plating inadequate.[1] Tests of 24-pounder shot against a target faced with poorly fastened iron bars at Strasbourg in September, 1829, proved unsatisfactory.[2] In a report submitted to the *Conseil des Travaux*, March 9, 1833, Captain de Montgéry recommended experiments with heavy wooden targets faced with iron, to throw light on the possibility of armoring warships.[3] On June 13, 1834, the Council drew up a program for artillery experiments on the beach at Gavres, near Lorient, which should include tests of the penetration, in heavy oak targets both armored and unarmored, of every sort of projectile used in the navy.[4] The average penetration of 30-pounder solid shot in a massive oaken target tested in 1835 was 1.346 meters, while hollow shot fired with reduced charges penetrated to an average depth of only 0.63 meters.[5] A commission appointed by the French Minister of War carried on at Metz in 1834, 1835, and 1836 elaborate experiments on the penetration of projectiles in earth, rock, masonry, wood, cast and wrought iron, and lead. Wrought-iron plates of 36, 48, and .77 millimeters thickness, and blocks of cast iron, alike failed to show satisfactory resistance to solid shot.[6] The results of firing a 24-

[1] *Transactions and Report of the Special Committee on Iron between 21st January, 1861, and March, 1862*, p. 159; Captain H. C. S. Dyer, R.A., "Remarks on Iron Defences," *Minutes of Proceedings of the Royal Artillery Institution*, iii (1863), p. 29.

[2] Paixhans, *Force et faiblesse militaires de la France*, pp. 444–445.

[3] A.M., BB^8 1110, pp. 47–57; BB^8 1113, March 9 and May 23, 1833.

[4] BB^8 1113, June 13, 1834. The Council rejected de Montgéry's proposal to abandon Gavres for a proving ground to be established on the peninsula of Giens, near Toulon.

[5] Hélie, *Traité de balistique expérimentale* (2d ed., Paris, 1884, 2 vols.), i, pp. 196–199. Hélie, who for years served as the *rapporteur* of the Commission de Gavres, does not state whether any armored targets were tested there at this time. Neither does the official report, *Expériences d'artillerie exécutées à Gavre par ordre du ministre de la marine pendant les années 1830, 1831, 1832, 1834, 1835, 1836, 1837, 1838 et 1840* (Paris, 1841).

[6] *Expériences faites à Metz en 1834, par ordre du ministre de la guerre, sur les batteries de brèche, sur la pénétration des projectiles dans divers milieux résistans, et sur la rupture des corps par le choc: suivies du rapport fait, sur ces expériences, à l'Académie des sciences de Paris, le 12 Octobre, 1835, au nom d'une commission composée de MM. Dupin, Navier et Poncelet, rapporteur* (Paris, 1836); Col. Duchemin, "Expériences sur le tir en brèche et sur divers effets relatifs à ce tir. Extrait des deux premiers rapports de la commission formée à Metz . . ." *Mémorial de l'Artillerie*, iv (1837), pp. 253–298; Captains Piobert, Morin and Didion, "Mémoire sur la résistance

pounder against heavy cast-iron blocks at Olmütz in 1834 and 1835 indicated that cast iron was unsuitable for armor. Yet armor inclined at an angle of 45 degrees and formed of old cast-iron 24-pounder guns showed satisfactory resistance at La Fère in 1837.[1]

In the United States every rumor of war brought forth proposals for adding armored ships to the navy. During the diplomatic imbroglio with France in Jackson's second administration, the House of Representatives instructed its Committee on Naval Affairs to investigate the expediency of testing Uriah Brown's ironclad fireship.[2] Although this committee reported in March, 1836, in favor of experiments, the bill appropriating the necessary funds failed of adoption at this time.[3] The same fate befell the bill appropriating $75,000 for the construction of an armored ram proposed by Commodore James Barron, which this committee reported on February 4, 1835.[4]

When submitting a plan for the engines of steam warships in January, 1834, W. Kemble, agent for the West Point Foundry Association, suggested to Commodore John Rodgers, President of the Navy Board, that the machinery be placed so low as to expose above the deck only the cranks and crosshead. These he proposed to guard by a dome, covered with boiler-plate, "from which shot, under ordinary circum-

---

des corps solides ou mous à la pénétration des projectiles," *ibid.*, pp. 299–383; "Commission des Principes du Tir à l'Ecole de Metz. Extrait des troisième et quatrième rapports. Par MM. Piobert, Morin et Didion." *Ibid.*, v (1842), pp. 501–552; Douglas, *Naval Gunnery*, pp. 120–122. According to Brialmont, however, the French tested in 1835 a rolled iron plate 77 millimeters thick bolted to an oaken target, and found that the plate was not pierced by 12- and 24-pounder solid shot fired with charges of one and two kilograms, respectively, at a range of 20 meters. *Etudes sur la défense des états et sur la fortification* (Brussels, 1863, 3 vols.), i, p. xci, note.

1 Aïcha, *Panzerungen*, pp. 7–8; Brialmont, *Etudes sur la défense des états*, ii, p. 84. Cf. Paixhans, *Fortification de Paris* (Paris, 1834), pp. 179–180.
2 House Journal, 23d Congress, 2d Session, p. 156, January 2, 1835. This committee had reported on February 9, 1827, that nothing further should be done with Brown's proposal at that time; but on May 10, 1828, it recommended experiments, as did Major General Alexander Macomb and Brigadier General Bernard. *American State Papers, Naval Affairs*, iii, pp. 40, 141, 201–203. Congress, however, failed to act. *Ibid.*, iv, p. 876. See above, p. 9 and below, p. 53.
3 *Ibid.*, iv, p. 877.
4 *Ibid.*, iv, pp. 704–707. See Appendix B.

stances, would glance."[1] Three years later, Captain Matthew Calbraith Perry recommended to the Navy Commissioners that the engines of the *Fulton* be protected by inclined bulwarks shod with iron, "so as to cause all shot striking them from any direction to ricochet."[2] Heavy wooden bulwarks were, in fact, built up from her decks and beveled as a protection against the enemy's fire.[3]

When the extinction of the United States debt afforded the advocates of preparedness a brilliant opportunity in 1836, proposals to strengthen the national defences rained down upon Congress.[4] While rival experts were wrangling over the relative merits of forts, steam warships and floating batteries, Major General Edmund Pendleton Gaines, commanding the Western Division, suggested the construction of large flat-bottomed floating batteries 200 to 300 feet long and 90 to 150 feet wide, mounting 120 to 200 heavy guns. These strange craft were to be propelled by towboats and armored with "sheet-iron of immense thickness." In peace time they were to be used as barracks, hospitals, and military schools, or to be equipped with "a framework of *ploughs* and scrapers of iron" attached to their bottoms and used to deepen the ship channels![5] To the wise and to the foolish advocates of preparedness alike, Congress turned a deaf ear, and "deposited" the surplus revenue with the states.[6]

Five years later, however, the prospect of war with Great

---

[1] House Executive Document No. 423, 25th Congress, 2d Session.
[2] *Ibid.*, p. 56. Lieutenant W. F. Lynch of the *Fulton* suggested that her machinery "could be easily protected by cotton bales, or other light elastic materials, between it and the ship's side." Lynch to Captain M. C. Perry, February 15, 1838. *Ibid.*, p. 127.
[3] Stuart, *Naval and Mail Steamers*, p. 18.
[4] House Executive Document No. 243, 24th Congress, 1st Session; Senate Documents Nos. 412 and 495, 25th Congress, 2d Session; Senate Document No. 267, 25th Congress, 3d Session; Senate Documents Nos. 120 and 451, 26th Congress, 1st Session; Senate Document No. 227, 26th Congress, 2d Session; Senate Document No. 2, 27th Congress, 2d Session; *American State Papers, Naval Affairs*, iv, pp. 954–956.
[5] Senate Document No. 256, 26th Congress, 1st Session; House Executive Document No. 311, 25th Congress, 2d Session; House Executive Document No. 206, 26th Congress, 1st Session, pp. 143–148.
[6] See E. G. Bourne, *History of the Surplus Revenue of 1837* (New York and London, 1885).

Britain stirred Congress to action. In April, 1842, an initial appropriation of $250,000 for a shot- and shell-proof steamer, destined never to be completed, crowned the efforts of the tireless Stevenses. In the next ten years numerous tests of iron plates in England, France, and elsewhere on the Continent, failed to solve the problem of protection for warships. It does not appear, however, that the abortive American experiments in ironclad building had any notable influence on the policy of foreign powers. The same cause that led Stevens to propose and Congress to sanction the adoption of armor, impelled European governments to costly experiments in the forties and to the construction of ironclads in the following decade. That cause was the introduction of shell guns.

CHAPTER III

UNARMORED IRON WARSHIPS

GREAT BRITAIN introduced the unarmored iron warship, as she had introduced the first iron vessels and the first iron steamers. Her preëminent metallurgical industries facilitated this development, which was due primarily not to the wish for protection against shot and shell, but to the superiority of iron over wood as a material for shipbuilding.

In 1787 John Wilkinson introduced the use of iron for canal boats by constructing the *Trial*, a barge about seventy feet long weighing eight tons. The first iron steamer, the *Aaron Manby*, which had been constructed at Horsley in 1821, sent in parts to London, and assembled there, reached Paris in June of the next year, under the command of Captain, afterwards Admiral, Sir Charles Napier. Manby then shipped a second similar craft in parts for assemblage at Charenton, where two others were constructed forthwith for use on the Seine. Several English and French firms soon undertook iron shipbuilding. In 1838, the *Iron-Sides*, a sailing vessel of 260 tons, built at Liverpool by Jackson, Gordon, and Co., crossed the Atlantic.[1]

Preëminent among these early shipbuilders in iron was the firm of William Laird and Sons, of Birkenhead, which had to its credit in September, 1842, a total of forty-four iron vessels built or under construction.[2] John Laird, who had proposed a design for an iron frigate in 1836, found the East India Com-

---

[1] On the beginnings of iron shipbuilding see: De Montgéry, "Mémoire sur les navires en fer," *Journal des sciences militaires*, i (1825), pp. 488–507; Dupuy de Lôme, *Mémoire sur la construction des bâtiments en fer* (Paris, 1844), with atlas of plans (Toulon, 1843); John Grantham, *Iron as a Material for Ship-building* (London, 1842); W. S. Lindsay, *History of Merchant Shipping from 1816 to 1874* (London, [1876?], 2 vols.), ii, pp. 83–98, 187–189, 194 note, 226, 251–256, 450–452, 486–543, 599; A. W. Kirkaldy, *British Shipping, Its History, Organization and Importance* (London, 1914), pp. 31–38, 45–46, 65–67.

[2] Dupuy de Lôme gives particulars in tabular form, *op. cit.*, p. 6.

pany less conservative than the Admiralty. For the Company, he constructed in 1839 two iron paddle steamers; the *Phlegethon*, 161 feet in length, 26 feet beam, of four guns, 510 tons, and 90 horse power; and the *Nemesis*, 169 feet long, 29 feet beam, of 660 tons, and 120 horse power, armed with two 32-pounders on swivel carriages, using both shot and shell. The *Nemesis* subsequently carried five additional long brass 6-pounders and ten small iron swivels. Both these vessels did good service in the war with China.[1]

In 1842 Laird built for the Mexican Government the iron paddle frigate *Guadalupe* of 788 tons, 175 feet in length, 30 feet beam, and 180 horse power, with an armament of two 68-pounder pivot guns. At the same time Mexico had another light-draft steam frigate built in London, the *Montezuma*, 203 feet long, 24 feet beam, 1164 tons, and 280 horse power. The fitting out of these vessels, which sailed with English crews under the command of English officers, raised interesting questions of international law, foreshadowing the *Alabama* case.[2] On the outbreak of war between the United States and

[1] P.R.O., Adm. 12/371: 59–1; Adm. 12/413: 59–1; *Parliamentary Papers*, 1847–1848, xxi, no. 555, part i, pp. 647–651; A. F. B. Creuze, "On the Nemesis, private armed steamer, and on the comparative efficiency of iron-built and timber-built ships," *The United Service Journal and Naval and Military Magazine*, May, 1840; Dupuy de Lôme, *op. cit.*, pp. 5–6, 106–109; W. D. Bernard, *Narrative of the voyages and services of the Nemesis, from 1840 to 1843* (London, 1844, 2 vols.); Admiral Sir John Hay, *Lines from my Log-books* (Edinburgh, 1898), p. 182. A picture of the *Nemesis* destroying Chinese war junks is reproduced in Frank C. Bowen, *The Sea: its History and Romance* (London, [1925–1926], 4 vols.), iv, p. 57.

[2] E. D. Adams, *British Interests and Activities in Texas, 1838–1846* (Baltimore, 1910), pp. 83–93; *Diplomatic Correspondence of the Republic of Texas*, American Historical Association *Report*, 1908, ii, using index s.v. Guadalupe and Montezuma; *Parliamentary Papers*, 1847–1848, xxi, part i, no. 555, pp. 574–580. A. F. B. Creuze, principal shipwright surveyor under Lloyd's Register Book, stated that, at the time she was launched, the *Guadalupe* was the largest iron vessel that had ever been built. *Ibid.*, p. 607. A model of her may be seen in the Science Museum, South Kensington, and plans of her are reproduced in the atlas accompanying Dupuy de Lôme's *Mémoire sur les bâtiments en fer*. The figures in the latter work, pp. 5–6, 43, 103–105, differ slightly from those given for the *Guadalupe* and *Montezuma* in *Annales maritimes et coloniales*, xci (1845), pp. 254–255.

After Mexico purchased these vessels, Francis B. Ogden, the United States consul at Liverpool, proposed to Ashbel Smith that the Republic of Texas should have a large iron steam warship built, to carry two twelve-inch guns and four or eight smaller ones. Such a vessel, he declared, could destroy a dozen line-of-battle ships with ease and safety to herself, and "could reduce the citadel

Mexico in 1846 these ships, which had never been paid for, were transferred to a British firm and escaped to Havana.[1]

Advocates of iron construction argued that it increased strength, solidity, durability, and salubrity, reduced the fire risk, effected a great saving in hull weight, increased the cargo space, saved money in construction and repairs, and facilitated water-tight subdivision. It would make possible the building of much larger vessels, and the better utilization of the screw, which produced leaks in the sterns of wooden ships. They pointed out that several iron ships that had run aground had sustained remarkably slight injuries.

To the dyed-in-the-wool conservatives, however, the construction of ships out of a substance heavier than water seemed "contrary to nature." They declared that those iron ships that had run aground had done so on account of the effect of the metal on the compass, which rendered navigation hazardous. They rang the changes on the rapidity with which iron hulls became fouled with marine plants and animals, and predicted that artillery fire against the iron sides would have the direst results. Thanks to the elastic qualities of wood, on the other hand, the holes caused by solid shot often closed of themselves almost completely.[2]

Although the Admiralty rejected John Laird's proposal for an iron frigate in 1836, it gave him on February 4, 1839, an order for the iron paddle packet *Dover*, which was launched at Birkenhead the following year and employed on the Engglish Channel service. Six more small iron steamers were ordered in 1840 and 1841, including one for service on the American lakes. In January, 1844, the Board contracted for six iron steamers of 334 to 378 tons, the *Bloodhound, Harpy,*

---

of St. Juan d'Ulloa into a heap of ruins in a couple of hours." Ogden to Smith, December 8, 1844. Smith replied that if Mexico should renew hostilities, Texas would need such a ship. Professor W. C. Binkley kindly sent the writer a photostat and transcript of these letters from the originals in the Library of the University of Texas. Cf. Church, *Ericsson*, i, p. 152.

[1] Justin H. Smith, *The War with Mexico* (New York, 1919, 2 vols.), ii, p. 195.
[2] Besides the works of de Montgéry, Grantham and Dupuy de Lôme cited above, see R. Taylerson, *Iron Ship Building* (London, 1854); J. Scott Russell, *The Fleet of the Future: Iron or Wood?* (London, 1861), p. 20; and W. S. Lindsay, *History of Merchant Shipping from 1816 to 1874*, ii, pp. 83-97.

Jackall, Lizard, Myrmidon, and *Torch,* which carried a small armament, and were intended for use as tenders to flagships. After favorable reports had been received from the commanders of the iron warships *Nemesis* and *Guadalupe,* the Admiralty, despite the reluctance of the Surveyor, Sir William Symonds, and of his assistant, John Edye, ordered the construction of five steam frigates, the *Birkenhead,* a side-wheeler of 1405 tons, and the *Simoom, Vulcan, Greenock,* and *Megaera,* screw ships of 1953 to 1391 tons.[1]

Conclusions adverse to the use of iron as a material for warship building had been drawn from experiments made at Woolwich in August, 1840. An elastic composition of rubber and cork, nine inches thick, suggested by Lieutenant George Walter, R.M., failed to show merit either as a backing or as a covering for $\frac{5}{8}$-inch iron plates. Thirty-two-pounder shot fired with a charge of one pound at 40 yards range pierced the target, throwing out numerous small, jagged fragments.[2]

The advocates of unarmored iron warships had not, of course, alleged that these vessels would prove impenetrable to shot and shells. Their arguments dealt with the superior qualities of iron as a material for shipbuilding. Eight English experiments conducted between 1846 and 1851 convinced the Admiralty of the unsuitability of iron vessels for war service, and influenced decisively the course of naval construction in France as well as in Great Britain.

---

[1] Adm. 12/358: 59–1; Adm. 12/375: 91–1; Adm. 12/388: 97a; Adm. 12/402: 97a 1; Adm. 12/417: 97a 1; Adm. 12/429: 59–1; Adm. 12/432: 91–2 and 97a 1; Adm. 12/449: 97a 1; Surveyor's Submission Letter Book no. 10, May 11, 17, June 1, 12, August 25, 1841; February 23, 1842; *ibid.*, no. 11, May 9, July 23, 1844; *ibid.*, no. 12, September 9, 1846. Cf. *Parliamentary Papers,* 1847–1848, xxi, no. 555, part i, pp. lxvi, 123, 149, 174–182, 209, 574–580, 647–651, 677–680, 685–686; part ii, pp. 1025–1030; Clowes, *Royal Navy,* vi, p. 196; Captain E. Pellew Halsted, "Iron-cased ships ...," *Journal of the Royal United Service Institution,* v, p. 128 (March 4, 1861); James Napier, *Life of Robert Napier of West Shandon* (Edinburgh, 1904), pp. 153–156. The last-named work errs in stating that Napier's three steamers, the *Bloodhound, Jackall,* and *Lizard,* were the first iron vessels in the British service.

[2] *Transactions and Report of the Special Committee on Iron, between 21st January, 1861, and March, 1862,* p. ix; General Sir Howard Douglas, *A Treatise on Naval Gunnery* (5th ed., London, 1860), p. 122; Lieutenant George Walter, *Iron Ships for War or Peace* (London, 1850).

In the first of these experiments at Portsmouth, in 1846, the *Ruby*, a small iron steamer built of ¼-inch iron ribs and plates, was riddled by 8-inch and 32-pounder shot at a range of 450 yards. All the shot passed through both sides, punching out, in the nearer side, holes whose edges were generally smooth even when a rib was struck, and producing "few, but very severe" splinters. In the farther side the damage was much more serious. If the shot struck a rib, plates were torn off and injured to a considerable extent, and even when the projectile passed clean through between the ribs, the holes were hard to plug. When the target vessel was placed end-on to the guns, the shot "so tore the ribs and plates that it was evident that a similar vessel so situated would be in danger of being instantly sunk by one well directed shot." [1]

Tests of musketry, case, and grape shot in 1849 against iron plates ⅛- to ¾-inch thick and oak plank one to six inches thick did not show conclusively whether iron or oak of the thicknesses used afforded the best cover. The resistance offered by iron and oak to shot was as nearly as possible in the same proportion as their specific gravities, that is, as eight is to one. Although the holes made in oak planking always partially closed, those made through iron plates were "open and sometimes very jagged." The splinters from the iron plates were fewer but more dangerous than those from the oak.

Four experiments were made in 1850 on targets representing sections of the side of the iron steam frigate *Simoom*, with

---

[1] Adm. 12/461: 59–4a; *Experiments in H. M. Ship "Excellent" . . . from 1832 to 1854*, p. 233. Tests made in this same year 1846 to ascertain the effect of shot and shells on a steamer's funnel, indicated that it would be "very difficult to destroy funnels in action, and the holes may be readily stopped when steam is not up . . . and that shot passing through do little or no injury. . . . That in the event of the funnel being shot away, full speed can be got on the vessel to run her out of fire, or the steam may be worked expansively, and the vessel kept under perfect command, thus giving her a great superiority over a sailing ship that may be supposed to have lost a mast at the same time that the steam vessel did her funnel." *Ibid.*, pp. 55–59; Adm. 12/461: 59–4a.

When the *Lizard* was under fire in the Paraná in 1846, iron splinters caused several casualties. A "parasol plug" of tarred canvas and an iron frame was employed to stop shot holes. Douglas, *Naval Gunnery*, 5th ed., p. 125. Cf. Adm. 12/461: 59–4a; Adm. 12/481: 97a 1.

results very unfavorable to iron construction. It seemed evident that

the large, irregular, and at times very ragged holes that are made by shot in ships thus built of ⅜ iron ribs and plates, would be very difficult to stop, and therefore exceedingly dangerous if made near the waterline.

And that the number and destructive nature of the splinters produced by the breaking up of the shot would cause a few well directed shot to clear away whole guns' crews, and these two facts, more especially the last, must certainly condemn such ships as unfit for war purposes.

Little or no additional protection was afforded by filling in timbers between the ribs and planking overall on the inside, or by planking with two to four inches of fir outside the plates, or backing them with Kamptulicon, a composition of rubber and cork which proved an entire failure.[1]

Attempts were made at Portsmouth in July and August, 1851, to ascertain the effect of 8-inch and 32-pounder shot on vessels having plates of ⅜- or ½-inch iron with regular timbers throughout instead of iron ribs, and on vessels having ⅝-inch iron ribs with teak planking outside and inside, instead of iron plates. In both tests, after gun practice with 10-pound charges at 450 yards range against a target representing the nearer side of the ship, the target was reversed so as to represent the farther side of the ship, and fired at with reduced charges, to allow for the reduced velocity which a shot would have after traversing the first side. The conclusions were: "that all shot will pass through ⅜ inch iron without splitting, but that solid shot will sometimes, and hollow shot will very generally split on passing through ⅝ inch iron, with high charges"; that the injury to the farther side of an iron ship would be severe; and that even in a vessel planked with wood, shot striking iron ribs as compared with shot striking wooden timbers would cause more dangerous splinters and greater damage to the far side of the ship.[2]

[1] *Experiments in H. M. Ship "Excellent" ... from 1832 to 1854*, pp. 32–49; *Transactions and Report of the Special Committee on Iron*, pp. 161–162; Adm. 12/461: 59-4a; Adm. 12/509: 59-4a; Adm. 12/525: 59-4a. Cf. Douglas, *Naval Gunnery*, 5th ed., pp. 125–128; Walter, *Iron Ships for War or Peace*.
[2] Adm. 12/541: 59-4a; *Experiments in H. M. Ship "Excellent" ... from 1832 to 1854*, pp. 50–54; Douglas, *Naval Gunnery*, 5th ed., pp. 128–132, with three illustrations showing the damaged targets.

Convinced of the utter unsuitability of iron vessels for war purposes, the Whig administration which took office in mid-summer of 1846 directed that the iron steam frigates which the preceding Admiralty had ordered should be converted into transports.[1] According to an Admiralty order of June 24, 1850, the contractors for carrying the mails to and from North America, Malta, Alexandria, the East Indies, and China had been informed that no vessels begun after that date would be approved under the terms of the mail contract if built of iron "or of any material offering so ineffectual a resistance to the striking of shot." [2] Protesting bitterly against this order, the champions of iron steamers formed an association for testing the comparative merits of iron and wood, and strove to persuade the Admiralty to rescind its decision.[3] They pointed out, correctly enough, that the *Ruby* was a wretched specimen to have been selected for the tests in 1846, as her ribs were very wide apart, her deck had been partly removed, her plates were "no thicker than half-a-crown," and the rivets were "quite gone, especially internally." [4] Despite the strong prejudice against iron which prevailed at the Admiralty, several iron steamers were accepted under the various mail contracts,[5] and 58 of the 286 gun and mortar boats and vessels built by contract for the Royal Navy between 1854 and 1857 were constructed of iron.[6]

[1] Adm. 12/461: 59-4a; Adm. 12/465: 91-2; Adm. 12/481: 97a 1; Adm. 12/497: 91-1; Surveyor's Submission Letter Book no. 12, September 9, October 18, November 19, 1846; April 23, May 31, June 11, 14, 1847.

[2] Quoted in Surveyor's Submission Letter Book no. 18, October 11, 1856. Cf. the report of a committee appointed by the Board of Ordnance to inquire into the capabilities of merchant steam ships for war purposes. *Parliamentary Papers*, 1852–1853, lxi, no. 687.

[3] Adm. 12/461: 59-4a; Adm. 12/541: 59-1, 59-4a and 59-9; Adm. 12/544: 97a 1; Adm. 12/557: 59-1; Surveyor's Submission Letter Book no. 14, June 2, 1851.

[4] Adm. 12/461: 59-4a; *Parliamentary Papers*, 1847–1848, xxi, no. 555, part i, p. 540. According to a report from Chatham Yard October 17, 1842, the *Ruby* was "too slight for carrying stores or towing ships" and was capable only of towing lighters carrying workmen and light stores. Adm. 12/402: 97a 1.

[5] Surveyor's Submission Letter Book no. 18, October 11, 1856. Cf. *Parliamentary Papers*, 1852–1853, xcv, no. 121. In August, 1850, however, the Admiralty advised the Treasury to have nothing to do with iron vessels for the coastguard. Adm. 12/528: 97a 1.

[6] *Parliamentary Papers*, 1860, viii, no. 545, p. iii. Cf. Surveyor's Submission Letter Book no. 20, August 5, 1858.

The British experiments of firing against iron plates received wide publicity. Both France and the United States had followed Great Britain in constructing unarmored iron warships. Now they imitated her again, by turning away from iron for war steamers, after the prevailing British opinion had definitely condemned iron ships for all purposes of war.

In June, 1842, the Minister of Marine, Admiral Baron Duperré, had despatched to England, to study the latest methods of iron shipbuilding, a young officer destined to become the foremost naval constructor of the age. Born at Plœmeur, Morbihan, October 16, 1816, Stanislas-Charles-Henri-Laurent Dupuy de Lôme, after preparatory studies at the Collège de Lorient, had entered the École Polytechnique in 1835, passed into the school for naval constructors on his graduation two years later, and attained the rank of *sous-ingénieur* of the second class in November, 1841, at the age of twenty-five. After months of study in the principal British shipyards, notably with Messrs. Laird of Birkenhead, he submitted a report which, published in 1844 by order of the minister and accompanied by an admirable collection of drawings, became a shipbuilding classic. As a champion of iron he set forth its advantages over wood, traced in detail the development of iron shipbuilding in Great Britain, and described with a wealth of illustration the best methods of execution.[1]

Before this report was published, the Ministry already had ordered three small iron steamers for service in Guiana and Senegal, and several iron corvettes and despatch vessels. By the end of the year 1853, the French Navy had built, purchased, or contracted for eight iron corvettes, the largest of which displaced 950 tons, and thirty-five iron despatch vessels, ranging from small river paddle steamers of twenty to thirty horse power, up to craft of seven hundred tons displacement, carrying four 30-pounder shell guns.[2] Although

---

[1] *Mémoire sur la construction des bâtiments en fer.*
[2] According to a list compiled from the three-volume manuscript register, "Matricule des bâtiments à vapeur à flot," A.M., O DD [1] 10–12. For descriptions of

the French experiments in firing against iron plates at Gavres in the years 1843 to 1845 failed only by the narrowest of margins to demonstrate the great possibilities of armor,[1] French sentiment soon followed the predominant British opinion in turning against the unarmored iron warship.

In contrast to Great Britain and France, the United States built only three unarmored iron warships prior to the Civil War. Early in the forties Secretary Upshur favored the construction of iron ships, not merely on the ground of their superior durability and cheapness, but also to stimulate the American iron industry.[2] The Navy Department, which was looking at this time for opportunities to spend money beyond the Alleghenies, favored the construction of iron vessels on the western waters. Nevertheless, as in Great Britain and France, official opinion soon swung round to the view that unarmored iron vessels were unsuitable for war purposes.

The first American iron warship, U. S. S. *Michigan*, renamed in 1905 the *Wolverine*, served on the Great Lakes from 1844 to 1923, when she suffered her first serious accident, which led to her condemnation and conversion into an historic memorial at Erie. Her hull, engines, and boilers were built at Pittsburgh and transported in parts to Erie, Pennsylvania, where the ship was constructed and launched

---

some of these vessels see *Annales maritimes et coloniales*, c (1847), pp. 715–716; E. de Moras, "Quelques documents sur le matériel flottant des marines françaises et anglaises," *Nouvelles annales de la marine et des colonies*, ii (1849), pp. 363–396; J. Cros, "Considérations sur le matériel de notre flotte," *ibid.*, iv (1850), pp. 25–45, 77–130.

[1] See below, chapter iv.
[2] "It seems now to be no longer doubtful, that iron ships will answer all the purposes of coast and harbor defence, and, probably, also of ocean cruising. It is the wish of this Department to construct as many vessels as possible of this material. This is desirable, not only on account of its superior durability and cheapness, but because, by extending the use of it, the Government would afford a well-deserved encouragement to the industry of a large class of our people, and aid in developing and bringing into action, a most important part of our country's resources. Supplies of iron, to any extent, may be afforded by means of the Mississippi and its tributaries...." Upshur's report of January 31, 1842. Senate Document No. 98, 26th Congress, 2d Session. Upshur had recommended the construction of at least one iron warship in his annual report of December 4, 1841. Senate Document No. 1, 27th Congress, 2d Session, p. 382.

December 5, 1843.[1] She was not the first iron warship to serve on the inland waters of North America, for the iron steamer *Mohawk* of 176 tons had been built in sections in England by Fairbairn and Co. in 1841, delivered to the Admiralty, shipped to Canada, and there completed and launched on February 21, 1843.[2] Both the *Michigan's* tonnage of 582 tons and her original armament of six guns exceeded the stipulations of the Rush-Bagot agreement of 1817 limiting naval armaments on the lakes, and provoked some diplomatic correspondence, which led to a reduction of her armament to one gun.[3]

Meanwhile Lieutenant William W. Hunter, commanding the wooden war steamer *Union*, which had been built in 1842 to test his invention of horizontal submerged paddle wheels, had suggested in 1843 the introduction of a protective deck, similar to one proposed by Labrousse in France three years earlier.[4] He urged that the United States seize the command of the sea by building heavily armed iron steamers propelled according to his system, and rendered impervious to shot by means of a convex shield deck of iron or faced with iron.[5] Although the Navy Department did not adopt Hun-

---

[1] Stackhouse and Tomlinson of Pittsburgh built this vessel, whose hull was designed by Samuel Hartt. Senate Document No. 211, 27th Congress, 2d Session; House Document No. 199, 27th Congress, 2d Session; House Executive Document No. 65, 33d Congress, 1st Session, p. 77; Charles B. Stuart, *Naval and Mail Steamers*, pp. 26-28; N.D., Class 2, AD, "Alterations proposed Steamer Michigan ... 1845." Concerning the extraordinary length of service of this paddle steamer, due in part to her wintering in harbor, see the articles of Commodore E. B. Underwood, Lieutenant John P. Smart, and Lieutenant Commander Walter E. Brown in the United States Naval Institute *Proceedings*, l, pp. 597-602, 971-972, 1687-1694 (April, June, October, 1924), with picture facing p. 1693. Photographs of this vessel are also reproduced in Bennett, *Steam Navy*, i, facing p. 44, and in M. M. Quaife's "The Iron Ship," Burton Historical Collection *Leaflets*, November, 1928.

[2] P.R.O., Adm. 12/388: 97a; Surveyor's Submission Letter Book no. 10, May 11, 17, June 1, 12, 1841; *Parliamentary Papers*, 1847-1848, xxi, no. 555, part i, pp. 181, 209; part ii, pp. 1025, 1026.

[3] House Document No. 471, 56th Congress, 1st Session, pp. 19-28; J. M. Callahan, *The Neutrality of the American Lakes and Anglo-American Relations* (Baltimore, 1898), pp. 16, 18, 123-129, 132-134, 138.

[4] See below, pp. 44, 57, 64, 107, and Appendix B.

[5] Senate Document No. 244, 27th Congress, 3d Session; Senate Document No. 1,

ter's idea of a protective deck, it had a small iron steamer, the *Water Witch*, built at the Washington Navy Yard in 1843 and 1844, to serve as a water tank for the vessels at Norfolk. Her plans, drawn by John L. Porter of Portsmouth, Virginia, and her submerged wheels of Hunter's design, proved so unsatisfactory that she was cut in two, lengthened thirty feet, and fitted with a Loper propeller, which was replaced in 1847 by side paddle wheels. Since this patchwork craft, which was armed with three guns during the Mexican War, lacked both stability and strength, a wooden hull was ordered for her engines in March, 1852, and her old hull was condemned.[1]

Secretary Upshur gave Hunter's ideas a far more costly test by ordering the construction of the iron steamer *Alleghany*, of 989 tons and four guns, built by Joseph Tomlinson at Pittsburgh under a contract dated October 7, 1843. This vessel, whose construction was supervised by Hunter and Porter, was not ready to leave Pittsburgh until February 23, 1847. Owing to her peculiarities of design, her insufficient strength for ocean service, and the inefficiency of Hunter's propellers, she proved an utter failure and provoked much hostile criticism of the Navy Department.[2]

The Oregon controversy with Great Britain roused public interest in the navy. Recommending an increase of the steam fleet in his annual message of December 2, 1845, President Polk strongly recommended liberal appropriations for the construction of iron steam warships, stressing the fact that they could be built in the interior, and that, thanks to

---

28th Congress, 1st Session, pp. 557–561, with drawing which is also reproduced in Bennett, *Steam Navy*, i, p. 49.

[1] House Executive Document No. 65, 33d Congress, 1st Session, pp. 97–98; Bennett, *Steam Navy*, i, pp. 51–52; Lieutenant George F. Emmons, *The Navy of the United States* (Washington, 1853), pp. 30–31; Stuart, *Naval and Mail Steamers*, pp. 52–54.

[2] House Executive Document No. 65, 33d Congress, 1st Session, pp. 77–97; N.D., Unclassified Mss., bundle endorsed "Contract for Building Iron Steamer at Pittsburg, Pa., 1843;" *Bureau Letters*, Commodore Charles Morris to Secretary Mason, December 18, 1846, January 29, 1847; Bennett, *Steam Navy*, i, pp. 53–57; Emmons, *Navy of the United States*, pp. 34–35; Stuart, *Naval and Mail Steamers*, pp. 59–62, 101–103, 161–163.

their light draft, they could enter many harbors inaccessible to deeper vessels.[1]

In his annual report of December 1, 1845, Secretary Bancroft recommended that additional seagoing war steamers be constructed, after consultation of the most experienced builders, "and that doubtful novelties, especially such as conflict with the known laws of mechanical forces, should be disregarded."[2] The House Committee on Naval Affairs thereupon submitted inquiries to some leading shipbuilders and engineers, and received several proposals. A. J. Bergen offered to build an iron frigate of the first class to carry sixty guns, for $262,000.[3] John Ericsson replied to the committee's inquiries that

> with reference to the practicability of rendering an iron vessel shot-proof, I need hardly premise that the weight of a floating body is prescribed within such narrow limits as to preclude the introduction of extreme thickness in its sides. It is proved, moreover, not only by theoretical deduction, but amply by late experiments, that the momentum of heavy projectiles is so great as to render it impossible to make the vessel's side of sufficient thickness to prevent penetration.

He therefore proposed to render the effect of penetration harmless by means of a series of water-tight bulkheads fastened at the bottom to "a flat arch of sheet iron extending the entire length of the engine-room and attached to the ship's sides ... to be placed about three feet below the water line," and by numerous additional bulkheads fore and aft of the engine room. The flat arch resembled the convex protective deck earlier suggested by Labrousse and Hunter. Ericsson proposed that

> the bow should be made sharp, and composed of several layers of iron plates, presenting an aggregate thickness of about two inches, to continue for a distance of fifty feet from the bow, and extend some three feet below the water-line, and about seven feet above the gun-deck ...

He submitted the plan of such a craft, designed to fight bow-on, which he offered to build and furnish complete, save for

---

1 James D. Richardson, *A Compilation of the Messages and Papers of the Presidents* (Washington, 1896–1899, 10 vols.), iv, p. 413.
2 Senate Document No. 1, 29th Congress, 1st Session, p. 649.
3 House Report No. 681, 29th Congress, 1st Session, pp. 30–31. A. J. Bergen to Thomas Butler King, Washington, May 13, 1846.

stores and ammunition, for the sum of $415,000. This screw steamer, of 1200 horse power and about 1200 tons, was to have bulwarks of 5/16-inch iron; and the forward part of her deck, "and perhaps all the vessel" was to be covered with sheet iron. Ericsson specified that two semicircular railways for Paixhans guns should be laid on the main deck amidships, and that a twelve-inch gun should traverse on a circular railway at the stern. These proposed gun installations represent a partial solution of the problem of all-round fire, which was later solved by the Monitor turret.[1]

R. and G. L. Schuyler of New York declared that engines of at least 1200 horse power would be required for any vessel which would meet the committee's requirements of fifteen knots speed and sufficient displacement to permit an armament of six twelve-inch guns "ranging in full circles," besides two or four smaller guns. They offered to build two iron side-wheel steamers for $591,000 each, and submitted plans of a ship 241 feet long on the main deck, of 36 feet beam and 24 feet depth of hold, subdivided by iron bulkheads into eleven water-tight compartments, and with the engines "protected by coal bunkers or other means at the side, so as to be entirely free from shot."[2]

In their report of May 20, 1846, the committee unhesitatingly recommended iron as the best material for warship building. From the policy of the British Admiralty at that date, they concluded that wood would soon be abandoned for ships of war. Some persons, they observed, believed that the invention of shells and hollow shot had "produced a new era in naval warfare." Experiments had shown the destructive effect of these projectiles when lodged in wooden walls, and had indicated that a single ten- or twelve-inch shell, exploding at the water line, might sink a frigate or even a ship

---

[1] House Report No. 681, 29th Congress, 1st Session, pp. 17-23, Ericsson to Thomas Butler King, January 20, 23, May 21, 1846; Church, *Ericsson*, i, pp. 177-178.
[2] House Report No. 681, 29th Congress, 1st Session, pp. 24-26, R. and G. L. Schuyler to Thomas Butler King, New York, May 12, 1846. On January 17, 1846, they had proposed to build one or two side-wheel frigates of 1920 tons, to carry four Paixhans swivel guns on the upper deck and twelve 36-pounders on the main deck, for the sum of $460,000 for one, or $900,000 for two. N.D., *Miscellaneous Letters*.

of the line. Such projectiles, it was believed, would have far less effect on an iron ship, passing through both her sides and "leaving a smooth round hole, which could be easily stopped." The committee brought in a bill for the construction by private contractors of twelve iron steamers to carry six to eight heavy guns, and one iron frigate to carry sixty heavy guns.[1] In a second report, dated June 12, 1846, they proposed that the United States follow Great Britain in giving mail contracts to shipowners who would construct steamers suitable for conversion into efficient warships.[2] An act of March 3, 1847, appropriated $1,000,000 toward the construction of four first-class seagoing steam warships, and directed the Secretary of the Navy to contract with three steamship lines for the transportation of the mails in ships convertible for war purposes. The act did not specify whether iron or wood, screw propellers or paddle wheels, should be employed.[3]

Secretary Mason appointed a board to propose plans for the four steamers, composed of Commodores Charles Morris, Lewis Warrington, and Joseph Smith, Chiefs of the Bureaus of Construction and Repair, Ordnance, and Yards and Docks, together with Charles H. Haswell, engineer-in-chief, Francis Grice, chief naval constructor, John Lenthall and Samuel Hartt, naval constructors, and Charles W. Copeland, an engineer.[4] At its first sitting, March 23, the board decided, by the votes of Morris, Warrington, Smith, Grice, Lenthall, and Hartt, that at least three of the ships should be built of wood. The material for the fourth vessel was left for future consideration until May 3, when the board decided unanimously that it, too, should be of wood instead of iron.[5] This

[1] House Report No. 681, 29th Congress, 1st Session, pp. 1–9.
[2] House Report No. 685, 29th Congress, 1st Session.
[3] *Statutes at Large*, ix, pp. 187–188.
[4] N.D., *Bureau Letters*, Supplemental volume, 1847–1849, Charles Morris to J. Y. Mason, March 5, 1847; House Executive Document No. 65, 33d Congress, 1st Session, p. 112, J. Y. Mason to the board, March 22, 1847.
[5] *Ibid.*, pp. 114, 117. The board recommended that three steamers be built with side wheels, and one with a screw propeller, but with a different model from that of the *Princeton*. *Ibid.*, p. 114. The vessels thus built were the *Susquehanna*, *Powhatan*, *Saranac* and *San Jacinto*.

decision may have been influenced by the British experiments of 1846. Charles William Skinner, who succeeded Morris as Chief of the Bureau of Construction and Repair, in transmitting to Secretary Preston on July 8, 1850, a report condemning the iron steamer *Alleghany* as unfit for war purposes, declared that

> the bureau is of opinion that the material of which she is constructed prevents her being suited to the purposes for which she was designed. Recent experiments in Europe have demonstrated their inability to resist shot or shells, and the increased danger to a crew from fragments of iron beyond that of splinters from wood.[1]

[1] *Ibid.*, pp. 79-80. Frederick Perry Stanton of Tennessee deduced from the superior durability of iron an argument against its use for warship building. In his report from the House Committee on Naval Affairs, February 20, 1851, he asserted that "the power owning an iron navy would, in this age of discovery and invention, be liable to have it thrown into disuse any day by the introduction of some new principle, discovery or improvement." He preferred white oak to live oak, on the ground that the latter was too durable! House Report No. 35, 31st Congress, 2d Session.

CHAPTER IV

IRONCLAD PROJECTS OF THE FORTIES

AS THE destructive force of shell-fire against wooden walls became more clearly realized in the forties, the governments of the principal maritime powers made numerous efforts to find some means to keep out the shells. If the United States took the lead in making the first appropriation for an ironclad steam warship, the French, in a long series of careful experiments at Gavres, came very near to solving the problem of armor protection. A revulsion of feeling against armor at the close of the decade, however, postponed the effective solution until the Crimean War.

The war scare of 1841-1842 awakened Congress to the need of better coast defences. A joint board of army and navy officers met in New York in July, 1841, to superintend experiments conducted by Edwin A. and John C. Stevens, in the absence of their brother Robert in Europe. These tests indicated that wrought-iron boiler plates riveted together to form armor 4½ inches thick would resist 64-pounder solid shot fired with battering charges at 30 yards range. Both shot and shells broke into small fragments on striking the target. On August 13 the two brothers proposed, in a letter to the chairman of the joint board, the construction of a fast iron screw steamer, with a high-pressure engine and boiler placed below the water line. Iron armor four to six inches thick, set at an angle of 45 degrees, was to render her shot- and shell-proof. Rigged as an ordinary vessel, and fitted for use as a ram, she was to carry several breech-loading wrought-iron rifled guns of the largest caliber for firing shot and shell.[1]

In a memorial to Congress dated January 25, 1842, Robert Livingston Stevens urged the construction of a shot- and

---

[1] A three-page printed copy of this letter of E. A. and J. C. Stevens is in the *Ericsson Mss.*, i.

shell-proof steamer of not less than 1500 tons burden, faster than any warship then afloat, and armed with long guns adapted both to shot and to his elongated shells designed to explode after penetration. Movable screens would protect the portholes, which, since the bulwarks would be only four or five inches thick, need be "but little larger than the muzzle of a gun, and yet allow it to be fired at any angle." The ship was to have artificial ventilation, boilers adapted to anthracite fuel, and no rigging.[1]

Stevens's plan was recommended to the Secretary of the Navy on January 13 by the Board of Navy Commissioners, and to Congress on February 15 by the New York Chamber of Commerce. The report of the House Committee on Naval Affairs, presented by Francis Mallory of Virginia on March 15, urged "speedy and vigorous prosecution" of coast defences in view of the warlike preparations of Great Britain. Although wooden walls, however massive, could not resist the ravages of Paixhans shells, Stevens's vessel, with no spars and sail, would present scarcely a vulnerable point.[2]

After this hearty endorsement, Congress delayed no longer. The Act of April 14, 1842, authorized the Secretary of the

[1] The principal printed sources concerning the Stevens war steamer are: House Report No. 448, 27th Congress, 2d Session; Senate Report No. 129, 32d Congress, 1st Session; Senate Executive Document No. 34, 37th Congress, 2d Session; House Executive Documents No. 23 and No. 121, 37th Congress, 2d Session; the annual reports of the Secretary of the Navy; and three pamphlets: Edwin Augustus Stevens, *The Stevens Battery, Memorial to Congress, Merits of the Battery as Unanimously Admitted by the Board of Examiners, Opinions of Experts and Results of Experiments Disproving the Objections of the Majority.* ([N. Y., 1862], 71 pp.); New Jersey, Commissioners on the Plan of the Stevens Battery, *Report of the Commissioners . . . with a report of the engineer in charge* [George B. McClellan], (Trenton, 1870, 6 pp.); New Jersey, Commission Appointed to Effect the Sale of the Stevens Steam Battery, *The Stevens Iron-clad Battery*, (New York, 1874, 46 pp.).

The earlier accounts by R. H. Thurston, *The Messrs. Stevens of Hoboken* (Philadelphia, 1874); J. E. Watkins, *Biographical Sketches* (Washington, 1892); and F. de R. Furman, ed., *Morton Memorial, A History of the Stevens Institute of Technology* (Hoboken, 1905); have been superseded by Turnbull, *John Stevens*, ch. xviii. Although the author of that work has used unpublished materials in the Navy Department and in the possession of the Stevens family, he seems to have made no use of the numerous manuscripts concerning the Stevens battery which are preserved in the Library of the Stevens Institute of Technology and in the archives of the Bureau of Construction and Repair.

[2] House Report No. 448, 27th Congress, 2d Session.

Navy to contract with Robert L. Stevens for the construction of a war steamer, on his plan, at a total cost not exceeding the average cost of the *Missouri* and *Mississippi*; and appropriated $250,000 towards carrying out the project.[1]

Pursuant to this act, Secretary Upshur contracted with Stevens, February 10, 1843, for a vessel principally of iron, "shot and shell proof against artillery now in use on board vessels of war, viz., from 18-pounders to 64-pounders; to be propelled by the submerged machinery called Stevens's circular sculls." She was to be not less than 250 feet long, but as much longer as Stevens might choose to make her, 40 feet beam, and 28 feet deep amidships. Four or more condensing engines, of a combined force at least 50 per cent superior to that of the *Missouri* and *Mississippi*, and wholly out of the way of shot, were to drive her faster than any existing American steam warship. She was to have air-tight fire rooms, with artificial blast, and six or more large guns designed principally to fire shells. The hull was to be built of iron plates averaging half an inch in thickness, with an iron upper deck, and side armor 4½ inches thick composed of wrought or rolled iron plates, tapering off below the water line. Stevens reserved the right "of varying the size of any and all the parts of said war steamer or her machinery provided, however, that they shall not be made less than herein expressed." [2]

Soon convinced that he could not launch a vessel of this size and description, Stevens began the excavation of a dry dock big enough to build her in and float her out. At the same time he conducted experiments on the propeller, developing one which replaced the Ericsson screw on the *Princeton*.[3] Little else had been done,[4] when, on November 14, 1844,

---

[1] *Statutes at Large*, v, p. 472.
[2] The text in Senate Executive Document No. 34, 37th Congress, 2d Session, varies slightly from that of the manuscript and press copies in N.D., Class 2, AC, folder labeled "Stevens War Steamer."
[3] See above, p. 14.
[4] Charles W. Skinner, Chief of the Bureau of Construction, Equipment and Repair, to Secretary W. B. Preston, August 17, 1849, Executive Document No. 5, 31st Congress, 1st Session, p. 446; "Memorandum of the claim of Robert L. Stevens

Stevens concluded with Secretary John Y. Mason a second contract extending the time of completion two years from that date, agreeing on the sum of $586,717.84 to be paid as the mean average cost of the *Missouri* and *Mississippi*, and defining with more precision the particulars of the ship and her equipment.[1] A supplementary agreement, December 11, established prices for labor and for use of machines, and allowed Stevens cost plus 33⅓ per cent on all unwrought materials.[2]

Under this second contract, bills to the amount of $31,043.66 had been approved when, on December 5, 1845, Secretary George Bancroft directed Stevens to spend no more money on the steamer until he furnished a plan of it to the Bureau of Construction, Equipment, and Repair. Stevens stopped work and went to Europe for his health. In a memorial to Congress dated January 31, 1851, he asserted that he had "furnished his general plan in his original contract, and a detailed plan in the contract of November, 1844." The descriptive passages in these contracts, however, were not "plans" of the sort wished by Bancroft. John Lenthall, Chief of the Bureau of Construction and Repair, reported on May 18, 1860, that "the records of this Bureau do not show

 against the United States," January 31, 1851, N.D., Class 2, AC; Stevens Letter Book, Stevens Institute of Technology.

1 The depth should be measured from the upper deck, whether of iron or wood; the boilers should bear a proof of thirty pounds to the square inch; and the plates and ribs of the iron work of the hull should be made of wrought or rolled iron. Stevens should provide whatever equipment should be necessary for the operation of the ship in New York harbor, receiving additional payment for shot and shells. The Secretary was to appoint an agent to receipt for all materials purchased, which would then be marked as property of the United States. When approved bills had been paid to the amount of $500,000, two examiners named by Stevens and the Secretary, who should select a third in case of disagreement, were to state whether she could be finished at a total cost of $586,717.84. If they concluded that a larger sum would be necessary, "such deductions and reservations shall be made and withheld from all or any subsequent bills presented ... as ... will be sufficient to cover the probable excess ..." On completion of the vessel, a board similarly appointed should determine whether all the terms of the contract had been fulfilled. Stevens was to give to the United States a mortgage on his establishment at Hoboken, as security for fulfilment of his part of the agreement. He forwarded this mortgage to Mason, December 31, 1844. N.D., *Miscellaneous Letters*.

2 Senate Executive Document No. 34, 27th Congress, 2d Session. Press copies are in N.D., Class 2, AC.

that any plans or explanations further than named in the contract were furnished by the Contractor."[1]

In 1845 and 1846 the possibility of war with Great Britain or Mexico stimulated the zeal of several American inventors. James Robertson of New York submitted to the Navy Department a vague proposal for vessels "impervious to water and Balls of the Enemy."[2] Charles Warren of Boston proposed a flat-bottomed steam gunboat of 350 tons "to besiege St. Juan of Ulloa." She was to be built of heavy timbers, with a sloping roof plated with iron "to roll off shot and shells," and with shields fore and aft of iron bars six inches thick, "presenting a convex surface, suspended on pivots to swing either way when struck...."[3] James Stimpson of Baltimore offered to sell the model of a ship combining "self-protection, celerity of action and certain destruction of the enemy."[4] Jonathan Morrill of Amesbury, Massachusetts, suggested a plan for a shot-proof ram.[5] Commodore Thomas ap Catesby Jones's model and plans for a river and harbor defence vessel were commended by Samuel Humphreys and four engineers, despite "a want of ventilation in the deck and sides."[6] Charles H. Haswell, engineer-in-chief, reported adversely on the proposal of James C. Patton of Petersburg, Virginia, for an iron screw steamer with an arched shot-proof deck and with cylinders to take in water and depress the vessel till her guns were nearly on a level with

---

[1] Senate Executive Document No. 34, 37th Congress, 2d Session, p. 11; N.D., Class 2, AC; John Lenthall to Secretary Isaac Toucey, May 18, 1860, *Bureau Letters*.
[2] N.D., Unclassified Mss., "Report of Board of Naval Officers, in relation to whether any changes should be made in the armament of vessels of the Navy," Robertson to George Bancroft, May 9, 1845; Robertson to W. M. Crane and others, May 16, 1845.
[3] B.C.R., *Miscellaneous Letters*, xii, Warren to George Bancroft, July 11, 1845. This letter is to be found with the correspondence for July, 1846.
[4] *Ibid.*, x. Stimpson wrote to President Polk, January 1, 1846, that a single ship of this kind, which he had proposed to naval officers in Jackson's second administration, "could clear our coasts of the combined Fleets of all Europe." It would prevent "maratime wars ever after, and thus Great Britain will shrink down to the size of her own little island."
[5] *Ibid.*, x, January 25, 1846.
[6] B.C.R., *Engineers and Constructors Letters*, i, Samuel Humphreys to Commodore Morris, February 4, 1846; Charles H. Haswell, Charles W. Copeland, John Faron, Jr., and A. Hebard to Commodore Morris, February 10, 1846.

the water.[1] John Holder sought to serve his "adopted country" by writing from Manchester, England, to the American Minister at London, suggesting the conversion of Mississippi River steamboats by building them higher, giving them a false keel, packing them with compressed cotton, and covering them with sheet iron, to sweep the Gulf.[2]

Meanwhile Uriah Brown, now a resident of Alton, Illinois, had renewed in 1846 his proposal to build an impregnable fireship, about 250 feet long and 60 feet wide, entirely of iron, designed to project liquid fire. This vessel was to present "in no part of her surface an angle of more than 18 or 20 degrees to the *point blank* line of an enemy's fire," for she would have "the appearance of a wedge, the acute angle of which is formed at or near the water's edge by the meeting of corresponding inclined planes, composing the sides and circular ends of the deck and lower parts of the vessel." All the hatchways and other necessary openings were to be made in the flat top deck and were to be protected during action by strong iron gratings. On this deck, moreover, were "ball-proof iron observatories ... provided with starred loop-holes." The House Committee on Naval Affairs reported that it had several times investigated this project, which had been "highly recommended by the Navy and Engineer departments, as well as by gentlemen of deserved scientific reputation." The committee brought in a bill, which became section 7 of the Naval Appropriation Act of March 3, 1847, appropriating $10,000 for experiments to test both Brown's liquid fire and his shot-proof steamship. The inventor exhausted all the appropriation for the test of his liquid fire, which took place on October 16, 1847, and proved unsatisfactory. In spite of Brown's arguments for a test of his idea of inclined armor, Secretary Mason declined to recommend a further appropriation.[3] As Mason's predecessor, George

---

[1] *Ibid.*, ii, Charles H. Haswell to Commodore Morris, June 11, 1846.
[2] B.C.R., *Miscellaneous Letters*, xii, John Holder to McLane, June 9, 1846.
[3] N.D., *Miscellaneous Letters*, Robert Smith to George Bancroft, June 8, 1846; *Bureau Letters*, L. Warrington to George Bancroft, June 10, 1846; House Report No. 36, 29th Congress, 2d Session; *Statutes at Large*, ix, p. 173; House Executive Document No. 8, 30th Congress, 1st Session, pp. 1306–1308; Senate Document No. 1, 30th Congress, 1st Session, p. 953.

Bancroft, had ordered work stopped on the ironclad projected at Hoboken, on account of the failure of Robert L. Stevens to submit plans, no further work on armored vessels was undertaken in the United States until the revival of Stevens's project in 1852.[1]

That Stevens's proposal influenced the introduction of ironclads in Europe to an important degree is doubtful. The news that the American Congress had voted money for an ironclad may have aroused somewhat greater interest in an idea already old. One of the numerous British armor tests of the forties seems to have been inspired by a report of a similar experiment in America. Robert L. Stevens discussed his project with friends abroad, at least one of whom, Scott Russell, became an ardent advocate of ironclads. Yet the scanty and unimportant references to Stevens's project in the British and French naval archives do not indicate that American ideas had much influence on the policy of those governments. The cause of their experiments in the forties and of their construction of ironclads in the fifties was the introduction of shell guns.

The 12-inch wrought-iron gun named the "Oregon," which John Ericsson had brought from England for installation on the *Princeton*, sent a solid cast-iron shot through a wrought-iron target 4½ inches thick in 1842.[2] It may have been this test which Lord John Hay witnessed at New York and later described to the Select Committee on Navy, Army, and Ordnance Estimates in 1848, when he declared that shot had passed through laminated plates built up of half-inch iron, and "knocked them all to pieces." According to his testimony the Americans had tried "every sort of wood, and leather, and every description of thing" to resist the shot, but without success.[3]

The vulnerability of the engines and boilers of the early steam warships led to numerous suggestions for their protec-

---
[1] See below, pp. 211–219.
[2] Church, *Ericsson*, i, pp. 123–124, ii, p. 116; Ericsson, *Contributions to the Centennial Exhibition*, p. 403.
[3] *Parliamentary Papers*, 1847–1848, xxi, no. 555, part i, p. 159.

tion by various sorts of armor, sometimes combined with a special arrangement of the coal bunkers. On December 23, 1841, the Admiralty appointed a committee of master shipwrights "to consider the best mode of strengthening ships of war and to recommend improvements, to give greater power of attack and defence, without interfering with the powers of sailing."[1] Among the proposals of this sort received by the Admiralty between 1839 and 1843 was one from an inventor named Belmano, whose suggestion of laminated armor was tested at Portsmouth in 1842 and 1843 and proved wholly unsatisfactory. Laminated iron armor 5¼ inches thick, made up of fourteen plates ⅜ of an inch thick riveted together, was firmly fixed to a butt equal in thickness to the side of a line-of-battle ship at the bends. Eight-inch hollow shot and 32-pounder solid shot fired with ten-pound charges at a range of 400 yards broke all the plates and passed through the woodwork. At the same range twenty-eight iron plates riveted together to make seven inches of armor, firmly fastened to a butt eighteen inches thick, failed to stop eight-inch shot. The first shot penetrated halfway through the plates; the second, striking in nearly the same place, drove the damaged portion of the armor straight through the wooden backing and twenty yards beyond.[2]

After examining several plans for protecting the machinery of steam warships from shot, and conferring with some of the inventors, the Surveyor of the Navy reported on January 14,

---

[1] Adm. 3/265.
[2] P.R.O., Adm. 12/398: 59–4; Adm. 12/402: 97a 1; *Experiments in H. M. Ship "Excellent,"* ...*from 1832 to 1854*, pp. 26–27. Cf. *Nautical Magazine*, December, 1842, pp. 863–864; *Annales maritimes*, 1843, unofficial part, i, pp. 92–94. According to Bowen (*The Sea*, iv, p. 35), "Delmeno" demonstrated the advantages of iron armor in the United States early in the forties by tests which led the Admiralty to undertake similar experiments. In a lecture before the Royal United Service Institution, March 4, 1861, Captain E. Pellew Halsted, R.N., stated that the experiment made at Portsmouth in 1842 was intended to "verify results said to have been obtained in America ..., it was not connected with and did not furnish results bearing on, the construction of the iron frigates." His account of the tests differs in important respects from the official reports cited above. *Journal of the Royal United Service Institution*, v, p. 129.

The writer has found no trace of Belmano or Delmeno in the Navy Department archives.

1843, that the plans generally consisted of "various modifications of shields of iron, combined with springs, caoutchouc, horse hair, or other elastic substances." In one case the inventor estimated the weight of the armor at about twenty-six tons, in another case more than 101 tons. The Surveyor believed that "whatever protection might be found, on experiment, to be given by any of these Plans, the apparatus would occupy so much space, and involve so enormous an increase of weight, as to render the adoption of them entirely out of the question in H. M.'s Steam Vessels."[1] Although the flood of proposals for shot-proof ships steadily mounted,[2] the remaining experiments of the British Navy in firing against iron plates in the forties were not designed to ascertain the possibilities of armor, but to test the suitability of unarmored iron vessels for war purposes. The revulsion of feeling against these unarmored iron ships after 1846 brought with it an increased prejudice against all proposals for the adoption of armor.[3]

Experiments in firing against iron armor intended for use in fortifications were conducted at Waalsdorp in Holland in 1843, at Turin by Cavalli in 1845, at Woolwich between 1846 and 1850, at West Point by General Totten in the years 1853 to 1855, and by Brialmont and others in Belgium in the fifties.[4] With a view to cuirassing their warships on the Danube the Austrians, in the summer of 1855, fired 6- and 18-pounder field pieces against both vertical and inclined targets faced with iron.[5] The most interesting experiments

[1] Submission Letter Book no. 11. For the proposals, see Adm. 12/358: 59–4; Adm. 12/385: 59–4; Adm. 12/398: 59–4; Adm. 12/402: 97a1.
[2] Adm. 12/413: 59–1; Adm. 12/417: 97a1; Adm. 12/432: 97a1; Adm. 12/445: 59–1 and 59–4a; Adm. 12/461: 59–1, 59–8, and 59–9; Adm. 12/493: 59–1 and 59–4a; Adm. 12/497: 97a1; Adm. 12/525: 59–4a; Adm. 12/557: 59–1; Submission Letter Books no. 12, May 29, November 6, 1846, September 17, 1847; no. 14, October 12, 1849.
[3] See above, pp. 36–40.
[4] Aïcha, *Panzerungen*, pp. 8–11; Brialmont, *Etudes sur la défense des états*, ii, pp. 77–92; Douglas, *Naval Gunnery*, pp. 408–417; Alexander L. Holley, *A Treatise on Ordnance and Armor* (New York, 1865), pp. 624–625, 626–628; Joseph G. Totten, *Report . . . on the Effects of Firing with Heavy Ordnance from Casemate Embrasures: and also the Effects of Firing against the same Embrasures . . .* (Washington, 1857).
[5] Aïcha, *Panzerungen*, p. 9.

of this period, however, were those conducted by the French at Gavres between 1843 and 1845.

These resulted from the proposals of a brilliant young naval officer, Nicolas-Hippolyte Labrousse, who in 1840 submitted to the Minister of Marine the first of his long series of proposals for ironclad rams.[1] Although the *Conseil des Travaux* threw cold water on the project, the *Conseil d'Amirauté*, composed of some of the senior officers of the service, recommended that tests be made at Lorient to simulate ramming, by sliding a chest weighing fifty to sixty tons, armed with a ram, down an inclined plane to strike targets of wood, of iron, and of wood plated with iron.[2] On February 27, 1843, the minister ordered the desired tests, as well as experiments with gunfire against coal bunkers and targets representing sections of a steamer's side. On October 19 following, a series of questions was submitted to special commissions to be formed in each of the five principal ports. Among them were the merits of Labrousse's ram project, the problem whether some types of steamers should be built of iron instead of wood, and the question whether some of them should be protected by armor in their most vulnerable parts. The *Commission supérieure centrale des bâtiments à vapeur*, composed of officers of all branches of the service headed by the minister, Vice Admiral Baron Mackau, Vice Admiral Baron Hugon, and the Prince de Joinville, was created on October 22 to examine the replies to this questionnaire, together with the report of the Gavres Commission as to the tests at Lorient.[3]

---

1 [Nicolas-Hippolyte Labrousse], *Notice sur les travaux scientifiques et les services du contre-amiral Labrousse* (Paris, 1866), pp. 5–6, 63–64. See above, pp. 42, 44, and Appendix B.
2 A.M., BB⁸ 1116, June 16, 1842; BB⁸ 1122, June 21, 1848; A.N., BB⁸ 872, Nov. 4, 1842.
3 A.M., BB⁸ 1117, June 1, 1843; *Annales maritimes et coloniales*, lxxx, pp. 1045–1050, 1092. Before the results of these projected tests were known a small commission headed by the Prince de Joinville urged that steamers confine themselves to end-on fighting, and that their engines and boilers be protected by transverse coal bunkers 1.5 meters thick. They doubted the practicability of weighting a ship with iron side armor, and argued that if the armor were confined to the bow and stern the motive power would be exposed to fire at certain angles. *Ibid.*, lxxv (1844), pp. 5–32. Captain Verninac Saint-Maur, a member of the *commission*

In the long series of experiments on the beach at Gavres, near Lorient, the targets were generally larger, heavier, and more firmly planted than those used in England. The ordinary French target, to which iron plates were screwed, was of solid oak, six meters high by twelve meters broad, formed of heavy posts bolted together, set down into the sand, and firmly buttressed. The firing tests which began July 27, 1843, showed that no ordinary coal bunkers could give adequate protection. Solid shot fired from a long 30-pounder with five kilograms of powder at 10 meters range penetrated 3.43 meters of coal. Similar shot pierced 59 cm. of oak plus 2.79 meters of coal, as well as 59 cm. of oak, plus 11 mm. sheet iron, plus 2.83 meters of coal. When 27 cm. shells with a bursting charge of 3.2 kilograms were fired at an oak wall 59 cm. thick, backed by two meters of coal plus a bulkhead of 12 mm. sheet iron, the projectiles or their fragments never reached the sheet iron, but were found in the coal at a depth of never more than 1.4 meters. Shells generally exploded while passing through the outer wall of oak.[1]

Conclusions adverse to iron shipbuilding were drawn from experiments made in February, 1844, with 30-pounder solid shot fired obliquely with charges of 2½ kilograms against 12 mm. sheet iron fastened by vertical angle-irons against a wall of oak. The shot broke all the angle-irons which they struck and produced in the plates rents varying from 40 to 90 cm. in length and 8 to 16 cm. in breadth. Even when they struck the iron at an angle of only five degrees, the rent was 40 cm. long. When an angle-iron was struck the rivets fastening it to the plates were often broken or torn out for the space of a meter, producing a hole that would have caused a serious

supérieure centrale des bâtiments à vapeur, declared that neither armor nor coal bunkers could protect the engines of steamers satisfactorily. *Ibid.*, pp. 227–228. In February, 1845, this commission was reorganized and divided into two sub-commissions, the first of which was headed by the Prince de Joinville. *Ibid.*, lxxxix, p. 151. Cf. Joinville, *Vieux Souvenirs, 1818–1848* (15th edition, Paris, 1894), pp. 362–365.

[1] Reports of the Gavres Commission, December 16, 1843, and November 4, 1845, *Mémorial de l'artillerie de la marine*, 1st series, iii (1864), pp. 265–286, 368–369; Hélie, *Balistique expérimentale*, i, pp. 193–195; ii, pp. 378–379.

leak below the water line. The fragments of iron thrown off from the target resembled the deadly grapeshot.[1]

Further experiments prescribed by an order of January 26, 1844, indicated the worthlessness of an inner bulkhead of sheet iron, as well as of 10 cm. of oak planking backed by 12 mm. of iron as a covering for ordinary ships' sides. On the other hand, several important tests pointed the way to better protection. The commission noted that 12 mm. sheet iron sufficed to break up all shells save those fired with reduced charges. Moreover, nine sheets of 12 mm. iron broke up a solid 30-pounder shot moving at 378 meters per second, though the fragments passed through the target; while twelve similar sheets broke up a similar shot at 450 meters velocity, stopping all the fragments.[2]

At the request of the Prince de Joinville, a new series of tests of nine targets of oak, of iron, and of different combinations of oak and coal, of iron and coal, and of oak, iron and coal, began at Gavres in August, 1844. By using 30-pounder solid shot striking the targets at only 10 meters range with a velocity of 450 meters per second, the commission gave to the guns an advantage which it frankly admitted would be extremely rare in actual warfare. Armor which proved inadequate under these drastic tests, the commission observed, might well be impenetrable under ordinary battle conditions. A thickness of 1.8 meters of solid oak, or three times the thickness of the sides of a steam frigate of 540 horse power, was required to stop the shot. The 30-pounder shot always broke up when it struck armor made up of eight, ten, or twelve layers of 12 mm. sheet iron. The fragments traversed eight layers, and some of them pierced ten, but none passed through armor of twelve layers. Even that maximum protection, however, was so badly damaged by the test as to afford no security. Per square meter of surface, this target of twelve sheets of iron weighed 1120 kilograms, as compared with about 1800 for the minimum impenetrable wall

---

[1] Report of the Gavres Commission, April 29, 1844, *Mémorial de l'artillerie de la marine*, 1st series, iii, (1864), pp. 301-308, 371-372.
[2] *Ibid.*, pp. 294-301, 310-312, 316-317.

of oak, and with even heavier weights for such of the combination targets as resisted shot.[1]

At this stage of the problem, the man who was destined to solve it for seagoing ships submitted his first ironclad project. Representing as it does the first phase in the evolution of the seagoing ironclad in the mind of its creator, Dupuy de Lôme's proposal dated February 20, 1845, is of the highest interest. To render steam warships superior to sailers, he argued, we must reduce sails to the auxiliary rôle and install machinery of great power. Since engines of this force cannot be placed far enough below water to be out of the way of plunging shot, protection is indispensable. The minimum impenetrable thickness of oak, 1.8 meters, would render the hull far too heavy. In a steamer 68 meters long, and of 2400 tons displacement, however, the weight saved by constructing the hull of iron instead of wood might be used for a belt of laminated iron armor 166 mm. thick and 2.4 meters wide extending around the water line. This reinforcement of the 11 mm. skin of the ship would give far more than the necessary protection. By reducing the thickness of the armor to the minimum required, we might extend the armor to protect part or all of the gun deck. Fast steamers of this type mounting a few heavy guns behind shot-proof bulwarks could overcome any type of wooden ship and force any passage however well defended by land batteries.

He therefore submitted plans and specifications for a steamer of 28 guns and 600 horse power fitted with Smith's screw and designed for eleven knots speed with a mean draft of 5.5 meters and an immersed midship section of 53.234 square meters. Her displacement would be 2366 tons, length 68.3 meters, beam 13 meters, depth 6.54 meters, and height of battery amidships 2 meters. Six layers of 15 mm. sheet iron, not merely placed one upon the other as in the tests at Gavres, but solidly riveted together and backed by angle-irons, would girdle the ship from 1.50 meters below to .90 meters above the water line, rising to the beam line of the

[1] Report of November 21, 1844, *ibid.*, pp. 336–368; Dislère, *Marine cuirassée*, p. 7.

upper deck for the space of 40 meters amidships. Athwartship coal bunkers fore and aft of the engine room would afford some additional protection. He estimated the cost of the hull at 1,068,000 francs, or 1110 francs per ton; and requested tests of 9 cm. armor at Toulon.[1]

On May 12 Dupuy de Lôme submitted a program for experiments with direct and oblique fire at 80 meters range against two targets 104 mm. and 96 mm. thick, each formed of eight layers of sheet iron. Baron Mackau, who had been inclined at first to order armor tests at Toulon, refused his consent on June 9, on the advice of de Coisy, the inspector general of naval artillery. The latter had pointed out that fragments of solid shot had traversed ten sheets of 12 mm. iron at Gavres.[2] Nevertheless Mackau on July 3 directed the Gavres Commission to experiment with oblique fire against targets composed of varying numbers of 10 mm. plates with and without intervals between the layers. These tests, carried out in September and October, showed that the intervals between the plates were a disadvantage. The results, at 10 meters range, were unfavorable to laminated armor. Even when the projectile was stopped by the layers of iron, it damaged the armor beyond repair, indicating that such protection would be promptly destroyed by solid shot.[3] Commenting on these results, the *Conseil des Travaux* declared

---

[1] A.M., 6DD¹ 2, dossier 24; Dislère, *Marine cuirassée*, pp. 8–9. The ship was to carry 600 tons of coal for fourteen days steaming, and provisions for two months for 400 men.
  Since the completion of the writer's researches in the Archives de la Marine, M. Olivier Guihéneuc has published the text of Dupuy de Lôme's project of February 20, 1845, with a brief summary of the correspondence concerning it, in an interesting article, "Les origines du premier cuirassé de haute mer à vapeur, Le plan de Dupuy de Lôme en 1845," in *La revue maritime*, April, 1928, pp. 459–482. He points out inaccuracies in the treatment of this project by Xavier Raymond in *Les marines de France et d'Angleterre*, pp. 136–139, and by the Prince de Joinville in *Vieux souvenirs*, pp. 418–420, but he commits the grave error of describing the plan of 1845, which he reproduces, as the "Plan d'ensemble de la *Gloire*." The latter vessel was not a "belt-and-battery" ship like that projected in 1845, for her armor belt extended from stem to stern as a protection for the gun deck as well as the water line. See the plans of the *Gloire* in Admiral Pâris, *Souvenirs de marine*, iv, nos. 182–186.

[2] A.M., 6DD¹ 2, dossier 24.

[3] Report of October 31, 1845, *Mémorial de l'artillerie de la marine*, 1st series, iii, (1864), pp. 355–363.

that the inclined targets which had been tested presented no advantage for protecting steamers from gunfire.[1]

Provision for two floating batteries with hulls of wood and iron was made in the ordinance of September 23, 1845.[2] The naval committee of the Chamber of Deputies, in their report of April 1, 1846, observed that in the tests at Gavres sheet iron was terribly damaged by shot, even when struck at very sharp angles of incidence. They concluded that, for the present, it must be assumed that iron was unsuited for the construction of warships, unless some special system of armor protection such as that proposed by Dupuy de Lôme should prove satisfactory. At their suggestion, however, the great naval program of 1846 included an appropriation for the two floating batteries, which the committee conceived as purely defensive vessels, propelled by engines of 400 horse power, incombustible and unsinkable, if that were possible, but in any event heavily armed and protected by bulwarks hard to penetrate.[3] In submitting the amended bill to the Chamber of Peers, Baron Mackau remarked that each of the floating batteries would carry 40 to 50 guns, and would cost 1,150,000 francs. He promised that the forms and dimensions of their hulls would be worked out without delay.[4]

On December 9, 1846, Mackau ordered the preparation in the ports of plans for screw floating batteries for coast defence able to steam at a speed of six knots. They must draw not more than five meters of water, must carry a more powerful armament than any sailing frigate or seagoing steamer, and must resist shot better than an ordinary ship of the line. Of the proposals submitted in response to this order, that of *sous-ingénieur* Gervaize was the most important. He recommended a vessel 70 meters long and 13.5 meters beam, built wholly of iron, with engines of 580 horse power, a maximum draft of 4.66 meters, thirty guns, at least eleven knots speed, and sufficient strength for use as a ram. Laminated armor

---

[1] A.M., BB⁸ 1118, December 27, 1845.
[2] *Annales maritimes et coloniales*, lxxxix, pp. 882, 897.
[3] *Procès-verbaux des séances de la Chambre des Députés*, 1846, iv, appendix, pp. 179, 190–191.
[4] *Moniteur*, April 28, 1846, pp. 1135–1136; *Annales maritimes et coloniales*, xcvi, pp. 9–10, 71–73. Cf. *ibid.*, xciv, p. 914.

154 mm. thick composed of 20-mm. plates divided in three groups each separated by Z-shaped frames, extended from 1.5 meters below the water line to the beam line of the gun deck, while similar armor 97 mm. thick protected the battery. At the same time *sous-ingénieur* de Gasté proposed a wooden floating battery of 50 guns, 586 horse power and 9½ knots speed, 60 meters long, 16.8 meters beam, a draft of 4.95 meters, and wooden walls protected by bands of iron 25 mm. thick spaced 5 cm. apart.[1]

The *Conseil des Travaux* declined to recommend either of these projects; but asked for new experiments at Gavres to ascertain whether shot striking the laminated armor proposed by Gervaize at an oblique angle would, as they feared, tear it to pieces. Their opinion, they took pains to point out, did not imply the rejection of the idea of iron armor, but simply a delay for the purpose of further experiments. At their suggestion the minister added to the program for the floating batteries the following conditions. They must carry 60 guns mounted in two covered batteries, have rounded extremities and a bottom designed to permit running aground without injury, and a protection of bands of iron 2 to 3 cm. thick. Though equipped with an engine of 400 to 450 horse power, they were to fight only when stationary.[2]

Before these tests could be held, however, the *Conseil des Travaux* decided to abandon all ideas of ironclad construction. On November 17, 1847, it reported that during the interval which had elapsed since the first proposal for armor tests the idea of using iron as a material for warships had met with less and less favor, owing to numerous facts noted in France as well as in England pointing to the lack of durability and propensity to fouling of iron hulls. Instead of being adopted for a certain class of warships, iron hulls now

---

[1] A.M., 6 DD¹ 2, dossier 44; 6 DD¹ 38, dossier 834; Dislère, *Marine cuirassée*, p. 10. On June 19, 1847, the minister directed the *Conseil des Travaux* to hold two sessions weekly instead of one, if needed to complete the report on these two projects, since the floating batteries must be laid down during the year 1847. A.M., DD¹ 127, no. 48.

[2] A.M., BB⁸ 1120, June 23, 1847; 6 DD¹ 38, dossier 835, program as modified July 12, 1847. See also BB⁸ 1121, July 28, 1847, regarding delays in the experiments at Gavres, which it was hoped to undertake as soon as possible.

seemed likely to prove of very restricted use, and perhaps would be entirely abandoned.[1]

Thus French official opinion, like the English, had swung from partiality to iron construction to prejudice against it. This prejudice comes out clearly in much of the naval literature of the day, and in the testimony given during the official investigation of the navy in 1850.[2] Together with the drastic economy forced by the financial stringency following the Revolution of 1848, it doomed all projects for costly experiments and shipbuilding novelties, including the ram project of Labrousse.[3]

Between 1846 and 1854 nine French inventors submitted projects of armored ships to the Ministry of Marine. Most of them were vague, and apparently the work of persons unfamiliar with the navy and with shipbuilding. Not one of them had any influence on the evolution of the armored ship, though two of the inventors, a Parisian engineer named Aubert and Frédéric Billot, a lawyer of Arles, both claimed the French ironclads of 1854 as their invention. These projects show, however, that some men outside the naval service realized the existence of the problem of protecting ships against the new ordnance. When this problem became acute, at the outbreak of war in 1854, the impulse for its solution was to come from the Emperor himself.[4]

---

[1] A.M., BB⁸ 1121. Thus the *Conseil des Travaux* did not approve the project of a partially armored floating battery submitted by Pierre-Felix Le Grix, the director of naval construction at Lorient, submitted on October 7, 1847, and March 9, 1848. A.M., 6 DD¹ 38, dossier 835; BB⁸ 1122, March 29, 1848.

[2] *Assemblée Nationale, Enquête parlementaire sur la situation et l'organisation des services de la marine militaire ordonnée par la loi du 31 octobre 1849* (Paris, 1851, 2 vols.), ii, pp. 53, 84, 143, 184–185, 233; Du Bourg, *Les Principes et l'organisation de la marine de guerre* (Paris, 1849), p. 313, cited in Douglas, *Naval Gunnery*, p. 121, note; speech of Vice Admiral Grivel in Chamber of Peers, July 17, 1845; report of Captain Count E. Bouët-Willaumez, April 24, 1847, published in *Annales maritimes et coloniales*, c (1847), pp. 715–716; E. de Moras, "Quelques documents sur le matériel flottant des marines française et anglaise," *Nouvelles annales de la marine et des colonies*, ii (1849), pp. 363–396; J. Cros, "Considérations sur le matériel de notre flotte: amélioration à introduire dans le régime de nos arsenaux," *ibid.*, iv (1850), pp. 25–45, 77–130.

[3] See Appendix B.

[4] See below, p. 70; A.M., BB⁸ 1119, October 28, 1846; BB⁸ 1121, October 27, 1847; BB⁸ 1126, January 5, 1850; BB⁸ 1130, May 19, 1852; DD¹ 196, August 8 and 26, and October 13, 1853; BB⁸ 1134, April 29, 1854; A.N., GG¹ 76, dossier 69; Billot, *Les hippiscaphes* (Paris, 1855).

Meanwhile the development of the French steam navy in the forties roused in England an alarm which outlived both the July Monarchy and the Second Republic. Already the introduction of heavy shell guns in the navies of France and the United States in the thirties had forced on the British Navy a transformation of armament.[1] Now, by rendering warships less dependent on winds and tides, steam seemed to have bridged the Channel. British advocates of preparedness raised the specter of invasion, and clamored for naval increases, harbors of refuge, costly fortifications, a larger army, and a reorganized militia. The suspicions engendered by this armament race mounted, like a series of waves, until France and Great Britain found themselves at war, not with each other, but with a common enemy.

During the Eastern crisis of 1839 to 1841 the increased strength of the French Navy provoked sharp comment across the Channel. Although Palmerston professed confidence in the ability of the British fleet to control the seas if France began hostilities, other members of the Cabinet feared defeat in the early stages of a naval war, and Palmerston himself showered on the French government questions and complaints concerning their augmented naval forces. Melbourne, indeed, is said to have intimated to Louis-Philippe, by means of a letter written to King Leopold of Belgium, that if France persisted in her hostile armaments England would sweep them from the seas.[2]

Despite the *entente cordiale* established by Aberdeen, Peel, and Guizot, the progress of the French steam navy caused apprehensions across the Channel. In the summer of 1844, when the Pritchard affair in Tahiti and the French attack on Morocco brought France and Great Britain to the brink of war, British readers devoured several editions of an indis-

---
[1] See above, p. 26.
[2] Lord Dalling and E. Ashley, *Life of Viscount Palmerston* (3rd ed., London, 1871–1874, 3 vols.), ii, pp. 306–309, 327–329; Vicomte de Guichen, *La crise d'orient de 1839 à 1841 et l'Europe* (Paris, 1921), pp. 179, 200, 273, 354, 397, 445; Sir Herbert Maxwell, *Life of Clarendon* (London, 1913, 2 vols.), i, pp. 199, 215, 218; L. C. Sanders, ed., *Lord Melbourne's Papers* (London, 1889), pp. 464–469, 487; *A Portion of the Journal kept by Thomas Raikes* (2d ed., London, 1856–1858, 4 vols.), iv, pp. 109–112.

creet pamphlet recently published by the son whom Louis-Philippe now honored with the command of the French naval expedition to Tangier and Mogador. In this "Note sur l'état des forces navales de la France," the Prince de Joinville argued that steam had lessened the handicap from which the French Navy had hitherto suffered on account of her smaller seafaring population. Although the French steam navy was still sadly inferior to the British, its development would permit a naval war "of most daring aggression." While one French fleet won mastery in the Mediterranean, skilful cruisers would harry Britain's far-flung commerce, and another force, crossing the Channel by night, might inflict on the enemy coasts unparalleled losses and suffering.[1]

When Palmerston, in the van of the alarmists, told the House of Commons that the Channel was no longer a barrier but simply "a river passable by a steam bridge," Peel retorted that two nations could play at that game, and pointed to England's great superiority in both merchant and war steamers. Privately, however, the Prime Minister expressed alarm at the state of British defences, and showed such zeal for greater naval and military expenditures that Aberdeen once submitted his resignation in protest. When the *entente cordiale* evaporated in the heat produced by the Spanish marriages, and the French Chambers passed the great naval program of 1846, providing ninety-three million francs for new construction, there developed an invasion scare little short of a panic.[2]

When the Whigs returned to power in 1846 Palmerston declared to his colleagues that France could throw twenty to

---

[1] Guizot, *Mémoires pour servir à l'Histoire de mon temps* (Paris, 1872, 8 vols.), vii, chs. xl, xli; Major John Hall, *England and the Orleans Monarchy* (London, 1912), pp. 351-368; Paul Thureau-Dangin, *Histoire de la monarchie de juillet* (Paris, 1884-1892, 7 vols.), v, ch. vi. Joinville's pamphlet, which first appeared in the *Revue des Deux Mondes*, May 15, 1844, ran through several French and English editions.

[2] Hansard, *Parliamentary Debates*, 3rd series, lxxxii, cols. 1223-1233; Richard Cobden, *The Three Panics* (6th ed., London, 1862), pp. 1-14; C. S. Parker, *Life and Letters of Sir James Graham* (London, 1907, 2 vols.), ii, pp. 17, 154; C. S. Parker, *Sir Robert Peel* (London, 1891-1899, 3 vols.), iii, pp. 196-218, 395-412; Thureau-Dangin, *Monarchie de juillet*, vi, pp. 195-196.

thirty thousand men across the Channel in steamers in a single night. While the Cabinet discussed the erection of new coast defences and the reconstitution of the militia, the public was suddenly aroused by the publication early in 1848 of a letter written nearly a year before by the Duke of Wellington to Sir John Burgoyne, Inspector-General of Fortifications. Deploring his inability to spur the government to adequate efforts the Duke asserted that the development of steam navigation had exposed all parts of the British coasts to invasion and insult, and that from Dover to Portsmouth there was not a spot on the coast, save immediately under the fire of Dover Castle, "on which infantry might not be thrown on shore at any time of tide, with any wind, and in any weather."[1]

The brief panic produced by this letter was promptly stilled by Russell's proposal of an increase of fivepence in the income tax in a year of financial distress, and by the fall of Louis-Philippe. The British naval and military estimates declined to the lowest point since 1841. As the French naval appropriations were likewise curtailed, and the new Prince-President gave assurances of peaceful intentions, the outcries of British alarmists fell on deaf ears.[2] In January, 1849, the French Government offered to make "almost any reduction" in naval armaments the British might suggest, provided the British did so "upon somewhat the same relative scale." Palmerston replied that the British Government had already determined on a considerable reduction, but that Great Britain could never fix the amount of her Navy with reference to the force maintained by any single Power.[3] After

---

[1] Dalling, *Palmerston*, iii, ch. x; G. P. Gooch, *Later Correspondence of Lord John Russell* (London, 1925, 2 vols.), i, ch. ix; Maxwell, *Clarendon*, i, p. 287; Spencer Walpole, *Life of Lord John Russell* (2d ed., London, 1889, 2 vols.), ii, pp. 13–30; Lieut. Col. George Wrottesley, *Life and Correspondence of Field Marshal Sir John Burgoyne* (London, 1873, 2 vols.), i, pp. 427–428, 434–451, 467–482. Cf. Lord Dundonald and H. R. Fox Bourne, *Life of Thomas, Lord Cochrane, Tenth Earl of Dundonald* (London, 1869, 2 vols.), ii, pp. 260–262.

[2] E. B. de Fonblanque, *Life and Labours of Albany Fonblanque* (London, 1874), p. 57; Evelyn Ashley, *Life of Viscount Palmerston* (London, 1876, 2 vols.), i, pp. 250–253; Sir Francis Head, *The Defenceless State of Great Britain* (2d ed., London, 1850); Wrottesley, *Burgoyne*, i, pp. 486–491; P.R.O., Adm. 12/509: 52–5.

[3] Normanby to Palmerston, January 17, F. O. 27/840; Palmerston to Normanby, January 25, no. 47, F. O. 27/834.

Louis-Napoleon's *coup d'état* of December 2, 1851, however, the British scaremongers carried all before them. Amid a flood of sensational pamphlets and speeches which swept the country into a major panic, Palmerston carried an amendment strengthening Lord John Russell's proposed militia bill, and caused the fall of the Whig Prime Minister who had lately dismissed him. On April 23 he assured the House of Commons that fifty or sixty thousand French troops "might be collected at Cherbourg before you knew anything of the matter," and transported to British soil in a single night. "All our naval preparations, be they what they might, could not be relied on to prevent the arrival of such an expedition." With a better grasp of the power of the fleet to defend the coasts, the Admiralty hastened preparations to ward off a surprise attack. The proclamation of the Empire in France roused memories of an earlier invasion scare, and produced "an Electric effect upon the whole Country." As late as February 12, 1853, *Punch* published a cartoon of an ass with its tail turned to a row of French guns, and braying "No Danger." This was "very disrespectfully dedicated to the Peace Society." Yet in little more than a year the French and British fleets were fighting side by side in the defence of Turkey. This new-found comradeship, however, could not still mutual suspicions for long. In the course of the joint operations against Russia was born a new type of warship, carrying within its armored sides the germs of a still fiercer and costlier rivalry.[1]

---

[1] Hansard, cxx, col. 1104; P.R.O., Adm. 12/557: 52–5; Mabell, Countess of Airlie, *Lady Palmerston and Her Times* (London, 1922, 2 vols.), ii, p. 149. See also A. C. Benson and Viscount Esher, eds., *Letters of Queen Victoria* (1st series, London, 1907, 3 vols.), iii, pp. 452, 481, 482; Gooch, *Russell Correspondence*, ii, pp. 89, 91; Vicomte de Guichen, *Les grandes questions européenes et la diplomatie des puissances sous la Seconde République française* (Paris, 1925-1929, 2 vols.), ii, pp. 430, 438, 448; Reginald Lucas, *Lord Glenesk and the "Morning Post"* (London, 1910), pp. 137, 138; Earl of Malmesbury, *Memoirs of an Ex-Minister* (2d ed., London, 1884, 2 vols.), i, pp. 354, 356–357, 359–360, 362, 364; Sir Theodore Martin, *Life of the Prince Consort* (London, 1875–1880, 5 vols.), ii, pp. 433–445; Walpole, *Russell*, ii, pp. 176–177. Cobden's assertion in his *Three Panics*, pp. 15–39, that French naval preparations at this time were greatly exaggerated was borne out by Philip Taylor, the founder of the Forges et Chantiers de la Méditerranée. J. K. Laughton, ed., *Memoirs of Henry Reeve* (London, 1898, 2 vols.), i, p. 282.

CHAPTER V

THE CRIMEAN WAR

FOR more than three decades prior to the Crimean War the most progressive ordnance officers had predicted the disastrous effect of shell-fire against wooden ships. They pointed to the results of several experiments in firing shells against wooden targets, and to successful instances of the use of shells in minor wars.[1] After experimental shell practice in 1838 against the three-decker *Prince George*, at 1200 yards range, the commander of the British gunnery ship *Excellent* reported that it was clear that shells would be much more destructive to wooden hulls than the same number of solid shot, since those which hit but did not explode produced effects equal to those of solid shot, while those which exploded after passing through the side did the work not merely of solid shot but of grape and canister as well, and at the same time caused great inconvenience to the enemy by smoke, and threatened to set his ship on fire. Shells which exploded in the wooden sides, moreover, "would produce large and irregular fractures which it would be very difficult to stop up," so that the enemy must send his crew to their pumps, since "mere plugging could not stop such holes."[2]

Although shells from coast batteries at Eckernförde in April, 1849, destroyed the Danish line-of-battle ship *Christian VIII*, and a frigate,[3] the first great demonstration to open the eyes of the public to the deadliness of the new projectiles was the annihilation of the Turkish fleet at Sinope, November 30, 1853. According to the testimony of the Austrian consul at Sinope, reported a few days later by the com-

---

[1] See above, pp. 17, 20, 23, 25, 26, 29. Cf. Thiroux, *Réflexions et études sur les bouches à feu de siège, de place et de côte* (Paris, 1849), p. 133.
[2] *Experiments in H. M. Ship "Excellent,"* . . . *from 1832 to 1854*, pp. 12-15.
[3] Hovgaard, *Modern History of Warships*, p. 7; C.-F. Allen, *Histoire de Danemark*, (tr. by E. Beauvois, Copenhagen, 1878, 2 vols.), ii, pp. 335-336. See the lithograph reproduced in Bowen, *The Sea*, iv, p. 63.

mander of the French frigate *Mogador*, a Turkish force composed of seven frigates, three corvettes, and two steamers was lying at anchor in some disorder, when a Russian squadron of six ships of the line, two sailing frigates, and two steamers entered the harbor about noon. At half past one a sharp action commenced. Although the Turkish vessels fought bravely, they were overpowered by the heavy guns of their enemy, and within two hours they were completely destroyed, save for one steamer which made its escape.[1]

After this crushing disaster to the Turkish arms, General Paixhans found a ready hearing for his observations on the effectiveness of the Russian shell guns and the vulnerability of large wooden ships.[2] Napoleon III, convinced that the Russian fleets would avoid an action at sea and take refuge under the guns of their fortifications, hesitated to risk his wooden ships of the line against coast batteries of Paixhans guns. Believing that ordinary bomb vessels would fail to reduce the Baltic forts, he called for plans of light-draft floating batteries, carrying a few heavy guns, and armored sufficiently to protect them against shell-fire. These craft he thought might cross the shoals under fire, outflank the outer forts covering Cronstadt, and attack them from their weak side. Garnier, the inspector general of naval construction, Guieysse, a naval constructor, and Commander Favé, an artillery officer serving as the Emperor's aide-de-camp, set

[1] "Aussi, après deux heures de combat, leur destruction était-elle complète; mais pas une d'elles n'amena son pavillon, et, soit par le feu de l'ennemi, soit par l'incendie qu'allumèrent leurs propres équipages, les sept frégates turques, les trois corvettes et un des deux bâtiments à vapeur, avaient sauté, coulé, ou échoué à la côte quand la nuit vint couvrir de son ombre, cette scène de carnage et de destruction. Le second bâtiment à vapeur, parvint à s'échapper.... Il a fallu d'ailleurs que le tir des Russes ait été, ou peu soutenu ou peu exact, pour qu'ils aient mis tant de temps à réduire la flottille turque.... On cite entr'autres la frégate —— qui a résisté près de deux heures au feu de deux vaisseaux avant de faire explosion...." Report of the commander of the *Mogador*, December 8, 1853. A.N., BB⁴ 692. Cf. Vice Admiral Hamelin's report of December 10 in A.N., BB⁴ 690.

[2] See his "Observations sur l'incendie, dans la mer noire, des bâtiments turcs par la flotte russe," in the *Moniteur*, February 21, 1854. The third section of the *Conseil des Travaux*, however, refused to admit that the disaster at Sinope was due principally to the use of shell guns, and attributed it to the superior number of the Russian guns. A.M., BB⁸ 1134, June 3, 1854.

to work on this problem in the spring of 1854. The original idea suggested by the Emperor was to protect the vessels by chests filled with shot.[1]

On May 5 Garnier reported that, although the form of the battery would depend on the kind of armor which would finally be adopted, he and Guieysse had agreed that, with a length of 36 meters, 13.4 meters beam, and 2.5 meters draft, the vessel could support armor formed of shot-cases a foot thick ["pourrait avoir pour blindage un coffre à boulets de 0m.30."][2] Three days later he stated that the battery should have the shape of an ordinary vessel, with the scantling of a large corvette. To obtain light draft, however, and sufficient room for working the guns, the beam should be large; and to present as small a surface as possible to the enemy's fire, the length should be reduced as much as the requirements of navigability would permit. He proposed six ports on a side and an armament of eight guns, six of which should be worked on the side facing the enemy, and the others used to defend the opposite side or the bow and stern. This steam battery should be protected, from a certain distance below water to the upper deck, with armor composed of wood, iron plates, and shot, or in any other fashion indicated by firing tests which would be undertaken at Vincennes to find the combination which would give the requisite protection with the least weight. He estimated the displacement at about 950 tons, and the cost, even though the battery be built of the cheapest wood, at four hundred to five hundred thousand francs. Ships of this sort could not be completed before the weather closed the Baltic to navigation, but they might be made ready for the campaign of 1855.[3]

Although the original object was the creation of a shell-proof, not a shot-proof vessel, the tests now carried out warranted the hope that armor would prove invulnerable by

---

[1] The brief, impressionistic account of the origin of the French armored floating batteries which was published in the *Moniteur*, November 12, 1855, must be revised in the light of the unpublished correspondence for 1854 and 1855 in A.M. Cf. Favé, *Etudes sur le passé et l'avenir de l'artillerie*, vi, p. 296.
[2] A.M., 7 DD¹ 65.
[3] *Ibid.*, Garnier to Ducos, May 8, 1854.

more shot than were likely to strike the same spot in a prolonged action. These experiments were made at Vincennes, instead of at the naval proving ground at Gavres, to enable the Emperor to watch the testing of his theories.[1] In these tests a target composed of 12-mm. sheet iron backed by two layers of wood 172 mm. thick separated by 4-and 6-pounder solid shot, satisfactorily resisted 30-pounder shot and 22-centimeter shell at 300 meters range. But solid iron plates of 10 and 14 cm. thickness proved far superior both to this shot-case protection and to laminated iron armor. The importance of heavy wooden backing for the plates was clearly indicated.[2]

A target faced with iron plates ten cm. thick was penetrated to the wood backing only after having been hit fourteen times within one square meter by 30-pounder solid shot fired at 300 meters range with charges of ten pounds of powder. This result seemed wholly satisfactory.[3] In the tests of two plates, one of ten and one of fourteen cm. thickness, the first withstood nine and the second thirteen hits before they were split into irregular fragments, which were still held fast to the wooden backing by the armor bolts.[4]

On July 17 the French Minister of War informed Lord Cowley, the British Ambassador at Paris, that the problem of gun-proof vessels had been solved and that plans for a light-draft gunboat with sheet-iron armor would soon be sent by the French to the British government. Cowley concluded

---

[1] *Moniteur*, November 12, 1855.
[2] Dislère, *Marine cuirassée*, pp. 11, 171. Dislère gives the thickness of the plates on the French floating batteries of 1854–1855 as 110 mm. But the contemporary documents cited below fix the thickness at 10 cm.

Sir Charles Wood testified before the select committee on the Board of Admiralty, May 28, 1861, that "it is a curious thing that the iron-plates, which are supposed to be of French invention, were, in fact, suggested by our dockyard officers. They were sent over to inspect a scheme which the French had of having musket balls enclosed between two coats of iron as a protection against shot. Two of our dockyard officers were sent over in communication with the French Government to see what they were doing, and they suggested that it was far better to substitute a solid plate for the French design. . . ." *Parliamentary Papers*, 1861, v, no. 438, p. 338.

[3] A.M., 1 DD¹ 213, Ducos to Vice Admiral Parseval, commanding the Baltic fleet, August 11, 1854.
[4] A.M., 7 DD¹ 99, Garnier's note of January 25, 1855, for Cherbourg.

that, if this proved true, both Cronstadt and Sebastopol would fall.[1]

Late in July, Ducos, the Minister of Marine, ordered the construction of ten steam floating batteries, with iron armor ten centimeters in thickness over all their deadworks. In order to have them ready for sea in April, 1855, they were to be built as a rush job in the Government yards on the Atlantic with wood of inferior quality, since these vessels were for temporary use only. Ducos assigned two to Cherbourg, four to Brest, two to Lorient, and two to Rochefort. The batteries, whose length was 42.8 meters, beam 13.1 meters, and draft 2.36 meters, were each to carry twelve 30-pounder guns, nine of which could be fought on a side.[2]

Doubting the capacity of the French ironworks to complete sufficient armor plate for ten floating batteries before the opening of the 1855 campaign, the French Government hastened to suggest that its British ally undertake the construction of some of the ships of this new type.[3] While this negotiation was pending, the French Minister of Marine contracted for armor and for engines, and decided to build only five ironclads. On August 28, Ducos approved contracts with the two firms of Petin, Gaudet and Company of Rive de Gier, and Schneider and Company of Le Creusot, who were each to make the plates for one side of each of the floating batteries.[4] At the same time he ordered from Schneider and

---

[1] Colonel F. A. Wellesley, *The Paris Embassy during the Second Empire* (London, 1928), p. 55. Hereafter cited as Wellesley, *Cowley*.

[2] A.M., 1 DD¹ 209, Ducos to Lorient, July 29, 31, August 2, 1854; 1 DD¹ 211, Ducos to Cherbourg, Brest, Rochefort, August 17; 1 DD¹ 213, Ducos to Vice Admiral Parseval, August 11; 7 DD¹ 65, Ducos to Brest, July 31. To Lorient was assigned the task of laying off the detailed plans and making the patterns for the iron plates for all the vessels.

As outletters from the Minister of Marine to the principal ports were uniformly directed to the naval prefect, they are cited as "to Brest," etc., instead of "to Préfet Maritime, Brest."

[3] A.M., 1 DD¹ 213, Ducos to Vice Admiral Parseval, August 11, 1854; Ducos to Drouyn de Lhuys, Minister of Foreign Affairs, August 16; 1 DD¹ 211, Ducos to Cherbourg, Brest, Rochefort, August 17; 7 DD¹ 65, Drouyn de Lhuys to Ducos, August 15; Charles Baudin, French Chargé d'affaires at London, to Drouyn de Lhuys, August 23. Copy transmitted by Drouyn de Lhuys to Ducos, August 24.

[4] A.M., 1 DD¹ 208, No. 165, August 28, 1854.

Company five high-pressure engines of 150 horse power each, which it was hoped would give these screw steamers a speed of about six knots.[1] On September 1 Ducos fixed the number of ironclads to be built at five, of which two were to be constructed at Lorient, and one each at Cherbourg, Brest, and Rochefort. To permit the installation of sixteen 50-pounder guns, the plans were altered to add 10.05 meters amidships.[2]

On August 15 Drouyn de Lhuys had transmitted to Ducos a despatch from Charles Baudin, the French chargé d'affaires at London, stating that Sir James Graham, the First Lord of the Admiralty, would study the French plans for floating batteries as soon as the specifications were translated. He would then take the matter up with Sir Baldwin Walker, the Surveyor of the Navy, and would send him to Paris, if the French government wished, to confer with the French artillerists and naval constructors. If an agreement was reached as to the efficacy of the proposed system, the Admiralty would at once order the construction of its share of the program, as the French requested.[3] Eight days later Baudin reported that Sir Baldwin Walker, wishing to propose certain improvements which he thought would render the batteries stronger and less costly, would visit Paris about September 1 to discuss these changes with Ducos and to agree with the French minister on the details of the project, of which the Admiralty was ready to undertake half.[4]

Sir James Graham expressed to Baudin in an interview on September 16 his entire willingness to cooperate in building the floating batteries. In view of the considerable expense

---

[1] A.M., 7 DD¹ 65, contract with Schneider and Company, signed August 21, approved August 28, 1854.
[2] A.M., 1 DD¹ 211, Ducos to Lorient, Brest, Cherbourg, Rochefort, September 1 and 2, 1854.
[3] A.M., 7 DD¹ 65.
[4] *Ibid*. Prince Albert visited Napoleon III at Boulogne, September 4-8, 1854. Two days after his return he dictated to General Grey the following memorandum: "He [Louis-Napoleon] had likewise had experiments carried on as to the power of resistance of wrought-iron, which proved that, at a given angle, a small thickness, like two inches, would resist any shot — the shot splitting. He thought an application of this to floating batteries to be the way of taking Cronstadt without any loss. The project has been communicated to the English Admiralty for consideration." — Martin, *Prince Consort*, iii, p. 116.

involved, however, he thought it necessary to test the proposed armor in England. Seven or eight years earlier, he explained, another Board had ordered a rather large number of iron warships which later experience proved unsuitable for war. He did not wish to expose himself to the reproach of having hastily undertaken new construction of a similar nature. Hence, despite the favorable report of Sir Baldwin Walker, the satisfactory tests at Vincennes, and the extraordinary thickness of the armor proposed, he had ordered some large targets constructed at Portsmouth representing a section of the projected ironclads. If, as he expected, the experiments succeeded, the Admiralty would immediately order the construction of these armored vessels. Graham invited Ducos to send the inventors of the proposed system to attend the experiments at Portsmouth.[1]

The experiments made at Portsmouth on September 26 and 27, 1854, convinced the Admiralty of the merits of the French project. Seven plates, each 9 feet by 15 inches, and 4½ inches thick, of wrought iron made from the best scrap, were bolted to four inches of fir planking, attached to a substantial butt. Of ten 32-pounder solid shot which struck the target at 360 yards range, the greatest indentation caused by any one round was two inches. Two rounds which struck in nearly the same spot caused an indentation of 2¼ inches and slightly cracked the plate. "Four rounds struck one plate, cracked it through in four places, bulged it in 3½ inches, and sprung one of the diagonal braces directly in the rear." The wooden backing suffered no material injury. "All the shot that struck the plates broke up and fell back." Two 68-pounder solid cast-iron shot, at 1250 yards range, each cracked a plate right across, without materially injuring the

---

[1] A.M., 7 DD¹ 65, Baudin to Drouyn de Lhuys, September 16, 1854. Copy, confidential, transmitted to Ducos. The latter replied that he would send representatives to watch the experiments, which would not contradict the results obtained at Vincennes, but might perhaps show some facts of value. A.M., 1 DD¹ 213, Ducos to Drouyn de Lhuys, September 19. Garnier and Guieysse were sent to Portsmouth, with instructions to note any new facts relating to the quality of iron most suitable for the plates, and the best method of applying the armor. A.M., 1 DD¹ 212, Ducos to Garnier, September 22. Favé was to have attended the tests, but did not go. A.M., 7 DD¹ 65, Garnier to Ducos, September 26.

backing. Continued firing with 68-pounder shot at 400 yards range nearly destroyed the target.[1]

The British Admiralty thereupon agreed to construct five armored floating batteries on the French plan, provided that the French Navy would build ten mortar vessels, without steam power, to carry 13-inch mortars, and twenty steam gunboats, to match the same number of similar vessels projected by the British for service in the campaign of 1855.[2] The British would furnish plans for the ten French mortar vessels; and each government would remain free to select its own plans for the gunboats, provided they should have about the same draft, speed, and armament.[3] Applying to the Treasury for a supplemental credit for this new construction destined for the attack on Cronstadt and Sveaborg, Sir James Graham declared that "it may contribute powerful aid to the speedy and honourable conclusion of the War; and the means of attack, which we now provide, will at all times be most useful and available for the defence of our own Shores and Harbours . . ."[4] Gladstone readily agreed to the expendi-

---

[1] *Transactions and Report of the Special Committee on Iron between 21st January 1861, and March, 1862*, pp. x, 160. Garnier reported from Portsmouth, September 26 and 27, that Admiral Berkeley was satisfied with the tests and that Sir Baldwin Walker was impatient to receive the new plan which had been laid down at Lorient. A.M., 7 DD¹ 65.

Sir Thomas Maitland wrote to Captain Mends from Portsmouth on November 16 that the trials just made showed that iron plates 4½ inches thick "will resist *all shot* except the 68-pounder fired with 16-pound charge, and they must be within 400 yards; at 900 yards the 68-pound shot did not destroy the plates." B. S. Mends, *Life of Admiral Sir William Robert Mends* (London, 1899), p. 363.

[2] For this agreement see A.M., 1 DD¹ 212, Ducos to Garnier, September 30, 1854, describing an interview with Lord Cowley; and P.R.O., Adm. 1/5632, Admiralty Board minutes of September 29 and 30, 1854. Cf. A.M., 1 DD¹ 213, Ducos to Guieysse, October 10, 1854.

[3] A.M., 7 DD¹ 65, Garnier to Ducos, London, October 4, 1854.

[4] P.R.O., Adm. 1/5632, September 30, 1854. Sir Baldwin Walker's estimates of the expense, including the conversion to screw steamers of five small line-of-battle ships, were as follows:

	Hulls	Machinery	Totals
5 Floating batteries	£225,000	£41,250	£266,250
20 Gunboats	86,400	66,000	152,400
10 Mortar vessels	21,060	00,000	21,060
5 Line-of-battle ships	43,750	55,000	98,750
Total	£376,210	£162,250	£538,460

ture for these vessels, which Lord Cowley believed destined "to lay the whole northern coast of Russia smack and smooth next summer."[1]

When one considers the force of naval traditions perpetuating the memory of former conflicts, and the fact that the French and British fleets were potential rivals for the first rank at sea, the hearty cooperation of the allied navies during the Crimean War is noteworthy. Not only were plans for floating batteries, mortar vessels, and gunboats exchanged, but naval constructors of each power were permitted to inspect the methods of the other.[2] The French sought with success the plans of the famous British 68-pounder gun.[3] Napoleon III himself gave to Lord Cowley, for transmission to the Admiralty, a project he had devised for transforming wooden ships of the line into ironclads capable of attacking coast defenses. The British Ambassador deemed "particularly gratifying ... the readiness with which his Majesty imparts plans for rendering more efficient a branch of our service, of which France might, almost without causing surprise, retain feelings of jealousy and caution."[4]

---

[1] Philip Guedalla, ed., *Gladstone and Palmerston* (New York and London, 1928), p. 100; Wellesley, *Cowley*, p. 58.

[2] Sir Baldwin Walker visited France in the spring of 1854 to exchange ideas concerning gunboats; and the Chief Constructor, Isaac Watts, came over in the autumn to inspect the construction of the French ironclads. The French naval constructors Molle, Mangin, Garnier, Guieysse, Sabatier and Pastoureau, and the Captain of Naval Artillery Sapia, made tours of inspection in England in 1854 and 1855. A.M., 1 DD¹ 213, Ducos to the French Consul General at London, June 21, 1854; 1 DD¹ 211, circular to Brest, Cherbourg, Lorient and Rochefort, November 29, 1854, concerning Watts's visit; instructions to Molle and Mangin, June 20, 1854; 1 DD¹ 212, Ducos to the *Direction du Personnel*, December 1, 1854; 1 DD¹ 218, Hamelin, Minister of Marine, to Brest and Rochefort, August 13, 1855.

[3] A.M., 1 DD¹ 213, Ducos to Drouyn de Lhuys, November 20, 1854.

[4] P.R.O., Adm. 1/5633, Cowley to Clarendon, November 19, 1854, no. 1393, enclosing letter of Napoleon III to Cowley, of the same date, which enclosed a copy of the Emperor's note to Ducos of November 16. For the text of this note, see Appendix C.

Sir Baldwin Walker reported that the British block ships then being converted would be fitted in accordance with the Emperor's suggestions, except that their topsides would not be plated with wrought iron. The additional weight for armor, he argued, would increase their draft from 22 to nearly 25 feet, and would bring their lower deck ports within three feet of the water. The manufacture and application of the proposed iron armor, moreover, would require so much time that he doubted whether the ships could be got ready for service early in the spring. Adm. 1/5633.

So great were the difficulties encountered in the novel work of manufacturing the four-inch iron plates that the last instalments were not finished by Schneider and Company until May 8 nor by Petin, Gaudet and Company, until May 12, 1855.[1] Meanwhile, in consequence of a British decision to augment the heating surface with a view to increased speed, Ducos ordered two additional boilers for each floating battery.[2] In solving the many problems raised by the new type of construction, Garnier and Guieysse continued to play the leading rôles.[3] The latter, who had prepared the plans for the batteries, determined their internal arrangements and rig, in collaboration with Captain Dupré, recently assigned to the command of the *Tonnante*. In view of the limited displacement of the floating batteries, it seemed impossible to find space for all the objects necessary both for the outward passage and for combat. The vessels were therefore equipped with three temporary masts, to be landed on arrival at the theater of hostilities, when most of the munitions and part of the crew would be transferred from a transport.[4] There was never any question of these ironclads making a voyage alone: they were to be towed by steam frigates to the scene of hostilities, make their way to their post of combat under their own steam power, and then fight at anchor.[5]

The first of the five French floating batteries, the *Tonnante*, was launched at Brest on March 17, 1855, followed by the *Dévastation* at Cherbourg, April 17, the *Lave* at Lorient, May

[1] Slowness in transmitting patterns and specifications from the Government yards had occasioned some delay at the outset. In view of the extraordinary efforts of the manufacturers, and the novel character of the work, the Ministry of Marine imposed none of the penalties for delay which had been stipulated in the armor plate contracts. A.M., 1 DD¹ 215, decisions of January 22, February 3, March 3, April 10, May 7 and 18, September 5 and November 5, 1855.
[2] A.M., 1 DD¹ 214, Ducos to Schneider and Company, October 9 and 27, 1854; 1 DD¹ 213, Ducos to Guieysse, October 17; 1 DD¹ 208, decision of October 27; 7 DD¹ 65, supplementary contract with Schneider and Company, November 15.
[3] Ducos congratulated Garnier on having taken the largest part in the introduction of the new type. A.M., 1 DD¹ 212, December 11, 1854.
[4] A.M., 7 DD¹ 65, reports of December 2 and 29, 1854. A copy of the former is in A.N., BB⁴ 1038, in a folder dated 1856.
[5] A.M., 1 DD¹ 216, Hamelin to Cherbourg, June 26, 1855; 7 DD¹ 65, note from Garnier to the *Direction du Matériel*, November 15, 1855; Dupré's report of December 2, 1854; Rear Admiral Lavaud to Ducos, December 13, 1854.

26, the *Congrève* at Rochefort, June 1, and the *Foudroyante* at Lorient, June 2.[1] Of the British ironclads, which had been begun by private contractors a month or two later than the French, the *Meteor* and *Thunder* were launched by Messrs. Mare at Blackwall, April 17, and the *Glatton* and *Trusty* by Messrs. Richard and Henry Green at Blackwall on April 18 and May 3. A fire in Scott Russell's shipyard at Millwall destroyed the *Aetna* on the night of May 3.[2]

To the great disappointment of the French, the first trials of their floating batteries showed them to be excessively hot and ill-ventilated, hard to steer, and inferior in speed to the similar British ironclads. Despite the increase in boiler capacity, which it was hoped would give them 225 horse power in all, the French high-pressure engines proved disappointing. To remedy the defects, Guieysse hastened to England to inspect the ironclads there; and various propellers were tested in the French ports. After some experimenting, the French batteries were each fitted with three rudders and two leeboards.[3]

These ugly, flat-bottomed vessels with rounded bow and

---

[1] A.N., BB[5] 49, "Registre des mouvements par catégorie de bâtiments, 1855;" A.M., 7 DD[1] 101, *Tonnante*; 7 DD[1] 99, *Dévastation*; 7 DD[1] 96, *Lave*; 7 DD[1] 65, *Congrève*; and 7 DD[1] 107, *Foudroyante*.

[2] P.R.O., Submission Letter Book no. 17, October 4 and 9, 1854, and May 4, 1855. The dates of launching are given in *Parliamentary Papers*, 1876, xlv, no. 297.

[3] While the British tests showed a speed of 5.77, the *Tonnante* made only 3.2 knots. The *Lave* averaged 3.795 knots in her trials on June 7, 1855. A.M., 7 DD[1] 96; *devis d'armement* of the *Lave*; 1 DD[1] 216, Hamelin to Lorient, telegram, June 3; 1 DD[1] 218, circular to Cherbourg, Brest, Lorient and Rochefort, June 20; 1 DD[1] 220, Hamelin to Garnier, June 22; 1 DD[1] 217, Hamelin to Brest, June 8, and telegram, July 6; 7 DD[1] 65, Hamelin to De Chabannes, June, 1855; Rear Admiral de Chabannes, London, to Hamelin, June 2 and 6; Garnier to Dupuy de Lôme, June 8 and 9; Garnier to Hamelin, June 16, transmitting Guieysse's observations on the English floating batteries. Commenting on the fact that the sail area of the British batteries was only about 700 square meters, compared with 1100 for the French, Guieysse observed that: "Les Anglais d'ailleurs ne devant envoyer leurs batteries que dans la Baltique la question de la voilure a beaucoup moins d'importance pour eux, que pour nous qui avons de plus longues traversées à faire. . . . Leur embossage doit se faire avec de moyennes ancres de 800 à 1.000 kilos. La chaine de l'avant passera par un écubier debouchant sous l'eau comme l'avait proposé M. le directeur des constructions navales au port de Brest." Thus these batteries anticipated the *Monitor* in placing the hawse hole under water to protect the anchor chain from the enemy's fire. Wrought-iron gratings were designed to cover the hatches during an action.

stern were 51.05 meters long between perpendiculars, 13.14 meters wide, with a moulded depth of 2.63 meters, a mean draft of 2.54 meters, a displacement of 1575 tons, and a height of battery of 90 cm. They carried sixteen 50-pounder guns, and a crew of 280.[1] Wrought-iron armor four inches thick protected their topsides and extended 70 cm. below the water line.[2] In a table of values of the French fleet, drawn up in March, 1856, the cost of the five floating batteries is given as 6,580,000 francs.[3] The four English batteries, with wooden hulls and four-inch armor like the French, ranged from 1469 to 1538 tons, builder's measurement, with a length between perpendiculars of 172 feet 8 inches to 173 feet 6½ inches, and an extreme breadth of 43 feet 11 inches to 45 feet 2½ inches. To avoid increasing their mean draft above 8 feet 9 inches, their projected armament of 68-pounders of 95 hundredweight was reduced from sixteen guns to fourteen. The first cost of the British batteries averaged £58,528.[4] At least one of the French batteries had an improvised armored conning tower, which appeared to Admiral Lyons to be an indispensable advantage.[5]

[1] A.M., 7 DD¹ 99, *devis d'armement* of the *Dévastation*, 1855. The statistics for this vessel in the *Mémorial du génie maritime*, 1863, ii, p. 737, give the height of midship battery port as 1.005 meters, the sail area as 1055 square meters, and the displacement when fully equipped as 1668.681 tons. The variations from these figures in the *devis d'armement* of the four other French floating batteries are insignificant.
　　The sail plan of the *Dévastation* and a picture of the *Tonnante* are reproduced in the article by Commandants de Balincourt and Vincent-Bréchignac, "La Marine française d'hier, Les cuirassés. I. Batteries flottantes," in *La revue maritime*, May, 1930, pp. 577-595.
[2] A.M., 7 DD¹ 65, "procès verbal d'armement et des emmenagements de la batterie flottante *Congrève*," August 2, 1855.
[3] A.M., 1 DD¹ 235, "avant projet de Budget pour 1857," March 25, 1856.
[4] *Parliamentary Papers*, 1863, xxxvi, nos. 86 and 237; *ibid.*, 1876, xlv, no. 297; P.R.O., Submission Letter Book no. 17, May 15, 1855; A.M., 1 DD¹ 217, Minister of Marine to Brest, April 4, 1855; ships' books of *Aetna, Glatton, Meteor, Thunder, Trusty*, Admiralty Library. The builder's measurement of the *Trusty* was 1469 tons, her displacement 1672 tons. For the different ways of measuring tonnage see W. H. White, *Manual of Naval Architecture* (2d ed., London, 1882, 2 vols.), i, ch. ii.
[5] In his comparison of the French and British batteries, Sir Edmund Lyons wrote that "The last point of difference, the 'safe guard' (I do not know what else to call it), speaks for itself. It seems to me one of two things, either a safeguard or plurality of captains." Captain S. Eardley Wilmot, *Life of Lord Lyons* (London, 1898), p. 363. Cf. *Nouvelles annales de la marine*, April, 1860, p. 260. This article

By March, 1855, the exigencies of the Sebastopol campaign had made it clear that neither the French nor the British government "could well spare or transport to the Baltic troops enough to accomplish any important operation."[1] Palmerston therefore on April 9 explained to the Queen that the program for the Baltic campaign must be reduced to what could be done by ships alone. Although the allied naval forces would suffice "to coop up the whole Russian Fleet in its Ports during the season when the Baltic is navigable," it seemed unwise to risk them in attacks against Sveaborg and Cronstadt. Even if the walls of the former fortress were demolished and its batteries silenced, the place could not be held by the allies, and the two Russian ships of the line there would have been lightened and removed to interior waters beyond reach. Cronstadt had been so much strengthened by batteries commanding the approaches and by dams and submarine stockades obstructing the channels that an attack by ships of the line seemed foredoomed to failure.

It remains to be ascertained by local investigation whether an attack might not be made with better chance of success by the Gunboats and floating batteries now constructing, especially if they could be armed with some of the very large Cannon and Mortars which have been suggested by different Inventors, or it is possible that the Submarine vessel constructing by Sir James Fox may be available against the Fleet in Cronstadt. If a large army could have been sent to the Baltic and if the Swedish army could have been subsidized to co-operate with the allies Sweaborg and Helsingfors might have been taken, and even Petersburgh might have been threatened, but means are wanting for such an undertaking, because all available Land Forces are required for the Black Sea.[2]

---

states that at Kinburn the captain of the *Dévastation* "ayant jugé sa présence indispensable sur le pont, fit entourer le tronc du grand mât de sa batterie d'un manchon mobile en tôle. Cet écran, dont il eut lieu de reconnaître l'efficacité, donna à son pointage une précision et une certitude à laquelle il ne pouvait antérieurement prétendre." Both the French and the English batteries were equipped with gutta-percha speaking tubes.

1 *Windsor Mss.*, xxv, G. 26, Palmerston to Queen Victoria, March 18, 1855.
2 *Windsor Mss.*, xxvii, G. 28, Palmerston to Queen Victoria, April 9, 1855. Professor Herbert C. Bell has generously permitted the writer to quote his transcripts of this and the foregoing letter of Palmerston to the Queen. Cf. Martin, *Prince Consort*, iii, pp. 231–234; Admiral John Moresby, *Two Admirals* (London, 1909), p. 168; Sir George Douglas and Sir George Dalhousie Ramsay, eds., *The Panmure Papers* (London, 1908, 2 vols.) i, pp. 154, 156–159, 165.

On May 11 Admiral Hamelin, who had recently become Minister of Marine on the death of Ducos, ordered the *Congrève, Lave,* and *Tonnante* to prepare for service in the Black Sea. Orders dated June 14 directed the *Congrève, Dévastation,* and *Foudroyante* to make ready to be towed to the Baltic. On July 9, however, the destination of the *Dévastation* was changed to the Black Sea. She left Cherbourg on August 10 towed by the *Albatros*, preceded by the *Tonnante*, which had left Brest July 30 towed by the *Darien*, and by the *Lave*, which had left Lorient August 6 towed by the *Magellan*. Despite their wretched nautical qualities, the ironclads weathered a storm in the Bay of Biscay, and safely joined the Black Sea Fleet in Kamiesch Bay between September 12 and 23, after stops at Cadiz, Algiers, Malta and Constantinople.[1] The British batteries *Glatton* and *Meteor*, which had been ordered on July 20 to prepare for service in the Baltic, were ordered to the Black Sea early in August, but reached Kinburn a few days too late to take part in the attack.[2] The remaining ironclads do not seem to have been ready in time for use in the campaign of 1855 in the Baltic. On August 16 the *Thunder* and *Trusty* were ordered to be placed in reserve at Sheerness; and the *Congrève* and *Foudroyante* were laid up for the winter during the course of September.[3]

Although they arrived too late to participate in the final

---

[1] A.N., BB5 49. See also the *devis d'armement* of the three vessels in A.M., 7 DD1 96, 7 DD1 99, and 7 DD1 101. H. Langlois, an officer of the *Dévastation*, described the outward voyage in the *Revue des Deux Mondes*, February 1, 1858, pp. 588–609. The *Tonnante* stopped also at Corunna, and the *Lave* at Gibraltar.

[2] P.R.O., Adm. 12, Index 4798, out-letters, Secretary's Department, *s.v. Glatton* and *Meteor*, July 20, August 7, 1855; A.M., 7 DD1 65, Admiral Bruat to Admiral Hamelin, October 26, 1855, reporting the arrival of the two British ironclad batteries at Kinburn the day before, somewhat in need of repairs.

Like their French models, the British floating batteries were rigged simply as an auxiliary to steam during the voyage. "It was intended that all the rigging, spars, bulk heads, and unnecessary coals and every other weight not required when in action should be previously removed, so as to bring the Batteries to their constructed lines and raise their ports to the intended height for effectively fighting the guns." P.R.O., Submission Letter Book no. 17, July 21, 1855.

[3] Adm. 12, Index 4798, Out-letters, Secretary's Department, *s.v. Thunder* and *Trusty*, August 16; Submission Letter Book no. 17, August 11, 1855; ships' books, *Thunder, Trusty*; A.N., BB5 49. See also the *devis d'armement* of the *Congrève* and *Foudroyante* in A.M., 7 DD1 65, and 7 DD1 107.

bombardment of Sebastopol, the three French floating batteries did not have to wait long for their baptism of fire. An allied council of war at French headquarters on September 29 decided to carry out Napoleon III's proposal for an attack on the fortress of Kinburn, commanding the estuary formed by the waters of the Bug and the Dnieper, whose capture would block the despatch of Russian troops and supplies by water from Nikolaev and Kherson, and threaten the rear of the Russian army in the Crimea. An allied fleet of ten ships of the line, the three French ironclads, seventeen frigates and sloops, three corvettes, four despatch boats, twenty-two gunboats, eleven mortar vessels, and ten transports, under the command of Admirals Bruat and Lyons, carrying eight thousand troops commanded by Generals Bazaine and Spencer, left the bases near Sebastopol on October 6 and 7, and appeared off Odessa on the 8th. Detained there by fog, the fleet did not make the short run across to Kinburn until October 14.[1]

On the long, narrow sand spit of Kinburn, opposite Ochakov, fifteen hundred Russian troops under General Kokonovitch held three fortifications, consisting of a quadrangular stone fort with bastions at the four angles, mounting fifty guns, some in casemates and some *en barbette*, and two sand batteries mounting ten and eleven guns, nearer the tip of the promontory. On the night of the fourteenth, five English and four French gunboats entered the mouth of the Dnieper and ran past the forts, despite a cross fire from Kinburn and Ochakov. On the following morning the troops landed about three miles south of the fortress, cutting off the defenders

[1] The orders issued during the Kinburn expedition by Jurien de la Gravière, Admiral Bruat's chief of staff, are preserved in A.N., BB⁴ 1791 and 1792. Numerous reports concerning the expedition may be found in A.N., BB⁴ 692, 697, 698, and 699, and in A.M., 7 DD¹ 65, 96, 99 and 101. See also H. Langlois, "La Dévastation, Épisodes et souvenirs de la Guerre d'Orient," *Revue des Deux Mondes*, February 15, 1858, pp. 737–774; Baron de Bazancourt, *L'Expédition de Crimée, La Marine française dans la Mer Noire et la Baltique* (Paris [1858]), ii, pp. 177–214, 395–399; Eardley-Wilmot, *Lyons*, pp. 358–372; Clowes, *Royal Navy*, vi, pp. 469–474; Richild Grivel, *Attaques et bombardements maritimes avant et pendant la guerre d'Orient* (Paris, 1857), pp. 53–55; H. W. Wilson, *Ironclads in Action* (London, 1896, 2 vols.), i, pp. xxxi–xxxvi.

from all hope of retreating along the neck. Unfavorable weather delayed the attack until the morning of the seventeenth, when the allied squadrons took up positions determined on after soundings taken by Captain Spratt of the *Spitfire* and Lieutenant Cloué of the *Brandon*. On the night of the sixteenth, Ensign de Raffin of the *Dévastation* had placed three buoys to guide the floating batteries before his boat was detected and driven off by a heavy fire.[1]

The French ironclads, which had landed their masts before quitting the Crimea, and had been towed across the Black Sea, got under way at 8 A.M. under their own power, and led the fleet into action. Although the original plan had directed them to take station at 600 meters range, if they found sufficient depth of water, the *Dévastation*, *Lave*, and *Tonnante* anchored between 8.45 and 9.30 A.M. at ranges of 877, 975 and 1150 meters from the fortress. The *Dévastation*, which had been under fire for about twenty minutes, engaged the principal fort at 9.06, followed by the *Lave* and *Tonnante* at 9.30 and 9.42. The ironclads were supported by the gunboats, which took station near them as soon as the Russian fire slackened, and by a well-directed long-range fire from the mortar vessels.

It was on the *Dévastation* that the Russian 24-pounders concentrated their heaviest fire. Twenty-nine shot rattled off her four-inch armor and thirty-five plowed furrows in her deck of heavy oak. One shell, however, entered the battery through the imperfectly protected main hatch, and two more through the ports, killing two men and wounding thirteen others. The *Lave* suffered no casualties and no injuries to her plates; but fragments of two shot which entered the ports of the *Tonnante* wounded nine men. Of sixty-six shot which struck the latter, fifty-five slightly dented the plates, ten swept the deck, and one cut the main-piece of the starboard rudder.

In about four hours of fighting, the *Dévastation* fired 1265

---

[1] A.N., BB⁴ 692, folios 228–229, "Remarks on the fortifications of the Kinburn Channel," by Captain Spratt; Bruat to Hamelin, October 17 and 18, 1855, printed in De Bazancourt, *op. cit.*, ii, pp. 395–399; Langlois, *op. cit.*, pp. 744–745.

shot and shell, the *Lave* 900, and the *Tonnante* 1012. Their picked crews made excellent practice, setting the fort on fire, silencing most of its guns, and breaching the wall in several places. At noon the ships of the line got under way, anchored at 1600 meters from the enemy, and poured in a heavy fire, while six British and three French frigates steamed up the Dnieper and opened fire on the forts from the rear. Encircled by an overwhelming fire, with all hope of escape cut off by the allied troops on the neck, General Kokonovitch surrendered at 1.25 P.M.[1]

Bruat warmly praised the work of the three ironclads, which seemed to him to have fulfilled all the Emperor's hopes. "On peut tout attendre de l'emploi de ces formidables machines de guerre," he reported.[2] He nevertheless pointed out that since the heaviest guns to whose fire they had been exposed were long, cast-iron 24-pounders, the experience gained on October 17 furnished only a presumption as to their capacity to withstand the fire of 50- or 68-pounder solid shot. In view of the small depth of the indentations caused by the 24-pounder shot, however, it seemed evident that 30-pounder shot, at 1000 to 1200 meters, could do the batteries no damage.[3]

In a letter to the First Naval Lord, Sir Maurice Berkeley, on October 20, Sir Edmund Lyons expressed "golden opinions" of the French floating batteries, whose plates showed only "a few rust-like marks where the shot struck and bounded off." Shells were said to have broken up on striking the armor before they had time to explode. Although he suggested that the mortar vessels and gunboats had contributed more to the capture than the floating batteries, and argued that the *coup de grâce* had been given by the ships of the line,

---

[1] A.N., BB⁴ 692, folios 224–225 verso, "Plan of attack upon Kinburn;" BB⁴ 1792, nos. 993, 1030, 1040; BB⁴ 697, 698, 699, reports of the commanders of the three floating batteries; Lyons's despatch of October 18, 1855, in Eardley-Wilmot, *Lyons*, pp. 364–367. The casualties in the British ships amounted to only two wounded.
[2] Bruat to Hamelin, October 17 and 18, *Moniteur*, October 21, November 5, 1855; De Bazancourt, *op. cit.*, ii, pp. 395–399.
[3] Bruat to Hamelin, October 26. A.M., 7 DD¹ 65.

he deemed it certain that the ironclads, though prevented by shallow water from taking their intended station within 600 yards of the fort, would in two or three hours' more firing have "brought the walls down by the lump" and rendered the whole sea-face accessible. He remarked that nothing heavier than 24-pounders were fired at them, and that it was not certain that the Russian powder was of the first quality.

> Still you may take it for granted that floating batteries have become elements in amphibious warfare, so the sooner you set about having as many good ones as the French the better it will be for you. . . . The French no doubt go great lengths in their praises of this favourite weapon of their Emperor's; but make all the allowance you please for that, and there will still remain too much in favour of it to admit of its being discarded without a fair trial.[1]

On the day after the victory Lyons's flag captain confided to his diary that the French floating batteries were "perfect." Solid shot simply indented the plates a trifle, and "shell broke against them like glass." Cronstadt and Sveaborg now seemed doomed. "This is the way to make war; destroy your enemy and save yourself." [2]

The British Admiralty promptly increased the number of their floating batteries, ordering in November the construction at Chatham dockyard of the wooden-hulled armored battery *Aetna* of 1588 tons, builder's measurement, in place of the ironclad of that name burned on May 3. This ship of 200 horse power mounted sixteen 68-pounders and cost £50,297. She was launched April 5, 1856, moored in the Thames in 1861 for river defence while the forts were under repair, fitted as a police ship at Sheerness in 1865, and finally taken to pieces at Chatham in 1873.[3] In December, 1855, the Admiralty ordered from private contractors three floating batteries on a new plan, to be ready for sea by April 15 or May 1, 1856. These vessels, a little over 186 feet long between perpendiculars and 48 feet beam, with a draft slightly less than 9 feet, and engines of 200 horse power, ranged from 1954 to

---

[1] Eardley-Wilmot, *Lyons*, pp. 368–369.
[2] Mends, *Mends*, p. 302.
[3] She was 186 feet long between perpendiculars, 43 feet 11 inches beam and 8 feet 2 inches draft. Ship's book, *Aetna*.

1973 tons builder's measurement, and each originally carried sixteen 68-pounder guns. They had iron hulls, with iron ribs covered by ⅝-inch skin plating. Their topsides, which tumbled in sharply, were protected by 4-inch wrought-iron armor backed by only five or six inches of oak, whereas the *Meteor* class had four times as much oak backing behind the 4-inch armor. Comparative tests with 32- and 68-pounder guns against the *Meteor* and *Erebus* in October and November, 1858, indicated the superior resisting powers of the former, and the advantage of heavier wooden backing than was given to the iron-hulled batteries. Of the latter, the *Erebus*, launched by Napier and Sons at Glasgow on April 19, 1856, cost £82,039; the *Thunderbolt*, launched by Samuda Brothers at Millwall on April 22, cost £80,230; and the *Terror*, launched by Palmer Brothers at Newcastle on April 26, cost £81,556. As the termination of the war averted the projected campaign of 1856 in the Baltic, these vessels never received their baptism of fire.[1] The *Terror* was sent to Bermuda in 1857; the *Erebus* and *Thunderbolt* were never commissioned.[2]

During the years 1854 to 1856, seventy-three inventors submitted to the British Admiralty projects for the construction or improvement of shot-proof ships and floating batteries; while twenty-three inventors submitted similar proposals to the French Ministry of Marine.[3] Though none of these was adopted, the number of projects shows a great in-

---

[1] Cf. Douglas and Ramsay, *Panmure Papers*, ii, pp. 56–57, 62, 91; Fitzmaurice, *Granville*, i, p. 132; Martin, *Prince Consort*, iii, pp. 429, 485; Colonel Willoughby Verner and Captain E. D. Parker, *The Military Life of H. R. H. George, Duke of Cambridge* (London, 1905, 2 vols.), i, pp. 88–91; Wellesley, *Cowley*, pp. 86–87.

[2] Ships' books, *Erebus, Terror, Thunderbolt*, Admiralty Library; P.R.O., Submission Letter Book no. 18, November 16, 23, December 22, 24, 26, 27, 1855, January 10, 12, 19, May 26, July 18, 1856; *Parliamentary Papers*, 1863, xxxvi, nos. 86 and 237; *ibid.*, 1876, xlv, no. 297; *Transactions and Report of the Special Committee on Iron between 21st January, 1861, and March, 1862*, pp. xi, 172–173, 175; J. D'Aguilar Samuda, "On the Construction of Iron Vessels of War Iron-cased," *Transactions of the Institution of Naval Architects*, ii, pp. 8–10, and plate 1; Napier, *Life of Robert Napier*, pp. 197–198, with a picture of the *Erebus*.

[3] From lists compiled from P.R.O., Submission Letter Books nos. 17 and 18; and A.M., BB^8 1135, 1136, 1137, 1138 and 1139; 1 DD^1 207, 213, 214, 216, 221, 222, 236. See also, for a proposal by the Earl of Rosse, Wrottesley, *Burgoyne*, ii, pp. 47–49, 418–419. Cf. *David Napier, Engineer* (Glasgow, 1912), pp. 27–28, 121–122.

crease of interest in the problem of the ironclad. Several of these inventors suggested the construction of double-ended ships, with rudders fore and aft; others advocated the use, with or without iron, of cork, compressed cotton, gutta-percha, and india rubber, as a protection against shot. The only two of these projects which seem to have had any influence on the evolution of the ironclad ship were those of Cowper Phipps Coles, representing the first stage of development of his ideas for a battleship turret,[1] and of J. Scott Russell, which had some influence, often exaggerated, on the design of the *Warrior*.[2]

Five of these inventors raised unfounded claims that the floating batteries of 1854 to 1856 were their invention. On the strength of two patents of 1853 for vague improvements in the use of iron,[3] John Clare, Jr., a produce broker of Liverpool, demanded five per cent of the value of the *Erebus*, *Terror*, and *Thunderbolt*, and later of the *Warrior* and subsequent ironclads. Although the Admiralty denied infringement and refused compensation, Clare, who described himself as "the greatest patriot and inventor of this iron age," received £100 in 1859 from the Royal Bounty Fund. When allowed to bring suit for damages, by petition of right, he lost his case in February, 1863, and published a violent pamphlet.[4] His French contemporary, Aubert, who had proposed in March, 1854, the use of corrugated-iron armor, did not have his day in court. His persistence in claiming twenty-four per cent of

---

[1] See below, pp. 185–195.
[2] Russell advocated "vessels with sharp bows for speed, with shot-proof coating amidship, with transverse shot-proof bulkheads, with longitudinal strengthening, with a recessed side for armour and backing, with all their guns on one deck, and with a deck overhead, forming the corvette class, or frigate of single deck." *Transactions of the Institution of Naval Architects*, ii, p. 21. For Scott Russell's share in the design of the *Warrior*, see below, p. 130, note 1.
[3] British patent specifications nos. 2042 and 2062, 1853.
[4] See Clare's *Life Preserving Ships* (London, [1860]), and *Clare versus the Queen* [London, 1863]; P.R.O., Adm. 12/624: 91-1; Submission Letter Books no. 18, February 20, July 18, 1856, and no. 21, July 8, 20, September 6, December 20, 1859, February 28, 1860. The entries in Adm. 12/669 concerning Clare are humorous. Messrs. Samuda and Scott Russell testified at the trial that they had, for many years before Clare's patents, built ships on the principles which he claimed to be his own.

the credit for the "invention" of the ironclad batteries of 1854, while conceding only fourteen per cent to the Emperor, eventually got him into trouble with the police.[1] Hamelin had patiently explained to him the undoubted fact that the French experiments in 1843, 1844, and 1845 had made clear, among other facts, all those that Aubert thought he had discovered as to the capacity of armor to resist solid shot and shells.[2]

For use in shoal water several British and French naval officers proposed that guns be mounted on rafts more or less protected from shot, and the Russians actually constructed fifteen armored rafts towards the close of this war.[3] Many of the British and French gunboats constructed at this time had sheet-iron screens of various sorts as protection against musketry fire, much as did the so-called "tinclads" used on the Mississippi River during the Civil War. Several naval constructors proposed to give these gunboats more elaborate protection by means of heavier armor and inclined walls.[4]

At the outbreak of the war, Naval Constructor Gervaize revived his project of 1847 for an ironclad ram and floating battery. The project for a floating battery was rejected, as inferior to the plans of Guieysse; but both the *Conseil des Travaux* and the special commission of 1855 on the recon-

---

[1] In 1872, under the Third Republic, Aubert complained to the Minister of Marine that: "Pour plaire à Napoléon III, on lui a attribué l'invention des murailles en fer à l'épreuve des boulets, en sorte qu'il ne me fut rien accordé et de plus, en 1861, je fus dévalisé de tous mes livres, brochures et manuscrits et avec défense de réclamer." A.N., GG¹, dossier 69; A.M., BB⁸ 1134, April 29, 1854; BB⁸ 1136, May 22, 1855; BB⁸ 1137, August 21, 1855; BB⁸ 1143, July 13, 1858.
[2] A.M., 1 DD¹ 263, July 28, 1858.
When the French General of Engineers Daullé declared that he had suggested to Napoleon III in April, 1854, the use of wrought iron to protect warships, the *Conseil des Travaux* concluded that Daullé had simply proposed an idea already old, without suggesting anything immediately applicable. A.M., BB⁸ 1135, August 26, 1854; BB⁸ 1136, January 30, April 10, 1855. For the English inventor, Nelson, see P.R.O., Submission Letter Books no. 17, S. 3051, and no. 20, April 25, 1859. The absurd claims of Frédéric Billot are presented in his *Les Hippiscaphes* (Paris, 1855), p. 51.
[3] See below, p. 185, note 3.
[4] A.M., BB⁸ 1135, October 8, 21, 26, November 18, 1854; 1 DD¹ 208, November 27, 1854; 1 DD¹ 216, Hamelin to Lorient, May 13 and 20, 1855, and to Rochefort, May 23, 1855; BB⁸ 1142, May 25, 1858; P.R.O., Submission Letter Book no. 20, October 25, 1858.

struction of the steam navy regarded with favor the proposal for an ironclad ram.[1] In February, 1855, Ducos called on the naval constructors in the five great ports and at Indret to submit projects for a steam ram sufficiently armored to be shot-proof near the water line and shell-proof above. No satisfactory project, however, was received before the end of the war.[2]

After the capture of Kinburn, numerous proposals were made, and some steps taken, to improve the French floating batteries.[3] To the French, the British iron-hulled batteries seemed the reverse of an improvement. Garnier commented on a detailed description of the *Erebus* which the French naval constructor Pastoureau sent from Glasgow, that this type of backing was so little suited to withstand hammering by solid shot that, before an action had long continued, the plates would be damaged, the rivets started, and the battery leaking.[4] The most important result of the battle of Kinburn, however, was to turn men's minds to the possibility of creating large seagoing ironclads. Among the first to use the experience of Kinburn as an argument for building larger armored vessels was the great Italian artillerist Giovanni Cavalli, one of the pioneers in the introduction of breech-loading rifled guns. In 1856 he proposed a floating battery of

---

[1] A.M., 6 DD¹ 2, dossier 44; 1 DD¹ 211, August 17, 1854; BB⁸ 1135, December 12, 1854; BB⁸ 1136, January 16, 1855; 1 DD¹ 218, circular to the five great ports, August 27, 1855.

[2] A.M., 1 DD¹ 218, circular to Cherbourg, Brest, Lorient, Rochefort, Toulon and Indret, February 5, 1855; 1 DD¹ 217, Hamelin to Toulon, November 28, 1855; BB⁸ 1136, March 13, 1855; BB⁸ 1138, March 11, 1856; 1 DD¹ 229, Hamelin to Cherbourg, April 25, 1856.

Vice Admiral Romain-Desfossés had reported in favor of the ram idea, May 7, 1854. A.N., BB⁸ 837, *Conseil d'Amirauté*, May 12, 1854.

[3] A.M., 7 DD¹ 101, Dupré's report, October 22, 1855; 7 DD¹ 65, reports of Garnier, November 15, 1855, Montaignac de Chauvance, January 6, 1856, Sochet, January 12, 1856; Brest commission, September 12, 1856, Dupré, September 18, 1856; 7 DD¹ 107, report of Thomeuf and Bonie, January 9, 1856; BB⁸ 1140, February 25, 1857, discussion of d'Harcourt's report; 1 DD¹ 218, circular to Cherbourg, Brest, Lorient and Rochefort, December 12, 1855; BB⁸ 1139, October 21, 1856; 1 DD¹ 228, to Cherbourg, Brest and Toulon, November 10, 1856. See also A.N., BB⁴ 1038, report of Rear Admiral Pellion, February 20, 1856. Cf. Xavier Raymond, "La marine militaire à vapeur," *Nouvelles annales maritimes et coloniales*, xvi (1856), pp. 26–54, 104–120, 154–163, 226–236.

[4] A.M., 7 DD¹ 65, March 28, 1856.

1500 tons and a larger ironclad of 24 guns and 1600 tons, or of 36 guns and 2400 tons. For both types he advocated hulls entirely of iron, inclined sides, a sort of corrugated-iron armor, and sufficient strength to permit use as a ram. Cavalli argued with force that the creation of large ironclads was inevitable, thanks to the development of the metallurgical and shipbuilding industries.[1] What he predicted, Frenchmen of equal vision and the requisite genius in naval construction were soon to make a reality.

[1] Jean Cavalli, *Mémoire sur divers perfectionnements militaires* (Paris, 1856), pp. 93–114.

CHAPTER VI

THE FIRST SEAGOING IRONCLAD FLEET

ON August 11, 1855, the *Commission supérieure centrale* charged with the program for the French steam fleet proposed the creation of a force of forty fast screw line-of-battle ships each carrying 70 or 90 guns, twenty frigates, thirty corvettes, sixty despatch-vessels, a steam ram, and sufficient transports for an expeditionary force of 32,000 men.[1] The cost of this vast force of wooden steam warships was estimated at 272,440,000 francs.[2] Eighteen months later, convinced that the new rifled guns recently tested at Lorient would greatly increase the power of ordnance and render imperative the adoption of armor, the first section of the *Conseil des Travaux* boldly proposed that all work on wooden warships be stopped.[3] Indeed not one French wooden ship of the line was laid down after 1855.[4]

Even before the successful demonstration of iron walls at Kinburn, Napoleon III, alarmed at the damage suffered by his wooden ships in the bombardment of Sebastopol on October 17, 1854, had proposed the transformation of wooden ships of the line into ironclads, to reinforce his newly projected floating batteries.[5] Captain de Montaignac of the *Dévastation*, on his outward voyage to the Black Sea in August, 1855, predicted the feasibility of armored seagoing frigates.[6] After the action at Kinburn, and especially when the close of the war gave French naval constructors more

---

1 A.M., 1 DD¹ 218, circular to the five great ports, August 31, 1855.
2 This figure was raised to 292,708,800 francs to permit an increased number of transports sufficient for an expeditionary force of 40,000 men. A.M., 1 DD¹ 219, nos. 38 and 39, November 1 and 23, 1855. Cf. A.N., BB⁸ 98, folios 225–226, 236–243. For the revised figures see A.M., 1 DD¹ 241, November 25, 1857.
3 A.M., BB⁸ 1140, January 13, 1857.
4 A.M., 1 DD¹ 275, September 22, 1860. See Appendix E.
5 See above, p. 77, and Appendix C.
6 A.M., 7 DD¹ 99, report dated Cadiz, August 20, 1855.

leisure for new studies, projects for larger and faster ironclads fit for sea service came thick and fast. Rear Admiral Pellion, Captain Dupré, and Lieutenant Duseutre advocated a new type of armored ship, equipped with a ram, capable of meeting the enemy at sea and harassing his coasts.[1] Before the close of 1856 naval constructors Guesnet, Marielle, and de Ferranty and Lieutenant Béléguic submitted projects for fast ironclad frigates of 20 to 34 guns, ranging from 1800 to 4009 tons displacement.[2]

The *Conseil des Travaux* pointed out that the success of the first French ironclads and the improvements of which they were susceptible indicated that the composition of the fleet would soon be profoundly modified by the introduction of new types which united a certain degree of invulnerability with high speed and seaworthiness. The new ships must be considered from three points of view: coast defence, cruising warfare, and attack on the enemy's coast. Though the Council declined to approve any ironclad plan until further studies and experiments were made of the best mode of constructing and fastening the ship's sides, it nevertheless laid down, in its discussions of the various projects submitted in 1856, certain

---

[1] Pellion's report of February 20, 1856, is in A.N., BB⁴ 1038. For the views of Dupré and Duseutre see A.M., 6 DD¹ 22, dossiers 486 and 488; BB⁸ 1139, October 28, 1856; BB⁸ 1140, March 24, 1857; Dislère, *Marine cuirassée*, pp. 15–16.

[2] The projects of the three naval constructors are well summarized by Dislère, *op. cit.*, pp. 16–19. The originals, with the comments of the *Conseil des Travaux*, are in A.M., 6 DD¹ 22, dossiers 487, 490; BB⁸ 1139, July 22, 1856; BB⁸ 1140, January 20, 1857. For Béléguic's project see 6 DD¹ 22, dossier 500, and BB⁸ 1140, January 20, 1857.

Guesnet proposed a frigate of 2861 tons, 26 guns, 600 horse power, and 12 to 13 knots speed, with a length of 68.5 meters, 14.4 meters beam and 5.7 meters draft. He adopted a pointed stern to simplify the manufacture of the armor plates. He proposed experiments on the moment of inertia, which the minister authorized him to undertake. A.M., 1 DD¹ 242, Hamelin to Cherbourg, January 14, 1857.

Marielle submitted a memorandum arguing that armored frigates would soon replace wooden ships of the line as capital ships, and proposed an ironclad of 2973 tons, 600 horse power, 20 guns, and 12 knots speed, with a length of 65 meters, 13.4 meters beam and 5.6 meters draft.

De Ferranty proposed a frigate of 4009 tons, 34 guns, 800 horse power and 13 knots speed, with a length of 70 meters, 15.66 meters beam and draft of 6.77 meters.

Béléguic, whose proposal was a mere sketch compared with the carefully studied projects of the naval constructors, suggested a vessel of 1800 tons, 32 guns, and 11 knots speed, 60 meters long and 13 meters beam.

general principles to guide the construction corps. First and foremost it emphasized speed, declaring thirteen knots to be the minimum, so that the ironclad might always be able to choose its range and position. The Council agreed with Dupré that the adoption of a hull entirely of iron would increase rigidity and dispense with caulking, but observed that the Vincennes experiments indicated that shocks transmitted from the armor would gravely damage the inside plating. Armor at least 10 cm. thick must cover all the topsides and extend at least 1.5 meters below the water line. To permit fighting the guns in rough weather, the height of the gun ports above the water must be at least two meters. The ironclad should be rigged as a corvette for cruising, and have her screw well protected. To fulfil all these conditions, even the displacement of 4000 tons suggested by de Ferranty was deemed too small.[1]

A new series of experiments at Vincennes in 1856 on plates of cast steel one to eight cm. thick, furnished by Frederick Krupp of Essen, the Bochum Works, and Jackson Brothers, Petin, Gaudet and Company, as well as on plates of bronze seven to eleven cm. thick, seemed to indicate that iron alone was suitable for armor plate.[2] At the request of the Commission which presided over these tests, orders were issued in October, 1856, for new tests of iron plates ten and eleven centimeters thick, of three different types of iron: "fer doux et nerveux; fer dur à grains fins, fer à nerf et à grains."[3] Before these were carried out, the *Conseil des Travaux* drew up on December 23, 1856, a program for studies in the ports of projects for ships' sides at least as resistant as those of the first floating batteries, and if possible more dur-

---

[1] A.M., BB⁸ 1139, July 22, October 28, December 23, 1856; BB⁸ 1140, January 20, March 24, 1857.
[2] A.M., 1 DD¹ 219, no. 37, November 8, 1855; 1 DD¹ 215, no. 225, November 14, 1855; 4 DD¹ 6, contract with Jackson Brothers, Petin, Gaudet and Co. December 21, 1855; 1 DD¹ 217, January 4, June 27, July 2, 14, December 5, 1856; 1 DD¹ 235, Hamelin to the Minister of Finance, April 7, 1856; 1 DD¹ 234, Hamelin to president of Vincennes Commission, April 14, May 5, 21, 1856, and to Garnier, October 3, 10, 1856; A.N., BB⁸ 92, folio 124, Hamelin to Napoleon III, November 9, 1855.
[3] A.M., 1 DD¹ 233, Hamelin to the director of the La Chaussade iron works, at Guérigny, October 27, 1856.

able, more easily repaired, less liable to leaks, and more likely to withstand ramming.[1] The projects submitted by twenty naval constructors in response to this call proved somewhat disappointing, for most of them suggested only slight modifications of the system adopted in 1854. The general idea was a wooden hull protected by iron plates eleven or twelve centimeters thick fastened by various methods to a substantial wooden backing. Several proposed to strengthen the armor by reducing the number of bolt holes; others suggested methods of caulking to reduce leaks. De Gasté recommended plates 8 inches thick with deep grooves to reduce their weight. Antoine preferred two layers of iron, each 9 cm. thick, separated by 4 inches of oak. The *Conseil des Travaux* thought it unnecessary to order tests of the various proposals based on wooden hulls, but recommended tests at Vincennes of the project of Camille Audenet, the best of the proposals for armoring iron hulls, which was eventually adopted for the frigate *Couronne*.[2]

At the end of March, 1857, the Emperor himself had taken a hand in the game. Aiming to get the same resistance offered by a flat plate 10 cm. thick, with only 77 to 80 per cent as much weight, Napoleon III ordered tests of several styles of corrugated and grooved plates of his own design.[3] In the experiments at Vincennes in the autumn of 1857, these plates of the Emperor's proved inferior to the

---

[1] A.M., 1 BB⁸ 1139, December 23, 1856.

[2] A.M., BB⁸ 1140, opinion of the *Conseil des Travaux*, June 30, 1857. Eighteen of the original projects are preserved in A.M., 6 DD¹ 23, dossier 501.

[3] A.M., 1 DD¹ 248, note by Dupuy de Lôme, March 30, 1857, "sur les fers ondulés pour blindages ... conformément aux indications qui m'ont été exposées par S. M. l'Empereur." In the margin of the draft of a despatch to the iron works of La Chaussade, March 31, ordering six of the proposed plates, are two very rough sketches of cross sections of the plates. 1 DD¹ 245.

A despatch to the inspector general of naval construction June 3, 1857, describes the plates to be tested at Vincennes as follows: "1° 6 plaques de fer plat ...; 2° 6 plaques cannelées, avec vide intérieur, de 2.50 de longueur, 17 cm. de largeur, 130 mm. au plus épais et 30 mm. aux pattes qui ont 30 mm. de hauteur. Les boulons seront placés au milieu du mamelon présentant la plus forte épaisseur. 3° 6 plaques semblables aux précédents, mais sans vide intérieur. 4° 6 plaques cannelées, avec vide intérieur et pattes venant s'appliquer les unes sur les autres; mêmes dimensions en longueur et épaisseur que les précédentes; pattes

ordinary armor.[1] So did a target provided at the expense of its designer, the well-known Bordeaux shipbuilder, Arman.[2] At the same time the Vincennes Commission experimented with the three types of iron plates ordered from the imperial iron works of La Chaussade in October, 1856, and with plates of hard iron from Fourchambault, "qui se rapproche de l'acier puddlé et qui est plus dur que le fer de grosse forge."[3] The commission also carried out comparative tests of rolled plates, hammered plates, and plates that had been both rolled and hammered. Its report showed that the plates made in the La Chaussade works from Fourchambault iron were the best yet developed.[4] The target representing the system of armor and wood backing proposed by Audenet for ironclads with iron hulls successfully withstood solid shot of

de 6 cm. de chaque bord et vide intérieur de 5 cm. Les boulons seront mis au milieu des pattes. . . ." 1 DD¹ 247.
  See further: 1 DD¹ 245, to the iron works of La Chaussade, April 27, May 30, July 10, August 12, 21, 1857; 1 DD¹ 247, to the inspector general of naval construction, July 11, 22, 1857.

[1] "L'Empereur, qui se faisait rendre compte de toutes ces études de la façon la plus détaillée, nous fit essayer concurremment avec les plaques pleines des fers à nervures saillantes qui donnèrent des résultats dont les conséquences seront peut-être utilisées un jour, quoique les plaques planes aient été préférées à cette époque." [Dupuy de Lôme], *Notice sur les travaux scientifiques de M. Dupuy de Lôme* (Paris, 1866), p. 35.

[2] A.M., 1 DD¹ 246, letters to Arman, August 10, September 4 and 28, 1857; 1 DD¹ 247, to the Vincennes Commission, August 11 and September 4, 1857.
  Arman's later record as a builder of ironclads for the French and the Confederate navies renders his earlier activities of some interest. The firm of Courau and Arman of Bordeaux was bankrupt in 1848. (A.M., 1 DD¹ 140, "Note pour la commission des machines et de l'outillage," February 15, 1848). Arman's system of mixed construction for merchant vessels and unarmored warships was well known by the time of the Crimean War. A report of the *Conseil des Travaux* on this method of combining wood and iron is in A.M., BB⁸ 1128, June 4, 1851. In A.N., GG¹ 74 are two rejected projects by Arman for a screw despatch vessel of 180 horse power in 1852, and for a steam frigate of 60 guns and 500 horse power in 1853, both of mixed construction. During the Crimean War Arman and Company contracted with the French government to build two transports of 160 horse power, *La Gironde* and *La Dordogne*; and the hulls of two despatch vessels, *le Prégent* and *le Renaudin*. A.M., 1 DD¹ 211, to *Commissaire général*, Bordeaux, August 23, 1854; 1 DD¹ 233, to *Chef de Service*, Bordeaux, May 26 and December 10, 1856. Soon after the close of the war, Arman contracted with the Russian government for three ships to be built at Bordeaux on his system: the frigate *Svetlana*, the corvette *Baian*, and a pleasure yacht for the Emperor. A.M., 6 DD¹ 88, dossier 2385. For some of Arman's later activities, see below, pp. 103, 104, 113, 114.

[3] A.M., 1 DD¹ 247, to Garnier, July 11, 1857.
[4] *Ibid.*, July 7, 28; 1 DD¹ 241, December 30, 1857.

THE FIRST SEAGOING IRONCLAD FLEET

wrought iron and of steel from 30-pounder and 50-pounder guns. These tests, which led to the adoption of Audenet's plans for the armored frigate *Couronne*, had one other important result. The old system of bolting the armor to the wooden backing, which had the serious defect that frequently the bolts broke and the nuts flew off when the plate was struck by a projectile, was now superseded by the use of screws (*vis à bois*), first employed on the *Gloire*.[1]

Though the Vincennes experiments were to continue for several years, they had already produced sufficient data for the solution of the problem of the fast seagoing ironclad; and the man destined to solve it was now at his post. The appointment on January 1, 1857, of Dupuy de Lôme as *Directeur du Matériel* — a post corresponding to that of Surveyor of the Navy or Chief of the Bureau of Construction and Repair in the British and American navies of that day — marks one of the outstanding dates in the history of naval architecture. The man whose rules for iron shipbuilding had for more than a decade been the standard for French shipyards, who had submitted his first plan for a seagoing ironclad as early as 1845, now at the age of forty took the key position in the Ministry of Marine and set his hand to the great revolution. As an English master of the craft well said: "In boldness of conception and in executive skill he takes the first place among the naval constructors of our time."[2] In 1847, when most of the opponents of paddle wheels still advocated the screw simply as an auxiliary of sail power, he had proposed his famous 92-gun screw ship of the line of 960 horse power, which, launched at Toulon May 18, 1850, and known in those days of revolutions and *coups d'état* as *le 24 Février, le Président*, and *le Napoléon*, astonished the world by its perfection and by its remarkable speed of 13.86 knots. When the Anglo-French fleet was baffled in the Dardanelles, September

---

[1] A.M., 1 DD¹ 245, to the director of the La Chaussade iron works, August 7, 21, September 18; 1 DD¹ 247, July 13, October 7, 16, 1857; *Notice sur Dupuy de Lôme*, pp. 35-36.
[2] Nathaniel Barnaby, *Naval Development in the Century* (London, 1904), p. 63. For his early career, see above, pp. 40, 61, 62.

22, 1853, by head winds and current too strong for the low-powered engines of the ordinary capital ships of that day, she had triumphantly steamed up the straits, towing behind her the French flagship *Ville de Paris* of 112 guns.[1]

In the autobiographical sketch which he published in 1866 in support of his candidacy for the Académie des Sciences, Dupuy de Lôme stated that when, in November, 1856, he was ordered to collaborate with Rear Admiral Jurien de la Gravière and de Lavrignais, then *Directeur du Matériel*, in a report on the transformation of the fleet, he was already convinced that the real lesson of Kinburn was the creation of ironclads for the high-seas fleet. He had already conceived the plan of a fast seagoing frigate sufficiently armored to withstand at close range the heaviest guns afloat. Arguing that the substitution of these ironclad frigates in place of the fast wooden ships of the line in the program proposed by the commission of 1855 would constitute an advance of the French Navy in the direction of a balance of power at sea, he persuaded his colleagues to leave room, in their report on the transformation of the fleet, for the possible substitution of these ironclads as units equivalent to the ships prescribed by the 1855 program.[2]

The considerable number of writers on naval history and naval architecture who have assumed that the *Gloire* was designed by the simple process of taking the plans of the *Napoléon*, suppressing one deck with its guns, and devoting the weight thus saved to armor, would have done well to note the pains taken by Dupuy de Lôme, in his autobiographical sketch, to refute this idea. In England the idea prevailed for many years that the *Gloire* was merely a wooden warship that had been razeed, armored, and re-named. As a matter of fact, the *Gloire* was an entirely new ship, built from the keel up, and her principal dimensions and general construction were "profoundly modified" from those of the *Napoléon*.[3]

---

[1] Tramond and Reussner, *Histoire maritime*, p. 57; De Bazancourt, *L'Expédition de Crimée*, i, pp. 14–19.
[2] *Notice sur Dupuy de Lôme*, p. 34.
[3] *Ibid.*, p. 38. Sir Philip Watts, in his paper, "Warship Building (1860–1910),"

Convinced that in an action between two ships that were equal in speed, armor protection, nautical qualities, and radius of action the smaller ship would have the advantage, Dupuy de Lôme sought from first to last in his designs for ironclads to solve the problem with the smallest possible dimensions. Fixing the displacement of the *Gloire* at 5620 tons, 500 tons more than that of the *Napoléon*, he proposed nevertheless to obtain equal speed from the same horse power, by giving his ironclad six meters more length on the water line than his wooden masterpiece, with practically the same beam and draft. Thanks to the finer lines, he obtained, despite the increased tonnage, an immersed midship section of only 101 square meters compared with 99 square meters for the *Napoléon*. The elimination of one deck and great increase in the weight of the ship's sides raised problems of transverse strength which Dupuy met by introducing a layer of sheet iron under the wooden upper deck, strongly fastened throughout to the sides of the vessel. The combination of increased weight with reduced height necessitated the most careful study of the problems concerning the center of gravity, the moment of inertia, and the probable pitching, rolling, and turning qualities of the new type of ship.[1]

Dupuy declared that a single such ironclad, in the midst of a whole fleet of wooden ships of the line, would resemble a lion among a flock of sheep.[2] On March 4, 1858, Hamelin ordered three ironclad frigates of 900 horse power laid down at once in government yards, two at Toulon and one at Lorient.[3] In an interesting report approved by the minister on April 16, Dupuy de Lôme argued that, for the moment, it was inadvisable to concentrate on a single type of ironclad. Any project that met the three tests of sufficient impenetrability, sufficient strength for use as a ram, and speed and

---

Institution of Naval Architects *Transactions*, liii (1911), p. 294, seems to have been the first British writer to correct this error.

[1] *Notice sur Dupuy de Lôme*, pp. 37-39; *devis d'armement* of the *Gloire*, A.M., 7 DD¹ 170, reproduced in *Mémorial du génie maritime*, 1860, ii, pp. 354-383.
[2] *La Grande Encyclopédie*, s.v. Dupuy de Lôme.
[3] A.M., 1 DD¹ 254. Dupuy drafted the orders for the minister's signature. 1 DD¹ 257, 1 DD¹ 259, March 4, 1858.

radius of action equal to the *Napoléon*, deserved serious consideration. He proposed that his plan for wooden-hulled ironclads, already adopted for the *Gloire* and *Invincible*, which were to be built at Toulon, should not serve for all of the armored vessels to be laid down in 1858, but that the ideas of other constructors be tested. He therefore suggested that Audenet's plans for an iron-hulled armored vessel should, if approved by the *Conseil des Travaux*, serve for the ironclad to be laid down at Lorient.[1]

Arguing that iron hulls would be more quickly constructed, stronger, more easily adapted for use as rams, less likely to leak, and capable of water-tight subdivision, Audenet had proposed a frigate of 5890 tons, and 900 horse power, with armor of 8 or 10 cm. thickness, according to whether the strake was above or at the water line, backed first by 10 cm. of teak, then by an iron lattice-work 34 mm. thick, followed by 28 cm. of teak, resting on the hull of 20-mm. iron. On June 8 the *Conseil des Travaux* approved the plan, with certain modifications, insisting that the displacement be increased to permit the stowage of provisions for ninety days, while maintaining a height of battery of 2.06 meters, which the Council deemed the minimum admissible. Audenet's revised project, increasing the displacement to 6114 tons, and strengthening the stem for ramming, was despatched to Lorient on September 1, with the minister's approval, to serve for the frigate *Couronne*.[2]

Two days later Hamelin ordered a fourth ironclad, soon named the *Normandie*, to be laid down at once at Cherbourg

---

[1] This report, preserved in A.M., 1 DD¹ 254, April 15, 1858, and in the *Couronne* dossier in A.C.N., is printed in full in Appendix D.

[2] A.C.N., *Couronne* dossier; A.M., BB⁸ 1142, June 8, 1858; 1 DD¹ 254, June 30, 1858; 1 DD¹ 262, to Audenet, June 30, 1858; BB⁸ 1143, August 17, 1858; 1 DD¹ 257, to Lorient, September 1 and 24, 1858.

For the complicated system of armor adopted, see the descriptions by Audenet, A.M., 6 DD¹ 23, dossier 501; by the first section of the *Conseil des Travaux*, BB⁸ 1142, June 8, 1858; by Captain Penhoat of the *Couronne*, March 1, 1862, in the *Couronne* dossier in A.C.N.; and by Vice Admiral Pâris in *L'Art naval à l'Exposition universelle de Paris en 1867* (Paris, 1870), pp. 85–86, 104, and plate 6, figures 1, 2, 3, and 4.

on the plans of the *Gloire*.[1] Four more ironclad frigates, one to be built at Cherbourg, one at Brest, and two at Toulon, headed the list of new construction to be undertaken in 1859, which Dupuy submitted and Hamelin approved on October 30, 1858. The list for 1859 comprised no wooden ship bigger than a frigate, for the ironclads now replaced the wooden screw ships of the line in the French program for transforming the steam fleet. In his submission of October 30 the *Directeur du Matériel*, wishing to get as many new ideas as possible on the ironclad problem, called for new projects from these members of the construction corps best able to present a solution. He left them wide scope for their proposals, stipulating only that they should have a minimum speed of 12½ knots, an ample supply of coal, food for four months, and water for two.[2]

Before any contract was signed for armor plate for any of these eight ironclads, a new series of experiments took place at Vincennes. Plates 10 to 12 cm. thick from several French ironworks using ores of different qualities, as well as some steel plates furnished by Stirling Begbie of London, were tested by the commission, which was now headed by the new inspector general of naval construction, Prétot. At the same time, scraps of wire rope were tried without success as a backing for plates, at the suggestion of the Emperor.[3] The armor tests showed that

une plaque composée d'une première couche de 5 à 6 cm. de fer nerveux bien corroyé sur laquelle sont encollées une série de tôles très douces légèrement soudées entr'elles de manière à former un feuilleté compact et bien lié, constitue le meilleur blindage aujourd'hui connu. ...."[4]

---

[1] A.M., 1 DD¹ 254, September 3, 1858; 1 DD¹ 255, to Cherbourg, September 3, 1858.

[2] A.M., 1 DD¹ 254, October 30, 1858; 1 DD¹ 253, circular to the five great ports, October 30, 1858. This program for 1859 prescribed that during the year Cherbourg and Lorient should also continue or finish the *Normandie* and *Couronne*, while Toulon should continue the *Invincible* and finish the *Gloire*.

[3] A.M., 1 DD¹ 245, to Guérigny, December 30, 1857; 1 DD¹ 260, to the same, January 13, 1858; 1 DD¹ 261, to the inspector general of naval construction, January 11; to the Vincennes Commission, January 28, August 6, 20; to the Commission des machines et de l'outillage, July 21, 1858; 1 DD¹ 254, January 6, July 28, 1858; 1 DD¹ 264, January 17, 1859; 1 DD¹ 263, to Pieux-Aubert, October 4, 1858.

[4] A.M., 1 DD¹ 254, December 8, 1858.

On the recommendation of the Vincennes Commission, the Minister of Marine, instead of confining the manufacture of the plates to the government plant at Guérigny, instituted further competitive tests at Vincennes, and divided the orders for plates between several private firms, of which Petin, Gaudet and Company of Rive de Gier played the leading rôle at this period.[1]

These contracts generally stipulated for deliveries within four, seven, or ten months, subject to penalties for delay. If the one plate from each lot of twenty-five or fifty which was tested by gunfire at Vincennes proved inferior to certain standard plates established by tests there on February 23, 1859, October 17, 1859, and September 29, 1862, the whole lot was to be rejected. The prices were slightly less than those of 1854. The Government, wishing to distribute its orders as widely as possible, did its best to encourage bidders and contractors. But the tests of the sample plates led to so many rejections in these early years that Petin, Gaudet and Company, who had best solved the difficult technical problems involved, had almost a monopoly of the business.

Since the close of the Crimean War the problem of coast defence had attracted considerable attention in France. In March, 1857, the *Conseil des Travaux* concluded that the defence of Cherbourg in time of war would require eight ironclad floating batteries, at least six fast ironclads suited for use as rams, and numerous gunboats.[2] Although the wooden hulls of the floating batteries of 1854 proved to be in surprisingly good condition when examined in 1862,[3] they had so generally been believed decayed that in September, 1858, the Minister of Marine ordered plans prepared at Cherbourg for new hulls of greater solidity and better nautical qualities to receive the old armor and engines. In rejecting a plan of this sort submitted by *sous-ingénieur* Antoine of Cherbourg

---

[1] A.M., 1 DD¹ 254, December 8, 1858; 4 DD¹ 6. For a brief description of the difficulties and technical methods adopted see Dislère, *Marine cuirassée*, pp. 177–185.

[2] A.M., BB⁸ 1140, March 14 and 17, 1857.

[3] *Mémorial du génie maritime*, 1863, i, p. 227.

the *Conseil des Travaux* reported on March 29, 1859, that the experiments made in England in firing against the batteries protected with 4-inch plates and the tests at Vincennes proved that 68-pounder shot would pierce the existing batteries at five to six hundred meters. The Council therefore recommended that floating batteries be built with iron instead of wooden hulls, so that the weight thus saved might be devoted to increasing the armor from 10 cm. in thickness to 12 cm.[1]

During the war with Austria in 1859, the *Dévastation, Lave,* and *Tonnante* formed part of the Mediterranean Squadron, though their service in the Adriatic involved no fighting.[2] On May 11 of that year Dupuy de Lôme proposed plans for two armored floating batteries, one with a wooden, the other with an iron hull.[3] Despite the opinion expressed by the *Conseil des Travaux* on March 29 in favor of iron hulls, the French government contracted with Arman for the construction at Bordeaux of four wooden-hulled ironclad batteries, the *Paixhans, Palestro, Peiho,* and *Saigon,* on Dupuy de Lôme's plans. These screw vessels of 14 guns and 150 horse power were somewhat smaller than the French ironclads of 1854, but made seven knots instead of four. Their displacement was 1365 tons, length 46.4 meters, beam 14.04 meters, and mean draft 2.65 meters. Their armor was 12 cm. thick at the water line, and 11 cm. for the three upper strakes. They were not finished until 1861 and 1862.[4]

Most of the many French gunboats built at this period had some armor, usually in the form of a gun shield on the for-

---

[1] A.M., BB⁸ 1143, September 14, 1858; BB⁸ 1144, March 29, 1859; 1 DD¹ 255, to Cherbourg, September 20, 1858; 1 DD¹ 259, to Toulon, December 17, 1858; 1 DD¹ 265, to Cherbourg, April 26, 1859.
[2] A.N., BB⁵ 53.
[3] A.M., 1 DD¹ 264.
[4] Hamelin contracted for the *Paixhans* on May 20 and for the *Palestro, Peiho,* and *Saigon* on July 15, as the Commission on Coast Defence had asked for four new floating batteries. A.M., 1 DD¹ 264, June 1, July 1, 14, 1859; 1 DD¹ 268, to Commissary General, Bordeaux, August 13, November 21, 1859; A.N., BB⁵, 55, 56; *Bulletin officiel de la marine,* 1861, ii, pp. 92–96; *Notice sur Dupuy de Lôme,* pp. 48–49. The dimensions given above, from the *Mémorial du génie maritime,* 1861, ii, pp. 19–22, 37–40, do not agree with those of De Balincourt and Vincent-Bréchignac, "La marine française d'hier," pp. 583, 587.

ward deck. In December, 1858, seemingly with a view to war with Austria in the following spring, the French Government ordered eleven sectional wooden steam gunboats, ten from the Société des Forges et Chantiers de la Méditerranée, and one from Arman, each to carry one gun behind a curved shield of 4-inch armor. Five of these vessels, Numbers 6 to 10, were shipped in parts to Lake Garda, assembled at Desenzano with a view to an attack on Peschiera, and presented to the King of Sardinia when the war was abruptly ended.[1] The problem of giving at least partial armor protection to small vessels at this time called forth a large number of plans,[2] of which the most interesting was that of the iron sectional floating batteries designed at short notice by Dupuy de Lôme for service on the lakes and rivers of Italy.

On May 24, 1859, Napoleon III telegraphed from Alexandria to ask Dupuy de Lôme whether two floating batteries for river service not more than 24 meters long and of not more than one meter draft could be speedily built, each to mount a single rifled 12-pounder forward and to carry sufficient armor for protection against field pieces. Two such batteries, the Emperor declared, might render the most brilliant service, destroying the bridges of the Austrians while he attacked them in front. "What I ask is difficult, but the result would be immense. How much time would be needed?"[3] After a rapid interchange of telegrams, Hamelin ordered from the Société des Forges et Chantiers de la Médi-

---

[1] Of these eleven *chaloupes canonnières*, Dupuy de Lôme designed Nos. 1 to 10 which had a rudder at both ends, and Captain Dupouy designed No. 11, the one built by Arman. Schneider and Company furnished the armor. A.M., 1 DD¹ 254, December 17, 22, 30, 1858; DD¹ 264, January 7, 17, 1859; 1 DD¹ 269, to Toulon, April 15, 1859; 1 DD¹ 264, July 27, 1859; 1 DD¹ 272, to *Direction du Personnel*, May 20, 1859; 1 DD¹ 273, to Rear Admiral Dupouy, "commandant supérieur de la flotille intérieure d'Italie," August 8, 1859; 4 DD¹ 6, contract with Schneider and Company, January 14, 1859; A.N., BB⁵ 53.

[2] A.M., BB⁸ 1141, November 24, 1857; 1 DD¹ 269, to Toulon, April 23, 1859; 1 DD¹ 273, to vice admiral commanding Mediterranean squadron, June 29, 1859; 1 DD¹ 264, July 1, 1859; BB⁸ 1146, February 7, April 3, June 12, 1860; 1 DD¹ 282, to *Conseil des Travaux*, April 27, July 2, 1860; 1 DD¹ 281, circular to the five great ports, July 2, 1860; 1 DD¹ 275, October 1, 1860; BB⁸ 1147, November 20, 1860; BB⁸ 1148, March 12, 1861; BB⁸ 1149, September 18, December 10, 1861. See also Dislère, *Marine cuirassée*, pp. 119–120, 132–133.

[3] A.M., 7 DD¹ 245.

terranée, on May 31, five floating batteries which, as the Emperor phrased it, were to make him "master of the whole course of the Po."[1]

These were iron twin-screw vessels of 32 horse power and 142 tons, loopholed for musketry and armed with two 24-pounder breech-loading rifled guns firing ahead. They were 22 meters long, 7.7 meters beam, and of one meter draft. Petin, Gaudet and Company furnished the 2-inch iron armor, which with its wooden backing was believed to be proof against the Austrian 12-pounder field pieces. Each vessel was built in fourteen sections, to bolt together, with a sheet of vulcanized-rubber packing in each joint. The largest section of the hull weighed five tons.[2]

Although sixty days had been allowed for their construction, Battery No. 1 was built, taken to pieces, and loaded on board the *Cacique* in 37 days, reaching Genoa July 7 on the eve of the armistice. After its return to Toulon, this battery was put together in 87 hours, was tested in the harbor, where it steered well and showed an average speed of 4.4 knots, and was taken apart again in 30 hours.[3]

---

[1] *Ibid.*, Hamelin to Dupuy de Lôme, May 31, 1859, transmitting an extract from a letter from the Emperor; *Il carteggio Cavour-Nigra dal 1858 al 1861* (Bologna, 1926–1929, 4 vols.), ii, p. 213.

[2] A.M., 1 DD¹ 273, to Rear Admiral Dupouy, June 25, 1859.

[3] A.M., 7 DD¹ 245, reports of August 5 and 11, 1859. Besides the carton devoted to these vessels, 7 DD¹ 245, see 1 DD¹ 273, telegrams to the Emperor, May 24 and 30, 1859; 1 DD¹ 274, to Compagnie des Forges et Chantiers, May 28, 31, June 3, July 1, 1859; 1 DD¹ 264, June 10, 12, 15, July 1, December 2, 1859; 1 DD¹ 275, January 20, 1860; A.N., BB⁵ 53; *Notice sur Dupuy de Lôme*, p. 50; De Balincourt and Vincent-Bréchignac, "La marine française d'hier," p. 594. Dislère, in his account of these batteries, describes a proposal made by Forfait in 1798 to construct a "corvette démontable" for the expedition to Egypt. *Marine cuirassée*, pp. 137–142.

Twenty unarmored iron sectional gunboats, Nos. 12–31, on a plan by Dupuy de Lôme, were ordered in October, 1859, from the Société des Forges et Chantiers. Nearly all of these were shipped to China, and assembled there. A.M., 1 DD¹ 264, October 15, 21, 1859; 1 DD¹ 265, to Cherbourg, December 19, 1859; 1 DD¹ 269, to Toulon, October 17, 1859, stating that each gunboat would have a 20 horse power engine, and would be shipped in 15 sections; 1 DD¹ 272, to the *Direction du Personnel*, December 16, 1859; 1 DD¹ 274, to Compagnie des Forges et Chantiers, October 17, 1859; 1 DD¹ 275, June 6, October 7, 1860; 1 DD¹ 286, April 25, 1861, loss of Nos. 17 and 26; A.N., BB⁵ 54. See also, *Mémorial du génie maritime*, 1860, i, p. 141; and *Journal des Débats*, January 24, 29, February 7, March 12, 19, 24, 1860.

When Hamelin called for new projects for the four armored frigates to be laid down in 1859, eight naval constructors responded. De Moras proposed a vessel of 7967 tons, 1200 horse power, and more than 13.5 knots speed, carrying twenty-eight 50-pounders on her main deck, and twenty-eight 30-pounder rifles on her upper deck. Armor protected her water line and lower deck from stem to stern, but, on her upper deck, covered only 35 meters of her sides amidships. Sochet pushed still further the idea of protecting only part of the hull. He proposed a wooden vessel armored at the water line, with thirty-eight guns concentrated amidships on two decks, behind armor. For the unarmored extremities, the hull was to be of iron instead of wood, to reduce the fire hazard. Aurous and de Coppier proposed ironclads with iron hulls like the *Couronne*; Dorian and de Gasté, frigates resembling the *Gloire*. Guieysse advocated a reduction of beam which seemed to the *Conseil des Travaux* to imperil stability. Courbebaisse submitted a plan for a ship of 6851 tons with armored sides inclined at an angle of 45 degrees, which the Council deemed wholly unsuitable for fighting at sea, though perhaps admissible in a floating battery for harbor defence.[1] Hamelin pointed out that the Vincennes tests showed that no appreciable advantage was gained by inclining the armor unless the angle was less than 45 degrees. In that case the advantage due to the slope of the armor would hardly compensate for the increased weight as compared with vertical protection. Courbebaisse's doubts as to the possibility of protecting vertical sides seemed to the minister exaggerated, since plates of 11 and 12 cm. had withstood very satisfactorily the fire of 50-pounder shot at 20 meters range, with charges equal to one-third the weight of the shot.[2]

The *Conseil des Travaux* declined to approve any of these eight plans; and Hamelin rejected the projects for armored ships of the line of 6440 and 10,700 tons displacement sub-

---
[1] A.M., BB⁸ 1144, April 26, June 28, 1859; 6 DD¹ 22, dossier 490.
[2] A.M., 1 DD¹ 265, to Cherbourg, June 15, 1859.

mitted a little earlier by naval constructors Aurous and Legrand.[1] On April 26, 1859, the Council proposed the following conditions: length of about 90 meters, immersed midship section of 100 square meters, displacement of about 7000 tons, armor of 12 cm. thickness at the water line and of 11 cm. above, 44 guns on the main deck and six in an armored redoubt on the upper deck, engines of 1000 horse power, reduced sail area, supplies of water for two weeks, provisions for two months, and 200 rounds of ammunition per gun. As the Council believed that only iron hulls were sufficiently solid and durable for armored ships, it expressed the opinion that as many of them should be provided in the ironclad program as the available supply of French metal workers would permit.[2]

Vice Admiral Count Bouët-Willaumez, the naval prefect at Toulon, and the naval constructors at that port, together with Captains Labrousse and Gicquel des Touches and naval constructors Sochet and Joyeux at Cherbourg and Guieysse and de Roussel at Brest, all submitted projects for armoring wooden ships of the line. Although the temptation to utilize existing ships was strong, and the minister seemed several times on the point of adopting this policy, the French finally decided that the proposed transformation would produce only mediocre vessels, not worth their cost, and therefore confined their appropriations for armored vessels to new construction.[3]

---

[1] A.M., 6 DD¹ 22, dossier 483; 1 DD¹ 259, to Toulon, October 11, 1858; 1 DD¹ 273, to Legrand, February 9, 1859. Dislère summarizes the proposals of de Moras, Sochet, Aurous and Legrand in his *Marine cuirassée*, pp. 76–78.

[2] A.M., BB⁸ 1144.

[3] A.M., 1 DD¹ 244, to Toulon, May 22, 1857; 1 DD¹ 255, to Cherbourg, February 6, July 21, 26, 1858; BB⁸ 1142, May 25, 1858; BB⁸ 1144, January 25, June 28, 1859; 1 DD¹ 265, to Cherbourg, February 7, 1859; 1 DD¹ 266, to Brest, July 4, 1859; 1 DD¹ 273, to Gicquel des Touches, July 6, 1859; BB⁸ 1145, July 5, October 31, 1859; 6 DD¹ 22, dossier 474; 6 DD¹ 23, dossier 506; *Notice sur Labrousse*, pp. 25–26, 80. In a long memorandum dated September 21, 1861, Bouët-Willaumez pointed out that if wooden line-of-battle ships were to be used in war again, they must either be armored or they would be forced to seek safety from the ironclad frigates by flight, if flight were possible. As twenty-five of the existing thirty-seven French steam ships of the line were in good condition, he pressed the minister to authorize their transformation. Although a conference at Toulon

Of the four ironclads scheduled to be laid down in 1859, Dupuy de Lôme proposed on June 10 that one be built on the plan submitted by de Moras, which should be altered to meet the objections of the *Conseil des Travaux*. For the remaining three he submitted a new plan of his own, drawn up after receipt of confidential information from England as to the plans of the proposed British ironclads. Believing it indispensable that the French ironclads excel all rivals in speed, and at least equal them in number of guns, and fearing lest the new British vessels surpass in these respects the French ironclads already under construction, he had hastened to design a new type with more guns, speed and bunker capacity. He proposed a vessel of 6724 tons, 52 rifled 30-pounder guns, 1000 horse power, and an estimated speed of 14 knots, with a length of 86 meters, a breadth of 17.34 meters, and a draft of 7.83 meters. This ship, resembling what was later called in England the "belt-and-battery" type, was armored from end to end at the water line and the orlop deck, above which the armor was limited to a section amidships. The guns were concentrated amidships on the main and upper decks behind the armor, and were protected from a raking fire by shot-proof transverse bulkheads. This arrangement placed half the guns at an increased elevation, and lightened the extremities of the vessel. A conical ram was added, designed to pierce any enemy ship that was struck even at moderate speed.[1]

Hamelin rejected the revised project of de Moras, which failed to suit the *Conseil des Travaux*; and decided to commence only two ironclads in 1859, both on the new plan by Dupuy de Lôme. The *Magenta*, laid down at Brest June 22,

of Hamelin, Dupuy de Lôme, the Naval Prefect and the six naval constructors at the port, led to revised projects for converting wooden ships into ironclads, none was finally adopted. See the endorsement in Dupuy de Lôme's hand on the memorandum of Bouët-Willaumez. A.M., 6 DD¹ 23, dossier 506.

[1] A.M., 1 DD¹ 264, June 10, 1859. An unsigned memorandum in English, with French translation, headed "Renseignemens sur les nouvelles frégates cuirassées anglaises. (Communiqué par S.M. le 11 avril 1859)" is in 6 DD¹ 88, dossier 2355. The document in English, apparently a copy, headed "Private and confidential. Rough particulars of 6 iron cased screw frigates [Béliers cuirassées] about to be built," contains important particulars about the *Warrior* class, and terminates as follows: "N.B. Full specification and drawing can be supplied."

and the *Solférino*, laid down at Lorient June 24, 1859, were both launched just two years to a day from the date on which their construction was begun.¹ Most of the ironclad projects submitted by French naval constructors since 1856 had contemplated the use of the vessel as a ram.² Although a long series of proposals for rams had been rejected, they may have had some influence on the adoption of that weapon by Dupuy de Lôme in the *Magenta*, *Solférino*, and later ironclads. On January 25, 1859, the *Conseil des Travaux* had concluded that only new and specially designed vessels would be suitable for use as rams, and that the ram itself must be so constructed as to permit striking the enemy ship under water at the stem or stern, and if possible disabling its propeller.³ To meet these conditions Dupuy de Lôme gave the *Magenta* and *Solférino* rams which projected sharply under water and were covered with a steel cone weighing 14,000 kilograms which was strongly supported by many of the heaviest longitudinal timbers in the ship.⁴

Meanwhile work on the *Gloire*, *Invincible*, *Normandie*, and *Couronne* progressed steadily. Although the original plans had called for plates in three layers, the Vincennes experiments caused the rejection of laminated armor and the adoption of plates 11 cm. thick for the eight upper strakes, and 12 cm. thick for the five lower.⁵ Despite the difficulties presented by her novel construction the *Gloire* was built on schedule time. Her launching, which the original orders to Toulon had set for the end of 1859 or the beginning of 1860, actually took place on November 24, 1859. She made a most favorable impression in her first trials in August and September, 1860, and while escorting the Em-

---

1 A.M., 1 DD¹ 264, June 10, July 1, 1859; BB⁸ 1145, August 30, 1859; 7 DD¹ 139; 7 DD¹ 197; 1 DD¹ 270, to Brest and Lorient, July 1, 18, October 31, 1859.
2 See especially A.M., BB⁸ 1140, April 28, 1857; 1 DD¹ 262, to Labrousse, July 19, 1858; 6 DD¹ 22, dossier 474; *Notice sur Labrousse*, pp. 25–26, 80. For earlier projects see above, pp. 27, 48, 57, 63, 64, 89, 90, 91, 92, 93, 99, 100, 102, and Appendix B.   3 A.M., BB⁸ 1144.
4 *Notice sur Dupuy de Lôme*, pp. 41–43; A.M., 4 DD¹ 6, contract with Petin, Gaudet and Co., September 13, 1861. Cf. Lullier, *Essai sur l'histoire de la tactique navale* (Paris, 1867).
5 A.M., 1 DD¹ 259, to Toulon, March 20, August 27, 1858; 7 DD¹ 170.

peror and Empress to Algiers later in the same month. Using only half her boilers she easily made 11 knots without the help of her sails, and under full steam she made a maximum speed of 13.1 knots and an average speed of 12.31 knots for ten hours. Against a gale of wind and heavy sea she made 10 knots, pitching very little and showing no signs of straining. Her triumphant designer estimated that her 675 tons of coal would suffice for more than 27 days at 8 knots, 14 days at 11 knots, or 7 days at full speed; and declared that in steaming and nautical qualities she equalled or surpassed the best wooden steam ships of the line afloat.[1]

On this revolutionary vessel, whose successful trials sounded the knell of the wooden capital ship, sails played a more subordinate rôle than on the British ironclads built to cope with her. The *Gloire* was a three-masted vessel of 5617.936 tons displacement, 900 horse power and 36 guns, 77.89 meters long on the water line, 17 meters beam, and with a mean draft of 7.758 meters. Sacrificing the ability to fight anywhere on the seven seas which had characterized the sailing ship of the line, and postulating that his new creation was "not destined to act far from European waters," Dupuy de Lôme drastically reduced her canvas to a total of 1095.31 square meters. Although her sails would help her while steaming under certain circumstances, they were not designed to play an important part in the ship's movements.[2]

---

[1] A.M., 7 DD¹ 170, September 7, 1860. Later favorable reports indicated that she rolled a good deal and shipped considerable water in bad weather. In five voyages between Algiers and Toulon in 1860 she covered 3308 miles without a single accident or forced stop. *Ibid.*, March 20, 30, May 27, August 12, 24, 27, 1861; A.N., BB⁵ 54, 55; *Mémorial du génie maritime*, 1860, ii, pp. 354–383.

[2] 7 DD¹ 170, report of September 7, 1860, and original *devis d'armement* of the *Gloire*. The latter was reproduced in the *Mémorial du génie maritime*, 1860, ii, pp. 354–383. The bottom of the *Gloire* was sheathed with copper, separated from the iron armor by a groove 3 cm. wide filled with a composition of red lead, coal tar, and bisulphate of mercury. A.M., 7 DD¹ 170, report of Dorian, the naval constructor in charge, December 10, 1861.
Of the contemporary descriptions of the *Gloire*, all more or less inaccurate, the best are: *Journal des Débats*, January 15, 1860; *Nouvelles annales de la marine et revue coloniale*, April, 1860, pp. 259–260, and February, 1861, pp. 95–98; *Journal des sciences militaires*, October, 1860, pp. 156–160; Xavier Raymond, *Les marines de France et de l'Angleterre, 1815–1863*, pp. 140–161. Her plans are reproduced in Pâris, *Souvenirs de marine*, iv, nos. 182–186. See also *Notice sur Dupuy de Lôme*, pp. 37–40.

Her sister ships, the *Normandie* and *Invincible*, were launched on March 10, 1860, and April 4, 1861, soon followed by the *Magenta* and *Solférino* on June 22 and 24. Although Audenet's revised plans for the iron-hulled ironclad *Couronne* had been approved by Hamelin on September 1, 1858, nearly eight months before the Admiralty approved the plans of the *Warrior*, the French vessel was not begun until February 14, 1859, nor launched until March 28, 1861, almost four months after the *Warrior's* launching. If it be fair to classify the large and high-powered Stevens battery with these vessels rather than with the floating batteries of the Crimean War, three powers share the honors of priority in developing the iron-hulled seagoing ironclad. The United States made the first appropriation for such a vessel, but it was never finished. Of the successful vessels of this type France was the first to begin and Great Britain the first to complete one.[1]

The *Couronne*, a strong and seaworthy ship of 6076 tons displacement and 900 horse power, mounted 40 guns. She was 80 meters long on the water line and 16.7 meters beam, with a mean draft of 7.6 meters and a midship section of 101.86 square meters. In her trials her best speed was 13 knots. In addition to her side armor, described above, she was protected against plunging fire by an armored deck of 12-mm. sheet iron, supported on heavy beams of iron and wood backed by pine planking. Although this deck was much heavier than those of the other French ironclads it failed to extend over the engines and boilers, where there were large openings for the smokestack and to admit air and light to the fire and engine rooms.[2]

On September 22, 1860, Dupuy de Lôme submitted a report of capital importance in naval history. In view of the great success of the *Gloire*, and of the obvious superiority of armored frigates to the largest wooden warships, he remarked

---

[1] A.M., 7 DD¹ 95, 113, 139, 197; A.C.N., *Couronne* dossier; A.N., BB⁵ 54, 55, 56; *Mémorial du génie maritime*, 1862, ii, pp. 223-238; See above, pp. 48-52, 54, and below, pp. 131, 158, 159, 211-219.
[2] A.C.N., *Couronne* dossier; A.N., BB⁵ 56; *Mémorial du génie maritime*, 1861, i, pp. 119-122; 1862, ii, pp. 223-238.

that France might congratulate herself on having laid down no wooden ship of the line since 1855. Now the way was clear for a great ironclad program. To her six seagoing and nine coast-defence ironclads built or building, France must add twenty seagoing ironclads for the active fleet, ten for the reserve, and eleven armored floating batteries. Since the national finances and the capacity of the shipyards did not permit undertaking all these ships simultaneously, he proposed that ten seagoing ironclads, nine with wooden hulls and one of iron, should be laid down at once and pushed to completion within eighteen months, and that eleven armored floating batteries should be undertaken simultaneously.[1]

Hamelin promptly approved the program, giving France a total of sixteen seagoing and twenty coast-defence ironclads built, building, or authorized.[2] Though many details in design and construction remained to be solved, the great revolution in French building policy was now complete. For the ten new frigates, the French experts now debated the details: the proper height of battery,[3] the best type of conning tower,[4] narrower gun-ports,[5] and the proper rig for these vessels "not

---

[1] Dupuy's report printed in Appendix E is in A.M., 1 DD¹ 275.

[2] A.M., 1 DD¹ 281, circular of September 25, 1860; 1 DD¹ 282, to *Conseil des Travaux*, October 3, 1860.

[3] After a canvass of the opinions of the *Conseil d'Amirauté*, the *Conseil des Travaux*, the naval prefects, and other superior officers, the Emperor himself, adopting the advice of a majority of the *Conseil des Travaux*, fixed the height of battery at two meters. A.M., 6 DD² 23, dossier 507; 1 DD¹ 281, circulars of September 25, October 3, 1860, November 16, 1860; BB⁸ 1147, October 15, 1860.

[4] The conning tower or "blockhaus" of the *Gloire* was an unroofed two-story affair about twelve feet high, placed just forward of the mizzen-mast, and abaft the bridge, and armored with wrought-iron plates four inches thick. A.M., 4 DD¹ 6, December 2, 1859; *Nouvelles annales de la marine et revue coloniale*, April, 1860, pp. 259–260. The models of the *Solférino*, *Flandre* and *Gloire* in the *Musée de la Marine* at the Louvre, all show conning towers. Those of the *Solférino* and *Flandre* are roofed and placed just abaft the funnel. Serious attention was given to the problem of repelling boarders. For discussions on this point and on conning towers, see A.M., BB⁸ 1146, March 20, April 24, 1860; BB⁸ 1148, June 18, 1861; BB⁸ 1149, October 15, 1861; BB⁸ 1150, June 10, 1862; 1 DD¹ 281, to Brest and Lorient, March 14, 1860; 1 DD¹ 278, to Lorient, April 7, 1860; 7 DD¹ 95, note of de Robert, July 20, 1861.

[5] A.M., BB⁸ 1144, June 21, 1859; 1 DD¹ 266, to Brest, November 16, 1859; BB⁸ 1146, April 24, 1860; 1 DD¹ 277, to Brest, July 18, 1860. *Notice sur Labrousse*, pp. 55–56, 87.

destined for action far from European waters."[1] New tests at Vincennes and Gavres, which form an important chapter in the contest between ordnance and armor, led to the adoption of plates 15 cm. in thickness.[2] To fulfil the new conditions, Dupuy de Lôme, with the advice of the *Conseil des Travaux*, slightly enlarged and modified the plans of the *Gloire*, creating a new type, of 5800 tons and 1000 horse power. This plan served for all of the ten ironclad frigates whose construction was ordered on November 16, 1860: the wooden-hulled *Flandre*, at Cherbourg; *Gauloise*, *Magnanime* and *Valeureuse* at Brest; *Surveillante* at Lorient; *Guyenne* at Rochefort; *Provence*, *Savoie* and *Revanche* at Toulon; and the iron-hulled *Héroïne* at Lorient.[3] In striking contrast to the later building policies of the two nations, this first French ironclad fleet was far more homogeneous than the British fleet which was designed to cope with it.

Had the state of the French iron industry and the number of her skilled workers in metals permitted, few or none of the new ironclads would have had wooden hulls. The *Conseil des Travaux*, which greatly preferred the use of iron, obtained its adoption for the eleven projected floating batteries. As Napoleon III wished these new coast-defence vessels to be smaller than those already built, five government naval constructors and Arman submitted projects ranging from 1060 to 1295 tons and carrying six to ten guns. The project of *sous-ingénieur* Lemoine of Lorient for a vessel with guns mounted in a central battery alone met with favor. Various modifications enlarged and transformed this plan into two: one for the *Arrogante*, *Implacable*, and *Opiniâtre*, built by Gouin and Company at Nantes, and the other, somewhat shorter and broader, for the *Embuscade*, *Refuge*, *Protectrice*,

---

[1] A.M., BB⁸ 1146, March 20, May 29, 1860; BB⁸ 1147, August 28, October 30, 1860; 1 DD¹ 276, to Cherbourg, January 9, June 15, 1860; 1 DD¹ 286, March 2, 1861; A.C.N. *Couronne* dossier, letter from the naval prefect, Lorient, October 10, 1861; *Notice sur Labrousse*, p. 27.
[2] See below, p. 209.
[3] A.M., 6 DD¹ 23, dossier 507, note of Dupuy de Lôme, October 27, 1860; BB⁸ 1147, October 30, 1860; 1 DD¹ 275, November 16, 19, 1860; 1 DD¹ 281, circulars of November 16 and December 29, 1860.

and *Imprenable*, built by Arman at Bordeaux. For financial reasons the Minister of Marine, Count Chasseloup-Laubat, on November 28, 1861, suspended the orders for building the four remaining floating batteries of the 1860 program, which had been allotted to government yards.[1]

Both technical and financial difficulties greatly retarded the execution of the French program of 1860. Realizing how much French public and private yards had to learn from the British in iron shipbuilding, the government, between 1857 and 1861, sent eight naval constructors to study British methods. Captain Pigeard, the French naval attaché at London, did his best to supplement the reports of these constructors, three of which were reproduced in the *Mémorial du génie maritime* for the benefit of the whole corps. Much had to be done in the way of training personnel and introducing machine tools before France could readily build the iron hulls which so many of her naval constructors preferred.[2]

The financial burdens entailed by ironclad building soon slowed up construction. The *Gloire* cost 4,797,901 francs; the *Normandie*, 4,800,836; the *Invincible*, 4,987,097; the *Cou-*

[1] A.M., 1 DD¹ 282, to *Conseil des Trauvaux*, October 3, 1860; BB⁸ 1147, October 30, 1860; 1 DD¹ 275, November 16, 19, 1860; 1 DD¹ 281, circular of November 16, 1860; BB⁸ 1148, April 30, 1861; BB⁸ 1149, July 9, November 26, 1861; 1 DD¹ 298, November 30, 1861; 7 DD¹ 233, January 31, August 14, September 13, November 28, 1861; January 16, February 20, May 16, 1862; BB⁸ 1150, January 7, 1862; 1 DD¹ 305, June 16, July 19, October 30, December 12, 1862; 7 DD¹ 234; *Mémorial du génie maritime*, 1866, i, pp. 251–253; De Balincourt and Vincent-Bréchignac, "La marine française d'hier," pp. 583, 589–595; Jean Destrem and G. Clerc-Rampal, *Catalogue raisonnée du musée de la marine* (Paris, 1909), p. 283; Dislère, *Marine cuirassée*, p. 121. The model of the *Arrogante* in the naval museum at the Louvre shows a central battery with nine ports on a side, and three ports forward and three aft.

Early in 1861 Arman had presented a project for an ironclad frigate of 7250 tons and 40 guns, with its extremities cut down to the level of the gun deck, leaving a central battery surmounted by two fixed turrets. This plan, which was rejected by the *Conseil des Travaux*, seems to bear no resemblance to the Confederate States ram *Stonewall* built by Arman in 1863 and 1864.

[2] For the missions of Audenet in 1857, Masson, Piedvache and LeGrand in 1858, Forquenot and Calla in 1859, and Jaÿ and Lebelin in 1861, and for the reports of Pigeard, see A.M., 6 DD¹ 32, dossier 507; 6 DD¹ 89, dossier 2406; 1 DD¹ 262, to Ministre des Affaires étrangères, July 5, 1858; 1 DD¹ 273, to Forquenot, July 15, 1859; 1 DD¹ 284, to Jaÿ, December 21, 1860; *Mémorial du génie maritime*, 1860, i, pp. 83–100, 121–140; 1861, i, pp. 153–238; 1862, i, pp. 203–302; *Le moniteur de la flotte*, October 22, 1857.

ronne, 6,019,095. Some began to ask whether France, in attempting to outstrip England by the introduction of a new type, had not merely transferred the competition to a basis on which length of purse and superior metallurgical and industrial development gave Britain enormous advantages.[1]

At all events, between 1854 and 1860, Napoleon III had inaugurated a great revolution in naval architecture. In the combats at Hampton Roads the French saw little more than a tribute to the foresight of their naval constructors, their ministers, and the Emperor himself. Make what allowances we will for the exaggerations of courtiers and for the shrewdness of naval constructors who furthered their ends by proclaiming the ironclads as the Emperor's own creation, the contemporary French view that Napoleon III played a great rôle in the introduction of the armored ship is fully warranted. As an artillerist he appreciated the problem raised by the introduction of shell guns. He was quick to see the need of new types of ship, and unwavering in his support of experiments to perfect them. For the execution of his grand design, he picked the right man, and backed him with the necessary funds and with a personal interest that swept aside all obstacles. The great revolution in naval construction was due to the will of Napoleon III and to the genius of Dupuy de Lôme.

[1] A.M., 7 DD¹ 95, 113, 170; A.C.N., *Couronne* dossier.

CHAPTER VII

GREAT BRITAIN ENTERS THE RACE

AMONG naval powers the weaker have a more obvious interest in revolutionizing naval warfare than have their stronger rivals. If a power which already enjoys the command of the seas takes the lead in introducing a novel type of ship destined to supplant the capital ship of the day, it runs the risk of converting its existing fleet into junk and giving its rivals a fresh start with the slate wiped clean. When the dominant power can build ships faster than its weaker rivals, and can hope to overtake them rapidly if a lead be momentarily conceded, the argument for conservatism in construction policy becomes all the stronger. Combating the *Dreadnought* policy of Admiral Sir John Fisher in the Committee of Imperial Defence, Sir George Clarke, now Lord Sydenham of Combe, argued in vain that it should be an axiom of British policy "never to lead in ship construction but always to follow with something better."[1] In 1856 as in 1906 Great Britain owed command of the seas to a large force of capital ships which a revolution in naval construction might render obsolete over night. Then as later her shipbuilding facilities permitted her to hope to overtake rapidly any rival whose naval constructors might devise a new and better type of ship. In 1856, when the success of the armored floating batteries at Kinburn had raised the problem of seagoing ironclads, the Admiralty did not rush to the fore with a mid-century *Dreadnought*. It left to the French the task of rendering Britain's wooden walls as obsolete as the trireme.

The keynote of the Admiralty's policy during the two years following the close of the Crimean War is found in the report or "submission" of the Surveyor of the Navy, Sir Baldwin Walker, to the Admiralty on June 22, 1858.

[1] Colonel Lord Sydenham of Combe, *My Working Life* (London, 1927), p. 209.

Although as I have frequently stated it is not to the interest of Great Britain possessing as she does so large a navy to adopt any important change in the construction of ships of war which might have the effect of rendering necessary the introduction of a new class of very costly vessels until such a course is forced upon her by the adoption by Foreign Powers of formidable ships of a novel character requiring similar ships to cope with them, yet it then becomes a matter not only of expediency but of absolute necessity.[1]

A trickle of ironclad projects from inventors, soon to become a flood, had already begun to reflect the growing public interest. The British received six projects of this sort in 1857, twenty-one in 1858, and fifty in 1859.[2] Between May 1, 1859, and May 1, 1862, the number of proposals and plans "for the purposes of shot-proof ships" received by the Admiralty amounted to five hundred and ninety.[3] Among the earliest of these suggestions, the most interesting was that of Vice Admiral Sir Charles Napier, who proposed in September, 1857, to take an old three-decked ship, cut her down to a frigate, apply the weight thus saved to iron armor, and fit her with 10-inch guns. The Surveyor reported, however, that such ships would prove costly to convert and of short duration, with adequate stability but insufficient height of battery. Sir Baldwin Walker believed, moreover, that no iron-hulled ironclads would be suitable for any service which would preclude their being frequently docked to have the bottoms cleaned, until more effectual means had been discovered to prevent fouling.[4]

Sir Charles Wood, First Lord of the Admiralty from March, 1855, to March, 1858, in Palmerston's first administration, believed that armored ships had received no "real trial" at

---

[1] P.R.O., Controller of the Navy, Submission Letter Book no. 20. Printed in *Parliamentary Papers*, 1861, v, no. 438, p. 231.

[2] Based on lists compiled from Adm. 12/637, Adm. 12/653, and Controller of the Navy, Submission Letter Books nos. 19, 20 and 21. For those of the inventors who also applied for patents, see *Patents for Inventions, Abridgments of Specifications, Class 113 . . . 1855–1866* (London, 1905), s.v. Armor and Armor-plating, and War-Ships.

[3] *Parliamentary Papers*, 1862, xxxiv, no. 392. Of these 590 proposals, all were referred in the first instance to the Controller's department; 85 were subsequently submitted to the Committee on Iron Plates, 19 to Captain Hewlett, commanding the gunnery ship *Excellent*, and one to a special committee.

[4] P.R.O., Controller of the Navy, Submission Letter Book no. 19, October 13, 1857.

Kinburn, since the guns of the fort were "very small" and few in number. The suitability of ironclad floating batteries for service in shoal water he nevertheless deemed to be established "beyond an experiment."[1] To throw light on the problem of the seagoing ironclad the Admiralty requested the War Department to test the relative merits of hammered and rolled iron plates, and of iron and steel, for casing ships' sides. In these experiments, conducted at Woolwich in December, 1856, and April, May, and June, 1857, wrought-iron shot proved far more destructive than cast-iron shot. A 2-inch steel plate offered no effectual resistance. Between the rolled and hammered plates of 4-inch iron there was little to choose. Both offered a good resistance to cast-iron 68-pounder shot at 600 yards, but were broken up when the blows were repeated, or when the range was reduced to 400 yards.[2]

Shortly before Sir Charles Wood left the Admiralty in March, 1858, the Surveyor submitted a rough design for a 26-gun corvette with armor plates four inches in thickness from the upper deck "to about five feet below the load water line." This vessel of 5600 tons displacement and 800 nominal horse power was to be 280 feet long, of 58 feet beam and 25 feet 3 inches draft, with a midship port ten feet above the water and an estimated speed of twelve knots. The cost of her hull and engines was estimated at £200,000, that is, about £80,000 more than for an ordinary wooden vessel with the same armament and engine power. Before any definite plan for ironclads could be submitted, however, Sir Baldwin Walker thought two points remained to be decided: first, how could their bottoms be kept clean, particularly on for-

---

1 *Parliamentary Papers*, 1861, v, no. 438, "Report from the Select Committee on the Board of Admiralty," testimony of Sir Charles Wood, May 28 and 31, 1861, in reply to questions 2881–2884, 3153, 3154.
2 P.R.O., Controller of the Navy, Submission Letter Books no. 18, March 18, April 18, May 9, July 4 and 11, 1856, and no. 19, January 1, 1857; Adm. 12/621: 59–4a; Adm. 12/637: 59–4a; Adm. 1/5724, copy of Report of Ordnance Select Committee, August 29, 1859; *Transactions and Report of the Special Committee on Iron between 21st January, 1861, and March, 1862*, hereafter cited as Special Committee on Iron, *First Report*, pp. x, 165–167. Further tests of heavy cast-iron blocks in 1857 threw little fresh light on the problem. *Ibid.*, pp. x, 163–164.

eign stations where dockyards were lacking; and second, what thickness of the recently invented homogeneous metal would resist not only ordinary shot but also "those more formidable projectiles invented by Mr. Whitworth."[1] Despite the fact that the subject of seagoing ironclads had been under consideration for a year or more, the Board was not yet ready for a vote on the matter, although a sum of money had been taken in Vote No. 10 of the navy estimates "which might have been applied to that object [an experimental ironclad] in 1858, if we had gone on with it."[2]

The Conservative Board of Admiralty headed by Sir John Pakington[3] took office on March 8 at a tense moment in Anglo-French relations. Orsini's attempt to assassinate Napoleon III by means of a conspiracy organized in England provoked an outburst of mutual animosity in France and Great Britain which brought to a climax two years of increasing discord. As in the aftermath of a greater war, hearty cooperation against a common enemy had been followed by serious friction in the execution of the peace treaty. French readiness to concede points to the beaten Russians proved as distasteful to British opinion of that day as did, to a later generation of Frenchmen, the British interest in the rehabilitation of Germany after 1919. As the signs of rapproche-

---

[1] *Parliamentary Papers*, 1861, v, no. 438, p. 338. The copy of the original in the Controller's Submission Letter Book no. 19, is dated March 3, 1858. On Whitworth's projectiles see below, pp. 125, 197, 205, 206. "Homogeneous iron is a variety of cast-steel, containing a small proportion of carbon, and is intermediate, in that as well as in other respects, between malleable iron and cast-steel." *Experiments with Naval Ordnance, H.M.S. "Excellent"* (London, 1866), p. 130, note.

[2] Testimony of Sir Charles Wood, May 28, 1861, *Parliamentary Papers*, 1861, v, no. 438, p. 338. In response to the question "Can you give a date when the question of iron ships like the 'Warrior' was first submitted to the consideration of your department?" Isaac Watts, Chief Constructor of the Navy, declared in February, 1861: — "I should think somewhere about three years ago; but it originated with the Controller's department; it was not referred to that department." *Parliamentary Papers*, 1861, xxvi, no. 2790, "Report of the Commissioners appointed to inquire into the control and management of Her Majesty's naval yards . . .," p. 377.

[3] Vice Admiral William Fanshawe Martin, Vice Admiral Sir Richard Saunders Dundas, Rear Admiral Alexander Milne and Captain James Robert Drummond were the Sea Lords; Lord Lovaine, the Civil Lord; Henry Thomas Lowry Corry, First Secretary; and William Govett Romaine, Second Secretary. *London Gazette*, March 9, 1858; W. L. Clowes, *The Royal Navy*, vii, p. 2.

ment with Russia multiplied, rumors of a Franco-Russian alliance became rife.[1] One of the first special minutes of the new Board of Admiralty contained the significant remark: "When determining upon the number of ships, and upon the Naval Force generally, which England should have, it should be borne in mind that the navies of France and of Russia may very probably be combined against her."[2]

Far from maintaining a two-power standard at sea, however, Great Britain had allowed France to attain parity in fast screw ships of the line. The launching of Dupuy de Lôme's *Napoléon*, of 900 horse power, in May, 1850, and of H. M. S. *Agamemnon*, of 600 horse power, in 1852, had started a race for supremacy in screw line-of-battle ships. England answered France's program of ships of this class with a greater program of her own. In the work of building new ships and converting old ones to the screw, however, the Crimean War, with its demands for great flotillas of light-draft gunboats, seriously hampered England's progress. Although Palmerston, at the height of the *Entente cordiale*, was unwilling to relax Britain's defensive arrangements designed to cope with a possible French invasion,[3] the exigencies of the Crimean War led Great Britain to slacken her construction of capital ships, just as the exigencies of the World War led the United States to shelve her great capital-ship program of 1916 in order to speed the construction of smaller craft. Soon

---

[1] On Franco-Russian relations in these years, see: *Extrait des Mémoires du Duc de Morny, Une Ambassade en Russie, 1856* (4th ed., Paris, 1892); V. Boutenko, "Un projet d'alliance franco-russe en 1856," in *Revue historique*, July–August, 1927, pp. 277–325; F. Charles-Roux, *Alexandre II, Gortchakoff, et Napoléon III* (Paris, 1913); S. Goriainov, "Les étapes de l'alliance franco-russe," in *Revue de Paris*, January 1, February 1, 15, 1912; Kurt Rheindorf, *Die Schwarze-Meer-(Pontus-)Frage vom Pariser Frieden von 1856 bis zum Abschluss der Londoner Konferenz von 1871* (Berlin, 1925); H. Rothan, "L'entrevue de Stuttgart," in *Revue des deux mondes*, December 1, 1888, January 1, 1889; A. Stern, *Geschichte Europas seit den Verträgen von 1815 bis zum Frankfurter Frieden von 1871* (Berlin, 1894–1924, 10 vols.), viii, pp. 183 ff.; L. Thouvenel, *Trois années de la question d'orient, 1856–1859* (Paris, 1897).

[2] Adm. 3/266, March 27, 1858. Sir Baldwin Walker's submission of November 13, 1858, argued that the British fleet ought to be large enough to cope with France and Russia combined. Controller of the Navy, Submission Letter Book no. 20.

[3] G. P. Gooch, ed., *The Later Correspondence of Lord John Russell*, ii, p. 171, Palmerston to Russell, September 23, 1854.

after his entry into office, in March, 1858, Pakington received from Sir Baldwin Walker a submission urging redoubled efforts to increase the screw fleet.[1] On July 27 the Surveyor declared that

> although a few years ago we were far ahead of them [the French] in respect of screw line of battle ships, they are now for the first time equal to us and unless some extraordinary steps are at once taken to expedite the building of screw ships of the line, the French at the close of next year will be actually superior to us as regards the most powerful class of ships of war.... [2]

Two days later the Board placed on record "the deep sense they entertain of the importance of the facts stated with regard to the present equality of the French Navy with that of Great Britain, and the certain superiority which France will in a few months have obtained," and concluded that the Board "would incur the most serious responsibility if they delayed to call the attention of H. M. Gov^t to this unprecedented condition of the British Navy as compared with that of France, irrespective of those of other countries in Europe."[3]

Thanks to the utmost pressure from the Tory Board of Admiralty, the number of completed screw line-of-battle ships rose from 29, in the spring of 1858, to 40 in midsummer of 1859.[4] At the same time Pakington grappled with the grave problem raised by the construction of the *Gloire* and

---

[1] P.R.O., Controller of the Navy, Submission Letter Book no. 19, March 24, 1858.

[2] P.R.O., Controller of the Navy, Submission Letter Book no. 20, July 27, 1858. See also "Report of a Committee appointed by the Treasury to Inquire into the Navy Estimates, from 1852 to 1858, and into the Comparative State of the Navies of England and France," January 6, 1859, in *Parliamentary Papers*, 1859, xiv, no. 182; and the speeches of Sir John Pakington, Sir Charles Wood, and Admiral Sir Charles Napier in the House of Commons, February 25, 1859, Hansard, 3rd series, clii, cols. 882–927. For an able, hostile analysis of the figures presented by the advocates of greater preparedness, see Cobden, *The Three Panics*.

[3] Adm. 1/5698, minute of July 29, 1858. In the same bundle is a memorandum by Admiral Martin, November, 1858, arguing that "We shall not be safe until our absolute naval means greatly exceed those of France. We must remember that a combination against us is highly probable, that we have many remote dependencies to defend, that the force of France is concentrated, and that our existence depends upon success." Cf. *Letters of Queen Victoria*, iii, p. 378, Queen Victoria to Derby, August 2, 1858.

[4] *Parliamentary Papers*, 1859, xiv, no. 182; speeches of Sir John Pakington, February 25, 1859, and of Lord Clarence Paget, July 8, 1859, Hansard, 3rd series, clii, cols. 904–908; cliv, cols. 904–905.

her consorts.[1] On April 22, 1858, Captain R. S. Hewlett of the gunnery ship *Excellent* reported concerning some experiments with land batteries cased with iron which he had witnessed at Woolwich on the previous day. A wrought-iron plate, 6 feet square and 8 inches thick, was placed nearly upright, leaning against some iron blocks which were backed by heavy blocks of granite. Cast-iron and wrought-iron 68-pounder shot, at a distance of 600 and 400 yards, soon cracked and broke up the poorly supported plate. Hewlett, however, concluded that "iron plates afford a considerable protection, for it might very likely occur during an action, that no number of shot would strike near any one point, and that if it did do so, that it would only tend to weaken that particular point, the other parts of the vessel still retaining its original strength." He believed that if the plate had been firmly bolted to a ship's side "the result might not have been so immediate," and he recommended experiments with 4-inch iron plates backed by some elastic substance and fastened to a section of the side of a vessel.[2] In accord with this suggestion, and with a request from the Surveyor for tests of plates of homogeneous metal, which he believed to have double the strength of ordinary iron, the Admiralty ordered experiments at Portsmouth on various plates attached to the old wooden vessel *Alfred*.[3]

Before these tests took place, Sir Baldwin Walker's submission of June 22, 1858, declared the construction of sea-going ironclads to be "of the highest importance not only as regards the supremacy of the British Navy but even the safety of the country." As noted above, the Surveyor re-

---

[1] In his testimony given May 31, 1861, Sir Charles Wood stated that he had been to the Admiralty that morning, and found that the first news received there of the French ironclads was a communication from France, dated May 5, 1858, stating "that the two steam battery frigates to be built at Toulon, are to be called the 'Gloire' and the 'Invincible'." A second despatch from Paris on June 7 reported "that they are also laying down the first timbers of an iron-sided frigate to be called the 'Gloire'." *Parliamentary Papers*, 1861, v, no. 438, p. 364. Cf. P.R.O., Adm. 12/653: 52–5 and 59–1.
[2] Adm. 1/5691: A. 818. Cf. Special Committee on Iron, *First Report*, pp. x, 174.
[3] Controller of the Navy, Submission Letter Book no. 19, April 20 and 24, May 4, 22 and 27, 1858; Adm. 12/653: 59–1 and 59–4a.

marked that it was not sound policy for Great Britain to begin to introduce a new class of costly ships until such a course was forced on her. Now, however,

> ... this time has arrived. France has now commenced to build frigates of great speed with their sides protected by thick metal plates and this renders it imperative for this country to do the same without a moment's delay.

He therefore proposed to build two wooden-hulled ironclads in the government yards at Chatham and Pembroke, and to contract with private builders for four iron-hulled armored vessels to be constructed "on a principle similar to that adopted in the iron floating batteries built during the last war but with fine lines and great power." The objections to iron vessels based on their rapid fouling "would not apply to vessels such as those under consideration which are intended for home or Channel service where there are always facilities for docking."

The Surveyor therewith submitted a design of a screw vessel of 1000 horse power, 12¾ knots speed, and 6096 tons displacement, carrying 26 guns and "covered from the upper deck to six feet below the load line with metal plates four inches in thickness." He estimated the cost of the two wooden ironclads of this type at £197,560 each and that of the four armored iron vessels at £193,340 each.[1]

The Surveyor's submission of June 22, 1858, and the news of the progress of the French ironclads made Sir John Pakington "very anxious ... mortified and vexed." He determined to redress the loss of time, in some degree, by building British ironclads with such great care that they should be superior to their French prototypes. No body of men, he declared two years later, "could have been more unanimous on any subject than the Board of Admiralty was upon the necessity of using every effort to recover the ground which had been lost."[2] At the suggestion of the Secretary, Henry

---

[1] Controller of the Navy, Submission Letter Book no. 20.
[2] Testimony before the Select Committee on the Board of Admiralty, May 14, 1861, *Parliamentary Papers*, 1861, v, no. 438, pp. 232–235.

Thomas Lowry Corry, the Board decided on July 29 that part of the appropriations for the next year should be devoted to "at least two wooden frigates being coated with iron." [1]

Tests of 68-pounder shot at ranges of 400, 200, and 100 yards against plates fastened to the side of the *Alfred* at Portsmouth in August showed the superiority of wrought-iron plates to those of homogeneous metal and of steel, as then manufactured. Slabs of vulcanized india rubber, much vaunted as armor then and later by inventors of "shot-proof" ships, failed utterly. Captain Hewlett reported that no shot that struck the wrought-iron plates actually penetrated the ship's side, even at 100 yards. In one spot three feet in length by two feet broad, eight projectiles struck close together, fracturing the armor but failing to penetrate the backing. "On the inside, in a line with that spot, no very great injury is done to the ship's side, and possibly not a man would have been wounded." Pointing out that so concentrated a fire would have knocked an unarmored ship to pieces, he concluded that the experiments

> tend to shew the immense advantage ships clothed with wrought iron have over one not so protected; it puts a vessel with a few heavy guns more than on a par with the *heaviest 3-decker* supposing she has more speed, and . . . under such circumstances . . . the issue of an action could not long remain doubtful.

Such vessels would also be most valuable in engaging batteries, since they could take station at a distance of 400 yards "with almost impunity," and in all probability could make a breach before being compelled to retire.[2]

Observing that projectiles which struck near the edge of a plate did most damage, Captain Hewlett proposed further tests of larger plates and suggested placing a layer of india rubber between the iron and the wooden backing. Continued experiments, might, he hoped, explain why some wrought-iron plates proved more resistant than others made by the same manufacturers under apparently similar circum-

---
[1] Adm. 12/653; Adm. 1/5698.
[2] Adm. 1/5691: A. 1744, Hewlett to Admiral Seymour, August 20, 1858.

stances.¹ From the August tests the Surveyor concluded that 4-inch plates of common wrought iron "appear to afford a reasonable amount of protection," but that no decision as to building armored vessels could be reached until it was ascertained whether such plates could resist the elongated shot fired by Whitworth's rifled guns, which he thought would probably be found to have much greater penetrating power both above and under water.²

In the first British test of rifled ordnance against armor at Portsmouth in October, 1858, against 4-inch iron plates attached to the side of the *Alfred*, three cast-iron shot from a Whitworth 68-pounder at 350 and 400 yards cracked the plates and started the bolts fastening them to the hull, but caused indentations of only ⅝ to 1⅛ inches. The only wrought-iron shot that struck the armor before the gun burst passed right through the plate and the ship's side, which here measured 6 or 7 inches of oak planking.³

---

1 *Ibid.*

2 Controller of the Navy, Submission Letter Book no. 20, September 30, 1858. Iron bars 4 inches thick, about 4½ inches wide and 4 inches apart, bolted to the side of the *Alfred*, with the spaces between the bars filled in with African oak, afforded insufficient protection. Shot fired against homogeneous iron 2 inches thick, fastened to the ship's side and covered with 3 inches of African oak, passed through the sheathing, the plate, and the ship's side at every round. *Ibid.*, March 12, 1859; Adm. 1/5691: A. 1744; *Experiments with Naval Ordnance, H.M.S. "Excellent,"* p. 130.

3 In addition to Captain Hewlett's reports in Adm. 1/5691, the official sources for the British armor tests of 1858 are: Controller of the Navy, Submission Letter Book no. 20, June 23, July 12, 28 and 30, August 4, September 4, 22 and 30, October 1, 23 and 28; Adm. 12/653: 59–1 and 59–4a; Adm. 13/7, July 27, 29, August 3, 30, September 4, 5, 13, 28; Special Committee on Iron, *First Report*, pp. xi, 169–170, 172–173, 175–176; *Experiments with Naval Ordnance, H.M.S. "Excellent,"* pp. 133–136; *Parliamentary Papers*, 1863, xi, no. 487, "Report from the Select Committee on Ordnance," July 23, 1863, pp. 416–417.

Besides these official reports of the British experiments in firing against armor, one may note the following: Captain H. Dyer, R.A., "Remarks on Iron Defences," in *Minutes of Proceedings of the Royal Artillery Institution*, iii, 29 ff.; Captain A. Harrison, R.A., "Results of experiments with projectiles against iron armour," *ibid.*, iv; Captain T. Inglis, R.E., "The Application of Iron to Defensive Works," in *Papers on Subjects connected with the Duties of the Corps of Royal Engineers* (1862). Both Dyer and Harrison served as secretary of the Special Committee appointed to inquire into the application of iron for defensive purposes. The account of these British experiments in Alexander L. Holley, *A Treatise on Ordnance and Armor* (New York, 1865), consists in extracts from Dyer and Inglis. The leading British opponent of the introduction of ironclads, General Sir

Further experiments that same month demonstrated the importance of weight in projectiles destined to attack armor. A single 68-pounder shot did almost as much injury to the armor and more damage to the woodwork and frame of the target ship than five 32-pounder shot that struck close together. Comparing these results with a confidential report from Colonel Claremont, the British military attaché at Paris, on the French armor tests, Captain Hewlett noted the superior penetration of wrought-iron shot from the British 68-pounders as compared with that of steel shot from the French 50-pounders. The results of the tests, however, gave great encouragement to the advocates of armor. Wrought-iron plates 4 inches thick resisted perfectly both cast-iron 68-pounder shot and wrought-iron shot weighing 72 pounds, fired with full service charges at 400 yards range. At 200 and 100 yards the projectiles had greater effect, but none passed completely through, save those striking in holes previously made. Even at twenty yards the cast-iron shot failed to penetrate, but the wrought-iron shot passed through the ship's side, showering the deck with splinters and fragments of iron. Hewlett believed these experiments were "sufficiently conclusive as to the almost invulnerability of the common wrought iron plates at the shortest distances," and predicted that a fast ironclad, carrying a few heavy guns, would have "an immeasurable advantage over Ships of any size not so clothed." If she were to be supplied with Martin's shells, filled with molten iron heated in a cupola installed on board, he thought it impossible to say what havoc she might work among an enemy's fleet.[1]

Experimental firing against the floating batteries *Erebus* and *Meteor* in October and November demonstrated the importance of heavy wooden backing for the plates. Those of the *Erebus*, backed only by 5 or 6 inches of oak and the ⅝-inch iron skin of the vessel, suffered much more damage

---

Howard Douglas, gave a partisan account of the experiments in the fifth edition of his *Treatise on Naval Gunnery* (London, 1860), pp. 396–408, with striking illustrations.

[1] Adm. 1/5691: A. 1748, Hewlett to Admiral Seymour, October 15, 1858.

than those of the *Meteor*, a wooden-hulled battery on the French model, with 25 inches of oak behind the armor. At no time during the firing at the *Meteor* did it appear that the inconsequential damage inboard would have caused any inconvenience to the men working her guns.[1]

In a sensational report as to the French strength in wooden capital ships, Sir Baldwin Walker had argued in July that the French ironclads, if not met by similar ships, "would still further increase their superiority as regards the most formidable class of ships of war." [2] Renewing his plea for increased naval strength on November 13, he observed that, if the experiments which were then being made at Portsmouth led to the construction of armored vessels,

> they must be regarded as an addition to our force as a balance to those of France, and not as calculated to supersede any existing class of ship; — indeed no prudent man would at present consider it safe to risk, upon the performance of ships of this novel character, the naval supremacy of Great Britain.[3]

In the ensuing discussions at the Board Admiral Martin, a staunch advocate of increasing the size of the heaviest guns carried by ships of the line, argued that "they may possibly have to deal with iron-plated ships, and to such an encounter their present hollow shot guns are quite unequal." Corry objected strongly to treating the ironclad problem as one simply for future discussion, contending that it demanded immediate attention and that it was, "in some degree, at least, already ripe for decision." Although he agreed with the Surveyor that it would be unsafe to risk Britain's naval supremacy on the performance of ships of this novel character, he argued on the basis of Hewlett's reports that iron plates well backed by wood were "a complete protection against ordinary guns, and penetrable only by a description of shot not now in use in any Navy." Ships thus armored would have an enormous

---

[1] Adm. 1/5691: A. 1742 and A. 1743. Captain Hewlett thought that the iron-hulled *Erebus* "might possibly stand a good deal of battering" at 800 yards, but that she could not withstand the fire of heavy guns at much less distance.
[2] Controller of the Navy, Submission Letter Book no. 20, July 27, 1858.
[3] *Ibid.*, November 13, 1858.

advantage over wooden ships, "which might be sunk by a single broadside from guns of the description now in ordinary use." Corry carried his point as to the necessity of depriving France of the advantage due to the exclusive possession of "this formidable arm." On November 27 the Admiralty directed Sir Baldwin Walker to submit a project for a "wooden steam man of war to be cased with wrought iron 4½ inches thick," and the Navy Estimates presented on February 5, 1859, included the sum of £252,000 for two armored frigates to be built by contract.[1]

In response to the Admiralty order of November 27 the Surveyor four days later proposed the construction of a vessel with the scantling of an 80-gun ship, capable of fourteen knots under steam alone, with 34 guns on her main deck, two guns on her upper deck, bunker capacity for seven days under full steam, and stowage for provisions for 500 men for three months and water for one month.[2] Believing that iron was the most suitable material for the hull, especially in view of the difficulty experienced in obtaining timber, he proposed that the iron armor should be backed by substantial woodwork "so as to afford about the same resistance to the passage of shot, independently of the iron plates, as would obtain in a wood-built vessel." To obtain the high speed desired he recommended great length, fine lines, and an engine of 1000 horse power. The estimated cost for hull and engines was about £250,000.[3]

At his suggestion the master shipwrights in the government dockyards and some of the most experienced of the private shipbuilders in iron were invited to submit designs to meet these conditions. The Surveyor's department stipulated that the armor should extend from the upper deck to five feet below the load water line, and that the midship port must be at least nine feet above water. Although an iron

---

[1] Adm. 1/5698, November, 1858; Controller of the Navy, Submission Letter Book no. 20, December 1, 1858; *Parliamentary Papers*, 1859, xiv, no. 42, p. 55; Hansard, 3rd series, clii, pp. 910–911.
[2] Controller of the Navy, Submission Letter Book no. 20, December 1, 1858.
[3] *Ibid.*, January 14, 1859.

hull seemed preferable in strength and in durability, plans for a wooden ship would be considered. Adopting an idea proposed by the well-known private shipbuilder, John Scott Russell, Sir Baldwin Walker pointed out that, although in a wooden-hulled ship the armor must extend from the stem to the stern, in an iron ship the side armor might be confined to about two hundred feet of the middle part of the vessel, joined fore and aft by strong athwartship bulkheads "covered also with 4½ inch plates to extend down to about 5 feet below the plates on the sides." The unarmored ends should be subdivided into as many water-tight compartments as practicable, to afford strength for ramming and security against damage by collision or shot. He now specified stowage for provisions for 550 men for four months and water for six weeks. The ship was to be masted and rigged as an 80-gun ship, protected by an upper deck of ⅝-inch iron covered with 3 inches of Dantzic fir, and equipped with engines able to produce a speed of 13½ knots under steam alone.[1]

In response to this call the Admiralty received from eight private shipbuilders and six master shipwrights of government yards fifteen plans for ships ranging from 340 to 430 feet in length, 4887 to 7544 tons burden, and 6507 to 11,180 tons displacement. The nine plans submitted by the private builders, and the two proposed by Lang and Henwood, master shipwrights at Chatham and Sheerness, called for iron hulls; the other four dockyard officers preferred wooden ironclads.[2] Rejecting all these designs, the Board of Ad-

---

[1] *Ibid.*, January 27, 1859. Printed in *Parliamentary Papers*, 1861, xxvi, no. 2790, p. 20.

[2] Palmer and Company submitted two plans, only one of which is noted in the table on p. 64 of Sir Nathaniel Barnaby's *Naval Development in the Century* (Toronto, etc., 1904). That table errs in not listing the plans by Cradock and Chatfield as to be built of wood. An analysis of the fifteen plans submitted by the Surveyor, April 28, 1859 (Controller of the Navy, Submission Letter Book no. 20), is printed in *Parliamentary Papers*, 1861, xxvi, no. 2790, pp. 21–22. On October 18 and 19, 1860, Sir Baldwin Walker testified that "most of the members of the Board of Admiralty came to my department and examined all the models, and after they had examined them and gone into the whole of the question in the fullest way, they decided upon building the 'Warrior,' and tenders were called for." *Ibid.*, pp. 7, 20–22, 26. Cf. *Parliamentary Papers*, 1861, v, no. 438, pp. 233–234, 237–

miralty adopted the plans prepared by the Surveyor's department in 1858, called for tenders, and on May 11, 1859, accepted the offer of the Thames Iron Shipbuilding Company of Blackwall, to construct one ironclad frigate at £31.10.0 per ton, builder's measurement. She was to be launched within eleven months, and to be completed for sea, except masting, within three months more.[1]

In the autumn of 1858 the Admiralty had despatched two members of the Surveyor's department, Large and Sweeny, to France to obtain particulars of the warships under construction there, particularly of the ironclads.[2] A report laid before Parliament early in January pointed out that the French had laid down no wooden line-of-battle ships since 1855, and that they had four ironclads under construction, with two to four more projected. "So convinced do naval men seem to be in France of the irresistible qualities of these ships, that they are of opinion that no more ships of the line

---

238, and xxvi, no. 2790, pp. 227–228; Controller of the Navy, Submission Letter Book no. 20, December 23, 1858, February 3, 19, 22, March 4, 18, 23, 24, 25, 1859; Adm. 12/669: 59–1; Napier, *Life of Robert Napier*, pp. 209-211; J. D'Aguilar Samuda, "On the Construction of Iron Vessels of War Iron-cased," in *Transactions of the Institution of Naval Architects*, ii, pp. 8–17.

For a proposal to protect the magazines of wooden ships by iron plates, see Controller of the Navy, Submission Letter Book no. 20, October 28, November 5 and 10, and December 22, 1858.

[1] *Ibid.*, March 20, 21, 23, 25, April 28, 30, May 10, 12, 13, 14, 1859; Adm. 12/669: 59–1.

When the Admiralty rejected his tender on account of price and time required for completion, Scott Russell complained that his rôle as a pioneer advocate of ironclads entitled him to special treatment. The Admiralty rejected this claim, when the Surveyor reported that Russell was not alone in 1855 in thinking that vessels of this class would be introduced into the Royal Navy, and that none of the "main features of the plan which has been adopted originated with him with the exception of omitting the protecting plates from the bow and stern and introducing transverse shot proof bulkheads for the protection of the midship part of the vessel. All the other features such as fine lines for speed, general arrangement of the skin of the iron hull and the extensive introduction of longitudinal iron webs and iron decks were in such general use that any constructor would it is believed consider himself free to adopt them if he felt inclined to do so. Fine lines for speed cannot in fact be regarded as having originated with any one individual. It has been gradually developed from the earliest date of steam navigation." Submission Letter Book no. 20, June 17, 1859; Adm. 12/669: 59–1.

[2] Controller of the Navy, Submission Letter Book no. 20, September 24, 1858; January 28, March 10, 1859.

will be laid down, and that in 10 years that class of vessels will have become obsolete." [1] At the same time the first British tests of steel shot, from an Armstrong rifled 32-pounder against the 4-inch plates of the floating battery *Trusty*, led Captain Hewlett to renew his pleas for the construction of ironclads.[2]

In his speech on the Navy Estimates, February 25, 1859, Sir John Pakington informed the House of Commons that the progress of the French ironclads and the results of the British armor tests had convinced the Admiralty that "whatever be the cost ... it is our duty to lose no time in building at least two." [3] Sir Charles Wood, the principal speaker of the Opposition, observed concerning the proposed ironclads that "everybody knew that the greatly increased power of ordnance rendered it necessary that something should be done to meet it in some way or other." [4] Admiral Sir Charles Napier wished three ironclads built instead of two.[5] Sir Francis Baring thought it was "possible that the great steel ships might not answer all the expectations ..., still we ought not to lose the advantage of any possible success by which their construction might be attended. All this would cost a great deal of money, and he was afraid the expense would not be temporary, but would have to be continued over more years than the present." [6]

After approving the plans of the first British seagoing ironclad, the famous *Warrior*, on April 29, the Board of Admiralty had succumbed to misgivings. They were so "startled and astonished" at the great size and cost of the vessel that they reconsidered the whole question, with a view to reducing the armor from $4\frac{1}{2}$ inches to $2\frac{1}{2}$. After a week's delay, they surrendered on May 6 to the arguments of Cap-

---

[1] "Report of a Committee appointed by the Treasury to Inquire into the Navy Estimates, from 1852 to 1858, and into the Comparative State of the Navies of England and France," *Parliamentary Papers*, 1859, xiv, no. 182, pp. 15, 16, 19, 21.
[2] Adm. 12/669: 59–1, January 10, 1859; *Experiments with Naval Ordnance, H.M.S. "Excellent,"* p. 151.
[3] Hansard, 3rd series, clii, cols. 910–911.
[4] *Ibid.*, 922.   [5] *Ibid.*, 925.   [6] *Ibid.*, 941.

tain Hewlett and of the Surveyor in favor of the heavier armor belt and the large displacement required to float it. In view of the great cost involved, however, Pakington decided to begin no more than two seagoing ironclads before the success of the first could be tested. Indeed, he had not yet let the contract for the second armored frigate when he retired from office in June, 1859, after the fall of Lord Derby's ministry.[1]

Even before the terms of peace with Russia were signed the British had become critical of French leanings towards the enemy. When the French sided with the Russians in questions growing out of the execution of the peace treaty, Sir James Graham declared that "'the new love is proclaimed, while cold excuses only are offered to the discarded old love."[2] Palmerston deemed it "quite evident that our marriage with France will soon end in a separation on account of *Incompatibilité des moeurs.*"[3] In these altered circumstances the progress of the French fleet provoked increasing alarm.

As a concession to the popular demand for lower taxes, the Cabinet reduced the army and navy estimates for 1857, despite the strong objections of the Queen and Prince Albert.[4] At Osborne, in August, 1857, Louis Napoleon did his best to breathe new life into the alliance, although he admitted to Palmerston that the feeling in France towards England was not good, and that a quarrel with her would be popular there.[5]

The great efforts of the Conservative Board of Admiralty to prepare England against a sudden attack by France were far from satisfying British popular demands, which by the

[1] See Pakington's memorandum of May 6, 1859, in Adm. 1/5716, and his testimony before the Select Committee on the Board of Admiralty in May, 1861. *Parliamentary Papers*, 1861, v, no. 438, pp. 178, 199–200.
[2] Stanmore, *Sidney Herbert*, ii, p. 60, Graham to Herbert, November 15, 1856. Cf. Fitzmaurice, *Granville*, i, pp. 186 ff.; Greville, *Journal*, ii, pp. 56 ff.; Maxwell, *Clarendon*, ii, pp. 131 ff.; Martin, *Prince Consort*, iv, pp. 28 ff.; and the works cited above, p. 120, note 1.
[3] Philip Guedalla, *Palmerston* (London, 1926), p. 385, Palmerston to Clarendon, December 10, 1856.
[4] Duke of Argyll, *Autobiography and Memoirs* (London, 1906, 2 vols.), ii, pp. 72–73; Martin, *Prince Consort*, iv, pp. 17–20, 78.
[5] T. W. Riker, "The Pact of Osborne," in *American Historical Review*, January, 1929; Wellesley, *Cowley*, p. 131, Clarendon to Cowley, September, 1857.

summer of 1859 reached an extraordinary pitch. Even while French and British troops fought side by side in the mud of the Crimea the suspicions rife during the war scare of 1852 were not entirely stilled. Lord Malmesbury deplored England's failure to leave all the land operations to the French and to monopolize the naval operations for herself. She would thus have assured her maritime ascendancy against the French as well as the Russians, and have concealed the shortcomings of her military system.[1] As it was, the French public thrilled at the first-rate showing of the French Black Sea fleet and conceived the extravagant notion that the British Army was lacking in everything but valor. As a friend of the English alliance, Tocqueville deplored the loss of British prestige in the eyes of Parisians "of every rank and of every shade of political opinion." To an English friend he complained that

> the heroic courage of your soldiers was everywhere and unreservedly praised, but I found also a general belief that the importance of England as a military Power had been greatly exaggerated; that she is utterly devoid of military talent, which is shown as much in administration as in fighting; and that even in the most pressing circumstances she cannot raise a large army.
>
> Since I was a child I never heard such language. You are believed to be absolutely dependent on us; and in the midst of our intimacy I see rising a friendly contempt for you, which if our Governments quarrel, will make a war with you much easier than it has been since the fall of Napoleon.[2]

French pride and confidence in her strength on sea as well as on land help to explain not only the zeal of Napoleon III in developing the fleet in the years following the Crimean War but also the British alarm at that striking development. A generation of Englishmen who regarded British command of the seas to be as natural and as vital to their prosperity as the rising of the sun in the heavens, found it novel and disturbing to learn that any Frenchmen considered that France would have an even chance with her great rival in war at

---

[1] Malmesbury, *Memoirs*, ii, pp. 34–36, Malmesbury to Stanley, October 21, 1855.
[2] M.C.M. Simpson, ed., *Correspondence and Conversations of Alexis de Tocqueville with Nassau William Senior from 1834 to 1859* (London, 1872, 2 vols.), ii, p. 91, January 22, 1855.

sea.[1] In a conversation with Nassau Senior in April, 1858, Admiral Mathieu, Hydrographer of the French Navy, ridiculed the attempts of the *Moniteur* to minimize the great efforts France was making to increase her strength at sea. Vaunting the improvement in *matériel*, gunnery, and morale, he remarked that though French naval officers in former years had dreaded a naval war, owing to disparity of force, now they were "confident, and eager to try their hands."[2] Not even the friendly conduct of the Emperor during the Indian mutiny silenced British suspicions. Lamenting that England was "*disgracefully unprepared*," and was "now existing as a nation by the grace of Louis Napoleon," Clarendon instructed Cowley to report the exact state of the French Navy, with their means of transport: "In short, what they could do *at once*, on a declaration of war."[3]

When Anglo-French relations were dangerously strained in the exciting days following Orsini's attempt on the life of Napoleon III, and the *Moniteur* printed addresses of French colonels who demanded to be led to London to hunt down the assassins in their dens, the Emperor relieved the tension by naming the Crimean hero, Marshal Pélissier, his ambassador in London.[4] On March 31 Napoleon III wrote to King Victor Emmanuel that his relations with England were better, but that French animosity against that power was increasing daily.[5] The visit of Queen Victoria and the Prince Consort to Cherbourg in August, instead of rejuvenating the alliance,

---

[1] Even Cobden, the great champion of peace and disarmament, declared that if France should seek to equal or surpass Great Britain in naval armaments, "there is no amount of expenditure which this country would not bear to maintain our due superiority at sea." *The Three Panics*, p. 127.

[2] M. C. M. Simpson, ed., *op. cit.*, ii, pp. 198–202. Cf. Ashley, *Palmerston*, ii, p. 193; and Mends, *Mends*, p. 331.

[3] Wellesley, *Cowley*, p. 136. The Emperor resented the British suspicions, and especially a defiant speech by Palmerston at the Lord Mayor's banquet, November 9. *Ibid.*, pp. 130–131, 138–141; Ashley, *Palmerston*, ii, pp. 138–140.

[4] General Derrécagaix, *Le Maréchal Pélissier, Duc de Malakoff* (Paris, 1911), ch. xxi; Greville, *Journal*, ii, pp. 157–158, 162–170, 179, 181; Malmesbury, *Memoirs*, ii, pp. 94–115, 140–141, 151; Martin, *Prince Consort*, pp. 196–199; E. Ollivier, *L'Empire libéral* (Paris, 1895–1915, 17 vols.), iii, pp. 466–471; Stern, *Geschichte Europas*, viii, pp. 286–292; Wellesley, *Cowley*, ch. vii.

[5] *Il carteggio Cavour-Nigra*, i, p. 83.

led to increased suspicion of French armaments. The royal pair during a visit a year before had regarded the new works in progress at Cherbourg as "grave cause for reflection." Now at the sight of the fortified roadstead filled with French warships they renewed their pleas for more ships and coast defences. "The war preparations in the French Marine are immense!" wrote Prince Albert. "Ours despicable! Our Ministers use fine phrases but they do nothing. My blood boils within me." [1]

Under the spur of excitement the press was no more inclined than was the Prince to do justice to the efforts of the Admiralty. While the *Times* loosed its thunderbolts at the great French naval base,[2] Palmerston urged the editor of the *Morning Post* "not to underrate its importance as a point of aggression against us. ... The only value of Cherbourg and its only intention is that it is a secure place d'armes where a fleet and army may assemble" for the invasion of England.[3] His visit to the Emperor at Compiègne in November, however, reassured him as to Louis Napoleon's good intentions towards England. While sounding his noncommittal guest as to the British attitude in the event of war between France and Austria, the Emperor expressed dislike of Russia and assured Palmerston that the whole system of naval warfare had changed and that the French would build no more large ships.[4]

If these private assurances quieted the suspicions of the great Whig leader, nothing lessened the alarm of the Court and of the Board of Admiralty. Malmesbury wrote to Cow-

---

[1] Martin, *Prince Consort*, iv, pp. 115-123, 263-278. Cf. Malmesbury, *Memoirs*, ii, pp. 128-130; Maxwell, *Clarendon*, ii, p. 164.

[2] *E. g.*, July 13, August 9, 1858. As to the bitterness evoked in France by these attacks see Martin, *Prince Consort*, iv, p. 277. Cf. *Punch*, July 13, August 7, 14, 1858.

[3] Lucas, *Lord Glenesk and the "Morning Post,"* pp. 142-146, August 19, 1858.

[4] Wellesley, *Cowley*, p. 166. This was true as concerned wooden ships, but highly misleading as to the French ironclad program. Palmerston wrote Delane, March 2, 1859, that he did not "share the belief that the French Emperor meditates an attack upon England," although he admitted that the French armaments were strong enough to "successfully strike a blow by no means agreeable to us." Dasent, *Delane*, i, p. 317.

ley on October 26 that "there is a party, and its name is Legion (for it is composed of every party and some Governments) striving to drive England and France into a war. . . . A complete plan for the invasion of England by Admiral de la Gravière, made in 1857, is in my possession. It is satisfactory to know that they only meant to stay a week, and to be nearly sure that not a man would have returned."[1] In a vain attempt to dispel such fears, Disraeli, then Chancellor of the Exchequer and leader of the House of Commons, sent his private secretary, Ralph Earle, on a confidential mission to the Emperor in December, to assure him that Disraeli contemplated "the possibility of the eventual increase of his dominions . . . but all this should be attempted with the sanction, or at least with the sufferance, of England, not in spite of her." To regain the good opinion of the English people, Disraeli believed that Napoleon would be prepared "to make great sacrifices, to force free trade in France, perhaps even to reduce his marine." Earle was therefore instructed to propose that the Emperor make a public statement expressing surprise that England should look with jealousy on his efforts to restore the French Navy "to its ancient and proper force," and assuring the British

that France seeks no undue supremacy on the sea; that she wishes to enter into no rivalry with England; . . . [and] that there would be no jealousy in France if the English fleet were twice the strength of that of France.

If he gave such an assurance, and a French war with Austria should follow, British public opinion

would prevent interference in the quarrel, and no one would be persuaded, which otherwise, as in old days, would be the case, that an Austrian war was a good distraction from a French invasion from Cherbourg, and therefore that Austria should be encouraged and supported by England.[2]

Although Earle reported that the Emperor agreed to make such a declaration in his speech at the opening of the Chambers, that utterance proved vague and unsatisfactory.[3] Dis-

[1] Malmesbury, *Memoirs*, ii, pp. 140-141.
[2] Monypenny and Buckle, *Disraeli*, iv, pp. 215-226.
[3] *Ibid.*, pp. 219-220, 226; *Oeuvres de Napoléon III*, v, pp. 73-77, February 8, 1859. Cf. his letter to Queen Victoria, February 14, in Martin, *Prince Consort*, iv, pp.

raeli's incursion into the diplomatic field served only to irritate his colleague Malmesbury. To the great relief of the Queen the Cabinet on January 18 had already agreed to a great addition to the effective force of the navy.[1] Pakington's announcement that the naval estimates would involve a "reconstruction" of the navy provoked some alarm abroad and such great expectations at home that the champions of preparedness, not content with the largest vote of men which had ever been proposed in the House of Commons in time of peace, were "positively disappointed" to find the estimates for shipbuilding increased only £1,000,000.[2] When rumors of a Russo-French alliance became rife on the eve of the war between France and Austria,[3] the Admiralty heavily reinforced the Mediterranean fleet, which was concentrated at Malta ready for sea to keep a close watch on the French, and mobilized a new fleet in the Channel, in consequence of the attitude assumed by Russia.[4]

As the war in Italy progressed, excitement in England as to Napoleon's next move reached fever pitch. Palmerston deplored the abuse of the Emperor by the English press, observing that although he might have unavowed schemes hostile to British interests, it was folly to hasten a rupture.[5] Some of the wild stories of French projects of invasion which fed the public anxiety originated with French enemies of the Emperor,[6] and sovereigns fearful of his power. Leopold I of Belgium, ever alert to the opportunity for sowing distrust of his powerful neighbor, told Disraeli that "We must take care

---

368–371. For the Emperor's views at this time as to British neutrality, see his letter to Walewski printed in Ollivier, *L'empire libéral*, iii, pp. 537–542, at p. 540.
[1] *Letters of Queen Victoria*, iii, pp. 395, 399.
[2] Stanmore, *Sidney Herbert*, ii, p. 168, Herbert to Gladstone, February 19, 1859; Hansard, 3rd series, clii, cols. 882–913. Cf. Vitzthum von Eckstaedt, *St. Petersburg and London in the Years 1852–1864* (London, 1887, 2 vols.) i, 321, 331; and the full-page drawings in *Punch*, February 19, 26, March 5 and May 14.
[3] Ernest d'Hauterive, ed., *Napoléon III et le Prince Napoléon, Correspondance inédite* (Paris, 1925), pp. 118–127; Charles-Roux, *Alexandre II, Gortchakoff et Napoléon III*, pp. 241–247.
[4] Adm. 3/267, minutes of April 18, 19, 26; Martin, *Prince Consort*, iv, pp. 432, 435; *Letters of Queen Victoria*, iii, p. 420.
[5] Wellesley, *Cowley*, p. 182, Palmerston to Cowley, May 8.
[6] *Ibid.*, p. 165.

that 'Rule Britannia' does not become an old song." [1] Pius IX warned the British representative at the Vatican. "Prepare and take care of yourselves in England, for I am quite certain the French Emperor intends sooner or later to attack you." [2]

Tennyson voiced the public alarm in the *Times* of May 9, calling for recruits for the Volunteer Rifle Corps.[3]

> There is a sound of thunder afar,
> Storm in the South that darkens the day,
> Storm of battle and thunder of war,
> Well, if it do not roll our way.
>   Storm! storm! Riflemen form!
>   Ready, be ready to meet the storm!
>   Riflemen, riflemen, riflemen form!
>
> Be not deaf to the sound that warns!
> Be not gull'd by a despot's plea!
> Are figs of thistles, or grapes of thorns?
> How should a despot set men free?
>   Form! form! Riflemen form!
>   Ready, be ready to meet the storm!
>   Riflemen, riflemen, riflemen form!
>
> Let your Reform for a moment go,
> Look to your butts and take good aims.
> Better a rotten borough or so,
> Than a rotten fleet or a city in flames!
>   Form! form! . . .
>
> Form, be ready to do or die!
> Form in Freedom's name and the Queen's!
> True that we have a faithful ally,
> But only the Devil knows what he means.
>   Form! form! . . .

[1] Monypenny and Buckle, *Disraeli*, iv, p. 255. Cf. Malmesbury, *Memoirs*, ii, p. 345; and Baron Beyens, *Le Second Empire vu par un diplomate belge* (Paris, 1924–1926, 2 vols.), i, pp. 102, 363–391.

[2] *Letters of Queen Victoria*, iii, 458, Odo Russell to Lord John Russell, July 17, 1859.

[3] On the Volunteer Movement, which enrolled 170,000 men by May, 1861, see: — Cecil S. Montefiori, *A History of the Volunteer Forces from the Earliest Times to the Year* 1860 (London, 1908); Robert Potter Berry, *A History of the Formation and Development of the Volunteer Infantry* (London, 1903), part i, section 4; W. H. Russell, *Rifle Clubs and Volunteer Corps* (London, 1859); Stanmore, *Sidney Herbert*, ii, pp. 386–393; Colonel Willoughby Verner and Captain E. D. Parker, *The Military Life of H. R. H. George, Duke of Cambridge* (London, 1905, 2 vols.), i, pp. 272–277.

When thousands of volunteer riflemen were flocking to the colors to defend Britain's shores, the partial success of the Conservative Board of Admiralty in building wooden ships of the line, conducting experiments with armor, and ordering a single ironclad, fell far short of popular expectations. The progress of ordnance had made each wooden ship a potential death trap. To the experts in charge of the armor tests, the best 4½-inch plates seemed to promise indispensable protection. Although their reports convinced the Admiralty of the need of building experimental ironclads, they left many questions as to the nature of plates, backing and design still unsolved. Just at the moment when rapid progress seemed most necessary, if the lead conceded to the French was to be regained, the fall of the Conservative ministry in June, 1859, put England several more months behind in the race.

CHAPTER VIII

THE PASSING OF THE WOODEN CAPITAL SHIP

IN THE two years from June, 1859, to June, 1861, the ironclad supplanted the wooden vessel as the capital ship of the major European navies. If England had fought both France and Russia in 1859 the British fleet would have found itself outnumbered in wooden steam ships of the line, and wholly lacking in completed seagoing ironclads. To meet this double threat the Admiralty increased its ironclad program from one ship to four before the end of 1859, and rushed to completion enough wooden screw line-of-battle ships to attain the desired two-power standard in 1861. The successful trials of the *Gloire*, however, which were followed immediately by the great French ironclad program of 1860, again forced the Admiralty's hand. Between October, 1860, and August, 1861, Great Britain not only increased her ironclad program from four to fifteen seagoing ships; she also suspended the construction of large wooden ships except for the purpose of casing them with iron. When England thus followed France in discarding wooden ships from the line of battle, the day of the wooden capital ship had ended.

It was in the full tide of popular excitement over the Italian War that the Whig Board of Admiralty took office. Alarmist speeches in Parliament raised the specter of invasion. The venerable Lord Lyndhurst described the French Navy as "aggressive in its character," declared that reliance could not be placed in the Emperor "because he is in a situation in which he cannot place reliance on himself," and closed his declamation with the phrase, *Vae victis!*[1] In the House of Commons Horsman proposed a loan for completing the na-

---

[1] Hansard, 3rd series, cliv, cols. 616–627, July 5, 1859. The Earl of Hardwicke advocated a fleet of 100 ships of the line, and Lord Ellenborough declared that "we are under circumstances the most perilous which have occurred for the last half century." *Ibid.*, cols. 638–640, 643–646.

tional defences, in what Cobden called "the great panic speech of the session."[1] Under the spur of popular excitement the Admiralty ordered more ironclads and, before the spring of 1861, raised the number of wooden capital ships afloat to 53, with fourteen others in process of building or conversion.[2] Public opinion, however, roused by Parliament and by the press, demanded more than ships.[3] A Royal Commission on the Defences of the United Kingdom submitted a unanimous report on February 7, 1860, declaring that "the nation cannot be considered as secured against invasion if depending for its defence upon the fleet alone." They proposed an expenditure of £10,850,000 for fortifications in the next four years, and £1,000,000 for ironclad harbor-defence vessels.[4]

---

[1] *Ibid.*, clv, cols. 676 692, July 29, 1859. For attempts to allay the public excitement, see the speeches of Bright and Cobden in *ibid.*, cols. 190–203, 704–717, and Cobden's hostile analysis of the speeches of the alarmists in *The Three Panics*, pp. 52–128.

[2] Lord Clarence Paget in the House of Commons, March 11, 1861, Hansard, 3rd series, clxi, col. 1773.

[3] Among the alarmist books and pamphlets engendered by the invasion scare may be noted: *Admiralty Administration, its Faults and Defaults* (London, 1861); "Forewarned, but not Forearmed," *Letters on the Invasion and Defence of Britain* (London, 1858); Lieut. Col. Alexander, R.M.A., *The Command of the Channel and the Safety of our Shores* (London, 1860); George Parker Bidder, *The National Defences* (London, 1861); W. A. Brooks, *The Defence of Portsmouth by Means of Advanced Sea Works* (London, 1861); Hans Busk, *The Navies of the World* (London, 1859); Captain Cowper Phipps Coles, R.N., *Our National Defences* (London, 1861), and *Spithead Forts, Reply to the Royal Commissioners' Second Report on our National Defences* (London, 1861); T. Hewitt Key and Alexander W. Williamson, *Invasion Invited by the Defenceless State of England* (London, 1858); John Laird, *Letters to "The Times" on Iron Ships of War and Coast and Harbour Defences* (n.p., 1859); David Urquhart, *The Invasion of England* (London, July, 1860).

[4] *Parliamentary Papers*, 1860, xxiii, no. 2682. On the origin of this commission, which was appointed on August 20, 1859, see Stanmore, *Sidney Herbert*, ii, pp. 269–273. For a searching criticism of its conclusions, see Vice Admiral P. H. Colomb, *Memoirs of Admiral Sir Astley Cooper Key* (London, 1898), pp. 288–300. A War Office committee appointed to consider the best form of a floating battery for harbor defence had already reported on December 23, 1858, in favor of the construction of four armored floating batteries, on two different plans. When this suggestion was referred to the Admiralty, Pakington had replied that the efforts being made to increase the navy rendered it inadvisable to undertake the building of such batteries at that time. Adm. 1/5724, January 24, 1859. The fourth edition of J. Scoffern's *Projectile Weapons of War* (London, 1859), p. 366, described the armored floating batteries built during the Crimean War as worthless, on account of their rolling and their bad sailing and steaming.

In the Cabinet Gladstone fought a losing battle against the general desire for greater army and navy appropriations.[1] Sharing in large measure Cobden's scornful view of the invasion scare, that "a delusion more gigantic, or a hoax more successful, was never practised on the public mind since the days of Titus Oates," [2] he sought in vain to quiet the fears of his friend Sidney Herbert at the War Office, who insisted that war with France was probable, perhaps imminent. The joint Anglo-French expedition to China seemed to the Secretary of State for War no guarantee of the stability of the alliance, but rather a decoy to strip England of troops and leave her open to invasion. In reply to his sensational memorandum demanding extensive fortifications, Gladstone justly retorted that England's best reliance was a fleet in command of the Channel, and added that "an immense series of preparations for war" has a "predisposing power ... in begetting war." [3] When Palmerston and a majority of the Cabinet sided with Herbert, Gladstone's hints of resignation left the Prime Minister unmoved.[4] He wrote to the Queen that he hoped to overcome Gladstone's objections to the fortifications bill, but if that should prove impossible, "it would be better to lose Mr. Gladstone than to run the risk of losing Portsmouth or Plymouth." [5]

Since the death of Wellington in 1852 Palmerston had stood out as the foremost champion of large armaments in England. He assured Gladstone that "the two great objects" which he had had "always before him in life" were the suppression of the slave trade and putting England in a state of defence.[6] Although he had not shared the fears of a French invasion in the spring and summer of 1859, he saw

[1] But see below, pp. 173, 178, 321.
[2] J. A. Hobson, *Richard Cobden, The International Man* (London, 1919), p. 263.
[3] Stanmore, *Sidney Herbert*, ii, ch. vi; John Morley, *Life of William Ewart Gladstone* (New York, 1911, 3 vols.) ii, ch. iii, and appendix.
[4] Philip Guedalla, ed., *Gladstone and Palmerston, Correspondence ... 1851–1865* (New York and London, 1928), pp. 58–59; Fitzmaurice, *Granville*, i, pp. 380, 386. Cf. Maxwell, *Clarendon*, ii, p. 220.
[5] Martin, *Prince Consort*, v, p. 99. For an early forecast of this dissension, see Malmesbury, *Memoirs*, ii, p. 191.
[6] Morley, *Gladstone*, ii, p. 45.

no reason why the reduction of the French land and sea forces to a peace footing, which was announced in the *Moniteur* late in July, should lead to reduction of the British estimates.[1]

The Emperor did his best to disarm the suspicions of England and to enlist her aid to extricate himself from the impasse into which his Italian policy had led him. In a long conversation with Cowley early in August he complained of the British fears of invasion, denied that France was to blame for the naval rivalry, and impressed the British ambassador with his sincere attachment to the English alliance.[2] Primarily to remove the deep distrust felt by the British public, the Emperor braved the wrath of the French protectionists and approved the negotiations which led to the Commercial Treaty of January 23, 1860.[3] Palmerston's lukewarmness towards this treaty was due in part to fear lest it lead to a relaxation of efforts for national defence. He was concerned that the reductions in revenue incident to the treaty might furnish Gladstone with additional arguments against large appropriations for ships, troops and forts. By a *tour de force* of jingoistic reasoning, he argued that the commercial treaty would render preparations for defence more necessary than before, since free trade would strengthen France and make

---

[1] Hansard, 3rd series, clv, cols. 543, 669–670. Vitzthum reported that the statement in the *Moniteur* had "only increased the distrust already prevailing" at London. "People fear reciprocity — an invitation to England to discontinue now her coast defences, if she does not wish to expose herself to the suspicion of aggressive designs . . ." *St. Petersburg and London*, i, p. 376. Cf. the full-page drawings in *Punch*, July 9, 30, August 6, 13, 20; and Wellesley, *Cowley*, p. 187.

[2] Martin, *Prince Consort*, iv, pp. 470–472; Wellesley, *Cowley*, pp. 187–189. But see Malmesbury, *Memoirs*, ii, p. 211.

[3] Cobden declared that nine tenths of Napoleon's motives for approving the treaty "were political rather than politico-economical; he aimed at conciliating the English people, and I did not hesitate to assure him that if he entered without reserve on the Free Trade path, it would be taken as a proof of his pacific intentions by the British public." Greville, *Journal*, ii, p. 315. See also John Morley, *Life of Richard Cobden* (Boston, 1881), ch. xxix, especially pp. 474, 482, 483, 485–486; Hobson, *Richard Cobden*, p. 251; Wellesley, *Cowley*, p. 193; Gooch, *Later Correspondence of Lord John Russell*, ii, pp. 250–252. Fresh light on these negotiations is thrown by Professor Arthur Louis Dunham in his scholarly monograph, *The Anglo-French Treaty of Commerce of 1860 and the Progress of the Industrial Revolution in France* (Ann Arbor), 1930, chs. iii–v.

her increasingly dangerous as a neighbor, unless she could see that England was impregnable![1]

In November Palmerston wrote to Lord John Russell that till lately he had had

> strong confidence in the fair intentions of Napoleon towards England, but of late I have begun to feel great distrust and to suspect that his formerly declared intention of avenging Waterloo has only lain dormant ... he has been assiduously laboring to increase his naval means, evidently for offensive as well as defensive purposes; and latterly great pains have been taken to raise throughout France, and especially among the army and navy, hatred of England, and a disparaging feeling of our military and naval means.[2]

Early in January, it is true, he would have been ready, but for the opposition of a majority of his colleagues, to agree to an alliance with France pledging mutual assistance if Austria should use force in Italy.[3] As soon as the French intention to annex Nice and Savoy became apparent, however, Palmerston's suspicions of Louis Napoleon became inveterate. He now believed that the Emperor's appetite for territorial acquisitions would come with eating, and that he would seek Russian aid first to dismember the Turkish Empire, and then to obtain the Rhine frontier and perhaps Belgium.[4]

The Emperor's hopes of winning British public opinion by means of the commercial treaty were dashed to the ground by the outburst of British jealousy and suspicion provoked by his annexation of Nice and Savoy.[5] His resentment found

---

[1] P.R.O., G.D. 22: 21, Palmerston to Russell, January 14, February 5, 1860. Cf. Parker, *Graham*, ii, pp. 392–393; and Argyll, *Autobiography and Memoirs*, ii, p. 154.

[2] Ashley, *Palmerston*, ii, pp. 187–189. He warned the Duke of Somerset that at the bottom of Napoleon's heart "there rankles a deep and inextinguishable desire to humble and punish England," and that "he is now stealthily but steadily organizing his naval means." *Ibid.*, p. 190.

[3] *Ibid.*, pp. 174–180; Fitzmaurice, *Granville*, ii, p. 369; Guedalla, *Gladstone and Palmerston*, pp. 120–121; Martin, *Prince Consort*, v, pp. 7–9, 19–20; Maxwell, *Clarendon*, ii, pp. 199–204, 206–207; Morley, *Gladstone*, ii, p. 14; *Letters of Queen Victoria*, iii, pp. 488–491.

[4] P.R.O., G.D. 22: 21, Palmerston to Russell, March 15, May 5, 1860. Cf. *Il Carteggio Cavour-Nigra*, iii, pp. 230–231, 240–241, 262, 270.

[5] Hansard, 3rd series, clvi, cols. 573–609, 1933–1970, 2143–2146, 2228–2264; clvii, cols. 1–3, 91–102, 245–246, 343–354, 707–711, 751–761, 1169–1189; *Parliamentary Papers*, 1860, lxvii, "Correspondence respecting the Proposed Annexation of Savoy and Nice;" "Further Correspondence relating to the Affairs of Italy,"

vent in an angry scene with Cowley on March 6, which evoked memories of some of the outbursts of the first Napoleon.[1] Amid the cheers of the House of Commons, Lord John Russell declared that, since "such an act as the annexation of Savoy is one that will lead a nation so warlike as the French to call upon its Government from time to time to commit other acts of aggression," Great Britain should be ready to act with other powers to maintain the peace of Europe against the French.[2]

Both the indictment and the threat gave great offence in France.[3] Palmerston and Count Flahault coolly discussed the possibilities of war and invasion.[4] The Prime Minister calmed the excited French ambassador, Persigny, however, by assuring him that Russell's apparent threat did not mean that England intended to form a hostile coalition, unless French aggressions should provoke one.[5] The great champion of preparedness sought Britain's security, not in defensive treaties which would tie her hands,[6] but in stronger national defences.

That Gladstone could propose to abandon the paper duty and in the same breath object to the new fortifications on the ground of a deficiency of revenue, seemed to the Prime Minister a two-faced stand, supported only by the fallacies of

---

parts iii vi; *Il Carteggio Cavour-Nigra*, iii, p. 101; Martin, *Prince Consort*, v, pp. 9-12, 20, 26-33, 44-51, 58-62; Maxwell, *Clarendon*, ii, pp. 208-212; Vitzthum, *St. Petersburg and London*, ii, pp. 2-6; Wellesley, *Cowley*, pp. 196-206.

[1] *Letters of Queen Victoria*, iii, pp. 497-501; Martin, *Prince Consort*, v, pp. 38-43; Wellesley, *Cowley*, pp. 200-201. Cowley met the attack with great dignity and the Emperor apologized.

[2] Hansard, 3rd series, clvii, cols. 1252-1258, March 26.

[3] *Il Carteggio Cavour-Nigra*, iii, p. 227; Malmesbury, *Memoirs*, ii, pp. 225-226; Martin, *Prince Consort*, v, pp. 71-72; L. Thouvenel, *Le Secret de l'Empereur* (Paris, 1889, 2 vols.), i, pp. 99, 120-121, 123-124, 126.

[4] Ashley, *Palmerston*, ii, pp. 190-192; Martin, *Prince Consort*, v, pp. 72-74. Cavour was concerned at the Anglo-French tension. N. Bianchi, *La Politique du Comte Camille de Cavour de 1852 à 1861* (Turin, 1885), p. 361.

[5] P.R.O., G.D. 22:21, Palmerston to Russell, April 1, 1860. Cf. Martin, *Prince Consort*, v, p. 72.

[6] P.R.O., G.D. 22:21, Palmerston to Russell, March 5, 1860; Ernest II, Duke of Saxe-Coburg-Gotha, *Aus meinem Leben und aus meiner Zeit* (Berlin, 1887-1889, 3 vols.), iii, p. 63; Martin, *Prince Consort*, v, p. 86.

Bright and arguments worthy of a schoolboy.[1] He assured the Chancellor of the Exchequer that a sudden French attack on the dockyards might paralyze the British Navy for more than half a century, and reduce England to the rank of a third-rate power.[2] When the Cabinet at last agreed on a compromise which left the Prime Minister a substantial victory, Palmerston introduced the fortifications bill in a provocative speech, raising the specter of invasion and asserting that the armaments of France both on land and sea were "disproportionate to her necessities of defence." [3]

Louis Napoleon kept his temper and risked his popularity at home to return a soft answer.[4] On August 1 *The Times* reprinted from the *Moniteur* an imperial manifesto in the form of a letter to Persigny, urging Palmerston and his colleagues to "lay aside pitiful jealousies and unfounded distrust," and declaring that his one thought since the peace of Villafranca had been to live on good terms with all his neighbors, especially with England. Insisting that his army and fleet were no menace to anyone, he asserted that his steam navy "is far from being even adequate to our wants and the number of steamers is far short of that of Louis-Philippe's sailing ships."

Punch reflected the depth of British distrust in a full-page drawing, "Injured Innocence and his Billet-Do," which depicted the Emperor as a wolf in sheep's clothing.[5] Suspicions of France continued to spring up in Russell's mind as rapidly as weeds in fertile soil.[6] Persigny told the editor of the *Morning Post* that, though the Emperor wished peace with England, French public opinion might force him into war unless

---

[1] P.R.O., G.D. 29: 19, Palmerston to Granville, May 21; and 22: 21, Palmerston to Russell, May 27.
[2] Guedalla, *Gladstone and Palmerston*, p. 116.
[3] Argyll, *Autobiography*, ii, pp. 163–166; Guedalla, *Gladstone and Palmerston*, pp. 146–148; Parker, *Graham*, ii, pp. 395–399; Hansard, 3rd series, clx, cols. 17–33. He suggested that £9,000,000 be spent on fortifications in the next three or four years; and proposed an immediate expenditure of £2,000,000, which Parliament promptly granted.
[4] Nassau William Senior, *Conversations with M. Thiers, M. Guizot and other Distinguished Persons during the Second Empire* (London, 1878, 2 vols.), ii, p. 365.
[5] August 11, 1860.
[6] Thouvenel, *Le Secret de l'Empereur*, i, p. 323, Thouvenel to de Flahault, December 13, 1860. Cf., however, Gooch, *Russell*, ii, p. 267.

the British government expressed confidence in him and avoided all attempts to organize a coalition against France. He added that, with the existing state of naval and military forces of the two countries, the result of war would probably be unfavorable to England, whose dockyards might be destroyed by French ironclads. When this was reported to Palmerston, he wrote Persigny that England as well as France could apply science and the mechanical arts to war, but that she had the advantage, not only in coal, iron, and industrial development, but also in the superior tenacity of her fighting forces.[1]

It is easier to smile at the exaggerated fears of an invasion of England than to fathom the motives underlying Louis Napoleon's naval policy. That he at any time desired war with England is hard to believe. Lord Malmesbury's verdict in 1852 "that he is convinced that war with England lost his uncle the throne, and that he *means* to try *peace* with us," seems a just one.[2] Apart from the diplomatic advantages of the British alliance, the sympathies of the British press and the support of British financiers might be deemed important aids in his domestic policy.[3] Why then should he take the surest means of rousing British jealousy and antagonism by threatening the maritime supremacy of the mistress of the seas?

In the years following the Crimean War, the Emperor must have often felt the British alliance to be stricken with sterility. He complained to Disraeli that the alliance should work both ways, France assisting England in her policy and receiving aid in return, but that Palmerston "seems always to think that the first condition of the alliance should alone prevail."[4] If the Emperor was already contemplating the

---

[1] Ashley, *Palmerston*, ii, pp. 192–198.
[2] Malmesbury, *Memoirs*, i, p. 357.
[3] Martin, *Prince Consort*, iii, p. 122; Vitzthum, *St. Petersburg and London*, i, pp. 136, 212. As to the financial factor, see Boutenko in *Revue historique*, July–August, 1927, pp. 300–303, 317–320, and Pierre Dupont-Ferrier, *Le marché financier de Paris sous le Second Empire* (Paris, 1925).
[4] Monypenny and Buckle, *Disraeli*, iv, p. 57. Cf. Thouvenel, *Le Secret de l'Empereur*, i, p. 348.

acquisition of territory on the Rhine,[1] the outburst of British hostility over the annexation of Nice and Savoy was a harsh warning. Indeed the thwarting of French ambitions seemed to have become a major preoccupation of British policy.[2] Under the circumstances it would not be strange if something similar to Admiral von Tirpitz's conception of a *Risikoflotte* should have taken shape in the mind of Louis Napoleon.[3] If the exigencies of domestic politics should lead him to further attempts at expansion which involved a sharp clash of French and British interests, might not the existence of a strong French fleet lead England to stop and count the cost, especially if she had not yet regained the lead in ironclad building which she had allowed France to obtain? In conversation with the Confederate agent, John Slidell, on July 25, 1862, the Emperor

regretted to say that England had not properly appreciated his friendly action in the affair of the *Trent*, that there were many reasons why he desired to be on the best of terms with her, but the policy of nations necessarily changed with circumstances, and that he was consequently obliged to look forward to the possible contingency of not always having the same friendly relations as now existed.[4]

It was Lord Cowley's belief that the desire to maintain national prestige explained the large French armaments. "There is one paramount notion in the Emperor's mind — that the Bourbon and Orleans Dynasties were both lost through their having allowed France to drop in the scale of Nations." On account of jealousy of England, French pride would, Cowley thought, be less touched by a reduction of the

---

[1] Besides the introductory remarks in Hermann Oncken, *Die Rheinpolitik Kaiser Napoleons III von 1863 bis 1870 und der Ursprung des Krieges von 1870/71* (Stuttgart, 1926, 3 vols.), i, pp. 11 ff., and Beyens, *Le Second Empire*, i, pp. 85–86, 312–317, see the admirable article of Albert Pingaud, "La politique extérieure du Second Empire," in *Revue historique*, September–October, 1927, pp. 48–55, 60–61.

[2] P.R.O., G.D. 22: 14, Palmerston to Russell, February 8, 1861.

[3] Alfred von Tirpitz, *Erinnerungen* (Leipzig, 1919), pp. 55, 80–81, 91, 105–106, 109, 153–155, 167, 179, 192–193.

[4] *Official Records of the Union and Confederate Navies in the War of the Rebellion*, 2d series (Washington, 1921–1922, 3 vols.), iii, p. 484.

army than of the navy.[1] Could a Napoleon safely do less for the fleet than had Louis-Philippe?

Convinced though they are of the importance of sea power for themselves, British observers have sometimes been over-ready to describe the fleets of other nations as mere luxuries, maintained primarily for prestige. It is safer, perhaps, to let a Frenchman explain the French naval requirements. Seldom have they been more cogently stated than by the distinguished admiral, Jurien de la Gravière, in writing to a friend in the British Navy in November, 1860. Arguing that France and England had no serious reasons for war, and would be wise enough to live in peace, he concluded that

> the great subject of disagreement is the increase which each nation is making in her navy. *You* wish to be incontestably masters of the sea, and to fear neither us nor any maritime coalition; we do not object to this pretension up to a certain point. We should not wish, however, that your security should be such, that you should imagine yourselves able to treat us in any way you like.

If British naval supremacy enabled her to blockade and destroy French ports and ravage her coast, would not France have as much reason for alarm as England had "when menaced with an impossible invasion?"

> How, then, are we to avoid such a danger, if not by increasing our Navy? We are too rich, too industrious, too dependent on other nations, to face indifferently the prospect of a blockade like the one that Russia had to submit to during two years.[2]

We have several accounts [3] of a conversation between Napoleon III and Bismarck in 1857, during which the Emperor is said to have expressed the desire to make the Mediterranean almost a French lake, and to bolster up the second-rate fleets to create a balance of power at sea. As Bismarck described the interview to Lord Loftus on July 29, 1870, Napoleon expressed a desire

> to see Prussia enlarged, and more especially to see her become a maritime Power which, in conjunction with France and the second-rate maritime

---

[1] Wellesley, *Cowley*, p. 239, January 10, 1862.   [2] Mends, *Mends*, p. 331.
[3] Conveniently assembled in Robert Pahncke, *Die Parallel-Erzählungen Bismarcks* (Halle, 1914), pp. 53-59.

Powers, would be enabled to cope with England. He wished for the independence of the sea, and that no one power should be mistress on that element. He proposed to Bismarck to take Hanover, and to annex the Elbe Duchies to Prussia, as a means of increasing her maritime strength. . . .[1]

According to another version Napoleon III stated that

> Eine viel pikantere Befriedigung würden die Französen in einer Ausdehnung der Seegrenze finden. Er denke nicht daran, das Mittelmeer zu einem französischen See zu machen, 'mais à peu pres.' Der Französe sei kein Seemann von Natur, sondern ein guter Landsoldat, und eben deshalb seine Erfolge zur See ihm viel schmeichelhafter . . . Es müsse für Preussen wunschenswert sein, sein Gebiet durch die Erwerbung Hannovers und der Elbherzogtümer zu konsolideren. Für eine solche Kombination sei es aber erförderlich, dass Preussen seine Marine verstärke. Es fehle an Seemachten zweiten Ranges, die durch Vereinigung ihrer Streitkräfte mit den französischen das jetzt erdrückende Übergewicht Englands aufhoben . . . .[2]

Contemporary evidence to support these statements of Bismarck is not lacking. The Emperor's eagerness to strengthen maritime powers of the second rank attracted British attention. At Osborne in August, 1857, Louis Napoleon sounded Palmerston and Prince Albert as to a plan to unite Denmark with Sweden, and give Prussia Holstein with the harbor of Kiel.[3] Nor was the Prussian Navy the only object of imperial favor. Despite the unusual precautions taken to keep secret the plans of the *Gloire*, the Naval Prefect at Toulon was authorized to show the Grand Duke Constantine, at the time of his visit in December, 1858, both the ironclads under construction there, and even to let him examine the plans and copy the figures as to weights and dimensions.[4] British susceptibilities were touched when Cavour permitted the Russians to establish a naval base at Villafranca.

---

[1] *Diplomatic Reminiscences of Lord Augustus Loftus*, 2d series (London, 1894, 2 vols.), i, p. 130. In the first fortnight of the Franco-Prussian War, Bismarck might be suspected, of course, of exaggerating France's determination to rival England at sea. Here he places this interview with Louis Napoleon two years too early.

[2] H. von Poschinger, *Ein Achtundvierziger; Lothar Buchers Leben und Werke* (Berlin, 1890–1894, 3 vols.), iii, pp. 152–157. Cf. the other accounts assembled in Pahncke, *loc. cit.*, and Bismarck, *Gedanken und Erinnerungen* (Stuttgart, 1898, 2 vols.), i, pp. 193–194.

[3] Martin, *Prince Consort*, iv, p. 110. The Emperor told Prince Albert that Palmerston had not objected to the plan, but Palmerston gave the Prince a different version of the conversation. *Ibid.*, 113.

[4] A.M., 1 DD¹ 259, December 22, 1858.

Malmesbury instructed Cowley to ask Walewski whether France wished Russia to become a maritime power in the Mediterranean. The Russians, he declared, were

> trying to get ports in Spain, Sicily and Egypt, like Villafranca — that is military ports.... When the Emperor pretended to Clarendon that he did not know where Villafranca was, it was clearly a *comédie*.[1]

The effect of the unification of Italy on the command of the seas roused great interest on both sides of the Channel. Lord John Russell advised the Queen in November, 1860, that "if France were to sway the united Navies of Genoa and Naples, and Great Britain to look on from fear or apathy, or excessive love of peace, she might soon have to defend her possessions of Malta, Corfu, and Gibraltar."[2] One of Prince Albert's numerous anti-French memoranda was provoked by a sensational speech of Prince Napoleon in March, 1861, demanding the overthrow of the treaties of 1815. The Prince, who aspired in vain to the command of the French fleet,[3] declared to the Senate that

> if there be any position which can strengthen us against England, it is to make ourselves the centre of all the secondary Navies. When I say this, I am only citing one of the axioms of the traditional policy of France.... For if you think that all the secondary navies ought to be grouped around that of France, it is evident, that if the Italians have a navy, this will be a gain for France. Do not be deceived on this head. English statesmen know it well.[4]

As early as September, 1852, a speech of Louis Napoleon at Marseilles proposing to make the Mediterranean a French lake, provoked a protest from Lord Cowley.[5] At Osborne, five years later, the Emperor assured Prince Albert that he aimed to make of the Mediterranean not a French lake, as Napoleon I had wished, but a European lake. "Spain might have

---

[1] P. Matter, *Cavour et l'Unité Italienne* (Paris, 1922–1925, 3 vols.), iii, p. 43; Malmesbury, *Memoirs*, ii, pp. 147–148, January 11, 1859.
[2] *Letters of Queen Victoria*, iii, p. 524. Cf., *ibid.*, p. 545, and Maxwell, *Clarendon*, ii, p. 201.
[3] Ernest d'Hauterive, *Napoléon III et le Prince Napoléon*, pp. 209, 385.
[4] Martin, *Prince Consort*, v, pp. 301–302. Palmerston deemed this speech additional proof of the need of better defences. Gooch, *Russell*, ii, pp. 273–274.
[5] Wellesley, *Cowley*, p. 7.

Morocco, Sardinia a part of Tripoli, England Egypt, Austria a part of Syria — *et que sais-je?* ... France herself wanted an outlet for her turbulent spirits."[1] Palmerston rejected all ideas of a partition of North Africa and grew suspicious of French designs on Morocco.[2] In one quarter of the Mediterranean after another, in Genoa,[3] in Sardinia,[4] in Catalonia, and in the Balearic Islands,[5] French annexations were scented. The French expedition to Syria after the massacres of 1860 roused fears of the partition of Turkey.[6] As French sea power increased, British hostility to the Suez Canal project grew more bitter.[7] Palmerston declared that "the first week of a war between France and England would see 15,000 or 20,000 Frenchmen in possession of the canal, to keep it open for them and shut for us."[8] Unlike his critics at that time and since, the Prime Minister recognized the fact that from 1858 to 1863 France, thanks to her extraordinary efforts in shipbuilding, might hope to command the Mediterranean in the event of war.

Unfortunately for Palmerston's projects of national defence, the change of ministry which restored him to power in June, 1859, caused a delay in the development of British

---

[1] Martin, *Prince Consort*, iv, p. 110.
[2] Maxwell, *Clarendon*, ii, pp. 300–301; Gooch, *Russell*, ii, pp. 241–242; Ashley, *Palmerston*, ii, pp. 125–127, 166–167; Greville, *Journal*, ii, pp. 270–271.
[3] *Parliamentary Papers*, 1861, lxvii, no. 2757, "Further Correspondence relating to the Affairs of Italy," part vii, nos. 15, 18, 20.
[4] *Ibid.*, nos. 15, 18, 20, 33, 35; P.R.O., G.D. 22: 56, Palmerston's memorandum of March 2, 1861; and 22: 21, Palmerston to Russell, June 10, 1861; Hansard, 3rd series, clxiv, cols. 1189–1242; Martin, *Prince Consort*, v, pp. 360–362. In a conversation with King William I of Prussia in October, 1861, Louis Napoleon ridiculed these British suspicions. Karl Ringhoffer, *Im Kampfe für Preussens Ehre, Aus dem Nachlass des Grafen Albrecht v. Bernstorff* (Berlin, 1906), pp. 440–441.
[5] Ashley, *Palmerston*, ii, p. 187.
[6] Besides the extended debates in Hansard, 3rd series, clix-clxiii, see P.R.O., G.D. 22: 21, Palmerston to Russell, July 19, 20, 22, 1860; and 22: 14, Palmerston to Russell, March 12, 1861; *Parliamentary Papers*, lxix, nos. 2715, 2720, 2728, 2734, and 1861, lxviii; Thouvenel, *Le Secret de l'Empereur*, i, pp. 328, 344, 391, 440, 445; ii, pp. 35, 124; Sir Alfred Lyall, *The Life of the Marquis of Dufferin and Ava* (London, 1905, 2 vols.), i, ch. xiv; Camille de Rochemonteix, *Le Liban et l'expédition française en Syrie (1860–1861)*, (Paris, 1921).
[7] On British antipathy to the Suez Canal project see H. L. Hoskins, *British Routes to India* (Philadelphia, 1928), chs. xii-xiv, and Hussein Husny, *Le Canal de Suez et la politique égyptienne* (Montpellier, 1923), pp. 165–306.
[8] Ashley, *Palmerston*, ii, p. 327, December 8, 1861.

naval policy. Weeks and months elapsed before the new Admiralty Board [1] could familiarize itself with the results of earlier experiments and agree on a forward policy for building ironclads. Experiments at Portsmouth in May had proved compressed cotton to be an unsatisfactory backing for armor, and had upset the early belief in the superiority of rolled-over forged iron plates.[2] When Sir John Pakington, on July 29, asked the intentions of his successors concerning the further armor tests ordered by his Board and the second ironclad which he had expected to order, Lord Clarence Paget, the new Secretary of the Admiralty, replied that the experiments had been delayed owing to slow work by the firm which was making the various plates, but that they would be proceeded with immediately. A second ironclad would not be constructed, however, "till the result of the experiment in the first case had been brought to a conclusion." [3]

In proposing the construction of additional wooden line-of-battle ships, much against his own judgment, Paget found himself in an embarrassing position. More than a year earlier he had declared in the House of Commons that

> he was persuaded, and it was the general opinion of the naval profession, that line-of-battle ships were not destined to play an important part in future naval wars. It was believed that these ships would be superseded in the line-of-battle, and more particularly in attacking forts, by ships with one tier of heavy guns and their sides cased with iron.[4]

When the Admiralty rejected in August his proposal to substitute three ironclads for three of the new wooden capital ships recently ordered, he submitted his resignation, but was

---

[1] The Duke of Somerset became First Lord of the Admiralty, Vice Admiral Sir R. S. Dundas, Rear Admiral Frederick Thomas Pelham, Captain Charles Eden and Captain Charles Frederick, Sea Lords, and Samuel Whitbread, M.P., Civil Lord. Rear Admiral Lord Clarence Paget was First Secretary and W. G. Romaine continued as Second Secretary. *London Gazette*, June 28, 1859; Sir John Henry Briggs, *Naval Administrations, 1827 to 1892* (London, 1897), p. 141.

[2] Report of Captain R. S. Hewlett, May 19, 1859, Adm. 1/5708: A. 863; Submission Letter Book no. 20, February 23, April 30, May 6, June 10; *ibid.*, no. 21, October 28, November 18, 1859. Additional iron plates were ordered for another trial. Adm. 12/669: 59-1, June 10, 1859.

[3] Hansard, 3rd series, clv, col. 657. Experiments on sailing vessels, he answered Pakington, would depend on the results of the experiments with armor.

[4] *Ibid.*, cxlix, cols. 929–930, April 12, 1858.

persuaded by Palmerston to withdraw it.[1] Gladstone warmly endorsed the idea of substituting ironclads for wooden vessels, but Palmerston supported the Admiralty's efforts to regain a heavy predominance in wooden capital ships.[2]

Tests of various types of armor fastened to the side of the wooden vessel *Undaunted* began at Portsmouth in August, 1859. They indicated that both steel and puddled steel, as then manufactured, were inferior to rolled iron. The rolled-iron plates 4½ inches thick furnished by Palmer and Company of Newcastle proved slightly superior to those of hammered iron produced by the Thames Iron Shipbuilding Company. As the latter company, however, could not roll plates of that thickness, they forged those for the *Warrior* under the hammer. Plates of less than 4 inches proved quite inadequate. Laminated armor, resembling that adopted for many vessels during the American Civil War, appeared to be inferior to solid plates of the same thickness. Although the ship's side was not penetrated when covered by six thin iron plates riveted together to make 4 inches of armor, the shot nevertheless broke through all the plates and drove them several inches deep into the hull.[3] Captain Hewlett again reported that the results of his experiments demonstrated the value of plating ships of war.[4]

Still more impressive were the tests of Armstrong's 70-pounder rifled gun against the 4-inch plates of the floating battery *Trusty*, at ranges of 200 and 400 yards. After two days' firing, there were "only one or two screw nuts off, and a very few bolts started" on the inside of the vessel. Hewlett concluded that the plates were "invulnerable against the first blow of a shell and nearly in every case from a solid shot

---

[1] *Parliamentary Papers*, 1861, xxvi, no. 2790, p. xlv; Sir Arthur Otway, *Autobiography and Journals of Admiral Lord Clarence E. Paget* (London, 1896), p. 193.
[2] Guedalla, *Gladstone and Palmerston*, pp. 113–114, 158, 228; Hansard, 3rd series, cxlix, cols. 934–938.
[3] *Ibid.*, clxii, col. 1063; *Parliamentary Papers*, 1861, xxxviii, no. 347; Submission Letter Book no. 21, August 23, 1859; Adm. 1/5708: A. 1829; Special Committee on Iron, *First Report*, p. 176; *Experiments with Naval Ordnance, H.M.S. "Excellent,"* p. 131.
[4] Adm. 12/669: 59–1, August 15, 1859.

of the heaviest description; and therefore there can be no doubt of the advantage of these 4 Inch iron clothed ships, which I consider we cannot urge on too rapidly in their construction...."[1] Sir Baldwin Walker agreed that

> the "Trusty" having stood so well, there would appear to be no good grounds for questioning the efficiency of the 4½-inch plates which it is proposed to place on a much more substantial backing of solid timber to be attached to the iron plating of the iron cased frigates building, unless guns of much greater penetrating power should be invented.[2]

Concerned at what then seemed the great size and cost of Pakington's armored frigate, which on October 5 was designated the *Warrior*, the Whig Board of Admiralty set its heart on producing a smaller type of seagoing ironclad. In defence of this course they argued that it was desirable to try another class in order to see their relative advantages, and they anticipated that the Commission on National Defences [3] would recommend some smaller ironclads for coast defence. Great Britain, moreover, had at that time only two docks big enough to contain vessels of the size of the *Warrior*.[4]

To meet the wishes of the Admiralty Sir Baldwin Walker submitted on September 21 a project for a vessel of 5223 tons burden, with the same beam, draft, and height of battery as the *Warrior*, but with the length reduced to 335 feet and the armament reduced from 36 guns to 22. Pointing out, however, that the reduced size would permit engines of only 800 horse power, giving an estimated speed of twelve knots, the

---

[1] Adm. 1/5708: A. 2021, October 3, 1859. Later tests of the plates of the *Trusty*, however, showed them to be brittle and very inferior both to the 4-inch plates tested on the *Undaunted*, and to the 4½-inch plates more recently tested. See the report of the Special Committee on Iron Plates and Guns, March 13, 1860, reproduced in Special Committee on Iron, *First Report*, pp. 185-199, and also Adm. 1/5732, Hewlett's report of October 1, 1860; A.M., 6 DD¹ 23, dossier 507, Pigeard's report of October 10, 1860; *Parliamentary Papers*, 1861, xxvi, no. 2790, p. 70; Douglas, *Naval Gunnery* (5th ed., London, 1860), pp. 221, 414, 420-422.

[2] Submission Letter Book no. 21, November 19, 1859. The Surveyor here stated, with regard to a point raised by Hewlett, that he believed that a red-hot shot or liquid iron which lodged in the wooden backing between the iron hull and the armor might smoulder for a short time, but the fire, he thought, would soon go out for want of air.

[3] See above, p. 141 and below, pp. 160, 170, 188.

[4] *Parliamentary Papers*, 1861, v, no. 438, pp. 6-7, testimony of the Duke of Somerset, April 16, 1861.

Surveyor argued that this speed, scarcely exceeding that of full-powered wooden capital ships, would not enable the ironclads to choose their range and always

> to avoid a close action with them, and the serious consequences which might be the effect of their concentrated broadsides with the improved heavy artillery of the present day, nor would such a speed be sufficient to enable these frigates to force a passage in the event of its being necessary to throw in supplies in the face of a superior force.[1]

In response to this strong argument the Board yielded for the moment, and decided to build the second ironclad frigate on plans similar to those of the *Warrior*. After calling for tenders from four leading shipbuilders, they awarded the contract early in October to Robert Napier and Sons, who agreed to build her on the Clyde within twelve months at £37.5.0 per ton. In January she was named first the *Invincible*, and then, definitively, the *Black Prince*.[2]

Before the award of this contract, the results of the experiments on the *Undaunted* and *Trusty* had shown that armor could withstand heavy guns of the latest pattern. The Admiralty now, with the Prime Minister's approval, pressed the Surveyor again for the design of a smaller type of ironclad. In response Walker submitted on November 24 the plans for a class of ship of 3,668 tons burden, "suited for Channel and Home Service." These vessels, 280 feet long, of 54 feet beam, and 25 feet draft, were designed to carry 16 guns with 7½ feet height of midship port. Engines of 600 horse power would give them a speed of 10¾ knots. They were to carry coal for eight days at full speed, and provisions for 400 men

---

[1] The estimated cost for the smaller vessel was £210,524 for hull and engines, compared with £262,100 for the *Warrior*. As ironclads would last many years, "certainly much longer than ordinary ships of war," Walker argued that they must have "a superiority of speed which, even when diminished in a few years by the progress of improvement, will still enable them to perform the intended services." Otherwise they would be of no use save for harbor defence, for which cheaper vessels, such as the eight existing floating batteries, would serve. Submission Letter Book no. 21.

[2] *Ibid.*, September 23, October 5, 1859, January 14, 1860. See also Napier, *Life of Robert Napier*, pp. 211-214. Palmer and Company had submitted a lower bid, but required 16 or 18 months for delivery.

PASSING OF THE WOODEN CAPITAL SHIP 157

for twelve weeks. The Surveyor proposed that six vessels of this type be built by contract, pointing out that

> as it is probable that iron cased ships will in any future war play an important part, and as several ships of this description are in course of construction in foreign ports, it seems most desirable if not absolutely necessary, to lose no time in building at least an equal number.[1]

When the Admiralty promptly applied for authorization to build two such ships, Palmerston reminded the Chancellor of the Exchequer of the great progress the French were making with ironclads. Gladstone "entirely and cordially" concurred with Somerset's request, and again urged that work on some wooden capital ships be discontinued in favor of ironclad building. Palmerston admitted that iron plating "will certainly stand any shot beyond 4 or 500 yards, and ships so armed would therefore beyond those distances have an immense advantage over ships not protected in the same manner." He was not yet ready to abandon the wooden capital ship, however, for "whether Iron plated ships will stand such shot as improved Science will bring to bear against them remains to be seen, but even then it will be some Time before they can be completed in sufficient Numbers by any Power to constitute the Main arm of Naval Warfare."[2]

According to the contracts which were awarded on December 14 to Palmer and Company of Newcastle-on-Tyne and Westwood, Baillie and Company of Millwall, these smaller ironclads were to be delivered on March 14, 1861, and December 14, 1860, and were to be completed while the engines were being installed. These sister ships were named the *Defence* and the *Resistance*.[3] This pair of ironclads, like the *Warrior* and *Black Prince*, was designed by Isaac Watts, the Chief Constructor of the Navy. All four were iron vessels protected amidships for more than half their length, and

---

[1] Controller of the Navy, Submission Letter Book no. 21.
[2] Guedalla, *Gladstone and Palmerston*, pp. 113–114.
[3] Submission Letter Book no. 21, December 3 and 14, 1859, January 14, 1860. Palmer's price was £43 per ton; Westwood, Baillie and Company's, £44. See also *Parliamentary Papers*, 1861, v, no. 438, p. 36, and xxvi, no. 2790, p. **xxxii**; and Hansard, 3rd series, clvi, col. 980 and clvii, col. 2037.

from their upper deck to five feet below the water line, with 4½-inch iron plates backed by 18 inches of teak. Except for the *Couronne*, whose plans were finally approved by the French Minister of the Marine September 1, 1858,[1] and for the abortive Stevens battery, they were the first seagoing ironclads to be designed with iron hulls. Unlike the *Couronne*, however, which was armored from stem to stern like the *Gloire*, both ends of the first four British ironclad frigates were wholly unprotected by armor, but were subdivided into water-tight compartments, so fitted as to enable water being admitted to increase their immersion.[2] At both extremities of their side armor were armored transverse bulkheads.

The *Warrior*, a handsome ship-rigged vessel of 6109 tons, builder's measurement, and about 9000 tons displacement, had an overhanging bow, concealing a strong stem of ram form.[3] She was 380 feet 2 inches long, 58 feet 4 inches extreme breadth, and 26 feet 2 inches maximum draft when first fitted for sea, October 4, 1861, with a height of midship port of 9 feet 4 inches. Her depth of hold was 21 feet 1 inch, and the area of her midship section 1218 square feet. Her engines of 1250 nominal horse power gave her a speed of 14.354 knots. Her armament as ordered September 28, 1860, comprised thirty-four 68-pounders on the main deck, with two 68-pounder guns on pivots and four 40-pounder Armstrongs on slides and carriages for the broadside on the upper deck. After several changes, it comprised in May, 1862, twenty-six 68-pounders and eight 110-pounder Armstrongs on the main deck, with two 110-pounder and four 70-pounder Armstrongs on the upper deck. She carried 579 seamen and boys, and 125 marines. In 1861 an elliptical blockhouse, armored with 4-inch plates and loopholed for musketry, was placed under the after bridge.[4]

1 The *Couronne* was launched March 28, 1861, three months later than the *Warrior*. The British had been the first to adopt iron hulls for armored floating batteries. See above, pp. 86–87, 111.
2 *Parliamentary Papers*, 1862, xxxiv, no. 262.   3 See Appendix B.
4 Ship's book of the *Warrior*. There are excellent plates of the *Warrior* in J. Scott Russell, *The Modern System of Naval Architecture* (London [1865], 3 vols., folio), vol. iii; and in W. J. M. Rankine, ed., *Shipbuilding, Theoretical and Practical*

Imperial War Museum photograph. Copyright reserved.

H.M.S. *WARRIOR*

The novel form of construction, together with several additions to the original design, caused great delay in the building of the *Warrior*. Instead of being launched on April 11, 1860, and completed in the following July, according to contract, she was not launched until December 29, 1860, nor commissioned until August 1, 1861. Forging the massive stern-post caused much difficulty. Furthermore, while she was under construction, the Admiralty decided that all the armor plates must be tongued and grooved for additional strength, and that the size of her gun ports must be reduced. Her sister ship, the *Black Prince*, was not launched until February 27, 1861, nor commissioned until June 18, 1862.[1] Her speed at the measured mile was 13.604 knots. Her total cost was £357,579; that of the *Warrior*, £357,291.[2]

The *Defence* and *Resistance*, armored amidships like the *Warrior*, had bows of a conspicuous ram form, with the point close to the water line. For better security when ramming, they had lower masts and bowsprits of iron. The *Defence* was launched April 24, 1861; delivered on September 7, nearly six months late; commissioned December 4; and finished Febru-

---

(London, 1866); and interesting models in the Science Museum, South Kensington, and the Royal Naval Museum, Greenwich. Of the many descriptions of this famous vessel, those by E. J. Reed in his *Our Iron-Clad Ships* (London, 1869), and his *Shipbuilding in Iron and Steel* (London, 1869), are noteworthy. No one observed the *Warrior* with greater care and interest than the French Naval Constructors, Jaÿ and Lebelin, whose reports are preserved in the *Mémorial du génie maritime*, 1861, i, and 1862, i, with accompanying sketches.

[1] "Copy of correspondence between the Admiralty and the contractors who built the 'Warrior,' in reference to the non-fulfilment of their contract within the stipulated time," *Parliamentary Papers*, 1861, xxxviii, no. 207; *ibid.*, 1863, xxxvi, nos. 83 and 237; Submission Letter Book no. 21, *passim*; Admiralty 12/701: 59–1; Admiralty 12/705: 91–2. See also, Napier, *Life of Robert Napier*, pp. 211–214, with picture of the *Black Prince*, facing p. 208. There are brief reports on the *Black Prince* by the French Consul at Glasgow and by Naval Constructor Lebelin in the *Mémorial du génie maritime*, 1860, ii, p. 409, and 1862, i, pp. 211–213. A half model of her is preserved in the Science Museum, South Kensington. G. L. Overton, in the catalogue of that collection, *Water Transport, III, Steam Ships of War*, p. 36, says of the *Black Prince* that "The constructional difference from the 'Warrior' was in the above-water form of her fore-part, where the breadth from the main deck upwards was somewhat less, which afforded a more graceful appearance."

[2] *Parliamentary Papers*, 1866, xlvi, nos. 76 and 526. The ship's book of the *Warrior*, however, gives the original cost of her hull and machinery as £356,693 and the total cost, exclusive of armament and coal, as £377,292.

ary 12, 1862, at a total cost of £237,614. She made 11.356 knots in her first trials, and 11.612 later. The *Resistance* was launched April 11, 1861; delivered December 5, nearly a year after the date stipulated in the contract; commissioned July 2; and completed August 21, 1862, at a total cost of £242,695. Her speed at deep draught at the measured mile was 11.832 knots. The armament first ordered for these vessels in November, 1860, consisted of sixteen 68-pounders for the main deck, and two 68-pounder pivot guns and four 40-pounder Armstrongs on the upper deck.[1]

The testimony of leading naval officers before the Royal Commission on the Defences of the United Kingdom in October and November, 1859, was practically unanimous that forts could not prevent ironclad ships from forcing a passage through a clear channel, unless the ships came under a concentrated fire at close range.[2] To supplement land defences, a committee of naval officers appointed by the Commissioners proposed stationary floating batteries protected by 4½-inch iron plates, and steam floating batteries similarly armored, of about 2000 tons and 10 knots speed, capable of use as rams.[3] The Commissioners disapproved of stationary floating batteries, but unanimously recommended the expenditure of £1,000,000 on ironclad steam vessels for harbor defence.[4]

[1] Ship's books of *Defence* and *Resistance*; Adm. 12/701: 59–1, May 18, 1861; returns from the Controller's office in *Parliamentary Papers*, 1862, xxxiv, no. 432; 1863, xxxvi, no. 83; 1866, xlvi, nos. 76 and 526. A report by Lebelin on the *Defence* is in the *Mémorial du génie maritime*, 1862, i, pp. 211–219.

[2] "Report of the Commissioners appointed to consider the defences of the United Kingdom," February 7, 1860, *Parliamentary Papers*, 1860, xxiii, no. 2682, testimony of Vice Admiral Sir Richard Dundas, Rear Admirals Sir Michael Seymour and Sir Thomas Maitland, and Captains Bartholomew James Sulivan and Richard Strode Hewlett. General Sir John Fox Burgoyne, Inspector General of Fortifications, testified that he had "no great confidence in iron-plated vessels. I think that improvements in artillery will go on faster than improvements in fortifying the sides of ships; and . . . even with iron-plated vessels the decks remain open . . ." *Ibid.*, p. 40. The Commissioners were: Major General Sir H. D. Jones, Major General D. A. Cameron, Rear Admiral George Elliot, Major General Sir Frederic Abbott, Indian Army, Captain Astley Cooper Key, Colonel John Henry Lefroy, and James Fergusson. See above, p. 141.

[3] *Ibid.*, pp. 63–64. The committee was composed of Rear Admiral Sir Thomas Maitland, and Captains E. Gardiner Fishbourne, Arthur A. Cochrane, M. S. Nolloth, and Cowper P. Coles.

[4] *Ibid.*, pp. ix–x, xviii–xix.

Anticipating this demand the Admiralty insisted on the preparation of designs for ironclads still smaller than the *Defence* and *Resistance*. Sir Baldwin Walker replied with a frank *non possumus*. The advantages of iron-hulled over wooden-hulled ironclads, he observed, were greater strength and durability, and the possibility of leaving the extremities of an iron ship unarmored, so as to obviate the difficulty of plating curved surfaces and of placing heavy weights over the fine ends. The protected middle portion, however, must have sufficient buoyancy to float the vessel even though her unprotected bow and stern were riddled with shot. There was no way, he argued, of attaining this, combined with other essential features of a sea-service ship, in vessels smaller than the *Defence*. She and her sister ship were, he pointed out, smaller than the French armored frigates, and were "not fit for general service," although well adapted for coast defence. "Any attempt to construct ships smaller than these intended to combine all the properties essential for seagoing ships would end in disappointment." Despite their slow speed and small height of ports the existing floating batteries seemed well adapted for harbor defence, but they "of course are altogether unfit to be relied on for coast defence."[1]

Not to be denied, the Admiralty called on the master shipwrights in the dockyards for a "detailed report as to the best class of seagoing steam vessels for coast defence, carrying two or four heavy guns, and cased or partially cased with 4½-inch iron plates."[2] Seven master shipwrights attempted to solve the problem, but not one found an answer that satisfied the Surveyor's department. Isaac Watts and his assistants, Joseph Large and Richard Abethell, failed to discover in the several designs anything new that seemed to warrant adoption. They adhered to the view that no seagoing ironclads smaller than the *Defence* and *Resistance* could be suitable for

---

[1] Submission Letter Book no. 21, December 28, 1859. For these reasons the scientific officers of the Controller's department deemed it impossible to make a ship exactly conforming to the conditions proposed by the Commissioners on the Defences of the United Kingdom. *Parliamentary Papers*, 1861, v, no. 438, p. 70.

[2] Submission Letter Book no. 21, December 31, 1859; *Parliamentary Papers*, 1861, xxvi, no. 2790, p. 227.

coast defence. Even those two vessels, capable of little over eleven knots speed, they thought

cannot be regarded as fit to contend, under all circumstances, and more especially in fine weather, with vessels like "La Gloire," constructed with comparative disregard to strength and endurance, and with very low ports, in order to obtain great speed.

Strength of hull and height of ports, however, they regarded as the paramount qualities.[1]

In this same report of December 11, 1860, the three naval constructors rejected another project which had begun to attract public attention. The idea of protecting ships by inclined armor, which had been proposed repeatedly in the United States since 1812,[2] may possibly have received an impetus from the fact that the sides of the iron-hulled British floating batteries built in 1855–1856 sloped inward considerably. At all events, in the years 1858 and 1859 two Englishmen patented the idea and six other men sent projects for inclined armor to the Admiralty, which were rejected by the Surveyor.[3] Captain Adderley Willcocks Sleigh, late of the Royal Navy, obtained letters patent dated July 7, 1858, for "improvements in the construction of floating sea barriers or artificial beaches, break-waters and batteries," by inclined planes which might be plated with iron.[4] And on November 1, 1859, Josiah Jones, Junior, a Liverpool shipbuilder, obtained letters patent for "improvements in shipbuilding." His specification filed on April 30, 1860, explained that by

combining thick protecting plating of metal with a ship, the sides and ends of which are considerably inclined, a structure is obtained which will resist shot much more effectually than the floating batteries hitherto constructed

---

[1] Submission Letter Book no. 21, December 11, 1860. Richard Abethell, the master shipwright of Portsmouth yard, had been detailed to assist the Surveyor's department in the examination of these plans. *Ibid.*, November 9, 1860. See also, for O. W. Lang's proposal of January 31, 1860, *Parliamentary Papers*, 1861, xxvi, no. 2790, p. 227.

[2] See above, pp. 9, 31, 48, 52, 53, and below, pp. 215, 219, 226–228.

[3] For the projects of Messrs. D. Brown, Crispin, Hogg, Hughes, Hyde, and Morton, see Submission Letter Book no. 20, December 7, 1858, February 5, 1859; and *ibid.*, no. 21, December 15, 1859. Three projects of Mr. Turner, the master shipwright of Woolwich yard, which were rejected December 11, 1860, also had considerable tumble-home.

[4] British Patent Office, 1858, no. 1529.

... I prefer that the sides of the ship should incline outwards from the centre line of the ship until they rise up to the water line; also, that at this point they should make a sharp angle, bend or round, and from this point upwards that they should incline inwards towards the centre line...

The angle, however, might come either above or below the water line. Although steel or wrought iron was preferred for the ribs or framing, other materials might be used.[1]

Anticipating, as so many other inventors had done, the design of the *Merrimack*, Jones submitted to the Admiralty six plans for ships ranging from 205 to 400 feet in length, and 2800 to 10,000 tons displacement, protected by 3½-inch armor inclined at an angle of 40 degrees. In his report of August 20, 1858, as to the experiments on the *Alfred*,[2] Captain Hewlett stated that two 68-pounder shot at 200 yards distance, striking the plates at an angle of 40 degrees, "did not at that angle glance off, but did almost as much injury as those striking direct...."[3] Tests made at Portsmouth in 1860, however, with 68-pounder cast-iron shot fired at 200 yards range against a substantial butt on Jones's system, covered with 4½-inch wrought-iron plates inclined at an angle of 52 degrees, showed

that the principle of inclining plates intended to resist heavy shot has been most successfully established, for, not only is the penetration under these circumstances less than half that when the plates are perpendicular, but the effect on the woodwork supporting the plates has been very slight in comparison with the effect when the plates are on the side of the ship.[4]

The three naval constructors, Watts, Large, and Abethell, however, objected that the excessive tumble-home would reduce the space of the weather deck so as to make it scarcely available for working the ship; would prevent fixing the channels to the proper spread for supporting the masts effectively; would admit the seas on board in rough weather and diminish stability at large angles of inclination; would require larger gun ports; and "would make the 'between decks' a most un-

[1] British Patent Office, 1859, no. 2491.
[2] See above, p. 124.   [3] Adm. 1/5691: A. 1744.
[4] Report dated H.M.S. "Excellent," August 4, 1860, in Special Committee on Iron, *First Report*, pp. xi, 180–184. Cf. the London *Times*, October 16, 1860.

comfortable residence for the ship's company and a very inconvenient place for working the guns." They concluded that

taking weight for weight, there is no advantage, as regards resistance to horizontal shot, in the inclined side over the vertical side; whilst any shot striking the former less obliquely, as for instance, those fired from an elevated battery or a three deck ship, or during the heeling of the ship towards the enemy, would meet with less resistance than if striking a ship with vertical sides under similar circumstances.[1]

Meanwhile, throughout the year 1860, the current of opinion in favor of ironclad ships grew steadily stronger. The speakers before the newly founded Institution of Naval Architects seem to have been unanimous in favor of the new departure.[2] The debates in Parliament reflect the growing public interest in armored warships, and the growing anxiety lest France had taken too long a lead in the new course.[3] Tradition has it that the dockyard officers were numbered among the bitterest opponents of the introduction of armor. Yet Richard Abethell, master shipwright of the Portsmouth yard, thought that the future tendency would be to build ironclads, not ships of wood. He preferred iron to wood for the hulls of armored vessels; and declared that there was "no doubt about their behaving well in a heavy sea."[4] Oliver

---

[1] Submission Letter Book no. 21, December 11, 1860. Cf. *Transactions of the Institution of Naval Architects*, ii, pp. 65 ff.

[2] *Transactions of the Institution of Naval Architects*, i (1860). Nathaniel Barnaby, then a draftsman in the department of the Controller of the Navy, declared that the *Warrior* and *Black Prince* would be "the strongest, the safest, and the swiftest men-of-war that ever swam; the latest step in the progress of invention in naval architecture . . . the sides of these ships are sufficiently strong to resist the most powerful ordnance yet constructed, under all ordinary circumstances. . . . Such ships are, however, far too long ever to be used as rams. . . ." *Op. cit.*, p. 154.

[3] Cf. the speeches of Lord Clarence Paget, Sir John Pakington, Sir Charles Napier, Whitbread, G. Ridley, and Sir Morton Peto, in the House of Commons, February 13, April 9, April 19 and August 20, 1860, Hansard, 3rd series, clvi, cols. 980, 985, 989, 996, 1138, 2029, 2032, 2033–2037; clx, col. 1589–1590. The only member who expressed doubts of the policy of building ironclads was Sir William Jolliffe, *ibid.*, col. 2032, April 19, 1860. Sidney Herbert declared that forts must be the main reliance for harbor defence, since "At present we know little as to the way of making them [floating batteries] invulnerable by iron coating." *Ibid.*, clx, col. 39, July 23, 1860.

[4] *Parliamentary Papers*, 1861, xxvi, no. 2790, p. 326, testimony before the Royal Commission on Dockyards, December 11, 1860.

William Lang, master shipwright of Chatham yard, likewise testified concerning ironclads that "we have made the ship almost invulnerable, and it is clear that under equal circumstances wooden ships would stand no chance at all with them."[1] Yet there were still doubts whether an iron ship could serve everywhere that a wooden ship could. Sir Baldwin Walker told the Dockyard Commission in October, 1860, that he doubted very much whether ironclads "will ever replace a class of ship." If foreign powers had them, England must have them, although it was still to be proved that they would answer in every respect. He was sure, however, that they "would do good service on particular occasions," such as home defence and general Channel service.[2]

The successful trials of the *Gloire*, followed by the first rumors of the great French building program of 1860,[3] induced the Admiralty to expand its ironclad program from four to seven ships. On September 28, 1860, Sir Baldwin Walker, now styled Controller, instead of Surveyor, of the Navy, proposed the construction of one ironclad like the *Warrior* in Chatham dockyard and two similar ships by contract. He warned the Admiralty that it was of the utmost importance that England should show her determination not to be outstripped in any class of warship, and argued that, although the *Warrior* had not been tried, there was "no reason for believing that she will not answer all the purposes for which she was designed."[4]

Although the Admiralty approved this proposal for building three new ships like the *Warrior* and *Black Prince*, they revealed their uncertainty by directing the Controller to report how such vessels could be utilized, as transports or other-

---

[1] *Ibid.*, p. 220, November 28, 1860.
[2] *Ibid.*, p. 29.
[3] See above, pp. 109–113. For an early rumor of the great French ironclad program, see the London *Times*, October 15, 1860.
[4] Submission Letter Book no. 21. If the docks then being lengthened at Devonport and Pembroke had been completed he would have proposed that the two latter ships be built there. Lord Clarence Paget favored the policy of building the ironclads of wood in the government dockyards instead of iron by private contract. *Parliamentary Papers*, 1861, xxvi, no. 2790, p. xxxiii, June 29, 1860. Cf., *ibid.*, pp. 26, 214, 229, 423.

wise, "in case it should be deemed advisable at any time to strip off the Armour plates."[1] Indeed none of these three ships was built on the original plan. Before awarding the contracts for the two ships which were to be built in private shipyards the Board gave rein to their hobby and demanded a new design for a type smaller than the *Warrior* but with a greater extent of armor. To meet these views Walker submitted on January 10, 1861, the design of a coast-defence ironclad of 4063 tons, 32 guns, and 800 horse power, to carry 30 guns on the main deck, which was to be protected by 4½-inch armor from end to end. Under the main deck to about five feet below the water line, the armor was to extend only to within 30 feet of the stem and 35 feet of the stern port. In the hope of improving the seagoing qualities of the ship, the water line was thus left unprotected at both the bow and the stern. Contracts for two ships of this type were awarded on January 25 to Napier and Sons and to Westwood, Baillie and Company.[2] These vessels, the *Hector* and *Valiant*, were 280 feet long, 56 feet 3 inches beam, with a mean draft of 24 feet 8 inches and a bow of ram form. Although the contract called for delivery complete on July 25, 1862, the *Hector* was not launched until September 26, 1862, nor completed for sea until February 22, 1864. She cost £283,822 and made a speed of 12.36 knots in her time trials. In the autumn of 1861 Westwood, Baillie and Company threw up the contract for the *Valiant*, which was completed by the Thames Iron Shipbuilding Company. She was launched October 14, 1863, and completed for sea September 15, 1868. Her speed was 12.633 knots.[3]

On the same day that the Board approved the contracts for the *Hector* and *Valiant*, the Admiralty seems to have come to the conclusion that the types previously ordered had inadequate protection at the water line, leaving the steering gear

---

[1] Submission Letter Book no. 21, October 15 and 24, November 10, 1860.
[2] Adm. 1/5774; Adm. 12/701: 59–1; Adm. 12/705: 91–2. See also *Parliamentary Papers*, 1861, xxvi, no. 2790, p. 377.
[3] Ship's book, *Hector*; Adm. 12/701: 59–1; Adm. 12/705: 91–2; Adm. 12/720: 91–2; returns from the Controller's office in *Parliamentary Papers*, 1862, xxxiv, no. 432; 1863, xxxvi, no. 83; 1866, xlvi, nos. 76 and 526; 1874, xxxviii, no. 99.

H. M. S. *ACHILLES*

Imperial War Museum photograph. Copyright reserved.

exposed.[1] For it was on that date that they directed the Controller to prepare drawings for a vessel with sufficient additional length "to bear plating round the extremities above and below the water line only, the plating round the main deck being confined as in 'Warrior' to a certain portion of the sides."[2] Of this "belt-and-battery" type the Chatham-built ironclad, *Achilles*, became the first example. She was a ship of 6121 tons, builder's measurement, and 9525 tons displacement, 380 feet long, 58 feet 3½ inches beam, and 26½ feet mean draft, with engines of 1250 horse power and a speed of 14.343 knots. She was launched December 23, 1863, and completed for sea November 26, 1864, at a total cost of £444,380.[3]

The successful trials of the *Gloire* made many critics impatient of the slow progress of the British in building ironclads.[4] A writer in the October issue of the *Quarterly Review*

---

[1] Sir Nathaniel Barnaby, who in 1861 was draftsman in the Controller's department, pointed out in his *Naval Development of the Century*, pp. 68–69, that "the wooden line-of-battle ships, with which the designers of these first iron-cased ships were familiar, had required no special water-line protection ... they had a lower or gun deck about four feet above the water-line, and an orlop deck about three feet below the water-line. Between these two decks the ship's sides were stouter than in any other part, and shot did not easily perforate them. ... The 'wing-passages' on the orlop were clear, from end to end of the ship, and they were patrolled by the carpenter's crew who were provided with shot plugs of wood and oakum and sail cloth with which to close any shot holes. As against disabled steering gear there were spare tillers and tiller ropes, and only injury to the rudder head itself was serious. But a steam-ship, built of iron, and having only a single propeller was very different. Such a ship must keep control of her steering power; and shot holes between wind and water at the end of the ship might create inconvenient changes of trim." Barnaby attributes the change in the design of the *Achilles* to Sir Edward Reed.

[2] Adm. 12/701: 59–1, January 25, 1861. Cf. Robinson's submission of May 3, 1862, Adm. 1/5802.

[3] Ship's book, *Achilles*; Adm. 12/701: 59–1; Adm. 12/705: 91–2; Adm. 12/717: 59–1; Adm. 12/720: 91–2; returns from the Controller's office in *Parliamentary Papers*, 1862, xxxiv, no. 432; 1866, xlvi, nos. 76 and 526; 1874, xxxviii, no. 99. Her armament, by Admiralty order of May 3, 1861, was to consist of 50 guns: thirty-four 100-pounder Armstrongs on the main deck; with two 100-pounder Armstrongs on revolving carriages, eight 100-pounder Armstrongs on slides and carriages, four 40-pounder Armstrongs on truck carriages and two 32-pounders on truck carriages, on the upper deck. It was reduced to 30 guns, however, in 1862, by removing all the upper-deck guns except two 110-pounder Armstrongs.

[4] "With one voice the country demands in justice to its seamen, as to its own dearest interests, that not another hour should be lost in turning our vast resources to account in providing iron ships." *Admiralty Administration, Its Faults and De-*

asserted that "it would be extremely difficult to find any one among the younger officers of the service, who are either likely to command or to be called upon to serve in wooden ships, who is not of opinion that their day is gone...." [1] Prince Albert complained to Lord John Russell that

> it is a perfect disgrace to our country, and particularly to our Admiralty, that we can do no more than hobble after the French, turning up our noses proudly at their experiments and improvements, and, when they are established as sound, getting horribly frightened, and trying by wasting money to catch up lost time, and all the while running serious risk of our security.

The Prince warned the Duke of Somerset that numerical equality with the French would still be "real inferiority," since Russia, a possible ally of France, had begun to build ironclads, and Great Britain would need some armored ships for detached service. If England, as the Prince believed, required ironclads to defend Malta, Gibraltar, and other foreign ports as well, the number she ought to possess was "very great indeed." [2]

As the rumors of the great French building program of 1860 multiplied, the advocates of ironclads redoubled their efforts to prove that the day of wooden line-of-battle ships was at an end. In February, 1861, they hailed with delight the "conversion" of their most redoubtable opponent, General Sir Howard Douglas, who had hitherto thrown the weight of his immense prestige against the construction of ironclads.[3] In a letter of February 26, read before the In-

---

faults (two editions, London, 1861), 1st ed., p. 54. Cf. "Iron-Clad Ships of War," in *Blackwood's Edinburgh Magazine*, November–December, 1860.

Captain Pigeard, the French naval attaché in London, sent to the Minister of Marine on October 10, 1860, an interesting analysis of British opinion as to ironclads and the new ordnance, which emphasizes the impetus given by the successful trials of the *Gloire*. A.M., 6 DD¹ 23, dossier 507.

[1] At p. 290 of the American edition.
[2] Martin, *Prince Consort*, v, pp. 256–257, December 8, 10, 1860. Cf. Dasent, *Delane*, ii, pp. 14–17.
[3] General Sir Howard Douglas, *On Naval Warfare with Steam* (London, 1858); *A Treatise on Naval Gunnery* (4th ed., London, 1855; 5th ed., London, 1860); *A Postscript to the Section on Iron Defences*, contained in the 5th Edition of 'Naval Gunnery' (London, 1860). Cf. S. W. Fullom, *Life of General Sir Howard Douglas* (London, 1863), ch. xxxix. The most detailed answer to Douglas's earlier writings on the subject of ironclads was John Scott Russell's *The Fleet of the Future: Iron*

stitution of Naval Architects two days later, the aged artillerist maintained his objections to unarmored iron ships and to ironclads built wholly of iron. Though contending that iron-cased ships were not absolutely invulnerable, he conceded at last that "so long as our neighbours — the French — persist in building iron-cased ships, we *must* do so likewise, and that in a manner to keep well ahead of anything the French or any other power may do for aggressive purposes." British fleets in future, he "confidently" declared, must be built like the French, with wooden bottoms and iron-cased sides.[1]

The appointment of Rear Admiral Robert Spencer Robinson as Controller of the Navy, on February 7, 1861, promised greater activity in the introduction of ironclads. On the day before he assumed his new duties, Robinson had submitted to the Dockyard Commission a memorandum deploring the delays in introducing armored vesesls. He combatted the doctrine

> that it was not for England . . . to take the lead in adopting inventions, which would go far to render the expenditure already incurred in a great measure useless. . . . Superiority on the sea is vital to our national existence, and five years ago an invention for resisting to an immense extent the destroying power of projectiles, was applied to ships with a large measure of success. It surely needs no argument to prove that the country most interested in and most affected by the invention was that which should have taken the lead in ascertaining its merits and perfecting its application.

He asserted that if the same British experiments which began in 1858 had been commenced two years earlier,

> we might have been in 1858 in the exact position with regard to iron-plated ships which we now occupy in 1861, possibly with fewer wooden ships, but unquestionably with a far more formidable naval force and with a more judicious expenditure of some of those vast amounts of money which we have been considering.[2]

---

or Wood? (London, 1861), in which he proposed the construction of a fleet of ironclads of ten different classes. Cf. Russell's paper, "On the Professional Problem Presented to Naval Architects in the Construction of Iron-cased Vessels of War," in *Transactions of the Institution of Naval Architects*, ii (1861), pp. 17–42, February 28, 1861.
1 *Ibid.*, pp. 2, 6.
2 *Parliamentary Papers*, 1861, xxvi, no. 2790, pp. 600–601.

On February 8 the First Sea Lord, Vice Admiral Sir Richard Dundas, recommended the substitution of iron-cased ships for the new fortifications authorized at Spithead. He proposed the conversion of sailing or steam ships of the line into coast-defence ironclads carrying 30 heavy guns, and capable of steaming seven or eight knots. Lord Herbert referred the proposal to the Commissioners for the Defences of the United Kingdom, who adhered to their program for mixed defences, consisting of iron-cased ships and iron-cased forts.[1]

In response to demands for an increase in the British ironclad program Lord Clarence Paget promised the House of Commons on February 28 that if the Admiralty "found much more progress made over the water or among any other nation in building these ships," they would propose to match them.[2] As a matter of fact alarming news had already reached the Board, for on February 9 the Foreign Office had transmitted a report from Captain Hore, the naval attaché at Paris, stating that the Emperor had ordered ten seagoing ironclads of the largest class laid down that year, in addition to the six already launched or nearly completed, and that a special credit of 100,000,000 francs had been opened for their completion.[3]

[1] *Ibid.*, 1861, xxxvi, no. 219, pp. 2–3. General Burgoyne remarked of iron-cased vessels that "although they would clearly require much more battering than a timber ship, which would give them an enormous advantage over the latter in action, it is a very bold expression to call these sides (as they have hitherto been denominated) invulnerable." *Ibid.*, p. 15.

The forts designed for erection on the shoals at Spithead were each to be "constructed for 120 guns, in four tiers; of iron 10 inches in thickness from low-water mark, unless it is found expedient to carry the foundations of solid granite up to high-water mark ... They will thus be individually in every respect invulnerable to any species of projectile, and impregnable by any force of ships that can be brought against them, or by any conceivable mode of assault. Their vertical walls, 60 feet in height, will render them inaccessible by boarding ..." *Ibid.*, pp. 6–7. For the controversy as to the relative merits of ironclad ships and forts, see also Captain Cowper Phipps Coles, *Our National Defences* (London, 1861), and *Spithead Forts, Reply to the Royal Commissioners' Second Report on the National Defences* (London, 1861); and George Parker Bidder, *The National Defences* (London, 1861).

[2] Hansard, 3rd series, clxi, col. 1155.

[3] Recent French orders for two additional floating batteries were also reported, according to the summary of this Foreign Office letter in the minute of the naval members of the Board of Admiralty, February [?] 13, 1861, next cited.

This challenge led the naval members of the Board of Admiralty to record in a special minute their unanimous opinion on the necessity of immediate counter measures. "Otherwise the spring of 1862 might see the French in possession of such a fleet of iron-cased ships as would give them the command of the Channel." They proposed to ask for authority to contract for "not less than ten sea going iron-cased ships and also to commence at once to adapt ten or more of the steam line-of-battle ships for casing with iron plates."[1]

The Queen heartily favored the proposed increase in ironclads, objecting only that it was not large enough to give a sufficient preponderance over the French. Gladstone, however, strongly protested against demanding a fresh outlay of three million pounds within three weeks of the submission of the annual estimates, and deplored especially the suggestion that the sum be raised by a loan. Although he doubted whether the British yet had sufficient "knowledge and experience, with respect to several most important questions of construction and use" of ironclads "to justify immediate decision on the immense orders now proposed," he favored an increase in the appropriation for armored vessels if it might be offset by reductions in expenditure for wooden ships. As a solution, he suggested transferring some of the appropriations for wooden ships to the construction of wooden-hulled ironclads like the French. Palmerston retorted that

as to transferring to Iron Ships the Sums taken in the Estimates for Wooden ones, . . . that would go a very little Way and would deprive us of some Things which are still essential.[2]

Palmerston was soon to make clear his views on wooden ships on the floor of the House of Commons. There the provision of the extraordinary sum of £949,371 for timber in the Navy Estimates for 1861–62 aroused fierce opposition.

---

[1] Although the copy of this minute in Adm. 1/5765 is dated "13.1.61." it cites the Foreign Office letter of February 9. Perhaps February 13 was the correct date of this minute.

[2] *Letters of Queen Victoria*, iii, p. 554; Guedalla, *Gladstone and Palmerston*, pp. 157–160.

Lord Clarence Paget pointed out that the stock of timber had been greatly depleted by the recent activity in wooden ship building.

It is not that we are going to expend this timber, but what we want is to lay in a stock of it ... for duty on distant stations, where there are no means of getting docks, we must at present maintain our wooden ships. If an iron ship were for a couple of months in an equatorial latitude, her bottom would become like a lawyer's wig.[1]

Lord Palmerston declared that the House

must not suppose that iron ships will wholly supersede those of wood. We may depend upon it that, in case of war, wooden line-of-battle ships will play their part, and that an important part, especially on distant stations. You cannot send the iron ships to keep the sea for any length of time where they cannot clean their bottoms.

Even ironclads, he observed, required much wood for their decks and for the backing behind their armor.[2]

W. S. Lindsay, who led the unsuccessful attack on the timber estimates, moved an amendment on April 11 that any further expenditure on the construction of wooden line-of-battle ships or on their conversion from sail to steam should be deferred. Although his motion met with general approval, he withdrew it when Paget stated that the Admiralty had no intention at present of proceeding with the construction or completion of line-of-battle ships, although they wished to finish the four then undergoing conversion from sail to steam, and to get them out of the docks as soon as possible.[3]

In this debate Sir Morton Peto had suggested that any ministry who should send wooden ships of the line to sea to oppose invulnerable iron ships would deserve impeachment.

[1] Hansard, 3rd series, clxi, cols. 1741, 1745, March 11, 1861.
[2] *Ibid.*, clxi, col. 1790; clxiii, col. 38, March 11, May 23, 1861.
    The recent "Report from the Select Committee on the Navy (Gun and Mortar Boats)," revealing the defects in the small vessels built of unseasoned timber during the Crimean War, gave point to the demands for an increased stock. *Parliamentary Papers*, 1860, viii, no. 545.
[3] Hansard, 3rd series, clxii, cols. 417-479, clxiii, cols. 30-51.
    The proposal to build one of the new ironclads in a government yard instead of by contract was likewise assailed unsuccessfully. *Ibid.*, clxii, col. 417; clxiii, cols. 59-65. Cf. the "Report of the Commissioners appointed to inquire into the Control and Management of Her Majesty's Naval Yards," *Parliamentary Papers*, 1861, xxvi, no. 2790.

No one who studies the Admiralty papers for 1861 and notes the desperate efforts to increase the British ironclad program is likely to believe that the Board relied on wooden ships to oppose the French armored vessels. No longer did they disregard such warnings as those of Captain H. J. W. Jervis, that under such conditions "wooden line-of-battle ships would be nothing better than mere slaughterhouses." Both their actions and their memoranda clearly show that by the spring of 1861 they were convinced that, except on distant stations where ironclads were not yet threatening to put in an appearance, the day of the wooden capital ship had passed.[1]

Although the naval members of the Board of Admiralty had demanded that the British program of seagoing ironclads be increased immediately from seven ships to at least twenty-seven, Gladstone's opposition to the heavy expenditure involved held the actual increase in the program down to nine new armored ships, instead of twenty. On May 8 the Controller submitted that, as the further building of wooden line-of-battle ships had been suspended, the frames of some of them should be made ready to receive 4½-inch iron plates. He proposed to begin with the *Royal Oak* at Chatham, which he estimated could be converted at a cost of £211,850 into an armored frigate of 50 guns and 1000 horse power, which would be a sufficiently good sea boat to go to the Mediterranean if required, with a maximum speed of at least 12.4 knots. She was to be plated throughout with 4½-inch iron, "except for a small portion of the Counter, and at the round of the Bows," where he believed thinner plates "would be perfectly shell-proof, and in many instances deflect the greater part of the Shot." He proposed to give the ship an elliptical stern, to facilitate carrying the armor belt around the stern at the height of the main deck. Admiral Robinson deemed it needless to remind the Board "that every maritime power in Europe is advancing in this direction, and that

---

[1] Hansard, 3rd series, clxii, cols. 431, 460. For a different view see Albion, *Forests and Sea Power*, pp. 403–410.

unprotected wooden Ships cannot contend with success against their iron coated rivals." [1]

Shortly after approving this project for the *Royal Oak* the Admiralty received news that, of the ten French ironclad frigates of the 1860 program, eight had already been begun and a ninth was to be laid down as soon as the necessary slip was vacant. France thus had fifteen seagoing ironclads built, building, or immediately to be laid down, and a sixteenth authorized, while only seven such British vessels were under construction. To obtain equality "in this decisive arm of modern warfare," the Admiralty, on May 23, urged on the Cabinet the necessity for immediate construction of more iron-plated vessels of the first class, with such improvements as experience had suggested. The Board were "convinced that none but the most vigorous and energetic measures will prevent the command of the Channel at an early date falling into the hands of the French Emperor." [2]

Admiral Robinson, the Controller, submitted that

without adverting in a spirit of jealousy to the progress which every Naval Power in Europe is making in the direction of protecting their military Navy by Iron Plating, it is evident that a complete revolution has taken place in the requirements of Naval Architecture, and that an ordinary Ship of War unprotected by Iron Plates, is certain to be destroyed in action even by any wooden Ship of the same force as herself.

Believing that the need for abandoning construction of wooden ships was "manifestly urgent," he proposed that the frames of four more wooden line-of-battle ships besides the *Royal Oak* should be cased with iron, even though these wooden-hulled ironclads would be "in every way inferior" to iron-built ships like the *Achilles*.[3]

Admiral Dundas, the First Sea Lord, pointed out that France would have six ironclads afloat in the summer of 1862

---

1 Adm. 1/5774; Guedalla, *Gladstone and Palmerston*, pp. 161 ff.
2 Adm. 1/5765; Adm. 12/701: 59–1.
3 Adm. 1/5765, May 22, 1861. Robinson objected to completing the four wooden frigates then undergoing conversion from sail to steam, on the ground that in action with any European navy they would certainly be destroyed, and that their size would make them too costly for use "where modern science had not yet penetrated."

"of classes with which her Government appear to be content," while Great Britain would have ready to oppose them not more than four ships "of classes with which we are perhaps less well contented, and of which two only can be considered as well adapted for seagoing purposes. . . ." Although it would be impossible to reach a wholly satisfactory solution of the ironclad problem without further information and experience, no further delay could be risked. Prompt action might avert a rupture to which France might be tempted if she enjoyed clear superiority at sea. With the concurrence of the other Sea Lords he proposed that six more iron-hulled ironclads be built at once by contract, that the frames of two more ships of the line be cased with iron, and that two teak ships of the *Ganges* class be razeed and plated with iron.[1]

The Duke of Somerset lamented the necessity of ordering more ironclads before the Admiralty had more information as to the best design and best type of armor that could be adopted. Although the cheapest way of obtaining rapidly some additional ironclads would be to cut down some teak-built ships and fit them with engines and armor, he believed that they would not be seagoing ships and would thus prove inferior to the French armored frigates. If the frames of partially completed line-of-battle ships like the *Royal Oak* were put up, given additional length, and plated with iron, those ships would be equal to the French wooden ironclads, but would have many of the same defects and could not be expected to last. Although they would be inferior to the *Warrior*, and justly open to criticism as indicating a "retrograde movement," some of them could be built without exceeding the estimates for 1861–1862. Until a new style of armor could be tested,[2] Somerset objected to applying to Parliament for a supplementary vote for five or six more iron-hulled ironclads. A demand for an immense outlay on ships of this sort before the *Warrior* had been tried at sea might be deemed preposterous. If the Board, moreover, should adopt a new type of armor in preference to that of the *Warrior* before that

[1] Adm. 1/5765. [2] See below, pp. 201–206.

ship had her trials, Parliament might "fairly refuse to entrust the board with means of making new experiments at such a cost."

The political objections to such a demand, moreover, would be equally strong. Parliament would ascribe it "to some new distrust, at a moment when a good understanding with France may most usefully tend to the removal of difficulties in our relations with the United States."[1]

Within the next four days, however, the Admiralty concluded that further ironclads must be ordered without waiting for tests of new types of armor. On May 27 Somerset ordered the frames of four more line-of-battle ships besides the *Royal Oak* — the *Caledonia, Ocean, Prince Consort* and *Royal Alfred* — prepared for plating with iron in government yards. And on May 30 he directed that six iron-hulled ironclads should be put up in frame only, pending experiments with new methods of applying the armor. These vessels, whose plans were later radically altered, were originally intended to be 14-knot "belt-and-battery" ships of the *Achilles* class, with a water-line belt six feet wide extending around the ship, and with forty guns behind armor on the main deck and ten on the upper deck.[2]

The news that the French had actually commenced building the ironclads of their great 1860 program caused an outburst of criticism in Parliament. Sir John Pakington declared that Great Britain was "rapidly becoming the second maritime power of Europe." Lord Clarence Paget sought to reassure the House by announcing the plan for five new wooden-hulled ironclads. Distinguishing these from razeed vessels, he explained that they were "not to be cut down, because they are not yet built up." Taking the timbers prepared for five new 90-gun ships, the frames of only two of which had been laid down, they would construct wooden hulls, lengthened about twenty feet, and case them from stem to stern like the *Gloire*. With regard to cutting down completed ships

---

[1] Adm. 1/5765, May 23, 1861.
[2] Adm. 1/5765, May 27; Adm. 1/5744, May 31; Adm. 12/701: 59–1; Adm. 12/705: 91–2.

of the line, "a measure which probably ere long will have to be undertaken with a view to casing them with iron," he pointed out that their displacement was in general too small to permit them to carry a heavy armament, or serve for more than coast defence. In the House of Lords Somerset explained the reluctance of the Admiralty to build more ironclads until the forthcoming trials of the *Warrior* and the experiments of the new committee on iron plates [1] should throw fresh light on the best ship design and the best armor to meet the new rifled projectiles. Believing that "next year we ought to have better ships than three-deckers cut down would give us," he was "unwilling to advance too fast, because . . . we can advance much more efficiently by waiting a little longer." [2]

Nevertheless French competition forced the pace. Palmerston was the more alarmed at the lead the French had obtained because of his conviction that the design of the first British seagoing ironclads was "sadly wrong in Principle," since a considerable part of their sides, towards the extremities, consisted of nothing more than a thin skin of ¾-inch iron. Despite their athwartship armored bulkheads and the water-tight subdivision of their unprotected ends, he believed that the *Gloire* would promptly smash their bow and stern to pieces and render them "a Mere Box floating on the Water, . . . Waterlogged and . . . comparatively unmanageable." He had therefore "repeatedly and strongly remonstrated with the Duke of Somerset against this Paste Board Construction of our so called Iron Ships of War," and had carried his point that the newer British ironclads should be armored from stem to stern.[3]

[1] See below, pp. 201–206.
[2] Hansard, 3rd series, clxiii, cols. 49, 412–427, 524–539, 685–686, 903–915. As for wooden ships, Somerset pointed out that no three-decker had been ordered to be built since January, 1855. Two of them were launched in 1859, but these had been finished for a long time. "The last two-decker ordered was by the late Government in 1859. The present board have ordered none . . . we have converted sailing ships of the line into steam-ships, and we have ordered small vessels." *Ibid.*, cols. 910–911. Cf. his memorandum of June 7 and his letter to Russell of June 12, 1861. G. D. 22: 24.
[3] Guedalla, *Gladstone and Palmerston*, pp. 181–187, Palmerston to Gladstone, July 21, 1861. After thoroughly inspecting the *Warrior* Palmerston thought better

After Gladstone had successfully opposed Palmerston's proposal to issue a million pounds of terminable annuities to pay for some of the proposed ironclads, Lord Clarence Paget on July 26 presented to the House of Commons a supplementary estimate for £250,000, part for the plating and engines of the five wooden ironclads, and part for a first instalment of the new armored iron ships. As for the latter, he proposed that the Admiralty be empowered to contract for not more than six such ships, leaving the Board free "either to make a greater progress with a smaller number, or to proceed very slowly with the whole six." During the current financial year, ending March 31, 1862, the Admiralty proposed to push these ships no faster than would permit their profiting by the trials of the *Warrior* and by the experiments at Shoeburyness. The latter, it was thought, might indicate the desirability of thicker plates with thinner backing, or even of dispensing with the wooden backing altogether. Admitting that the total future cost of the ironclad program, beyond the current year's estimates, would reach £2,455,251 exclusive of the labor on the *Achilles*, Paget pointed out that

> it is no use denying that the whole world is commencing the construction of these ships. Every maritime nation has completely given up the thought of building wooden line-of-battle ships.

Although Lindsay questioned at first the accuracy of the reports of French activity, and, with Disraeli's support, suggested an agreement with France to limit naval armaments,[1] the House voted the supplementary estimates without a division.[2]

After calling for tenders for six new iron-built ironclads, the Admiralty decided to push more rapidly ahead with a

---

of her. "She is better protected fore and aft than I had imagined but still her armor plating ought to have been carried along her whole length." He opposed sending her to Mexico lest her merits and defects become at once apparent to the French. P.R.O., G.D., 22: 21, Palmerston to Russell, October 6, 1861.

[1] See below, p. 322.
[2] Guedalla, *Gladstone and Palmerston*, pp. 172–174, 180; *Parliamentary Papers*, 1861, xxxviii, no. 450; Hansard, 3rd series, clxiv, cols. 1629–1686. Cf. Cobden, *The Three Panics*, pp. 128–139.

H. M. S. *MINOTAUR*

Imperial War Museum photograph. Copyright reserved.

smaller number, and on August 31 ordered three from the Thames Iron Shipbuilding Company, John Laird and Sons, and Mare and Company. The contracts left the Admiralty at liberty to alter the arrangement of the plating within three months without additional charge. Although these vessels, soon named the *Minotaur, Agincourt,* and *Northumberland,*[1] were first described as "belt-and-battery" ships of the *Achilles* class, they were twenty feet longer, and had a 5½-inch armor belt, tapering to 4½ at the bow and stern, extending the whole length of their sides from five feet below the water line to the level of the upper deck. These powerful vessels of 6621 tons burden and 1350 horse power were originally designed to mount forty 100-pounder Armstrong guns on the main deck and ten on pivots on the upper deck.[2] As Admiral G. A. Ballard has pointed out, they were "the longest and largest single screw fighting ships ever built, as well as the longest and largest to carry their heaviest guns mounted between decks. They were also the only fighting ships ever rigged with five masts."[3]

On November 11, 1861, E. J. Reed, who was soon to be retained by the Admiralty and shortly afterwards made Chief Constructor, submitted a project for a rigged armored screw corvette of what was later known as the "central battery" type, of 2250 tons and 600 horse power. He proposed to build an iron ship of stout scantling, to carry four masses of armor: (1) a belt of 6-inch armor extending entirely around the ship from three or four feet below, to one or two feet above the load water line; (2) a deck covered with ¾-inch iron at the height of the upper edge of the water-line armor

---

[1] For a short time prior to October 18, 1861, the two first were named *Elephant* and *Captain.* Adm. 12/701: 59–1; Adm. 12/705: 91–2.
[2] Adm. 1/5774, May 31, August 1, 5, 31, 1861.
 These three vessels, which were 400 feet long, 59 feet 3½ inches beam, and of over 10,000 tons displacement, were launched in 1863, 1865, and 1866, and completed for sea in 1867 and 1868. *Parliamentary Papers,* 1862, xxxiv, no. 432; 1866, xlvi, nos. 76, 526; 1874, xxxviii, no. 99. Cf. E. J. Reed, "The Iron-Cased Ships of the British Navy," *Report* of the British Association for the Advancement of Science (1861), xxxi, part ii, pp. 232–239.
[3] See his admirable description of these ships in *The Mariner's Mirror,* October, 1929, pp. 291–407, and January, 1930, pp. 48–57.

belt; (3) an armored central battery on the upper deck containing six 68-pounder pivot guns; (4) a "large trunk," constructed of 6-inch armor rising from the armored deck below to the center of the battery, to protect the passage of the gunners and of the ammunition. The vulnerability of part of the upper works of the vessel was, Reed believed, more than offset by the "immense advantage" gained by the saving of weight, which could permit the attainment of great speed and handiness "without resorting to extravagant dimensions."[1]

Although this project, which seemed to meet the Admiralty's desire for a smaller class of ironclad than any yet constructed, was favorably reported upon on January 20, it was not definitely approved till April. Before the battle of Hampton Roads, however, the Admiralty had added a sixteenth ironclad to its program, having decided on January 14 to construct a mastless vessel of 2529 tons mounting twelve breech-loading rifled guns in six turrets on Coles's system.[2]

In the eighteen months between the trials of the *Gloire* and the battle of Hampton Roads the British Admiralty had not reached the conclusion that wooden warships were useless for every purpose. They still maintained that on distant stations, where iron bottoms would foul and no docks existed, wooden ships would continue to serve. As far as home waters were concerned, however, they recognized at last that France, taking the lead in ironclad construction, had revolutionized naval architecture. In 1861 the British "suspended the building of large wooden ships except for the purpose of casing them with iron,"[3] and laid down eleven new seagoing ironclads, a larger number, indeed, than they began in the two years following the combat of the *Monitor* and the *Merrimack*.

[1] Adm. 1/5774, November 11, 25, 1861; Adm. 1/5804, April 14, 16, 1862; Adm. 12/720: 91–2. Reed acknowledged the assistance of Nathaniel Barnaby, of the Controller's department, in constructing the design, and stated that a shipbuilder of Deptford named Lungley had a patent for the plan in its general form, "as it sprang up originally in connection with a Patent of his for unsinkable iron ships," the specification of which Reed had drawn. See British Patent Office, 1861, no. 206.   [2] See below, ch. ix.
[3] Reply to a request of the Turkish government for information concerning ironclads, Adm. 12/705: 91–1, October 4, 1861.

CHAPTER IX

THE ORIGINS OF THE TURRET SHIP

THE year 1861 is memorable in British naval history not merely for the passing of the wooden capital ship and for the jump in the Admiralty's ironclad program from four to fifteen seagoing ships, but also for the first successful experiments with a revolving turret for an armored battleship. Before the *Monitor* faced the *Merrimack* in Hampton Roads a British naval officer had devised and patented a practicable system of installing guns in revolving turrets, had seen his project triumphantly vindicated by severe tests under the fire of heavy ordnance, and had convinced the Admiralty of the wisdom of ordering an experimental multiple-turret ironclad.

The idea of revolving gun platforms was indeed an old one. Ericsson often ridiculed the popular belief as to their novelty, asserting that "this obvious device" of installing guns on a revolving platform, open or covered, "dates back to the first introduction of artillery." An instructor had taught him about 1820 that "under certain conditions a position assailable from all sides should be defended by placing the guns on a turntable."[1] He stated in 1884 that "a house or turret, turning on a pivot for protecting apparatus intended to throw warlike projectiles" was a device known to the ancient Greeks, and that he could not recall any period of his life at which he did not know of its existence.[2]

The revolving platforms of the "Maximilian towers" at Lintz were well known to artillerists.[3] As early as 1805 Sir

---

[1] John Ericsson, "The Building of the 'Monitor,'" in *Battles and Leaders of the Civil War* (New York, 1888–1889, 4 vols.), i, pp. 730–744, at p. 738.
[2] Church, *Ericsson*, ii, p. 114.
[3] General Sir Howard Douglas, *Observations on Modern Systems of Fortification* (London, 1859), pp. 143–145. Cf. his *Postscript to the Section on Iron Defences* (London, 1860), p. 26, note.

Howard Douglas had proposed a method of traversing guns in any direction, in a circular battery.[1] The *Nautical Chronicle* in that same year described a "turning impregnable battery, impervious to shot or bombs," invented by a Scotsman named Gillespie, which it was believed would be equally serviceable in floating batteries. Two years later the *Transactions* of the Society for the Promotion of Useful Arts in the State of New York contained an illustration of a circular revolving floating battery designed by one Abraham Bloodgood, who argued that shot would glance from this circular tower, and that its guns "would be more easily worked than is common, as they would not require any lateral movement." As the battery revolved, each of its guns would be brought to bear "successively, as fast as they could be loaded, on objects in any direction."[2] Such all-around fire was sought by Colonel John Stevens in his design of a saucer-shaped ironclad during the War of 1812;[3] and by a French architect named Baltard, who published a brochure in 1831 advocating the installation of "batteries tournantes" on the bow and stern of gunboats, as well as in land defences.[4]

Somewhat similar to Bloodgood's proposal was the project of Theodore R. Timby, a native of New York State, who filed at the United States Patent Office on January 18, 1843, a caveat for a "'Metallic Revolving Fort' to be used on land or water, and to be revolved by propelling engines located within the same and acting on suitable mechanism." His proposed tower, which was to contain several floors with tiers of guns arranged radially, was designed to turn on friction rollers. Timby later asserted that he had exhibited his plans to Napoleon III in 1856 and had "received some encouragement, but without practical results." On September 30, 1862, he obtained a patent for "improvement in revolving battery tower . . . for defensive and offensive warfare,

---

[1] See his *Treatise on Naval Gunnery* (5th ed., London, 1860), p. 191, note.
[2] John Ericsson in *Battles and Leaders of the Civil War*, i, p. 739.
[3] See above, p. 9.
[4] Baltard, *Essai sur la Fortification* (Paris, 1831), pp. 44–45, 58–61, and plates 19, 21 and 27.

whether placed on land or water." After the battle of Hampton Roads Timby received from Ericsson's partners a handsome royalty on each of the monitors they constructed. He had not had the slightest influence, however, either on the adoption by the United States and Great Britain of turreted warships, or, as far as available evidence goes, on the design or construction of the original *Monitor*. His claim to the invention of her revolving turret deserves slight consideration.[1]

Angered by statements made in Parliament challenging his claim to priority in the invention of the turret, Ericsson sent to Secretary Welles on June 28, 1862, copies of plans and specifications of "an Impregnable Battery and Revolving Cupola, constructed by me and presented to his Majesty Emperor Napoleon III in the year 1854." He enclosed an extract from a communication which he said he had forwarded from New York City to the Emperor on September 26, 1854; and which, he declared, had been "at once acknowledged by his Majesty." The extract described an iron vessel with a triangular midship section and with a deck, plated with 3-inch sheet iron, which "curved both longitudinally and transversely with a spring of 5 feet," and projected eight feet over the rudder and screw propeller. "Reflecting telescopes, capable of being protruded or withdrawn at pleasure," would afford "a distant view of surrounding objects."

---

[1] For statements of the case for Timby, see A. H. Guernsey, "The Revolving Tower and Its Inventor," *Harper's Magazine*, January, 1863, and Francis B. Wheeler, *John F. Winslow, LL.D., and the Monitor* (Poughkeepsie, N. Y., 1893), pp. 54–66, 241–248. Professor William Hovgaard dismisses the claims of Timby's supporters in his article "Who invented the Monitor?" in the *Army and Navy Journal*, November 27, 1909, xlvii, p. 357.

Ericsson wrote to R. B. Forbes, November 29, 1884, that: "Timby having stated in his patent that the invention was intended 'for land or water' (meaning, of course, that like many other forts it might be built in the water), claimed, as soon as the *Monitor* had proved a success, that I had infringed. My generous partners in the *Monitor* enterprise, desirous of securing an interest in the grand revolving turret, which they supposed would be employed to protect *every* harbor in the country, at once took Timby by the hand, and paid him a sum of money, partly taken out of my pocket. Timby got his original patent reissued in such form that my disinterested partners imagined that they held my patent. Civil engineers of the highest standing at once prepared drawings of my friend's harbor defence turrets; but practical Lincoln, well advised by my friend Fox, could not see that the safety of the country demanded the immediate erection of Timby's turrets." Church, *Ericsson*, ii, p. 115.

Amidships rose a "semi-globular turret of plate-iron, 6 inches thick, revolving on a column and pivot by means of steam power and appropriate gear work." In a calm or light winds an entire fleet of sailing ships would find themselves at the mercy of a single craft of this sort, which would be immune from boarding, "since the turret guns, which turn like the spokes of a wheel, may keep off and destroy any number of boats by firing slugs and combustibles. . . ." [1]

Ericsson destroyed most of his papers of a date prior to 1862. In his *Contributions to the Centennial Exhibition*, published in 1876, he said of the plan of 1854 that

> the Emperor promptly acknowledged the receipt of these documents through Gen. Favé [his aide-de-camp], whose letter commences with the following flattering sentence:
> "L'Empereur a examiné lui-même avec le plus grand soin le nouveau système d'attaque navale que vous lui avez communiqué.
> "S. M. me charge d'avoir l'honneur de vous informer qu'elle a trouvé vos idées très-ingénieuses et digne du nome célèbre de leur auteur." [2]

When inventors sent projects to Napoleon III the usual practice was for one of his aides to transmit the papers to the Ministry concerned, which then reported its opinion. A prolonged search has failed to reveal any reference to this proposal of Ericsson's in the archives of the French Ministry of Marine. It certainly had no influence on the French iron-

---

[1] N.D., *Miscellaneous Letters*, June, 1862, iii. An engraving of the proposed vessel accompanies the letter to Welles. This is similar to plate 42 in Ericsson's *Contributions to the Centennial Exhibition*. In vol. i of the *Ericsson Mss.* are two documents headed "Monitor of 1854. List to whom Engravings sent." Among the names on the list are those of Lord Clarence Paget, Lord Palmerston, Captain Cowper P. Coles, and the Duke of Somerset. Church published in facsimile two pencil drawings, covered with calculations, purporting to be the originals of 1854. *Ericsson*, i, pp. 238–239. The extract of the letter to Napoleon III which Ericsson forwarded to Welles in 1862 is printed in the *Eclectic Magazine* for August, 1862, pp. 568–569; in the *Report of the Secretary of the Navy in relation to Armored Vessels* (Washington, 1864), p. 13; and in Ericsson's *Contributions to the Centennial Exhibition*, p. 410.

[2] *Op. cit.*, p. 410. Church gives a translation agreeing with this text and continuing as follows: "but the Emperor thinks that the result to be obtained would not be proportionate to the expenses or to the small number of guns which could be brought into use. Although not disposed to make use of your inventions the Emperor appreciates all their merit, and directs me to thank you for this interesting communication." Church, *Ericsson*, i, p. 241.

THE ORIGINS OF THE TURRET SHIP 185

clads of 1854, which were designed and ordered prior to September 26.[1]

Still another inventor, Delaporte père, a blind inmate of the hospital of the Quinze-Vingts at Paris, proposed in 1855 a gunboat equipped with several circular platforms carrying guns. Each platform, covered with a hemisphere of iron, was to revolve on a railway turntable. The idea, though crude and undeveloped, resembles Coles's patent of 1859.[2]

During the Crimean War the obvious advantages of lightdraft vessels for approaching the Russian coast defences led to several proposals to mount guns on rafts more or less protected from shot. By far the most interesting of these was the work of a nephew of Admiral Lyons, Commander Cowper Phipps Coles, who mounted a 32-pounder gun on a raft, christened the "Lady Nancy," to attack Taganrog in the Sea of Azov in June, 1855.[3] Not long after this successful

---

[1] See above, pp. 70–74. Discussing in 1873 the turrets of Coles and Ericsson, Dislère abandoned the problem of priority, in view of the vagueness of the information concerning Ericsson's first attempts. He pointed out that the *prames* of the Boulogne flotilla of Napoleon I had their guns installed in the middle of the deck on a revolving platform carrying a bulwark [bastingage] pierced by a narrow aperture through which protruded the muzzle of the gun. "Si ce n'est pas là le principe, l'idée mère de la tourelle, c'est tout au moins celle de la demi-tourelle." *Marine cuirassée*, p. 49. The drawings of the *prame* "La Ville de Mayence," however, which Edouard Desbrière published in his *Projets et Tentatives de Débarquement aux îles Britanniques*, iii, facing p. 90, show five ports on a side and two bow ports, for the twelve guns of that vessel.

[2] A.M., BB⁸ 1137, December 12, 1855.

[3] While commending the "Lady Nancy" raft, Sir Baldwin Walker observed that "It is however but fair to Commander Boyd of the 'Royal George' to state that he constructed a raft on the same principle last year in the Baltic which was inspected by Admiral Sir Charles Napier, and a model of it was forwarded to this office, and afterwards returned to Commander Boyd." Submission Letter Book no. 17, July 14, 1855.

Somewhat similar rafts were proposed in France by Rear Admiral Pénaud, Colonel Hier, and a sea captain named Geoffroy. A.M., BB⁸ 1136, April 17, 1855; 1 DD¹ 219, Hamelin to Pénaud, May 1, 1855; BB⁸ 1136, January 23, 1855; 1 DD¹ 214, Ducos to Geoffroy, September 27, 1854.

According to some notes and plans in A.M., 6 DD¹ 88, dossier 2388, transmitted by the Directeur du Matériel to Garnier on December 13, 1856, the Russians built fifteen armored rafts prior to May, 1856, on plans devised in 1855 by the Grand Duke Constantine, General Todleben and Major Shestakov of the Russian Navy. These batteries each consisted of eleven flat boats 68 feet long, fastened together by transverse beams planked over to form a deck from which rose a wall first inclined, then vertical, plated with sheet iron. These batteries, each carrying four 80-pounder guns, were to be towed into position for river and harbor defence by gunboats.

experiment, Coles saw the French floating batteries in action at Kinburn, and there "first became impressed with the necessity for iron-cased ships."[1] The fact that the casualties on the French ironclads came from shot entering the ports, suggested the desirability of a different system for mounting the guns. Coles at once designed another raft, composed of empty casks, and provided with a hemispherical iron shield over a 68-pounder gun. The small portion of the raft thus exposed to horizontal fire was to slope at an angle of 40 degrees, and to be faced with 4-inch iron. After a committee of officers appointed by Lyons had reported favorably on the project, November 13, Coles was ordered to England, where he proposed that the Admiralty construct a number of these rafts, one-third of them to be fitted with steam power, for operations against Cronstadt. The Chief Constructor, Isaac Watts, however, reported unfavorably on the project, arguing that the shell-proof cover over the gun would protect only a small portion of the deck, and that the proposal to fight the raft with its deck awash "would be most hazardous and unsafe," owing to lack of stability.[2]

When Captain Coles, some six years later, saw the sketch of the *Monitor* in the New York *Herald* of March 11, 1862, he sent to Lord Clarence Paget the following comparison of his drawing submitted to the Admiralty in 1855 with Ericsson's successful creation:

> It will be seen that my vessel has a double bottom and is capable of being immersed when going into action from 4 ft. 6 to 5 ft. 3, she is sharp at both ends, has a formidable prow, and a projection of iron to protect the rudder and screw, in fact the only difference is that my vessel is smaller, and of less draught of water, the shield is spherical instead of a vertical cylinder, and was not then on a turntable — a port being considered sufficient for training, such a small vessel itself being so readily turned, at the same time being less complicated.[3]

---

[1] Remarks by Coles before the Institution of Naval Architects, February 28, 1861. *Transactions*, ii, p. 45.

[2] Controller of the Navy, Submission Letter Book no. 17, July 14, 1855; *ibid.*, no. 18, October 29, 1855, and January 22, 1856; S. Eardley-Wilmot, *Life of Lord Lyons*, pp. 304–305, 403; Cowper Phipps Coles, "Shot-Proof Gun-Shields as adapted to Iron-Cased Ships," *Journal of the Royal United Service Institution*, June 29, 1860, iv, pp. 280–290.

[3] Adm. 1/5802, March 31, 1862.

Though this raft plan met with no encouragement from the Admiralty, it is memorable as the germ of the revolving turret, for which Coles filed his first patent specification on March 30, 1859.

After the rejection of his raft project in January, 1856, Coles had continued to wrestle with the problem of protecting guns and gun crews. By March, 1859, he had become convinced of the advantages of a revolving turret. He now sent to the Admiralty and to the War Office drawings of his armored shields fitted upon turntables adapted for use in large vessels and in forts.[1] His letters patent of March 30, 1859, described "an apparatus for defending guns and gunners in ships of war, gun boats, and land batteries."

> My Invention consists of a large convex shield covered all over with thick iron, and mounted upon a platform or frame which is capable of revolving after the manner of a turntable, and which also carries the gun upon any suitable carriage. An aperture is formed in the shield to allow the muzzle of the gun to pass through it, and this aperture is somewhat larger vertically than horizontally, in order to admit of the elevation and depression of the gun, the lateral aim being secured by the rotation of the platform.
>
> I do not limit myself to any precise form or mode of construction, but, I prefer to make the shield hemispherical, and to construct it of a wooden frame with timbers in vertical planes, placed close together, the whole being covered with thick iron plates.

According to his specification filed on September 30, the shield or turret was to be "large enough in some cases to cover two or even more than two guns side by side and parallel to each other." It was to be revolved on conical rollers, spherical balls, or otherwise, by means of a hand wheel and gearing, although "sometimes ... I employ any other suitable means for the purpose."[2]

When Coles proposed in the spring of 1859 to apply his "shotproof hemispherical screen" to guns placed on the upper deck of iron-cased ships, the Surveyor raised several objections, and declared that the plan "could not be successfully applied except to a very large ship." He thought it ob-

[1] *Ibid.*
[2] British Patent Office, 1859, no. 798.

vious that the gun, together with its heavy shield, could not be worked as easily and as rapidly as the gun alone, especially in a seaway.

> Further as these guns with their screens are to be ranged at the midship fore and aft line of the deck they could only occupy the intervals of space between the masts and funnel and other necessary middle line fittings of the vessel while the spread of the shrouds for the support of the masts would very considerably restrict the degree of training of several of the guns, either therefore the number of the guns must be small or the ship must have great length. . . .[1]

Despite these objections his project awakened sufficient interest at both the War Office and the Admiralty to induce them to finance the construction of an experimental turret, which was begun in Scott Russell's shipyard in 1859.[2]

The committee of naval officers appointed by the Commissioners on the Defences of the United Kingdom examined a plan prepared by Scott Russell for an ironclad mounting twelve guns in Coles's revolving cupolas, but, although they recognized that it offered several advantages, notably the reduction in the size of the ports and the great protection against being raked, they did not recommend the construction of a vessel of this specific form.

On June 15, 1860, Coles took out a patent for "Improvements in iron-cased ships of war," constructed so as to be "particularly well adapted to receive" his revolving turrets.

> My Invention consists in forming iron-cased ships of war with two sides or a double side at that part of the ship which is protected by the iron casing, the inner side being inclined inwards at a considerable angle, and cased with thick metal, and the outer side being for the purpose of completing the external form of the vessel according to any approved design, and for affording the requisite deck accommodation between it and the upper

---

1 Submission Letter Book no. 20, March 19, April 25, 1859.
2 *Ibid.*, no. 21, October 19, 1859. This submission is inserted at page 529, following a submission of December 31, 1860. See also Admiralty 12/669: 59-1, September 26 and 27, 1859, and Admiralty 12/701: 59-1, January 11 and 21, 1861. Russell asserted that he "constructed Captain Coles's shield, and . . . many of its peculiar arrangements are mine." See his *The Fleet of the Future in 1862* (London, 1862), p. 47. Coles acknowledged the aid and encouragement given him in 1855 by the celebrated engineer Brunel. *Journal of the Royal United Service Institution*, iv, p. 290. Lord Clarence Paget in 1862 gave the credit for first taking up Coles's invention to General Peel of the War Office. Hansard, 3rd series, clxvi, cols. 762–763.

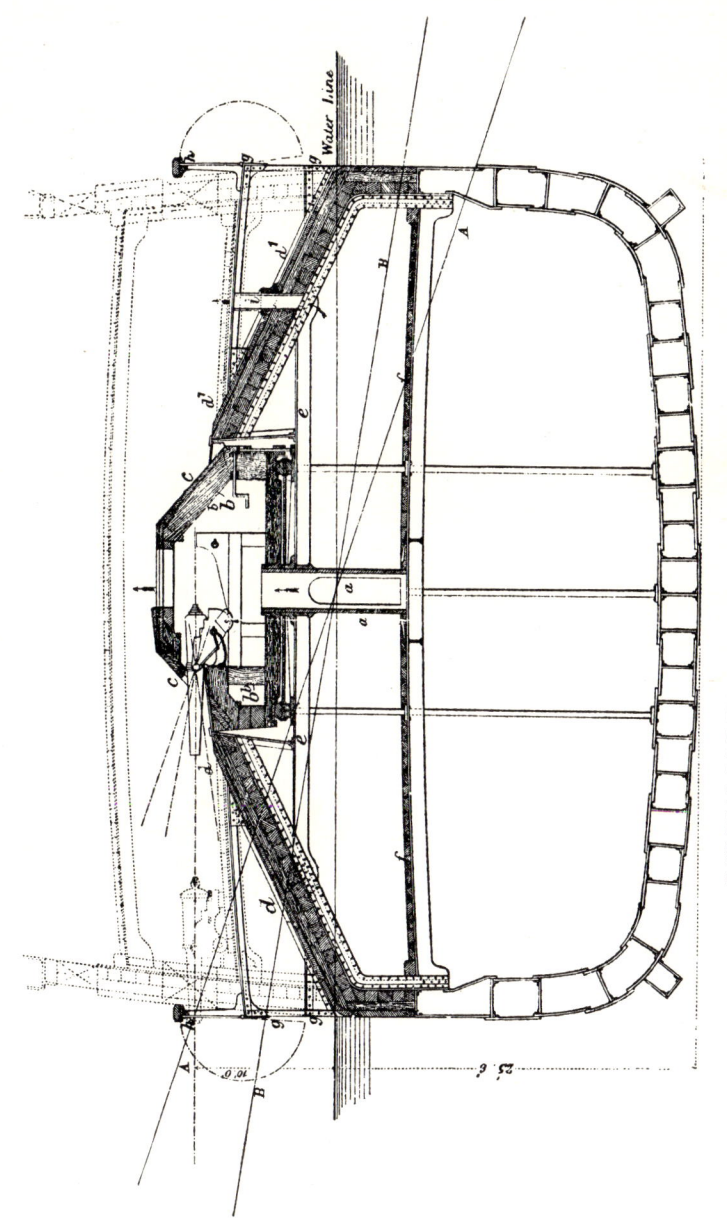

COLES'S SPECIFICATION OF JUNE 15, 1860

portion of the defended side. The outer side is to be of iron and should be constructed as lightly as is consistent with the required strength.[1]

In an address before the Royal United Service Institution, June 29, 1860, Coles explained his system, in which only the upper portion of the turret was exposed to the enemy's fire, as the lower part was sunk into the deck and protected by an armored glacis sloping at an angle of 40 degrees. He advocated the construction of fifteen ironclads able to steam at twelve miles an hour, each carrying eighteen guns in nine "shields."

An enormously strong ship is thus obtained — not weakened, as are ordinary ships, by numerous portholes, but having a continuous side, with the weights placed amidships instead of at the sides.... three of these shield ships would be equal to ten 3-deckers.... In future our fleets must fight in armour; and supremacy afloat must depend henceforth on superior ability to produce the new ships required.[2]

Coles submitted to the Admiralty in September and October, 1860, two projects for turreted ironclads, one similar to the ship he had described to the members of the Royal United Service Institution, the other with a vertical side cased with 4½-inch plates as high as the main deck waterway. The three naval constructors, Watts, Large, and Abethell, reported that, in comparison with other ironclads,

1st. Capt. Coles cannot obtain greater invulnerability without an increase of weight, except as regards the smallness of his ports.

2nd. In a given space fore and aft the total number of guns he can stow is not greater than can be stowed on *each side* of an ordinary ship.

3rd. He cannot, except for a portion of his guns, obtain the great training he speaks of, but he can sweep the deck of boarders.

4th. He obtains greater facilities for taking aim at a moving object.

5th. His plan does not give a steadier platform.

6th. His alleged economy of manual labor at the guns requires to be practically tested.

7th. He does not obtain greater strength of structure.

8th. He does not diminish the required breadth of beam.

... In conclusion ... while ships with the ordinary arrangements for fighting them can, we conceive, be made practically invulnerable, and to a large extent secure from casualty by means of small ports, we do not think

---

[1] British Patent Office, 1860, no. 1462.
[2] "Shot-Proof Gun-Shields as adapted to Iron-Cased Ships," *Journal of the Royal United Service Institution*, iv, pp. 280–290. With nine illustrative figures.

it advisable to recommend the adoption of Capt. Coles' form of ship, which, independently of her peculiar description of armament and mode of protection, labors under every disadvantage in point of efficiency as a seagoing man of war.[1]

While the technical staff of the Controller's department was pouring cold water on Coles's projects, ardent supporters entered the lists in his behalf. *Blackwood's Magazine* for December, 1860, contained an enthusiastic description of his proposed "shield ship," which was hailed as the best ironclad yet projected, and as more than a match for two wooden three-deckers. With the help of diagrams illustrating the revolving turrets and inclined armor the anonymous author expounded the advantages of the turret ship over the *Gloire* and *Warrior*.[2] Far stronger support was soon forthcoming. The plans for a turret ship had been laid before Prince Albert, who gave Coles six interviews and "advice of the greatest benefit . . ., for he had previously turned his attention to the same subject, and . . . was thoroughly conversant with all the mechanical details involved in the execution of my plan."[3] On December 10 the Prince Consort urged Somerset to order the construction of one of Coles's ships "*at once*, with such modifications as may be suggested to him." Prince Albert agreed with the First Lord that "it would not be prudent to restrict ourselves to vessels of this novel construction, but we should give the country the benefit of possessing some such. . . . Should Captain Coles's plan succeed, his ships will be vastly superior to those we are now building. . . ."[4]

At the suggestion of the War Office the Admiralty early in 1861 ordered that the experimental turret, begun in Scott

---

[1] Submission Letter Book no. 21, December 11, 1860.
[2] *Loc. cit.*, pp. 643–649.
[3] Coles to the Editor of *The Times*, March 31, 1862, published April 5. J. Scott Russell asserted that "long before" the adoption of the turrets of Coles and of Ericsson, the Prince Consort "had matured an analogous system. These plans were known to the writer, who afterwards had to undertake the construction of the first Coles' cupola, which did its work so well in the 'Trusty,' as to establish the success of the system which his Royal Highness had already initiated, and of which he was magnanimous enough to cede the whole public credit to Captain Cowper Coles, who also had done the same thing in a somewhat different way." *The Modern System of Naval Architecture*, i, p. xxvii.
[4] Martin, *Prince Consort*, v, p. 258.

Russell's shipyard in 1859, should be completed at Woolwich.[1] On March 14, moreover, the Board approved the proposal of the new Controller, Rear Admiral Robinson, "to complete and try this Invention in as perfect and thorough a manner as possible." The turret was to be erected in the ironclad floating battery *Trusty*, which was to be taken to Shoeburyness and fired at, to test the applicability of the turret "to all the purposes of warfare ashore and afloat." Coles was forthwith detailed to attend to the preparation of his revolving "shield" for the ensuing trials.[2]

The severe tests to which the turret was exposed in the *Trusty* proved a triumph for the inventor. In a very favorable report on September 19 Captain Ashmore Powell described it as "one of the most formidable inventions adapted to naval warfare, as well as coast defences, that has ever come to my notice." He pointed out that "the cupola gun beats the gun between decks in every description of firing, but it shows its decided superiority when the object is moving or the ship veering about ... twelve rounds were fired at different targets in a quicker time than has ever before been recorded." Exposed to the fire of a 68-pounder smooth-bore, and of 40- and 100-pounder Armstrong rifled guns, "at the conclusion of the practice, although the shield [turret] had been struck 33 times, it worked with the same ease as before."[3]

The effect of these tests on the First Lord of the Admiralty was reported by Palmerston to Russell on September 24.

I saw Somerset today who is in great glee at the success of Capt. Coles's cupola covers for cannon on a ship's deck. These iron domes from under

---

[1] Adm. 12/701: 59–1, January 11, 21, 29, 1861.
[2] Adm. 1/5774, nos. 170, 180; Adm. 12/701: 59–1; Adm. 1/5756, August 15, 1861.
[3] *Parliamentary Papers*, 1866, xlvi, no. 267. Cf. *Experiments with Naval Ordnance, H.M.S. "Excellent,"* pp. 110–115.

The French naval constructor Lebelin, who examined this turret after the return of the *Trusty* to Woolwich, reported that it was covered with plates 11 centimeters thick tongued and grooved and applied lengthwise of the turret wall, and bolted to the heavy wooden backing. The turret worked satisfactorily throughout the tests, and the plates in general resisted very well, even when the shot struck on a joint. *Mémorial du génie maritime*, 1862, i, pp. 295–296. Cf. *Revue maritime et coloniale*, March, 1862, pp. 552–556.

which heavy guns are to fire have been pounded at from short distance by all the heaviest guns we have and nothing has made any impression on them. Somerset thinks that comparatively small iron cased ships armed in this way with all their guns, perhaps 16 on deck, and without any port-holes and therefore low in the water, will prove formidable ships of war ...[1]

To discover whether two 100-pounder Armstrong guns could be worked as well in a Coles turret as the one 40-pounder just tested, the Admiralty at once ordered the construction of a wooden model of a cupola, mounting the two heavy guns, and had it installed in the hulk *Hazard*. The tests on February 18 and 21, March 1 and June 17, 1862, proved very satisfactory.[2] The task of designing a seagoing ironclad adapted to this type of gun mounting, however, proved far more difficult.

On September 25, a few days after the successful experiments with the turret in the *Trusty*, the Controller was ordered to consult with Coles and to report the approximate dimensions of a flush-deck ironclad to carry four heavy Armstrong guns in two turrets.[3] When Coles proposed the construction of a ship of 5600 tons displacement to carry at least sixteen 100-pounders "under cupolas," Paget informed him that the Board was "not prepared to experimentalize on so large and expensive a scale."[4] Nevertheless on October 23 the Controller submitted figures on two types of double-turreted ironclads, the first a vessel 240 feet long, of 2600 tons displacement, 400 horse power, and an estimated speed of 11 knots, the second of 300 feet in length, 3893 tons displacement, 500 horse power, and 11 or 11½ knots speed. The Chief Constructor, Isaac Watts, pointed out, however, that as the smaller vessel did not have sufficient displacement to permit the armor on the transverse bulkheads being carried more than two feet six inches below the water line, her engines,

[1] P.R.O., G.D. 22: 21. The writer is indebted for this quotation to his generous friend, Professor Herbert C. Bell.
[2] Adm. 12/701: 59–1; Adm. 12/717: 59–1; Adm. 3/269, special minute, September 28, 1861; *Parliamentary Papers*, 1863, xi, no. 487, pp. 447–449, 451; *Experiments with Naval Ordnance, H.M.S. "Excellent,"* pp. 115–117.
[3] Adm. 12/701: 59–1.
[4] *Parliamentary Papers*, 1871, xlii, c. 271, p. 43, October 7 and 10, 1861.

boilers and magazines would be greatly exposed to a raking fire. He deemed the iron on her inclined sides "too thin to offer effectual resistance to shot, being only equivalent to 4½ ins. vertical plates *without backing.*" In the larger design the armor and backing were equivalent to 6½ inches of iron, and the plating on the transverse bulkheads might be carried much lower. The protected portion of the ship, however, bore

> so small a proportion to the whole displacement that any serious damage to the extremities of the hull below the water would probably result in the sinking of the ship ... the band at the water line offers but slight protection against such damage. For although it might prevent a shot entering between wind and water, yet a raking shot entering above the band with a dip of about 3°, and a broadside shot with a dip of only 7° might pass out on the other side below the Armour.

Both he and the Controller believed these two types to be too small to afford adequate security against heavy ordnance.[1]

Admiral Robinson remarked that

> the protection afforded by the Cupola to the gun's crew is complete, and far more effective against vertical as well as horizontal fire than that obtained by iron plating applied to the general form of ships sides; and the offensive power of guns in these shields is also considerably greater than that possessed by guns mounted in the ordinary way and fired through Port holes.

To his mind, however, the turret ships must be plated all round as heavily as any other ship, and carry the weight of the turrets in addition. If they were to do this, and attain adequate speed, the displacement and the expense *per gun* would be greater than in any ship yet designed. For that reason he concluded that the limitation of the turrets to two was "probably the most disadvantageous mode possible" of applying Coles's system. A large ship carrying eight or ten shields, on the other hand, "might prove a match in mere fighting for the 'Warrior.'"[2]

Impressed by these arguments for an increased number of turrets, the Admiralty decided on January 13, 1862, to build

---

[1] Adm. 1/5774.
[2] *Ibid.* Robinson added that "up to this time" Coles had "not clearly determined whether an inclined or vertical side is to be part of his plan."

at once a vessel on Coles's system as the sixteenth seagoing ironclad of their building program.[1] The estimates for 1862–1863, introduced by Lord Clarence Paget on February 24, provided £120,000 for the construction of a mastless ironclad of 2529 tons burden and 500 horse power, to carry twelve breech-loading rifled guns in six of Coles's cupolas. This "totally novel class of vessel" was proposed in the hope of solving the problem of an efficient light-draft ironclad for coast defence.[2] In submitting plans for this ship, shortly before the news of the fight between the *Monitor* and the *Merrimack* reached England, the Controller declared that

> her dimensions are small but it is difficult to see how she could be much damaged in action, and looking at her only as a fighting machine in smooth water what class of ship yet built could hope to come victoriously out of a contest with her?[3]

The Admiralty at once approved these plans and called for tenders, reserving the right within three months to alter without additional charge the thickness of the wood backing from 9 to 18 inches, and to diminish the iron plating from 5½ to 4½ inches.[4] Thus before the first news of the battle of Hampton Roads had crossed the Atlantic, the Admiralty had approved the plans of the *Prince Albert*, the first ancestor of the modern multiple-turret battleship. If further testimony to Coles's right to share the honor of introducing the armored turret were required, it might be found in the surprising

---

[1] The Board decided to take £120,000 in the estimates for 1862–1863, and a probable sum of £60,000 in those of the following year, for this purpose, in addition to £30,000 required for the ship's engines. Adm. 1/5795; Adm. 12/720: 91–2.

[2] Hansard, 3rd series, clxv, col. 662.

[3] Adm. 1/5802, March 14, 1862. Her estimated displacement of 4020 tons permitted her to carry an armor belt extending "4 feet amidships and 3 ft. 6 inches forward and aft below the load water line to 7 feet above it terminating at the height of the battery on upper Deck," which consisted of ¾-inch iron covered with 4-inch plank. The six turrets on the upper deck were to be covered with 4-inch iron plates backed by sixteen inches of teak, unless projected experiments proved that increasing the thickness of the plate would permit the backing to be omitted. If the ship were required to go on a long sea voyage, "she would be rigged for the occasion and when on the spot where her services would be required, her masts and rigging would be taken out of her."

[4] Adm. 1/5802, March 17, 1862; Adm. 12/717: 59–1.

fact, hitherto overlooked, that in the autumn of 1861, while ordering a single *Monitor* to be built on contract subject to drastic guarantees, the United States Navy Department proposed the construction of a whole fleet of double-turreted ironclads on Coles's system.

CHAPTER X

ORDNANCE AND ARMOR IN 1861

ALTHOUGH German gunsmiths had produced rifled small arms and cannon at the close of the fifteenth and in the early part of the sixteenth century, and Robins had calculated and explained the ballistics of rifled guns as early as 1742, rifled ordnance was not perfected and introduced into ships of war until the years following the outbreak of the Crimean War. The influence of these new weapons on the history of the ironclad ship, prior to the battle of Hampton Roads, presents three phases. First, the destructive powers of the new guns proved an irresistible argument in favor of the adoption of defensive armor. Secondly, during several years of experiments, wrought-iron plates 4½ inches thick resisted the best of the old guns and the first of the new so successfully that France, England, and the lesser maritime powers began large programs of ironclad warships. Thirdly, the temporary success of the 4½-inch plates led the makers of ordnance to redouble their efforts. By the close of 1861, the success of the latest guns indicated the need for still heavier armor. The see-saw contest between the guns and the plates was on in earnest.

After centuries of very slow development, naval ordnance passed in the second half of the nineteenth century through a series of transformations, multiplying its power many fold from decade to decade. Sensational advances in metallurgy, in the construction of guns and projectiles, in the mechanical application of power, and in the chemistry of propellants, crowded close on one another. The activity of gunmakers had reached fever heat several years before the opening of the American Civil War. The long-established balance between offence and defence, upset by the introduction of horizontal shell-fire, now seemed utterly destroyed by the development of still more powerful weapons in the half decade before 1860.

The introduction of the muzzle-loading rifled gun of sixteen centimeters, model 1855, in the French fleet contributed powerfully to the decision of the Ministry of Marine to adopt defensive armor. It was the tests of the new rifled guns at Lorient which led the *Conseil des Travaux* to propose that all work on wooden warships should be stopped.[1] In England the invention of powerful rifled guns by William Armstrong and Joseph Whitworth, together with great improvements in the construction of shells, led to the direst predictions of the fate of unarmored warships. Admiral Sir Charles Napier declared in the House of Commons that

> no human being could tell what would be the result of the next naval action. At the first broadside a hole as large as a wheelbarrow would be made in a ship's side, and everybody knew that to prolong a contest under such circumstances would be utterly impossible. It has been repeatedly proved that nothing could resist molten iron, and that the ship so struck would be burnt. It was probable that in the first naval action which was fought, both fleets would be almost annihilated....[2]

The introduction of armor, however, promised for a time to tip the scales heavily in favor of the defence. The numerous tests made in France, England, Austria, Denmark, Prussia and Italy indicated that wrought-iron plates 4½ inches thick, backed with wood, would under ordinary circumstances afford adequate protection against the best of the old smoothbores and the first of the new rifled guns. The experimenters now devoted themselves to testing the relative merits of rolled and hammered plates, of steel and iron, and of the products of various manufacturers, and to ascertaining the best methods of fastening the plates, as well as the possibility of decreasing the wooden backing or dispensing with it

---

[1] A.M., BB⁸ 1140, January 13, 1857. Cf. *ibid.*, BB⁸ 1136, January 30, 1855; A.N., BB⁸ 883, March, 1855, and BB⁸ 885, March 6, 1855; *Mémorial de l'artillerie de la marine* (1865), pp. 141–154, report of the Gavres Commission, February 15, 1855; *ibid.*, 2d series, i, pp. 478, 483, and ii, pp. 359, 397.

[2] Hansard, 3rd series, clvi, col. 1138, February 16, 1860. Cf. Cobden, *The Three Panics*, p. 138; *Quarterly Review*, October, 1860, pp. 290–291.

altogether.[1] The temporary superiority of the 4½-inch armor over the best guns of the day proved of enormous importance in the evolution of naval architecture. During this phase not merely France and England but the maritime powers of the second rank began the construction of armored vessels.

The great Italian artillerist Giovanni Cavalli, whose proposals for ironclads in 1856 have already been noted, influenced Cavour to adopt the armored ship as the basis of the new Italian Navy.[2] The armored iron corvettes *Terribile* and *Formidabile* of 2700 tons displacement, 400 horse power, and 20 guns, were constructed by French shipbuilders at La Seyne, and launched in 1861. In that year the Italian government contracted with William H. Webb of New York for the wooden ironclads *Re d'Italia* and *Re di Portogallo*, of 5700 tons displacement and 800 horse power. These vessels, designed with sides sloping inward and protected from stem to stern by a belt of 11 cm. armor, were launched at New York April 18 and August 29, 1863.[3]

The Austrian Navy, under the command of the unfortunate Archduke Ferdinand Maximilian, promptly entered the race with the armored wooden frigates *Drache* and *Salamander* of 2824 tons displacement, 26 guns, and 500 horse power, which were laid down in 1860 and launched in the following year. Three larger wooden ironclads, the *Kaiser Max*, *Prinz Eugen*, and *Don Juan d'Austria*, were begun in 1861 and launched in March, June, and July, 1862.[4]

[1] Reports of the Austrian, Danish, Prussian, and Italian experiments may be found in P.R.O., Adm. 1/5798, January 31, 1862; Adm. 12/701: 52–9, 52–23, 59–1, 59–4a. Cf. Aïcha, *Panzerungen*, pp. 20–27, 31–36.
[2] *Scritti editi e inediti del generale Giovanni Cavalli* (Turin, 1910, 4 vols.), ii, pp. 221–235. Cavalli advocated inclined armor. See above, pp. 90–91.
[3] Josef Fleischer, *Geschichte der K. K. Kriegsmarine während des Krieges im Jahre 1866* (Vienna, 1906), pp. 4–6; J. F. von Kronenfels, *Das Schwimmende Flottenmaterial der Seemächte* (Vienna, 1881), pp. 367–369, 383; C. Randaccio, *Storia delle marine militari italiane* (Rome, 1886, 2 vols.), ii, pp. 16–25, 37; *Revue maritime et coloniale*, March, 1862, p. 549; New York *Herald*, April 19, August 30, 1863.
[4] Austria likewise had one or more armored floating batteries. Fleischer, *Kriegsmarine*, pp. 24–27; von Kronenfels, *Flottenmaterial*, pp. 427–440, 456; *Journal des sciences militaires*, March, 1862, pp. 449–451; November, 1862, pp. 285–305; *Revue maritime et coloniale*, September, 1862, pp. 25–36.

Spain and Russia likewise entered on the new course. In 1860 Don Justo Gayoso advocated the creation of a fleet of nine ironclad frigates, to give Spain an advantage over the backward United States Navy.[1] The Spanish government in the following year began the construction at Ferrol of the wooden ironclad *Tetuan* of 6200 tons displacement; and ordered from the Société des Forges et Chantiers de la Méditerranée the iron-hulled ironclad *Numancia*, of 7200 tons and 40 guns.[2] On June 19, 1861, the Russian government determined to order an ironclad in England, the contract for which they awarded on November 16 to the Thames Iron Shipbuilding Company, the builders of the *Warrior*. This armored iron vessel of 3300 tons displacement, the *Pervenetz*, had a ram bow and sides sloping sharply inward. Orders for the conversion into ironclads of the wooden frigates *Sebastopol* and *Petropavlosk* were issued on June 26 and October 29, 1861. And on March 19, 1862, a few days before the receipt of the news of the battle of Hampton Roads, the Russians contracted with the English shipbuilder, Mitchell, for the construction at St. Petersburg of a fourth ironclad, the *Netrone Menia*, on plans resembling those of the *Pervenetz*, save that the tumble-home began, not at the water line, but a few feet above.[3]

Holland had already converted one sailing ship of the line and four frigates into partially armored floating batteries.[4] In 1859 the Société des Forges et Chantiers de la Méditerranée constructed for the Egyptian Navy a light-draft, twin-screw gunboat, the *Rahmanyeh*, built of sheet steel, with con-

---

[1] *Estudios sobre la marina militar de España* (Ferrol, 1860), ch. v.
[2] Both these vessels, which were launched in 1863, had engines of 1000 horse power and armor 13 centimeters thick. E. Heriz, *Memoria sobre los barcos acorazados* (Barcelona, 1875), pp. 49-50; *Nouvelles annales de la marine et revue coloniale*, May, 1861, pp. 311-312; September, 1861, pp. 180-182; *Mémorial du génie maritime*, 1864, ii, pp. 501-503; Pâris, *L'art naval à l'exposition de Paris en 1867*, pp. 15, 174-185, 667-668 and plate 19; P.R.O., Adm. 12/701: 52-21.
[3] De la Planche, *Les navires blindés de la Russie* (Paris [1865]), pp. 4-9; Heriz, *Memoria*, pp. 43-44; von Kronenfels, *Flottenmaterial*, pp. 484-489, 496-498; P.R.O., Adm. 1/5774, May 14, 1861; Adm. 12/701: 52-14; Adm. 12/717: 52-14.
[4] S. P. L'Honoré Naber, ed., *Het Leven van een Vlouthouder, Gedenkschriften van M. H. Jansen* (Utrecht, 1925), p. 339.

siderable tumble-home and an armored shield forward.[1] Two years later, Arman built for the Viceroy of Egypt the wooden armored gunboat *Egyptienne*, destined for the defence of Alexandria.[2] And in this same year, 1861, both Prussia and Turkey were gathering information with a view to the construction or purchase of ironclad warships.[3]

While the lesser maritime Powers were beginning the construction of ironclads, hundreds of proposals for improvements in armor poured in upon the British Admiralty. Some advocated the use of steel, of homogeneous metal, or of iron with its outer surface case-hardened. Others preferred lead, wire rope, hemp matting, or alternate bars of iron and wood. While many suggested new ways of fastening the armor to its wooden backing, others advised doing away with the backing altogether, and putting the wood in front of the plates. A few thought corrugated armor would afford adequate resistance with reduced weight. For the best material to back the plates, springs, hides, rubber, cork, and iron tubes all had their champions. In the world of inventors, the idea of inclining the armor had a *succès fou*.[4]

On March 13, 1860, the Special Committee on Iron Plates and Guns, which had been conducting experiments against armor since the previous September, reported to the War Office that vessels protected by wrought-iron plates of 4½

---

[1] A.M., 6 DD¹ 88, dossier 2392, reports of *sous-ingénieur* Orsel and M. Verlaque, October 8 and 29, 1859. This vessel of 86 tons displacement was destined for service on the Nile.

[2] *Ibid.*, dossier 2393, reports of the naval prefect, Toulon, and of Lieutenant Lagougine, who commanded the *Egyptienne* on her voyage to Alexandria, June 30 and September 30, 1861; *Nouvelles annales de la marine et revue coloniale*, September, 1861, p. 190.

[3] P. R. O., Adm. 12/701: 52–23; 52–24, 59–1. The Prussian government asked for copies of the reports of British armor tests, and carried out experiments on English plates at Berlin. The Turkish government obtained from the British Admiralty estimates of the cost of building two ironclads in Great Britain.

[4] P.R.O., Controller of the Navy, Submission Letter Book no. 21; Adm. 12/701: 59–1; Adm. 12/717: 59–1; British Patent Office, *Abridgments of Specifications, Class 113, 1855–1866* (London, 1905); Special Committee on Iron, *First Report*, pp. xii–xiii.

Of the numerous advocates of inclined armor at least five — Hamilton, Jones, Pickering, Sharp and Sleigh — claimed priority in its "invention." See above, pp. 7, 9, 28, 31, 48, 52, 53, 61–62, 87, 89, 91, 106, 162–164; and also De Morhange, *Sur les navires cuirassés* (Paris, 1863), pp. 52–53, 57–62.

inches thickness were, "to all practical purposes, invulnerable against any projectile that can at present be brought to bear against them at any range." To insure the full resistance of the plates this committee deemed it "of great importance that they should be backed as strongly as possible, and firmly bolted and nutted."[1]

Impressed by the success of the ironclad floating batteries built during the Crimean War, Sir John Fox Burgoyne, the Inspector General of Fortifications, had proposed in 1856 a series of experiments on wrought-iron embrasures for fortifications, somewhat more elaborate than the embrasures in use in the United States. These tests, which were carried out in 1859 and 1860, led the Ordnance Select Committee to report that there was "very good ground for believing" that iron screens or targets would resist the heaviest shot and would prove "of the greatest value in protecting casemates."[2]

The chief burden of the British armor tests in the years 1861 to 1864 fell on the Special Committee on Iron, appointed by the War Office with the concurrence of the Admiralty on January 12, 1861, to investigate the problem of "the application of iron to the purposes of Land Fortifications and the protection of ships' sides from shot." This committee, which came more immediately under the direction of the Admiralty after July 22, 1861, began its labors by collecting the records of previous armor tests, and by taking the testimony of numerous military and naval officers, engineers, shipbuilders, and iron manufacturers. The committee began a long series of experiments at the new proving ground at Shoeburyness

---

[1] This committee was dissolved on April 28, 1860, and its business transferred to the Ordnance Select Committee. Its report cited above is printed in Special Committee on Iron, *First Report*, pp. 185 ff.

[2] *Minutes of Proceedings* of the Royal Artillery Institution, ii, pp. 327–332; Special Committee on Iron, *First Report*, pp. xi–xii, 201–204; *Second Report*, pp. 32–36; Wrottesley, *Burgoyne*, vol. ii, p. 356. For the American experiments in firing against wrought-iron embrasures in the years 1853 to 1855 see General Joseph G. Totten, *Report on the effects of firing with heavy ordnance from casemate embrasures: and also the effects of firing against the same embrasures* (Washington, 1857), and the adverse criticisms of General Sir Howard Douglas in his *Naval Gunnery* (5th ed., London, 1860), pp. 408–417. Cf. Brialmont, *Etudes sur la défense des états*, ii, pp. 77–79, 81, 84–89. For later British experiments see Special Committee on Iron, *First Report*, pp. xix–xxi; Adm. 12/701: 59–1.

on April 23, and on August 3 submitted a preliminary report recommending wrought-iron plates of not much more than five inches in thickness, but of the largest superficial dimensions obtainable. No kind of steel or of steely iron, such as puddled steel or homogeneous iron, appeared to possess "any good resisting qualities when made in large masses," for any degree of hardness seemed to "carry with it a corresponding degree of brittleness under sudden concussion."[1]

The report of March 27, 1862, was more specific. Copper, the committee declared, offered too little resistance; steel and steely iron proved too brittle. The best plates yet furnished were of wrought iron of the softest quality, produced by the Lowmoor Iron Company, the Thames Iron Shipbuilding Company, John Brown and Company, the Pontypool Iron Company, and Beale and Company. It had not proved necessary to employ the most costly kinds of iron to make the best armor plates. With suitable care and powerful machinery good plates could be obtained at moderate cost either by hammering or rolling, or by combining the two processes. The softness of the iron and its freedom from internal strain were so important that, with all plates produced under the hammer, pains must be taken to anneal the finished plate. For the manufacture of satisfactory rolled plates "enormous compressing power" was indispensable.[2]

Laminated armor, the committee declared, proved "in

---

[1] Special Committee on Iron, *First Report*, pp. ix, 154–155. This committee was composed of Captain John C. Dalrymple Hay, R.N., chairman; Major William D. Jervois, R.E.; Brevet Colonel W. Henderson, R.A.; Dr. John Percy, F.R.S.; William Fairbairn, F.R.S.; and William Pole, F.R.S. Its four reports of March 27, 1862, February 24, 1863, February 26, 1864, and August 17, 1864, are of capital importance. Cf. "Correspondence on Iron Armour between the Chairman of the Royal Commission on Scientific Education and Members of the Iron Armour Plate Committee," *Parliamentary Papers*, 1877, lii, no. 228; and Admiral Sir John C. Dalrymple Hay, *Lines from my Log-Books* (Edinburgh, 1898), pp. 231 ff.

[2] Special Committee on Iron, *First Report*, pp. xiv–xv, 176, 207, 221. Concerning the difficulties encountered in the first stages of the armor-plate industry see "Return of Makers' Names, and Mode of Manufacturing the Armour Plates of the 'Warrior,' 'Black Prince,' 'Resistance,' and 'Defence'; the Quantities of Iron or Armour Plates Condemned, and the Date and Reason of their Condemnation," *Parliamentary Papers*, 1861, xxxviii, no. 347; *Experiments with Naval Ordnance*, H.M.S. "Excellent," pp. 137–141; Adm. 12/701: 59–1.

every case far weaker than solid plates of similar thickness." Corrugation appeared to weaken the plates.

All tongueing and grooving, or any departure from plane-edges, is a source of weakness to each particular plate; is liable to assist in destroying neighbouring plates which would not otherwise be affected by a blow, and has structural disadvantages, in preventing facility in repairing a damaged ship, or changing a damaged plate.[1]

Elaborate tests of inclined as compared with vertical armor indicated that the former afforded no advantage if the plate had to be made thinner to compensate for a larger exposed area. The committee did not contend that a 4½-inch plate would not offer greater resistance, especially to spherical shot, when placed obliquely than when placed vertically. It concluded, however, that a given weight of iron would afford more protection if disposed in vertical plates than if disposed in thinner plates, of necessarily greater surface, placed obliquely to protect the same vertical area.[2]

Much attention was paid to the possibility of eliminating or greatly reducing the wood backing behind the armor. Experiments with two targets designed to dispense with the wood backing altogether demonstrated that

however much the armour plates may be supported by direct contact with a rigid backing of iron, and however desirable it may seem to exclude wood or other perishable materials from them, yet the concussion is so injurious to the fastenings of a rigid structure, that, in the present state of our knowledge, it would be unwise to recommend the abandonment of the wood backing.[3]

---

[1] Special Committee on Iron, *First Report*, pp. xiii, xvi, xviii, xx, xxi. In its preliminary report of August 3, 1861, the committee had expressed "grave reason to doubt whether the tongue and groove at the edge of the plates, as hitherto applied in the 'Warrior' and other plated ships, may not be a disadvantage rather than a benefit." *Ibid.*, p. 155. In October, 1861, the Admiralty dispensed with the tonguing and grooving of the plates for the *Hector* and *Valiant*. Adm. 12/701: 59-1. Cf. *Mémorial du génie maritime*, 1862, i, pp. 293-294.

Two targets formed of "6 layers of ½-inch corrugated bars interlaced with ½-inch bars passing through the spaces formed by the corrugation," one target made of steel and the other of iron, proved unsatisfactory. *Experiments with Naval Ordnance, H.M.S. "Excellent,"* p. 130.

[2] Special Committee on Iron, *First Report*, pp. xi, xvi, 155, 227, 236. Cf. Adm. 12/701: 59-1; Hansard, 3rd series, clxiii, col. 1059; *Parliamentary Papers*, 1863, xi, no. 487, pp. 440-443; *Mémorial du génie maritime*, 1862, i, p. 295; De Morhange, *Sur les navires cuirassés*, pp. 57-59.

[3] Special Committee on Iron, *First Report*, pp. xiii, xvi-xvii, xxii-xxiii. For the proposal of Joseph D'Aguilar Samuda to dispense with wooden backing and to incor-

Wrought-iron plates 4½ and 6 inches in thickness, unbacked save for their edges resting against upright timbers of fir, were so severely damaged by solid cast-iron shot fired from 126-pounder and 100-pounder Armstrong guns at Shoeburyness in the summer of 1861, that Captain Hewlett submitted a strong report on the importance of wood backing.[1] For the three new ironclads, *Agincourt*, *Minotaur*, and *Northumberland*, however, the Admiralty reduced the wood backing to nine inches, instead of the eighteen inches behind the plates of the *Warrior*, while increasing the thickness of the armor plates from 4½ to 5½ inches.[2]

If the problem confronting the Admiralty had been merely the production of armor to resist the French 50-pounders or the British 68-pounder 4¾-ton gun, its solution would have been relatively easy. Wrought-iron plates 4½ inches in thickness would have served the purpose. But the new rifled ordnance was being developed so rapidly that no one knew what the next month might bring forth. "The ship may be cased with armor which today is shot-proof; but tomorrow it may be pierced with ease by shot or shell thrown by some new iron monster."[3]

---

porate 6-inch armor plates into the structure of the vessel, see Controller of the Navy, Submission Letter Book no. 21, March 30, 1860; Adm. 1/5774, May 14, 1861; British Patent Office, 1861, No. 1005; J. D'A. Samuda, "On the Form and Materials for Iron Plated Ships, and the points requiring attention in their Construction," *Minutes of Proceedings* of the Institution of Civil Engineers, xxi, pp. 187-256, January 28, 1862. Cf. Special Committee on Iron, *Second Report*, p. x. On the interest shown by the Admiralty in other systems of plating see Adm. 1/5774, May 2, 1861; Adm. 1/5765, Somerset's memoranda of May 23, 27, 1861; Hansard, 3rd series, clxiii, col. 912; Adm. 1/5769, July 27, 1861; Adm. 12/701: 59-1,59-4a. Cf. British Patent Office, 1860, no. 1805; 1861, nos. 152, 1198.

Covering armor plate with four inches of wood reduced considerably the damage from shot; but the wooden covering could easily be ripped off by shellfire. Special Committee on Iron, *First Report*, pp. xiii, xvii; *Experiments with Naval Ordnance, H.M.S. "Excellent,"* p. 142. Cf. Controller of the Navy, Submission Letter Book no. 21, March 30, 1860.

1 Adm. 1/5756: A. 1726, July 4, 1861; Special Committee on Iron, *First Report*, pp. 221-222. A 68-pounder solid shot which struck the unbacked portion of a plate over one of the ports of the target ship *Sirius* at Portsmouth a few weeks earlier had done similar damage. Adm. 1/5756, July 10, 1861.

2 Adm. 12/720: 91-2, January 25, 27, 1862; Adm. 1/5802, March 12, 1862.

3 Nathaniel Barnaby, "On Mechanical Invention in its Relation to the Improvement of Naval Architecture," *Transactions* of the Institution of Naval Architects, i, p. 154, March 3, 1860.

As a matter of fact no shell penetrated a 4½-inch plate until the trials of Whitworth's 70-pounders and 150-pounders in September, 1862.[1] In October, 1858, one of Whitworth's flat-headed hexagonal 70-pounder shot, whose diameter was only 5¼ inches, had punched a clean hole through a 4-inch plate fastened to the side of the *Alfred*, which here measured only six or seven inches of oak planking. The 4-inch plates of the floating battery *Trusty* withstood their first tests from rifled guns remarkably well, but later showed themselves brittle and quite inferior.[2] In January, 1861, however, a 70-pounder flat-headed steel bolt from a Whitworth rifled gun at 200 yards range dented and cracked, but failed to penetrate, a 4½-inch plate fastened to the side of the frigate *Sirius*.[3] In the following July Captain Hewlett of the *Excellent* declared that it was generally believed by the experts at Shoeburyness that 4½-inch plates with wooden backing "would stand the first blow of a projectile from any of the guns (rifled or otherwise) that are at present constructed."[4] Against a target representing the side of the *Warrior*, tested at Shoeburyness in October, 1861, at 200 yards range, both the 68-pounder smoothbore and the 110-pounder Armstrong rifled gun proved ineffective, though they demonstrated the disadvantages of tonguing and grooving the plates. At that range, Captain Hewlett thought the Armstrong gun inferior to the smoothbore. The Committee reported that

one 140-pounder shot caused the plates struck to buckle, and bent one rib. Three 100-pounder shot striking near together still further buckled the plate, and slightly cracked it. Two 68-pounders cracked the plate and broke two bolts. Four 200-pound shot from the Armstrong 100-pounder, with reduced charges, buckled the plate, and broke one tongue and groove for a length of 2½ feet, but did no further damage. Three 100-pounders, fired in salvo, and hitting the same plate, broke a hole 18 inches by 9 inches, and cracked the plate across. A 140-pounder, fired in the same

---

[1] *Experiments with Naval Ordnance, H.M.S. "Excellent,"* p. 152; Special Committee on Iron, *First Report*, pp. xxi, 246–247; *Second Report*, pp. viii, 82, 85; *Parliamentary Papers*, 1863, xi, no. 487, pp. 374–375.
[2] See above, pp. 131, 154–155.
[3] Special Committee on Iron, *First Report*, pp. xi, 168; *Parliamentary Papers*, 1863, xi, no. 487, p. 554.
[4] Adm. 1/5756: A. 1726, July 4, 1861.

salvo, sheared another tongue and buckled the plate. Lastly a steel-jacketed shot, flat-ended, striking near where other shot had struck, broke the plate through. In all, 3229 lbs. weight of shot struck.[1]

Although these experiments in 1861 scarcely justified the boasts of the makers of rifled guns, the rapid developments in ordnance greatly impressed the Admiralty. The Duke of Somerset stated in the House of Lords that he had insisted on the *Achilles* having sufficient displacement to carry at least 6-inch plates, but that now he no longer felt sure that even such armor would prove invulnerable.[2] For the three new ironclads, *Agincourt*, *Minotaur*, and *Northumberland*, the Admiralty ordered plates of 5½-inch iron, with nine inches of wood backing, instead of 4½-inch plates with eighteen inches of backing as in the *Warrior*.[3]

Whether or not iron plates would stop every sort of solid shot, it seemed obvious that something must be done to keep out the shells. When Roebuck declared in the House of Commons that one of his constituents had offered to build a gun which would throw a thousand pounds of shot through the sides of the *Warrior* "as easily as through blotting-paper," Lord Clarence Paget replied that even if this could be done

that would not alter the merits of iron-cased ships as compared with wooden ones. If they had only shot to deal with the superiority of the former might not be so marked, but unfortunately they had to deal with shell, and especially of a new kind of shell, filled with liquid iron, which was very murderous, and very destructive to wooden ships. The main superiority of the iron-cased ships was that they were safe against shell.[4]

The Admiralty spurred on the gunmakers to produce "monster" ordnance, in the belief that one "might as well throw marbles against our iron-sides" as shot of small caliber.[5] If

---

[1] Special Committee on Iron, *First Report*, p. xxi; Adm. 12/701: 59–4a, October 30, 1861.
[2] Hansard, 3rd series, clxiii, cols. 908–912, 1059, June 11, 14, 1861.
[3] See above, pp. 175–179.
[4] Hansard, 3rd series, clxiii, cols. 64–65, May 23, 1861. Shells filled with molten iron were more feared at this time than hot shot. On the effect of such shells on the wooden frigate *Undaunted* see Douglas, *Naval Gunnery* (5th ed., London, 1860), p. 228, note; and Barnaby, *Naval Development*, pp. 139–140. Cf. Adm. 1/5766, December 18, 1861; Adm. 1/5842, December 29, 1863.
[5] Lord Clarence Paget in the House of Commons, February 24, 1862. Hansard, 3rd series, clxv, col. 659.

these guns should outstrip armor in the race, however, as Hewlett justly observed, that would not "affect the question of building iron plated ships, for they must always have a vast superiority over wooden ones."[1]

In the French armor tests, neither steel nor homogeneous metal plates, of both foreign and domestic manufacture, proved as resistant as wrought iron.[2] Nor did the Emperor's suggestion of armor composed of a network of hawsers, or of compressed sailcloth, prove satisfactory.[3] On the other hand, the manufacturers of wrought-iron plates improved the quality of their product. Their plates of 11 and 12 centimeters resisted so well the fire of the heaviest French guns and of British 68-pounders that the Ministry of Marine, for a brief period in July, 1860, contemplated diminishing their thickness to 10 and 11 centimeters.[4] The success of the plates, however, spurred the ordnance experts to greater efforts.

In the experiments at Gavres in 1860 with the 16-cm. muzzle-loading rifled gun, model 1858, both shells and cast-iron shot proved wholly ineffective against plates 11 and 12 centimeters thick. Wrought-iron shot, especially those with a steel head, produced deeper dents, but failed to pierce the plates. Hammered cast-steel shot, weighing 45 kilogrammes, penetrated the plates, but did not pass through the wooden backing, even though the timbers were in bad condition.[5]

Rear Admiral Comte de Gueydon, the naval prefect at Lorient, in transmitting the report of the Commission de

---

[1] Adm. 1/5756, March 7, 1861.
[2] A.M., 1 DD¹ 274, to Edward Rowcliffe, London, November 21, 1859; 4 DD¹ 6, contract with Petin, Gaudet and Co., December 2, 1859; DD⁴ 1109, extracts from the minutes of the Vincennes Commission, May 21 and June 4, 1860.
[3] A.M., 1 DD¹ 282, to Vincennes Commission, March 23, 1860; 1 DD¹ 276, to naval prefect, Cherbourg, April 2, 4, 11, 1860.
[4] A.M., 1 DD¹ 281, circulars to Cherbourg, Brest, Lorient and Toulon, July 20 and 27, 1860; 1 DD¹ 285, to Petin, Gaudet and Co., August 2, 1860.
  The French naval authorities maintained their opposition to inclined armor. A.M., 1 DD¹ 271, to the Vincennes Commission, January 31 and April 8, 1859; BB⁸ 1148, April 9, 1861. See above, pp. 62, 106. For later experiments see the *Mémorial de l'artillerie de la marine*, 2d series, iii, pp. 48-84, 278-280, 301.
[5] "L'artillerie et les murailles cuirassées," *Mémorial de l'artillerie de la marine*, 2d series, ii, pp. 101-106.

Gavres, argued that only guns of greater calibers, say 18 or 20 centimeters, would prove effective against armor. Nevertheless, the inspector general of naval artillery objected to the introduction of such large projectiles, which he deemed too heavy for gunners to handle. Inspired by the reputed success of Whitworth's armor-piercing bolts of only 5¼ inches diameter, he pinned his faith on guns of 14 and 16 centimeters caliber, with heavier charges and increased velocities.[1]

To permit the adoption of these increased charges French artillerists had already taken up an old idea which was now winning great favor in Europe. The strengthening of cannon by hoops or bands dates from the origin of artillery itself. In 1833 Captain A. Thiéry of the French Army proposed to strengthen guns by wrought-iron bands from the trunnions to the breech. Three years later Colonel Fredericks of the Liège foundry applied such reinforcement to two cast-iron field pieces with success. When John Ericsson came to the United States in 1839, he brought with him a 12-inch wrought-iron gun, called the "Oregon," which was similarly reinforced by two tiers of hoops. Improvements of this nature were patented by Benjamin Chambers, Daniel Treadwell and Robert P. Parrott in the United States, July 31, 1849, December 11, 1855, and October 1, 1861. Captain Alexander Theophilus Blakely, whose British patent bore date of February 27, 1855, made a contribution in demonstrating mathematically and reducing to a working system the application of hoops. Colonel Treuille de Beaulieu introduced hoops of puddled steel with such great success that the French Navy, on November 3, 1859, adopted this system for all its rifled guns. Spain, Holland, Italy, Russia, Sweden, and Norway adopted similar methods.[2]

---

[1] A.M., DD⁴ 1109, De Gueydon to de Chasseloup-Laubat, December 13, 1860; *Mémorial de l'artillerie de la marine*, 2d series, i, p. 131; ii, pp. 66–70, notes of the inspector general of naval artillery, February 3 and 14, May 7, August 25 and 31, 1860, and April 10, 1862.
    For a comparison of British and French rifled guns at this period, see Xavier Raymond, "Le canon Armstrong et le canon Whitworth," *Journal des Débats*, March 21, 1860.

[2] A. Thiéry, *Application du fer aux constructions de l'artillerie* (Paris, 1834 and 1840); *Journal des sciences militaires*, viii (1834); *Mémorial de l'artillerie de la*

In 1861 the Gavres Commission tried three new guns against 11- and 12-cm. plates. One was a lengthened muzzle-loading rifled gun of 14 centimeters; the others, *la Marie-Jeanne* and *la Nivernaise*, were breech-loading steel rifled guns of 16 centimeters, reinforced with steel hoops. For the breech mechanism, Treuille de Beaulieu had adopted the interrupted screw, patented in the United States in 1853 by John P. Schenkl and Adolph S. Saroni.[1] The first gun proved ineffective against armor; the two others pierced the target only when firing shot of 80 kilogrammes with excessive charges. Both the Commission and the inspector general were forced to admit the necessity of larger calibers.[2]

Already, however, the progress of rifled ordnance had convinced the French naval authorities of the need of thicker armor. An order of the Minister of Marine, Count Chasseloup-Laubat, on December 30, 1861, prescribed a water-line belt of 14 centimeters thickness for the new floating batteries.[3] For the ten seagoing ironclads laid down in 1861, the maximum thickness of armor was fixed at 15 centimeters.[4]

When the news of the battle of Hampton Roads crossed the Atlantic, more than forty seagoing ironclads, thirty armored coast-defence vessels, and eighteen partially protected gunboats, were already built, building, or authorized in Europe.

---

marine, 1863, pp. 129 ff.; *ibid.*, 2d series, iv, pp. 81-125; xii, pp. 266 ff.; J. Schmoelzl, *Les canons rayés* (Paris, 1865), pp. 112-113; Holley, *Ordnance and Armor*, pp. 1-81, 87, 240-281, 837-874; Church, *Ericsson*, i, p. 123; Colonel Rogers Birnie, Jr., *Gun Making in the United States* (Washington, 1907), ch. i.

1 "Le système de fermeture de culasse, basé sur l'emploi d'une vis à filets interrompus, est aujourd'hui généralement désigné en Europe sous le nom de système français; mais il est en réalité d'origine américaine. Le premier brevet demandé pour ce mode de fermeture a été pris aux Etats-Unis, le 16 août 1853, par John Schenkl et Adolphe Saroni." *Mémorial de l'artillerie de la marine*, 2d series, v, p. 315. Cf. Holley, *Ordnance and Armor*, pp. 608-610.

An American named Castmann had built six such guns at Boston for the British government in 1855; but the workmanship was too crude to permit introduction in the British service. These guns had a screw with six sectors. Treuille de Beaulieu first adopted one with four in 1859, but the French soon changed to the screw with six sectors.

2 *Mémorial de l'artillerie de la marine*, 2d series, ii, pp. 69, 107-116; iv, p. 97.

3 A.M., BB⁸ 1150, January 7, 1862; 7 DD¹ 233, report of Dupuy de Lôme, January, 1862; 4 DD¹ 6, contract with Petin, Gaudet and Co., October 31, 1862.

4 A.M., 4 DD¹ 6, contracts with Petin, Gaudet and Co., July 3 and October 9, 1863.

The makers of rifled ordnance, whose first successes had given a powerful impetus to the introduction of ironclads, were on the eve of fresh triumphs in the race between the guns and the plates. Already the leading naval powers had perceived the necessity of introducing armor thicker than four and a half inches to resist the new elongated projectiles.

CHAPTER XI

MALLORY'S IRONCLAD POLICY

WHILE the European Powers were thus engaged in revolutionizing naval architecture, the United States did not complete a single ironclad until its peace was rudely disturbed by civil war. Except for the unfinished Stevens war steamer, the proposals of inventors and of far-sighted naval officers went unheeded. Indeed the refusal of so progressive and inventive a nation as the United States to abandon wooden vessels was used as an argument by the British opponents of the introduction of ironclads.[1]

Fortunately for the Union cause, Congress had authorized in 1854, 1857, and 1858 the construction of nineteen wooden steam warships.[2] Its sole appropriation for an ironclad, however, served only to push the Stevens battery one stage further towards a completion destined never to be attained.[3]

When Secretary John Y. Mason returned to the Navy Department in the place of George Bancroft, Robert L. Stevens had obtained in September, 1848, a renewal of his contract with four years' extension of time.[4] Nevertheless, in August, 1849, after bills to the total amount of $75,689.04 had been approved, of which sum $16,329.44 represented the advance allowed to Stevens above the cost of unwrought materials, Secretary William Ballard Preston refused to make further payments. In his annual report, December 1, he pointed out that "no precise plan has yet been submitted by the contractor to the department, and no progress has been made in the

---

[1] *The Saturday Review*, March 29, 1862, cited in *Littell's Living Age*, May 10, 1862.
[2] For descriptions of these ships see Bennett, *Steam Navy of the United States*, 2d ed., i, ch. x. Cf. O.R.N., 2d series, i; and the interesting criticism of these vessels by Donald McKay in the Boston *Commercial Bulletin*, November 17, 1860.
[3] For the early history of this projected ironclad see above, pp. 48–52.
[4] Senate Executive Document No. 34, 37th Congress, 2d Session, p. 10. Stevens renewed the mortgage; and on February 13, 1849, agreed on the same prices and rates of payment as before.

construction of the vessel beyond the purchase and delivery of certain quantities of iron." [1]

On being notified by Commodore Skinner, Chief of the Bureau of Construction, in January, 1851, that the Navy Department, considering the contract void, "designs to sell shortly the materials collected for that purpose," Stevens petitioned Congress, requesting that his contract be reaffirmed and continued in force. He declared that

when the contractor was first arrested in his work by Secretary Bancroft, he was in advance and liable for material, principally for heavy plates of iron from Pennsylvania, to about $40,000, which was subsequently paid to him. He is now in advance about $36,000, also for heavy iron plates, tubes for the boilers, &c., from England.[2]

Senator Stockton's report from the Senate Committee on Naval Affairs, March 16, 1852, simply echoed Stevens's memorial, and declared his ironclad to be "that very sort of war-steamer which the service requires." [3] A clause in the Naval Appropriation Act of August 31, 1852, "authorized and required" the Secretary of the Navy "to have completed with the least possible delay, the war-steamer contracted for with Robert L. Stevens . . .; and the balance of the appropriation heretofore made, which has been carried to the credit of the surplus fund, shall be used for that purpose." [4]

Work could now proceed in earnest. Bills approved in 1853 totaled $22,568.67; those in 1854, $148,277.99. An act of March 3, 1855, appropriated a second two hundred and fifty thousand dollars, which had all been expended by De-

---

[1] Executive Document No. 5, 31st Congress, 1st Session, pp. 434, 447. Congress omitted to act on the matter until 1852. Senate Report No. 129, 32d Congress, 1st Session.
 Charles W. Skinner, Chief of the Bureau of Construction and Repair, reported on August 17, 1849, that no plan of the vessel had been submitted to the Bureau, and that the demand for one had been relinquished for reasons assigned by Secretary Mason. He stated that no money had been paid by the Department under the original contract, but that $42,630.47 had been paid under the first renewal, and $33,058.57 under the second renewal. Executive Document No. 5, 31st Congress, 1st Session, pp. 446–447.
[2] N.D., "Memorandum of the claim of Robert L. Stevens against the United States," Washington, January 31, 1851. 3 pages [printed].
[3] Senate Report No. 129, 32d Congress, 1st Session.
[4] *Statutes at Large*, x, p. 101.

cember 14 of that year.[1] So extensive had been the alterations in the original project, however, that the vessel was not yet half completed.

In the years that had elapsed since the conception of Stevens's project, the progress of ordnance had led him to modify his plans. Ericsson's 12-inch wrought-iron gun had pierced a target of 4½-inch wrought iron in 1842.[2] Six years later R. L. Stevens told the English shipbuilder, John Scott Russell, that experiments had convinced him that "six inches thick of plates of iron bolted to the outside of a wooden ship, formed a perfect protection against the heaviest artillery then in use." [3]

In explanation of the great cost of his ironclad compared with the sum fixed in the contract, Stevens pointed out that the vessel partially built in 1854 and 1855 was much larger and higher powered than that first projected. Her hull was nearly four times and her 6¾-inch armor nearly three times the weight of the battery contracted for in 1843. The government now, he asserted, required an ability to resist shot of 125 pounds instead of 64; and a great increase of engine power was necessary if the vessel was to overtake the improved vessels of her day. The new ironclad was a slender vessel of 4683 tons, 420 feet long, 45 feet beam, with eight vertical, overhead-beam, condensing engines of 8600 horse power, designed to drive two independent screw propellers. In January, 1856, Stevens declared that he could complete her for service in twelve months more, if sufficient funds were provided.[4]

---

[1] *Statutes at Large*, x, p. 676; Senate Executive Document No. 34, 37th Congress 2d Session, p. 11.

[2] Church, *Ericsson*, i, p. 123.

[3] J. Scott Russell, *The Fleet of the Future in 1862* (London, 1862), p. 55. Shortly before his death in 1856, R. L. Stevens renewed his experiments with a 10-inch gun against an iron target. Stevens Letter Book, in the library of the Stevens Institute of Technology, R. L. Stevens to Commodore Joseph Smith, March 26, 1856.

[4] F. de R. Furman, *History of the Stevens Institute of Technology*, pp. 127–131, E. A. Stevens to Secretary J. C. Dobbin, December 22, 1856. For the dimensions of the vessel see House Executive Document No. 23, 37th Congress, 2d Session, p. 2, and Lenthall to Dobbin, May 9, 1856, N.D., *Bureau Letters*.

A board appointed on February 19, however, estimated that, in addition to the half million already paid, the further sum of $812,033.68 would be required to complete the vessel. In his annual report, December 3, 1857, Secretary Toucey stated that Robert L. Stevens, who had died in 1856, and his executor [Edwin A. Stevens] had expended on the vessel the sum of $702,755.37.[1] Toucey suggested compliance with the executor's request that the sum of $86,717.84, the balance of the contract price, which had been appropriated by Act of August 16, 1856, should "be paid to him from time to time as an equal amount in work and materials shall hereafter be put upon the vessel."[2] No action, however, seems to have been taken.

Not even the existence of civil strife and the possibility of a foreign war sufficed to bring the Stevens battery to completion. Soon after the outbreak of the Civil War, Edwin A. Stevens, the New Jersey authorities, and others, showered requests on the Navy Department for an appropriation to finish the ironclad lying half built at Hoboken. Captain Hiram Paulding, who was ordered by Secretary Welles to examine the vessel, reported on July 2 that her model was "exceedingly good." Although she would draw too much water to permit her to attack any of the Confederate defences, save perhaps at Pensacola and, "by some assistance in lightening," on the lower Mississippi, Paulding thought she would be useful "more with reference to any foreign — than domestic troubles," and recommended that a further examination and report should be made by a board of officers.[3] In response to a suggestion by Welles in his report of July 4, 1861, Congress authorized him, by a joint resolution approved on July 24, to appoint a board to examine the

---

1 Including the $500,000 paid them by the government. The statement made by Edwin A. Stevens to the examining board in 1861, showed an expenditure, up to that date, of $228,435.87 over and above the government payments. House Executive Document No. 23, 37th Congress, 2d Session, p. 8.
2 Executive Documents, 35th Congress, 1st Session, ii, part iii, p. 582.
3 N.D., AD., copy of Paulding to Welles, July 2, 1861.

MALLORY'S IRONCLAD POLICY 215

Stevens vessel and to report at the next meeting of Congress upon the expediency of completing her.[1]

As the proposal made by the Stevens brothers in 1841 was for a vessel with inclined sides, and the plans described by Edwin A. Stevens and illustrated in his memorial of 1862 show sloping armor, some writers have assumed that these later plans represented the ship built in 1854–1856. The board which examined the battery at Hoboken in 1861, however, stated that Robert L. Stevens had designed her with vertical armored sides. This board began its work on November 1 by requesting plans and descriptions of the vessel, which were furnished on December 10. It then became apparent that Edwin A. Stevens

has materially changed the plans from what appears to have been originally intended. Instead of the vertical sides above water, clothed with armor and pierced with gun ports, which seems to have been the design of Robert L. Stevens, the plans presented to us bear date of November, 1861, and resemble the inclined armor-plated ships, the designs of which have been patented in England by Captain Adderly Sleigh, in July, 1858, and by Mr. Josiah Jones in November, 1859, ... with some important exceptions.

The board reported that

it now remains to complete a small portion of the plating near the bow and the stern; put in the beams and decks; attach a fore and aft box keelson to the floor timbers amidships throughout the whole length of the vessel; make the flue connexions and chimney to the boilers; connect the engines, and add a few wanting pieces; put in floor plates to engine and fire rooms; make and attach the propeller shaft bearers to the outside of the vessel; supply the propellers; put in the required bulkheads; apply the armor and the machinery for loading and working the guns; and to manufacture the guns themselves.

The naval members of the board, however, regarded the project with disfavor. The plans received from Edwin A. Stevens on December 10 depicted a twin-screw iron vessel of 5000 tons and 8600 horse power, 420 feet long, of 53 feet beam, and 20 feet 6 inches ordinary load draft. On going into action, she was to take in sufficient water ballast to sink her two feet deeper and decrease the area to be protected by

[1] Senate Executive Document No. 1, 37th Congress, 1st Session, p. 96; *Statutes at Large*, xii, p. 328.

armor. A central casemate whose inclined sides and ends were plated with 6¾ inches of iron, was covered by a flat bomb-proof deck, on top of which seven huge 15- or 18-inch guns were mounted on revolving platforms. These guns were pointed and loaded by steam machinery operated by gun crews in the casemate below. An armored deck, a foot below the water line when the ship was in fighting trim, protected those parts of the ship fore and aft of the central casemate. Below the knuckle, the underwater armor belt, 3½ inches thick, extended from stem to stern, to a depth of four feet below the water line. Stevens estimated that the ship could be completed in four months at a cost of $783,294, in addition to the $500,000 which the government had appropriated in former years. The majority of the board, however, Commodore S. H. Stringham, Commodore William Inman, Captain Thomas A. Dornin, and Chief Engineer Alban C. Stimers, reported on December 24 that, though approving many features of the battery, they deemed its completion inexpedient. They declared that the method of mounting her guns, and that of sinking the vessel beyond her load draft, were untried; that if shot pierced her unarmored extremities above the bomb-proof deck, the inrush of water would sink the ship; and above all, that her hull was so deficient in strength that "the action of the waves would cause her to writhe and twist to an extent that would soon open the seams of her light iron sides." The eminent civilian member of the board, however, Professor Joseph Henry, stated in a minority report that "although the vessel may not be a convenient or safe ship for long voyages, she might be made of sufficient strength to withstand the exposure to which she would be subjected, and to efficiently perform the service required."[1]

[1] House Executive Document No. 23, 37th Congress, 2d Session; [Edwin A. Stevens], *The Stevens Battery, Memorial to Congress* [1862]. Stevens wrote to the board of examiners on November 7 that the vessel had been originally planned for the defence of New York, but that he had "since decided on an alteration of the plan by completing the unfinished portion of the vessel to adapt her to the defence of the whole country." Stevens Letter Book. Cf. *ibid.*, July 11–December 25, 1861; N.D., *General Letter Book* no. 66, Welles to E. A. Stevens, October 22, De-

Undeterred by the unfavorable report of the examining board, Stevens collected further endorsements from shipbuilders and engineers, conducted experiments demonstrating the resistance of sloping laminated armor, and submitted a lengthy memorial to Congress.[1] To demonstrate some of his theories he fitted up at his own expense the iron steamer *Naugatuck* for the Treasury Department in the winter of 1861–1862. According to his memorial to Congress this craft, 100 feet long, 20 feet beam, and 7 feet depth of hold, was turned end for end in 75 seconds by the reversing of one of her two screw propellers. In fifteen minutes she took in sufficient water ballast to sink her 2 feet 10½ inches, and pumped the water out in eight minutes. She joined the North Atlantic blockading squadron in Hampton Roads in April, and took part in all the naval operations there until her one 100-pounder Parrott rifled gun burst in the attack on Drewry's Bluff, May 15, 1862.[2]

cember 28, 1861, March 21, 1862; N.D., *Miscellaneous Letters*, E. A. Stevens to Welles, October 17, and to G. V. Fox, December 2, 1861. Peter Cooper wrote to President Lincoln on September 4, 1861, urging the completion of the vessel. *Ibid.* The *Scientific American* endorsed the project in a long, illustrated article on August 31, 1861, pointing out that the Stevens brothers had proposed inclined sides long before Coles, "the reputed father of the scheme," had patented his invention. "But the Stevens plan omits the objectionable feature of Capt. Coles's plan — the revolving houses covering the guns, and thus adding to the height, weight and steepness of the sides."

The most interesting modern verdict on the Stevens project is that of Professor William Hovgaard, in his *Modern History of Warships* (London, 1920), p. 6.

[1] *The Stevens Battery, Memorial to Congress, Merits of the Battery as Unanimously Admitted by the Board of Examiners, Opinions of Experts and Results of Experiments Disproving the Objections of the Majority* ([n.p., 1862] 71 pp.). Cf. *Scientific American*, January 18, 1862, pp. 41, 42, 43.

[2] She later served in North Carolina waters. O.R.N., vii, using index, *s.v. Naugatuck*; O.R.N., 2d series, i, p. 215. See also Stevens Letter Book, E. A. Stevens to S. P. Chase, July 16, October 10, 1861. E. A. Stevens wrote to Chase, June 2, 1862, that "such of her principles as have been tested have proved entirely successful — On her recent passage up the James River, and in the attack on Fort Darling her ability to submerge the whole hull under the water not only prevented her being struck by a single shot, but enabled her to pilot the other vessels of the fleet up the river, as she pumped out her water apartments and in that way got afloat whenever she ran aground. The plan of placing the gun 'en barbette' and the crew below the water line prevented a large loss of life which otherwise must have followed the bursting of her gun. — The two independent propellers have given the most positive evidence of their usefulness in enabling her to turn quickly in narrow channels." (*Ibid.*) Cf. N.D., *Executive Letters*, W. L. Hodge to Welles,

After the battle of the *Monitor* and *Merrimack*, Stevens's hopes of completing his ironclad rose high. The naval appropriation act of April 17, 1862, included $783,294 for the completion of the vessel, with a proviso, however, "that said money shall not be expended unless the Secretary of the Navy is of opinion that the same will secure to the public service an efficient steam battery." A second board, composed of Captain Charles H. Davis of the Navy, Colonel Richard Delafield of the Army, Naval Constructor Pook, Samuel V. Merrick of Philadelphia, and Moses Taylor of New York, reported in May against the completion of the vessel on Stevens's plans, but stated that she might be made satisfactory by means of "modifications rendered necessary by recent important changes in the art of war." Deeming this report "vague and inconclusive," Welles declined to proceed without authorization by Congress, and the joint resolution approved July 17, 1862, relinquished all interest of the United States in the vessel to the heirs of Robert L. Stevens.[1]

Stevens made several unsuccessful attempts to sell his ironclad to the Federal government on condition that she be finished on his "general plan," but he refused to consent to have "Mr. Timby's towers, commonly known as Ericsson's towers, put on her."[2] In December, 1863, he wrote to Charles B. Sedgwick, chairman of the House Committee on Naval Affairs, that Assistant Secretary Fox "approved of the Model and many of the principles (particularly the sinking property) of the Battery and wished she could be added

September 28, 1861, with Welles's reply, October 1, in N.D., *Executive Letter Book* no. 14.

Models of the Stevens battery and of the *Naugatuck* are preserved at the Stevens Institute of Technology. For a side-elevation of the latter, see Furman, *op. cit.*, p. 127. Cf. Turnbull, *John Stevens*, pp. 428–431; and *Scientific American*, March 29, 1862, p. 202.

[1] N.D., AD, Welles to Captain Charles H. Davis, May 5, 7, 1862; Stevens Letter Book, pp. 199–202; Senate Executive Document No. 34 and House Executive Document No. 121, 37th Congress, 2d Session; *Statutes at Large*, xii, pp. 380, 628. In Turnbull's *John Stevens*, pp. 425–427, the two examining boards are treated as one.

[2] Stevens Letter Book, E. A. Stevens to Joseph P. Bradley, March 1, 1863. As to Timby, see above, pp. 182–183.

to the Navy..."[1] Stevens was never able, however, to come to terms with Welles. On his death in 1868 he bequeathed her to the State of New Jersey, which was permitted by a special act of Congress to accept the gift,[2] together with one million dollars for her completion. Although this money was spent in 1869 and 1870, under the supervision of General George B. McClellan, the Stevens battery was never launched, and was finally broken up in 1881 and sold as junk.[3]

Although the Navy Department confined its appropriations for armored vessels in the fifties to the Stevens battery, other proposals were not lacking. In 1852 Lieutenant John A. Dahlgren, then engaged in transforming the armament of American ships of war, proposed several methods of armor protection, by using "an iron ribbing *externally*, with such stowage of coal *within* as the ship permits; using also an interior arrangement of thin plates calculated to give a harmless direction to projectiles, that is, from vital parts...." But, as he pointed out when renewing his proposals in December, 1860,

the means that I requested to complete the data necessary for the design of the armature not being furnished, and no notice being taken of any suggestions, the opportunity was lost to this country of initiating one of the most important inventions that has occurred in naval affairs, the idea of which was suggested by Paixhans in 1825....[4]

The writings of Major John Gross Barnard of the Engineer Corps reflect the change of expert opinion in Great Britain

---

[1] Stevens Letter Book, December 14, 1863.
[2] Joint Resolution approved July 1, 1870. *Statutes at Large*, xvi, p. 383.
[3] N.D., AC, "Stevens War Steamer," Report of John A. Bolles, Naval Solicitor, May 2, 1877; New Jersey, Commissioners on the Plan of the Stevens Battery, *Report of the Commissioners on the Plan of the Stevens Battery ... with a Report of the Engineer in Charge* [George B. McClellan] (Trenton, 1870); (New Jersey, Commission Appointed to Effect the Sale of the Stevens Steam Battery), *The Stevens Iron-clad Battery* (New York, 1874). Among the numerous pay rolls, account books, check books and vouchers for the construction of the battery which are preserved at the Stevens Institute of Technology is an officer's pay roll showing that General McClellan's salary in 1869 and 1870 was $1000 a month. Cf. Furman, *op. cit.*, pp. 131–135.
[4] Executive Document No. 25, 36th Congress, 2d Session; M. V. Dahlgren, *Memoir of John A. Dahlgren*, pp. 246–248.

and the United States. In 1859 he regarded the experience of Kinburn as inconclusive. Two years later, discussing the recent British armor tests, he declared that "the probability that ships-of-war will soon be mostly clad in plates of iron, invulnerable to solid shot," called for the introduction of guns of "extraordinary calibre" for coast defence. To smash through inclined armor would require even heavier projectiles.

> Certain it is that the successful introduction of iron-clad vessels by one nation will *compel* their adoption by others who would not be driven from the ocean.

Barnard deemed Coles's cupolas "probably worth trial," and thought that, if not found successful, they might lead to "something of the kind which *will* be." A 14-gun ship on Coles's system seemed to him "far more formidable . . . than . . . a 100-gun three-decker."[1]

When the London *Times* of January 11, 1861, expressed surprise at the failure of the United States to notice "the one question which has absorbed for months past the thoughts of the maritime Powers of Europe . . . *the invention of iron-cased ships*," the Philadelphia *Press* observed:

> It is a curious fact that the United States . . . should be charged with being behind the age. Yet there is a good prima facie case. . . .
> It is more than probable that, and without much further delay, if we intend to have a national and naval force worthy of our power and pretensions, we shall have to follow suit, and build iron-cased vessels, as France and England have done, and are doing. Before the end of this year, France will have *eight* and England *six* such vessels. How many are *we* to have? . . .[2]

Despite its absorption in fateful domestic issues, Congress did not overlook entirely the revolution in naval architecture. On January 19, 1861, the Senate, at the suggestion of Grimes of Iowa, requested the Navy Department to furnish a "detailed estimate of the expense of building and equipping a steel or iron cased gun-boat of the capacity and armament

---

[1] *The Dangers and Defences of New York* (New York, 1859), pp. 30, 54–55; *Notes on Sea-coast Defence* (New York, 1861), pp. 28, 48, 52–55.
[2] Reprinted in the *U. S. Naval Gazette*, March 23, 1861.

of the ... *Iroquois*."[1] John Lenthall, Chief of the Bureau of Construction, to whom Secretary Toucey entrusted the report, stated that the *Iroquois* measured 1016 tons and carried six guns and two howitzers.

> The least thickness of iron plating that should be put on, is thought to be 3 inches and from the weight of this plating, the additional strength that must be given to the hull in order to sustain it, and from the elevated position of the weights, a larger vessel than the 'Iroquois,' will be required to carry the same equipment and armament.

Basing his estimate on the *Iroquois*, Lenthall figured that a single-deck vessel drawing 15 feet and plated with 3 inches of iron would measure 1500 tons and cost $558,000.[2]

Though the Naval Appropriation Act of February 21, 1861, included the sum of $1,200,000 for seven wooden screw sloops, whose draft should not exceed fourteen feet, Congress voted no money for ironclads at this session.[3] South Carolina, however, lost no time in testing armor ashore and afloat. Early in 1861 the Secessionists erected at Cummings Point on Morris Island a formidable battery, constructed of heavy timber inclined at an angle of 40 degrees, and faced with bars of railroad iron.[4] At the same time Captain John Randolph Hamilton, formerly of the United States Navy, constructed a crude floating battery, with a sloping side facing the enemy

---

[1] *Congressional Globe*, 36th Congress, 1st Session, col. 463. Cf. *ibid.*, col. 846.
[2] N.D., *Bureau Letters*, February 4, 1861.
[3] *Statutes at Large*, xii, p. 151.
   In the debate on this measure Representative Freeman H. Morse of Maine, Chairman of the House Committee on Naval Affairs, urged the construction of three new ships every year, some of them to be ironclads. He declared that in less than two years France and England would have "their entire navies clad in iron armor;" and that a single armored frigate could sink the entire American fleet. *Congressional Globe*, February 20, 1861.
[4] The Charleston *Year Book* for 1883 at page 549 states that Colonel C. H. Stevens, Twenty-fourth South Carolina Volunteers, began the erection of this battery, as a private citizen. Cf. Alfred Roman, *The Military Operations of General Beauregard* (New York, 1884, 2 vols.), i, p. 37, where it is stated that the inclined surface was "to be properly greased when ready for action." Sketches of this battery may be found in O.R., 1st series, i, p. 165, and in the accompanying atlas, plates 1 and 2. Major P. F. Stevens, Superintendent of the Citadel Academy, Charleston, commanded this battery in April, 1861.
   Captain J. G. Foster, the engineer officer in Fort Sumter, reported on February 5 that "the idea of covering the bomb-proof with iron and giving it an inclination is no doubt derived from the Sardinian method for forming the sides of a man-of-war, so as to deflect the shot." *Ibid.*, p. 165. See above, pp. 90-91.

similarly protected by railroad iron. General Abner Doubleday, a captain in Fort Sumter in 1861, stated in 1876 that "the State Militia had a great prejudice against it, and could not be induced to man it. They christened it 'The Slaughter Pen,' and felt certain it would go to the bottom the moment we opened fire upon it."[1] At all events, on the night of April 10, the battery was towed to the west end of Sullivan's Island, and beached behind a stone breakwater, which protected its water line from ricochet shots.[2] Major Anderson thought it was "admirably placed for pouring a murderous fire upon any vessel attempting to lay alongside our left flank, and also well situated for enfilading the flanks of this work."[3] In the attack on Fort Sumter, the two 42- and two 32-pounders mounted on this stranded raft, under the command of Lieutenant Joseph A. Yates, threw 470 shot, enfilading the fort at about 2100 yards with some effect. This battery was repeatedly hit, "resisting all the shot (32-pounders) which had struck it, with the exception of one, which had passed through the narrow angular slope just below the roof."[4] Against the ironclad land battery on Cummings Point, whose three 8-inch Columbiads did considerable damage to Fort Sumter, the Union fire did no more than to put one port shutter out of commission. The shot generally rattled off the sloping iron sides "like peas upon a trencher." Sloping ar-

---

[1] *Reminiscences of Forts Sumter and Moultrie in 1860–'61* (New York, 1876), p. 128. A photograph of this floating battery is reproduced on page 239 of the volume which Major James Barnes contributed to the *Photographic History of the Civil War* (New York, 1912, 10 vols.), vi. Years after the war, Colonel Joseph A. Yates stated that "the battery was substantially built, flat, heavily timbered on her shield, with railroad iron laid on it — two courses of rails turned inward and outward, so as to form a pretty smooth surface. The bags of sand represented on the deck were to counterweight the guns, which were 32- and 42-pounders. She was struck many times, several shot going entirely through the shield." *Battles and Leaders of the Civil War*, i, p. 66, with a picture of the battery based on a sketch by Yates.

[2] Journal of Captain J. G. Foster, April 11, 1861, in O.R., 1st series, i, p. 17. Foster reported to General Totten, on March 6, that the armor being placed on the raft was "railroad *strap-iron* instead of the T rail. This has a cross-section of about three-fourths or one inch by two inches or two and a half inches." *Ibid.*, p. 191.

[3] Anderson to Thomas, April 11, 1861. *Ibid.*, p. 250.

[4] Foster's journal, April 12, in *ibid.*, p. 19; reports of Lieut. Col. R. S. Ripley, April 16, and of Miles and Manning, April 15, *ibid.*, pp. 43, 63.

mor, so often advocated in the previous half century, had proved its value for the first time on American soil. Inclined sides became the characteristic feature of Confederate ironclads.[1]

Stephen Russell Mallory, Secretary of the Navy of the Confederate States of America, still remains something of an enigma. Born on the Island of Trinidad in 1813, the son of a civil engineer from Reading, Connecticut, and of an Irish mother, he grew to manhood at Key West, an orphan with little schooling. There he served as inspector and collector of customs, and achieved distinction as a lawyer. He fought as a volunteer in the Seminole War, and represented Florida in the United States Senate from 1851 to 1861, serving as Chairman of the Committee on Naval Affairs.[2]

As Secretary of the Confederate Navy, he became highly unpopular. The vitriolic Edward A. Pollard declared that Mallory, prior to 1861, had been "the butt of every naval officer in the country." Pollard harped on the "notorious inefficiency" of the Confederate Navy Department, describing the Secretary as "remarkable for his obtuseness, slow method, and indifferent intellect," and ignorant "even of the geography of Kentucky and Tennessee."[3] Despite all the bitter criticisms of Mallory's administration, however, Scharf's verdict on the Confederate Secretary seems far nearer the truth:

---

[1] Doubleday, *Reminiscences*, p. 151; Roman, *Beauregard*, p. 37; O. R., 1st series, i, pp. 39–49, 54–56, 165, 316. Cf. J. Thomas Scharf, *History of the Confederate States Navy* (2d ed., Albany, N. Y., 1894), pp. 657–658; Samuel Wylie Crawford, *The Genesis of the Civil War, The Story of Sumter* (New York, 1887), pp. 210, 292, 301, 399, 429–430; Edward A. Pollard, *The First Year of the War* (New York, 1863), pp. 51, 54; Captain O. L. Spalding, "The Bombardment of Fort Sumter, 1861," in American Historical Association *Report*, 1913, i, pp. 187–188, 202.
  W. S. Lindsay commented on the Charleston ironclad battery in the House of Commons, May 23, 1861. Hansard, 3rd series, clxiii, col. 25. As he pointed out, iron was also used to strengthen the defences of Fort Sumter. O. R., 1st series, i, pp. 179–180, 184, 216, 293. See also Commander W. M. Walker to Commodore Paulding, April 15, 1861, in N.D., *Commanders Letters*.

[2] Scharf, *op. cit.*, p. 29, note.

[3] *The First Year of the War* (New York, 1863), pp. 236–237, 267. Cf. Pollard's *Life of Jefferson Davis* (Philadelphia, 1869), p. 224, note; and John B. Jones, *A Rebel War Clerk's Diary* (Philadelphia, 1866, 2 vols.), i, pp. 43, 354; ii, pp. 6, 15.

He was a gentleman of excellent sense, unpretending manners, and probably conducted his department as successfully as was possible with the limited naval resources of the South.... He could not command success, but he deserved it by faithful and diligent labor, and by intelligent and discreet effort.[1]

In view of the progress that had already been made in ironclad construction in Europe, Mallory cannot rank as a great innovator in naval architecture. He stated in 1865 that he had "never entertained a doubt" that armored ships were suitable only for harbor and coast defence.[2] Within these limits, however, he clearly perceived the importance of ironclads to the South.

In his report of April 26, 1861, Mallory proposed "to adopt a class of vessels hitherto unknown to naval services," that is, wooden ships suitable for commerce destroying,

built exclusively for ocean speed, at a low cost, with a battery of one or two accurate guns of long range, with an ability to keep the sea upon a long cruise and to engage or to avoid an enemy at will....[3]

Two weeks later he submitted a strong plea for armored vessels. Reviewing the experiments of Robert L. Stevens, and the introduction of ironclads in France and England, he declared that he regarded

the possession of an iron-armored ship as a matter of the first necessity. Such a vessel at this time could traverse the entire coast of the United States, prevent all blockades, and encounter, with a fair prospect of success, their entire Navy.

If to cope with them upon the sea we follow their example and build wooden ships, we shall have to construct several at one time; for one or two ships would fall an easy prey to her comparatively numerous steam frigates. But inequality of numbers may be compensated by invulnerability; and thus not only does economy but naval success dictate the wisdom and expediency of fighting with iron against wood, without regard to first cost.

Naval engagements between wooden frigates, as they are now built and armed, will prove to be the forlorn hopes of the sea, simply contests in which the question, not of victory, but of who shall go to the bottom first, is to be solved....[4]

[1] Scharf, *op. cit.*, p. 30, and note; cf. E. Channing, *History of the United States*, vi, p. 498.
[2] Mallory to A. G. Brown, Chairman of the Committee on Naval Affairs of the Confederate States Senate, February 18, 1865. N.D., VN, Class 2.
[3] O.R.N., 2d series, ii, p. 51.
[4] O.R.N., 2d series, i, pp. 740-743, Mallory to C. M. Conrad, Chairman of the

As the Confederate Congress promptly appropriated two million dollars for the purchase or construction in France or England of "one or two war steamers of the most modern and improved description,"[1] Mallory despatched Lieutenant James H. North on this mission. Observing that the *Gloire* "is regarded as the most formidable ship afloat," Mallory naïvely proposed to buy her, or one of her sister ships.

> The views and disposition of the French Government are understood to be favorable to our cause, the recognition of our independence at an early day is expected, and it is thought that arrangements might be made with it for the transfer to our Government either directly or through some friendly intermediary of one of the armored frigates of the class of the *Gloire*.

If the French government declined this proposal, North was to seek permission for the construction of one ironclad in France and one in Great Britain. If they were designed to carry only six or eight heavy guns, such as the breech-loading Armstrong rifles, Mallory thought the appropriation of two millions would suffice. North should consult Captain Cowper Coles, and other recognized authorities, and examine the *Warrior*.

> We want a ship which can not be sunk or penetrated by the shell or shot of the U. S. Navy at a distance at which we could penetrate and sink the ships of the enemy, and which can not be readily carried by boarders.[2]

Mallory promptly despatched Captain Duncan N. Ingraham on the difficult quest of wrought-iron plates two to three inches in thickness,[3] and on June 10 directed Lieutenant John M. Brooke " to aid the department in designing an ironclad war vessel, and framing the necessary specifications."[4] As to just what followed, there is a sharp conflict of testi-

---

Committee on Naval Affairs, C. S. House of Representatives, May 8, 1861. This letter is also printed in *ibid*., ii, pp. 67–69, with date of May 10, 1861. Cf. *ibid*., i, p. 793. The numerous errors in detail concerning the French and British navies do not weaken the force of Mallory's argument.

1 Act of May 10, 1861, printed in O.R.N., 2d series, ii, p. 66.
2 *Ibid*., pp. 70–72, Mallory to North, May 17, 1861.
3 *Ibid*., p. 72, Mallory to Ingraham, May 20, 1861. Cf. *ibid*., i, pp. 791–792.
4 *Ibid*., ii, p. 174, Mallory's report of March 29, 1862.

mony, for Brooke, a distinguished officer in the old navy, whose invention of a deep-sea sounding apparatus had been adopted by the United States government; E. C. Murray, who built the Confederate ironclad *Louisiana*; and Naval Constructor John L. Porter, all claimed the design of the *Merrimack* or *Virginia* as their own.[1]

John L. Porter had been employed by the United States Navy Department, at the request of Lieutenant William W. Hunter, in the construction of the unsuccessful iron steamers *Water Witch* and *Alleghany*. In his article dated October, 1887, in *Battles and Leaders of the Civil War*,[2] he stated that in April, 1846, while superintending the construction of the latter ship at Pittsburgh, he "conceived the idea of an iron-clad, and made a model with the exact shield which I placed on the *Merrimac*." According to his son's statement in 1892, this plan of 1846 contemplated an iron vessel of nineteen feet draft and forty feet beam, whose sides sloped inward at an angle of 45 degrees from the knuckle, which was two feet below the water line. Three inches of inclined armor covering "all of the vessel above the water line and to a depth of four feet below it," the designer deemed sufficient to withstand the heaviest ordnance of that day. "The ends beyond the shield

---

[1] Porter's case is set forth briefly in his article in *Battles and Leaders of the Civil War*, i, pp. 716–717, and at length in *A Record of events in Norfolk County, from April 19th, 1861, to May 10th, 1862* (Portsmouth, Va., 1892), ch. xlvii, by his son, John W. H. Porter. Brooke contributed a brief statement to *Battles and Leaders of the Civil War*, i, pp. 716–717 (1887); and published a reply to Porter in the Southern Historical Society *Papers*, xix, pp. 3–34 (January, 1891). For the testimony of Brooke and Murray before a joint special committee of the Confederate Congress to investigate the affairs of the Navy Department, see O.R.N., 2d series, i, pp. 757, 783–788. Murray testified that he "went to Montgomery and submitted a plan of a vessel to the department last April 12 months [1861]. I furnished the plans of the *Merrimack*, though, by some jeremy diddling, it is attributed to Lieutenant Brooke."

As to the merits of Brooke's deep-sea sounding apparatus, see the letter of Captain D. N. Ingraham, Chief of the Bureau of Ordnance and Hydrography, to Secretary J. C. Dobbin, January 17, 1857. N.D., *Bureau Letters*.

For the tradition in the Wise family that Governor Henry A. Wise played some part in the designing of the *Virginia*, see Henry A. Wise, *Seven Decades of the Union* (Philadelphia, 1876), pp. 279–282; John S. Wise, *The End of an Era* (Boston and New York, 1899), pp. 191, 193; and B. H. Wise, *Life of Henry A. Wise* (New York, 1899), p. 317.

[2] Vol. i, p. 717.

were constructed upon the same incline (as to their sides) as the shield, and the deck forward and aft of the shield was protected with armor plate." As wrought-iron port shutters were also provided, "the resisting surface was to have been entirely of iron." On examining those plans, Lieutenant Hunter suggested the adoption of an iron protective deck, to be built below the gun deck, for added protection against plunging fire. Porter added this feature to his drawings, and despatched them to the Navy Department, which "took no further notice of them than to acknowledge their receipt, but Mr. Porter transferred them to his book of naval designs which he retained and still has in his possession." [1]

A careful search in the archives of the Navy Department and of the Bureau of Construction and Repair has failed to reveal these plans, or any reference to them in the correspondence of Hunter and Porter with either the Department or the Bureau. In the autumn of 1847 Porter presented himself at Washington for examination for an appointment as naval constructor, but failed to pass.[2] He obtained the appointment later, and superintended the building of the *Powhatan*, *Constellation*, *Colorado*, *Seminole*, *Pensacola*, and other vessels, before his resignation from the service on May 1, 1861.[3]

It is perfectly clear, at all events, that the idea of an ironclad with inclined armor was already an old one in 1846. D'Arçon's batteries of 1782 and the *Fulton the Second* had had sloping sides of heavy timbers. Inclined iron armor had been proposed by Ochoa in Spain in 1727, by Congreve in England in 1805, and in the United States by Gregg and by Brown,

---

[1] John W. H. Porter, *op. cit.*, pp. 327–328.
[2] N.D., *General Letter Book* nos. 38 and 39, J. Y. Mason to John L. Porter, September 13 and October 6, 1847.
[3] John W. H. Porter, *op. cit.*, p. 329. Charges of "gross neglect of duty" in constructing the *Seminole*, which were preferred against Porter in 1860, were not sustained. N.D., Miscellaneous Mss., "Papers concerning the charges of Lieut. William P. A. Campbell vs. John L. Porter, 1860"; *General Letter Book* no. 63, Toucey to Porter, October 3, 1860. Porter's letter of resignation, dated Portsmouth, Va., May 1, 1861, is endorsed "Dismissed 15 May 1861," in accord with Welles's policy of refusing to accept the resignations of officers believed to intend to join the Confederate forces. *Resignations and Dismissals*, 1861, no. 109.

during the War of 1812, by the Stevens brothers in 1841, by Warren in 1845, and by Patton in 1846. Congress had several times considered Brown's project, had described it in public documents, and in 1846 had appropriated $10,000 in order that it might be tested. The numerous projects for inclined armor in England, France, and Italy in the fifties, which provoked wide discussion, attest the popularity of the idea on the eve of the American Civil War. The sloping iron batteries built at Charleston in 1861 were no novelties. Nor need we be surprised at Secretary Mallory's statement that, in June of that year, Constructor Porter and Lieutenant Brooke "adopted for their casement a thickness of wood and iron and an angle of inclination nearly identical."[1]

Constructor Porter and his son have strenuously maintained that Mallory's memory played him false when, in his report of March 29, 1862, he awarded to Brooke the credit of the original design of the *Merrimack* or *Virginia*. For the really novel feature of her construction, the extension of the bow and stern beyond the shield under water, Brooke obtained a Confederate patent on July 29, 1862. Porter did not claim the *extended* submerged ends as part of his proposals. His son explains that Brooke's patent "was not contested by the builder of the *Merrimack*, because no one would have thought of building such a vessel with submerged ends except as a matter of necessity, for it left the crew no space to exercise."[2]

When the Federal forces evacuated the Norfolk Navy Yard on the night of April 20, 1861, the steam frigate *Merrimack* "was sunk and burned to her copper line and down through to her berth deck, which, with her spar and gun decks, were also burned."[3] On May 30 she was raised and

---

[1] Report of March 29, 1862, in O.R.N., 2d series, ii, p. 174. For the earlier history of inclined armor see above pp. 7, 9, 28, 31, 48, 52, 53, 61–62, 87, 89, 91, 106, 162–164, 207, note 4, 215, 219.

[2] John W. H. Porter, *op. cit.*, pp. 343, 357; Brooke, "The Virginia, or Merrimac: her Real Projector," in Southern Historical Society *Papers*, xix, pp. 8–30. Brooke testified in February, 1863, that "the object of having these parts of the vessel submerged was to gain speed and to have buoyancy without exposing the hull, and to avoid increasing the draft of water." O.R.N., 2d series, i, p. 784.

[3] Commissioner Wm. H. Peters to Governor John Letcher, Navy Yard, Gosport,

placed in the dry dock.¹ Chief Engineer William P. Williamson, Brooke and Porter reported to Mallory on June 25 that in obedience to his order they had carefully examined "the various plans and propositions for constructing a shot-proof steam battery." It was their opinion that the *Merrimack*, which was so damaged by fire as to be useless for any other purpose without very heavy expense for rebuilding,

> can be made an efficient vessel of that character mounting [ten] heavy guns [two pivot and eight side guns of her original battery], and from the further consideration that we can not procure a suitable engine and boilers for any other vessel without building them, which would occupy too much time. It would appear that this is our only chance to get a suitable vessel in a short time. The bottom of the hull, boilers, and heavy and costly parts of the engine being but little injured reduces the cost of construction to about one-third of the amount which would be required to construct such a vessel anew.

They estimated the cost of the transformation at roughly

> about [one hundred and ten thousand dollars], the most of which will be for labor, the materials being nearly all in the navy yard, except the iron plating to cover the shield.
> The plan to be adopted in the arrangement of the shield for glancing shot, mounting guns, arranging the hull, etc., and plating to be in accordance with the plan submitted for approval of the department. . . .²

Mallory promptly directed Porter to make a plan for the new *Merrimack* ³ soon to be renamed the *Virginia*. According to Porter's story, the Secretary approved this plan on July 11, giving him the following order addressed to the commandant of the Norfolk Navy Yard:

Va., October 19, 1861, O.R.N., 2d series, ii, p. 110. For the earlier history of this ship, see Charles H. Davis, "History of U. S. Steamer *Merrimack*," *New England Historical and Genealogical Register*, xxviii, pp. 245–248 (1874).

1 O.R.N., v, pp. 801, 804. Captain S. Barron reported to Governor Letcher on June 10 that the value of the *Merrimack*, in her partially burned condition, was not less than $250,000. *Ibid.*, p. 806.

2 O.R.N., 2d series, ii, pp. 174–175. The omissions in that text are supplied above in brackets from the text given in John L. Porter's letter of March 29, 1862, to the Richmond *Examiner*, reprinted in Southern Historical Society *Papers*, xix, pp. 11–12. Mallory's report of July 18, 1861, which stated that "the cost of this work is estimated by the constructor and engineer in charge at $172,523," was probably based on a revised estimate submitted after further examination. O.R.N., 2d series, ii, p. 78.

3 Cf. Brooke's testimony in O.R.N., 2d series, i, p. 784; and Porter's in Southern Historical Society *Papers*, xix, p. 12.

You will proceed with all practicable dispatch to make the changes in the form of the *Merrimac*, and to build, equip and fit her in all respects according to the design and plans of the constructor and engineer, Messrs. Porter and Williamson. . . .[1]

Porter at once assumed all the duties of constructor, and "originated all the interior arrangements;" Williamson overhauled and improved the engines; and Brooke supervised the manufacture of the armor plates at the Tredegar Works in Richmond, tested inclined targets, determining "interesting and important facts... of great importance in the construction of the ship," and designed hooped rifled guns for her armament.[2]

Although the Confederate authorities knew of the English experiments on inclined armor, they "were without accurate data . . . and were compelled to determine the inclination of the plates and their thickness by actual experiment."[3] Experiments conducted by Lieutenants Brooke and Catesby Jones at Jamestown Island showed that the 3-inch armor first proposed for the *Virginia's* shield was inadequate. When a target formed of wood about 24 inches thick, faced with three layers of one-inch plates, inclined at an angle of about 30 degrees with the horizon, was tested at about 300 yards range, 8-inch solid shot "penetrated the iron and entered 5 inches into the wood." A new target covered with two layers of 2-inch plates proved more satisfactory, and led to the adoption of that thickness of armor. Eight-inch shot and 9-inch shell shattered the outer plates and cracked the inner ones, "but the wood was not visible through the cracks in the plating."[4]

---

[1] John L. Porter to the Editor of the Richmond *Examiner*, March 29, 1862, published April 3, and reprinted in Southern Historical Society *Papers*, xix, p. 12. Mallory's letter of July 11, 1862 [1861] is not printed in the O.R.N.

[2] Mallory's report of March 29, 1862, O.R.N., 2d series, ii, p. 175. His statement that Brooke's banded rifled guns were "of a class never before made," is extraordinary, in view of the widespread use of guns of this type in Europe. They were, for example, the standard gun of the French Navy in 1861. See above, pp. 14, 208–209, and also N.D., BG, "Heavy rifled guns, Development by Lieut. John M. Brooke, C.S.N.;" and Holley, *Ordnance and Armor*, p. 76. Cf. Kathleen Bruce, *Virginia Iron Manufacture in the Slave Era* (New York and London, 1931), pp. 354–355.

[3] Mallory's report of March 29, 1862. O.R.N., 2d series, ii, pp. 175–176.

[4] Brooke's testimony, February 26, 1863. *Ibid.*, i, pp. 785–786. Mallory's report of July 18, 1861, stated the original intention to "shield her completely with 3-inch

When the Confederate blockade runner *Fingal* ran into Savannah in November, 1861, the Union vessels bottled her up so tight that she never ventured forth again until, converted into the ironclad ram *Atlanta*, she fell a victim to the *Weehawken*. In the meanwhile, some Englishmen in her crew made their way to Norfolk and sought to pass through the Union lines in order to reach a northern port and find passage home. General Wool and Secretary Seward, however, decided that if these men had been so eager to visit the Confederacy that they ran the blockade, they might as well stay there. Nothing daunted by this refusal, eight men from the *Fingal* and from the British steamer *Camilla* rowed through the Union blockading fleet in Hampton Roads, one dark night in April, and boarded the British sloop of war *Rinaldo*. Here the engineer of the *Fingal*, J. Anderson, told Captain Hewett of the *Rinaldo* so interesting a story of the Confederate ironclad, which he had recently visited at Norfolk, that he was given a free passage to England, on condition that he tell the Lords of the Admiralty what he had seen. The written description of the *Virginia* which he gave to Hewett is as follows.[1]

> Of course you are aware that her guns are on the original berth deck — which she was burnt down to, by the Federals when they evacuated Norfolk.
> You ascend the roof by means of a rope ladder, and at once see the difficulty there would be in boarding her, the roof laying over at such an angle. On the top of the roof there is a kind of platform or grating, on which you can travel to either end, and which is formed in such a manner so as to give ventilation below, and at the same time shot proof.

---

iron, placed at such angles as to render her ball proof." *Ibid.*, ii, p. 78. On October 29, 1861, Nelson and Asa Tift acknowledged receipt of a "report of the experiment made by Captain Jones, commanding at Jamestown, with 8-inch shot and 9-inch shell, on a target 527 yards distant, covered with railroad iron (T), double and locked by reversal. Captain Jones is doubtless right in his conclusions; first, that flat iron, in three layers, 1 × 8 inches, is better than railroad iron for covering batteries; second, that the railroad iron was not sufficiently fastened, and we think the experiment was not a satisfactory test for this reason...." *Ibid.*, i, p. 578.

[1] P.R.O. Admiralty 12/717: 52–25; Admiralty 1/5787: P. 492, Commander Hewett to Sir A. Milne, May 10, 1862. The eight men escaped from Norfolk on the night of April 26–27. Anderson had "been all through the 'Virginia' when in dock, and since her appearance on the 11th ult." [April 11].

On the gun deck, which had to be lighted by means of lanterns, the guns were not placed opposite one another as the space becomes contracted by the sloping of the roof, and when run in, they are amidships; if they were opposite, loading would be a matter of great difficulty. There are 4 heavy smooth bore guns on each side, and one very heavy rifled gun in the bow, and another in the stern of the same description, for these two pivot guns there are 6 ports, 3 at each end, the whole of the pivot and broadside ports can be closed in action, by means of shields, made of 3 inch iron, they are on the outside and are worked from within by means of small chains.

The funnel casing took up a good deal of valuable room. Over the heavy woodwork of the casemate were lengths of iron 2 inches thick, and about 7 inches broad — placed fore and aft, and over that, is placed another layer of the same size, but laid cross to the other, — making the resisting surface 4 inches of iron, — which is held together by counter-sunk bolts — shewing a very smooth surface. Below the roof and against the ship's side, (under the water line), there is but one layer of iron running fore and aft, and about 4 feet deep, — except where the boilers and engines are — which place is protected by iron knees 2 inches thick, being bitted above, and greatly strengthening that part.

Her stem was strapped with 2-inch iron, "building together the stem-head," over which was fixed the ram, of malleable iron, "standing out from the stem about 20 inches, and about the same in depth, 6 inches broad, and square at the point." Her original cast-iron ram had broken off and remained in the side of the *Cumberland*.

Her submerged after part was admitted to be her weakest part, for if she were struck there by a ram it was believed that her stern post or screw would be disabled, rendering her unmanageable. Her roof, or casemate, had resisted well, receiving very small damage from ricochet shot. Direct hits, however, had a much better effect, starting the bolts, and bursting the segments, piercing through the outside layer of iron — then making an indentment on the inside layer which arrested its course, there were 7 or 8 such like shots. One advantage is apparent in having a covering so built in segments, for when one is damaged, it can easily be replaced by another. The pilot house is placed forward, on the top part of the roof, covered over with a conical shield, which was struck — but made little impression. The quality of the iron used is indifferent, partly owing to the hurried way it was manufactured, great difficulty was experienced in collecting the requisite quantity,

C. S. S. *VIRGINIA*

From the original sketch in Adm. 1/5819: P. 184.

— many objections to her build were formed, it was thought she would sink too low in the water &c, but it proved otherwise as an immense quantity of ballast had to be taken on board. . . .

While fifteen hundred workmen hastened to complete this most famous of Confederate ironclads,[1] various other Southerners strove to create armored or partially armored vessels for the defence of the western rivers. Some of these were river steamers strengthened for use as rams, with light plating protecting the bows or the boilers and engines. The most interesting Southern "tinclad" was the ram *Manassas*, the work of John A. Stevenson, a steamboat captain and commission merchant of New Orleans. After failing to interest Mallory in a project for an ironclad ram in the early days of the war, Stevenson took the tugboat *Enoch Train*, which had been built in Boston in 1855, strengthened her bow, and gave her a turtle-back deck covered with thin iron plates. For his attack on the Union vessels *Richmond*, *Vincennes*, *Preble*, and *Water Witch* at the head of the Passes in the early morning of October 12, 1861, Commodore Hollins requisitioned the ram, and placed Lieutenant A. F. Warley in command. The *Manassas*, appearing out of the darkness "somewhat like a huge whale," struck the *Richmond* and stove in three planks about two feet below the water line, making a hole about five inches in circumference, but doing no very serious damage. Though the shock cost the *Manassas* her smokestacks, and put one engine temporarily out of commission, she managed to crawl upstream, while her consorts chased the Union vessels down to the mouth of the Mississippi.[2] When Farragut's

---

[1] Mallory's report of February 27, 1862, in O.R.N., 2d series, ii, p. 152.
[2] For the construction of the *Manassas* see O.R.N., 2d series, i, pp. 259, 454, 472–473, 709, 722, 724–725; and C. W. Read, "Reminiscences of the Confederate States Navy," in Southern Historical Society *Papers*, i, p. 334 (May, 1876). Admiral David D. Porter's account of the action, or lack of it, at the mouth of the Mississippi, seems in part even more severe on the Union commanders than the facts warrant. *Naval History of the Civil War* (New York, 1886), pp. 89–91. Cf. O.R.N., xvi, pp. 703–730a. Mrs. Katharine V. Hart of Colorado Springs kindly permitted me to consult the diary of Lieutenant John E. Hart, who was on the *Vincennes* at this time. See also James Morris Morgan, "The Pioneer 'ironclad,'" in the *Proceedings* of the United States Naval Institute, October, 1917, pp. 2275–2282.

fleet forced its way past Forts Jackson and St. Philip, on April 24, 1862, Warley rammed the *Brooklyn* with little effect, thanks to the chains which protected her sides. The *Manassas*, riddled by shot and shell as if she had been made of paper, was set on fire and destroyed.[1]

Contracts for two far more formidable craft were awarded to John T. Shirley of Memphis, Tennessee, on August 24, 1861. Though he agreed to build them within four months, Shirley found such grave difficulties in getting iron and labor that, when the Union fleet neared Memphis, the *Arkansas* had received only part of her armor, the *Tennessee* none at all. To prevent their falling into the hands of the enemy, the latter was burned on the stocks; and the former was towed up the Yazoo. Here she was completed for her brief but glorious career under the command of Lieutenant Isaac Newton Brown.[2]

On September 16, 1861, Mallory awarded to E. C. Murray, a shipbuilder of New Orleans, the contract for the ironclad *Louisiana*, to be built by January 25, 1862, at a cost of $196,000. This vessel, which was 264 feet long and 62 feet beam, had a sloping casemate covered with railroad iron. Her flat upper deck, however, was so lightly protected that a single shell, falling perpendicularly upon it, might have sufficed to sink her.[3] When towed from New Orleans to Fort St.

---

[1] Warley testified that the *Manassas* was covered with half-inch iron. *Proceedings of the Court of Inquiry, relative to the Fall of New Orleans* (Richmond, 1864), p. 79. Captain Mitchell stated that "the iron in her was very thin, being not more than an inch and a half in thickness." O.R.N., 2d series, i, p. 454. She carried one 32-pounder carronade, firing right ahead. There is a lurid picture of her, with flames bursting from her sides, in Senate Executive Document No. 56, 37th Congress, 2d Session. See also O.R.N., xviii, pp. 182, 302, 336–345. For a drawing and a picture of her, see *ibid.*, p. 335, and facing p. 344. The latter is reproduced in O.R.N., 2d series, i, facing p. 259.

[2] O.R.N., 2d series, i, pp. 248, 268, 508, 722–723, 747, 779–783, 794–795, 798, 801. Cf. Scharf, *op. cit.*, pp. 303 ff.; C. W. Read, *op. cit.*, pp. 347 ff.; George W. Gift, "The Story of the Arkansas," Southern Historical Society *Papers*, xii, pp. 48 ff. (January, 1884).

[3] Testimony of Lieut. A. F. Warley, who joined the *Louisiana* on April 25. *Proceedings of the Court of Inquiry, relative to the Fall of New Orleans*, p. 77; O.R.N., 2d series, i, pp. 258, 434, 754–762. Pictures of the *Louisiana* may be found in Scharf, *op. cit.*, p. 266, and in Senate Executive Document No. 56, 37th Congress, 2d Session; and drawings of her, in O.R.N., xviii, pp. 287, 288.

Philip on April 20-21, her machinery was incomplete, her motive power imperfect, and her battery of 16 guns improperly mounted. Unable to leave her moorings on the 24th of April, she brought six of her guns to bear on Farragut's fleet, and withstood the Union fire without serious damage. When the forts surrendered four days later, the officers of the *Louisiana* completely destroyed her.[1]

Two natives of Mystic, Connecticut, Nelson and Asa F. Tift, who had gone south in boyhood and had become intimate friends of Stephen Mallory, built what promised to be the most formidable of Confederate ironclads. Nelson Tift of Georgia had been a merchant, an editor, president of a railroad, and a member of the Georgia State Convention. His brother Asa had been a merchant in Key West for over thirty years. At the outbreak of war, believing the chief weakness of the Confederacy lay on the water, the brothers sought to devise a new style of shipbuilding, eliminating the curved frames, crooks and knees which required the services of skilled ship carpenters. In their plan for the ironclad *Mississippi*,

all the surfaces are flat, or in straight lines, except the four corners, which connect the two ends of the ship with the sides. There is no frame. The work is made solid the required thickness. It is commenced at the bottom and completed as the work goes up. But few skilled ship carpenters are required; the greater part of the work may be done by house carpenters.[2]

In August, 1861, after a board of naval officers had approved this plan, Mallory accepted the Tifts' offer to serve without compensation as navy agents in the construction of the vessel. The difficulties they encountered in building this ship on the outskirts of New Orleans throw a flood of light on the chief obstacles in the way of a Confederate navy: the lack of iron works, of machine shops, and above all, of engine builders.[3] For their casemate, the brothers first adopted an

---

[1] O.R.N., xviii, pp. 289-304, 309-331; O.R.N., 2d series, i, pp. 441, 443, 455-457, 525. Cf., C. W. Read, *op. cit.*, pp. 341-342.
[2] O.R.N., 2d series, i, pp. 547, 549, 762.
[3] O.R.N., 2d series, i, pp. 431-809, using index *s.v. Mississippi*. Cf. *Proceedings of the Court of Inquiry, relative to the Fall of New Orleans, passim*; C. W. Read, *op.*

angle of 36 degrees with the horizon, later changed to 30 degrees. After a difficult search, they obtained rolled-iron plates from Scofield and Markham, of Atlanta.

> The method of covering with iron is with 3 plates of 1¼ inches each thick for the upper angle; two lengthwise making joints, and one up and down, covering the whole. The lower angle, one plate lengthwise and one up and down, on the sides between the angle single two plates lengthwise, on the upper deck and the level part fore and aft a single plate 1¼ inches thick, the knuckle forward of cast iron. . . .[1]

Despite the utmost efforts of her projectors, who strove in vain to overcome the delays engendered by two strikes, the *Mississippi* was unfinished on April 25. In the panic caused by Farragut's passage of the forts, enough tugs to tow her upstream could not be had, and the powerful battery, designed for twenty heavy guns, was burned by the naval officers in charge. The unfortunate Tifts, heartbroken at their failure, were nearly lynched by an infuriated crowd at Vicksburg.[2]

On January 7, 1862, the South Carolina Convention appropriated $300,000 for the ironclad ram later named the *Chicora*, which was built at Charleston by James N. Eason for $263,892. At about the same time, the Confederate ironclad *Palmetto State* was begun at Charleston under the supervision of Flag-officer Duncan N. Ingraham.[3] Mallory promptly ordered the construction of two more ironclad gunboats at New Orleans, to be fitted as rams and to mount four guns each.[4] As a crowning act of faith in the ironclad system, he proposed, on March 4, 1862, the construction of

> fifty light-draft and powerful steam propellers, plated with 5-inch hard iron, armed and equipped for service in our own waters, four iron or steel-

---

cit., p. 347; Rear-Admiral W. M. Parks, "Building a War Ship in the Southern Confederacy," U. S. Naval Institute *Proceedings*, xlix, pp. 1299–1307 (August, 1923); Bruce, *Virginia Iron Manufacture*, pp. 366–369. Two diagrams of the vessel may be found in O.R.N., xviii, pp. 355, 356.

1 O.R.N., 2d series, i, p. 583.   2 *Ibid.*, p. 509.
3 *Journal of the Convention of the People of South Carolina Held in 1860, 1861 and 1862* (Columbia, S. C., 1862), p. 789; Charleston *Year Book*, 1883, pp. 550–553; O.R.N., 2d series, i, pp. 250, 262. A picture of the *Palmetto State* faces p. 262. There is a photograph of the *Chicora* in the *Photographic History of the Civil War*, vi, p. 239.
4 O.R.N., 2d series, ii, p. 150.

clad single-deck, ten gun frigates of about 2,000 tons, and ten clipper propellers with superior marine engines, both classes of ships designed for deep-sea cruising. . . .[1]

Aware, in general terms, of the progress that Europe had been making so rapidly in the introduction of armored vessels, Mallory had staked the success of the Confederate Navy on two well conceived projects: the creation of commerce destroyers like the *Alabama*, and the construction of ironclads to break the blockade and carry the war to the enemy. Thanks to the deficient industrial resources of the South and to the movements of the Northern forces, the words "too late" sum up the history of many of his projected ironclads. If his ambitious shipbuilding programs could have been completed, the Confederate Navy might have altered the whole course of the war. *Dis aliter visum*.

[1] O.R.N., 2d series, i, p. 796, Mallory to Davis, March 4, 1862.

CHAPTER XII

THE NORTH SEEKS A SOLUTION

THE legend that the Union Navy Department prior to the battle of Hampton Roads was excessively skeptical of the merits of ironclads, and particularly skeptical of the advantages of turrets, has been as popular in the United States as the kindred myth that the combat between the *Monitor* and *Merrimack* led the European powers to undertake the introduction of ironclad warships. Failing to examine the voluminous unpublished materials in the archives of the Navy Department, the Bureau of Yards and Docks, and the Bureau of Construction and Repair, American historians have persistently misrepresented the policy of the Federal authorities. A few writers seem to have suspected that the Bureau of Construction had an ironclad policy other than mere negation. As to what that policy was, however, they seem no better informed than the rest.

Yet in addition to the *Monitor*, *Galena*, and *New Ironsides*, — three ironclads which had recently been begun, — and in addition to the nine armored vessels being built at the expense of the War Department on the western waters, the Bureau of Construction and Repair proposed on November 29, 1861, the construction of twenty ironclads at a cost of $12,000,000. The specifications for these vessels, hitherto overlooked by historians, called for armored wooden ships, each carrying two cylindrical turrets on Captain Coles's system. Secretary Welles included the request for the twelve millions in his annual report, December 2, 1861. The Act of February 13, 1862, which had been hung up for weeks in the Senate, appropriated ten millions for not more than twenty ironclads. In its advertisement published February 24, 1862, twelve days before the battle of Hampton Roads, the Navy Department showed its partiality for turreted ironclads by requiring that all these armored vessels, except those for

Mississippi service, must have guns which trained "to all points of the compass without change in the vessel's position." [1]

Prior to March, 1862, Lincoln's administration received more than one hundred proposals for ironclad ships. Even before the fall of Sumter half a dozen such communications had reached the Navy Department.[2] Elias Hasket Derby of Boston, who had proposed to Secretary Toucey on January 16 the improvisation of an ironclad for the relief of Fort Sumter, renewed his proposal to Secretary Welles on March 20. Anticipating the construction of ironclads for the South, he deemed immediate action by the Union imperative.[3] On March 12, Lieutenant David D. Porter proposed the protection of wooden warships by means of longitudinal bars of wrought iron two inches thick, bolted to the sides, and placed three inches apart. He recommended an arched "shield deck" of light plate iron as a protection for the machinery.[4] The great shipbuilder, Donald McKay, who had been advocating the immediate construction of ironclads in a series of articles in the Boston *Commercial Bulletin*, offered on March 21 to submit plans of an iron-cased frigate of 36 guns, with 12 knots speed and 24 feet draft, and an iron-cased corvette of 14 guns, with 10 knots speed and 16 feet draft.[5] On another

---

1 New York *Herald*, February 24, 1862, advertisement dated February 20, 1862.
2 List compiled by the writer from N.D., *Miscellaneous Letters*, 1861–1862; *Officers' Letters*, 1861–1862; *Inventions, Examining Board, and Permanent Commission*, 1861–1865, vol. i.
3 N.D., *Miscellaneous Letters*. Derby contributed an interesting article on "Mail-clad Steamers" to the *Atlantic Monthly* for August, 1861. Cf. Derby to Commodore H. Paulding, August 6, 1861, *Miscellaneous Letters*.
4 "Our ships-of-war would meet with certain defeat if they came in contact with any one of the vessels lately built [by Great Britain and France], the outsides of which are covered with plates of steel. The plan of using steel *plates* I consider objectionable, inasmuch as it loads the vessels down too deep with the weight of iron, and experience will prove that they will be unserviceable as sea going, ships-of-war, though they may answer perfectly for harbor, or coast defense." Porter to Welles, *Officers' Letters*, March, 1861.
5 McKay to Welles, March 8 and 21, 1861, *Miscellaneous Letters*, April, 1861, ii, enclosing articles published November 17 and December 1, 1860, and March 16, 1861, in the Boston *Commercial Bulletin*. McKay, who had visited the English and French Navy yards in 1860, declared in these articles that "it is at this day generally acknowledged that no naval power that will not lose entirely her authority on the seas, should be without a number of these [iron-cased] frigates for

of these first ironclad projects of the war Commodore Hiram Paulding, a trusted adviser of Secretary Welles, endorsed a recommendation that an armored vessel be built "for service of blockade, and to pass down the Mississippi." [1]

After Major Anderson's surrender, proposals for ironclads came thick and fast. Of the score or more of these projects which advocated sloping armor, it is worth noting that eight originated prior to Mallory's orders for the conversion of the *Merrimack*.[2] The most interesting of these, submitted by Donald McKay on April 20, proposed a 12- or 16-gun screw corvette of 2390 tons displacement and 14 feet draft, whose engines of 200 nominal horse power would give her an estimated speed of 6½ to 8 knots. Her water-line armor belt tapered from 4½ inches thick amidships to 3½ inches thick at the ends of the vessel; and the next row of plates tapered from 4 to 2½ inches. Amidships rose a casemate 135 feet long, whose ports were protected by strong iron shutters, and whose sides sloped at an angle of 42 degrees with the horizon. Half-inch iron covered the deck and the roof of the casemate, whose sloping sides were protected by armor tapering from 3½ inches thick at the bottom to 2½ inches thick at the top. Her wooden hull was to be 24 inches thick at the load-line. McKay provided merely a jury rig and masts to steady the ship in a seaway and enable her to save coal on blockade duty. He asserted that the British tests of Jones's inclined armor had demonstrated the resisting power of that system,

---

defensive purposes . . . the steam fleet of the United States is hardly equal to that of third-rate European powers. . . ." He ridiculed the Stevens war steamer, as "one of the most shameless humbugs of the nineteenth century." *Loc. cit.*, Nov. 17, 1860. "The times for line-of-battle ships are over . . . they will be no match for a heavily armored, fast, iron-cased frigate . . . no ships constructed on the old system are capable of sustaining fifteen minutes' fight with one of these invulnerable monsters without being blown to pieces." *Loc. cit.*, March 16, 1861.

[1] Charles Blood to Commodore Paulding, Buffalo, April 12, 1861, *Miscellaneous Letters*.

[2] James Robinson to Welles, April 13; John N. Lawrence to Welles, New York, April 15, 30; P. Slater to Lincoln, Westfield, Fayette Co., Iowa, April 18; P. Slater to Wm. Vandever, May 11; W. H. Wood to Welles, Hudson, N. J., May 6; M. R. Fletcher to Welles, Cambridge, Mass., June 3, 14, July 26, August 6, November 6; Henry Preston Sinnell to Welles, Philadelphia, June 10; R. S. Harris to Lincoln, Galena, Ill., June 26. *Miscellaneous Letters*, 1861.

and argued that the general introduction of ironclads by England and France made it "'a necessity for us to follow in the same lines regardless of the higher cost, if we do not want to lose all prestige on the seas." [1]

These projects poured in upon a Department struggling with the gravest difficulties. The confusion incident to a change of administration was heightened many fold by the resignations due to secession and to the outbreak of hostilities. Four of the five bureau chiefs, to be sure, served throughout the war. The numerous resignations among their subordinates, however, created a feeling of uncertainty and distrust, and disorganized the administration of the Department for some time. In the Bureau of Ordnance and Hydrography, for example, every person save the draftsman and the messenger quit his post at the outbreak of war.[2]

Faced with the task of creating a fleet to blockade 3500 miles of coast, called upon to solve at short notice a score of problems demanding an immediate solution, it is small wonder that the Department hesitated in the first months of the war to embark on an ironclad program. From the endorsements on the projects of inventors, one can glean the views of the bureau chiefs in the spring of 1861. Captain A. A. Harwood, the new Chief of the Bureau of Ordnance and Hydrography, thought

it would be hazardous to rely upon new models of vessels, however plausible, at a critical time and intended to effect decisive results.

The experience of the Navy proves beyond a doubt that wherever the construction of vessels of war have been entrusted to persons not intimately versed in the requirements of a man of war, however able in other respects, the result has been uniformly a failure in some vital point. . . .[3]

---

[1] McKay to Welles, April 20, 1861, accompanied by endorsements from Glidden and Williams, Henry Wilson, and F. H. Morse. *Miscellaneous Letters.*

[2] Harwood to Welles, February 27, 1862. N.D., *Bureau Letters.* The resignation of Harwood's predecessor as chief of the Bureau of Ordnance, G. A. Magruder, dated April 22, 1861, is endorsed "Dismissed, 15 May, 1861." *Resignations and Dismissals.* See also, Charles O. Paullin, "A Half Century of Naval Administration in America, 1861–1911," in U. S. Naval Institute *Proceedings*, December, 1912, and March, 1913. The act of July 5, 1862 increased the number of bureaus in the Navy Department to eight. *Statutes at Large*, xii, pp. 510–512.

[3] Endorsement dated May 7, 1861, on the letter of P. Slater to Lincoln, April 18, 1861. N.D., *Miscellaneous Letters*, May, 1861, vol. ii.

John Lenthall, Chief of the Bureau of Construction and Repair since 1853, declared that "an iron vessel built for mercantile purposes cannot be properly converted into an efficient ship of war." He deemed ramming "a very old idea constantly being revived. It is not recommended to the consideration of the Department." Two of his endorsements on May 11 stated that

> the necessarily large size, the cost and the time required for building an iron cased steam vessel is such that it is not recommended to adopt any plan at present. . . .
>
> The subject of iron clad vessels with inclined sides has been freely discussed in the European mechanical journals, but their draft of water, cost, and the time required in the introduction of a new system render it inexpedient at this time to commence such vessels which will require very careful consideration.

Lenthall recognized that the problem must be taken up later, however. By November he had not only reached the conclusion that complete armor protection was far preferable to the British system of casing little more than half the length of the vessel; but he also had completed the specifications for a fleet of double-turreted ironclads.[1]

As naval operations on the western rivers were at first deemed within the sphere of the Army, not the Navy, it fell to the War Department to order the first Union ironclads. Soon after the surrender of Fort Sumter, Attorney-General Bates, perceiving the great need for gunboats in the west, summoned his friend James B. Eads of St. Louis, an expert on Mississippi River craft, to Washington for a conference. Eads proposed that the government establish a base at Cairo, blockade Confederate commerce, and convert a snag-boat owned by the Missouri Wrecking Company, in which he had been interested, into an armed steamer protected by cotton bales. Secretary Welles referred the proposal to the War Department, and sent Captain John Rodgers and Naval Con-

---

[1] See Lenthall's endorsements on the following letters: E. H. Derby to Welles, March 20; H. Maranville to Welles, Akron, Ohio, August 27; John Westwood to Welles, Cincinnati, May 4; W. H. Wood to Welles, May 6; John N. Lawrence to Welles, April 30; Merrick and Sons to Welles, Philadelphia, November 2. *Miscellaneous Letters*, 1861.

structor Samuel M. Pook west to assist the army authorities in improvising a flotilla. Rejecting Eads's snag-boat, Rodgers purchased three wooden steamers at Cincinnati, the *Conestoga, Lexington* and *A. O. Tyler*, re-named the *Taylor*, which became the nucleus of the great Mississippi River fleet.[1]

On June 1, Lenthall submitted to General Totten, of the Engineer Corps, a plan for a wooden paddle steamer of 436 tons and five feet draft, carrying four 8-inch guns, to serve as a basis for designing the river fleet. With the pessimistic comment that "it does not seem to be practicable to make an armed steam vessel for the Mississippi that will be very efficient," he advised the War Department to consult some western steamboat constructors and to rely on Pook for any necessary modifications of the plan.[2] As Totten and Lieutenant General Scott endorsed the project, the Quartermaster General advertised for bids, and on August 7 awarded to Eads the contract for seven gunboats, to be completed by October 10, 1861, at a cost of $89,600 each. These wooden vessels of 512 tons, 175 feet long and 50 feet beam, each mounted thirteen guns in a casemate with sloping ends and sides. The hull, divided into fifteen water-tight compartments, enclosed a single paddle wheel in the stern. As for armor, the specification simply stipulated that

it is intended to protect the boiler and engines of this vessel with iron plates of sufficient thickness, and placed in a suitable position to protect them from injury from the effect of shot or shell, for which purpose seventy-five tons of iron plating have been estimated.

Iron two and a half inches thick covered the sloping bow casemate and the inclined sides abreast of the engines, leaving more than half of the topsides unarmored. A conical ar-

---

[1] O.R.N., xxii, pp. 277–284; *Welles Papers*, xlv, Eads to Welles, May 8, 1861. Cf. Charles B. Boynton, *The History of the Navy during the Rebellion* (New York, 1867–1868, 2 vols.), i, pp. 498 ff.; James B. Eads, "Recollections of Foote and the Gun-Boats," in *Battles and Leaders of the Civil War*, i, pp. 338 ff.; Louis How, *James B. Eads* (Cambridge, [c. 1900]), ch. ii.

[2] O.R., 3rd series, ii, pp. 814–815.

mored pilot house, insufficiently protected, proved a death-trap for several brave Mississippi pilots.[1]

Eads disclaimed all responsibility for any share in the design of these vessels, which he built on the plans of Naval Constructor Pook.[2] Despite his utmost efforts, he was unable to complete the seven ironclads, the *St. Louis* (later re-named *De Kalb*), *Carondelet*, *Cincinnati*, *Louisville*, *Mound City*, *Cairo*, and *Pittsburg*, until December and January.[3] Meanwhile General Frémont, without the approval of the War Department, had ordered two river steamers converted into ironclads. The first of these, the snag-boat which Captain Rodgers had earlier rejected, was transformed by Eads on plans of his own into the most powerful of the western ironclads of 1862, the *Benton*, mounting sixteen guns in a sloping casemate protected with 3½ inches of iron on the bow, and with thinner plating on the sides, wheel-house and stern.[4] The second, the river steamer *New Era*, was purchased on September 20 from the Wiggins Ferry Company of St. Louis at a cost of $20,000 and converted into the ironclad gunboat *Essex*, mounting five guns.[5] Together with the *Cincinnati*,

---

[1] O.R., 1st series, lii, pp. 164–168; 3rd series, ii, pp. 792, 816–832, 837; O.R.N., xxii, p. 314; Eads, *loc. cit.*; O.R.N., 2d series, i, pp. 49, 52, 58, 129, 180.

[2] O.R., 1st series, viii, pp. 368–369; 3d series, ii, p. 820. Cf. How, *op. cit.*, p. 33. On November 12, 1861, Dr. Robert King Stone, of Washington, wrote to Secretary Welles that his patient, Mr. Pook, "one of the oldest and most respected of your naval constructors," was suffering, as a result of overwork and poor health, from the hallucination that he had committed a great breach of trust concerning the purchase of a vessel, and was to be hanged. This Samuel M. Pook, who became a naval constructor in January, 1841, was placed on the retired list August 15, 1866, and died in 1878. He is not to be confused with Samuel H. Pook, the designer of the *Galena*, who was appointed assistant naval constructor, May 17, 1866, retired April 15, 1871, and died in 1889. *Welles Papers*, xlviii; E. W. Callahan, ed., *List of Officers of the Navy of the U. S.* (New York, 1901), p. 440.

[3] O.R., 1st series, viii, pp. 367–369; 3rd series, ii, p. 832; O.R.N., xxii, pp. 320, 368, 378, 386–388, 390–391, 395, 431–435, 438–439, 441–456, 459, 462–474, 493–495, 502–504. The *Carondelet*, *St. Louis*, *Louisville*, and *Pittsburg* were built at St. Louis; the *Mound City*, *Cincinnati* and *Cairo*, at Mound City, Ill. Cf. Boynton, *loc. cit.*; How, *loc. cit.*

[4] O.R.N., xxii, using index, *s.v. Benton*; O.R.N., 2d series, i, p. 44, with picture; Eads, *loc. cit.*; O.R., 1st series, viii, p. 369.

[5] O.R.N., 2d series, i, p. 79; O.R.N., xxii, using index, *s.v. New Era* and *Essex*. Vol. vi of the *Photographic History of the Civil War* contains photographs of the *Pittsburg*, *Cincinnati*, *Louisville*, *Benton* and *Essex*.

Carondelet, and *St. Louis*, she took part in the capture of Fort Henry, receiving a shot through her boiler which put her out of action. The *St. Louis, Carondelet, Louisville,* and *Pittsburg* were considerably damaged in the attack on Fort Donelson.[1] When the Union gunboats *Conestoga, Tyler,* and *Lexington* pushed up the Tennessee River after the fall of Fort Henry, they found at Cerro Gordo, Tennessee, the abandoned steamer *Eastport*, which the Confederates had been converting into an ironclad gunboat. This prize was towed downstream, completed, and added to the Union fleet on the western waters.[2]

Shortly before the special midsummer session of Congress, Commander Dahlgren had submitted to the Secretary of the Navy the latest news of the large ironclads under construction in Great Britain and France.[3] In his report of July 4, 1861, Welles pointed out that

> much attention has been given within the last few years to the subject of floating batteries, or iron-clad steamers. Other governments, and particularly France and England, have made it a special object in connexion with naval improvements; and the ingenuity and inventive faculties of our own countrymen have also been stimulated by recent occurrences toward the construction of this class of vessels. The period is perhaps not one best adapted to heavy expenditures by way of experiment and the time and attention of some of those who are most competent to investigate and form correct conclusions on this subject are otherwise employed.

He recommended the appointment of a competent board to investigate and report on this important matter. It would be for Congress to decide whether, "on a favorable report," they would order "one or more iron-clad steamers, or floating batteries to be constructed, with a view to perfect protection from the effects of present ordnance at short range." [4]

In response to Welles's report Senator Grimes of Iowa introduced on July 19 a bill directing the Secretary of the Navy

---

[1] O.R., 1st series, vii, pp. 120 ff.; O.R.N., xxii, pp. 534 ff. Cf. Admiral D. D. Porter, *Naval History of the Civil War*, chs. xiv, xv.
[2] O.R.N., xxii, and O.R., 1st series, vii, using index *s.v. Eastport*; O.R.N., 2d series, i, p. 77.
[3] *Welles Papers*, xlvi, June 26, 1861. Dahlgren mentioned twelve British and fourteen French ironclads.
[4] Senate Executive Document no. 1, 37th Congress, 1st Session, p. 96.

to appoint "a board of three skilful naval officers" to investigate plans of armored steamships or steam batteries, and appropriating $1,500,000 for the construction of one or more if the board reported favorably. This measure was enacted on August 3, after a narrow escape from shipwreck when the House inserted an amendment which might have permitted the application of the appropriation to the completion of the Stevens battery. As the Senate firmly opposed the amendment, the House finally yielded. In this debate Grimes stated that he had introduced the bill at the instance of the Navy Department because

it was supposed to be possible that a conflict with some foreign Power might grow out of our present complications, and that in that event it might be important to provide armored batteries, floating steam batteries, for the defense of the various harbors along our sea-coast. I think the experiments in France and England and in this country, have demonstrated that, however valueless or however valuable armored ships may be as cruisers, they certainly are destined to be valuable for the defense of harbors. . . . The batteries can be constructed . . . at from $150,000. to $200,000. each.

If the proposed board concluded that these ships would be serviceable, the Senate Committee on Naval Affairs wished to construct two for the defence of New York, and one each for Philadelphia, Boston, Portland, Baltimore, and the other harbors on the Atlantic coast.[1]

Welles promptly published an advertisement, dated August 7, calling for

offers from parties who are able to execute work of this kind, and who are engaged in it, of which they will furnish evidence with their offer, for the construction of one or more iron-clad steam vessels of war, either of iron or of wood and iron combined, for sea or river service, to be of not less than ten nor over sixteen feet draught of water; to carry an armament of from eighty to one hundred and twenty tons weight, with provisions and stores

---

[1] *Congressional Globe*, 37th Congress, 1st Session, cols. 205, 218, 230, 235, 236, 243, 256–257, 274, 276, 277, 344–346, 357, 363–364, 371, 382, 384–385; *Statutes at Large*, xii, p. 286. Grimes declared on July 30 that "it is a very problematical question whether any vessel can be constructed of iron that can become a cruiser, or that can pass up and down the coast. The sole purpose of this bill is to enable the Secretary of the Navy to construct some floating steam batteries that can take position on either side of a harbor, or in the center of a harbor, to resist the ingress of vessels of war."

for from one hundred and sixty-five to three hundred persons, according to armament, for sixty days, with coal for eight days. The smaller draught of water, compatible with other requisites, will be preferred. The vessel to be rigged with two masts, with wire-rope standing rigging, to navigate at sea.

A general description and drawings of the vessel, armor, and machinery, such as the work can be executed from, will be required.

The offer must state the cost and the time for completing the whole, exclusive of armament and stores of all kinds, the rate of speed proposed, and must be accompanied by a guarantee for the proper execution of the contract, if awarded.

Persons who intend to offer are requested to inform the department of their intention before the 15th August, instant, and to have their propositions presented within twenty-five days from this date.[1]

On August 8 Welles appointed Commodore Joseph Smith, Chief of the Bureau of Yards and Docks, senior officer of the ironclad board, with Commodore Hiram Paulding and Commander Dahlgren as his associates. At Dahlgren's own request, he was relieved from this service shortly after, and Commander Charles H. Davis appointed in his place.[2] Both Smith and Paulding were close friends and advisers of the Secretary, with long and distinguished records. The personal relations of Welles and Smith, who had each been made chief of a navy bureau in 1846, were not only friendly but intimate. Commodore Smith, as Welles wrote years later, "in addition to great nautical and civil experience, possessed a singularly mechanical and practical mind. On him devolved, ultimately, the chief responsibility and supervision of the execution of the plans adopted" for the *Monitor*, *Galena* and *New Ironsides*.[3] Paulding, who was serving as chief of the recently improvised "office of detail," assigning officers to duty, had already recommended the construction of an iron-

[1] *Report of the Secretary of the Navy in Relation to Armored Vessels* (Washington, 1864), p. 2.
[2] Welles to Smith, August 8, 1861. As printed in *ibid.*, p. 2, Davis's name stands as one of the original appointees. The original manuscript in the Navy Department Archives, however, gives Dahlgren as the third member of the board, with Davis's name inserted in pencil. On August 20, Welles wrote to Smith that "Commander Dahlgren has been relieved from the Board on Ironclad vessels, at his own request, and Commander Chas. H. Davis has been ordered to report to you in his place." *Letters to Heads of Bureaus*, iv, pp. 11, 16.
[3] "The First Iron-Clad Monitor," in *The Annals of the War* (Philadelphia, 1879), pp. 17-31.

clad.[1] His assistant in the "office of detail," Davis, one of the most progressive officers in the service, had already demonstrated his scientific attainments by his work for the Coast Survey and by editing the *American Ephemeris and Nautical Almanac* from its establishment in 1849.[2]

The three members of the board on ironclad vessels, which met at Washington on September 5,[3] recommended on September 16 the construction of the three ironclads later named the *Monitor*, *Galena*, and *New Ironsides*. They approached the subject "with diffidence, having no experience and but scanty knowledge in this branch of naval architecture." Although the construction of ironclads was "zealously claiming the attention of foreign naval powers," opinions differed among naval and scientific men as to the wisdom of the policy. For coast and harbor defence the board deemed ironclads to be "undoubtedly formidable adjuncts to fortifications." No armored vessel, however, could "cope successfully with a properly constructed fortification of masonry." And the board was sceptical of the advantages and ultimate adoption of armor for cruising vessels. "But while other nations are endeavoring to perfect them, we must not remain idle."

Although "wooden ships may be said to be but coffins for their crews when brought in conflict with iron-clad vessels," their speed, which the board assumed would be superior, would enable them to choose their position and "keep out of harm's way entirely." They knew of nothing better than large and heavy spherical shot for destructive effects on ves-

[1] See above, p. 240. On August 4 Paulding had suggested that some small tugs recently purchased should be plated with boiler iron on the sides and equipped with a "*pepper box* cylinder" for the steersman, and used as "the flying artillery of the Navy," on the Confederate coast and rivers. *Welles Papers*, xlvii. Paulding, who seems to have resented Fox's influence with the Secretary, was soon transferred to the post of commandant of the New York Navy Yard. See his letter of August 21, 1861 to George D. Morgan, Welles's brother-in-law, in *ibid.*; and R. M. Thompson and Richard Wainwright, eds., *Confidential Correspondence of Gustavus Vasa Fox* (New York, 1918–1919, 2 vols.), i, p. 38.
[2] Paullin, *op. cit.*, xxxviii, pp. 1319, 1321; Captain Charles H. Davis, *Life of Charles Henry Davis, Rear Admiral, 1807–1877* (Boston and New York, 1899), chs. v, vii.
[3] N.D., *Bureau Letters*, Smith to Welles, September 2, 1861.

THE NORTH SEEKS A SOLUTION

sels, whether armored or not. Although rifled guns had greater range, the conical shot failed to produce the crushing effect of round shot. The board assumed that

> 4½-inch plates are the heaviest armor a sea-going vessel can safely carry. These plates should be of tough iron, and rolled in large, long pieces. This thickness of armor, it is believed, will resist all projectiles now in general use at a distance of 500 yards, especially if the ship's sides are angular. ... The tops of ships built of iron, we are told, wear out three bottoms; whilst the bottoms of those built of wood will outwear three tops. In deciding upon the relative merits of iron and wooden-framed vessels ... it would be well to try a specimen of each. ...

Although they had been informed that ironclads might be built more cheaply in England than in the United States, and that there were no mills in this country capable of rolling iron 4½ inches thick, which they considered superior to hammered plates, the board thought that the British government might prevent the delivery of ironclads built in that country, and they argued that "every people or nation who can maintain a navy should be capable of constructing it themselves."

As the first need of the North was invulnerable vessels of light draft "to penetrate shoal harbors, rivers and bayous," the board favored the construction of that class of vessels "before going into a more perfect system of large iron-clad sea-going vessels of war." Although the problem of armoring small vessels was difficult, they recommended

> that contracts be made with responsible parties for the construction of one or more iron-clad vessels or batteries of as light a draught of water as practicable consistent with the weight of their armor. Meanwhile, availing of the experience thus obtained and the improvements which we believe are yet to be made by other naval powers in building iron-clad ships, we would advise the construction, in our own dock-yards, of one or more of these vessels upon a large and more perfect scale, when Congress shall see fit to authorize it. The amount now appropriated is not sufficient to build both classes of vessels to any great extent. ...

Over and above the cost of the three ironclads recommended for immediate construction, $209,750 of the appropriation would remain unexpended. The board approved the general dimensions and armor of the vessel proposed by

Donald McKay, but thought the speed of six or seven knots slow. The price, $1,000,000, precluded its construction without a further appropriation. The board recommended that armor and heavy guns be placed at once on a river craft or scow, for service on the Potomac, and that Congress appropriate $10,000 for experimenting on iron plates of different kinds.[1]

Of the six different plans for turreted ironclads which inventors sent to the Navy Department prior to the battle of Hampton Roads, two were included in the seventeen proposals discussed by the ironclad board in their report of September 16. The first of these in date was submitted in May by C. W. Whitney of New York, and Thomas F. Rowland, in whose shipyard at Green Point, Brooklyn, the *Monitor* was later constructed. Their first specification, dated April 22, 1861, described a twin-screw iron vessel of about 750 tons displacement, 150 feet long, 30 feet beam, and 8 feet draft. An armor belt 5¼ inches thick composed of 1¼ inches of iron in three layers, backed by iron bars laid parallel to each other, with the spaces between the bars filled in with oak, extended for 110 feet amidships and protected the inclined sides of two diamond-shaped "gun-houses" installed "on the fore and aft centre line of the boat and attached to the main deck." Each of the two fixed "gun-houses" mounted an 11-inch gun worked through ports fitted with automatic shutters of 4½-inch wrought iron. Amidships was an armored pilot house, for the navigating officers and for a squad of riflemen to repel boarders. This vessel was to have all her machinery below the water line, to be ventilated by

---

[1] The board's report is printed in full in Senate Executive Document No. 1, 37th Congress, 2d Session, iii, pp. 152–156; in the *Report . . . in Relation to Armored Vessels*, pp. 3–7; in Senate Executive Document No. 86, 40th Congress, 2d Session, pp. 3–6; and in Bennett, *Steam Navy of the U. S.*, i, pp. 264–272. The original manuscript report, dated Bureau of Yards and Docks, 16 September 1861, is in *Bureau Letters*, 1862, vol. iii, instead of in the corresponding volume for 1861.
On December 18, 1861, Commodore Smith wrote privately to Flag Officer Foote, "Have you seen my report on iron-clad vessels? It is printed in advance of the Documents by many of the papers. The public feeling took a great interest in the subject. I had two co-adjutors but I did all the work." N.D., Area 11, folder labeled 1860–1862.

gratings in the top of the "gun-houses" and by two fan blowers driven by an auxiliary engine, and to be provided with tanks and pumps to take on or discharge water ballast. Whitney and Rowland offered to build her in five months for $220,000, guaranteeing a speed of ten knots.[1]

They soon, however, modified their plans to include two revolving turrets on Coles's system, in lieu of the fixed "gun-houses," and offered to construct the ship in four months for $110,000. The revolving "cupolas" were to be fifteen feet in diameter if breech-loading guns could be obtained, or twenty feet in diameter for muzzle-loaders. Each turret was to be provided with four ports for use if anything prevented the working of the turntables. Whitney wrote to Commodore Smith on July 25 that

> from the peculiar and angulated shape of the battery, not one shot in 500 will strike it point blank, or at an angle that can do the slightest damage. ... The weight of armor and domes we find upon accurate calculation to be 230 tons and not 270 as you estimated it. ... We have as you know the strongest testimonials, from practical and scientific men who have examined our plan, among them the lamented Captain Ward, Commodore Breese and others. Captain Harwood's objection that our plan was novel and his opinion that the revolving cupolas would not work, based upon an opinion of Sir Howard Douglas (an "Old Fogy" of the first water) ought not to outweigh the opinion of men who are regarded as more progressive at home and abroad.

To Harwood's objection that such a ship could not be built for $110,000, Whitney replied with an offer to furnish bondsmen.[2]

Two days later Smith replied that the Secretary would presumably appoint a board to examine models of ironclads, but expressed a "doubt if your model meets with success."[3] His forecast was correct, for the board's verdict of September 16 on the modified proposal was unfavorable, on the ground that a ship of the dimensions stated — 140 feet long, 28 feet

---

[1] Rowland to Welles, May 17, 30, 1861, N.D., *Miscellaneous Letters*; *Welles Papers*, xlvi; B.C.R., 80-11-28 A-C.
[2] N.W.R., vol. 2599.
[3] *Ibid.*, vol. 2633. Cf. Whitney and Rowland to Smith, September 4, 1861, and Smith's reply of September 6, in *ibid.*, vols. 2599, 2633.

beam, 13½ feet depth of hold, and 8 feet draft — would not bear the weight and possess stability.[1]

After this rebuff Rowland withdrew from the project and undertook the construction of the *Monitor*, as a subcontractor.[2] Whitney persisted, and soon after the battle of Hampton Roads he succeeded in obtaining a contract for the ironclad *Keokuk*.[3] A letter which he wrote to Smith on March 17, 1862, throws much light on the origin of his plan. In his idea of revolving turrets he admits that he followed the plans proposed by Coles. When he visited Washington in the summer of 1861

> Commodore Paulding expressed himself much pleased with my plan and model, and told me that instead of one the government needed a dozen of them at once, and in my presence, before a board of which you were chairman, he urged its adoption, Secretary Welles having expressed his willingness to order its construction if your board approved of it. Captain Davis and others of the board were in favor of it. . . . I was dismissed principally as I understood afterwards, through your opposition and Mr. Lenthall's who insisted, as in the case of the Ericsson Battery, that the armor would carry my boat under. . . . [4]

In September Whitney returned to Washington with his model "somewhat changed" to meet Smith's objection as to the possibility of revolving a turret weighing 40 tons,

> although Ericsson revolves one on the same principle weighing 140 tons. Commodore Paulding again did all he could for me, and Captain Davis told me that he had always liked my plan. You Sir, as chairman of the committee again threw me overboard, but not without a plank to lay hold of in the shape of a promise . . . that when more ironclads were needed, as you said they would be shortly, you would give me a chance. . . . [5]

---

[1] *Report . . . in Relation to Armored Vessels*, p. 6.
[2] According to Church's version, which does not mention Whitney, nor the relation of his plan to that of Coles, or to the *Keokuk*, Rowland took the model to Washington, where his project met with a prompt rejection. Returning to New York he was invited to call on Ericsson. "There he was shown the model sent to Napoleon in 1854, and satisfied that he could claim no priority for his idea of a turret. He was next informed of the order received from the Government for an iron-clad battery. Then turning to him, Ericsson said, 'You want money; I want fame. You can do the mechanical work on this vessel in your ship-yard, but it is my conception, and it must be understood that it was built here in my parlor. . . .'" *Ericsson*, i, p. 258.
[3] See below, p. 306.   [4] See below, pp. 263–265.
[5] N.W.R., vol. 2603. Whitney was the New York agent for the ironworks of Abbot and Son, Baltimore. His father-in-law was a partner of Mayor Opdyke of

THE NORTH SEEKS A SOLUTION   253

The other proposal for a turreted ironclad considered by Commodore Smith's board was that of John Ericsson.[1] The story of its presentation is so closely intertwined with that of the ironclad *Galena*, that the two may best be narrated together. In the summer of 1861, Cornelius Scranton Bushnell of New Haven, Connecticut, President of the New Haven, New London, and Stonington Railroad Company, sold two steamers to the Navy Department, and offered to construct several ironclads.[2] Although he had the assistance of Samuel H. Pook, a naval constructor of Boston, in preparing his plans, Bushnell, on the advice of Cornelius H. Delamater, of New York City, sought further help from John Ericsson. On August 17 Delamater gave Ericsson Bushnell's sectional plan of his ironclad, with a request "to construct a midship section of 36 feet extreme beam and of such a form as will accomodate the steam machinery." Ericsson sent Bushnell the desired plan the same day, remarking that he had followed his intentions as far as practicable, but had placed the extreme beam further below water

in order to present a considerable slope of the side immediately above water. The armor I have marked as carried 4½ feet below water line. Less will not answer during the slightest rolling of the vessel. You will notice also that I have placed the gun deck 4 feet instead of 3 feet above the water line in order to obtain sufficient space below for the boilers. I need not remind you that owing to the extraordinary rise of floor, the height under deck at a very short distance from the midship section diminishes very rapidly. Your plan evinces, on the part of the constructor, a perfect acquaintance with laws of hydrostatics. The great difficulty of protecting

New York. He submitted endorsements of his plan by numerous officers and civilians, including the Union Defense Committee of New York City.

[1] For accounts by Welles of the origin of the *Monitor*, see his *Diary*, i, pp. 213-215; his letter of July 25, 1868, printed as Senate Executive Document No. 86, 40th Congress, 2d Session; and *Annals of the War*, pp. 17-31. Bushnell's statement, written in March, 1877, and approved by Ericsson and Welles, may be found in William S. Wells, *The Original U. S. Warship "Monitor"* (2d ed., New Haven, 1906). For accounts by Ericsson, see his *Contributions to the Centennial Exhibition* (New York, 1876), chs. xxviii, xxxii-xxxiv, and *Battles and Leaders of the Civil War*, i, pp. 730-744. In preference to these accounts, which were written long after the events narrated, the present narrative is based largely on contemporary documents, the greater part of which are here used for the first time.

[2] Senate Executive Document No. 1, 37th Congress, 2d Session, iii, p. 140; Bushnell to Commodore Smith, July 24, 1861, N.W.R., vol. 2599.

the upper part of a floating body by heavy materials, is the unavoidable top weight and tendency to tip over. This difficulty can only be met by such a form of vessel as you propose. Stevens' floating battery with the intended "2000 ton armour" in addition to guns etc., would turn round, like a barrel, in the water with a weight attached to its *intended* top. . . .[1]

A week later Bushnell wrote to Smith that he had "the whole work under contract for the construction of ironclad gunboats and progressing finely." To his suggestion was apparently due the form of the guarantee clause in the contracts of October, 1861. Smith replied the next day that the board thought favorably of Bushnell's proposal for building ironclads, "especially as you propose a substantial guarantee to refund such portion of the cost of the vessel which may be advanced by the Government as she progresses, in case of failure." Bushnell declared that "we have no hesitation of giving bonds in any amount to refund the money advanced provided we do not live up to our contract."[2]

September 3, the last day for the submission of plans to the ironclad board,[3] was now fast approaching. On August 29, Ericsson wrote to President Lincoln, proposing to construct within ten weeks "a vessel for the destruction of the rebel fleet at Norfolk and for scouring the Southern rivers and inlets of all craft protected by rebel batteries." Five days later he sent to Commodore Smith's board his plans for an ironclad mounting a single revolving turret.[4]

According to statements made by Bushnell, Ericsson and Welles years later, when Bushnell visited Ericsson for advice concerning the *Galena* the latter

produced a small dust-covered box, and placed before me the model and plan of the *Monitor*, explaining how quickly and powerfully she could be built, and exhibiting with characteristic pride a medal and letter of thanks received seven years previously from Napoleon III. . . .

At the close of this interview Bushnell is said to have taken the model immediately to Welles at Hartford, where the

[1] B.C.R., 28–6–3.
[2] Bushnell to Smith, August 21, 24; Smith to Bushnell, August 22. N.W.R., vols. 2599, 2633. See above, p. 247.
[3] Smith to Bushnell, August 26, 1861. N.W.R., vol. 2633.
[4] Church, *Ericsson*, i, pp. 246–247, 274–275.

Secretary was spending a few days.¹ Welles thought the proposal possessed some extraordinary and valuable features tending to the development of certain principles, then being studied, for our coast and river blockade, involving a revolution in naval warfare. The twenty-five days for receiving proposals had, I think, expired; but I was so interested in this novel proposition that I directed Mr. Bushnell to proceed immediately to Washington, and submit the model to the Board for examination and report. But, deeming the subject of great importance, and fearing the Board would be restrained by the limit of twenty-five days, I immediately followed, and arrived in Washington almost as soon as Mr. Bushnell with the model.²

Welles left Hartford on the twelfth and, after stopping to visit the New York and Philadelphia Navy Yards, reached Washington on the evening of Saturday, September 14.³ In the meantime Bushnell had reached Washington and had enlisted the aid of John Flack Winslow, a partner in the Albany Iron Works at Troy, N. Y., and John A. Griswold, a banker of the same city. Both were men of capital and political influence, who had agreed to furnish the armor for Bushnell's own ironclad if he obtained a contract. The three of them, armed with a letter of introduction from Secretary Seward, laid Ericsson's project before President Lincoln, who, at once impressed with the plan, agreed to meet them the next day at the Navy Department. In the ensuing discussion at the Department, Lincoln is said to have observed, "All I have to say is what the girl said when she put her foot into the stocking, 'It strikes me there's something in it.'"⁴ Smith and Pauld-

1 Bushnell to Welles, March 9, 1877, in Wells, *op. cit.*, p. 12.
2 *Annals of the War*, p. 19. In his letter of July 25, 1868, Welles stated that when he urged Bushnell to hasten from Hartford to Washington he assured him "that in case of unavoidable delay beyond the time limited for receiving proposals, an exception should be made in favor of this novel invention of a submerged vessel with a revolving turret, and that it should be embraced among the plans on which the opinion of the board would be required." Senate Executive Document No. 86, 40th Congress, 2d Session. Cf. *Diary of Gideon Welles*, i, p. 214, January 3, 1863.
3 Welles to Mrs. Welles, September 15, 1861. *Welles Papers*, xlvii.
4 Bushnell to Welles, March 9, 1877, in Wells, *op. cit.*, p. 14. Cf. Francis B. Wheeler, *John F. Winslow, LL.D., and the Monitor*, pp. 21–25, 52–54. This work, and the letter dictated by Winslow in September, 1891, which it contains, exaggerate the rôles of Winslow and Griswold and treat both Ericsson and Bushnell unjustly. The contemporary evidence indicates that Ericsson, not Winslow, played the chief part in converting the ironclad board.

ing regarded the project with some favor, but Davis, according to Bushnell's story in 1877, told him that he "might take the little thing home and worship it, as it would not be idolatry, because it was made in the image of nothing in the heaven above, or in the earth below, or in the waters under the earth." [1]

To overcome this opposition Bushnell hastened to New York and persuaded Ericsson to go to Washington and explain his proposal to the board.[2] Ericsson's arguments won the day. On September 15 he reinforced his oral statements with a written explanation of his "Impregnable Battery." As its immersed midship section was only 312 square feet, he argued that an engine of 400 horse power would easily give a speed of nine statute miles. Supporting his exposition with an illustrative sketch he declared the stability of his vessel to be "30 times greater than the weight of the turret." As the turret was balanced from below, there was "not even a tendency to disturb the enormous stability which we have established." To the question whether the turntable would stand the recoil, he replied that there was no turntable.

> The wooden beams or slides supporting the gun carriages are secured directly to the side of the turret. The recoil therefore is received by the entire mass of the turret. The friction rollers work on axles, the bearings of which are secured in the deck, and the turret itself rests on those rollers. The light grating on which the gunners stand is attached to the wooden beams and to the inside of the turret.
>
> The turning of the turret only requires force enough to overcome the friction of the steel rollers on which it rests. The upright spindle of 9 inches diameter has more than tenfold the strength requisite for that purpose and for the purpose of preventing the turret from sliding side ways during the vessel's rolling at sea.

He estimated the weight of iron in the vessel and turret at something over 420 tons. Four ventilating tubes 28 inches in diameter and 8 feet high would suffice for ventilation under ordinary circumstances. When the vessel was in action, powerful blowers worked by separate engines would draw fresh air in "through the turret roof, under the turret,

---

[1] Wells, *loc. cit.*   [2] *Ibid.*, pp. 14-15, 21, 31.

through the holes in the pilot house and holes inside the turret." Part of this air drawn in would pass through the fires, while part went directly by side conductors to the chimney abaft the turret.[1]

Ericsson seems to have had little difficulty in converting the ironclad board, for on the very next day following his written explanation, they recommended the construction of one vessel on his plans. Their report of September 16 described his proposed ironclad as 172 feet long, 41 feet beam, 11½ feet depth of hold, and of 1255 tons displacement. She was to be built in 100 days, at a price of $275,000, and was to make nine statute miles per hour. This project, the board declared,

> is novel, but seems to be based upon a plan which will render the battery shot and shell proof. We are somewhat apprehensive that her properties for sea are not such as a sea-going vessel should possess. But she may be moved from one place to another on the coast in smooth water. We recommend that an experiment be made with one battery of this description on the terms proposed, with a guarantee and forfeiture in case of failure in any of the properties and points of the vessel as proposed.[2]

When the New York *Herald* on April 25, 1862, savagely attacked Welles for alleged delays in adopting the *Monitor*, Ericsson protested to James Gordon Bennett that his paper had done the Secretary a great injustice.

> A more prompt and spirited action is probably not on record in a similar case than that of the Navy Department as regards the *Monitor*. The committee of naval commanders, appointed by the Secretary to decide on the plans of gunboats laid before the department, occupied me less than two hours in explaining my new system. In about two hours more the committee had come to a decision. After their favorable report had been to the Secretary, I was called into his office, where I was detained less than five minutes. In order not to lose any time, the Secretary ordered me to "go ahead at once." Consequently, while the clerks of the department were engaged in drawing up the formal contract, the iron which now forms the keel plate of the Monitor was drawn through the rolling mill.[3]

---

[1] Memorandum signed J. Ericsson, Washington, September 15, 1861. N.W.R., vol. 2599.
[2] *Report . . . in Relation to Armored Vessels*, p. 5. Cf. Ericsson to E. P. Dorr, November 16, 1877, in Church, *Ericsson*, i, pp. 252–253, and his article in *Battles and Leaders of the Civil War*, i, p. 731.
[3] *Report . . . in Relation to Armored Vessels*, p. 14.

Commodore Smith wrote privately to Ericsson on August 18, 1862, that he claimed no credit for the *Monitor* system of ironclads "but that of adopting the first one *without delay* after a brief conference with you and sleeping *one night* over the plan; and for such improvements" as he had suggested for the later monitors.[1]

In a formal notice to Ericsson on September 21, 1861, approving his proposal of the original *Monitor*, Commodore Smith, to whose care Welles had entrusted all matters concerning the three ironclads to be built by contract, pointed out that there were some deficiencies in Ericsson's specification, and that "some changes may be suggested and a guarantee required."[2] Ericsson replied that his specification was meant to bind the contractor to furnish complete equipment, including a condenser for making fresh water and a collapsible India-rubber boat to be stored below for use in case the ordinary boats secured to the deck were destroyed. He had given particular attention to the construction of "a temporary rigging to be put up in case of need," which he trusted would merit Smith's approval.[3]

Ericsson, Bushnell, Griswold, and Winslow each took a one-fourth interest in the venture.[4] Winslow's reluctance to agree to the drastic guarantee demanded by the Department delayed the signing of the contract until October 4. When the partners submitted a substitute for Smith's draft of the guarantee, the Commodore refused to yield. His draft, he insisted,

> required nothing which you said the vessel would not perform, and upon your warranty to that effect, the contract was awarded to you.... You have modified the contract so that the government cannot expose the vessel to [the] very danger contemplated by you till after she shall have been accepted. So soon as the vessel is ready for service the government

---

1 *Ericsson Mss.*, ii. 2 *Ibid.*, i.
3 Ericsson to Smith, September 21, 1861. N.W.R., vol. 2600. Two days later Ericsson authorized Bushnell "to amend and complete my specification of an impregnable floating battery, in accordance with any request of Commodore Smith." Ericsson to Smith, September 27. *Ibid.*
4 Wells, *op. cit.*, pp. 20–21, 33; Church, *Ericsson*, i, p. 257; Wheeler, *op. cit.*, pp. 53–54.

THE NORTH SEEKS A SOLUTION 259

will send her on the coast and put her before the enemy's battery in the service for which you intended her. No other test can be made to prove the vessel and her appointments, than that to which both parties agreed to expose her; in fact it is the gist of the intentions of the contracting parties.

As the plan was novel, the designer had been required to warrant its success. The government would not receive the vessel unless allowed the stipulated ninety days for tests, although "it was understood that she should be subjected to no exposure which she was not intended by you to stand."

> Placing the vessel before an enemy's battery would test its capacity to resist shot and shell, that is the least of the difficulties I apprehend in the success of the vessel, but it is one of the properties of the vessel which you set forth as of great merit. . . . It would be the height of folly to set her up as a mark to expend ammunition on, when it could be sent home to the enemy at less expense. . . .[1]

The report of the ironclad board on September 16 had recommended that the contract for a single 12-knot ironclad, "on the rail and plate principle," be awarded to Bushnell, who apparently had originated the form of the guarantee by which the contractors agreed to refund the instalments paid by the government if their vessels proved failures. His ironclad was described as 180 feet long, 12⅔ feet depth of hold, and 10 feet draft, to be completed in four months for $235,250. The board feared that she would not "float her armor and load sufficiently high, and have stability enough for a sea vessel," but they recommended her, subject to a guarantee of those qualities.[2]

Welles forwarded to Bushnell on September 19 a contract which required a guarantee of the vessel's stability and speed, but not of her invulnerability to shot.[3] Bushnell returned the contract, duly executed as directed, on September 28, with the following observations:

> Captain Ericsson, Griswold, and myself, were better pleased with the wording of your contract for Ericsson's Battery, than with the one executed and sent forward, but Mr. Winslow had an idea that the three

---

[1] Smith to Ericsson, September 30. N.W.R., vol. 2634.
[2] *Report . . . in Relation to Armored Vessels*, pp. 6–7.
[3] N.D., *General Letter Book* no. 65; B.Y.D., *Contracts*, 1861, pp. 249–257; Smith to Bushnell, September 30, N.W.R., vol. 2634.

months, in the last clause, might be construed by other parties than yourself, as allowing three months to test the vessel in active service under the enemies fire before the Government would be justified in paying for, or accepting the same. I presume the contract sent forward will suit you just as well, or better, as it covers all points, and leaves the Government all the time they may ask in which to test the vessel in all respects. Other parties are desirous of taking the place of Mr. Winslow, and executing the contract you drew up, if it will please the Department better. . . . Both vessels are progressing finely.[1]

Ericsson deemed Smith's decision to test the *Monitor* under the enemy's fire before accepting her "perfectly reasonable and proper," and expressed the hope that her commander would be ordered "to save his powder until he is as near the rebel batteries as he can get." Except for his desire to retain Winslow in the enterprise "on account of his relations with certain members of the administration," he would not have agreed to Winslow's unsuccessful objections to Smith's draft of the guarantee. "After mature reflection," Winslow finally admitted the propriety of testing the vessel under the enemy's fire, but he pressed in vain for a reduction of the time stipulated for the tests. Meanwhile work proceeded on the steam machinery for the *Monitor*, and Winslow, Ericsson asserted, was "rolling the iron for the vessel itself, of a better quality, best scrap iron, than has yet been put into any vessel in this country."[2]

The contract for the *Monitor*, dated October 4, 1861, "between J. Ericsson, of the city of New York, as principal, and John F. Winslow, John A. Griswold, and C. S. Bushnell as sureties, on the first part, and Gideon Welles," provided for the construction of

---

[1] Bushnell to Smith, September 28. N.W.R., vol. 2600.
[2] Ericsson to Smith, October 2, 4, 8. N.W.R., vol. 2600. In supporting Winslow's plea for a reduction in the time allowed for the tests from three months to "such time as she can be fairly tested under the enemy's fire," Bushnell wrote to Smith, October 4: — "We are aware of the fact that we take upon ourselves an important responsibility in guaranteeing the success of this new means of National defence, and it is only the exigency of our present condition that would warrant such a step. . . ." *Ibid.* Winslow complained to Ericsson on November 26 that the *Scientific American* had stated that the contractors for the *Monitor* had guaranteed that she would withstand the fire of the enemy's batteries, and that she would not be accepted by the government until she was subjected to such proof. He declared that this was news to him. *Ericsson Mss.*, i.

an iron-clad shot-proof steam battery of iron and wood combined, on Ericsson's plan; the lower vessel to be wholly of iron, and the upper vessel of wood; the length to be one hundred and seventy-nine (179) feet, extreme breadth 41 feet, and depth 5 feet, or larger if the party of the first part shall think it necessary to carry the armament and stores required; the vessel to be constructed of the best materials and workmanship throughout, according to the plan and specifications hereto annexed, forming a part of this contract; and in addition to said specifications, the party of the first part hereby agrees to furnish masts, spars, sails, and rigging of sufficient dimensions to drive the vessel at the rate of six knots per hour in a fair breeze of wind. . . .

In addition to the specifications, the contractors were to furnish a condenser for making fresh water for the boilers. The vessel was to have space for provisions for one hundred persons for ninety days, with 2500 gallons of water in tanks, was to make eight knots under steam for twelve consecutive hours, and carry fuel for eight days' consumption at that speed. The contract stipulated that the deck of the vessel when loaded should be

eighteen inches above load line amidships; that she shall possess sufficient stability, with her armament, crew, and stores on board, for safe sea service in traversing the coast of the United States; that her crew shall be properly accommodated, and that the apparatus for working the battery shall prove successful and safe for the purpose intended, and that the vessel, machinery, and appointments, in all their parts, shall work to the entire satisfaction of the party of the second part.

The vessel should be completed and ready for sea in one hundred days, at a price of $275,000. As the work progressed, this sum was to be payable in instalments, from each of which 25 per cent was to be deducted and

retained until after the completion and satisfactory trial of the vessel, not to exceed ninety days after she shall be ready for sea.
And it is further agreed . . . that . . . in case the said vessel shall fail in performance of speed for sea service, as before stated, or in the security or successful working of the turret and guns with safety to the vessel and the men in the turret, or in her buoyancy to float and carry her battery, as aforesaid . . .

the contractors would refund to the United States the money that had been advanced to them within thirty days, the vessel meanwhile being held by the United States as collateral security. To meet the contractors' request that the time allowed for trial be reduced, Welles added a statement that

> after the battery shall be ready for sea, and be taken possession of by the government for the purpose of testing her properties as stipulated in the contract, such possession shall be regarded as accepting the vessel so far only as the workmanship and quality of materials are concerned, and that the test of the qualities and properties of the vessel as provided shall be made as soon thereafter as practicable, not to exceed ninety days, the reservation of twenty-five per cent. to be withheld until the test is made.[1]

Commodore Smith found his responsibility for the ironclads a heavy burden. To his friend Flag Officer Foote he wrote privately that he feared he should "burst" his reputation, on the ironclads, "as the Secretary has placed all the responsibility on me. . . ."[2] To Ericsson he expressed misgivings concerning the strength of the vessel, the size of the deck beams and turret shaft, the stability of the ship, the effect of her balanced rudder, her ability to float so great a weight of armor, the safe and successful working of the guns, and the effect of concussion on the men in the turret.[3] When the inventor submitted an elaborate scheme of ventilation by means of two centrifugal blowers, he retorted that

> your plan of ventilation appears plausible, but sailors do not fancy living under water without breathing in sunshine occasionally. I propose a temporary house be constructed on deck which will not increase the weight of the vessel more than eight or ten tons.[4]

His chief objection, however, seems to have been against the form of the hull. As is well known, the *Monitor* consisted of two vessels, an inner or lower hull of iron, and a raft-like upper vessel of wood and iron, overhanging the other. On October 21 Smith wrote to Ericsson,

---

[1] B.Y.D., *Contracts*, 1861, pp. 237–246. Printed in Senate Executive Document No. 86, 40th Congress, 2d Session, pp. 6–8; and in Wells, *op. cit.*, pp. 33–36. Cf. Smith to Ericsson, October 5, 1861. N.W.R., vol. 2634.
[2] October 18, 1861. N.D., Area 11, folder 1860–1862. On November 14 he declared to Foote, "I fear these iron-clad vessels will *bilge* my reputation." *Ibid.*
[3] Smith to Ericsson, October 5; Smith to Stimers, November 19, N.W.R., vol. 2634; Smith to Ericsson, October 19, 21, December 12, *Ericsson Mss.*, i. Cf. Church, *Ericsson*, i, pp. 264–271.
[4] Smith to Ericsson, October 19, 1861. *Ericsson Mss.*, i. Printed in Church, *Ericsson*, i, p. 268.

When I proposed to you in person to extend the width of the lower vessel, your reply was that shot would penetrate 36 feet under water, and hence the necessity for plating the wooden vessel securely under water, drawing in the lower vessel so that a shot passing under the plating of the wooden vessel could not by any possibility come in contact with the lower vessel. . . .

The more I reflect upon your Battery, the more I am fearful of her efficiency. You know from my remarks heretofore, why I object to the overhanging of the wooden vessel. It is a well established fact that strongly secured vessels with vertical sides will settle. What then will be the effect of the projection of your upper vessel over the lower one, loaded at either extremity with heavy plating. If the wooden vessel were to float by itself the iron plating would tend to settle her sides, so that the deck would, after a time, become much curved and finally break. The iron vessel in the centre of the wooden one will make this tendency still greater. I raise many objections, but I hope you will be able to overcome them all. . . .[1]

Considering the novelty of the design and the lack of experience in the United States in ironclad building, the misgivings of the gallant Commodore are by no means strange. Ericsson's confident replies silenced some of his objections. Defects in the original *Monitor* proved others to be altogether too well founded. The removal of some of these faults in later monitors was due largely to suggestions made by Smith himself. Despite his doubts, he steadfastly championed Ericsson's system against the other proposals for turreted vessels which were pressed on the Department in 1861 and 1862. On November 19, 1861, he declared to Stimers that he believed Ericsson's plan of turret to be "vastly superior to anything of the kind I have yet seen or heard described."[2]

Much fun has been poked at some of the Navy Department officials, notably Lenthall, for expressing their doubts of the ability of the *Monitor* to float.[3] Lenthall, who proposed in November, 1861, the creation of a whole fleet of double-turreted ironclads, needs no defence against the gen-

---

[1] *Ericsson Mss.*, i. Cf. Smith to Bushnell, October 22, N.W.R., vol. 2634.
[2] N.W.R., vol. 2634. Smith wrote to Stimers on December 3: "I have full confidence in Mr. Ericsson's ingenuity, skill and experience to enable him to overcome all difficulties and make his invention a success. . . ." *Ibid.*
[3] David D. Porter, *Incidents and Anecdotes of the Civil War* (New York, 1885), pp. 57–63; David D. Porter, *Naval History of the Civil War*, p. 121; Church, *Ericsson*, i, pp. 265–266; H. W. Wilson, *Ironclads in Action* (London, 1896, 2 vols.), i, pp. 11–12.

eral charge of "old fogyism." On the specific point of the calculations for the *Monitor*, historians have overlooked the fact that she was built on plans differing greatly from those first submitted by Ericsson. If an individual suddenly finds his income augmented at the same time that his living expenses are drastically reduced, the problem of keeping himself afloat financially assumes a very different aspect. In the same fashion, the problem of floating a vessel is radically altered when one increases its displacement and simultaneously cuts down the weight it has to carry. In submitting an amended specification on October 4, Ericsson pointed out that "the lower part of the vessel has been increased in length from 106 to 124 feet and made 18 feet instead of 16 feet wide at the bottom." This change in the dimensions of the lower vessel of course notably increased the total displacement. Shortly afterwards, he greatly reduced the weights his vessel was to carry. The original specifications provided for eight inches of iron on the turret, two inches on the deck, and a 6-inch armor belt, five feet wide, covering the sides of the upper vessel. Ericsson's revised project of October 19, 1861, reduced the deck armor from two inches to one, and the side armor from six inches to five, tapering below the water line to four and three inches in thickness.[1] Smith said he "would prefer the armor to be as specified, if the vessel can carry it." Nevertheless he

> was authorized by the Secretary of the Navy to say, that you can, at your discretion, reduce the thickness of the plating of the sides of the upper vessel as proposed, on condition that you guarantee the sides to repel shot, and deduct the cost pro rata to the whole cost of the plating and securing it to the vessel.

[1] Ericsson to Smith, October 19. N.W.R., vol. 2600. Cf. the calculations of the displacement of the *Monitor* in B.C.R., 80-11-26. The first of these unsigned papers figures the weight of the vessel at 171 tons above Ericsson's estimate, "increasing the draft $12\frac{3}{8}$ inches, and leaving the *deck only $5\frac{5}{8}$ inches above water-line*," even when 70 tons of masts, spars, rigging, boats, davits, furniture, galley, cooking apparatus and utensils were not included. The second paper estimates the weight saved by Ericsson's reduction of the deck and side armor to be 172 tons. The side armor, on the altered plan, was composed of three layers of one-inch iron covering the whole side, backed by one similar layer extending only 36 inches below the deck, and by an inner layer extending only 30 inches below the deck. The total weight of armor would then be 335 tons, instead of 507.

I am not surprised at your request to reduce weight of iron, as I think you must be satisfied the vessel will not float at the line you proposed without it, if then.[1]

He likewise authorized the reduction in the deck armor, but rebuked Ericsson's unconvincing argument that the specifications called for only one inch of iron on the deck, by pointing to the plan which had accompanied the rather ambiguous specification. On the plan, the 2-inch thickness was clearly indicated.[2]

To the various criticisms and suggestions sent to him, Ericsson replied with the greatest confidence, sending Smith several essays on stability, and assuring him that

there is no living man who has tripped me in calculation or proved my figures wrong in a single instance in matters relating to theoretical computation.[3]

He begged Smith

to rest tranquil as to the result; success cannot fail to crown the undertaking. Nothing is attempted not already well tried, or of so strictly mechanical a nature as to be susceptible of previous determination.[4]

On October 25, Ericsson, Winslow, Griswold, and Bushnell contracted with Thomas F. Rowland, of the Continental Iron Works, Green Point, Brooklyn, for the construction and launching of the vessel.[5] On the same day her keel was laid.

1 Smith to Ericsson, October 19, 21. *Ericsson Mss.*, i.
2 Ericsson to Smith, October 18, N.W.R., vol. 2600; Smith to Ericsson, October 23, *Ericsson Mss.*, i. Ericsson replied on October 24: "The plan to which you refer was never intended as a working drawing. It was originally intended merely as a diagrammatic and theoretical exposition of the *principle* of my battery before yourself and the other members of the committee appointed to decide on the ironclad vessels. It was, however, my intention, before I had looked closely into the subject, to make the deck plating *two* inches thick. On referring to my notes of the effect of the explosion of shells on level wooden platforms and the necessity of solid wood work under, rather than thick plating at the surface, I at once increased the strength of the deck by employing oak beams 10 inches square placed only 26 inches apart and deck planks 7 inches thick as more effective than thick plating. The great reduction of weight effected by the change, I need hardly say powerfully influenced me in adopting the heavy wood work in preference to the thick plating." N.W.R., vol. 2600.
3 Ericsson to Smith, September 27, October 14, 16, 17, 18, 23, 25, December 17. N.W.R., vols. 2600, 2601. Cf. Church, *Ericsson*, i, pp. 266–267.
4 October 17. N.W.R., vol. 2600.
5 The contract is printed and reproduced in facsimile in Wells, *op. cit.*, pp. 38–39, 54–56. Bushnell's signature was lacking. The partners were to furnish the ma-

The Novelty Iron Works of New York built the turret, and Delamater and Company of the same city, the engines. Charles De Lancy of Buffalo made the iron pendulums which served as port stoppers; and Abbott and Son of Baltimore, the Albany Iron Works of Troy, Holdane and Company of New York, and the Rensselaer Iron Works furnished the iron. Ericsson and Smith had hoped to get rolled plates of 4-inch thickness for the outer half of the turret; but nothing thicker than 15/16 or one inch could be had, without intolerable delay.[1] Smith estimated that the adoption of laminated armor formed of one-inch plates would reduce the resistance to shot "about one-fourth as compared to solid plates."[2]

Not even Ericsson's resourcefulness, energy and enthusiasm sufficed to complete the work by January 12, the date fixed by the contract. The ship was launched January 30, and commissioned on February 25, under the command of Lieutenant John L. Worden. Her two 11-inch Dahlgren guns had been commandeered from the gunboat *Dacotah*. Steam had been applied to the engines on December 31, and to the turret February 17. But the first trials of the vessel proved a dismal failure, to the dismay of the officials at the Navy Department, who were anxiously awaiting her arrival at Hampton Roads. Under feverish pressure, however, the defects in the engines and steering gear were remedied, and the *Monitor* left the New York Navy Yard at 10.30 A.M., March 6, escorted by the gunboats *Currituck* and *Sachem*, and the tugboat *Seth Low*.[3]

---

terials; and Rowland was to construct the ship for 7½ cents per pound of iron used.

[1] Ericsson to Smith, October 4, 8, 19, N.W.R., vol. 2600; Smith to Ericsson, October 5, N.W.R., vol. 2634, and October 11, *Ericsson Mss.*, i; Church, *Ericsson*, i, p. 259; Wheeler, *op. cit.*, pp. 28–33, with extracts from four letters from Winslow to Ericsson.

[2] Smith to Ericsson, October 19, *Ericsson Mss.*, i.

[3] N.D., *Bureau Letters*, October 19, 22, 1861; *Commandants Letters, Navy Yard, New York*, 1862, i, ii, *passim*; Fox to Ericsson, February 3, 1862, *General Letter Book* no. 67; *Officers Letters*, Jan.–March, 1862, using index, *s.v.* Worden; N.W.R., vols. 2601, 2602, 2634, 5068, *passim*; *Log of the U. S. S. Monitor*, February 25–March 6; *Ericsson Mss.*, i; O.R.N., vi, using index *s.v. Monitor*. See also the interesting reminiscences of Professor Charles W. MacCord, formerly chief draftsman for Ericsson, "Ericsson and his 'Monitor,'" in *North American Re-*

THE NORTH SEEKS A SOLUTION 267

All six instalments of the purchase price, less the 25 per cent reservation, had been paid by the Navy Department when the *Monitor* started for Hampton Roads.[1] The delays of the Treasury Department in meeting the drafts, however, had caused the contractors some embarrassment. Ericsson wrote to Smith that "in view of the large amount of funds thus called for from private sources, my contemplated organization and operation by what is called night gangs, has been to some extent frustrated."[2] The reservation, amounting to $68,750, was paid by warrant on March 14, 1862. Church states the cost of the *Monitor* to have been $195,-142.60, leaving a net profit of $79,857.40 to be divided among the four partners. Besides his one-fourth share, $19,964.35, Ericsson received $1000 for engineering services.[3] His lasting reward has been a nation's gratitude, richly deserved.

Though Bushnell rendered distinguished service in connection with the *Monitor*, little good can be said of his own ironclad, the *Galena*. This vessel, built with considerable tumblehome, was originally intended to have iron armor 2⅝ inches thick, formed of a combination of plates and rails, backed by 1½ inches of rubber, over her wooden sides. At the suggestion of Griswold and Winslow, the sub-contractors for the armor, however, the rubber was dispensed with and the thick-

---

view, October, 1889. Ericsson's letter of January 20, 1862, proposing the name of the vessel, is printed in Church, *Ericsson*, i, p. 254, note. Fox telegraphed him on February 1 that the Secretary agreed to the name. *General Letter Book* no. 67. Griswold declared to Ericsson, January 22, 1862, that he would have preferred the name "Ericsson Battery." *Ericsson Mss.*, i.

February was a busy month at the New York Navy Yard where the *Monitor* received her finishing touches. Paulding, the Commandant, reported on March 1 that "during the month of February twenty-five vessels mounting 122 guns have been fitted, equipped and got off from this Yard." *Commandants Letters, Navy Yard, New York*, 1862, vol. ii.

[1] Senate Executive Document No. 86, 40th Congress, 2d Session. The warrants were drawn by the Navy Department on November 25, December 3, December 17, January 3, February 6, and March 3.

[2] January 4, 1862. N.W.R., vol. 2602. Cf. Ericsson to Smith, February 6, 1862. *Ibid.* Smith replied that he had exerted his best efforts at the Treasury Department to speed the payments. N.W.R., vol. 2634, January 7, February 8, 1862. Cf. Griswold to Ericsson, January 3, 1862, *Ericsson Mss.*, i; and Church, *Ericsson*, i, pp. 269–270.

[3] *Ibid.*

ness of the iron increased to 3⅛ inches. This extended the whole length of the ship, at and near the water line, and rose amidships to the level of the port-sills. From the port-sills to the rail, and at the extremities of the vessel, was lighter armor. This screw steamer, mounting four 9-inch Dahlgren guns and two Parrott rifles, was launched on February 14, 1862, at Mystic, Connecticut, completed at Rowland's shipyard at Green Point, and commissioned April 21.[1] Flag Officer Goldsborough described her as

a most miserable contrivance — entirely beneath naval criticism . . . She is pretty good ram, and that, in general terms, is about the amount of her, unless she is kept bows on in fighting her guns. At best, however, she is a poor stick for an iron clad. Her moral is better than her physical effect![2]

After the action at Drewry's Bluff, May 15, 1862, in which she had 13 men killed and 11 wounded, her commander, John Rodgers, grimly reported: "We demonstrated that she is not shot-proof."[3]

The third of the three ironclads recommended by Commodore Smith's board, the *New Ironsides*, was a formidable vessel of 3486 tons, mounting eighteen heavy guns. Combining some of the features of both the *Gloire* and the *Warrior*, she formed a good example of the type known in the British Navy as the "belt-and-battery" class. Her wooden hull, 230 feet long and 56 feet beam, had sides which tumbled home at an angle of about 17 degrees. Tongued and grooved iron plates, 4½ inches thick, 15 feet long and 28 inches wide, protected her for 170 feet amidships, and also from stem to stern from 4 feet below to 3 feet above the load line.[4] Athwartship iron bulkheads between the spar and gun decks, and a layer of one-inch iron under the wooden spar deck, com-

---

[1] N.W.R., vols. 2600, 2601–2603, 2634, *passim*; O.R.N., 2d series, i, p. 90. In B.C.R., 28–6–3, are some drawings of, and calculations concerning, this vessel, accompanied by a letter of John Ericsson to Bushnell, September 11, 1861, stating that he had "examined the elements of stability of your intended steel clad vessel," and thought she would prove "not only sufficiently stable but what sailors call stiff."
[2] *Correspondence of G. V. Fox*, i, pp. 263, 272.
[3] O.R.N., vii, p. 357.
[4] The second, or lower, row of plates under water was three inches thick.

pleted her armor. The contractors, Merrick and Sons of Philadelphia, guaranteed a speed of 9½ knots, and delivery within nine months, for the sum of $780,000. They agreed to forfeit $500 per day for delay, and to refund all payments which had been advanced, if the ship failed in speed or other properties. Though she never attained the guaranteed speed, this bark-rigged screw steamer, which was commissioned on August 21, 1862, proved a great success. It is said that she participated in more days of actual fighting than any other ironclad of the Civil War.[1]

Meanwhile the flood of ironclad projects pouring in on the Navy Department had assumed such proportions that, at the close of December, Welles appointed a new board, headed by Commodore W. B. Shubrick, to examine the proposals. This board reported on February 28 that none of the plans they had examined merited adoption. They recommended, however, that a target be set up for tests of corrugated iron armor.[2] Of the scores of projects for armored vessels submitted prior to the battle of Hampton Roads, it is interesting to note that three more besides those of Whitney and Rowland, and Ericsson, were for turreted vessels. In August, Alfred Guthrie of Chicago brought to Commodore Smith models and drawings of a light-draft steam gunboat "either with or without four revolving shields of wrought iron in which may be planted two heavy cannon all worked from the inside secure from injury."[3] Lewis White of Dorchester, Massachusetts,

---

[1] *Report . . . in Relation to Armored Vessels*, p. 6; contract of October 15, 1861, with specification, in B.Y.D., *Contracts*, 1861, pp. 269–295; N.W.R., vols. 2599–2602, 2634, *passim*; O.R.N., vii–xvi, using index *s.v. New Ironsides*; O.R.N., 2d series, i, p. 159. Her plans may be found in B.C.R., 10-3-19, 78-12-18, 78-12-34, 107-9 -12 A–L. Cf. W. L. Barnes to Ericsson, February 17, 1862, in *Ericsson Mss.*, i; and Captain George E. Belknap, "Reminiscent of the 'New Ironsides' off Charleston," in *United Service*, January, 1879, pp. 63–82. Belknap states that she "never had a man seriously hurt in action." Fox wrote to Dupont, September 6, 1862, that "the Ironsides seems a success. Dahlgren's 11 in. gun with 30 lbs. powder at 76 feet glances from the 4½ plate placed at the same angle. And the same charge fired perpendicular only breaks the iron without penetration." *Correspondence of G. V. Fox*, i, p. 154.
[2] N.D., *Naval Examining Board*, December 27, 1861, February 28, 1862. Cf. Smith to Welles, December 21, 1861, *Bureau Letters*.
[3] Guthrie to Welles, August 16, September 6; Guthrie to President Lincoln, September 5. *Miscellaneous Letters*, 1861. Cf. *Letters on Inventions*, vol. i, no. 2.

submitted on January 25, 1862, several plans for ironclad vessels, including one for a double-turreted ship, dated August, 1861.[1] J. W. Norcross of Cicero, New York, declared in March, 1862, that he had been working on plans of a "revolving tower" for nearly ten years, and had submitted his project without success to Commodore Smith in the summer of 1861. His original design, he declared, comprised a vessel with three revolving and disappearing towers.[2] On August 31, 1861, John Murray Forbes wrote to a friend in England asking him to "get at the views of some experienced man" on a plan he had conceived for putting armor and turrets on two iron ships then on the stocks.[3] It would be interesting to know how many of these projects were influenced by the publication of Captain Coles's plans in 1860.[4] His idea of revolving turrets, at all events, took the Navy Department by storm in the autumn of 1861.

When John Laird stated in the House of Commons on March 27, 1863, that the Union Navy Department had asked his firm soon after the outbreak of the Civil War to submit bids and specifications for ironclad vessels and gunboats, Welles published a flat denial. He declared that no person had been authorized to apply to Laird or to any other foreign shipbuilder to build a vessel for the United States, and that when agents of foreign firms had submitted such proposals he had declined them in every instance.[5] Unpublished letters

---

[1] *Ibid.*, vol. i, no. 36. This inventor frankly confessed that he knew nothing of naval architecture.

[2] Norcross to Charles B. Sedgwick, chairman of the House Committee on Naval Affairs, March 14, 1862. B.C.R., 80-11-23. Norcross stated that he had obtained the dimensions of the *Monitor* from the foreman while she was on the stocks. Cf. the proposals of Willis and Co., of Cold Spring Harbor, Long Island, and Lemuel W. Wright of Palmer, Massachusetts. N.D., *Letters on Inventions*, i, no. 21, and *Miscellaneous Letters*, September 23, 1861.

[3] S. F. Hughes, ed., *Letters and Recollections of John Murray Forbes* (Boston and New York, 1899, 2 vols.), i, p. 245.

[4] See above, pp. 188-190.

[5] Hansard, 3rd series, clxx, cols. 70-71; Welles to Charles Sumner, May 19, 1863, New York *Herald*, August 7, 1863. A point of order prevented Cobden from reading this letter in the House of Commons on July 23. Hansard, clxii, col. 1259; London *Times*, July 24, 1863. Cf. *Letters and Recollections of J. M. Forbes*, ii, p. 25.

in the Navy Department, the Fox Papers and the Welles Papers, go far to explain this conflicting testimony, and indicate that Assistant Secretary Fox contemplated the construction by Laird for the Union Navy of two double-turreted ironclads somewhat resembling the two famous rams which Laird later built for the Confederates.

The policy of purchasing vessels abroad had been discussed more than once at the Navy Department since the outbreak of the war. John Fallon of Philadelphia transmitted to Welles on June 20, 1861, an offer from John Laird Sons and Company to construct gunboats for the United States; but Welles declined the proposal.[1] While on a visit to England in May and June, John T. Howard of New York obtained estimates from the Lairds for ironclad frigates and wooden gunboats, which he submitted on their behalf to the Navy Department in July. On July 30 he reported to the Lairds from Washington that he had had frequent interviews with the "Department of Naval Affairs" and had found the "Minister of the Navy . . . inclined to have an iron-plated ship built out of the country. . . ." He transmitted a memorandum which he had received from the Navy Department the previous evening, asking the Lairds to reply at once "stating if you will agree to build such a ship if desired, how soon and for how much, with such plans and specifications as you may deem it best to send me." The memorandum expressed a desire for the construction of an iron-plated floating battery planned for the sole purpose of entering ports guarded with batteries and forts which were 300 to 880 yards from the channel. She was to be a mastless vessel, with a draft not over fourteen feet, and must be proof against both horizontal and plunging fire. Her speed need not exceed six knots, but she must have a rudder at each end so placed as not to be liable to be disabled in passing the forts. She was to carry eight rifled guns weighing each about eight tons, two on each side, two on the bow, and two astern. "The ship

---

[1] *Welles Papers*, xlvi; Fallon to Dr. William Irvin, September 3, 1863, filed under "Chandler," in *Fox Papers*. Cf. Welles to Fox, August 19, 1863. *Ibid.*

to be finished complete, with guns and everything appertaining."[1]

Howard wrote to the Lairds on September 20 that "the Secretary was rather disappointed that you have not sent any response to the Memorandum in reference to a shell and shot-proof battery . . . intended to force an entry into Charleston Harbour . . .;" and again on October 25 that the Secretary "was very desirous to have you build the iron-plated or bomb-proof batteries. . . ."[2] In weighing this contemporaneous statement, one must bear in mind the natural tendency of brokers to exaggerate both their activity and the measure of their success. Welles's explicit denial of any such intention as Howard attributed to him is confirmed by statements made in 1863 both by Fox and by Charles B. Sedgwick, Chairman of the House Committee on Naval Affairs, who had introduced Howard to the Secretary in July, 1861.[3] Welles realized that American shipbuilders, as a result of the suspension of orders at the outbreak of the war, were so "clamorous for contracts . . . that we would have had terrible indignation upon us had we gone abroad for vessels, which I never thought of doing."[4]

Fox's version of the matter in 1863 was that Howard had called at the Navy Department in 1861 on behalf of Laird, whom he described as an English abolitionist eager to help the North by building vessels, especially ironclads.

> I told Howard what I told everybody else, that he might send plans and specifications, and I described to Howard what kind of an Iron clad I thought we ought to have. Howard subsequently sent some tracings when the subject was dropped, though I think a young Laird came over with renewed offers. The Department, however, never solicited, never requested, never purchased nor ever dreamed of obtaining a single vessel from abroad, on the contrary, the Secretary invariably set his face against

---

[1] *Appendix to the Case Presented on the Part of the Government of Her Britannic Majesty* [to the Geneva Tribunal of Arbitration, London, 1872, 7 vols.], v, pp. 204–210.
[2] *Ibid.*, pp. 213, 214.
[3] Sedgwick wrote to William Faxon, Chief Clerk of the Navy Department, on August 9, 1863, that Welles had "declined entering into any negotiation" with Howard in 1861. New York *Evening Post*, August 11, 1863.
[4] *Diary of Gideon Welles*, i, p. 291, May 2, 1863.

it. I don't know how far Howard went in his statements but he never had a shadow of authority and what conversation was held with him was by myself at his urgent solicitations but against my judgment....[1]

This account was supported by the recollections of W. H. Aspinwall, who stated that he had laid Laird's estimates before Fox in 1861, at Howard's request, and had transmitted to Howard a reply from Fox, "declining to buy or build abroad."[2]

Fox's unpublished letters, however, show indisputably that he gave Howard more encouragement than he was willing to admit in 1863. They indicate that the memorandum forwarded by Howard to the Lairds on July 30 was the work of the Assistant Secretary. On August 9 Howard sent the Lairds a copy of the Navy Department's advertisement of August 7, calling for offers to construct ironclads.[3] On the thirteenth Fox wrote to him: "I hope you have written out about the floating battery. I wish they would tender for two."[4] Meanwhile the Lairds had sent to Howard tracings showing a section of an iron cased frigate and the arrangement of engines in the British wooden screw gunboats, which he submitted to Welles some time previous to September 20.[5] On October 9, however, the Lairds informed Howard that, although they were still prepared to execute American orders for one or two gunboats, their engagements with the Admiralty for the construction of an iron cased frigate and of a large screw transport vessel would preclude their quick construction of "other vessels of this class, and we therefore decided not to tender to your Government for the vessels they require."[6] When Howard transmitted this letter to the Navy

[1] Fox to W. H. Aspinwall, April 24, August 27, 1863. Cf. Fox to G. W. Blount, April 17, 1863. *Fox Papers*.
[2] Aspinwall added that after this rebuff Howard took the estimates himself to Washington. Aspinwall to Fox, April 11, September 1 and 9, 1863. *Ibid.*
[3] *Appendix to British Case*, v, pp. 211-212. See above, pp. 246-247.
[4] Copy enclosed in letter of Howard to Fox, August 25, 1863, *Fox Papers*; New York *Evening Post*, February 13, 1897. Cf. *Appendix to British Case*, v, p. 212.
[5] *Ibid.*, pp. 210-213.
[6] *Ibid.*, p. 214. The original of this letter, with a tracing of the arrangement of engines in gunboats, is with Howard's letter of October 23, in N.D., *Miscellaneous Letters*. On October 12, however, the Lairds sent to the French Ministry of Marine a proposal to build ironclads for the French Navy, which was declined on November 5. A.M., 1 DD¹ 298.

Department on October 23, Fox replied that "what we proposed for them [the Lairds] to build was *iron clad* vessels, and not *Gunboats* as the latter are built in this country." On November 1 he informed Howard that

> we are making our own plans for boats such as I suggested to you, and shall soon be in the market. I wonder if we could not get some plates imported for a few of them. What do you think of it. Do you believe we could buy an entire Iron Frigate in England, all ready for sea. . . .[1]

Five days later the Assistant Secretary sent Howard a letter which throws a flood of light on the genesis of the Department's ironclad policy. He explained that "we are getting up models and plans of a floating battery such as described to you," and that, if the Assistant Secretary's ideas were adopted, the drawings would be sent to Howard, who would be commissioned to obtain the plates in England and to ship them at once.

> We propose a vessel of 205 feet in length, 47 feet beam, 12 feet draft; top flat, of 2-inch iron; sides 3 feet above the water, protected by 4½ inch iron; — two revolving towers of 4½ inch iron, each carrying one 11-inch gun.
> This is not a sea boat, but will steam six knots, and is constructed for the specific object I mentioned to you. We shall probably ask for the plates for the towers, which may be a little conical, and the sides; no others. I should like your address there, in case we should send abroad, and will ask you to talk with Laird and Son, as *time* is the great object.[2]

When Welles denied John Laird's statement to the House of Commons in 1863, the latter published the correspondence of his firm with Howard, whose name, however, he withheld.[3] After the publication of Sedgwick's letter to Faxon, Howard became restive and threatened to print the letters he had received from Fox in 1861. Although Welles and Fox gave their consent to the publication of the entire correspondence, Evarts and Sumner, whose advice was asked, feared that it would do harm; and Howard on their advice concluded to remain silent.[4] Welles confided to his diary some sharp com-

---

[1] Fox to Howard, October 29, November 1. Copies enclosed in Howard to Fox, August 25, 1863. *Fox Papers*; New York *Evening Post*, February 13, 1897.
[2] N.D., *Confidential Letters*, v.   [3] London *Times*, July 27, 1863.
[4] Howard to Fox, August 25, 28, September 5, telegram; Fox to Howard, August 27, September 5, telegram, September 6; Welles to Fox, August 5, 19, *Fox*

ments on Fox's officiousness.[1] The Assistant Secretary explained to his chief that

in '61 before Errickson gave us such an admirable inshore impregnable battery we had nothing, nor the offer of anything. Isherwood thought iron clads a humbug and Lenthal shrank from touching the subject. Just at that period when fatal days and months were passing I am aware that under Howards representations of the antislavery earnestness of this man, no one at the Dept objected to receiving plans, specifications and offers from any part of the world. I looked upon it as a means of obtaining something tangible to force Lenthal to work out our great want. My sentence would have been better to have omitted Laird's name and used built for build, but it is small capital to found an offer of the Dept upon as originally stated by Laird in Parliament. In the published correspondence by Laird, Howard does not aver that he has any authority, but he uses your office instead of mine and puts himself on a confidential relation unwarranted. . . .[2]

While the technical officers of the Navy Department were working out the details of Fox's plan to install two of Coles's revolving "towers" on ironclads of low freeboard, the Assistant Secretary investigated possible sources for a prompt supply of armor plate in the North. When an editorial in the *Boston Evening Transcript*, October 28, proclaimed the urgent need for armored vessels, and asserted that Boston could supply the Navy Department with thirty ironclad steamers in thirty days, the Assistant Secretary followed up the suggestion, only to find that the supply of iron at Boston had been greatly exaggerated.[3]

By the end of November John Lenthall, Chief of the Bureau of Construction and Repair, and Engineer-in-Chief B. F. Isherwood, spurred by the impatient Fox, had obtained the sanction of the Navy Department for the construction of a whole fleet of double-turreted ironclads on their own designs. In preference to Ericsson's turret they adopted Captain Coles's system, in which the base of the turret, instead of being exposed as in vessels of the *Monitor* type, was protected by a sloping armored glacis. Rejecting laminated armor,

Papers; Howard to Fox, August 27, telegram, N.D., *Miscellaneous Letters*; *Appendix to British Case*, v, pp. 215–216. Cf. J. M. Forbes to Welles, May 5, 1863, *Welles Papers*, liii; *Diary of Gideon Welles*, i, pp. 394–396. See also the article by John Raymond Howard in the New York *Evening Post*, February 13, 1897; and *Some Memories of John Tasker Howard* (N.Y. [?], 1909), pp. 46–47.
1 *Ibid.*, i, p. 401. 2 August 15, 1863, *Welles Papers*, liv.
3 W. P. Gregg to Fox, November 5, 8, 15, 28, 1861. N.D., *Miscellaneous Letters*.

they proposed large plates 3¼ inches thick for 15 feet at each end of the vessel, 3¾ inches thick for the next 15 feet, and 4¼ inches thick for the remaining 172½ feet amidships. The turret armor was to be composed of two layers of plates, three inches and two inches in thickness, backed by ten inches of oak. Two thicknesses of ¾-inch iron formed the deck armor.[1] Of the $16,530,000 for which Lenthall asked in his annual report of November 29, 1861, to be expended for purchase, alteration and construction of new vessels, twelve millions were required "for the construction and completion of twenty iron-clad vessels."[2]

In his annual report of December 2, 1861, Welles proposed this appropriation of twelve millions.[3] When Sedgwick introduced in the House on December 17 an appropriation of ten millions for these twenty ironclads, he stated that they would cost from $500,000 to $580,000 each. The plans, estimates and specifications for these vessels had been "under consideration for a long time in the Navy Department," had been prepared "with the utmost care," and "all perfected." These vessels, to be built on "an entirely new plan, and differing from any now being built," would be able to enter any harbor where there was more than twelve feet of water over the bar, and to run past any harbor defences without injury. The plans, which already had been "examined by the most competent ship builders in the country," were now "ready to go into the hands of the builders at any moment;" and competitive bids from private shipyards and from iron manufacturers had already been invited. The Navy Department hoped to have these vessels ready for service within four months. As a survey of the iron manufacturers of the country had shown that they could not furnish all the armor required within a year, some orders for plates must be placed abroad.[4]

1 The specifications for this class of vessels, hitherto overlooked by historians, are printed in full in Appendix F. Cf. Lenthall to Welles, March 13, 1862, *Bureau Letters*.
2 Senate Executive Document No. 1, 37th Congress, 2d Session, iii, p. 355.
3 *Ibid.*, pp. 22–23.
4 *Congressional Globe*, 37th Congress, 2d Session, cols. 123, 147–148.

This bill, which passed the House on December 19, without even a roll call, was held up in the Senate until February 7.[1] Meanwhile the Navy Department had sent specifications to most of the shipbuilders and ironmasters of the country, and had received numerous offers.[2] The replies of the ironmasters showed the impossibility of obtaining such large plates in the United States in the time desired, although several firms offered to construct the necessary machinery if the government would advance funds and guarantee large orders.[3] Welles, therefore, on December 21, despatched Daniel B. Martin, an engineer who had been superintending the construction of the *Galena*, to England, France and Belgium, in quest of armor plate.[4]

The news of Lenthall and Isherwood's plan caused great anxiety to Ericsson and his partners, who were hoping for further contracts for vessels similar to the *Monitor*. On December 17 Ericsson wrote to Commodore Smith asking him to point out to Secretary Welles that

> I made an elaborate drawing of a revolving turret thus supported on the point of the turret shaft, as early as 1854. This fact I can establish by the highest testimony and accordingly claim to have perfected this invention more than seven years before Captain Cole [sic] brought out his abortive scheme in England.[5]

Smith replied two days later, declining to interfere since he had not been consulted by the Department in regard to the new type of ironclads. His statement that the Department intended to use Ericsson's plan of turret on these twenty projected vessels is disproved by their specifications. He

---

[1] *Ibid.*, cols. 148, 697. See below, pp. 279–281.
[2] More than a dozen bids to construct one or more of these proposed ironclads may be found in N.D., *Miscellaneous Letters*, December, 1861, and January, 1862, and in B.C.R., *Miscellaneous Letters*, xliii.
[3] C. W. Whitney to Joseph Smith, December 5, 10, 11, 1861, N.W.R., vol. 2601; Samuel J. Reeves to Welles, December 20, 1861; Cooper, Hewitt, and Company, to Welles, December 23, 1861; W. P. Gregg to Fox, November 15, 1861. N.D., *Miscellaneous Letters*. Cf. Lenthall and Isherwood to Welles, March 17, 1862, *Bureau Letters*.
[4] Welles to Martin, December 21, 1861. *General Letter Book* no. 67. John A. Kernochan of New York, the American agent of the Mersey Steel and Iron Co., had sent Welles a price list of armor plates on July 24. *Miscellaneous Letters*.
[5] N.W.R., vol. 2601.

told Ericsson that he had known that the shaft supported the turret but had supposed that it was to

> bear and traverse on rollers also. The principle of the turret is old, but I presume your improved appurtenances may be patented and thus secure to you its advantages. If the Government use it in other vessels, you would have a claim for the patent, but I would recommend that it be fully tested before others are constructed, as there are several points about it which can only be settled by actual experiment.[1]

On December 23, Ericsson sent Secretary Welles a proposal to build six ironclads of an improved *Monitor* type, two of them to be delivered on April 30, and the rest on May 30, 1862. Though he mentions neither Lenthall, nor Isherwood, nor Coles, his whole letter is an interesting argument contrasting the merits of his own system with that of Coles, as advocated by the Bureau of Construction and Repair.[2]

Ericsson and his partners did not rest content with engineers' arguments alone. On December 25 Erastus Corning, a member of Congress and a partner of Winslow in the Albany Iron Works, wrote to Welles concerning the bill for twenty ironclads, that he was

> apprehensive that the plans adopted or proposed for adoption, are not such as will secure to the Government the very best result, and that the cost may be very much greater than it should be. . . . A few days delay may be far less important, than falling into either of the errors indicated. The friends who have brought this matter to my mind, have promised to submit their reasons in detail why hasty and immature action should not be had in determining this question, and will either transmit such to you direct or thro me at once. . . .[3]

Winslow hastened to Washington to interview the officials of the Navy Department. On January 6, while on his way back to Troy, he wrote to Ericsson that he thought he had accomplished something with "the powers" at Washington.

[1] N.W.R., vol. 2634. On December 10 Smith had written to C. W. Whitney: "The Navy Department, I believe, are about to build some ironclad vessels, to be plated with 4½ inch iron, but I have no knowledge of the plans, or any control in the matter." *Ibid*. Early in January Smith wrote that he understood "a number, at least twenty, armored gun boats besides the three armored vessels already under contract for, are to be constructed with all practicable despatch. . . ." Endorsement on letter of Craig Biddle, *Miscellaneous Letters*, January, 1862, i.
[2] This important letter is printed in full in Appendix G.
[3] N.D., *Miscellaneous Letters*.

At least the Navy Department will not authorize *more* than one or two boats on the Isherwood plan till ours is put in proof, and if that proof is satisfactory, I have a promise from the *very* highest source that we shall have all we want of the 20 to be built. This *ought* to satisfy us. . . .[1]

Four days later he sent a fuller report of his interview with Fox.

>While I cannot say that I found Mr. F. unfriendly, still there was at first a loftiness of manner toward us, and a confidence in the bureau plan, that was to me amusing; yet, finding him to be a really able man, and of controlling influence in matters relating to his bureau, I was determined he should either convert me to the bureau plan, or I would him to our plan, and therefore devoted all the time I could get him to appropriate to this object, and after more than five hours' consecutive discussion of all the points involved, I left him with an admission that he was only familiar with *sailing* and *defending* a ship; that, as to the mechanics and architecture incident to a ship or steamer building, he professed to know but little, and so far as the mechanical and other arrangements of the Ericsson battery were concerned, he would concede to me that it appeared to embody all the features of success, and if on trial this was demonstrated, ours would be the plan to be adopted. This was the substance and meaning of his parting assurances to me, and though it cost me hours of animated and earnest colloquial effort, yet I made a convert of him, as I think, and felt abundantly compensated.[2]

One is tempted to ask whether the political influence of Ericsson's partners had anything to do with the extraordinary delay of the passage of the ironclad bill by the Senate. After its passage by the House on December 19, it was referred by the Senate the next day to the Committee on Naval Affairs. When Senator John P. Hale of New Hampshire, the Chairman of the Committee, reported the bill on January 8 with amendments reducing the number of ships to twelve, there arose a bitter wrangle over his proposal that the President, not the Secretary of the Navy, be authorized to expend the money. Welles was under a heavy fire because his brother-in-law, George D. Morgan, whom he had employed to purchase vessels for the Government, had made $70,000 for five months' work by collecting a commission of 2½ per

---

[1] *Ericsson Mss.*, i. The endorsement gives the date as January 6.
[2] Church, *Ericsson*, i, pp. 277–278. Church does not state what the bureau plan was. On January 24 Griswold wrote to Ericsson from Troy: "I cannot imagine that the 'twenty gun boat' conspirators have ground for hope — certainly not if the 'Monitor' is *demonstrated* first." *Ericsson Mss.*, i.

cent from the sellers of the ships. This was the rate established by the New York Chamber of Commerce for ordinary commercial transactions of similar nature.[1] The Senate discussion of this affair delayed action on the ironclad bill, which was laid on the table on January 9. On February 3 Welles appealed to Hale to hasten the decision. Hale replied that the Committee, before acting on the bill, wished to know how many of these ironclads could be built in six months, and how many in a year; on what plan the Department proposed to build; what would be the cost of each ship; and to what particular use were the vessels destined. Welles explained on February 7 that the Department could probably build ten to twelve ironclads in the next six months, and "double or three times that number within a year." The Department did not intend "to confine itself exclusively to any particular plan yet offered," but would "avail itself of the experience which will be gained in the construction of those now going forward, one of which will be soon tested in actual conflict." The bids received for "those planned by the Department" ranged from $360,000 to $580,000 each. Captain Ericsson, "whose ingenious battery is now completed," had offered to build six similar vessels for $320,000 each. The Secretary earnestly recommended the appropriation of ten millions to build ironclads designed "to reduce all the fortified seaports of the enemy and open their harbors to the union armies."[2]

In the debate on the naval appropriation bill on February 4 Senator Grimes, a spokesman for the Navy Department, observed that some thought the proposed ironclads were

all to be built on one particular plan ... square at the ends and flat in the bottom; mere tubs. I believe it is proposed to build one or two of that description for some particular localities, but only one or two, and that the general idea is to build them very strong with iron, with sharp prows at

---

[1] Senate Report no. 9 and Senate Executive Document no. 15, 37th Congress, 2d Session. Cf. *Diary of Gideon Welles*, i, p. 487; and *Letters and Recollections of J. M. Forbes*, i, pp. 230–231, 289–290.

[2] *Congressional Globe*, 37th Congress, 2d Session, cols. 153, 219 ff., 245 ff., 619 ff., 696–697; Welles to Hale, February 3, 7, *Welles Papers*, xlix; N.D., *Letters to Congress*, xiii; Hale to Welles, February 5, *Miscellaneous Letters*.

each end, so that they can go forward either way, and can be used as rams, with a powerful engine; and with a cupola on the top, and one heavy gun ... they are not to be cruisers. ...[1]

After Hale read to the Senate Welles's explanation of February 7, the bill passed promptly the same day, and received the President's signature on February 13. It authorized the Secretary of the Navy "to cause to be constructed, by contract or otherwise, as he shall deem best for the public interest, not exceeding twenty iron-clad steam gunboats" and appropriated $10,000,000 for the purpose.[2]

It is interesting to note that the delays which had held up the bill in the Senate vanished as soon as Welles gave a guarded pledge of the sort so much desired by Ericsson's backers, that the Department would avail itself of the experience to be gained from the trial of the *Monitor* before completing its new program. W. L. Barnes, who was acting as agent for Ericsson and his partners in Washington, reported to Ericsson February 8 that the ironclad bill had passed the Senate, and that

> your plans are decidedly in favor. ... Commodore Smith is much pleased thus far, and favors you. I have telegraphed Winslow and Griswold to be here by Tuesday morning [February 11], at the latest. I wish it were so that you could be here though I do not think we will have any difficulty in securing say five more on your plans. I can hardly help congratulating you on the success which is so well nigh demonstrated and think your efforts will be highly appreciated. We shall bring strong influences to bear here.[3]

At the close of December and beginning of January the Bureau of Construction and Repair had made preparations for the construction of four of the proposed double-turreted ironclads in government yards. On December 23 Lenthall informed Paulding that "the Department has it in view to build one of the iron clad vessels" at New York. Within the next fortnight, he despatched specifications to the Comman-

---

[1] *Congressional Globe*, 37th Congress, 2d Session, cols. 621–622. Grimes said that Fox thought it doubtful whether sufficient iron could be obtained for ten ships within the year; and that probably not more than three or four could be built in time for use in this war.
[2] *Ibid.*, cols. 696–697, 710, 760; *Statutes at Large*, xii, p. 338.
[3] *Ericsson Mss.*, i.

dants at Philadelphia, New York, Charlestown and Kittery. On February 4 Paulding forwarded to Lenthall the following query, which he had just received from B. F. Delano, the Naval Constructor at the New York Yard.

> Your letter of the 3rd of January, 1862, says: "herewith enclosed you will find the dimensions by which the Naval Constructor will lay down on the mould loft floor the iron clad steamer which he will commence at once." I have to state the dimensions are laid down and are being taken from the floor to be sent to Washington as directed — but does the order mean that the vessel shall be commenced building at once? I so construe the order, and with your permission will lay down the blocks. . . .

Lenthall replied the next day that "you will not proceed any farther with that vessel than to send on the mould loft dimensions; do no other work." [1] The Department had at last decided not to proceed further with its ironclad program until the *Monitor* was tested. On February 13 Winslow reported to Ericsson from Washington that he and Griswold had

> had repeated interviews with Commodore Smith, and this morning saw Mr. Fox. . . . There is an evident determination not to commit the Department for any more batteries, of any sort, until ours is tried, and I would rather it should be so. If we are successful we shall have as many more to build as we shall have the ability to carry through.[2]

Martin's mission abroad in quest of armor and "towers" for five ironclads was wrecked largely by the Senate's delay in passing the "twenty gunboat bill." Reaching Liverpool on January 7, he found the British ironmasters deluged with orders "for armor plates from the French, Spanish, Russian, Austrian, and Italian Governments, beside what is being done for this Government [the British], which appears to be doing considerable in that line."[3] John Brown and Com-

---

[1] B.C.R., *Key, Commandants Navy Yards*, v, *passim*; Lenthall to Paulding, December 23, January 22, 27, February 5, *Letters to Commandants, New York*, iii; Paulding to Lenthall, January 20, 24, February 4, *Letters from Commandants, New York*, xxiv.

[2] *Ericsson Mss.*, i. On February 26 Bushnell wrote from Washington to Ericsson: "I found on enquiry that no plans, drawing or anything of the kind have been made yet for the proposed 20 iron clad vessels, in fact I have it from the highest authority that everything depends upon the test of your battery and that until after her trial nothing will be done. . . ." *Ibid.*

[3] Martin to Lenthall, January 9 and 21, 1862. B.C.R., *Miscellaneous Letters*, xliii.

pany of Sheffield were unwilling to undertake the contract "unless our Minister would come to some arrangement with the Government about allowing it to go out of the Country. This party has I know been to see the Government at London about it and I judge from his reply that they did not fully satisfy him."[1] Indeed, both the Home Office and the Admiralty, with a most delicate sense of the obligations of neutrality, which the British government did not invariably exhibit during this war, deemed the manufacture of armor plates for sale to the United States government illegal.[2]

The chief obstacle to Martin's success abroad, however, seems to have been his lack of funds. With orders pouring in from half a dozen governments, and prices rising, British ironmasters declined to make a contract without a guarantee of payment. This guarantee the fiscal agents of the United States, Baring Brothers, declined to give, for the Navy Department, owing to the Senate's delay in appropriating funds for the ironclads, had not sent the requisite instructions. Martin visited both Belgium and France, obtaining from Petin, Gaudet and Company an offer 12 per cent lower than their prices to the French government. They offered to furnish the "towers" complete for £50 per ton. James Jacks and Company, of Liverpool, asked £52 per ton, delivered on board ship. On February 15 Martin received orders from Lenthall to close up any contracts he had made in Europe and return to the United States. On account of the lack of funds, his mission had been fruitless, save for some information.[3]

It is of capital importance to note that the Navy Department, in February, 1862, was hesitating, not between the relative merits of wooden and armored ships, nor even between the relative merits of turreted and broadside ironclads. The issue lay between two types of turreted ironclads: the

---

[1] Martin to Lenthall, January 21. *Ibid.*
[2] P.R.O., Adm. 12/717, minute of January 16, 1862.
[3] The British ironmasters also objected to the short time allowed for delivery, and the necessity of bending the plates. Martin to Lenthall, January 21, 29, 30, February 6, 7, 15, B.C.R., *Miscellaneous Letters*, xliii; Martin to Welles, March 12, 1862, N.D., *Miscellaneous Letters.*

English system, devised by Coles and championed by Lenthall and Isherwood, and the Ericsson system. A week after the passage of the act authorizing twenty new ironclads, the Department issued an advertisement [1] for proposals for the construction of three classes of armored ships: one for service on the western rivers, one for harbor defence, and one for coast defence. Vessels of the second class were to carry "not less than from two to four eleven-inch guns;" those of the third class, "one or two fifteen or twenty-inch guns." On these two classes of ships the guns "are to train to all points of the compass without change in the vessel's position." It is difficult to imagine stronger evidence to show that the Navy Department, on the eve of the battle of Hampton Roads, was not skeptical of the merits of turreted ironclads.

[1] This advertisement stated that "the Department will consider any other propositions that may be presented in which the draft of water" does not exceed twelve feet.

CHAPTER XIII

HAMPTON ROADS

THOUGH the influence of the battles of Hampton Roads on the policy of European governments has been greatly exaggerated, few naval actions in history have made so profound an impression on the popular imagination. The combats of March 8 and 9 symbolized the passing of the old fleets and the coming of the new. Symbol they were, and not the cause, for they did not initiate the great revolution in naval architecture, they crowned it. They taught the man in the street what the naval constructors already knew: that shell guns had sounded the doom of the wooden navies of the world. On the chief problem confronting the naval constructors of Europe — the best design for *seagoing* ironclads — these battles threw little light. Nevertheless fate had provided for the first fight of ironclads so incomparable a setting that the *Merrimack* and *Monitor* have monopolized public attention in the United States, to the exclusion of the scores of ironclads then already built or building in Europe. The events of those two March days unfolded themselves with a dramatic simplicity never surpassed, while North and South hung breathless on the issue.

The governments at Washington and Richmond each had ample information concerning the other's ironclads. To the surprise of his partners and of the Navy Department, Ericsson had furnished the *Scientific American* with information for an excellent detailed description of the *Monitor*, for publication in its issue of November 23.[1] Two weeks earlier the

---

[1] This weekly seems to have been published prior to the date on its issues, for on November 16 Ericsson sent to Smith the issue describing the *Monitor*, suggesting "to the promoter of the enterprise to present a copy to the Secretary of State ... in view of its bearing on the harbor defences of the country." Four days later he explained that "it was my purpose to keep silent, but my refusal to give particulars gave great offence, and I had no alternative but to explain the structure or permit a most erroneous statement, damaging alike to the enterprise and the navy,

same periodical had published a rough sketch and description of the *Merrimack*, obtained from a mechanic who had worked on her transformation at Norfolk.[1] Every few days brought to the authorities at Washington fresh news of the progress of the Confederate ironclad.[2] To avert this menace, the Department considered several projects for an attack on Norfolk. A French inventor named Brutus de Villeroi undertook the construction of a submarine to attack the Confederate ironclad. Chief reliance, however, was placed on the *Monitor*.[3]

On February 13 Fox told Winslow that he should be at Fortress Monroe when the *Monitor* arrived there, "to witness her behavior in passing the batteries along Elizabeth River and Craney Island on her way up to Norfolk." Fox then expected her to leave New York early the next week, and he left to Ericsson the decision as to making a trial trip in the vicinity of New York.[4] In his narrative written in 1879, Welles stated that the Navy Department intended that the

> to go before the country . . . withholding correct information for another week would have brought out an injurious attack on the enterprise. Ericsson to Smith, November 16, 20, 1861, N.W.R., vol. 2601. Cf. Smith to Stimers, November 19, and Smith to Ericsson, November 18, 21, N.W.R., vol. 2634. These comments seem to refer to the long article in the issue dated November 23, rather than to the brief statement published November 16.
>
> In its issue of February 1, 1862, the *Scientific American* stated that the plan of erecting "an iron-plated tower or turret upon a small vessel, the sides of which should rise very little above the water . . . has been very extensively discussed in England by societies and in the mechanical papers. Captain Ericsson's battery is a modification of this turret device. . . ."

1 *Loc. cit.*, v, p. 304.
2 O.R.N., v, pp. 747, 748; vi, pp. 287, 333–334, 446, 482, 517–518, 535, 538, 540, 543–544, 627, 640, 659, 662, 663, 769–770; *Correspondence of G. V. Fox*, i, p. 428; *Diary of Gideon Welles*, i, p. 65; *Annals of the War*, p. 20; John A. Dix to Welles, October 21, 1861, N.D., *Miscellaneous Letters*.
3 For the projects for an attack on Norfolk, see *Correspondence of G. V. Fox*, i, pp. 243, 245–247, 397–400, 419–423. Cf. O.R.N., vi, pp. 651, 659, 740–741. Numerous letters concerning de Villeroi's vessel may be found in N.W.R., vols. 2600–2602, 2634. See also de Villeroi to President Lincoln, September 4, 1861, N.D., *Miscellaneous Letters*; Smith to Welles, October 16, with report of board of officers, July 7, *Bureau Letters*, September–December, 1861. This vessel, whose construction was greatly delayed, proved a failure. Cf. *Memoirs of Thomas O. Selfridge, Jr., Rear-Admiral, U.S.N.* (New York, 1924), ch. viii; and O.R.N., 2d series, i, p. 32. Several other proposals for submarines were made at this time.
4 Winslow to Ericsson, February 13, 1862. *Ericsson Mss.*, i. Cf. *Correspondence of G. V. Fox*, i, p. 244; ii, pp. 83, 94; and O.R.N., vi, p. 541.

Monitor, after steaming up the river to the Norfolk Navy Yard, should destroy both the dry-dock and the *Merrimack*. The hundred days expired on January 12, however; weeks passed, and still the *Monitor* was not ready.[1]

The delays in her completion and the fiasco of her first trials caused the gravest anxiety at Washington. Throughout February the Navy Department rained letters and telegrams on Ericsson, urging the despatch of the *Monitor* to Hampton Roads at the earliest possible moment.[2] When at last she left the New York Navy Yard for sea on February 27, she steered so badly going down the East River that her commander, Lieutenant John Lorimer Worden, found it necessary to put back.[3] Not daring to permit her to go to sea without one successful test, the Department ordered a further trial, which was made on March 3.[4] Despite the reassuring news of her success on that day, Welles on March 4 directed the senior officer at Hampton Roads, Captain John Marston of the *Roanoke*, not to let the *Monitor* go under fire of the enemies' batteries without further orders from the Department, "except for some pressing emergency." Her commander was to "exercise his men at the guns, and in all respects prepare for serious work."[5]

On the following day Welles suddenly changed his plans and telegraphed to Marston to send the *Monitor*, on its arrival at Hampton Roads, immediately to Washington. On the night of March 7 he also directed him to send the *St. Law-*

---

[1] *Annals of the War*, p. 20. Cf. *Diary of Gideon Welles*, i, p. 63.
[2] Fox to Ericsson, telegrams, February 3 and 21, N.D., *General Letter Book* no. 67; O.R.N., vi, p. 660; Smith to Ericsson, February 3 and 8, *Ericsson Mss.*, i; Smith to Worden, February 13; Smith to Stimers, February 19 and 24, N.W.R., vol. 2634. Cf. Barnes to Ericsson, February 17, *Ericsson Mss.*, i; Fox to Paulding, February 10; Welles to Worden, February 20, O.R.N., vi, pp. 627, 659.
[3] Paulding to Welles, telegram, February 26, *Commandants Letters*, Navy Yard, New York; O.R.N., vi, pp. 670, 673–674; T. F. Rowland to Ericsson, February 28, *Ericsson Mss.*, i.
[4] Smith to Stimers, March 1, N.W.R., vol. 2634; Paulding to Commander Francis W. Gregory, March 1 and 3, N.W.R., vol. 5068; Ericsson to Smith, March 4, N.W.R., vol. 2603. On February 28 Worden had requested "a board of three officers to accompany us on a trial trip of twenty-four hours, to test the steering qualities of the vessel after the present change is completed." O.R.N., vi, pp. 674, 676.
[5] O.R.N., vi, pp. 678–679.

rence, *Congress* and *Cumberland* at once into the Potomac River, using steam to tow them up. Marston was to consult with General Wool as to the disposition of the remaining vessels at Hampton Roads.[1] On March 8, however, Welles countermanded these orders, and directed Marston not to move the ships until Assistant Secretary Fox reached Old Point with further orders.[2]

On the basis of a memorandum of a conversation with Fox, Nicolay and Hay explain these orders as resulting from a sudden decision at Washington to attack the Confederate batteries on the Potomac so as to clear a passage for transports carrying McClellan's troops down the river. "The *Merrimac* was for the moment forgotten." When she was remembered next day the action was ordered to be suspended until Fox could reach Fortress Monroe and consult the naval officers in command.[3] All these eleventh-hour orders came too late to effect the desired concentration of forces in the Potomac. Welles's telegram ordering the *Monitor* to come direct to Washington reached the New York Navy Yard shortly after she and her consorts had departed for Hampton Roads.[4]

Despite the aid of the tug *Seth Low*, which took her in tow on leaving New York harbor, the *Monitor* twice nearly sank on her historic voyage. Stimers's statement to Ericsson that she proved "to be the finest seaboat I was ever in," may be taken, not as a sober statement of fact, but as evidence of the hero worship which endeared him to the inventor. A few days later Stimers reported to Commodore Smith that

we were not well prepared by calking for a gale of wind when we left New York, and moreover, our wind pipes were not high enough. I wanted Cap-

---

[1] O.R.N., vi, pp. 681, 686–687.   [2] *Ibid.*, p. 687.
[3] *Abraham Lincoln, A History* (New York, 1890, 10 vols.), v, pp. 221–222. The date at which Nicolay's conversation with Fox took place is not indicated. According to this account, the decision to send the wooden vessels and the *Monitor* to the Potomac was taken on the night of March 6. The telegram directing Marston to send the *Monitor* to Washington, however, which was forwarded by General Dix at Baltimore, was despatched from Washington on March 5 and received at Baltimore at 3.20 P.M. O.R.N., vi, p. 681.
[4] *Ibid.*, p. 682; Paulding to Welles, telegram, March 6, *Commandants Letters, Navy Yard, New York*.

tain Ericsson to make them the same height as the turret [nine feet], which would have prevented nearly all our difficulties, but he thought them high enough to prevent any mischief, and urged the inconvenience of stowing higher ones when we should go into battle.[1]

The little "cheese-box on a raft," on which mechanics had worked all night before her departure, encountered no difficulties until the afternoon of Friday, March 7, when a northwest gale, with a very heavy sea, caused even her consort the *Currituck* to ship large quantities of water. On the *Monitor*

the sea was breaking over our decks at a great rate, and coming in our hawse pipe forward in perfect floods. Our berth deck hatch leaked in spite of all we could do, and the water came down under the tower like a waterfall. It would strike the pilot house and go over the tower in most beautiful curves. The water came through the narrow eye-holes in the pilot house with such force as to knock the helmsman completely round from the wheel. At 4 P.M. the water had gone down our smoke stacks and blowers to such an extent, that the blowers gave out and the engine room filled with gas. . . .

Engineers Newton and Stimers, the latter a volunteer for the voyage, fought desperately to get the blowers to work until they fell unconscious, and were dragged by their comrades to the top of the turret. With the engines stopped, the crew set to bailing and passed buckets up through the tower, until the tug towed the *Monitor* inshore into smoother water, where her engines were started again at 8 P.M. Early Saturday morning, when the sea was "making a clean breach over the vessel," and pouring down the blowers, the wheel ropes "jumped off the steering wheel (owing to the pitching of the ship) and became jammed." Until the wheel ropes were put in working order half an hour later, the vessel sheered about "at an awful rate." At 6.45 A.M., seeing that the *Monitor* was showing a signal of distress, the commander of the *Currituck* "ran under her stern, when within hailing distance, the Captain wished us to stand in shore, and keep close to him, as his fires had repeatedly been extinguished, by the sea breaking over her." Soon, however, the gale moderated. "At 3 P.M.," so runs the log of the *Monitor*, "made Cape

---

[1] Stimers to Ericsson, March 9; Stimers to Smith, March 17. O.R.N., vii, pp. 26–27.

Henry light bearing S S W distance 11 miles and heard heavy firing in distance."[1]

On appointing Flag Officer Franklin Buchanan to the command of the James River Squadron on February 24, Secretary Mallory gave him no specific orders, but pointed out the wisdom of using the formidable powers of the *Merrimack*, now re-named the *Virginia*, as a ram in view of the great shortage of ammunition. He indulged the hope for "a dashing cruise on the Potomac as far as Washington." On March 7, he suggested a raid on New York in good weather, to "shell and burn the city and the shipping ... eclipse all the glories of the combats of the sea ... and strike a blow from which the enemy could never recover." If the Navy Yard and all the lower part of the city could be destroyed, "such an event, by a single ship, would do more to achieve our immediate independence than would the results of many campaigns...."[2]

One must remember, however, in considering the great panic caused by the exploits of the *Virginia*, that she was not a seagoing vessel. Her patched-up engines, which had been condemned in the Union service, would render any cruise at sea insanely hazardous. It is doubtful, moreover, whether her draft of twenty-two feet would have permitted her to cross the shoals in the Potomac below Washington. Despite these handicaps, however, she was destined to win undying fame in the sheltered waters of Hampton Roads.[3]

---

[1] Lieutenant S. Dana Greene to his mother, March 14, 1862, U. S. Naval Institute *Proceedings*, xlix, 1839 ff. (November, 1923); Isaac Newton to William Kelly, March 16, 1862, N.D., *Miscellaneous Letters*; log of the *Monitor*; private journal of William F. Shankland, commanding the U.S.S. *Currituck*, in Manuscripts Division, Library of Congress.

[2] O.R.N., vi, pp. 776–777, 780–781. Buchanan, one of the most distinguished officers of the old navy, had resigned in April, 1861, thinking his state, Maryland, was about to secede. Finding that he was mistaken, he sought re-instatement in vain in the Union service, declaring that "the circumstances which induced me, *very reluctantly*, to tender my resignation no longer exist, and I cannot voluntarily withdraw from a service in which I have passed nearly *forty seven* years of my life in the faithful performance of duty, as the records of the Navy Department will prove. I am ready for service." Buchanan to Welles, May 4, 1861. *Miscellaneous Letters*. Cf. Gideon Welles to Edgar T. Welles, May 9, 1861. *Welles Papers*, vol. xlv.

[3] William Harwar Parker and Catesby ap Rogers Jones in Southern Historical

This untried ironclad, whose green crew had had but a few days' training in handling her ten heavy guns, left Norfolk at eleven o'clock on the morning of Saturday, March 8. Accompanied by the gunboats *Beaufort* and *Raleigh*, she rounded Sewell's Point shortly before one o'clock, and steamed slowly towards Newport News. There lay at anchor the United States sloop *Cumberland*, mounting a heavy battery of twenty-two 9-inch smooth-bore guns, with one 10-inch smooth-bore and one 70-pounder rifle on pivots; and the frigate *Congress*, with the far less formidable armament of ten 8-inch and forty 32-pounder smooth-bores. Exchanging broadsides with the *Congress* as she passed, the *Virginia* rammed the *Cumberland* under the starboard fore channels. The mortal blow to the beautiful sloop cost the ugly iron monster more serious injuries than any others she received at the hands of an enemy. The shock wrenched from her bow her wedge-shaped cast-iron ram. And as the two vessels lay alongside, the gunners of the *Cumberland* aimed at the ports of their antagonist, shooting off the muzzles of two of her guns, and inflicting most of the casualties she received in the two days of fighting. Taking up a raking position, the *Virginia* poured in her shells until the *Cumberland*, whose gallant crew stood to their guns till the water rose about them, sank at last with her colors flying.[1]

Buchanan now ran his ship a short distance up the James River in order to turn her, and stood down for the *Congress*, which had made sail, slipped her cable, and run aground in-

Society *Papers*, xi (1883), pp. 37–38, 66, 67; *Diary of Gideon Welles*, i, pp. 61–67; *Annals of the War*, pp. 23–26; O.R.N., vii, pp. 74 ff.; Ray's letter of June 23, 1862, in Scharf, *Confederate States Navy*, 2d ed., pp. 224–228; records of the court martial of Tattnall, O.R.N., vii, pp. 790–799.

[1] The official reports of the action are collected in O.R.N., vii, pp. 3–73. The best of the later accounts by participants and eye-witnesses are listed below, in the bibliography. The most interesting of these are by Rear-Admiral Thomas O. Selfridge, Jr., a lieutenant on the *Cumberland*. See his "Story of the Cumberland," in the *Papers* of the Military Historical Society of Massachusetts, vol. xii, (1902), pp. 103–126; and his *Memoirs*, pp. 41 ff. Selfridge's statement that the *Virginia* rammed the sinking *Cumberland* a second time is corroborated by the report of Captain McIntire, of the Ninety-Ninth New York Infantry, who was serving on the *Congress*, and also by the commander of the French frigate *Gassendi*. O.R.N., vii, pp. 36, 66.

shore. Joined by the Confederate vessels *Patrick Henry*, *Jamestown*, and *Teaser*, the *Virginia* raked the *Congress* fore and aft with hot shot and shells that turned her decks into shambles. Lieutenant Pendergrast, who assumed command after the death of Lieutenant Joseph B. Smith, the son of the commodore, found his ship on fire in several places, and being unable to bring a single gun to bear on the enemy, struck his flag. While the *Beaufort* and *Raleigh* were alongside the *Congress*, taking off wounded and prisoners, a heavy fire from Federal forces on shore drove them off. Buchanan then sent his flag lieutenant, R. D. Minor, in a small boat to set the prize on fire. As fire was opened on this small craft, wounding Minor and some of his men, Buchanan recalled them and ordered the *Congress* destroyed by hot shot and incendiary shell. Of her total of 434 officers and men, 120 were reported killed or missing, or died on shore after the vessel was abandoned. She blew up shortly after midnight.[1]

As soon as the *Virginia* was sighted rounding Sewell's Point, the frigates *Minnesota* and *Roanoke*, at anchor near Fortress Monroe, got under way to join the *Congress* and *Cumberland*. The *Minnesota*, however, a sister ship of the old *Merrimack*, grounded in the north channel a mile or more from Newport News, and stuck fast. The *Roanoke*, dependent on tugs and her sails for motive power, as her shaft was broken, and the sailing frigate *St. Lawrence*, which came along a little later, both grounded, but got clear and sought refuge under the guns of Fortress Monroe. After setting the *Congress* on fire, the Confederates turned their attention to the stranded *Minnesota*. Fortunately for her, the *Virginia* drew too much water to come within a mile of her, and the untrained gunners of the big ironclad managed to hit the Union frigate only once. The *Jamestown* and *Patrick Henry*, however, did her a good deal of damage. When the Confederates withdrew at dark, the *Virginia* had lost two men

---

[1] Commander Radford of the *Cumberland*, who was absent serving on a court of enquiry on the *Roanoke* when the action began, reached Newport News on horseback in time to see his vessel sink. Of a crew of 376 officers and men, he reported 121 killed and missing. O.R.N., vii, pp. 20-22.

killed and nineteen wounded, including Flag Officer Buchanan, who turned over the command to Lieutenant Catesby ap Rogers Jones. Besides the loss of her iron prow, and of the muzzles of two of her guns, her armor was "somewhat damaged; the anchors and all flag-staffs shot away and smokestack and steam pipe were riddled."[1] This was no great price to pay, however, for the severe defeat inflicted on the Union forces. Confederate hopes were high for a still more decisive triumph on the morrow.

To the relief of the despondent Union forces, the *Monitor* reached Hampton Roads at nine o'clock Saturday evening, and soon proceeded to the assistance of the *Minnesota*. At eight the next morning, when the *Virginia* stood down to attack the stranded frigate, there began the first fight between ironclads, one of the strangest encounters on record. For four hours the two vessels fought, part of the time touching each other, without inflicting serious damage, and with only a single casualty. The two 11-inch smooth-bore guns in the Ericsson turret fired forty-one 168-pounder solid cast-iron shot, of poor quality, unfit for armor piercing. Specific orders prevented Worden from using charges heavier than fifteen pounds, less than half as much powder as was later used with safety. The *Virginia* fired little or nothing save shell, against which her adversary's armor afforded perfect protection. Despite the assistance of Chief Engineer Stimers in working the turret, the inexperienced crew found that aiming the guns was "almost impossible." Most of the *Virginia's* fire, on the other hand, passed completely over the low raft-like structure. In manœuvring for position, the light-draft *Monitor*, able to take refuge on the shoals, and to turn with far greater rapidity, showed to great advantage. The great length and draft of the *Virginia* in narrow channels with little depth of water under her rudder, made it hard to steer and turn her. Once she ran aground. Once, on the other hand, she did manage to ram her antagonist, but the absence of her beak rendered the blow more harmful to the attacker

[1] *Ibid.*, pp. 42, 46.

than to the attacked. As the *Virginia's* bow passed over the *Monitor's* deck "our sharp upper edged side cut through the light iron shoe upon her stem and well into her oak. She will not try that again. She gave us a tremendous thump, but did not injure us in the least. We are just able to find the point of contact." [1]

Twice Jones thought he had silenced the *Monitor's* fire. The first time she had simply hauled off into shoal water, to hoist a fresh supply of shot into the turret. The second time, shortly before noon, a shell from the *Virginia* broke one of the iron logs forming the *Monitor's* pilot house, forcing splinters of iron into the eyes of Lieutenant Worden. Temporarily blind, and believing that the pilot house was seriously disabled, the Union commander directed the pilot to sheer off, and sent for Lieutenant Greene, who took him to his quarters and then assumed command. As to whether the *Monitor* returned to the fray before the *Virginia* made for Norfolk, the sources are hopelessly in conflict. At all events, when the *Monitor* turned away, the men on the *Minnesota* felt their hour had come. The *Virginia*, however, was aleak forward; and her pilots insisted that if she did not return to Norfolk at once she could not cross the bar until the next day. Jones, who believed the *Minnesota* was too seriously damaged ever to move again, with the advice of his lieutenants gave the order to turn for home.[2]

Fox, who had arrived in time to witness the battle of the ironclads, telegraphed to McClellan that the *Monitor* had shown a "slight superiority," and that the "Merrimac was forced to retreat to Norfolk. . . ." Although she steamed away unaided, and her damage could not be ascertained, he thought she might have to lay up for a few days. "She is an

---

[1] Stimers to Ericsson, March 9. O.R.N., vii, p. 26.

[2] In addition to the contemporary documents collected in *ibid.*, see Greene's letter of March 14 to his mother, cited above. In the admirable collection on American naval history presented by Dr. Gardner Weld Allen to the Harvard College Library, is a typescript copy of a letter by Thomas W. Rae, Third Assistant Engineer of the *Minnesota*, written on March 17, 1862. The latest full discussion of the turning away of the *Monitor* is that of Dr. William Tindall, "The True Story of the Virginia and the Monitor," *Virginia Magazine of History and Biography*, January, April, 1923.

ugly customer and it is too good luck to believe we are yet clear of her." Union hopes were on the *Monitor*, which was all ready to renew the combat, "and this day's work shows that the 'Merrimac' must attend to her alone." [1]

Other witnesses of the fight were not so cautious in estimating the damages to the *Virginia*. In the excitement of the moment, it is small wonder that some of the combatants on the *Monitor* believed that they had crippled their opponent. Greene, Newton, and Stimers declared their shot had gone right through her.[2] With so promising a start, the legend of Hampton Roads grew rapidly. In 1874 Worden submitted on behalf of the officers and crew of the *Monitor* a petition for the award of the value of the *Virginia* as prize money. He declared that the *Monitor* had driven her antagonist back to Norfolk "in a condition so absolutely crippled and disabled that she was not afterwards fit for active or efficient service, but was, in fact, as the result of the encounter with the *Monitor*, finally destroyed as unable to take the sea and escape when Norfolk was destroyed by our forces." [3]

The *Virginia* set out on March 9 to destroy the *Minnesota*. Thanks to the *Monitor*, she failed to do so. In a larger sense the victory of the day was not of one ironclad over another, but of armor over guns. The injuries of the *Virginia*, which were principally received in her attack on the *Cumberland*, do not seem to have been very serious, save for the loss of her iron prow.[4] How she escaped more

[1] *Correspondence of G. V. Fox*, i, p. 435.
[2] O.R.N., vii, p. 27; Rae's letter of March 17, cited above; Scharf, *Confederate States Navy*, 2d ed., p. 207; Newton to Kelly, March 16, N.D., *Miscellaneous Letters*.
[3] The Committees on Naval Affairs of both the House and the Senate reported favorably on this petition in 1882. House Report no. 144, Senate Report no. 394, 47th Congress, 1st Session. Cf. the able adverse report of John G. Ballentine, of Tennessee, who had served in the Confederate Army, from the Committee on Naval Affairs, May 31, 1884. House Report no. 1725, 48th Congress, 1st Session. Ballentine's attack on the credibility of the affidavit made by James Byers in 1874, concerning the damages received by the *Virginia*, seems fully warranted.
[4] "We had run into the *Monitor*, causing us to leak, and had received a shot from her which came near disabling the machinery, but continued to fight her until she was driven into shoal water." Jones to Davidson, August 20, 1862. O.R.N.,

serious injury is somewhat of a mystery, for she was vulnerable at the water line. Jones had written to Brooke on March 5 that her draft would be a foot less than was first intended, for he had been ordered that morning not to take on any more ballast.

> The eaves of the roof will not be more than six inches immersed, which in smooth water would not be enough; a slight ripple would leave it bare except the one-inch iron that extends some feet below. We are least protected where we most need it, and may receive a shot that would sink us; a thirty-two-pounder would do it. The constructor should have put on six inches where we now have one.[1]

And Minor had informed Brooke on March 7 that "the edges of our plates are only five inches below the water." [2]

The principal work done on the *Virginia* after her return to Norfolk was not the replacement of a few damaged plates, or the fitting of iron port-shutters, or even the installation of a new ram; but the increase of her underwater armor belt from one to three inches in thickness. Mallory informed the Commandant of the Norfolk Navy Yard that "the original design in plating the *Virginia* was to bring the water two feet over the eaves of the roof or casemate, and this, the iron on her bends may accomplish. . . . Her bends and her propeller are her weak points." By the seventh of April, 440 plates had been added, "extending down the sides 3½ feet below the eaves, and extending for 160 feet from forward on both sides." The ship was out of the dock and her draft now met the Department's stipulations.[3] In August, 1862, the British vice-consul at Norfolk, Myer Myers, sent to Vice

vii, p. 59. The commander of the *Gassendi* reported that: "Le Merrimac m'a paru avoir reçu 50 ou 60 boulets, le tuyau était littéralement criblé et le mât de pavillon a été coupé. Aucun des coups n'a eu d'effets bien sérieux. La première plaque du blindage, quelquefois la seconde, était brisé, mais il n'y a eu nulle part de pénétration. Grace à l'inclinaison des surfaces, alors que le fer se brisait sous le choc, il n'y avait pas de courbure intérieure de la masse totale, comme cela a eu lieu pour la batterie Ericsson. La plaque, qui n'était pas brisée, restait à peu près intacte. Cependant, 2 coups, l'un au ras, l'autre au-dessous de la flottaison, ont fait éclater par le choc un morceau de bois à l'intérieur, mais dans aucun cas, le navire n'a fait d'eau." *Ibid.*, p. 68. Cf. O.R.N., 2d series, i, p. 634.
1 Southern Historical Society *Papers*, xix, p. 31 (January, 1891).
2 *Ibid.*, p. 32.
3 O.R.N., vii, pp. 761–764. Cf. Bruce, *Virginia Iron Manufacture*, p. 357.

Admiral Milne a memorandum on these improvements on the *Virginia*, which seems to have been written before her destruction. He pointed out that several of her plates, which were 8 feet long by 3½ wide, had been loosened by shot, and had curled up at the corners. As she was "hollow forward," she was not strong enough for her ram, and two of her forward beams were badly sprung. About thirty tons of timber had been inserted after her action, making her "nearly solid at, and near the bow."

> The ram was too long, it is now reduced and does not project more than half of its original length, 6 feet. It is amply secured with longer and stronger braces. About half the ram was carried away in the first blow with it on the Sh. "Cumberland," the remainder of it was loosened and broke when she ran with full force into the "Monitor," and the injuries to the ram caused a considerable leak in the "Merrimac" forward. The plate *below* the water line was only 1 inch thick. It was penetrated by a shell that entered the ship without exploding and hence caused no damage. The plates below water were increased to same thickness (3 inches) as those above. An additional plate making 4 inches was put over the wheel houses, and also on the ports made to close the portholes.
>
> Within a space of 8 feet, 2 of the plates were repeatedly struck and considerably dented by 11 inch shot, one of which carried away the muzzle of the bow gun. Most of the fragments flew *inside* without wounding any one, or doing injury.[1]

The panic in Washington and the cities of the Northern seaboard which followed the receipt of news of the destruction of the *Cumberland* and *Congress* is well known. Secretary of War Stanton at once advised the Governors of New York, Massachusetts, and Maine to prepare large timber rafts, protected by batteries, for the defence of their harbors. He also gathered a small fleet of canal-boats loaded with stone, to be sunk on the shoals of the Potomac below Washington if the *Virginia* appeared.[2] The battle between the *Monitor* and the *Virginia* did not end the alarm. Welles telegraphed the next

---

[1] P.R.O., Adm. 1/5788. With this is a report from Commander Algernon Lyons, of H.M.S. *Racer*, dated Fortress Monroe, August 8, 1862, describing both the *Monitor* and the *Virginia*. Lyons reached Hampton Roads April 1.

[2] O.R.N., vii, pp. 74–81. The account in the *Diary of Gideon Welles*, i, pp. 61–67, was written several years after the events narrated, as the editor points out. For a somewhat fuller version, see Welles's account in *The Annals of the War*, pp. 23 ff. Some allowance must be made for his animosity to Stanton.

day to Fox the President's orders that the *Monitor* "be not too much exposed,"⁵ and that she should in no event attempt to proceed to Norfolk unattended. Vessels loaded with stone should if possible be sunk in the channel of the Elizabeth River below Norfolk. The force at Hampton Roads was to be reinforced by the *San Jacinto, Dacotah, Sabine,* and a number of gunboats. He suggested that the *Minnesota* be detained until other vessels arrived.[1]

As a successful sortie by the *Virginia* might play havoc with the movement of McClellan's forces to the Peninsula, neutralizing the Confederate ironclad became an object of capital importance. Unwilling to rely on the *Monitor* alone, which might be disabled by accident, or by the thousand and one chances of single combat, the Union authorities concentrated in Hampton Roads a force of steamers, some of them hired for the purpose, to ram the *Virginia* if she sallied forth. Fox confessed shortly afterwards that "that confounded Merrimac has set like a nightmare upon our Department." The extreme caution shown by the Union forces on the occasions when the *Virginia* again came out and offered battle, suggests that the Navy Department, as well as Flag Officer Goldsborough, who commanded the forces in Hampton Roads, were influenced by the theory that containment of the enemy was equivalent to victory.[2]

When the *Virginia,* now under the command of Flag-Officer Josiah Tattnall, sallied forth on April 11, she was,

---

[1] O.R.N., vii, p. 83.

[2] *Correspondence of G. V. Fox*, i, pp. 120, 248-268, 274-276, 436-439. The despatches published in O.R., 1st series, v and ix, and O.R.N., vii, are summarized in Ballentine's report of 1884. House Report no. 1725, 48th Congress, 1st Session. Scharf gives a long, partisan account, with copious extracts from documents. *Op. cit.* ch. x. Paulding wrote privately to Welles on April 12 that unless the *Vanderbilt* or *Minnesota* could ram the *Virginia,* he greatly feared the result of her next sortie. "If now there shall be a want of resolution and skill, our naval force may be destroyed and even the great army at the mercy of the enemy for the gun boats cannot contend with the ironclad rebels. As for the Monitor, she is formidable but is not equal to the Merrimac. The Merrimac under full steam may in my belief run over her and this to my mind is a very simple problem. . . ." *Welles Papers*, vol. l. In a letter to his wife, July 20, Welles expressed his dissatisfaction with Goldsborough's conduct of operations in the previous spring. *Ibid.*

thanks to her underwater armor belt, improved ram, and set of port-shutters, a much more formidable craft than when she appeared on March 8 and 9. Goldsborough's forces showed extreme caution, permitting the consorts of the *Virginia* to capture three merchant vessels without striking a blow. Commander Hewett of the British sloop-of-war *Rinaldo* reported that the *Virginia* turned with surprising ease and was handled with great facility. He estimated her speed at a little over seven knots, somewhat faster than the *Minnesota* and about twice the speed of the *Monitor*. He deemed her much superior to the latter vessel, and declared that Goldsborough had agreed with him as to her superiority and had informed him that she "was not once penetrated" in the battles of March 8 and 9.[1] Although boarders would have a hopeless task on the well-slushed sloping sides of the *Virginia*, Hewett thought the *Monitor* could be easily taken by boarding, and that a concentrated fire directed against the perpendicular sides of her "cupola" would damage the machinery by which the "shield" was turned, and prevent its revolving. He declared that it was Tattnall's intention on April 11 to take the *Monitor* at any cost. On board the *Virginia* and the tugs and gunboats which accompanied her were 150 volunteers, ready to board Ericsson's ironclad, drive wedges "between the sliding parts of the tower," throw combustible chemicals down the ventilators, "and then stop them up with canvas which would most likely suffocate those on board." It was said that before the *Virginia* engaged the *Monitor* on March 9 she had expended all her solid shot. Now she was equipped with 120-pounder shot for armor piercing, of solid wrought iron and cast iron, square on the end, and with steel points. Hewett reported that the Confederate squadron on the eleventh "cruised about the Roads without opposition, the 'Virginia' occasionally going within range of the Federal guns on the Rip Raps, and Fortress Monroe, as well as those of the large squadron under the guns of the fortress. . . ." The *Monitor*, however, refused the challenge. The next day

[1] Cf. *Correspondence of G. V. Fox*, i, pp. 248–250.

the *Virginia* and her consorts steamed down to Sewell's Point and spent the day there, without provoking the Federal squadron to attack them.[1]

When General Johnston abandoned the lines at Yorktown on May 3, the authorities at Richmond ordered the evacuation of Norfolk. While preparations for this movement were in progress, the *Monitor* and several other Union vessels attacked the Confederate batteries on Sewell's Point on May 8, but retreated when the *Virginia* made her appearance.[2] Union troops began landing at Willoughby's Point on the night of the ninth, and occupied Norfolk the next day. On learning that enemy troops were approaching Norfolk, Tattnall ordered the *Virginia* to be lightened sufficiently to permit her to ascend the James River. When she had been lightened several feet, exposing her underwater belt, only part of which was plated with iron thicker than one inch, the pilots "declared their inability to carry 18 feet above the Jamestown Flats, up to which point the shore was occupied by the enemy." Deeming it impossible to bring the vessel down to fighting draft with the means at his disposal, Tattnall set fire to his vessel, which blew up a little before five o'clock on the morning of May 11. Although this act provoked bitter criticism, a court martial unanimously awarded Tattnall an honorable acquittal.[3] However necessary her

---

[1] Hewett to Milne, April 26, May 10, 1862. P.R.O., Adm. 1/5787. Portions of these despatches are printed in O.R.N., vii, pp. 224–225, 338. Cf. *ibid.*, pp. 219 ff., 753–754, 759–760; *Correspondence of G. V. Fox*, i, p. 264.

[2] The statement in the text is based on Tattnall's report which is corroborated by that of Hewett to Milne, May 10. Goldsborough gave a different version of the affair. O.R.N., vii, 331 ff. The extract from Hewett's despatch of May 10 printed in O.R.N., vii, 338, omits the following passage: "The firing on the part of the Federal squadron [against Sewell's Point, on May 8], was very indifferent, with the exception of the 'Susquehannah's,' which was somewhat better. This vessel received as part of her armament, the previous day, 2 100-pounder rifled Parrott guns." P.R.O., Adm. 1/5787.

[3] O.R.N., vii, pp. 335 ff., 787 ff.; O.R.N., 2d series, i, pp. 625, 633–635, 716–718. Cf. Nicolay and Hay, *Lincoln*, v, ch. xiii; and Scharf, *Confederate States Navy*, 2d ed., pp. 221–238. Hewett reported to Admiral Milne on May 22 that the Confederates had set the *Virginia* on fire at midnight of the tenth, when they found it impossible to lighten her to go up the James River. He stated that a ram and a small ironclad floating battery had been launched a few days before the evacua-

destruction may have been, it was a sorry ending for the first ship to prove in action the truth of Dupuy de Lôme's proud boast that a single ironclad, in the midst of a hostile wooden fleet, would resemble a lion amid a flock of sheep.

<blockquote>tion of Norfolk, and towed up to Richmond for completion. Their boilers and machinery were said to have been on board, but not placed in position. P.R.O., Adm. 1/5787.</blockquote>

CHAPTER XIV

THE CONSEQUENCES OF HAMPTON ROADS

ALTHOUGH it is not the purpose of this volume to trace in detail the development of the ironclad ship beyond the spring of 1862, an attempt must be made to estimate the influence of the *Monitor* and the *Virginia* on the progress of naval construction. On the general public, hitherto little aware of the revolution in naval architecture which the French had initiated, the sensational impression could scarcely be overstated. On the policy of the European governments, however, the influence of the *Monitor* and the *Virginia*, though notable, has been greatly exaggerated. The legend that these vessels inaugurated the introduction of ironclads is preposterous, for in March, 1862, nearly one hundred armored vessels were built or building in Europe. As Lord Sydenham well said of the *Monitor*: "to the employment of armor she may have given a fresh impulse; but no initiative."[1] Her success did give, however, a tremendous impetus to the use of the revolving armored turret.

The events of March 8 and 9 were not necessary to convince the Union Navy Department of the superiority of iron sides to wooden walls, or even of the advantages of armored turrets. They transformed, however, the little-known projects of the experts into the popular craze of the hour, and exerted on the building policy of the administration an influence which in one respect may be thought pernicious. So great was the need of light-draft ironclads suited for the immediate task in hand, the crushing of the Confederacy, and so popular was the *Monitor*, cheap, novel, and fresh from her dramatic struggle, that the opportunity for building a high seas ironclad fleet was largely overlooked.

That was not the fault of Lenthall and Isherwood. In a

[1] *Edinburgh Review*, January, 1893, p. 53.

long memorandum submitted to Secretary Welles on March 17, they pointed out that the recent change in the construction of warships, which had rendered the wooden ships of the European navies "nearly useless," now gave the United States the chance to "start equal with the first powers of the world in a new race for the supremacy of the Ocean." Without suffering, like our European rivals, a heavy loss of old stock and workshops, we should start "with matured plans embodying all the improvements and appliances of modern science, gained at the expense of the dear bought experience of our competitors." Combating the heresy that the United States should rely on coast defence alone, they championed the building of a fleet of "first class invincible ocean ships ... to preserve our coasts from the presence of our enemy's naval forces by keeping the command of the open sea with all the power it gives of aggression upon his own shores and commerce." By keeping our coasts clear, our seagoing fleet would enable our privateers to sally forth and bring home their prizes. Lenthall and Isherwood urged the creation of a large government establishment to manufacture armor plate and build steam engines and ironclads. These should be frigate-built iron ships strong enough to be used as rams, "clad with invulnerable armor plates, furnished with maximum steam power, and of a size larger than any vessel we now possess." With these should be a class of light-draft corvettes of the same character.[1]

This powerful appeal for an armored high seas fleet went for the most part unheeded. On March 25 Welles asked Congress to increase the appropriation for ironclads to $30,000,000. Next day he appointed Smith, Lenthall, Isherwood, and naval constructor Edward Hart to serve as a board to examine the proposals for armored vessels which had been submitted in response to the advertisement of February 20. By the end of June three casemate and twenty-four turreted ironclads were under construction in the North, and the list

[1] *Report of the Joint Committee on the Conduct of the War* (Washington, 1865, 3 vols.), iii, part ii, pp. 110–112.

soon rapidly lengthened.[1] Yet not until a generation later did the United States build a cruising ironclad fleet. During the Civil War attention was chiefly fixed on the requirements of the immediate struggle, which could be well met by building a powerful fleet of turreted ironclads of light draft and low freeboard. The ingenuity, novelty, and relative cheapness of the monitors, which were regarded as a typically American creation, gave them a great vogue in the North. Captain John Rodgers weathered a gale off Hatteras in the *Weehawken* in February, 1863. After the war the *Miantonomoh* visited Europe, and the *Monadnock* went to San Francisco. Despite these achievements, it seems clear that, although wonderfully serviceable in the shoal-water fighting of the Civil War, and adequate for harbor defence against any enemy of their time, they were slow and ill suited for all-around service against a European armored fleet at sea. Even the few ironclads designed during the war primarily with an eye to a possible conflict with a European power were not well endowed with sea-keeping qualities.[2]

Not the raft-like monitor, but the large multiple-turret ironclad of higher freeboard, was destined to rule the seas. From the standpoint of later development, the proposal made by Lenthall and Isherwood on March 19 to adopt Coles's idea of cutting down existing wooden ships and con-

---

[1] Senate Miscellaneous Document no. 70, 37th Congress, 2d Session; N.D., *Letters to Heads of Bureaus*, iv, pp. 71 ff.; Lenthall to Welles, July 30, 1862, *Bureau Letters*. These twenty-seven ironclads did not include the *Monitor*, *Galena* and *New Ironsides*.
  Photographs of many of the Civil War ironclads are reproduced in the admirable volume contributed by Colonel James Barnes to the *Photographic History of the Civil War*. For statistics of all, and pictures of some of them, see O.R.N., 2d series, i.

[2] For the unfavorable opinions of the French and British officers sent to examine them, see below, pp. 311, 316–317, 323–324, and P. Dislère, "Notes sur la marine des Etats-Unis," *Revue maritime et coloniale*, January, 1868, pp. 261–301. This article, which was also printed separately, reproduced the larger part of a confidential report by Dislère which appeared in the *Mémorial du genie maritime*, 1866, pp. 161–221. Dislère thought the *Dunderberg* and the *New Ironsides* were the only seagoing ironclads possessed by the United States. On the former vessel see *ibid.*, pp. 176–181; *Revue maritime et coloniale*, May, 1867, pp. 255–258; June, 1867, pp. 503–505; Pâris, *L'art naval à l'exposition universelle de Paris en 1867*, pp. 198–208, and plate 15; O.R.N., 2d series, i, p. 76.

verting them into armored all-big-gun ships with their guns mounted in several turrets aligned over the keel, is of great interest. They recommended that the wooden steam frigate *Roanoke*, a sister ship of the original *Merrimack*, be cut down, plated with iron, and armed with eight 12- or 15-inch guns in four "Cole towers." The result of installing three turrets on the *Roanoke*, however, was a failure. Her draft was too great for service in Confederate waters, as Fox had predicted, and she proved a wretched boat at sea.[1]

Four days after the combat of the *Monitor* and the *Virginia* Lenthall urged Welles to order the immediate construction of an ironclad "on the principles of the plan" for double-turreted ships which the Bureau of Construction and Repair had, with the sanction of the Department, proposed in the previous November.[2] Although the Department went no further with the suggestion for installing Coles's type of "towers," it nevertheless adopted the idea of double turrets for the ironclad *Onondaga*, built under contract by G. W. Quintard of New York, and in the course of the summer it ordered the construction of the four double-turreted wooden ironclads *Miantonomoh, Tonawanda, Monadnock,* and *Agamenticus* at the New York, Philadelphia, Charlestown and Kittery Navy Yards, on plans furnished by the Bureau of Construction and Repair. These plans resembled those proposed by the Bureau in November, 1861, save that the vessels were made larger to carry heavier armor and thicker turrets, which were constructed on Ericsson's, not on Coles's system. Late in 1863 four larger double-turreted wooden monitors were ordered, the *Quinsigamond, Passaconaway, Kalamazoo* and *Shackamaxon*, none of which was completed.[3] These

---

[1] N.D., *Bureau Letters*, March 19, 1862, with Fox's endorsement objecting to the proposed draft of 22 feet 9 inches; B.C.R., *Letters to New York*, vol. iii, and *Letters from New York*, vol. xxiv, *passim*; Paulding to Welles, March 31, April 27, 1862, *Welles Papers*, vols. xlix, l; Bennett, *Steam Navy*, i, p. 354; O.R.N., ix, pp. 83, 119, 419; O.R.N., 2d series, I, p. 193. In his *Guide to the Military History of the World War* (Boston, 1920), pp. 294–295, Captain Thomas G. Frothingham rightly emphasizes the historical significance of the idea underlying the transformation of the *Roanoke*, but fails to note its British origin.

[2] N.D., *Bureau Letters*, March 13, 1862. See above, pp. 275–276.

[3] Welles to Dahlgren, August 5, Welles to Lenthall, August 9, September 8, *Letters*

plans resembled those proposed by the Bureau in November, 1861, save that the turrets were on Ericsson's, not on Coles's system, and the vessels were made larger to carry heavier armor and thicker turrets.[1]

On March 17, 1862, C. W. Whitney renewed his proposal of 1861, suggesting that as the government had expressed a desire to try several plans, his vessel should carry two stationary turrets with three ports, instead of Coles's revolving turrets. He promptly obtained a contract for a vessel on his new plans, the *Keokuk*, whose armor of alternate bars of wood and iron covered with thin iron plates proved so vulnerable in the attack on Charleston, April 7, 1863, that she sank the next morning. Her commander, A. C. Rhind, reported that "she was struck ninety times in the hull and turrets, most of the shot piercing her — nineteen at and near the water line."[2]

Ericsson's plans were in such high favor after the battle of Hampton Roads that he and his associates soon obtained contracts for six improved monitors. On March 17 Commodore Smith suggested that in these vessels the lower hull should be built more strongly, the side armor plates should be much longer than those of the *Monitor*, and the pilot house and steering arrangements should be improved. The jog made where the upper vessel projected over the lower one must either be filled in with wood, or the side of the lower vessel must be shaped so as to give greater buoyancy, better speed and easy roll. The guns should be "of larger calibre, greater gravity, and unmistakable endurance." He believed

to *Heads of Bureaus*, iv. For correspondence concerning these vessels, see B.C.R., *Key, Commandants Navy Yards*, v, and *Key, Officers*, ii, under the name of Commodore F. H. Gregory. Numerous plans of these ships are preserved in these archives, and indexed under the name of the vessel. Cf. B.C.R., 80–10–13; Lenthall's circulars of July 9 and September 2, 1862, and January 12, 1863, N.D., AC, Boston Navy Yard, 1860–1870; G. V. Fox to B. F. Delano, September 16, 1863, *Fox Papers*; *Report of the Joint Committee on the Conduct of the War*, iii, part 2, p. 110; Bennett, *Steam Navy*, i, p. 400.

[1] See Lenthall's testimony in the *Report of the Joint Committee on the Conduct of the War*, iii, part ii, p. 110.

[2] O.R.N., xiv, using index, *s.v. Keokuk*. Her specifications and plans are preserved in B.C.R., 80–11–28, A–C. Numerous letters concerning her may be found in N.W.R., vols. 2603, 2634. See above, pp. 250–252.

that the deck of the *Monitor* was "too near the water to weather the coast, or even fight successfully in the Chesapeake bay...."[1]

In forwarding plans revised in accordance with these proposals Ericsson pointed out that the most important change made was "that of giving lines to the lower vessel resembling an ordinary vessel, yet retaining all the protecting features of the upper body." To comply with Smith's wishes the lower vessel was made 3 feet 8 inches wider than in the original *Monitor*, and the break where it joined the upper vessel was eliminated. The most important improvement, to Ericsson's mind, consisted in placing a cylindrical pilot house, six feet in diameter, on top of the turret. Air for the boilers and for ventilation was to be drawn down through the pilot house and the turret, to obviate the inconvenience experienced by the *Monitor* on her trip to Hampton Roads. The turret was to be supported by two transverse and two longitudinal bulkheads; the diameter of the propeller was to be increased from nine to twelve feet; and the fantail aft so modified as greatly to lessen the drag in the water, while preserving "the same complete protection to rudder and propeller as now."[2]

Smith insisted on March 22 that the new monitors should be at least 200 feet long and 46 feet beam, with a speed of nine knots. He preferred that the laminated turret and side armor be built up with 2-inch instead of one-inch plates, and wished to have two turrets on each boat, one to turn, mounting two 12-inch guns, and one fixed, mounting one 12-inch gun on a pivot carriage. When the inventor protested against the proposal for two turrets, Fox replied on March 28 that the fighting advantages of the double-turreted ship could not be overestimated. He proposed that Ericsson build one single-turreted monitor and furnish plans from which the government could have a larger vessel with two turrets constructed. Fox thought that a speed of ten knots could be obtained from these vessels, though Smith believed not more than nine knots might be hoped for.[3]

[1] *Ericsson Mss.*, i. [2] Ericsson to Smith, March 19, N.W.R., vol. 2603.
[3] *Ericsson Mss.*, i.

The upshot of these negotiations was that Ericsson contracted for six single-turreted monitors, later named the *Passaic, Montauk, Catskill, Patapsco, Lehigh,* and *Sangamon*.[1] He later obtained a contract for the large ironclads *Dictator* and *Puritan*, and furnished designs for numerous other monitors. Much against his wishes the *Puritan* was originally designed with two turrets.[2] After the loss of the *Monitor* at sea, December 31, 1862, and the narrow escape of the *Passaic* from the same fate, the Navy Department ordered that the overhang at the bow, sides, and stern be reduced in the later monitors.[3]

Ericsson deplored the reduction of the overhang, which he regarded as an essential protection against ramming.[4] The destruction of the *Cumberland* gave considerable impetus to ram projects at home and abroad. Charles Ellet, Jr., a distinguished civil engineer who had been advocating this idea for seven or eight years, at last obtained a hearing and improvised for the War Department the fleet of steam rams which he gallantly commanded in the naval victory off Memphis, June 6, 1862, in which he was mortally wounded.[5]

Great pains were taken by the inventor and the Navy Department to devise a better system for aiming the turret guns, which Fox remarked had been "almost impossible" in the original *Monitor*.[6] Ericsson admitted that, owing to "the

---

[1] For specifications and plans of these vessels see B.C.R., 26-8-16, 26-8-24, 80-11-24, 142-7-10. Numerous letters concerning the obtaining and execution of these contracts are in *Ericsson Mss.*, i, ii, and N.W.R., vol. 2603. On March 30, Ericsson assured Smith that the sides of the vessels of the *Passaic* class near the bulwarks would be "fully twice as strong as in the Monitor." Their laminated turret armor was eleven inches thick. N.W.R., vol. 2603.

[2] Ericsson, *Contributions to the Centennial Exhibition*, ch. xxxv; Church, *Ericsson*, ii, pp. 3-23, 35-43, 72. On the fiasco of the light-draft monitors, for which Ericsson was not responsible, see *ibid.*, pp. 23-33; *Report of the Joint Committee on the Conduct of the War*, iii, part ii; correspondence of Ericsson and Fox in *Fox Papers*, 1863-1865; and several folders in N.D., AC.

[3] Lenthall's circular of January 12, 1863, N.D., AC, Boston Navy Yard, 1860-1870; Fox to Ericsson, January 12, *Fox Papers*; O.R.N., viii, pp. 338-359.

[4] Ericsson to Fox, January 14, 1863. *Fox Papers*. Cf. Church, *Ericsson*, ii, pp. 10-11.

[5] O.R., 2d series, ii, and O.R.N., xxii, xxiii, using index *s.v.* Ellet, and Ram Fleet; *History of the Ram Fleet and the Mississippi Marine Brigade* (St. Louis, 1907).

[6] Fox to Ericsson, July 5, 1862. *Ericsson Mss.*, ii.

laborious and slow handling" of her pendulum stoppers, it had been necessary to turn the guns away from the enemy while loading, to protect the gunners. To eliminate this "pernicious practice," which led to much confusion and loss of time in finding the enemy's position after losing it at every fire, he devised port stoppers that might be closed in a few seconds.[1] His new system of firing the guns inside the turret, even when modified by the use of muzzle boxes to reduce the smoke in the turret, caused much dissatisfaction in the service and provoked an irresistible demand for the enlargement of the ports to permit the muzzle of the guns to protrude from the turret when firing, as in the original *Monitor*.[2]

The triumph of armor over guns at Hampton Roads gave rise to a long series of ordnance experiments which led to the introduction into the Union Navy of the 15-inch smoothbore gun. Fox, who believed that "the contest between the *Monitor* and the *Merrimac* showed that our present calibres are entirely inadequate to destroy such vessels," for a time championed the construction of 20-inch guns. The United States naval ordnance, which had "led all nations in the perfection of its smooth bore guns," must now, he declared, "keep pace and lead if possible in the production of smooth bore and rifled guns of such calibres and velocities as shall be irresistible against anything possible to construct which will cross the ocean."[3]

The battle of Hampton Roads stimulated ordnance experiments and ironclad building in the South as well as in the North. By February, 1863, the Confederates had eight ironclads in commission, and several more building at home and

[1] Ericsson to Fox, December 18, 1862. *Ericsson Mss.*, iii.
[2] Unsigned letter to Welles in Commodore Paulding's handwriting, New York Navy Yard, December 15, 1862, *Welles Papers*, lii; Ericsson to Fox, October 29, 30, Ericsson to Loring, November 27, Stimers to Ericsson, November 9, 26, Drayton to Dahlgren, December 10, Welles to Ericsson, November 16, *Ericsson Mss.*, iii; Ericsson to Fox, January 2, 1863, *Fox Papers.* Cf. *Correspondence of G. V. Fox*, ii, pp. 439-441; *Photographic History of the Civil War*, vi, pp. 159, 173, 179.
[3] Fox to Captain A. A. Harwood, May 15, 1862, N.D., *Letters to Heads of Bureaus*, iv. Cf. Welles to Harwood, May 21, *ibid.*; Fox to Ericsson, March 24, April 25, May 13, May 15, *Ericsson Mss.*, i, ii.

abroad.[1] Brooke designed a 10-inch smooth-bore gun capable of bearing 30-pound charges with perfect safety, but he doubted whether it would prove effective against eight inches of iron at distances exceeding 300 yards. The treble-banded 7-inch rifle, on the other hand, would penetrate six inches of iron at seven or eight hundred yards. Vertical or inclined sides of 4½-inch plate backed by 18 inches of oak seemed to him incapable of resisting the new ordnance; and inclining the armor a few degrees did "not materially lessen the effect of shot on iron." Brooke believed that a wall-sided or sloping-sided vessel "might drive off wooden vessels not armed with rifles bearing high charges, but the stronger ironclads of the north would be more effective when it came to close action." He deplored the lack of a seagoing ironclad to attack the blockaders. Arguing that vessels with inclined sides might be made seaworthy, he prepared drawings of such vessels to be constructed abroad. The Confederacy, he observed, lacked certain materials essential to the construction of ironclads. Confederate plating he judged inferior, "for our resources are not great." [2]

Reviewing his whole building policy in February, 1865, Mallory declared that he had never expected European or American ironclads to prove satisfactory seagoing vessels.

> The development of the power of heavy ordnance kept up with, but has far exceeded that of resistance of ships, and all attempts to combine invulnerability to shot, now in use with the essential requisites of a cruising ship have hitherto proved, and until naval architecture shall have wonderfully improved, must ever prove failures.

For river, harbor, and coast defence he believed that the later Confederate ironclads with a sloping shield, "though not the best where mechanical skill, machinery and supplies may be commanded at will," were the best that could have been adopted by the South and "in every respect . . . superior to

---

[1] "A List of the Confederate Steam Navy corrected to February 15th, 1863 in Commission," Adm. 1/5819, P. 199; O.R.N., 2d series, i, pp. 247-272.

[2] Brooke to Warley, January 4, 1863, N.D., AD. The inability of the Confederates to construct good marine engines hamstrung their ironclad building at home. See above, pp. 229, 235, 290. Cf. Dunbar Rowland, ed., *Jefferson Davis, Constitutionalist* (Jackson, Miss., 1923, 10 vols.), viii, p. 474.

the monitors of the Federals." In this same report, however, presented only seven weeks before Lee's surrender, he proposed the construction on the Chattahoochee River, at or near Columbus, Georgia, of a light-draft ironclad mounting two heavy guns in a revolving cupola.[1]

Abroad as well as at home, the combat of Hampton Roads stimulated the building of ironclads, evoked fresh experiments in ordnance, and called forth great interest in the revolving turret. It is important to distinguish, however, between the limited effect of the first fight between ironclads on the building policies of the foreign governments, and the vast effect of the dramatic struggle on popular opinion.

While the Austrians, Italians, Spanish, and Russians continued and increased their earlier ironclad programs, several other European and South American powers now began for the first time the construction of armored vessels.[2] France, which had not laid down a wooden ship of the line since 1855, regarded the battle of Hampton Roads as a striking testimonial to the sagacity of her Ministry of Marine. The great French ironclad program of 1860 tasked her shipbuilding resources so severely that France, prior to 1865, laid down only two additional ironclads, the corvette *Belliqueuse*, and the coast-defence ram *Taureau*, both begun in 1863. Primarily interested in seagoing vessels, the French regarded the first American ironclads with little favor. The success of the *Monitor*, nevertheless, stimulated French interest in the revolving turret.[3]

The news that a wooden frigate, cut down and armored, had swept all before it until confronted by a little ironclad built in a few months at a cost of less than £60,000, caused tremendous excitement in Great Britain, where popular in-

---

[1] Mallory to A. G. Brown, Chairman of the Committee on Naval Affairs, Confederate States Senate, February 18, 1865. N.D., VN, Class 2.

[2] The development of ironclads in the sixties may best be followed in Hovgaard, *Modern History of Warships*; Dislère, *Marine cuirassée*; Pâris, *L'art naval en 1867*; E. J. Reed, *Our Iron-clad Ships* (London, 1869); J. Scott Russell, *The Modern System of Naval Architecture*; von Kronenfels, *Flottenmaterial*.

[3] Dislère, *Marine cuirassée*, chs. ii–vi, and *Note sur la marine des Etats-Unis*; von Kronenfels, *Flottenmaterial*, pp. 289 ff.; *Notice sur Dupuy de Lôme*, pp. 48, 49–50.

terest in the navy was keenest. The conversion of the great mass of the British public to the importance of ironclads followed so closely on the heels of the conversion of British experts, that the public and the press failed to give the Admiralty credit for changing its ground in 1861. When spokesmen for the Admiralty pointed out that, in the preceding year, they had suspended the construction of wooden ships of the line, except for the purpose of casing them with armor, and that they now had, in addition to eight ironclad floating batteries, fifteen seagoing ironclads built or building, a large part of the public seems to have been too excited to listen. The London *Times* asserted that the ironclad problem had now been removed "from the region of theory to the region of fact;" and cried out that the British Navy had been reduced to two ships.[1] In the House of Commons, Bentinck exclaimed that

> we have learnt what if two months ago any man had asserted he would have been scouted as a lunatic; we have learned that the boasted navy of Great Britain, when opposed to iron vessels, is useless as a fighting navy.[2]

Russell wrote privately to Palmerston: "Only think of our position if in case of the Yankees turning upon us they should by means of iron ships renew the triumphs they achieved in 1812-13 by means of superior size and weight of metal."[3]

Observers were not lacking, however, to point out that the lessons of Hampton Roads had been largely discounted by European naval constructors, and that Great Britain had already made good progress in the transformation of her fleet. At the first news of the battle the London *Times* pointed out that, "both in defence and attack," the *Merrimack* had fulfilled "in the most complete manner" the expectations and calculations of European constructors. Wooden vessels had proved as helpless against iron ones as had been predicted, demonstrating that the reconstruction of the British Navy then under way had not commenced an hour too soon.[4]

---

[1] April 2 and 3, 1862.   [2] April 4, 1862. Hansard, 3rd series, clxvi, col. 601.
[3] E. D. Adams, *Great Britain and the American Civil War* (London, 1925, 2 vols.), i, p. 277.
[4] March 25, 26, 1862.

On learning that American newspapers were boasting that British naval supremacy was now at an end, the *Times* retorted that England was not as ill off as she seemed, and that her naval supremacy was "safe enough at present." Admitting that wooden ships no longer counted in the effective force of a fleet, Great Britain nevertheless had a force of ironclads superior, probably, to those of any other power, and certainly superior to those of the United States, for those were not seagoing vessels. England had fifteen iron-cased frigates under construction, eleven of which it was hoped would be afloat before the end of the year. If war had resulted from the *Trent* affair,

> we should never have left our smart frigates to be encountered by turreted Monitors. We should have sent the Warrior and her consorts across the Atlantic, and our supremacy would have been expressed as decidedly, though more compendiously than ever. We could have done the work of the Monitor and Merrimac together.[1]

The *Times* nevertheless clamored for the prompt conversion of several wooden ships into ironclads, and took to task the defenders of the Admiralty, alleging that they minimized the lessons of Hampton Roads. In the House of Commons on March 31 Sir George Lewis, the Secretary of State for War, declared that "in the opinion of the most experienced persons," the American engagement "throws little light upon the qualities of iron-clad vessels." The Secretary of the Admiralty, Lord Clarence Paget, observed that it had been well known for some time that ironclads would resist the best existing projectiles, "though how long that impenetrability will last, in view of the daily improvements of guns and projectiles, is a doubtful matter." The careful experiments at Shoeburyness had proved iron-cased ships to be much superior to wooden ones; and had caused the Admiralty to cease to build large wooden ships, and to begin the construction of ironclads. As for the merits of rams, he asserted that all the British iron-cased ships had been constructed with a view to enable them to run down an enemy.

[1] April 1, 1862.

He flatly denied that the time had come to abandon the construction of small wooden vessels for distant service.[1]

The speech of the Duke of Somerset, First Lord of the Admiralty, in the House of Lords on April 3, deserves close study. In his opinion the battle of Hampton Roads left the relation between armored and wooden ships unaltered, since "it was already the undivided opinion of all experienced men that where wooden ships met iron ships the former could not live." The American engagement, however, had made one great difference. Hitherto the Admiralty had expected to keep ironclads only for home service, relying on wooden frigates and corvettes for overseas service. Now, if other nations in distant seas were to follow the American example, Great Britain must be prepared to send her armored ships to all quarters of the globe.[2]

Some allowance must doubtless be made for the desire of the spokesmen of the Admiralty to put their previous policy in the best possible light. Nevertheless the distinction made by the Duke of Somerset really goes to the root of the matter. The action of the French in abandoning the construction of wooden ships of the line and beginning a seagoing ironclad fleet had forced the British cautiously to follow. When the successful trials of the *Gloire* in 1860 led to an enormous expansion of the French ironclad program, and to the adoption of ironclads by Austria, Italy, Spain, and Russia, the Admiralty had suspended the construction of wooden capital ships, and matched the great French program with a great ironclad program of its own. Until the summer of 1861, however, no power in North or South America or in Asia was building ironclads.[3] For service on distant stations the Ad-

---

[1] Hansard, 3rd series, clxvi, cols. 277, 284-285. Lindsay asserted on April 4 that "what the *Monitor* and *Merrimac* had done was nothing more than was known would take place years ago. It was well known that one iron ship would destroy a whole fleet of wooden ships." *Ibid.*, col. 618. See, however, the *Times*, April 2, 3, 5, 7.

[2] Hansard, 3d series, clxvi, col. 440. Cf. J. Scott Russell, *The Fleet of the Future in 1862*, p. 12.

[3] Work on the unfinished Stevens battery had ceased several years before. See above, pp. 212-214.

miralty felt it might still rely on wooden cruisers. After Hampton Roads, however, British ships might expect to encounter ironclads in every sea.

Palmerston assured the House of Commons that he was not surprised that the public at large, ignorant of the extent to which the government had investigated the ironclad problem, should have had their eyes opened by the American battle. Experiments had "naturally led the government for some time past to that conclusion to which the public has suddenly arrived" on the basis of the American news. He deemed the American ironclads poor models, far inferior to the British. As for turreted vessels, Coles's system would, Palmerston believed, "turn out most effectual for coast purposes," since "the experiments made on these cupolas are perfectly successful."[1]

On April 1 Admiral Robinson had advised the Board of Admiralty that sufficient experience had now been gained, "as to both the value and the practicability of protecting the batteries and waterlines of screw ships of war," to indicate that no such ship should henceforth be launched "without both these protections." In the interest of economy the Admiralty must "be satisfied for a year or two, while this great change is proceeding, with the number of wooden ships which we already possess." He recommended that all warships should have complete water-line protection and as large a battery behind armor as their displacement would allow. Although in the smaller ships not more than two guns could probably be so protected, "two guns in a ship that cannot be sunk and where the battery is protected will prove more than a match for twenty in an ordinary wooden ship." Reserving thirty-seven wooden screw ships of the line, to match those possessed by France, the British would have twenty additional vessels of this class, which "might be converted into formidable defences for the Channel, or equally formidable engines of offence, against neighbouring ports, or armaments." With this end in view he proposed to select

[1] Hansard, 3rd series, clxvi, cols. 606–608, April 4, 1862.

some of these ships, cut them down to their lower deck beams, and "put as many of Captain Coles Shields into them, as they would bear, plating them round, as it is proposed to do, in the new ship now building purposely for the reception of those shields." [1]

When the Board inquired whether some wooden vessels were not so far advanced that it would be better to complete them as wooden vessels, Robinson replied that no screw ships ought to be so completed until the possibility of converting them into satisfactory ironclads had been explored; but that the wooden despatch vessels under construction should be completed. To the query whether it would not be desirable to build some more wooden paddle steamers, he replied that none ought to be constructed for war purposes.[2]

The Admiralty, which had suspended the construction of wooden line-of-battle ships in 1861, now stopped work on all kinds of wooden ships except despatch vessels, and ships being converted into ironclads.[3] In 1862 they began the construction or conversion of five wooden-hulled armored vessels, and laid down the turreted ironclad *Prince Albert*, whose construction on Coles's system had been decided prior to the combat of the *Monitor* and the *Merrimack*. Eleven British ironclads were begun during 1861; only six, during 1862. In the three years preceding the battle of Hampton Roads, the Admiralty ordered sixteen seagoing ironclads, including the *Prince Albert*. In the three following years, they began the construction or conversion of twelve additional armored vessels, besides purchasing the two Laird rams which were being built for the Confederate Navy.[4]

The American ships had little or no influence on the design of these new British armored vessels, although the relation of Ericsson's ideas to the breastwork monitors which Sir Edward Reed brought out some years after the Civil War was obvious enough. The Admiralty took pains to collect detailed information concerning the Union and Confederate

---

[1] Adm. 1/5802.   [2] Adm. 1/5802, April 5, 1862.
[3] Adm. 12/720, April 1, 5, 7, 1862.
[4] *Parliamentary Papers*, 1865, xxxv, part ii, no. 367.

ironclads, but they were not favorably impressed. With regard to the Union ironclads built or building in November, 1862, the Controller, Admiral Robinson, reported that "there appears to be no novel or important principle elucidated by these constructions."

> The few that seem likely to possess sea going qualities are in no way superior to the French 'Gloire' or 'Invincible' or the ships of the 'Royal Oak' class.
> The greater number are mere rafts carrying very few heavy guns propelled at moderate speed, and though perfectly well adapted for the Inland Waters of that great Continent, and most formidable as Harbour Defences, are not in any sense sea going ships of War.

The Controller, however, had no wish to disparage the skill and industry displayed in their construction, or to undervalue the "enormous defensive power which has thus been developed," a power which he believed rendered the Americans "practically unassailable in their own waters." [1]

Although the tense relations of Great Britain and the United States at several times during the American Civil War forced the Admiralty to consider the problem of protecting British commerce against fast American raiders, the British built their ironclads during the years 1862 to 1865 with the French rather than the Americans in mind. The great French ironclad program of 1860, which had forced the Admiralty's hand in 1861, caused grave concern for several years thereafter. On February 11, 1863, Admiral Robinson submitted a long, confidential report to the Admiralty on the superiority of the French to the British armored fleet. The four French ironclads then available for hostilities, the *Gloire*, *Normandie*, *Invincible*, and *Couronne*, mounted 148 guns, of which 130 were behind armor, while the four completed British ironclads, the *Warrior*, *Black Prince*, *Defence*, and *Resistance*, mounted eighty protected and thirty-six unprotected guns. Although the two first-named British ships were faster than the French, the two latter, which would determine the fleet speed, were not. In the weather common in the Atlantic the superior height of their guns from the

---

[1] Adm. 1/5840, January 30, 1863.

water would give the British an advantage which would disappear in fine weather such as might be expected in the Mediterranean. So superior were the French ships, however, in the protection afforded their steering gear and "almost sheltered rudder," in the complete protection of their main-deck battery, and their greater quickness in turning, that the Controller believed that this supposed battle of four against four could not be said to be fought on even terms. "Against a superior force of artillery, superior speed, at least equal turning power, a lighter rig and a ship protected from end to end," the British squadron could "only set forth a higher battery, Guns further apart and smaller Port holes, — insufficient to turn the scale." England thus did not possess at that moment "an Iron clad squadron capable of fighting a duel with a French Iron clad squadron on equal terms."

France, however, would very shortly be reinforced by the *Solférino* and *Magenta*, which had already had their engines tried at sea; and England "not quite so soon" would have the *Royal Oak* and the *Hector*. Robinson deemed the *Hector* to be a fair match for the *Gloire*, and the *Royal Oak* to be the equal of any of the French ships, although in fine weather the double battery of the *Solférino* and *Magenta* might give them an advantage. Neither the *Defence* nor the *Resistance*, however, seemed to him a match for the French vessels. In a fleet action, six ships against six, the British force would be unequal to the French.

> The six French Ships have an advantage in average speed, in lightness of rig, in the average power of manoeuvering, the average height of their batteries would be lower, but the protected number of Guns would be greater, the English Artillery would be somewhat better placed, the French would have somewhat greater powers of training, and, balancing the inflammable and non-protected portions of the 'Magenta' and 'Solferino' by the non-inflammable but larger exposed surfaces of the English Ships, the duel between the squadron of six Iron clads of the two Countries could not be said to be fought on equal terms for us.

France, moreover, had ten improved *Gloires* of the 1860 program under construction, which Robinson thought could be at sea in two years if any pressure for their completion arose. If France completed five of these ships of the *Flandre* class by January, 1864, England would have ready to meet them the *Valiant*, sister-ship of the *Hector*, and the four iron-cased wooden ships, *Royal Alfred, Prince Consort, Caledonia*, and *Ocean*, which Robinson believed "equal either singly or collectively to any of the French Ships built or building at present for what may be considered the Line of Battle." In a fleet action, however, the French would have the advantage of greater homogeneity and greater fleet speed, and making every allowance for the superior height of the British guns and the speed of the *Black Prince* and *Warrior*, "the strife would on the whole be an unequal one for the English Fleet."

The Controller expected that by the end of 1864 France would have completed the last five ships of the *Flandre* class, and Great Britain would have made ready the *Achilles, Agincourt, Minotaur*, and *Northumberland*. He believed the *Achilles* would be "a match, unless under extraordinary circumstances, for any ship built or designed by France, — the 'Magenta' and 'Solferino' excepted." The other three British ships, "though very long for manoeuvering, would still fight an Action collectively and singly on terms not only of equality, but it is believed, with decidedly favourable chances against anything yet designed by France." Under these circumstances, in January, 1865, "compactness, and homogeneousness would be on the side of France — individual power on the side of England: — a decided superiority — nowhere."

The Controller admitted that the force of his argument as to the present and future inferiority of the British fleet was somewhat weakened by the discovery that the latest heavy shells could "penetrate all our present Armour Plated Ships at 800 yards," thereby somewhat diminishing the great difference between a partially and a wholly protected ship, and giving the partially protected iron ship an advantage over a wholly protected wooden-hulled ironclad. He emphasized, however, "the evils that must result in a general action at sea from the great variety of forms and power" of the British ironclads, compared with the French; and strongly urged the construction of five additional ships of the *Prince Consort* class, to be built of wood in the dockyards, and not converted from existing ships on the stocks. In addition to the ironclads of the battle fleet, Great Britain would have the armored cruisers *Research*, *Enterprise*, *Favorite*, and *Zealous*, whose conversion had been begun since the battle of Hampton Roads. With the completion of the cupola ships *Royal Sovereign* and *Prince Albert*, he believed the British Navy would equal the French in coast-defence ships.[1]

To the disgust of British advocates of the superiority of iron over wooden hulls for armored vessels, the Admiralty promptly ordered three wooden-hulled ironclads, the *Lord Clyde*, *Lord Warden*, and *Pallas*, and only one iron-hulled ship, the *Bellerophon*, laid down in 1863.[2] The Board's doubts as to the ability of the French to complete the ten ships of the *Flandre* class as rapidly as Admiral Robinson supposed, proved well founded. The *Provence*, the first of these ships to be finished, was launched on October 29, 1863, and ready for her trials in January, 1865. The *Flandre* and the iron-hulled *Héroïne*, launched in June, 1864, and December, 1863, were first tried at sea in May and July, 1865. The *Magnanime*, *Surveillante*, and *Valeureuse* were launched in August, 1864; the *Gauloise* and *Guyenne*, not until April and September, 1865.[3]

The British likewise built their ironclads more slowly than the Controller had anticipated. The *Royal Oak* was completed for sea on May 28, 1863; followed by the *Prince Consort*, *Hector*, *Research*, *Enterprise*, *Royal Sovereign*, and *Achilles* in the course of 1864. The *Caledonia* was completed for sea in July, 1865, followed in October by the Laird rams,

---

[1] Adm. 1/5840.
[2] Special minute of March 18, 1863, Adm. 3/271; submissions of March 12, 1863, Adm. 1/5840, and of May 23, July 20, 1863, Adm. 1/5841; Adm. 12/733: 59–1, 59–4a; *Parliamentary Papers*, 1863, xxxvi, no. 83; Hansard, 3rd series, clxix, cols. 1333–1390, clxx, cols. 898–919.
[3] *Mémorial du génie maritime*, 1865, pp. 27–32, 107–113; 1866, pp. 223–234; *Revue maritime et coloniale*, January, 1864, p. 196; August, 1864, pp. 821–823; September, 1864, p. 214; May, 1865, pp. 184–185; June, 1865, pp. 421–422; October, 1865, pp. 445–446; August, 1866, pp. 836–837; September, 1866, pp. 251–252.

now named the *Scorpion* and *Wivern*. 1866 saw the completion of the *Prince Albert, Favorite, Pallas, Bellerophon, Ocean, Lord Clyde,* and *Zealous*. Although the *Royal Alfred, Minotaur,* and *Lord Warden* were not finished until 1867; nor the *Valiant, Northumberland,* and *Agincourt*, until the last quarter of 1868, a spokesman of the Whig Board of Admiralty declared in July, 1866, that England then possessed a seagoing ironclad fleet "far superior to that of any other country," outnumbering the French by nineteen ships to sixteen of the first class completed, and mounting heavier guns.[1]

Thanks in large measure to Gladstone and other partisans of economy in the House of Commons, the transformation of the fleet was carried out in this period without great increase in the rate of naval expenditure. Although the sums voted in supply for the navy rose from £9,305,973 in 1857 to £12,779,726 in 1859, £12,836,100 in 1860, and £12,640,588 in 1861, they declined to £11,794,305 in 1862, and did not reach £11,000,000 in any year from 1863 to 1867.[2]

In terms of national jealousy and suspicion, however, the cost of the Anglo-French race in naval armaments was a heavy one. Palmerston devoured the reports of the British naval attaché in Paris, keeping them so long that the Admiralty repeatedly begged in vain that this information might come direct to them, instead of to the Foreign Office. Convinced that Napoleon saw in England the principal obstacle to his designs of conquest and aggrandizement, and built his ironclads against her, the aged prime minister demanded the maintenance of costly armaments to protect the nation from "the Crafty Spider of the Tuileries."[3]

In vain did Napoleon III seek to dissipate this exaggerated alarm. He complained to Malmesbury in April, 1861, that

---

[1] *Parliamentary Papers*, 1874, xxxviii, no. 99; Hansard, 3rd series, clxxxiv, cols. 1198–1206.

[2] *Parliamentary Papers*, 1863, xxxi, no. 534; 1867–68, xli, no. 112; Guedalla, *Gladstone and Palmerston*, pp. 235, 248, 270, 289, 293–308, 310–315, 320.

[3] See the copies of Hore's despatches of February 23 and December 29, 1863, and accompanying papers, in Adm. 1/5850 and Adm. 1/5901; Adm. 12/717: 52–5; Adm. 12/733: 52–5; Adm. 12/749: 52–5; Palmerston to Russell, November 11, 1861, October 27, 1862, G.D. 22: 21, 22: 14; Gooch, *Russell*, ii, p. 283; Guedalla, *Gladstone and Palmerston*, pp. 205–228, 270–271, 313–314, 324.

the British suspicions of his naval program were childish. "Let each build what he considers the right number," he declared. "You ought to have twice as many as I, as they are your principal protection." In a letter to the Queen of Holland which the latter communicated to Lord Clarendon in August, 1861, Napoleon hotly denied that either the French fleet or army were yet in proportion to the population or resources of the country.[1]

Several partisans of economy and friends of peace pointed out that the revolution in naval architecture afforded a remarkable opportunity for limiting naval armaments. While Emile de Girardin waged the battle of disarmament in France, Richard Cobden, whose zeal for economy and for international good will surpassed the accuracy of his knowledge of French naval preparations, fought tirelessly to curb British naval expenditures and to promote an international agreement. Disraeli denounced the "insane rivalry" which led to "bloated armaments," and insisted that France might be induced to agree to restrict warship building and accept British predominance at sea. Even Admiral Napier, whom Cobden dubbed a "professional monomaniac" of preparedness, expressed wonder that the British government had not come to an understanding with Napoleon III to limit naval competition.[2]

In January, 1861, Lord Clarence Paget, the Secretary to the Admiralty, devised a plan for limiting the French and British navies in such a way as to assure British superiority while effecting large savings for both countries. Palmerston returned his memorandum with the remark that there was "much truth in it," but that it was not "quite the sort of statement to be usefully shewn or repeated to the Emperor of the French." He deemed it inadvisable "either to make such a proposal to France, or to accept it if made by France to

---

[1] Malmesbury, *Memoirs*, ii, pp. 203–204; Maxwell, *Clarendon*, ii, pp. 241–242.
[2] Girardin, *Le désarmement européen* (Paris, 1859); W. H. Dawson, *Richard Cobden and Foreign Policy* (London, 1926), pp. 151–164; Gooch, *Russell*, ii, p. 262; Hansard, 3rd series, clv, col. 716; clvi, col. 989; clxiv, cols. 1678–1682; clxvi, cols. 1403–1428; clxvii, cols. 343, 373–382. See above, pp. 67–68.

us," since Great Britain must regulate her naval force with reference to other powers as well as to France.

In the next place, such an agreement with any foreign Power would shackle the free action and discretion of England in a manner which we would never submit to; and if such an agreement were made, there must be a perpetual inquisitorial watch kept up by each Power over the Dockyards and Navy of the other, in order to see that the agreement was not broken through, and this would lead to frequent bickerings, besides being intolerable to National self-respect.

If England, moreover, were now to suggest that she should have double the French force,

> the Emperor would laugh at us and say, 'By all means! I must have 20 or 24 Iron-cased ships — you are quite welcome to have 40 or 48, and I hope you will find money to build them; but do not expect that I am to sit with my hands across till you have done so!'[1]

Experiments with rifled ordnance in France and England in 1861 had already shown the need of armor plate thicker than $4\frac{1}{2}$ inches.[2] As the power of the guns increased, there followed demands for still better protection. In view of "the possibility of meeting more destructive Guns than those at present established on the Decks of Foreign Men of War," the Controller proposed on December 11, 1863, to strengthen the armor of ships of the *Lord Warden* class, whose two lower rows of plates were $5\frac{1}{2}$ inches thick, by adding an inner skin of $1\frac{1}{2}$-inch plates, to form a belt ten feet wide "round the whole of the ship comprising the battery."[3] In this phase of the race between the armor and the gun both France and England kept well posted as to American ordnance developments. Captain Pigeard, the French naval attaché at London, who was sent to the United States on a tour of observation, told the British naval attaché at Paris that "he did not

---

[1] Otway, *Paget*, pp. vi–vii. See above, pp. 67, 178. Cf. Ashley, *Palmerston*, ii, pp. 221, 335–341; Hansard, 3rd series, clv, col. 670. When Sir Morton Peto proposed such an agreement in the House of Commons, in July, 1861, Sir John Pakington declared that no surer course could be found "to lay the foundation of future misunderstandings and quarrels with France" than to define in a treaty the number of ships or the relative armaments which the two powers should maintain. *Ibid.*, clxiv, cols. 1634, 1638–1639.
[2] See above, pp. 201–209.   [3] Adm. 1/5842.

consider the Americans had surpassed or even equalled France or England in artillery, as far as the employment of heavy charges and thereby great initial velocities, but he was astonished at the numerous mechanical means they employed for working heavy ordnance." [1]

Although the battle of Hampton Roads did not inaugurate the era of ironclad warships, the success of the *Monitor* gave a great impetus to the adoption of the revolving armored turret. Several powers at once began the construction of turreted ironclads, some on Coles's plans, some on Ericsson's, some on French designs. Of those built on Coles's system, the most famous were the Danish double-turreted ship *Rolf Krake*, which did valiant service in the War of 1864; the single-turreted ship *Huascar*, of the Peruvian, and later of the Chilean, Navy; and the two double-turreted Laird rams, built for the Confederate Navy, and taken into the British service under the names *Scorpion* and *Wivern*. Light-draft turret ships appealed especially to Russia, which ordered from Napier and Sons the double-turreted ship *Smertch*, and had ten monitors constructed on Ericsson's system.[2]

The British Admiralty had decided on the construction of the multiple-turret ironclad *Prince Albert* on Coles's system and approved the plans before they learned the news of the battle of Hampton Roads. Reviewing the experiments which led to this decision, Somerset explained in the House of Lords, April 3, that the guns in the experimental cupola had been fired much faster than was possible with broadside guns, and that the cupola had withstood satisfactorily at short range

---

[1] Copy of Hore's report of May 16, 1864, in Adm. 1/5902.

[2] This development may be studied in the works of Dislère, Hovgaard, von Kronenfels, Pâris, and Scott Russell, cited above, p. 311, note 2. Both Dislère, *Marine cuirassée*, p. 30, and H. W. Wilson, *Ironclads in Action*, i, p. 33, note, state that the *Rolf Krake* was ordered in 1861; but correspondence noted in Adm. 12/717, April 22, August 11, 1862, indicates that the date should be 1862. Cf. Adm. 1/5840, April 29, 1863; A.M., 6 DD[1] 88, dossier 2399. Some material concerning Ericsson's relations with foreign governments is preserved in *Ericsson Mss*. Church's account in his *Ericsson*, ii, chs. xxiii–xxvi, "suffers from a want of proportion," often misses the significance of the facts, and metes out "palpable injustice" to Coles, as Lord Sydenham observed in the *Edinburgh Review*, January, 1893, pp. 53 ff.

Imperial War Museum photograph. Copyright reserved.

H.M.S. *WIVERN*

such a severe fire "as a vessel would hardly ever meet with, even in action." He had thought of trying the cupola in a wooden ship, cut down, but concluded that the new system would have a fairer test if, "in the first instance at least," it were tried in an iron-hulled vessel built expressly for the purpose on plans which had been adopted after consultation with the inventor, though with some important modifications of his hull design. Somerset declared his belief that this mastless turret ship would prove "the best form of vessel that we can have for the protection of our coasts," and that some rather smaller vessels might be constructed with advantage on the same principle. He proposed also to cut down some large wooden ships, plate them with iron, and fit them with cupolas.[1]

In addition to the *Prince Albert*, the contract for which was awarded to Messrs. Samuda of Millwall early in April, the Admiralty promptly ordered the wooden screw ship of the line *Royal Sovereign* of 131 guns and 800 horse power cut down for conversion into an armored turret ship at the Portsmouth yard.[2] On May 8 the Controller submitted plans for two iron-hulled coast-defence ironclads like the *Prince Albert* but considerably smaller, 180 feet long and 42 feet beam. He thought these vessels of 1385 tons and 250 horse power could make a speed of nine knots and could be built by contract for £83,100 each. Each was to carry two cupolas containing a single 12-ton Armstrong 156-pounder. As the French heavily outnumbered the British in coast-defence ironclads built or building, the Admiralty approved these plans but ordered further reports as to building these ships by contract.[3]

Admiral Robinson replied that, "considering how far behind our neighbours we are in the number of Iron plated ships of all classes," equality could not be attained without spending more money than Parliament had appropriated. He thought it best to build by contract the two small cupola

---

[1] Hansard, 3rd series, clxvi, cols. 437–439, 443; see above, pp. 190–192.
[2] Ships' books of *Prince Albert* and *Royal Sovereign*; P.R.O., Adm. 1/5802, April 7, 1862.
[3] Adm. 1/5802; Adm. 12/720: 91-2.

ships for Channel service, and to convert into ironclads some corvettes, frigates and line-of-battle ships now on the slips and in frame. Although there were grave doubts as to the durability of wooden-hulled ironclads, it was worth considering that the armored vessels against which the British were most likely to be engaged were almost all wooden-hulled.[1]

Although the Duke of Somerset wished to increase the number of ironclads both for coast defence and for service abroad, he deemed an application to Parliament for additional funds objectionable, since it "would incite and justify expenditure by France for a similar purpose." He therefore favored the conversion of ships in frame into ironclads in the government dockyards, and directed that, as soon as the vessels of the *Royal Oak* class were finished, the dockyards should undertake the conversion of other vessels, some for seagoing ironclads like the *Enterprise*, others for coast defence fitted with cupolas like the *Royal Sovereign*.[2]

As the size and power of the British naval guns rapidly increased, and muzzle loaders were preferred to breech loaders, Coles redesigned his cupola, increasing its diameter and adopting a cylindrical form instead of the original truncated cone. The *Prince Albert*, originally designed to mount twelve guns in six cupolas, each of which weighed about eighty tons, was built to carry four heavy guns in four turrets, each of which weighed 111 tons. The *Royal Sovereign* mounted five heavy guns in four turrets, instead of ten lighter guns in five cupolas as originally designed.[3]

Although Coles expressed to the Admiralty his "deep

[1] Adm. 1/5802, May 27, 1862.
[2] Sir Frederick Grey, the First Naval Lord, thought the dockyards should be employed in the conversion of seagoing vessels rather than in constructing vessels only applicable to coast defence. If the experimental cupola should withstand successfully the proposed battering by 150-pounder shot, he would favor the immediate construction by contract of the iron double-turreted ships proposed by the Controller. Adm. 1/5802, May 27, 28, 1862.
[3] Ships' books of *Prince Albert* and *Royal Sovereign*; P.R.O., Adm. 1/5802, April 8, July 4, July 26, 1862; Adm. 1/5840, March 19, 1863; Adm. 12/717; Adm. 12/720; Adm. 12/733: 59–1. Cf. *Parliamentary Papers*, 1866, xlvii, no. 395, pp. 12–19; and E. J. Reed, "On Iron Cased Ships of War," *Transactions* of the Institution of Naval Architects, March 26, 1863, p. 12.

mortification ... at the Americans' taking away the Palm of this invention" from England, he admitted that since the successful tests of his cupola in the *Trusty* in 1861 the Board had been "most anxious further to develope this invention."[1] He now asked £20,000 for his patent rights as far as they applied to ships or floating batteries; but accepted an arrangement by which the British government paid him £5000 for the expenses he had incurred, and promised him a royalty of £100 for every turret installed in a British ship or fort during the term of his patent. In the autumn of 1862 the Admiralty decided to permit him to make his own arrangements with private shipbuilders, who were offering him much larger sums for the right to install his turrets, on condition that the sanction of the Board be obtained in each case, and that the Admiralty be relieved of responsibility.[2]

The task of adapting Coles's turrets to seagoing, as distinct from coast-defence vessels, proved extremely difficult. If the deck of the turret ship were low, the Controller feared she would be swamped in a seaway. If it were high, great dimensions would be required to carry the weight of armor necessary and to afford proper stability. The presence of masts, rigging and sails, moreover, which the Admiralty still deemed indispensable in cruising vessels, limited the wide arc of fire which was the turret ship's peculiar advantage.[3] If the battle of Hampton Roads had helped to increase the interest of the Admiralty in Coles's ideas, the mishaps of the monitors at Charleston proved a distinct setback, leading the Admiralty to shelve the project of a seagoing turret ship until the *Royal Sovereign* or *Prince Albert* could be completed and tested.[4]

[1] Coles to Paget, March 31, 1862, Adm. 1/5802. Coles to the Editor of the *Times*, March 31, published April 5, 1862. Cf. Hansard, 3rd series, clxvi, col. 1936.
[2] Coles to the Secretary of the Admiralty, April 16, 1862, Adm. 1/5802; special minute of August 4, 1862, Adm. 3/270; Adm. 12/717: 59–1, 59–4a; Hansard, 3d series, clxvi, col. 2193.
[3] Controller's submissions of February 24, March 5, April 16 and 20, 1863, Adm. 1/5840; Adm. 12–733: 59–1; *Parliamentary Papers*, 1866, xlvii, no. 395, pp. 19–23.
[4] *Ibid.*, pp. 22–23; Controller's submission of June 27, 1863, Adm. 1/5841; Hansard, 3d series, clxx, col. 915.

To avert from his project the disfavor which the British visited on Ericsson's creations in 1863, Coles published a pamphlet discussing the reports of the Federal commanders at Charleston and contrasting his turrets with Ericsson's. He attributed the injuries of the Ericsson turrets to the use of laminated armor instead of thick plates with heavy wooden backing, and to the fact that the entire surface of the turret, nine feet in height, and of the superposed pilot house, was exposed to the enemy fire, while his turret had only four feet ten inches exposed, or less than half its height, since the base and working portion were protected on the lower deck. Instead of having its weight equally distributed on solid rollers at the periphery, as in Coles's system, the Ericsson turret did not work on rollers, but

being raised off the platform upon which it rests by the action of a wedge under the pivot it becomes wholly dependent for stability and support on the pivot round which it turns.... In addition to this cause of weakness, there is another, in the increased strain brought upon the pivot and turret by the position of the pilot-house on the top, which from its height, exerts a very great leverage upon it, and which is more severely felt from there being no bearing under the periphery of the turret.

While the Ericsson turret had "only *one* means of revolving, trusting entirely to steam," Coles, thanks to the free access from the lower deck to the platform of his turrets and the roller on which they worked, without exposure to fire, was able to supply four means of rotating the turret: rack and pinion inside the turret; rack and pinion outside, with a fixture on the lower deck; tackles; and handspikes shipped and manned like capstan bars.[1]

Ericsson never explained better his own system, as contrasted with Coles's, than in his letter to Welles, December 23, 1861. He objected to wooden backing to turret armor, since "there the impact of the shot not only depresses the wood in a radial direction but causes an enormous tangential strain on the wooden block nearly in the ratio of the chord to the versed sine." Destruction of the backing would be the

[1] *English versus American Cupolas, A Comparison between Capt. Coles's and Capt. Ericsson's Turrets* (Portsea, 1864). In the above quotations, references to the plates accompanying the text are omitted.

more certain because only short pieces could be employed in this curved structure. Believing that the vibration produced by the impact of heavy shot would derange any mechanism applied to the circumference of the turret, he condemned the employment of iron cogs or rack work at that exposed point and insisted that the mechanism for turning the turret must be applied at the center.[1]

Professor Hovgaard's verdict on the rival systems may be taken as high authority. He points out that jamming of the turret by projectiles entering at the foot of the turret wall, as occurred in the American monitors, notably in the attack on Charleston, "was not likely to happen" to Coles's turret. The latter, moreover,

> was always ready to turn, being mounted on a platform similar to a railway turntable, while the Ericsson turret had to be wedged up before it could move....
>
> The turret designed by Dupuy de Lôme and mounted in the *Cerbère* was similar to the Coles turret, but was superposed on a circular redoubt of somewhat smaller diameter, which formed the support of the roller part. The combination of turret and redoubt is a feature which is found in all modern installations, being necessitated by the claims to high freeboard. In the days of small, relatively low-freeboard ships, the Coles turret, partly sunk below an armor deck with a low center of gravity, formed the best solution and was most commonly used.[2]

In his long struggle to persuade the Admiralty to install his turrets on seagoing ships, Coles showed a dogged persistence and an irascible temper which remind one of Ericsson. He lacked, however, the astonishing resourcefulness and engineering knowledge of his Swedish rival. After the successful tests of his turrets in 1864,[3] the Admiralty, with much hesitation, laid down one rigged seagoing turret ship, the *Monarch*, and permitted Coles to design another, the *Captain*. Unhappily for Coles's fame he put to sea in this ill-fated vessel, which lacked sufficient stability to carry so much

---

[1] See above, p. 278 and Appendix G. When Fox sent him a plan of one of the Laird rams on Coles's system, Ericsson replied that "such a gingerbread affair must not come near our XV inch bulldogs in their impregnable kennels." September 26, 1863, *Fox Papers*.
[2] *Modern History of Warships*, pp. 402–403.
[3] *Parliamentary Papers*, 1866, xlvii, no. 395, pp. 12–19.

canvas, and met his death, September 7, 1871, in one of the most terrible disasters in naval history.[1] Despite his ill fortune, Coles is entitled to his full share of the honor of introducing the revolving armored turret. While Ericsson clung solely to the raft-like monitor with a single turret, and insisted that the day was not far distant "when two turrets on a vessel will be admitted to have the same advantages as two heads on the human body, or two suns in the heavens,"[2] Coles advocated both high- and low-freeboard vessels, with multiple turrets aligned over the keel. It was he, rather than Ericsson, who thus must be deemed the parent of the high-freeboard multiple-turret ironclad that since has ruled the seas.

Although the *Monitor* type of ship found few partisans in France, the revolving turrets proposed by Coles and Ericsson attracted great attention. In December, 1862, the *Conseil des Travaux* unanimously advised the Minister of Marine to order studies to be undertaken in the ports on the problem of installing turrets on board ship.[3] Lieutenant Farcy, Naval Constructor de Bussy, and others submitted projects for turreted ships; but the great French contribution to the development of the turret came from Dupuy de Lôme. He combined the turret with a circular armored redoubt, facilitating its installation on ships of high freeboard; and he likewise introduced the system of mounting guns *en barbette* on turntables.[4]

It is interesting to note that this first great improvement of the turrets of Ericsson and Coles was the work of Dupuy de Lôme. Clearly perceiving that the powerful shell guns introduced by Paixhans had upset the balance between offence

---

[1] *Ibid.*, 1866, xlvii, nos. 87 and 395; 1867–68, xlv, no. 26; 1870, xliv, no. 402; 1871, vii, no. 180, using index, s.v. "Captain;" xl, nos. 31, 37; xlii, c. 254, nos. 38 and 163; 1872, xiv, c. 477, c. 477–I, c. 489; xxxix, c. 487.

[2] Church, *Ericsson*, ii, p. 12.

[3] A.M., BB⁸ 1151, August 19, December 13, 1862. Cf. Cavelier de Cuverville, *Les bâtiments cuirassés* (Paris, 1865), p. 2.

[4] A.M., BB⁸ 1152, June 2, 1863; Dislère, *Marine cuirassée*, pp. 129–130; Hovgaard, *Modern History of Warships*, p. 403; Pâris, *Supplément à l'Art naval à l'exposition universelle de 1862* (Paris, 1864), pp. 1–39; Pâris, *Projet de navires de mer à tourelles* (Paris, 1868).

and defence, Dupuy as early as 1845 had designed a powerful seagoing ironclad. Fresh from his triumph with the *Napoléon*, he had been appointed to apply the lessons of the Crimean War to the reconstruction of the French fleet. New developments in ordnance reinforced his arguments for the necessity of armor; and the development of metallurgy furnished him with the means for a solution. He designed the first modern seagoing ironclad, and the world's first armored fleet. Paixhans, who foresaw the revolution which he did so much to create; Napoleon III, who picked the right man and backed him to the limit; and Dupuy de Lôme, who solved the problem of the seagoing ironclad, stand out as the three leading figures in the introduction of the ironclad warship.

APPENDICES

APPENDIX A

NOTES ON THE INTRODUCTION OF THE SCREW PROPELLER

IN reply to the assertions of John B. Emerson of New York, who sued him for alleged infringement of his patent for a propeller, Ericsson denied the charge. On March 8, 1845, he made an affidavit that his own invention was

> merely an improvement on the old fan wheel or smoke jack, which has been applied to purposes of propulsion for the last 50 years; and consists in cutting out the inefficient central part of the said instrument and inserting a broad and thin metallic cylinder or hoop to sustain the propelling planes, which planes are identical in form, twist and spiral curvature with the propelling planes of the propelling wheels patented by Benjamin M. Smith in the United States in the year 1829, and are therefore specifically disclaimed in the specification of this deponent's Letters Patent of 1838. And 2dly, said improvement consists in supporting the said cylinder by means of spokes, twisted in such a manner that they thread their way edgewise through the water and thereby obviating the great retardation which a spoke of any ordinary form would offer in passing through the water. . . .

Although Church mentions this affidavit, which is preserved in the first volume of the Ericsson Mss., he says nothing concerning the part of it quoted above. (*Ericsson*, i, p. 98.) Bourne, in his *Screw Propeller*, p. 78, had pointed out that

> on the 20th November, 1829, a patent was granted to Benjamin M. Smith, of Rochester, New York . . . for a new way of propelling vessels by the application of sculling wheels, or screw propelling wheels, at the stern. The wheels are made with six blades, like the vanes of a smoke-jack, and one is placed on each side of the stern — the two revolving in opposite directions. This arrangement of propelling wheels has since been introduced by Ericsson, for propelling barges on the canals and rivers of America, and is found to act in a satisfactory manner.

Ericsson wrote to Secretary John Y. Mason, February 26, 1847, admitting that

> there are disadvantages attending the hoop of my original propeller in a seaway. I have much pleasure in acknowledging that these were anticipated and pointed out to me by Commodore Morris already in the year 1840. I partially felt the force of that gentleman's remarks at the time, but not seeing any other way of making the propeller, I preferred sacrificing some efficiency under peculiar circumstances in order to secure strength

and lightness. Having in the meantime constructed a great number of propellers ... a plan ultimately suggested itself of bracing the blades diagonally in such a manner as to obtain even greater strength than by the employment of the hoop: the steamship *Massachusetts* is furnished with one of these improved propellers.

He concluded by strongly recommending the use of propellers of at least six blades. (*Ericsson Mss.*, i.)

When the town of Boulogne-sur-mer applied for authority to erect a statue to Sauvage as inventor of the application of the screw to steam navigation, the Minister of the Interior referred the matter to the Minister of Marine and received the following reply, dated April 7, 1864.

Je dois faire observer à Votre Excellence, que la priorité de l'invention de l'application de l'hélice à la navigation ne saurait être rigoureusement attribuée à Frédéric Sauvage, qui, dès 1823, a été devancé dans la recherche de la solution de ce problème par M. Delisle, capitaine du génie militaire français.

Toutefois, comme il est avéré que Frédéric Sauvage s'est imposé des sacrifices onéreux qui ont contribué à sa ruine en se livrant à des expériences interessantes de propulseurs hélicoidaux, et que cet homme ingénieux peut être considéré jusqu'à un certain point comme le promoteur en France de l'emploi de ce propulseur, je ne vois aucun inconvénient au point de vue de mon Département, à ce qu'il soit donné suite à la demande de la ville de Boulogne sur mer. (A.M., 1 DD¹ 331.)

G. Clerc-Rampal, in his remarkable article, "Les Lois générales de la construction navale," *Académie de Marine, Communications et Mémoires*, iii (1924), states that

En 1841 le constructeur havrais Augustin Normand mit en chantier un aviso de 376 tonneaux, le *Corse*, qui était muni d'une machine Woolf de construction anglaise, actionnant *l'hélice* tracée par Frédéric Sauvage.

And in his popular work *Le Navire*, he refers to this vessel as the first screw warship. The official *Matricule des bâtiments à flot*, however, while classifying le *Corse* as an *aviso* in use during the fifties, states that it was laid down in 1842 as the mail-steamer, le *Napoléon*, was transferred to the Navy by the Finance Ministry on November 26, 1850, for 189,557 francs, and was named le *Corse* on December 18, 1850. (A.M., 0 DD¹ 10, 175 verso.)

APPENDIX B

THE REINTRODUCTION OF THE RAM

The supplanting of oars by sail as the motive power for warships banished the ram, so important a weapon in ancient wars, from naval architecture and naval tactics. In much the same fashion the supplanting of sail by steam led to its reintroduction. The idea of reviving the ancient method of ramming occurred to numerous naval officers and inventors in the early days of steam navies. Frequently the sight of a steamboat collision gave rise to the suggestion. In June, 1823, Captain Delisle of the French engineer corps, whose important share in the development of the screw propeller has been already mentioned (above, p. 15 and Appendix A), proposed the conversion of a ship of the line into an armored screw steamer mounting heavy shell guns and equipped with "un énorme éperon, plein en bois, recouvert entièrement d'une très-forte armure en fer. Cet éperon offre une espèce de pyramide curviligne dont la base embrasse une partie de l'étrave et de l'avant du vaisseau; les arrêtes de cette pyramide sont aiguës et façonnées en dents de scie, son sommet formant la pointe de l'éperon est à un demi-mètre au-dessous de la ligne de flottaison." This vessel, he asserted, would sink any ship it could strike at five or six knots speed. As an alternative he proposed a double-ended screw-propelled ram, similarly armed and armored, of the size of an 120-to 130-gun ship. (See above, p. 27.) Four years later Captain Samuel Barron constructed a model of a machine ram which is now in the Naval Academy at Annapolis. (W. E. Griffis, *Matthew Calbraith Perry*, p. 127.)

Although the *Commission consultative des Travaux de la Marine* rejected in 1831 the ram project of a French inventor named Esquirol on account of the proposed method of construction, it observed that if steamers were to form a large part of future fleets, iron rams would be worth a trial. (See above, p. 27.) When relations between France and the United States were strained in Jackson's second administration, the House Committee on Naval Affairs recommended, on February 4, 1835, an appropriation of $75,000 for the construction of a "prow-ship," proposed by Commodore Charles Stewart. This strange craft, two hundred or two hundred and fifty feet long, and seventy or eighty feet wide, built of solid timbers, was to comprise three hulls, the center one of which was to contain three steam engines, of 150 horse power, driving side paddle wheels to revolve between the hulls. Protected by impenetrable wooden bulwarks, and a heavy deck overhead, with the whole exterior sheathed in such manner as to be "comparatively incombustible by ordinary means," she would attack hostile ships by striking them "two or three feet above the water and six or eight feet below its surface," with her solid "pyramidal prow," formed of hard wood logs covered with iron plates four to six inches thick in such fashion as to "produce a saw-shaped space upon the prow, and prevent the glancing of the vessel from her object." This ram, solidly incorporated by extending back at least fifty feet into the mass of the three vessels, so that no concussion even at a speed of eight or ten miles an hour might wrench it from its base, would be withdrawn from the enemy's side by reversing the paddle wheels. Congress, however, failed to act on the proposal. (*American State Papers, Naval Affairs*, iv, pp. 704-707.)

After learning of the effects of a collision between the *Fulton* and the brig *Montevideo* in the East River, August 28, 1839, Matthew Calbraith Perry proposed to the Secretary of the Navy that the *Fulton* be tested against a hulk, to ascertain the possibilities of ramming. When relations with Great Britain were strained by the Northeastern Boundary controversy, Perry "made preparations for securing the boilers and steam pipes of the Fulton," so that she might be used to run down an enemy. In November, 1850, he pressed on Secretary Graham the importance of this mode of attack, remarking that he claimed no credit for the originality of this invention, which had been utilized by the ancients, and suggested some years before by Commodore Barron." (Griffis, *Perry*, ch. xiv.)

Like Commodores Barron and Perry, Nicolas-Hippolyte Labrousse, who became the most persistent advocate of the ram in France, had noted the cutting force of a steamer's bow in collisions. In 1840 he proposed to the Minister of Marine the construction of two classes of rams, one for coast defence, the other for sea service. For the first class he recommended fast light-draft mastless screw steamers, whose bullet-proof convex deck, rising to a little over a meter above the waterline and plated over the engines with iron sheets one to two centimeters thick, sloped forward and ended in a conical ram of solid wood covered with bronze and solidly incorporated in the hull. With a quarter of the coal supply consumed, the point of the ram would be awash. The seagoing rams were to be paddle steamers of 450 horse power and normal type of hull, with heavily armored paddle boxes and a convex protective deck whose summit would be 50 centimeters below the water line. A hollow cone filled with powder placed at the apex of the prow would explode on penetrating the enemy's hull. In both types coal bunkers protected the machinery.

In the *Conseil des Travaux*, Labrousse's proposals met with little favor. Conceding that fast coast-defence rams might prove effective against light hostile craft such as ordinary steamers, the council pointed out the difficulties of ramming an enemy ship of nearly equal speed, deemed his suggestions for protection inadequate, held that rams would be of little use against stout ships of the line, and suggested that ramming might prove as disastrous to the attacker as to the enemy. The *Conseil d'Amirauté*, however, took the matter more seriously, and recommended tests at Lorient to ascertain the effect on walls of wood, of iron, and of wood plated with iron, of a chest weighing fifty to sixty tons, armed with a ram, and striking at speeds varying from one to five meters per second. (*Notice sur les travaux scientifiques et les services du contre-amiral Labrousse*, pp. 5–6, 63–64; A.M., BB[8] 1116, June 16, 1842; BB[8] 1122, June 21, 1848; A.N., BB[8] 872, November 4, 1842.)

A ministerial despatch of February 27, 1843, ordered the desired tests, and a circular of the 19th October following submitted Labrousse's proposal to special commissions which were to be formed in the five principal ports whose replies were to be submitted to the *Commission supérieure centrale des Bâtiments à Vapeur*, appointed three days later. (See above, p. 57.) The tests at Gavres in March and April, 1844, had surpassed his expectations. To ascertain the effects of ramming, without reproducing actual battle conditions, a large rectangular oak chest weighing fifty tons, terminating in a conical ram capped with cast iron, was slid down a greased inclined plane. Striking a heavy oak target at a speed of four meters per second, or about nine miles per hour, it penetrated twenty inches. At six meters per second, it penetrated twenty-eight inches. In a target covered with 12-mm. sheet iron, the penetration, with a speed of six meters per second, was twenty-five inches. In the following June, Labrousse submitted three projects for rams: one for coast defence, one for one month's sea service, and one for distant voyages. The Prince de Joinville, however, replied that "dans les discussions auxquelles ont donné lieu vos projects de navires à éperon, dans le sein de la commission, on n'a rien trouve à y dire: mais, comme nous avions quelques améliorations plus urgentes à obtenir, nous les avons laissés de côté, momentanément, pour ne pas demander trop à la fois." (*Notice sur Labrousse*, pp. 16–17, 54–55; Report of the Gavres Commission, May 6, 1844, in *Mémorial de l'Artillerie de la Marine*, first series, iii (1864), pp. 319–331.)

Believing that he had given his plans too much scope, Labrousse reduced them in 1847 to a single proposal to transform a 100-gun sailing ship of the line into a seagoing screw-propelled ram. The prow, ending in a bronze cone weighing five tons and projecting more than five meters beyond the stem, was to be solidly incorporated in the hull by prolonging the keel, the keelson and seven other principal timbers as integral parts of the ram. From the data obtained in the experiments of 1844, Labrousse argued that this 100-gun ship, weighing 4450 tons, and steaming at six knots speed, would smash a hole at least five meters in diameter in the side of a three-decker. (A.M. 1 DD^1 140, January 26, 1848; BB^8 1122, June 21, 1848.) Again, as in 1842, his project met with little favor in the *Conseil des Travaux*. The *Conseil d'Amirauté*, on the other hand, while opposing the transformation of a ship of the line, recommended that a ram bow on Labrousse's plans be built into a screw corvette of 200 to 320 horse power. The retrenchment forced on the French Navy at this period proved fatal to Labrousse's ram project. (See above, p. 64.) Despite this recommendation the Minister of Marine, de Tracy, declined on account of expense to permit the experiment. Though Rear Admiral Verninac and Vice Admiral Casy favored the construction of rams in their testimony during the parliamentary investigation of 1850, the government paid no further heed to ram or ironclad projects until the outbreak of the Crimean War. (A.M., BB^8 1122, June 21, 1848; DD^1 141, July 17, 1848; BB^8 1125, July 4, 1849; A.N., BB^8 878, August 6, 1849; *Notice sur Labrousse*, pp. 21–22, 61–76; Lullier, *Essai sur l'histoire de la tactique navale* [Paris, 1867], pp. 268–274; *Enquête parlementaire*, ii, pp. 73–75, 103.)

In Great Britain Commander Shuldham declared that he had

"invented" the ram in 1832. (Controller of the Navy, Submission Letter Book no. 20, September 25, October 11, November 15, 1858, April 7, 1859; Adm. 12/653.) Admiral Sir George Rose Sartorius, the leading British advocate of the ram, submitted proposals for a steam ram to the Admiralty in 1857, and for an armored steam ram in 1858 and 1859. The Surveyor, in recommending the rejection of these proposals, remarked in 1858 that "as soon as the building of vessels with armour plates has been determined on, the making of their extremities of a suitable form and of sufficient strength to enable them to perform such services without material damage to themselves may be accomplished." (Controller of the Navy, Submission Letter Book, no. 19, March 25, 1857; *ibid.*, no. 20, September 30, 1858, March 24, 1859; Adm. 12/669: 59–1, March 9, July 29, August 5, 1859.) There is an undated pamphlet by Sartorius, written soon after the battle of Lissa, *The Ram used simply as a projectile, without armour plating or artillery*, in the British Museum. From 1858 to 1862, inventors showered scores of ram projects on the Admiralty. Vice Admiral J. E. Walcott, in the House of Commons, August 3, 1860, advocated a reserve flotilla of steam gun and mortar boats, supported by a strong division of steam rams, 280 feet long. (Hansard, 3rd series, clx, cols. 668–670.)

APPENDIX C

PROJECT OF NAPOLEON III FOR ARMORING SHIPS OF THE LINE

On November 19, 1854, Lord Cowley, the British Ambassador in Paris, received the following note from the Emperor. (P.R.O. Adm. 1/5633. See above, p. 77.)

Milord. Je vous envoie une note que j'ai adressée au ministre de la Marine. Comme l'idée qui s'y trouve développée peut être d'une application utile dans la guerre actuelle, je vous prie de la communiquer à l'Amirauté anglaise afin qu'elle juge s'il y a un parti avantageux à en tirer. . . .

The enclosure, dated November 16, follows:

M. le ministre. La guerre maritime qui se poursuit aujourd'hui m'a suggéré de sérieuses réflexions que je suis bien aise de vous communiquer en vous priant de réunir une commission d'hommes spéciaux auxquels vous soumettrez ma lettre. Vous me ferez ensuite un rapport sur les observations qui vous auront été suggérées.

Il est un fait bien avéré, c'est que les vaisseaux sont destinés à se battre contre les vaisseaux ennemis et non contre les forteresses. En effet dans une guerre, comme dans un combat il faut se battre à armes égales; il faut que, sauf le courage et l'habileté, les chances soient les mêmes de part et d'autre. C'est ce qui a lieu sur terre.

On évite le combat tant que l'on n'a pas de chance probable de réussir. Ainsi l'on n'irait pas attaquer des fortifications avec de la cavalerie ou bien l'on n'irait pas sans chevaux s'engager dans des pays de plaines.

Dans un combat naval il en est de même. Les chances de gain ou de perte sont semblable des deux côtés. Si je risque ma flotte c'est avec l'espoir de détruire la flotte ennemie: je hasarde un capital immense, accumulé à grands frais, pour anéantir ce qui en a coûté autant à l'ennemi.

Mais dès que la flotte est employée à l'attaque d'une fortification, ces proportions changent complètement; car non seulement un vaisseau se trouvera inférieur à une batterie de terre, parceque ce vaisseau offre un grand but à atteindre tandisque la batterie de terre occupe un petit espace et se trouve protégée par des parapets mais encore l'enjeu est bien différent. J'aventure si c'est un vaisseau comme le Napoléon 5 millions, 1200 hommes et 100 canons contre une fortification en terre ou en pierre qui a coûté peu d'argent et sera garnie tout au plus d'une vingtaine de canons servis par un petit nombre d'hommes, la chance n'est donc pas égale.

Aussi qu'arrive-t-il de cette différence? c'est que les amiraux, comprenant la responsabilité qui pèse sur eux et les dangers qu'ils peuvent courir sans résultat décisif, ont l'air, aux yeux de l'Europe et de l'armée, de jouer un rôle peu en rapport avec leur importance et leur courage. En effet on voit, comme dans la mer noire, 25000 matelots et 3000 canons du plus gros calibre incapables d'ouvrir une brèche ou de faire un mal sérieux aux fortifications des Russes. Il en a été de même dans la Baltique.

De cette fausse position il résulte de graves inconvénients moraux et matériels. Le prestige de la marine en est affaibli. Les amiraux, blessés de leur inaction forcée et sentant, comme des hommes de coeur, le besoin d'agir sans vouloir cependant sacrifier la flotte, espoir de l'armée, puisque c'est elle qui la transporte et la fait vivre, se décident à des attaques sans résultat décisif, comme à Bomarsund, comme à Odessa, comme à Sévastopol; attaques qui entrainent des avaries graves pour nos vaisseaux sans faire un mal sensible à l'ennemi, car il suffit d'avoir la moindre notion d'artillerie pour savoir que des canons, tirant à 2000 mètres contre des fortifications, ne leur font aucun mal. On risque donc beaucoup contre rien.

En effet supposons 10 vaisseaux de 100 canons et 10 frégates à vapeur de 40, tirant sur un fort quelconque. Nous aurons 1400 canons et 16000 engagés avec un capital de 50 millions environ. Maintenant, comme la moitié seulement des canons peut tirer à la fois, nous aurons 700 canons employés, et si chacun lance 100 boulets et obus, on aura tiré en un jour 70,000 coups de canons qui, à 20 francs à coup coûteront à l'État 1,400,000 francs sans compter les avaries. Or, je le demande, cette dépense est-elle en rapport avec le résultat qui, si l'on reste à 1500 ou 2000 mètres sera nul, ou qui, si l'on avance à 400 mètres peut anéantir une partie de la flotte. Ainsi donc, dans l'état actuel des choses, si les vaisseaux lancent leurs projectiles à 2000 mètres, ils consoment leur munitions en pure perte; ils donnent au monde une fausse idée de leurs moyens. Si au contraire, ils s'approchent des fortifications, ils exposent l'État à des sacrifices trop considérables en proportion du but à atteindre. Car la plupart du temps, il serait parfaitement insensé de hasarder la perte d'une flotte pour la destruction de quelques forts.

Qu'y-a-t-il donc à faire ? Le voici.

Créer une flotte de siège capable de produire des effets décisifs et diminuer pour l'État les chances de perte en hommes et en argent.

On a déjà fait faire, d'après mes idées, des batteries flottantes qui, si elles ne sont pas complètement à l'abri des boulets pleins, sont certainement à l'abri des boulets creux, projectile le plus dangereux pour la marine mais cela ne suffit pas. Je voudrais qu'on choisit une dizaine de vieux vaisseaux hors d'état de rendre de bons services à la mer, on y placerait une petite machine à vapeur de la plus faible dimension, on y mettrait une mâture très légère pour pouvoir être démontée le jour de l'action, et les murailles de ce vaisseau seraient recouvertes d'une cuirasse de fer, dans le genre des batteries flottantes.

L'armement de la batterie basse se composerait de 25 canons de 60 [50?], celui de la batterie haute de 25 de 30; 10 canons seraient sur l'autre bord en réserve. Les poids pourraient être équilibrés pendant la marche. Sur le pont il n'y aurait point de canons. Le bastingage renforcé serait percé de meurtrières, derrière lesquelles seraient placés une vingtaine d'hommes armés de carabines à tige.

Examinons maintenant les effets que produirait ce nouveau vaisseau et quels sacrifices sa perte entrainerait. Nous avons dit que les vaisseaux tant qu'ils resteront à 1500 ou 2000 mètres de la place, ne produiront aucun effet, et que s'ils s'en approchent à 400 mètres, les sacrifices sont trop considérables en proportion du but à atteindre. Mon vaisseau au contraire, si on le place à 300 mètres de l'ennemi et s'il tire pendant dix heures à cette distance contre une fortification quelconque, y aura ouvert une large brèche et l'aura détruite de fond en comble. Qu'aurai-je risqué pour obtenir ce grand résultat? un vieux vaisseau qui, au lieu de valoir plusieurs millions, ne vaudra peut-être que 500,000 francs.

S'il est endommagé j'aurai perdu 60 canons au lieu de 100; 600 hommes au lieu de 1200, enfin juste le nombre d'approvisionnements dont il aura eu besoin pendant le combat. Son pont, dégarni de tout mât, de toute vergue, de toute voile et presque désert, offrira beaucoup moins de prise à l'ennemi. On risquera beaucoup moins pour obtenir beaucoup plus.

Je voudrais donc dans chaque escadre destinée à operer contre des fortifications qu'on disposât dès aujourd'hui des vaisseaux de ce genre qui, remorqués sur les lieux par des batteries à vapeur ou bien livrés à eux-mêmes viendraient donner à ces escadres une force irrésistible, permettraient de ménager notre veritable flotte de guerre et donneraient un moyen sûr à la marine de se joindre efficacement à l'armée de terre dans ses attaques contre les places maritimes.

APPENDIX D

DUPUY DE LÔME'S REPORT OF APRIL 16, 1858

In the volume of manuscript reports of the Directeur du Matériel for 1858, A.M., 1 DD¹ 254, this document bears date of April 15. The copy in the *Couronne* dossier preserved in A.C.N. is dated April 16, which is probably the day on which the report was submitted and approved. The report is signed "le Directeur du matériel Dupuy de Lôme," with the marginal note, "Ce rapport une fois approuvé par le ministre sera communiqué au conseil des travaux avec les plans en question." See above, pp. 99–100.

Il est superflu de s'attacher à démontrer aujourd'hui l'opportunité de construire pour prendre rang dans notre flotte de combat un bon nombre de navires à la fois rapides et aussi impénétrables que possible aux coups de l'artillerie la plus puissante. Cette question de principe a été résolue du jour où la possibilité d'allier des qualités nautiques avec impénétrabilité de muraille n'a plus été mise en doute, et les questions à résoudre à l'égard de cette classe de navire ne concerne plus que le choix à faire entre divers plans ainsi qu'entre divers modes de construction à employer tant pour la coque elle même que pour la partie cuirassée de la muraille.

Les expériences faites à Vincennes, quoi que se continuant encore, permettent déjà de fixer l'opinion sur l'efficacité des divers systèmes de cuirasses qui ont été essayés. Quant au mode de construction de la coque il suffit pour apprécier les divers projets présentés à cet égard de se laisser guider d'une part par les données générales en tout genre que fournit à notre époque l'art si avancé des constructions navales, et de l'autre par la considération des moyens que nos arsenaux maritimes possèdent ou qu'on y peut organiser.

Les résultats constatés après quelques années sur ces premiers navires cuirassés construits dans divers systèmes pourront seuls déterminer la choix à faire entre eux, si même alors on ne préfère encore utiliser à la fois nos divers moyens de production.

Pour le moment il me paraît rationnel de ne pas rechercher la préférence à donner à un système exclusif et de n'imposer à priori aux auteurs des projets de navires cuirassés que trois conditions générales: 1° l'impénétrabilité suffisante des murailles; 2° la solidité de l'avant avec une disposition permettant d'aborder un navire ennemi dans l'intention de le couler par le choc; 3° une marche à la vapeur au moins égale à celle de nos vaisseaux de 900 chevaux type Napoléon avec des approvisionnements en vivres et en combustible pour une durée au moins égale.

Tout projet de navire qui satisfera à ces conditions devra être examiné avec soin d'abord [au] point de vue des autres qualités que doit posséder un navire de mer et particulièrement en suite au point de vue de la puissance militaire comparée à son prix de revient et à la facilité d'exécution.

Le ministre désireux de mettre sans retard en chantier un certain nombre de frégates cuirassées m'a chargé de rediger à cet effet un plan que j'ai eu l'honneur de lui transmettre. Ce plan comporte une coque en bois et j'ai proposé à son excellence de ne l'appliquer qu'à une partie des navires cuirassés qui doivent être commencés en 1858, à fin d'exécuter les autres sur des plans différents que je savais à l'étude.

M. l'Ingénieur Audenet vient de terminer un projet de frégate cuirassée avec coque en fer et un système de muraille des hauts conforme à celui qui a déjà été recommandé par le conseil des travaux sur la proposition de ce même ingénieur. Ce mode de construction de muraille a depuis lors été expérimenté avec succès à Vincennes.

Le projet de navire de M. Audenet qui est conçu par ailleurs en vue des qualités nautiques requises me paraît donc être digne d'un examen approfondi. J'ai en conséquence l'honneur de proposer au ministre de le soumettre au conseil des travaux et, s'il était jugé satisfaisant, de le faire servir pour la frégate cuirassée qui doit être exécutée à Lorient.

J'ai l'honneur de proposer également de communiquer à cette occasion aux Conseil des Travaux, à titre de renseignement, 1° le dossier complet sur les expériences de cuirasses faites à Vincennes; 2° les plans et dessins de la frégate cuirassée de 36 canons et 900 chevaux qui sont déjà approuvées et qui s'appliquent aux deux frégates en chantier à Toulon.

APPENDIX E

DUPUY DE LÔME'S REPORT OF SEPTEMBER 22, 1860

The program of August 11, 1855, proposed by the Commission Supérieure Central headed by Admiral Parseval-Deschênes, is summarized above, page 92. This program, revised by a commission of three, Rear Admiral Jurien de la Gravière, the Directeur du Matériel, de Lavrignais, and Dupuy de Lôme, in November and December, 1856, became the report of January, 1857, which Dupuy discusses below. (See above, page 98.) The Conseil d'État, in a report approved by the Emperor November 23, 1857, fixed the sum to be spent for the transformation of the fleet at 234,992,000 francs, to be spread over fourteen years, beginning January 1, 1858. (A.M., 1 DD¹ 241, November 25, 1857; 1 DD¹ 247, note pour la Direction de la Comptabilité Générale, November 26, 1857.) Dupuy de Lôme's report of September 22, 1860, is in A.M., 1 DD¹ 275. See above, pp. 111-112.

Proposition de mettre en chantier 10 frégates cuirassées, 11 batteries flottantes et 6 frégates, corvettes et transports.

Frégates cuirassées. — Dans le rapport sur la transformation de la flotte, présenté à l'Empereur en Janvier 1857, et qui a reçu l'approbation de S.M., le nombre de nos vaisseaux à vapeur rapides est établi au chiffre de 40.

Ce chiffre est loin d'avoir été atteint, puisque la flotte actuelle ne comporte que 14 bâtiments de cette espèce, dont 12 à flot et 2 en chantier.

Il resterait donc, si l'on voulait réaliser le programme de 1857 à entreprendre la construction de 26 vaisseaux rapides.

A l'époque où ce programme a été conçu, le vaisseau à vapeur était considéré, par tous les marins, comme devant former le principal élément de la composition des armées navales.

Depuis lors, à la suite des progrès simultanés de l'architecture navale et de l'artillerie, les idées ont subi sur ce point une profonde modification. Conformément aux ordres du Ministre, 6 frégates à vapeur cuirassées de différents types ont été mises en chantier dans nos ports.

En attendant leur essai, les moyens de production disponibles dans les arsenaux ont été employés, soit à l'amélioration du matériel existant, soit à l'achèvement des navires ordinaires en construction et en transformation. Aucun nouveau vaisseau de ligne n'a été mis en chantier depuis 1855.

Aujourd'hui, les ports ont fait, en quelque sorte table rase des anciennes constructions qu'ils avaient à terminer, et, conformément aux ordres de S.E., je viens lui adresser des propositions sur les nouveaux bâtiments à construire.

Les expériences de l'une des frégates cuirassées, la *Gloire*, viennent d'avoir lieu à Toulon et leur bons résultats ont confirmé toutes les espérances. Il est, aujourd'hui, établi aux yeux de tous, que l'on peut réunir sur un même navire, aux qualités nautiques et à la vitesse de nos meilleurs bâtiments une résistance de muraille tellement supérieure à celle des coques ordinaires qu'on peut regarder comme certain, qu'avec une artillerie moindre, une frégate cuirassée l'emporterait facilement sur un vaisseau de ligne à muraille non protégée.

On doit donc se féliciter aujourd'hui de n'avoir pas poursuivi la construction des 26 vaisseaux à vapeur qu'il resterait à produire pour satisfaire au programme de 1857. Leur remplacement par un nombre égal de frégates cuirassées peut être hardiment entrepris. Cette convenance admise, et en tenant compte des 6 bâtiments de cette espèce déjà en chantier ou à flot, il resterait à construire 20 frégates cuirassées.

En réalité, ce chiffre doit être porté à 30, puisque dans son rapport, en date du 24 Mai 1860, la commission de défense des côtes a déclaré qu'en outre de la flotte active, il était nécessaire de posséder au moins 10 frégates cuirassées de réserve, spécialement destinées à la défense des cinq ports militaires.

En prenant pour base les ressources du budget normal voté pour 1861, et le personnel que comportent ces ressources et qui est déjà réuni dans les ports, il ne serait pas possible d'entreprendre d'un seul coup la construction de ces trente grands navires sans s'exposer à de grands retards dans leur achèvement. Je propose au Ministre de se borner pour le moment, à en commencer 10, savoir: 9 en bois et 1 en fer.

Je me suis assuré que dans les conditions précitées, l'exécution de ces 10 frégates peut être achevée dans 18 mois environ, en faisant en outre, la part des autres constructions de batteries flottantes et bâtiments inférieurs dont il sera question plus loin.

Conformément a l'intention exprimée par le Ministre, les frégates cuirassées en bois seraient exécutées sur les plans de la *Gloire*, sauf quelques améliorations dont ce type paraît encore susceptible. Ces améliorations consisteraient à porter la hauteur de batterie de 1m.88 à 2 m. et l'armement des gaillards de 2 à 4 canons rayés de 30, à réduire l'ouverture des sabords aux chiffres adoptés pour le *Magenta*, et le *Solférino*, à augmenter un peu l'immersion de la cuirasse a l'avant, enfin, à accroître le volume de carène de la quantité nécessaire, non seulement pour satisfaire aux modifications précitées, mais encore pour se reserver la faculté d'augmenter au besoin d'un centimètre l'épaisseur des plaques.

La frégate cuirassée construite en fer, serait exécutée sur un plan qu'il resterait à demander aux ports d'après un programme soumis au Conseil des Travaux en indiquant comme but à atteindre les résultats déjà constatés sur la *Gloire*.

Batteries flottantes. — Indépendamment des 10 frégates cuirassées spécialement destinées à rester dans les ports militaires, en cas de sortie de la flotte active, la commission de défense des côtes a demandé 20 batteries flottantes pour la défense de ces mêmes ports et de ceux du commerce.

Cinq de ces batteries ont été construites à l'époque de la guerre d'Orient,

4 sont en construction sur les chantiers de Bordeaux, 11 resteraient donc à exécuter. Je propose à Son Excellence, de décider que 6 d'entre'elles seraient construites en bois et 5 en fer, afin de profiter des ressources de l'industrie privée ainsi que de celles restant disponibles dans nos arsenaux.

Les batteries flottantes en construction à Bordeaux n'ayant point encore fait leurs essais, je proposerais au Ministre de mettre au concours dans les ports, d'après un programme rédigé par le Conseil des Travaux, les plans des deux types à créer.

Frégates, corvettes et Transports. — En dehors des bâtiments qui viennent d'être énumérés, Son Excellence a chargé de Conseil précité d'examiner les programmes de trois nouveaux types de navires qu'il paraît utile d'introduire dans la flotte et qui sont destinés au service des stations lointaines, ce sont:

1° — de petites frégates portant 22 canons de 30 rayés.
2° — des corvettes à barbette portant 16 canons de 18 rayés.
3° — des transports mixtes de 400 Tx.

Il conviendrait de mettre en chantier deux bâtiments de chacun de ces types, aussitôt après que leurs plans auront été tracés et approuvés. . . .

There follows a recapitulation of the 27 vessels to be laid down, and a table showing at which ports they were to be built.

APPENDIX F

THE NAVY DEPARTMENT PLAN OF 1861

The seven-page "Building Instructions for Iron-Clad Steam Battery," minuted in pencil "R. Powell, Dec., 1861" in B.C.R., 142–10–14, contain numerous references to the two "'Cole' towers" with which the vessel was to be equipped. The dimensions herein given are "length on deck, 216 ft. 2 in.; extreme breadth, 48 ft.; depth of hold amidships, 13 ft. 11 in."

With this is a paper headed "Dimensions to the outside of the Plank, that is to the inside of the iron plating. Iron Clad Steamer — January 7th, 1862. Dimensions for laying down the shape of the outside of the plank of the Hull, to which Iron Plates are to be prepared, fitted, etc., for the government of the United States of America — Length between perpendiculars 217 feet 9 inches, Beam 48 feet — Copy as sent to Mr. Martin at London, England."

In the same bundle are the following 4-page printed "Specifications of the Iron Armature and other Exterior Iron Work of a Steam Battery to be constructed for the United States." Another printed copy of this is in N.D., *Miscellaneous Letters*, December, 1861, i. See above, pp. 275–282.

Specifications of the Iron Armature and other Exterior Iron Work of a Steam Battery, to be Constructed for the United States

Side plating on the vessel. —

The length of curvature around the outside of the vessel (including both sides from stem to stern) is about 465 feet, the plating for which is to be in two widths, with proper shift for butts; each width to be 34 inches, and to have parallel sides. The thickness of the plates for 15 feet on each side of the vessel from each end is to be 3¼ inches; for the next 15 feet 3¾ inches, and for the remaining 172½ feet, 4¼ inches. The plating of 4¼ inches thickness must be in lengths of 15 feet 2 inches, except one piece of 7 or 8 feet. The length of 30 feet at each end (on both sides of the vessel) may be covered with four plates. All the plates to be made of first quality wrought iron scrap, and capable of sustaining a tensile strain of 55,000 pounds per square inch. The top edge of the upper width and the bottom edge of the lower width of plates to be smooth-finished to a fair uniform surface by the hammer or rolls; the other edges to be planed, but not tongued and grooved. All the plates are to be bent accurately to the form of the vessel, and to have close joints. The plates for being secured to the wooden hull are to be drilled along their top and bottom edges with holes of 1⅞ inch diameter. Distance from edge of plate to centre of holes 6½ inches. Distance from centre to centre of holes about 18 inches. Each hole is to be countersunk to a depth of 1¾ inch. Diameter of countersink on outside of plate 2¾ inches.

Bolts for side plating. —

For securing the side plating to the vessel there will be about thirteen hundred and sixty-six bolts of the first quality wrought iron, to be about 28 inches in length over all, and to be 1¾ inch diameter for the 4¼ inches thick plate, and 1½ inch diameter for the remaining plates; the heads are to be accurately turned to fit the countersink in plates, and the bodies are to be true to form. Each bolt, according to diameter, will have a *nut* 3½ or 3 inches square and 2¼ or 2 inches thick, screwed up against a wrought iron *washer* 5½ or 5 inches square and ¾ or ⅝ inch thick.

Deck plating. —

The deck of the vessel, with the exception of the spaces occupied by the towers and hatches, is to be covered with two thicknesses of rolled iron plates, each thickness to be ¾ inch. One thickness to be laid with the length of the plates fore and aft, the other thickness to have the length athwartship. All the plates to have a length of not less than 15 feet and a width of 3 feet, except at the endings and where the openings in the deck will not permit of such dimensions. A flange of 8 inches is to be turned down on the lower thickness all around the gunwale.

The deck plates are to be of the same quality of iron and of the same tensile strength per square inch as the side plates. Their edges are not required to be planed, but to be smooth, finished, fair and true from the rolls. Where they abut against hatch coamings or gunwale, they are to be planed. The plates are to be drilled with countersunk holes every 18 inches, the countersink to extend entirely through the upper plate. Diameter of holes, ¾ inch at bottom and 1½ inch at top. A row of bolts to be put 18 inches apart along the endings of the plates at the hatch coamings and at the gunwale.

There will be required a proper number of holes to be cut in the side and deck plates for bilge-pump discharges, ventilators, hawse holes, coal deckplates, deck lights, water closets, bolts for securing the anchors, boat davits, ring bolts, etc.

Bolts for the deck plates. —

To be ⅝ inch in diameter and 9 inches in length; to have a *nut* 1¼ inch square and ¾ inch thick, screwed up against a round wrought iron washer of 2¼ inches diameter, and ¼ inch thickness. Head of bolt to be turned to accurately fit the countersink in deck plates; body of bolt to be true to form.

Coamings for hatches. —

The hatches to be surrounded with wrought iron coamings, the lower part of which will consist of 4½ by 6 inches angle iron; the widest flange to be securely bolted to the deck. To the vertical flange will be rivetted a plate iron bulwark ¼ inch thick and 2½ feet high; the joints to be butted and strapped on the inside. All the rivetting to be countersunk flush. On the outer side of the upper edge of the bulwark there will be rivetted flush a band of bead iron 2 inches by 1 inch in section. A small piece of angle iron to be fitted inside the bulwark of the hatches at the top for sustaining the frame of the glazed covering.

Grating for hatches. —

A grating will be fitted over each hatch; it will be composed of wrought iron bars 6 inches by 1 inch in section, 4 inches from centre to centre, well tied together, and hinged to lift in halves when necessary. Between the bars there are to be cast iron *sockets*; web of socket, 6 inches by ½ inch in section; outside diameter of socket, 2¼ inches; diameter of hole in socket for bolt, 1⅛ inch. The socket bolts to be of wrought iron, 1 inch in diameter, and from 10 to 12 inches between centres. The smoke pipe grating is to be circular.

Deck stanchions. —

Around the gunwale of the vessel there is to be erected a row of wrought iron stanchions. They will be about 5 feet apart, and step in and pin to brass sockets. The *sockets* to be well secured to deck with four ⅝-inch diameter tap bolts of wrought iron. The stanchions are to be about 3 feet high and 1¼-inch in diameter at bottom, and will have three eyes each; the upper eye to receive a wrought iron railing rod of 1 inch diameter, which is to pass through and to be pinned to stanchion. The lower eyes to be fitted for a rope of ⅞-inch diameter, run through them and secured in a proper manner.

Towers. —

On the deck there are to be two cylindrical towers, composed of two thicknesses of wrought iron plates, securely bolted to a *backing* of oak 10 inches thick, the timbers of which are to be 6 feet 11 inches long, and arranged vertically, with tight joints in the direction of radii of the circle. Outside diameter of the towers 21½ feet. The *outside plates* to be 3 inches in thickness, and the *inside plates* to be 2 inches in thickness; all plates and appendages to be of first quality wrought iron scrap, capable of sustaining a tensile strain of 55,000 pounds per square inch. The outside of the tower to be four plates in height, each plate to be 26 inches wide and 16 feet 10½ inches long, making sixteen plates for each tower, of 3 inches thickness. Next to these plates, and breaking joints with them both vertically and horizontally, are the 2 inches thick plates, which, for each tower, consist in height of three rows 26 inches wide, one row 22 inches wide, and one row 13 inches wide, each row to be composed of four plates 16 feet 5 inches long.

APPENDICES 353

All the above plates to be accurately bent to the cylindrical form and planed on the four edges. The surfaces of the outer and inner plates to fit closely together. The inner plates are to be secured to the oak backing by *bolts* of 1 inch diameter with countersunk heads, square nuts, and washers. Each plate of the bottom row will have four 1 inch diameter bolts going through the backing, and eleven bolts of 1½ inch diameter passing through it from the outer plates. Each plate of the top row will have eleven bolts passing through it from the outer plates. The remaining inner plates will be secured to the oak backing by eight 1 inch diameter bolts each. Each plate of the two centre courses of outside plates are [*sic*.] to be secured to the inner plates and to the backing by twenty-two through *bolts* of 1½ inch diameter with countersunk heads, and square nuts on the inside of the backing. These nuts are to be screwed up against wrought-iron *bands*, which are to be three in number for each tower, and to extend entirely around it on the inside of the backing. The bands to be of plate iron 15 inches wide and ½ inch thick, in two pieces. Each plate of the top and bottom courses of the outside plates to be secured to the inner plates by eleven bolts of 1 inch diameter, and to the inner plates and backing by eleven bolts of 1½ inch diameter. Heads, nuts, etc., to be as described for the bolts of the centre courses.

At one place in the periphery of the tower there is to be cut for a gun a *port-hole* 24 inches wide and 41 inches extreme height, the top and bottom to be semi-circular. Around this hole, and on the inside of the inner plating, there is to be well secured a *washer* or frame, forged in one piece; section of iron of washer 15 inches wide and 3 inches thick.

On the top of the oak backing of each tower there is to be placed a plate of wrought iron to receive the feet of the rafters and purlins of the roof of the tower. This *plate* consists of two rings of 3 inches angle iron, one ring of flat iron 8 inches by ½ inch, and one band of flat iron 6 inches by ½ inch; all to be rivetted together and secured to the iron plating of the tower by the upper row of bolts.

The *roof* of each tower to be composed of two main *rafters* of wrought iron, 18 inches deep at the centre, 6 inches deep at the ends, 20 feet 6 inches long, and of the uniform thickness of 2 inches. These rafters to be separated by a space 38 inches wide. Extending from them to the sides of the tower will be one hundred and eighteen *purlins* of wrought iron, placed 4 inches between centres; purlins to have a section of 6 inches deep by 1 inch wide, and to be in lengths varying from 22 inches to 8½ feet. They will be placed at right angles to the main rafters, and will have one end turned down for bolting to them. Between the main rafters there are to be forty *pieces* of wrought iron 6 inches deep by 1 inch thick, having both ends turned down, so that the bolt which secures the purlin secures also the intervening piece between the rafters. Rafters to be secured to each other laterally by cast-iron sockets and wrought-iron bolts, as described for the gratings of the hatch.

Between and at the centre of the rafters for a length of 6¾ feet, there is to be left an *opening* for replacing the gun. This opening is to be covered with a *grating*, made in one piece, so as to be easily removable. The iron of the grating to be wrought slabs, 6 inches deep, 1 inch wide, and 4 inches from centre to centre.

The *deck* of *each tower* will consist of two wrought-iron girders, each 20 feet 6 inches long, and of a parallel depth of 12 inches. The thickness for a length of 5 feet at the centre, will be 3½ inches; thence it will taper to the ends to a thickness of 2 inches. Between these girders there are to be two wrought-iron *ties* of channel-plate form. Each tie to be of wrought iron, 3½ by 12 inches, and rivetted to the girders by ten rivets of 2 inches diameter, thus forming with the girders a rectangular eye or centre, 15 by 19 inches in the clear, for the upper end of the tower spindle. The ends of the girders are to be secured to the inside of the tower plating by *angle pieces* 18 inches each way, and 12 inches deep, each angle of each piece to have five *bolts* of 1½ inch diameter. The bolts which secure the angle pieces to the tower to have countersunk heads and square nuts; those which secure them to the girders to have square heads and nuts. From the sides of the girders, and at right angles to them, there will extend to the tower twelve wrought-iron *beams*, six to each girder, with their ends turned down to bolt to girder and tower with two bolts at each end of ⅞-inch diameter. On the top edge of the beams there will be secured by ⅝-inch diameter rivets, placed 9 inches between centres, a strip of 3 inches by 3 inches angle iron. Between the beams and on each side of the girders, there will be formed five *scuttles* by rivetting 3 inches by 3 inches angle iron, and flat iron 4 inches by ½ inch. The top flange of the angle iron is to have a ⅞-inch diameter hole drilled every 6 inches, to allow the bolts for holding deck plank of 4 inches thickness to pass through and be screwed up from beneath. The bolts for the deck plank to be ¾-inch in diameter, and 6 inches long, to have round heads, flush with plank, and square nuts.

Across the short beams there will be for each tower four *bars* of angle iron, 4 inches by 4 inches, and 20 feet 6 inches long, strongly secured to the angle iron on the beams; at the ends they will be bolted to the inside plates of the tower by angle pieces 12 inches by 12 inches, having four bolts of ⅞-inch diameter in each angle, to hold the gun-slides. At each end of the gun-slides there will be an iron strap 10 inches by ¾ inch, secured to the tower plating and to the slides by 1-inch diameter bolts.

Each tower rests on twelve wrought-iron *conical rollers*, 18 inches in diameter and 7 inches in width of face—face to be turned and polished. Each roller to have a steel *axle* 4 inches in diameter and 16 inches in length, supported in wrought-iron *brackets*, each secured to lower edge of inside tower plates by eight wrought-iron bolts and nuts 1¼ inch in diameter. The axles to be provided with hard gun-metal composition *boxes* properly secured between collars and furnished with a finished brass *oil-cup* each. *Journals of axles* to be polished and rolled. Brackets to be forged solid and have jaws slotted out. The rollers traverse on a finished wrought-iron *ring* made in two pieces, and secured to the deck every 18 inches by a wrought-iron bolt of 1¼ inch diameter, with a countersunk head and square nut beneath. The ring will have an outer diameter of 20 feet 9 inches, the width will be 12 inches, and the greatest thickness 4 inches; its top will conform to the face of the rollers.

There is to be one wrought-iron *spindle* to guide the tower; the upper end to be planed rectangular, 15 by 19 inches, and securely keyed in the eye formed by the girders and their cross-ties. The remaining length to be circular; diameter at top 12 inches; diameter at bottom 9 inches; length about 10 feet 3 inches. To have a hole of 3 inches diameter bored through its axis. To have a guide-block at top and bottom, bushed with hard gun-metal composition, finished. Journals in bushes to be polished.

Under the head of the spindle is a wrought-iron *plate* 3 inches thick and 28 inches diameter, with a groove turned in its lower side to rest on hard gun-metal composition balls.

The *main guide-block* of the spindle is of cast iron, bored and bushed with hard gun-metal composition ½ inch thick, and smoothly bored. Depth of block 18 inches; inner diameter of *bush* 12 inches; to be made with a *flange* 42 inches square to rest on the deck timbers of the vessel. Top of flange to be grooved to receive fifteen steel balls of 3 inches diameter. Between this flange and the wrought-iron plate there is to be a composition *ring* ¾ inch thick, having perforations to receive the balls and prevent them from touching.

The *lower guide-block* is to be of cast iron, turned and bushed with hard gun-metal composition ½ inch thick. Bush to be smoothly bored to a diameter of 9 inches, and a depth of 15 inches through the eye. Guide-block to have a flange at top 24 inches square by 2½ inches thick.

The flanges of both guide-blocks to be properly secured to their wood supports by wrought-iron *bolts* and nuts of 1¼ and 1½ inch diameter, and 16 and 18 inches in length.

Rack and pinions. —

On the outside of the two inches thick plating of the tower there is to be a cast-iron rack in twelve segments; each segment to be secured by eight wrought-iron bolts and nuts of 1¼ inch diameter; the metal to be stirling iron. The pitch line of the teeth in the rack will be about 21 feet 6 inches diameter, and the pitch of the teeth about 4 inches. Breadth of the teeth 9 inches; length of the teeth 2½ inches. The thickness of the body to be 1¾ inch; its breadth to be the same as that of the teeth — 9 inches.

There are to be two cast iron *pinions* of 26 inches diameter to pitch line; teeth to be of same pitch and breadth as those of the rack; hub to be bored 5 inches diameter. Pinions to be placed on opposite sides of tower on vertical shafts, one to be worked by a pair of steam engines, the other to be worked by means of a capstan.

Glacis. —

The base of each tower is to be surrounded with a glacis of iron plates bolted to timbers by blunt bolts. The *plates* are to be in two thicknesses of 1¼ inch each. The top plates to be in two courses of six each. The under plates to be in three courses of six each. The blunt *bolts* for fastening these plates to the timbers will be placed 18 inches between centres, and will be of wrought iron 1 inch in diameter with countersunk heads. The holes in the plates will be countersunk to receive the heads of the bolts. The interior diameter of the glacis will be 21 feet 8 inches; the exterior diameter will be 31 feet 6 inches. Height of glacis 26 inches above top of iron deck plating in the fore-and-aft direction.

Friction side-rollers. —

On the outside of the towers and beneath the inner edge of the glacis, there will be side-rollers of hard gun-metal composition, placed vertically to prevent lateral movement of tower. The rollers will be cylinders of 6 inches diameter and 9 inches length, held in suitable bearings and placed every 3 feet.

Water Closet. —

On each quarter of the vessel, at the height of the deck, there must be on each side a bar of wrought iron 4½ inches by 3 inches, so bent as to project one foot beyond the screw-propeller that it may be protected. Over this is to be built, on each side, a water closet of ¼ inch thick plate iron.

Conning or pilot-houses. —

At each end of the vessel, and upon its deck, there will be a *conning* or *pilot-house* of wrought-iron plates. It will be cylindrical in form, with a flat top. Interior diameter 24 inches; extreme height 46 inches; height above deck 28 inches. The sides to be constructed of one thickness of 4 inch plate, and one thickness of 2 inch plate, with smoothly fitting surfaces rivetted strongly together with 1½ inch diameter rivets. Each thickness to be in halves, and the joints at right angles to each other. The house to be thoroughly secured to the deck by an angle iron ring on the outside; angle iron to be 6 inches high by 8 inches on the deck, and secured by 1½-inch diameter bolts with countersunk heads; bolts to be 12 inches between centres. The cylindrical part will be let down through the deck, flush with the lower side of the deck beams, and will be bolted to these beams and to partners with eight 1¼ inch diameter bolts with countersunk heads and nuts.

On the inside of the cylinder, and within 3 inches of its top, will be rivetted an angle iron ring 6 by 6 inches, to which will be securely bolted a flat wrought-iron cover of 4 inches thickness, top of cover flush with top of sides of cylinder. Bolts for cover to be six in number, and 1 inch in diameter, with countersunk heads and nuts.

At 10 inches below the bottom of the cover the sides will be pierced with four tapering *peep-holes* of 2 inches diameter on outside of house, and 6 inches diameter on the inside; and 3 inches lower there will be four other peep-holes of the same sizes, put in at intermediate spaces between the upper ones. Holes to be made at the joints of the plates.

APPENDICES

Estimate of Weights for the Vessel

	Tons
Plating on sides	221.0
Plating on deck	248.2
Plating for glacis of two towers	40.6
Plating for two towers	116.3
Roofs for two towers	17.3
Decks for two towers and miscellaneous	48.2
Total	691.6

APPENDIX G

ERICSSON'S PROPOSAL OF DECEMBER 23, 1861

THE following is from an unsigned copy of Ericsson's letter of December 23, 1861, to Welles in N.D., Area 11, Folder 1860–62. See above, p. 278.

In conjunction with several patriotic citizens I respectfully propose to build for your Department six or more Impregnable gun boats or floating batteries of iron, similar in principle to the one which I am now constructing under your orders and contract dated 4th October 1861.

In tendering this offer I feel called upon to state my reasons for adhering to the precise form of the battery now nearly completed — a form which is the result of more than twenty years careful study. The subject naturally divides itself under three heads, viz.: The Impregnable Fort containing the armament, the vessel which supports the fort and lastly the means for propelling and directing the vessel. With your permission I will consider each in the order thus enumerated.

The Fort (Turret). I have adopted the plain cylindrical form in order that attack from all quarters of the compass may be resisted with equal certainty and in order that the building of the turret may not call for intricate workmanship. I have devised the flat roof placed somewhat below the top of the turret to insure perfect protection against the destructive effect of horizontal fire, the roof being perforated with a series of small holes to obviate any dangerous pressure and vibration of the atmosphere within the turret. The adoption of plate iron alone in the place of a combination of wood and iron was the result of the most thorough consideration of the subject. A wooden turret cased with two thicknesses of plate iron together 5 inches thick, as now advocated by some engineers will prove utterly inadequate to resist heavy ordnance at short ranges. The wooden lining under a vessel's side armor suffers the serious compression by the impact of heavy shot without detriment to the rest, not so in the wooden turret, there the impact of the shot not only depresses the wood in a radial direction but causes an enormous tangential strain on the wooden block nearly in the ratio of the chord to the versed sine — derangement and destruction to the wood work becomes the more certain since the sharp curvature permits only short pieces to be employed in the structure. The effect of a few broadsides of 11 or 12 inch solid shot on the proposed combined structure is not a matter of conjecture.

A structure composed entirely of plate iron will alone stand the test. With a turret composed of seven thicknesses of one inch plates properly overlapping each other firmly riveted together and protected by a single outer plating of 4 inch thickness, any of the iron clad European war vessels may be approached with perfect safety and if 12 or 15 inch solid shot be employed at short range those formidable vessels will prove unequal to the contest and inevitably be sunk. The application of the mechanism for turning the turret at the centre and not at the circumference is absolutely necessary. The vibration produced by the impact of heavy shot will derange any mechanism applied to the circumference. The expedient of employing cogs or rack work of case iron at that exposed point cannot be too severely condemned. It is well to bear in mind that while the destruction of a ships bulwark does not prevent the guns from being pointed at the enemy, here the destruction of the means of turning the turret brings instant defeat. The propriety of employing one turret containing two guns in preference to two turrets with one gun in each is quite evident since the former plan admits of fore and aft firing with *two* guns at all times so important during maneuvre while with two turrets only one gun can be employed during perhaps the most critical periods of the contest.

The Vessel. It is well known that the armor cannot be carried far down the sides without overloading, accordingly no adequate protection against plunging shot has hitherto been effected in armor clad vessels. The form of my battery, however, renders the hull impregnable against plunging shot as the lower body is brought so far under the armor clad part that shot before touching the sides must pass through more than twenty feet of water and then with spent force strike at an acute angle of 10 degrees. The armor of the vessel above water line is sustained by the whole of the massive deck presenting a solid backing behind the armor of forty feet thickness. The great extension of the upper impregnable vessel fore and aft entirely obviates the dangerous exposure during pitching to which other iron clad vessels are subject as shot will in such case pass entirely under the battery. The protection of the anchor, suspended as it is, in a well within the forward part of the impregnable upper vessel is another advantage secured by the form adopted.

Propeller and Rudder. Perhaps the most important feature of the battery is the absolute protection to the propeller and rudder, neither of which can by any possibility be struck by shot as they are placed entirely under the extending bottom of the upper impregnable vessel. The great imperfection of war vessels as hitherto constructed will not be revealed until actual naval combat, ship to ship, it will then be found that the first broadside delivered under the stern of a screw vessel, will utterly destroy the instrument of propulsion. A spent ball will in most cases suffice to cause sufficient derangement to check locomotion. Up to the present time we have been content to put the propeller out of sight merely. Actual warfare will soon prove that more is needed. Our gun boats or floating batteries, since they lack speed, size and many other potent elements of the large European iron clad war ships will be worthless unless absolutely impregnable and capable of carrying the heaviest ordnance. The battery under consideration I respectfully submit possesses the properties called for, requiring only increased substance of turret plate and to be armed with 15 inch guns to enable us to bid defiance to any war ship afloat. Having thus briefly stated my reasons for adhering to the peculiar form of battery now in course of completion under your orders, I most respectfully tender my offer to construct six or more of such batteries to be composed of iron and in all respects as regards form to be similar to the present battery. To be not less than 180 feet long, 41½ feet beam, 11½ feet depth of hold, to draw ten feet of water and to be capable of going at the rate of eight sea miles an hour. To be provided with a Turret made of plate iron eleven inches thick provided with gun slides and wrought iron carriages for fifteen inch guns. The vessel to afford requisite accommodation for crew and officers, ammunition stores coals and water. Each vessel to be delivered complete ready for active service in all respects excepting guns ammunition and stores, for three hundred and twenty-five thousand dollars. Two of the vessels to be delivered on the 30th of April and the remainder on the 30th of May 1862.

BIBLIOGRAPHY

BIBLIOGRAPHY

I. MANUSCRIPTS

France

The 284 volumes and cartons of French manuscripts consulted in the preparation of this work are preserved at Paris in the Archives de la Marine, 3, Avenue Octave-Gréard; in the Archives Nationales; and in the Archives du Bureau des Constructions Navales in the Ministry of Marine, Rue Royale. The investigator should consult the brief article, "L'état présent des archives et bibliothèques de la marine," which M. Charles Braibant, Chef du Service des Archives et Bibliothèques de la Marine, contributed to *Le bibliographe moderne*, xx, pp. 113-137 (July-December, 1920-1921).

Archives de la Marine

BB[8] 749, 750. *Direction du Cabinet*. Two cartons of in- and out-letters of the first bureau, 1854-1881, containing little on naval construction.

BB[8] 1106, 1107. Reports of the *Commission Consultative des Travaux de la Marine*, 1824-1831. Two volumes containing some material on the introduction of shell guns.

BB[8] 1108-1157. Reports and minutes of the *Conseil des Travaux*, the principal advisory body in matters of naval construction, for the years 1831 to 1865. Use of these fifty volumes of capital importance is facilitated by eight index volumes: BB[8] 1235-1238, 1245, 1246, 1248 bis, 1248 ter.

0 DD[1] 10-12. Three registers of vessels afloat or under construction, 1829-1857.

0 DD[1] 40. "Documents généraux relatifs aux divers types de bâtiments de la flotte française." A volume of statistical tables, the introduction to which, signed "Albaret, Ingénieur de la marine, 1er aout 1881," states that the figures are derived from the plans of the ships and from their *devis d'armement*.

1 DD[1] 127-333. Out-letters and reports of the *Direction du Matériel*, 1847-1864. Of this long series, which lacks any sort of index, 97 volumes have been examined for this study. Those containing reports to the minister of marine and circulars or other despatches to the great ports in which ironclads were under construction are of special importance. Many of the replies to these despatches may be found in the series 7 DD[1].

4 DD[1] 6. Contracts. Those with Petin, Gaudet and Co. and Schneider and Co. are important for the history of armor plate and marine engines.

6 DD[1]. Projects and reports. Cartons 2, 6, 22, 23, 27, 33, 38, 88 and 89 of this long series contain a large number of French projects for armored vessels, rams, and armor, together with valuable reports on foreign vessels.

A card catalogue of the series is preserved in the Archives du Bureau des Constructions Navales.

7 DD¹. Condemned vessels. This series, of capital importance, contains correspondence relating to each French ironclad, with her *devis d'armement*. The *Congrève* carton contains copies of the correspondence with the British government concerning the armored floating batteries built during the Crimean War. The cartons used for this study were: 7 DD¹ 65, *Congrève*; 96, *Lave*; 98, *Normandie*; 99, *Dévastation*; 101, *Tonnante*; 107, *Foudroyante*; 113, *Invincible*; 138, 139, *Magenta*; 170, 170 bis, *Gloire*; 196, 197, *Solférino*; 233–234, *Embuscade*; 245, armored batteries nos. 1–5. The *Couronne* cartons are still in the Archives du Bureau des Constructions Navales.

DD⁴ 1109–1111. *Direction du Matériel. Bureau de l'Artillerie.* 3 cartons, of which the first contains a few reports of the Vincennes Commission.

Archives du Bureau des Constructions Navales

The only documents concerning ironclads of the period treated in this work which remain in the Archives du Bureau des Constructions Navales are the cartons concerning the *Couronne*, and the card catalogue of the series 6 DD¹.

Archives Nationales

The manuscript inventory of the series Marine, BB⁴, BB⁵ and BB⁸, drawn up by M. Georges Bourgin, is an indispensable guide to these documents, of which the following proved most useful for this study.

BB⁴ 690–692, 694–695, 697–699, 1038. *Cabinet du Ministre. Bureau des Mouvements*, 1853–1856. Eight volumes and one carton, containing important information concerning the battle of Sinope, the Kinburn campaign, and the French armored floating batteries.

BB⁴ 1784–1792. Order books of Vice Admiral Bruat, containing additional information on the same subjects.

BB⁵ 48–56. Nine registers of movements of vessels, 1854–1862, containing brief extracts of orders and reports, as well as notes of movements.

BB⁸ 81–83, 85, 86, 89, 92–96, 98–99, 101, 108. *Cabinet du Ministre.* Correspondence, 1853–1856. These fifteen volumes contain very little concerning ironclads.

BB⁸ 853–900. *Conseil d'Amirauté.* Registre des délibérations, 1824–1869. Forty-eight volumes separately indexed, with a general index by subjects: BB⁸ 891 bis. The *procès-verbaux* on which these registers are based, are preserved in cartons BB⁸ 824–852. Although the *Conseil d'Amirauté* was the highest advisory body in the French Navy, it concerned itself rarely with problems of naval construction. Its minutes, however, contain some important discussion of Paixhans guns, Labrousse's ram projects, the introduction of rifled ordnance, and the best height of battery for armored frigates.

GG¹ 14–16, 19, 73–76, 99. Projects of inventors. These nine cartons contain nothing concerning ironclads, except some material on Aubert.

Great Britain

Although the Admiralty papers preserved in the Public Record Office have been heavily weeded, the entries in the Digests help to fill in the gaps. These remarkable manuscript digests, of which several large folio volumes exist for each year, contain abstracts of the in-letters of the Secretary of the Admiralty, and the directions of the Board concerning them. The topical headings under which all these are arranged are listed in the *Tables of Heads and Sections under which the Correspondence of the Admiralty Board is Digested* (London, 1870). The pertinent sections of 53 volumes of the Digest, covering the years 1839 to 1864, have been examined for this study, as well as the entries concerning shells in the volumes covering the years 1809 to 1838.

The copy of the *List of Admiralty Records preserved in the Public Record Office*, vol. i (London, 1904), in the Government Search Room of the Public Record Office at London, contains extensive ms. additions to the printed list. Of capital importance are the Submission Letter Books of the Controller of the Navy, who was styled the Surveyor until 1860. Volumes 10 to 15 and 17 to 21 of this series, covering the period from March, 1841, to June 30, 1853, and from June, 1854, to December, 1860, have been examined; but volume 16, embracing the submissions from July, 1853, to June, 1854, is missing. For the years 1861, 1862 and 1863, the reports of the Controller are preserved in Adm. 1/5774, 5802, 5804, 5841, 5842. This series contains the official proposals for ironclad vessels, together with reports on inventions submitted, and numerous other matters.

Of the other in-letters of the Secretary of the Admiralty, the reports of Captain R. S. Hewlett of the gunnery ship *Excellent*, contained in Adm. 1/5691, 5708, 5732 and 5756, threw fresh light on the experiments with ordnance and armor. Additional material of value was found in Adm. 3/265–272, special minutes, 1841–1867; Adm. 12/4798, 4799, indexes to out-letters of the Secretary, 1854–1856; and Adm. 13/7, secret orders and letters, 1855–1867.

The correspondence relating to foreign navies exchanged between the Admiralty and the Foreign Office is noted in the Digest volumes under the headings 52-5 (France), 52-9 (Italy), 52-14 (Russia), 52-21 (Spain), 52-23 (Austria and Germany), 52-25 (America), etc. The bundles of letters from the Foreign Office which proved specially important for this study were Adm. 1/5767, 5768, 5798, 5799, 5850, 5852, 5901–5903, 5952–5954. Despatches from the British commander-in-chief in American waters concerning the Union and Confederate Navies during the Civil War are preserved in Adm. 1/5759, 5787, 5788, 5819–5821, 5871–5873, 5922. An important confidential report on the United States Navy in April, 1864, which was printed for the use of the British cabinet, is in the Foreign Office papers at the Public Record Office, F.O.5, vol. 948.

Professor Herbert C. Bell most generously communicated to the writer some of his transcripts of the Russell and Granville papers preserved at the Public Record Office, and kindly permitted him to quote some of them that throw fresh light on British naval policy.

At the Admiralty Library, Whitehall, the ships' books of the armored floating batteries built during the Crimean War were consulted, and those of the *Achilles, Black Prince, Defence, Hector, Prince Albert, Resistance, Royal Sovereign, Scorpion, Warrior* and *Wivern*.

United States
Navy Department Archives

Since the publication of C. H. Van Tyne and W. G. Leland's *Guide to the Archives of the Government of the United States in Washington* (Washington, 1904), and of Robert W. Neeser's *Statistical and Chronological History of the United States Navy* (New York, 1909, 2 vols.), the records of the Secretary's office have been augmented and rearranged. Under the direction of Captain Dudley W. Knox, U. S. N., retired, the bound volumes, formerly arranged in series according to provenance, have been grouped according to dates. A large amount of material hitherto unclassified or newly acquired has been arranged in two series, one according to areas, the other according to subjects.

Of the bound volumes of manuscripts the following have been utilized for this study.

In-letters

Bureau Letters, 1846–1862. 33 vols.
Commandants Letters, New York Navy Yard. 1861, vol. i; 1862, vols. i and ii.
Commanders Letters, 1861. 6 vols.
Confidential Letters, 1861–1864. 1 vol.
Executive Letters, 1854–1863. 31 vols.
Inventions, Examining Board, and Permanent Commission, 1861–1865, vol. i.
Miscellaneous Letters, 1845–1846, 1861–1863. 68 vols.
Officers Letters, 1846–1847, 1861–1862. 37 vols.

Out-letters

Confidential Letters, vols. iv and v, October 20, 1857–September, 1863.
Executive Letter Books, vols. xiv–xvi, September 18, 1861–September 17, 1863.
General Letter Books, vols. xxxiv–xxxix, lxiii–lxvii, July 10, 1844–April 26, 1848, September 1, 1860–March 31, 1862.
Letters to Congress, vol. xiii, January 3, 1855–May 12, 1862.
Letters to Heads of Bureaus, vols. iii–iv, December 2, 1853–December 17, 1868.

In the same collection is the log of the *Monitor*.

In the material classified under Area 11: Headquarters, 1860–1862, is a folder containing numerous private letters of Commodore Joseph Smith to Flag Officer Foote. Among the documents classified according to subjects, valuable material was found in the series AC, AD, BG, and VN Class 2.

The papers of the Confederate States Navy Department, formerly preserved in the Adjutant General's Office, Old Records Division, were transferred to the Navy Department while this study was in progress. Nearly all those of importance have already been published, in the O. R. N. or elsewhere.

Of great importance for the history of ironclad ships are the numerous plans, specifications, and miscellaneous material preserved in the vaults of the Bureau of Construction and Repair building at the Washington Navy Yard. Extensive use of this material was facilitated by an elaborate card index. The bound manuscripts of the Bureau were found stored in the loft of the same building, in close proximity to a store-room containing painters' supplies.

The following "key" volumes which serve as indexes to the correspondence of the Bureau of Construction and Repair proved useful:

Officers, vols. i and ii, 1847–1865.
Commandants Navy Yards, vol. v, January, 1859–December, 1862.
Miscellaneous, vols. i and ii, 1847–1858.

The following volumes of the correspondence of this Bureau were consulted.

Letters from Commandant, New York, vol. xxiv, 1862.
Letters from Engineers and Constructors, vols. i–iii, 1845–1848.
Miscellaneous Letters, vols. x–xiv, xliii, 1846–1847, 1862.
Letters to New York Navy Yard, vol. iii, 1861–1866.

In 1861 and 1862 the Bureau of Yards and Docks played a great rôle in the introduction of ironclads into the United States Navy. Its manuscript records for this period, however, are practically inaccessible, for the present at least. When the old files of the Bureau were moved several years ago to the Navy Department building they were hopelessly jumbled together. Of the original documents of this Bureau for 1861 access was obtained only to the "key" of the correspondence for the years 1860–1865, and to one volume of contracts, containing those of the *Monitor*, *Galena*, and *New Ironsides*, with their specifications. When the Office of Naval War Records, however, was compiling materials for the O. R. N., copies of the Bureau papers were made and collated, but never published. These transscripts of the official correspondence of Commodore Joseph Smith, then Chief of the Bureau, which throw much new light on the policy of the Department in 1861 and 1862, are cited in this work as N. W. R. Vols. 2599–2603, covering the period from July 24, 1861, to March 31, 1862, contain letters from Bushnell, Ericsson, Merrick and Sons, Stimers, Whitney, and others connected with the construction of the first American ironclads. Vols. 2633 and 2634 contain out-letters to these persons, from May, 1861, to November, 1862. Vol. 5068, New York Navy Yard Papers, November 2, 1861–May 20, 1862; and vols. 5080, 5080½ and 5081, Philadelphia Navy Yard Papers, 1861–1862, also proved useful.

Other Collections

Volumes xliv–lvi of the Gideon Welles Papers in the Manuscripts Division of the Library of Congress contain many interesting private letters from leading naval officers, and numerous letters from Secretary Welles to Mrs. Welles and to his son Edgar, from 1861 to 1865. These are often accompanied by typescript copies, very badly done.

The Library of Congress has also the private journal of William F. Shankland, commander of the U. S. S. *Currituck*, February–December, 1862, which describes his voyage escorting the *Monitor* to Hampton Roads.

Among the manuscripts of the Naval History Society which are now deposited in the Library of the New York Historical Society, are the papers of Captain John Ericsson. W. C. Church, in his article, "John Ericsson, the Engineer," published in *Scribner's Magazine*, February, 1890, page 169, estimated the number of papers left by Ericsson at twelve or fifteen thousand. The first carton of the series suffices to hold all the correspondence that remains for the period from 1831 to April, 1862; the second contains letters from May to September, 1862. These consist almost entirely of in-letters, including many but not all of the official letters of Commodore Smith, and some very interesting private letters from Smith, Fox, and Ericsson's partners. Few copies of Ericsson's out-letters are preserved in these cartons.

Some valuable unpublished material was also found in the papers of Gustavus Vasa Fox, preserved in the same collection.

Most of the correspondence with survivors of the *Monitor* and others connected with that historic ship which is preserved in the Pierce Collection in the New York Public Library was written so long after the events described as to prove of slight value, save for a demonstration of the unreliability of recollection as a source of history.

Among the papers concerning the Stevens battery preserved in the Library of the Stevens Institute of Technology at Hoboken, New Jersey, are various account books, pay rolls and check books, and an important letter book covering all or part of the years 1843–1848, 1853–1856, 1861–1862.

II. PRINTED WORKS

No attempt is made in the following bibliography to cite again every book that has been named in the footnotes. Owing to limitations of space, works used for the diplomatic and political history of the revolution in naval architecture are omitted, as well as certain works of slight importance for this study or useful only for a single point in it.

BIBLIOGRAPHIES

List of Articles from Periodicals relating to the United States Navy collected by Gardner W. Allen and presented to the Harvard College Library. With a subject index. 2 vols. Typescript.

Admiralty Library. *Subject Catalogue of Printed Books*. Part I. Historical Section. London, 1912.

Library of Congress. *List of References on Shipping and Shipbuilding*. Washington, 1919.

Neeser, Robert W., *Statistical and Chronological History of the United States Navy.* 2 vols. New York, 1909. Vol. i.

New York Public Library. *A selected list of works in the library relating to nautical and naval art and science, navigation and seamanship, shipbuilding, etc.* New York, 1907.

Pollard, J., and Dudébout, A., *Architecture navale. Théorie du navire.* 4 vols. Paris, 1890–1894. Vol. i, pp. vii–liv.

Sawyer, Rollin A., Jr., *Naval architecture and shipbuilding. A list of references in the New York Public Library.* New York, 1919.

General P. Charbonnier, Inspecteur Général de l'Artillerie de la Marine, kindly placed at the writer's disposal an unpublished bibliography of French periodical articles concerning naval ordnance. The card catalogue of the Admiralty Library and the subject catalogue of the Conservatoire des Arts et Métiers at Paris also proved most helpful.

Newspapers and Periodicals

Annales maritimes et coloniales
Army and Navy Gazette
Blackwood's Edinburgh Magazine
Boston Commercial Bulletin
Boston Evening Transcript
Colburn's United Service Magazine
Journal des Débats
Journal des sciences militaires
Journal of the Franklin Institute
Journal of the Royal United Service Institution
London Gazette
London Times
Mariner's Mirror
Mechanics' Magazine
Mémorial de l'artillerie
Mémorial de l'artillerie de la marine
    General P. Charbonnier permitted the author to consult this important series, which was issued as confidential information for French naval artillerists.
Mémorial du génie maritime
    For access to this most valuable lithographed periodical an authorization from the Ministry of Marine is required. The set in the Bibliothèque Nationale is incomplete; but that in the Ecole d'Application du Génie Maritime is complete, with the accompanying atlases. Issued as confidential information for French naval constructors, it contains important data concerning French and foreign ironclads.
Minutes of Proceedings of the Institution of Civil Engineers
Minutes of Proceedings of the Royal Artillery Institution
Moniteur de la flotte
Moniteur universel

Nautical Magazine and Naval Chronicle
Naval and Military Magazine
Naval Chronicle
New York Evening Post
New York Herald
Nouvelles annales de la marine et des colonies
Österreichische militärische zeitschrift
Papers on Subjects connected with the Duties of the Corps of Royal Engineers
Punch
Revue des deux mondes
Revue maritime et coloniale
Scientific American
Southern Historical Society *Papers*
Spectateur militaire
Transactions of the Institution of Naval Architects
United Service Journal
United States Naval Gazette
United States Naval Institute *Proceedings*

Three scrap books of press clippings for the years 1866 to 1883, compiled by John Ericsson are preserved in the New York Public Library.

General Works

Adye, Captain Ralph Willett, *The Bombardier and Pocket Gunner.* 7th ed. London, 1813.
(Arçon, Jean-Claude-Eléonore de Michaud d'), *Conseil de guerre privé sur l'événement de Gibraltar en 1782.* 1785.
—— *Mémoire pour servir à l'histoire du siège de Gibraltar.* Cadiz, 1783.
Artiñano, G. de, *Arquitectura naval española.* Madrid, 1920.
Barnaby, Sir Nathaniel, *Naval Development of the Century.* London, 1904.
Benton, J. G., *Ordnance and Gunnery.* 2d ed. New York, 1862.
Bourne, John, *A Treatise on the Screw Propeller.* London, 1852.
Bowen, Frank C., *The Sea: Its History and Romance.* 4 vols. London, [1925–1926].
    Important for pictorial history.
Boxer, Lieutenant Colonel Edward M., *Remarks on the System of Ordnance calculated to prove the most efficient against Iron-clad Ships and Batteries.* Woolwich, 1862.
Brialmont, A., *Etudes sur la défense des états et sur la fortification.* 3 vols. Brussels, 1863.
Browne, Captain Charles Orde, *Armour and its Attack by Artillery.* London, 1887.
    This official text-book of the Royal Artillery Institution is too brief on the early experiments to be of much use in the present study.
Busk, Hans, *The Navies of the World.* London, 1859.
(Cavalli, Giovanni), *Scritti editi e inediti del generale Giovanni Cavalli.* 4 vols. Turin, 1910.

BIBLIOGRAPHY

Cavelier de Cuverville (Jules-Marie-Armand), *Les bâtiments cuirassés.* Paris, 1865.
Charnock, John, *An History of Marine Architecture.* 3 vols. London, 1800–1802.
Clerc-Rampal, G., "Les lois générales de la construction navale," Académie de Marine, *Communications et Mémoires,* iii (1924), No. 5.
Cobden, Richard, *The Three Panics.* 6th ed. London, 1862.
Custance, Admiral Sir Reginald, *The Ship of the Line in Battle.* Edinburgh, 1912.
Dahlgren, J. A., *Shells and Shell Guns.* Philadelphia, 1856.
De la Planche, Lieutenant, *Les navires blindés de la Russie.* Paris, [1865].
Dislère, Paul, *La marine cuirassée.* Paris, 1873.
Douglas, General Sir Howard, *A Treatise on Naval Gunnery.* 5th ed. London, 1860.
    His accounts of the armor tests of the fifties are biassed and often misleading.
—— *A Postscript to the Section on Iron Defenses contained in the fifth edition of "Naval Gunnery."* London, 1860.
—— *On Naval Warfare with Steam.* London, 1858.
Dupuy de Lôme, (Stanislas-Charles-Henri-Laurent), *Mémoire sur la construction des bâtiments en fer.* Paris, 1844.
Duro, Cesáreo Fernández, *Armada española desde la unión de los reinos de Castilla y de Aragón.* 9 vols. Madrid, 1895–1903.
—— *Disquisiciones Náuticas.* 6 vols. Madrid, 1876–1881.
Dusaert, Édouard, *Essai sur les obusiers.* Paris, 1842.
Fairbairn, Sir William, *Iron: its History, Properties, and Processes of Manufacture.* Edinburgh, 1861.
Favé (Général Ildephonse), and Bonaparte, Prince Louis-Napoléon (Napoléon III, Emperor of the French), *Etudes sur le passé et l'avenir de l'artillerie.* 6 vols. Paris, 1846–1871.
Fincham, John, *A History of Naval Architecture.* London, 1851.
Fleischer, Josef, *Geschichte der K. K. Kriegsmarine während des Krieges im Jahre 1866.* Vienna, 1906.
Garbett, Captain H., *Naval Gunnery.* London, 1897.
Gayoso, Don Justo, *Estudios sobre la marina militar de España.* Ferrol, 1860.
Glanz von Aïcha, Baron Emil, *Geschichtliche Darstellung der Panzerungen und Eisen Constructionen.* Vienna, 1873.
Grantham, John, *Iron as a Material for Ship-building.* London, 1842.
Halleck, Henry W., *Elements of Military Art and Science.* New York, 1846.
Hastings, Frank Abney, *Memoir on the Use of Shells.* London, 1828.
Hélie, Félix, *Traité de balistique expérimentale.* 2d ed. 2 vols. Paris, 1884.
Heriz, Enrique, *Memoria sobre los barcos acorazados.* Barcelona, 1875.
Hime, Lieutenant Colonel Henry W. L., *The Origin of Artillery.* London, 1915.
Holley, A. L., *A Treatise on Ordnance and Armor.* New York, 1865.

Hovgaard, William, *Modern History of Warships*. London and New York, 1920.
Jal, Auguste, *Archéologie navale*. 2 vols. Paris, 1840.
(Jansen, M. H.), *The Revolution in Naval Warfare*. London, 1867.
    A translation of the Dutch admiral's work, *De Omwenteling in het Zeewesen*.
Kronenfels, Captain J. F. von, *Das schwimmende Flotten-Material der Seemächte*. Vienna, 1881.
Lullier, C. E., *Essai sur l'histoire de la tactique navale*. Paris, 1867.
Miller, J. W., "The Development of Armor as applied to Ships," United States Naval Institute *Proceedings* (1879), pp. 513-536.
Naber, S. P. L'Honoré, ed., *Het Leven van een Vloothouder. Gedenkschriften van M. H. Jansen*. Utrecht, 1925.
Noble, Sir Andrew, *Artillery and Explosives*. New York, 1906.
Ogburn, William F., and Thomas, Dorothy, "Are Inventions Inevitable? A Note on Social Evolution," *Political Science Quarterly*, xxxvii (March, 1922), pp. 83-98.
Pâris, Admiral François Edmond, *L'art naval à l'Exposition de Londres de 1862*. 2 vols. Paris, [1863].
    A supplement of seventy-nine pages with eleven plates was published at Paris in 1864.
—— *L'art naval à l'exposition universelle de Paris en 1867*. Paris, 1870.
—— *Souvenirs de marine. Collection de plans ou dessins de navires et de bateaux anciens ou modernes existants ou disparus*. 5 vols. Paris, 1882-1892.
    An important collection of plans.
Penhoat, H., *Essai sur l'attaque et la défense des lignes de vaisseaux*. Cherbourg, 1862.
    By the captain of the *Couronne*.
Randaccio, C., *Storia delle marine militari italiane dal 1750 al 1860 e della marina militare italiana dal 1860 al 1870*. 2 vols. Rome, 1886.
Rankine, W. J. M., ed., *Shipbuilding, Theoretical and Practical*. London, 1866.
Raymond, Xavier, *Les marines de la France et de l'Angleterre, 1815-1863*. Paris, 1863.
Reed, E. J., *Shipbuilding in Iron and Steel*. London, 1869.
Robertson, Frederick Leslie, *The Evolution of Naval Armament*. London, 1921.
Russell, J. Scott, *The Modern System of Naval Architecture*. 3 vols. London, [1865].
    With important plans.
Scoffern, J., *Projectile Weapons of War and Explosive Compounds*. 4th ed. London, 1859.
Simpson, Lieutenant Edward, *A Treatise on Ordnance and Naval Gunnery*. 2d ed. New York, 1862.
    A textbook for the United States Naval Academy.
Smith, W. E., *The Distribution of Armour in Ships of War*. London, 1885.

Todleben, E. de, *La Défense de Sebastopol.* 2 vols. St. Petersburg, 1863–1870.
> Includes an account of the capture of Kinburn.

Taylerson, Robert, *Iron Ship Building.* London, 1854.
Thiroux, ——, *Réflexions et études sur les bouches à feu de siège, de place et de cote.* Paris, 1849.
Torr, Cecil, *Ancient Ships.* Cambridge, 1894.
Totten, Joseph G., *Report on the Effects of Firing with Heavy Ordnance from Casemate Embrasures: and also the Effects of Firing against the same Embrasures.* Washington, 1857.
Usher, Abbott P., *History of Mechanical Inventions.* New York, 1929.
Very, Edward W., "The Development of Armor for Naval Use," United States Naval Institute *Proceedings,* ix (1883), pp. 349–591.
—— "The Development of Rifled Ordnance," United States Naval Institute *Proceedings,* iii (1877), pp. 25–45.
Watts, Sir Philip, "Warship Building (1860–1910)," *Transactions of the Institution of Naval Architects,* liii (1911), part ii, pp. 291–337.
White, W. H., *A Manual of Naval Architecture.* 2d ed. 2 vols. London, 1882.
Whitworth, Sir Joseph, *On Guns and Steel.* London, 1873.
Wilson, H. W., *Ironclads in Action.* 2 vols. London, 1896.
—— *Battleships in Action.* 2 vols. London, [1926].

Works Relating More Particularly to the French Navy

(a) *Public Documents*

Assemblée Nationale. Enquête parlementaire sur la situation et l'organisation des services de la marine militaire. 2 vols. Paris, 1851.
Expériences d'artillerie exécutées à Gavre par ordre du ministre de la marine pendant les années 1830, 1831, 1832, 1834, 1835, 1836, 1837, 1838 et 1840. Paris, 1841.
Répertoire alphabétique des bâtiments de tout rang armés et désarmés par l'état. 1er Supplément, du 1er janvier 1829 au 31 décembre 1834. [Paris, n. d.]
—— *2e Supplément, du 1er janvier 1835 au 31 décembre 1844.* [Paris, n. d.]
—— *3e Supplément, du 1er janvier 1845 au 31 décembre 1854.* Paris, 1859.
—— *4e Supplément, du 1e janvier 1855 au 31 décembre 1868.* Paris, 1872.

(b) *Other Works*

Expériences faites à Brest, en janvier 1824, du nouveau système des forces navales proposé par M. Paixhans. Paris, 1837.
Expériences faites à Metz en 1834, par ordre du ministre de la guerre, sur les batteries de brèche, sur la pénétration des projectiles dans divers milieux résistans, et sur la rupture des corps par le choc. Paris, 1836.
Académie de Marine, *Communications et Mémoires.* Vols. i–. Paris, 1922–.

Bazancourt, Baron de, *La marine française dans la mer Noire et la Baltique.* 2 vols. Paris, 1858.
Bertrand, Emile, *Historique du vaisseau la Couronne.* Paris, 1894.
Bouët-Willaumez, Rear Admiral Count E., *Batailles de terre et de mer jusques et y compris la bataille de l'Alma.* Paris, 1855.
De Balincourt and Vincent-Bréchignac, Commandants, "La marine française d'hier. Les cuirassés. I. Batteries flottantes. II. Frégates cuirassées," *Revue maritime,* May, 1930, pp. 577–595; *ibid.,* March, 1931, pp. 289–317.
Destrem, Jean and Clarc-Rampal, G., *Catalogue raisonnée du musée de la marine.* Paris, 1909.
(Dupuy de Lôme, S. C. H. L.), *Notice sur les travaux scientifiques de M. Dupuy de Lôme.* Paris, 1866.
Grivel, Richild, *Attaques et bombardements maritimes, avant et pendant la guerre d'Orient.* Paris, 1856.
Guihéneuc, Olivier, "Les origines du premier cuirassé de haute mer à vapeur. Le plan de Dupuy de Lôme en 1845," *Revue maritime,* April, 1928, pp. 459–482.
Joinville (François-Ferdinand-Philippe-Louis-Marie d'Orléans), prince de, *Note sur l'état des forces navales de la France.* Paris, 1844.
—— *Vieux souvenirs.* Paris, 1894.
La Roncière, Charles de, *Histoire de la marine française.* 5 vols. Paris, 1899–1920.
Labrousse, H., "Des propulseurs sous-marins," *Revue générale d'architecture,* 1842, pp. 385–458, 500–532.
(——) *Notice sur les travaux scientifiques et les services du contre-amiral Labrousse.* Paris, 1866.
Montgéry, P. M. de, "Mémoire sur les navires en fer," *Journal des sciences militaires,* i (1825), pp. 488 ff.
Paixhans, Henri-Joseph, *Constitution militaire de la France.* Paris, 1849.
—— *Expériences faites par la marine française sur une arme nouvelle.* Paris, 1825.
—— *Force et faiblesse militaires de la France.* Paris, 1830.
—— *Fortification de Paris.* Paris, 1834.
—— *Nouvelle force maritime.* Paris, 1822.
Tramond, Joannès, and Reussner, André, *Eléments d'histoire maritime et coloniale contemporaine.* Paris, 1924.

WORKS RELATING MORE PARTICULARLY TO THE BRITISH NAVY

(a) *Public Documents*

In addition to the extensive naval material in the *Parliamentary Papers* and in Hansard's *Parliamentary Debates,* the following are important for this study.

Experiments in H.M. Ship "Excellent" . . . from 1832 to 1854. [London, 1854.]
Experiments with Naval Ordnance. H.M.S. "Excellent." London, 1866.

Extracts from the Reports and Proceedings of the Ordnance Select Committee. 6 vols. London, 1863–1869.
Patents for Inventions. Abridgments of Specifications. Class 113. Ships, Boats, and Rafts, Division I. Period A.D. 1855–1866. London, 1905.
Transactions and Reports of the Special Committee on Iron. [London, 1862–1864.]
    Four confidential reports of capital importance, March 27, 1862–August 17, 1864.

(b) Other Works

Admiralty Administration, its Faults and Defaults. London, 1861.
Catalogue of the Exhibits in the Royal Naval Museum, Greenwich. London, 1913.
On the new wants arising from the introduction of the Paixhans Gun in the Royal Navy. London, 1838.
Albion, Robert G., *Forests and Sea Power.* Cambridge, Mass., 1926.
Ballard, Admiral G. A., "The Black Battlefleet. British Battleships of 1870," *Mariner's Mirror*, xv (April, October, 1929), pp. 101-124, 391-407; xvi (January, April, July, 1930), pp. 48–67, 168–186, 212–238.
Bentham, M. S., *Life of Brigadier-General Sir Samuel Bentham.* London, 1862.
Bentham, Sir Samuel, *Naval Papers No. VII, containing Letters and Papers relative to the mode of Arming Vessels of War.* London, 1828.
Bernard, William Dallas, *Narrative of the Voyages and Services of the Nemesis, from 1840 to 1843.* 2 vols. London, 1844.
Bidder, George Parker, *The National Defences.* London, 1861.
Brassey, Sir Thomas, *The British Navy.* 5 vols. London, 1882–1883.
Briggs, Sir John Henry, *Naval Administrations 1827 to 1892.* London, 1897.
Chatfield, Henry, *Remarks on the Proposed Changes at the Admiralty and in the Dock-Yards consequent upon the Introduction of iron shipping into Her Majesty's Service.* Greenwich, [1863?].
Clowes, W. L., and others, *The Royal Navy.* 7 vols. London, 1897-1903.
Coles, Captain Cowper Phipps, *Captain Coles's Correspondence with the Admiralty on giving free publication to his views on Iron-clads.* Ventnor, 1866.
—— *A Comparison between Iron-Clad Ships with Broadside Ports, and Ships with Revolving Shields.* Portsea, 1863.
—— *English versus American cupolas. A Comparison between Captain Coles's and Captain Ericsson's turrets.* Portsea, 1864.
—— *Iron-Clad Sea-going Shield Ships.* [London, 1863.]
—— *Letters from Captain Cowper Coles to the Secretary of the Admiralty on Sea-going Turret Ships.* Portsea, [1865].
—— *Letters . . . and the Opinion of the Press on Turrets.* London, 1866.
—— *Our National Defences.* [London], 1861.
    This ran through at least four editions in 1861 and 1862.
—— "Shot-Proof Gun-Shields as adapted to Iron-cased Ships," *Journal of the Royal United Service Institution*, iv [1860], pp. 280–290.

—— *Spithead Forts. Reply to the Royal Commissioners' Second Report on our National Defences.* London, 1861.

—— *The Turret versus the Broadside System.* London, 1867.

Colomb, Vice Admiral P. H., *Memoirs of Admiral Sir Astley Cooper Key.* London, 1898.

Corbett, Sir Julian, *Drake and the Tudor Navy.* 2 vols. London, 1898.

Douglas, Sir Howard, *Observations on Modern Systems of Fortification.* London, 1859.

Eardley-Wilmot, Captain S., *Life of Vice-Admiral Edmund, Lord Lyons.* London, 1898.

Fairbairn, William, *On the Properties of Iron, and its Resistance to Projectiles at High Velocities.* [London?], 1862.

Fullom, S. W., *Life of General Sir Howard Douglas.* London, 1863.

Halstead, Captain Edward Pellew, *Iron-cased Ships.* [London, 1861.]

Hay, Admiral Sir John C. Dalrymple, *Lines from my Log-Books.* Edinburgh, 1898.

Laird, John, *Letters to "The Times" on Iron Ships of War and Coast and Harbour Defences.* [London], 1859.

Mallock, W. H., and Ramsden, Lady Gwendolen, eds., *Letters, Remains and Memoirs of Edward Adolphus Seymour, Twelfth Duke of Somerset.* London, 1893.

Mends, Bowen Stilon, *Life of Admiral Sir William Robert Mends.* London, 1899.

Moorsom, Captain William, *Remarks on the Construction of Ships of War, and the Composition of War Fleets.* Portsea, [1857].
    By an early advocate of ironclads.

Napier, James, *Life of Robert Napier of West Shandon.* Edinburgh, 1904.

Oppenheim, M., *A History of the Administration of the Royal Navy . . . from 1509 to 1670.* London and New York, 1896.

Otway, Sir Arthur, ed., *Autobiography and Journals of Admiral Lord Clarence E. Paget.* London, 1896.

Overton, G. L., *Catalogue of the Collections in the Science Museum, South Kensington: Water Transport, III, Steam Ships of War.* London, 1925.

Reed, E. J., *On Iron-Cased Ships of War, including a description of H.M.S. "Enterprise."* London, 1863.

—— *On the Modifications which the Ships of the Royal Navy have undergone during the present Century.* London, 1859.
    Reprint of an article in the *Mechanics Magazine*, December, 1858.

—— *Our Iron-Clad Ships.* London, 1869.

—— "The Iron-Cased Ships of the British Navy," *Report of the British Association for the Advancement of Science* [for 1861], London, 1862, part ii, pp. 232–239.

Russell, J. Scott, *The Fleet of the Future: Iron or Wood?* London, 1861.

—— *The Fleet of the Future in 1862; or England without a Fleet.* London, 1862.

Samuda, Joseph D'Aguilar, "On the Form and Materials for Iron Plated Ships," *Minutes of Proceedings of the Institution of Civil Engineers*, xxi (1861–1862), pp. 187–257.

Simmons, Captain T. F., *Ideas as to the effect of Heavy Ordnance directed against and applied by Ships of War*. London, 1837.
—— *A Discussion on the Present Armament of the Navy*. London, 1839.
Stephen, Leslie, and Lee, Sidney, *Dictionary of National Biography*. 66 vols. London, 1885–1901.
Symonds, Commander T. E., "On Constructing, Manoeuvring, and Propelling Screw Steamers for War," *Journal of the Royal United Service Institution*, vi (March 31, 1862), pp. 15 ff.
Walter, Lieutenant George, *Iron Ships for War or Peace*. London, 1850.
Wrottesley, Lieutenant Colonel George, *Life and Correspondence of Field Marshal Sir John Burgoyne*. 2 vols. London, 1873.

Works Relating More Particularly to the United States and Confederate States Navies

(a) *Public Documents*

In addition to the records of debates in the *Annals of Congress*, the *Register of Debates in Congress*, and the *Congressional Globe*, the appropriation acts in the *Statutes at Large*, and the messages and reports in the Congressional Documents, the following are important for this study.

American State Papers, Military Affairs, vol. i. Washington, 1832.
American State Papers, Naval Affairs. 4 vols. Washington, 1834–1864.
  For the years 1789 to 1836.
Appendix to the Case Presented on the Part of the Government of Her Britannic Majesty [to the Geneva Tribunal of Arbitration]. 7 vols. London, 1872.
Official Records of the Union and Confederate Navies in the War of the Rebellion. 30 vols. Washington, 1894–1922.
Proceedings of the Court of Inquiry, relative to the Fall of New Orleans. Richmond, 1864.
Report of the Joint Committee on the Conduct of the War. 3 vols. Washington, 1865.
Report of the Secretary of the Navy in relation to Armored Vessels. Washington, 1864.
  Some of the documents reproduced in this report from earlier Congressional Documents do not appear in full or in their original form.
The War of the Rebellion: a Compilation of the Official Records of the Union and Confederate Armies. 70 vols. Washington, 1880–1901.

(b) *Other Works*

Scores of accounts of the battles of Hampton Roads have been published by participants and eyewitnesses. Both the Allen Collection in the Harvard College Library and the Pierce Collection in the New York Public Library contain numerous examples of this literature. Most of them, written long after the events narrated, are of slight value save to historical critics seeking fresh evidence of the unreliability of recollection as a source of history. Only the best of the reminiscent accounts are listed among the following works.

"The Emperor Napoleon and Captain Ericsson," *Eclectic Magazine*, August, 1862, pp. 568–569.

History of the Ram Fleet and the Mississippi Marine Brigade. St. Louis, 1907.

"The 'Monitor' at Sea and in Battle," United States Naval Institute *Proceedings*, xlix (November, 1923), pp. 1839–1847.

    Lieutenant S. Dana Greene's letter to his mother, March 14, 1862.

Barnard, John Gross, *The Dangers and Defences of New York.* New York, 1859.

—— *Notes on Sea-coast Defence.* New York, 1861.

Belknap, Captain George E., "Reminiscent of the 'New Ironsides' off Charleston," *United Service*, January, 1879, pp. 63–82.

Bennett, Lieutenant Frank M., *The Monitor and the Navy Under Steam.* Boston and New York, 1900.

—— *The Steam Navy of the United States.* 2d ed. 2 vols. Pittsburgh, 1897.

Birnie, Captain Rogers, Jr., *Gun Making in the United States.* Washington, 1907.

Boynton, Charles B., *The History of the Navy during the Rebellion.* 2 vols. New York, 1867–1868.

Brooke, John Mercer, "The Virginia or Merrimac: Her real projector." Southern Historical Society *Papers*, xix (January, 1891), pp. 3–34.

Brown, Lieutenant Commander Walter E., "The Daddy of 'em all (U.S.S. *Michigan*)," United States Naval Institute *Proceedings*, l (October, 1924), pp. 1687–1694.

Bruce, Kathleen, *Virginia Iron Manufacture in the Slave Era.* New York, 1931.

Church, William Conant, *The Life of John Ericsson.* 2 vols. New York, 1891.

Davis, Rear Admiral Charles H., "History of the U. S. Steamer Merrimack," *New England Historical and Genealogical Register*, July, 1874, pp. 245–248.

Davis, Captain Charles H., *Life of Charles Henry Davis, Rear Admiral, 1807–1877.* Boston and New York, 1899.

Derby, Elias Hasket, "Mail-clad Steamers," *Atlantic Monthly*, August, 1861, pp. 227–235.

Dickinson, H. W., *Robert Fulton.* London, 1913.

Dislère, Paul, "Notes sur la marine américaine," *Revue maritime et coloniale*, January, 1868, pp. 261–301.

    This article reproduces the larger part of a confidential report by Dislère which appeared in the *Mémorial du génie maritime*, 1866, pp. 161–221.

Du Pont, H. A., *Rear Admiral Samuel Francis Du Pont, U.S.N.* New York, 1910.

(Eggleston, Captain John R.), "Captain Eggleston's Narrative of the Battle of the Merrimac," Southern Historical Society *Papers*, September, 1916, pp. 166–178.

Emmons, Lieutenant George F., *The Navy of the United States.* Washington, 1853.

BIBLIOGRAPHY 379

Ericsson, John, *Contributions to the Centennial Exhibition.* New York, 1876.
Furman, Franklin De Ronde, ed., *Morton Memorial. A History of the Stevens Institute of Technology.* Hoboken, N. J., 1905.
Gift, George W., "The Story of the Arkansas," Southern Historical Society *Papers,* xii (1884), pp. 48–54, 115–119, 163–170, 205–212.
Griffis, William E., *Matthew Calbraith Perry.* 2d ed. Boston and New York, 1890.
Guernsey, A. H., "Iron-clad Vessels," *Harper's Monthly,* September, 1862, pp. 433–446.
—— "The Revolving Tower and its inventor Theodore R. Timby," *Harper's Monthly,* January, 1863, pp. 241–248.
Hovgaard, William, "Who invented the Monitor?" *Army and Navy Journal,* xlvii (November 27, 1909), p. 357.
    Excellent brief statement dismissing Timby's claims.
How, Louis, *James B. Eads.* Cambridge, [1900].
(Howard, John Raymond?), *Some Memories of John Tasker Howard, 1808–1888, and his Wife, Susan Taylor Raymond, 1812–1906.* [New York?], 1909.
Hughes, S. F., ed., *Letters and Recollections of John Murray Forbes.* 2 vols. Boston and New York, 1899.
Johnson, Allen, and Malone, Dumas, eds., *Dictionary of American Biography.* Vols. i–. New York, 1928–.
Johnson, Robert Underwood, and Buell, C. C., eds., *Battles and Leaders of the Civil War.* 4 vols. New York, [1888–1889].
Jones, Captain Catesby ap Rogers, "Services of the 'Virginia' (Merrimac)," Southern Historical Society *Papers,* xi (1883), pp. 65–75.
Maclay, Edgar S., *History of the United States Navy.* 3 vols. New York, 1910–1917.
Maccord, Charles W., "Ericsson and his 'Monitor,'" *North American Review,* cxlix (October, 1889), pp. 460–471.
    By Ericsson's former chief draughtsman.
Marestier, Jean Baptiste, *Mémoire sur les bateaux à vapeur des Etats Unis d'Amerique.* Paris, 1824.
Meade, Rebecca Paulding, *The Life of Hiram Paulding, Rear-Admiral, U.S.N.* New York, 1910.
Miller, Francis T., ed., *The Photographic History of the Civil War.* 10 vols. New York, 1911.
    Volume vi, by Colonel James Barnes, contains excellent photographs of many Union and Confederate ironclads.
Morgan, James Morris, "The pioneer 'ironclad' [C.S.S. *Manassas*]," United States Naval Institute *Proceedings,* October, 1917, pp. 2275–2282.
New Jersey Commission appointed to Effect the Sale of the Stevens Steam Battery, *The Stevens Iron-Clad Battery.* New York, 1874.
New Jersey Commissioners on the Plan of the Stevens Battery, *Report of the Commissioners on the Plan of the Stevens Battery . . . with a report of the engineer in charge.* Trenton, 1870.

Newton, Virginius, "The Ram Merrimac," *Southern Historical Society Papers*, xx (1892), pp. 1–26.
Nicolay, John G., and Hay, John, *Abraham Lincoln. A History*. 10 vols. New York, 1890.
Paullin, Charles Oscar, "Naval Administration under the Navy Commissioners, 1815–1842," *United States Naval Institute Proceedings*, xxxiii (June, 1907), pp. 597-641.
—— "Naval Administration, 1842–1861," in *ibid.* (December, 1907), pp. 1435–1477.
—— "Half a Century of Naval Administration in America, 1861–1911," in *ibid.*, xxxviii (December, 1912), pp. 1309-1336; xxxix (March, 1913), pp. 165-195.
  This work was published in nine instalments, of which the first two cover the years 1861 to 1865.
Porter, Admiral David Dixon, *Incidents and Anecdotes of the Civil War*. New York, 1885.
—— *Naval History of the Civil War*. New York, 1886.
Porter, John W. H., *A Record of Events in Norfolk County, Virginia, from April 19th, 1861, to May 10th, 1862*. Portsmouth, Va., 1892.
Quaife, M. M., "The Iron Ship [U.S.S. *Michigan*]," *Burton Historical Collection Leaflets*, vol. vii (1928), no. 2.
Read, C. W., "Reminiscences of the Confederate States Navy," *Southern Historical Society Papers*, i (May, 1876), pp. 331-362.
Robinson, George H., "Recollections of Ericsson," *United Service*, January, 1895, pp. 10-26.
  By one of Ericsson's executors.
Rowland, Dunbar, ed., *Jefferson Davis, Constitutionalist*. 10 vols. Jackson, Miss., 1923.
Sargent, E., "Ericsson and His Inventions," *Atlantic Monthly*, July, 1862, pp. 68-81.
Scharf, J. Thomas, *History of the Confederate States Navy*. 2d ed. Albany, N. Y., 1894.
(Selfridge, Thomas O., Jr.), *Memoirs of Thomas O. Selfridge, Jr., Rear Admiral, U.S.N.* New York and London, 1924.
—— "The Story of the Cumberland," *Papers* of the Military Historical Society of Massachusetts, xii (1902), pp. 103-126.
S[hippen], E., "A Reminiscence of the First Iron-clad Fight," *Lippincott's Magazine*, February, 1878, pp. 218-226.
Stevens, Edwin Augustus, *The Stevens Battery*. (New York?, 1862.)
Stuart, Charles Beebe, *The Naval and Mail Steamers of the United States*. New York, 1853.
Thompson, R. M., and Wainwright, Richard, eds., *Confidential Correspondence of Gustavus Vasa Fox, Assistant Secretary of the Navy, 1861–1865*. 2 vols. New York, 1918-1919.
Thurston, Robert Henry, *The Messrs. Stevens, of Hoboken, as Engineers, Naval Architects and Philanthropists*. Philadelphia, 1874.
  Reprinted from the *Journal of the Franklin Institute*, October, 1874.
Tindall, William, "The True Story of the Virginia and the Monitor," *Vir-

ginia *Magazine of History and Biography*, xxxi (January, April, 1923), pp. 1–38, 89–145.

Tousard, Lieutenant Colonel Louis de, *American Artillerist's Companion*. 2 vols. Philadelphia, 1809.

Turnbull, Archibald D., *John Stevens: an American Record*. New York, 1928.

Welles, Edgar T., ed., *Diary of Gideon Welles*. 3 vols. Boston and New York, 1911.

    The first chapter, covering the events of the war prior to July, 1862, was written several years after the events narrated.

Welles, Gideon, "The First Iron-Clad Monitor," in *The Annals of the War*, Philadelphia, 1879, pp. 17–31.

Wells, William S., compiler, *The original United States warship Monitor. Copies of correspondence between C. S. Bushnell, John Ericsson and Gideon Welles, together with a brief sketch of Mr. Bushnell's life*. [2d ed., revised. 1906.]

Wheeler, Francis B., *John F. Winslow, LL.D., and the Monitor*. [Poughkeepsie, N. Y., 1893.]

    Based on an old man's faulty recollections.

INDEX

INDEX

A. O. Tyler (Taylor), 243, 245
Aaron Manby, 33
Abbott and Son, 266
Aberdeen, George Hamilton-Gordon, Earl of, 65
Abethell, Richard, 161, 163, 164, 189
Achilles, 167, 174, 176, 178, 179, 206, 319, 320, 366
Admiralty, British, 10, 13, 26, 34, 35, 36, 39, 45, 55, 74, 75, 76, 77, 86, 87, 111, 116, 117, 118, 119, 120, 121, 122, 123, 127, 128, 129, 130, 131, 132, 135, 137, 139, 140, 141, 153, 155, 156, 157, 159, 161, 162, 163, 165, 166, 168, 170, 171, 172, 173, 174, 175, 176, 177, 178, 179, 180, 181, 186, 187, 188, 189, 190, 191, 192, 193, 194, 200, 201, 204, 206, 231, 273, 283, 312, 313, 314, 315, 316, 317, 320, 321, 322, 325, 326, 327, 329, 341, 365
Aetna, 79, 86
Agamemnon, 120
Agamenticus, 305
Agincourt, 179, 204, 206, 319, 321
Alabama, 237
Albany Iron Works, 266
Albert of Saxe-Coburg and Gotha, Prince Consort, 74 n., 150, 151, 168, 190 and n.
Alfred, target ship, 122, 124, 125, 163, 205.
Alleghany, 43, 47, 226
American influence on European naval construction, 10, 15, 32, 54, 211, 213, 238, 285, 302, 304 n., 311–317, 323–324, 327, 330
Amphion, 15
Anchors, protection of, 79 n., 359
Anderson, J., 231
Anderson, Robert, 222, 240
Andréossy, Antoine-François, comte, 20
Antoine, Charles-Eugène, 95, 102
Archimedes, 13
Arçon, Jean-Claude-Eléonore de Michaud d', 7–8, 227
Ark of Delft, 6

Arkansas, 234
Arman, Jean-Lucien, 96, 103, 104, 113, 114
Armor
 backing, 9, 36, 55, 59, 72, 75, 87, 90, 95, 96, 97, 100, 101, 105, 111, 122, 126, 127, 128, 153, 158, 172, 193, 194, 197, 200, 203–207, 310, 328
 bronze, 5, 94
 copper, 202
 corrugated, 88, 91, 95, 200, 203, 269
 fastening, 93, 95, 97, 232
 for forts, 56, 170, 182, 201, 221
 homogeneous metal, 119, 122, 124, 200, 202, 207
 inclined, 5, 6, 7, 8, 9, 28, 30, 31, 48, 52, 53, 61, 62, 87, 89, 91, 106, 162–164, 190, 193, 198, 199, 200, 203, 207 n., 215, 216, 217, 219, 220, 221, 222, 223, 226, 227, 228, 230, 240, 242, 243, 250, 267, 268, 310
 iron. *See* Iron armor plates
 laminated, 54, 55, 59, 60, 61, 63, 72, 109, 154, 202, 217, 230, 232, 266, 275, 307, 308 n., 328
 lead, 4, 5, 6 n., 200
 steel. *See* Steel armor plates
 thickness of, 72, 73, 75, 80, 94, 95, 100, 101, 103, 107, 109, 113, 118, 119, 123, 126, 128, 194 n., 196, 197, 199 n., 200–203, 206, 207, 209, 210, 213, 221, 225, 230, 236, 240, 243, 249, 264–265, 267–268, 276, 296, 297, 308 n., 323
Armor plate manufacturers
 Abbott and Son, 266
 Albany Iron Works, 266
 Beale and Company, 202
 Begbie, Stirling, 101
 Bochum Works, 94
 Brown, John, and Company, 202, 282
 Holdane and Company, 266
 Jacks, James, and Company, 283
 Krupp, Frederick, 94
 Lowmoor Iron Company, 202
 Palmer and Company, 154, 156 n., 157

Petin, Gaudet and Company, 73, 78, 94, 102, 105, 283
Pontypool Iron Company, 202
Rensselaer Iron Works, 266
Schneider and Company, 73, 78, 104 n.
Scofield and Markham, 236
Tredegar Iron Works, 230
Armor tests, 23, 24, 28, 29, 36, 37, 38, 48, 54–61, 72, 75, 87, 94–97, 101–103, 122, 124–126, 154, 163, 201, 205–207, 209, 230
Armstrong, Sir William George, 197
Arrogante, 113
Aspinwall, W. H., 273
Atlanta, 231
Aubert, Louis, 64, 88, 89, 362
Audenet, Camille, 95, 96, 97, 100, 111, 114 n.
Aurous, Jules, 107
Austro-Hungarian Navy, 56, 197, 198, 282, 311, 314

Backing for armor, 9, 36, 38, 55, 56, 59, 72, 75, 87, 90, 95, 96, 97, 100, 101, 105, 111, 122, 126, 127, 128, 153, 158, 172, 193, 194, 197, 200, 203, 204, 205, 206, 267, 310, 328
Ballard, G. A., cited, 179
Baltard, Louis-Pierre, 182
Bancroft, George, 44, 51, 54, 211, 212
Barceló, Don Antonio, 7
Baring Brothers, 283
Baring, Sir Francis, 131
Barnaby, Sir Nathaniel, 164 n., 167 n., 180 n., 204 n.
Barnard, John Gross, 219, 220
Barnes, W. L., 281
Barron, James, 30, 338
Barron, Samuel, 337
Bates, Edward, 242
Baudin, Charles, 74, 75 n.
Beale and Company, 202
Beam of ships, 5, 28, 34, 45, 50, 60, 62, 63, 71, 73, 86, 93 n., 99, 103, 105, 106, 108, 110, 111, 118, 155, 156, 158, 166, 167, 213, 215, 217, 226, 243, 250, 251, 253, 257, 274, 307, 325, 360
Beaufort, 291, 292
Begbie, Stirling, 101
Béléguic, Eugène-Corentin, 93 and n.
Bellerophon, 320, 321
Belliqueuse, 311

Belmano, ——, 55
"Belt-and-battery" ships, 60, 61 n., 108, 109, 111, 167, 174, 176, 178, 179, 206, 238, 247, 248, 268, 318, 319, 320, 348, 366, 367
Bennett, James Gordon, 257
Bentham, Sir Samuel, 20, 21
Bentinck, G. W. P., 312
Benton, 244
Bergen, A. J., 44
Berkeley, Sir Maurice, 76 n., 85
Bertrand, Philippe-Etienne-Alphonse, 28
Billot, Frédéric, 64, 89 n.
Birkenhead, 36
Bismarck-Schönhausen, Otto E. L. Prince von, 149, 150
Black Prince, 156, 157, 159, 164 n., 165, 317, 319, 366
Blakely, Captain Alexander Theophilus, 208
Blood, Charles, 240 n.
Bloodgood, Abraham, 182
Bloodhound, 35
Boarding. See Tactics
Bochum Works, 94
Boilers, 11, 14, 41, 48, 49, 51 n., 54, 57 n., 78, 79, 110, 111, 193, 215, 229, 232, 233, 243, 245, 253, 261, 307, 338
Bomford, George, 22
Boston Evening Transcript, 275
Bottoms, protection of against fouling, 4, 5, 6 n. See also Fouling, Sheathing
Bouët-Willaumez, Louis-Edouard, comte, 107
Bourgois, Siméon, 16
Brandon, 84
Breese, Samuel L., 251
Brest, 25, 73, 74, 78, 82, 101, 107, 108, 113
Brialmont, Henri-Alexis, 56
Bright, John, 146
British Admiralty. See Admiralty, British
British Navy, 6, 8, 10, 11, 13, 15, 39, 56, 65–68, 76, 77, 80, 113, 114, 116, 120, 121, 122, 127, 131, 137, 140, 146, 169, 174, 239 n., 282, 312–323, 325
Broadside and turret ships, relative merits of, 186, 188, 189, 190, 191, 193, 283, 324
Bronze armor, 5, 94
Brooke, John M., 225, 226, 228, 229, 230, 296, 310

Brooklyn, 234
Brown, Isaac Newton, 234
Brown, John, and Company, 202, 282
Brown, Uriah, 9, 30, 53, 227
Browne, Lieutenant Colonel, 19
Bruat, Armand-Joseph, 83, 85, 364
Buchanan, Franklin, 290, 291, 292, 293
Bulkheads
  armored, 129, 130 n., 158, 177, 192, 268
  water-tight, 27, 44, 45, 100, 129, 158, 177, 243
Bureau of Construction and Repair, 51, 238, 278, 281, 305. *See also* Lenthall, John
Bureau of Construction, Equipment and Repair. *See* Bureau of Construction and Repair
Bureau of Ordnance and Hydrography, 241
Bureau of Yards and Docks. *See* Smith, Joseph
Burgoyne, Sir John Fox, 67, 160 n., 170 n., 201
Bushnell, Cornelius Scranton, 253–256, 258, 259, 260, 265, 267, 367
Bussy, Marie-Anne-Louis de, 330
Byers, James, 295 n.

Cairo, 244
Caledonia, 176, 319, 320
Captain, 329
Carcasses, 18, 20, 21
Carondelet, 244, 245
Carronades, 20, 21, 22 and n.
Casy, Joseph-Grégoire, 340
Catskill, 308
Cavalli, Giovanni, 56, 90, 91, 198, 221 n.
Cavour, Camillo, Count di, 150, 198
Center of gravity, 99, 329
"Central battery" ironclads, 179
Cerbère, 329
Chambers, Benjamin, 208
Charleston, 221–223, 228, 236, 271, 306, 327, 328, 329
Chasseloup-Laubat, François, comte de, 114, 209
Chauncey, Isaac, 8
Cherbourg, 20, 68, 73, 74, 78, 82, 100, 101, 102, 107, 113, 134, 135, 136
Chicora, 236
China, 34, 105 n., 142
Christian VIII, 69

Cincinnati, 244
Clare, John, Jr., 88
Claremont, Edward Stopford, 126
Clarendon, G. W. F. Villiers, Earl of, 134, 151, 322
Clark, Edward, 8
Clarke, Sir George (Lord Sydenham of Combe), 116, 302, 324 n.
Cloué, Georges-Charles, 84
Coal bunkers, 28, 45, 55, 57 and n., 58, 61, 108, 219, 339
Coast defence, 25, 49, 62, 93, 102, 112, 113, 155, 161, 166, 170, 191, 194, 220, 224, 246, 248, 284, 303, 311, 320, 325, 326, 327
Cobden, Richard, 134 n., 141, 142, 143 n., 322
Coisy, Nicolas-Marie de, 61
Coles, Cowper Phipps, 88, 160 n., 170 n., 180, 184 n., 185–195, 216 n., 220, 225, 238, 251, 252, 270, 275, 277, 278, 284, 304, 305, 306, 315, 316, 324, 326–330, 350
Colorado, 227
Columbiads, 9, 22, 222
Comet, 11
Commission consultative des Travaux de la Marine, 28, 337, 363
Commission on the Defences of the United Kingdom, 141, 155, 160, 161 n., 170, 188
Commission supérieure centrale des bâtiments à vapeur, 57, 92, 339, 347
Committee of Imperial Defence, 116
Committee on Coast Defence, 103 n.
Compass, effect of iron on, 35
Conestoga, 243, 245
Confederate States Navy, 96 n., 114 n., 221–237, 285–301, 309–311
Congress, 288, 291, 292, 297
Congrève, 79, 82, 362
Congreve, Sir William, 8, 227
Conning tower, armored, 53, 80 and n., 112 and n., 158, 232, 243–244, 248 n., 250, 294, 307, 328
Conseil d'Amirauté, 27, 57, 112 n., 339, 340, 364
Conseil des Travaux, 28, 29, 57, 61, 63, 70 n., 89, 92, 93, 94, 95, 100, 102, 103, 106, 107, 108, 109, 112 n., 113, 197, 330, 339, 340, 349, 363
Conseil d'État, 347
Constantine, Grand Duke of Russia, 150, 185 n.

388 INDEX

Constellation, 227
Continental Iron Works, 265. *See also* Rowland, Thomas F.
Copeland, Charles W., 46
Copper armor, 202
Copper sheathing, 110 n., 228
Coppier, Hyacinthe-Joseph de, 106
Corning, Erastus, 278
Corrugated armor, 88, 91, 95, 200, 203, 269
Corry, Henry Thomas Lowry, 124, 127, 128
Corse, 336
Cost of ironclads, 45, 51, 80, 86, 87, 92, 118, 123, 128, 130, 131, 156 and n., 157 n., 159 and n., 160, 166, 167, 173, 194, 214, 216, 218, 221, 229, 243, 250, 251, 257, 259, 261, 267, 269, 276, 280, 321, 325
Courbebaisse, Emile-Marie-Victor, 106
Couronne, 95, 97, 100, 106, 109, 111, 114, 158, 317, 364
Cowley, Henry Wellesley, Earl, 72, 77, 134, 135, 143, 145, 148, 151, 342
Crimean War, 3, 48, 69-91, 92, 102, 111, 116, 120, 133, 141 n., 147, 172 n., 185, 201, 331, 340, 364, 366
Cronstadt, projected attack upon, 70, 73, 74 n., 76, 81, 86, 87
Cumberland, 3, 232, 288, 291, 292, 295, 297, 308
Cupola system. *See* Coles, Cowper Phipps
Currituck, 266, 289, 368

Dacotah, 266, 298
Dahlgren, John A., 219, 245, 247 and n.
Danish Navy, 69, 197, 324
Daullé, General, 89 n.
Davis, Charles H., 218, 247 and n., 248, 252, 256
Deane, Sir Anthony, 6
Decks, iron, 27, 42, 44, 45, 50, 99, 106, 111, 129, 166, 179, 183, 216, 227, 233, 240, 264, 265, 276, 339
Defence, 157, 159, 161, 317, 318, 366
Delafield, Richard, 218
Delamater, Cornelius H., 253
Delamater and Company, 266
De Lancy, Charles, 266
Delano, B. F., 282
Delaporte, ——, 185
Delisle, Captain, 15, 27, 336, 337
Demologos, 10, 11

Derby, Elias Hasket, 239
Dévastation, 78, 80 n., 82, 84, 92, 103
Dictator, 308
Displacement, 14, 45, 71, 78, 80, 93, 94, 99, 100, 103, 106, 107, 110, 111, 123, 129, 132, 158, 163, 167, 177, 192, 193, 194 n., 198, 199, 206, 240, 250, 257, 264, 315
Disraeli, Benjamin, 136, 137, 147, 178, 322
D. L. F., Marquis, 27
Dockyard Commission, 165, 169
Dockyard Officers, opinions of, 164-165
Dockyards, 86, 97, 112, 117, 119, 123, 128, 146, 147, 161, 164, 165 and n., 172 n., 180, 250, 326
Don Juan d'Austria, 198
Dorian, Emile-Charles-Frédéric, 106
Dornin, Thomas A., 216
Doubleday, Abner, 222
Douglas, Sir Howard, 125 n., 168-169, 182, 251
Dover, 35
Drache, 198
Draft of ships, 8, 34, 62, 63, 71, 73, 80, 86, 93 n., 99, 103, 104, 105, 108, 110, 111, 118, 155, 156, 158, 166, 167, 214, 215, 217, 221, 226, 239, 240, 242, 243, 249, 250, 252, 259, 274, 276, 290, 293, 305
Dreadnought, 116
Drouyn de Lhuys, Edouard, 74, 75 n.
Ducos, Théodore, 73, 74, 75, 78, 82, 90
Dundas, Sir Richard, 153 n., 160 n., 170, 174
Duperré, Victor-Guy, baron, 40
Dupouy, Augustin, 104 n.
Dupré, Marie-Jules, 78, 93, 94
Dupuy de Lôme, Stanislas-Charles-Henri-Laurent, 4, 16, 40, 60, 61, 62, 95 n., 97, 98, 99, 101, 103, 104, 108, 109, 110, 111, 113, 115, 120, 301, 329, 331, 345-349
Duseutre (Jardin-), Auguste-Marcel-Zizim, 93
Dutch Navy, 6, 21, 199, 208
Dwarf, 13

Eads, James B., 242, 243, 244
Earle, Ralph, 136
Eason, James N., 236
Eastport, 245
Eckernförde, 69
Eden, Charles, 153 n.

INDEX

Edye, John, 36
Egyptian Navy, 199–200
Egyptienne, 200
Ellet, Charles, Jr., 308
Embrasures, iron, 182, 201, 221
Embuscade, 113
Engines, 11, 30, 41, 45, 48, 50, 54, 57 n., 60, 62, 63, 73, 74, 79, 86, 102, 107, 111, 118, 128, 129, 155, 156, 158, 167, 175, 178, 192, 199 n., 213, 215, 229, 230, 232, 233, 237, 240, 243, 256, 266, 273, 281, 290, 318, 338
    Confederate States Navy, 229, 235, 290, 310 n.
Enoch Train, 233
Enterprise, 320, 326
Erebus, 87, 88, 90, 126, 127 n.
Ericsson, John, vii, 12, 13, 14, 15, 16, 44, 50, 54, 181, 183, 184, 186, 208, 213, 218, 252, 253, 254, 256, 257, 258, 259, 260, 262, 263, 265, 266, 267, 269, 275, 277, 278, 280, 281, 282, 284, 285, 286, 287, 288, 289, 293, 299, 305, 306, 307, 308, 324, 328, 329, 330, 358, 367, 368
Escassi, Don Cayetano, 8
Esquirol, ———, 27, 337
Essex, 244
Evarts, William M., 274
Excellent, 69, 122, 205, 365

Facing, wooden, to armor plates, 38, 125 n., 200, 204 n.
Fairbairn, Sir William, 202 n.
Fairbairn and Company, 42
Fallon, John, 271
Farcy, Eugène, 330
Farragut, David Glasgow, 235, 236
Favé, Ildephonse, 70, 184
Favorite, 320, 321
Faxon, William, 272 n., 274
Ferdinand Maximilian Joseph, Archduke of Austria, 198
Ferranty, Achille-Auguste Zani de, 93 and n., 94
Fingal, 231
Fisher, Sir John, 116
Flahault, Auguste-Charles, comte de, 145
Flandre, 113, 318, 319, 320
Fletcher, M. R., 240 n.
Floating batteries, 3, 7, 8, 9, 10 n., 24, 25, 26, 31, 62, 63, 70–91, 92, 94, 102, 103, 104, 105, 106, 111, 112, 113, 114, 116, 118, 123, 126, 131, 141 n., 154, 160, 161, 162, 170 n., 182, 186, 191, 199, 201, 209, 221, 245, 271, 273, 274, 312, 327
Foote, Andrew H., 262, 366
Forbes, John Murray, 270
Forced draft, 14, 50
Ford, William Henry, 28
Formidabile, 198
Fortress Monroe, 286, 288, 292, 299
Forts, armored, 170, 182, 201, 221. *See also* Embrasures, iron
Foudroyante, 79, 82
Fouling, 35, 63, 117, 118, 123, 172, 180
Fourchambault, 96
Fox, Gustavus Vasa, 183 n., 218, 271, 274, 275, 279, 282, 286, 288, 294, 298, 305, 307, 308, 368
Fox, Sir James, 81
France
    naval rivalry with Great Britain, 24, 108, 115, 120, 121, 132–139, 140–152, 177, 321, 322, 325–326
    relations with Russia, 119, 120 and n., 132, 135, 137, 144, 150, 151, 168. *See* Crimean War
Francis B. Ogden, 13
Frederick, Charles, 153 n.
Fredericks, Colonel, 208
Frémont, John C., 244
French Navy, 4, 7, 11, 15, 16, 18, 24, 27, 40, 65–68, 76, 77, 80, 92, 98, 101, 107, 113, 114, 121, 130, 133–136, 140, 146, 147, 149, 170, 174, 208, 239 n., 282, 314, 315, 317, 318, 319, 322, 323, 325, 330–331, 340
Fulton, 31, 338
Fulton the Second, 227
Fulton, Robert, 8, 10
Funnels
    casing, 232
    effect of shot and shell on, 37 n., 296 n.
    telescopic, 14

Gaines, Edmund Pendleton, 31
Galena, 238, 247, 248, 253, 254, 267, 277, 367
Ganges, 175
Garay, Blasco de, 10 n.
Garnier, Gustave-Benoît, 70, 71, 75 n., 76 n., 77 n., 78 and n., 90
Gasté, Joseph-Alexandre-Adélaïde de, 63, 95, 106

Gauloise, 113, 320
Gavres, experiments at, 29, 41, 48, 57, 58, 59, 60, 61, 62, 63, 72, 113, 207, 209, 339
Gayoso, Don Justo, 199
Gervaize, Victor-Charles-Eudore, 62, 63, 89
Gicquel des Touches, Albert-Auguste, 107
Gillespie, ——, 182
Gilmer, Thomas W., 14
Girardin, Emile de, 322
Gladstone, William E., 76, 142, 143, 145, 154, 157, 171, 173, 178, 321
Glatton, 79, 82
Gloire, 4, 61 n., 97, 98, 99, 100, 101, 106, 109, 110, 111, 113, 114, 121, 122 n., 140, 150, 158, 165, 167, 176, 177, 180, 190, 225, 268, 314, 317, 318, 348
Goldsborough, Louis M., 268, 298 and n., 299
Gorgon, 11
Gouin and Company, 113
Graham, Sir James, 74, 75, 76, 132
Graham, William Alexander, 338
Great Britain
 naval rivalry with France, 65–68, 120, 121, 123, 127–128, 132–139, 140–152, 165, 167, 168, 169, 170–175, 177, 317–323
 relations with Russia, 120, 132, 137, 140, 144, 168. *See also* Crimean War
 relations with the United States, 42, 43, 48, 52, 148, 176, 283, 313, 317
Green, Richard and Henry, 79
Greene, Samuel Dana, 294, 295
Greenock, 36
Gregg, Thomas, 9, 227
Grenier, Captain, 28
Gribeauval, Jean-Baptiste Vaquette de, 20
Grice, Francis, 46
Griffiths, John Willis, 16
Grimes, James W., 220, 245, 246 and n., 280
Griswold, John A., 255, 258, 259, 260, 265, 267, 281, 282
Guadalupe, 34, 36
Guesnet, Achille-Antoine, 93 and n.
Gueydon, Louis-Henri, comte de, 207
Guieysse, Pierre-Armand, 70, 71, 75 n., 77 n., 78, 79, 89, 106, 107
Guizot, François-Pierre-Guillaume, 65

Gun carriages, 23 n., 34, 158, 167 n., 256, 307, 360
Gunboats, 6, 7, 9, 25, 52, 76, 77, 81, 83, 84, 85, 89, 102–105 n., 120, 199, 200, 209, 236, 242, 243, 254, 257, 266, 269, 270, 271, 273, 274, 281, 282, 298, 299
 sectional, 104–105
Guns. *See also* Armor tests, Ordnance
 breech-loading, 48, 90, 105, 158, 160, 167 n., 179, 180, 192, 194, 209, 225, 251, 326
 hooped, 14, 208, 209, 230 and n., 310
 rifled. *See* Ordnance, rifled
 shell. *See* Shell guns
Guthrie, Alfred, 269
Guyenne, 113, 320

Hale, John P., 279, 280, 281
Halsted, E. Pellew, 55 n.
Hamelin, François Alphonse, 82, 89, 99, 100, 101, 104, 106, 108, 111, 112
Hamilton, John Randolph, 221
Hampton Roads, 3, 4, 115, 180, 181, 183, 194, 199, 209, 217, 231, 238, 250, 252, 266, 267, 269, 284, 285, 287, 288, 290, 293, 295, 306, 307, 309, 311, 312, 313, 315, 320, 324, 327, 368
Harpy, 35
Harris, R. S., 240 n.
Hart, Edward, 303
Hartt, Samuel, 42 n., 46
Harwood, A. A., 241, 251
Hastings, Frank Abney, 11, 25
Haswell, Charles H., 15 n., 46, 52
Hay, John C. Dalrymple, 202 n.
Hay, Lord John, 54
Hazard, 192
Hector, 166, 318, 319, 320, 366
Height of battery, 60, 80, 94, 100, 112, 117, 118, 128, 155, 156, 158, 161, 162, 194 n., 364
Hélie, Félix, 29 n.
Henderson, William, 202 n.
Henry, Joseph, 216
Henwood, William, 129
Herbert, Sidney, 142, 164 n., 170
Héroïne, 113, 320
Hewett, William Nathan Wrighte, 231, 299
Hewlett, Richard Strode, 117 n., 122, 124, 126, 127, 131, 132, 153 n., 154, 155 n., 160 n., 163, 204, 205, 207, 365

INDEX

Hieron II, King of Syracuse, 4
Holdane and Company, 266
Holder, John, 53
Homans, Benjamin, 9
Homogeneous metal, 119, 122, 124, 125 n., 200, 202, 207
Hore, Edward George, 170, 321, 323
Horsman, Edward, 140
Hovgaard, William, cited, 329
Howard, John T., 271, 272, 273, 274, 275
Huascar, 324
Hugon, Gaud-Amable, baron, 57
Humphreys, Samuel, 52
Hunter, William W., 15, 42, 44, 226, 227

Implacable, 113
Imprenable, 114
Ingraham, Duncan N., 225, 236
Inman, William, 216
Institution of Naval Architects, 164, 169
Invention, multiple, 12, 15, 87, 117, 162, 181–195, 200 n., 239, 240, 250, 269–270. *See also* Patents
Invincible, 100, 109, 111, 114, 122 n., 156, 317
Iron armor plates, 5, 6, 7, 8, 9, 23, 26, 27, 28, 31, 48–51, 52, 53, 55, 56, 58, 59, 60, 61, 62, 63, 71, 72, 73, 78, 95, 99, 102, 109, 118, 122, 127, 128, 130 n., 160, 161, 171, 173, 174, 177, 183, 185 n., 187, 193, 194, 206, 212, 213, 221, 227, 233, 240, 243, 264, 265, 267, 276, 296, 297, 305, 306, 307, 310, 323
  cast, 29, 30, 118 n.
  corrugated, 88, 91, 95, 200, 203, 269
  hammered, 28, 29, 48, 50, 51 n., 74 n., 75, 80, 87, 96, 97, 118, 122, 124–126, 128, 153, 154, 163, 196, 197, 200, 202, 204, 207, 225, 249
  inclined. *See* Armor, inclined
  laminated, 54, 55, 59, 60, 61, 62, 63, 72, 109, 154, 202, 217, 266, 275, 307, 308 n., 328
  qualities required for, 94, 96, 101, 124, 197, 200, 202
  rolled, 50, 51 n., 96, 118, 153, 154, 197, 202, 236, 249, 266
Iron manufacturers. *See* Armor plate manufacturers
Iron, qualities of, required for armor, 94, 96, 101, 124, 197, 200, 202

Ironclads, iron-hulled, 48–52, 60, 62, 87, 91, 94, 95, 96, 100, 103, 106, 107, 111, 112, 113, 114, 117, 123, 126, 127 n., 128, 129, 157–160, 161, 162, 164, 169, 174, 175, 176, 198, 199, 206, 220, 239, 253–267, 273, 306–308, 313, 319, 320, 323, 325
Ironclads, wooden-hulled, 73, 78–80, 86, 95, 100, 102, 103, 107, 112, 113, 123, 127, 128, 129, 161, 169, 171, 174, 175, 176, 198, 199, 240, 267–269, 304–306, 313, 316, 319, 320, 325, 326
Iron-Sides, 33
Isherwood, B. F., 275, 277, 278, 279, 284, 302, 303, 304
Italian Navy, 90, 91, 151, 197, 198, 208, 221 n., 282, 311, 314

Jackall, 36
Jacks, James, and Company, 283
Jackson, Gordon and Company, 33
Jamestown, 292
Jervis, H. J. W., 17
Jervois, William D., 202 n.
Johnston, Joseph E., 300
Joinville, François-Ferdinand-Philippe-Louis-Marie d'Orléans, prince de, 57, 59, 66, 340
Jones, Catesby ap Rogers, 293, 294, 296
Jones, Josiah, Jr., 162, 163, 215
Jones, Thomas ap Catesby, 52, 230
Joyeux, Adrien-Charles, 107
Jurien de la Gravière, Jean-Pierre-Edmond, 98, 136, 149, 347

Kaiser Max, 198
Kalamazoo, 305
Kamptulicon, 38
Karteria, 11, 25
Keats, Sir Richard, 22 n.
Kemble, W., 30
Keokuk, 252, 306
Kinburn, 3, 80 n., 82, 83, 90, 92, 98, 116, 118, 186, 220, 364
Kokonovitch, General, 85
Korean "tortoise-ship," 6
Krupp, Frederick, 94

Labrousse, Nicolas-Hippolyte, 15, 16, 42, 44, 57, 64, 107, 338, 339, 340, 364
La Chaussade, 96, 102
Laclos, Pierre-Ambroise-François Choderlos de, 21

INDEX

Lady Nancy, 185
La Fère, 30
Laird, John, 33, 34, 35, 270, 271, 272, 273, 274, 275
Laird, John, and Sons, 179
Laird, William, and Sons, 33, 40
Laminated armor, 54, 55, 59, 60, 61, 62, 63, 72, 109, 154, 202, 217, 230, 232, 266, 275, 307, 308, 328
Lang, Oliver William, 129, 162 n., 164, 165
Large, Joseph, 130, 161, 163, 189
Lariboissière, Jean-Ambroise Baston, comte de, 21
La Salle, Jean de, 6
Lave, 78, 79 n., 82, 84, 85, 103
Lavrignais, Alexandre-Auguste-Gustave Robion de, 98, 347
Lawrence, John N., 240 n.
Lead armor, 4, 5, 6 n., 29, 200
Leake, Richard, 18
Legrand, Victor-Pierre-Justin-Léon, 107, 114 n.
Le Grix, Pierre-Félix, 64 n.
Lehigh, 308
Lemoine, Nicolas-Marie-Julien, 113
Length of ships, 8, 9, 13, 31, 34, 45, 50, 53, 60, 62, 63, 71, 73, 80, 86, 93 n., 99, 103, 104, 105, 107, 108, 110, 111, 118, 129, 155, 156, 158, 163, 166, 167, 192, 213, 215, 217, 243, 250, 251, 257, 259, 264, 274, 307, 325, 360
Lenthall, John, 46, 51, 221, 242, 243, 252, 263, 275, 276, 277, 278, 281, 282, 283, 284, 302, 303, 304, 305
Leonardo da Vinci, 5
Leopold I, King of the Belgians, 65, 137
Lewis, Sir George Cornewall, 313
Lexington, 243, 245
Limitation of naval armaments, 42, 67, 178, 322, 323
Lincoln, Abraham, 183 n., 254, 255
Lindsay, W. S., 172, 178
Lizard, 36
Lloyd, Vaughan, 22 n.
Loftus, Lord Augustus, 149
London *Times*, 220, 312, 313
Loper, R. F., 43
Lopez, Don Francisco, 8
Lord Clyde, 320, 321
Lord Warden, 320, 321, 323
Lorient, 29, 57, 58, 73, 74, 78, 79, 82, 92, 99, 100, 109, 113, 197, 207, 339

Louis-Philippe, King of the French, 65, 66, 67, 146, 149
Louisiana, 226, 234, 235
Louisville, 244, 245
Lowmoor Iron Company, 202
Lungley, C., 180 n.
Lyndhurst, John S. Copley, Lord, 140
Lyons, Sir Edmund, 80, 83, 85, 86, 185, 186

McClellan, George B., 219 and n., 288, 294, 298
Mackau, Ange-René-Armand, baron de, 57, 61, 62
McKay, Donald, 211 n., 239 and n., 240–241, 250
Magenta, 108, 109, 111, 318, 319, 348
Magnanime, 113, 320
Mail contracts, 39, 46
Maitland, Sir Thomas, 76 n., 160 n.
Mallory, Francis, 49
Mallory, Stephen Russell, 223, 224, 225, 228, 229, 233, 234, 235, 236, 237, 240, 290, 296, 310
Malmesbury, James Harris, 3rd Earl of, 133, 135, 137, 147, 150, 321
Manassas, 233, 234
Manby, Aaron, 33
Mangin, Amédée-Paul-Théodore, 77 n.
Maranville, H., 242 n.
Mare and Company, 79, 179
Marielle, Jules, 93 and n.
Marsh, James, 8
Marston, John, 287, 288
Martin, Daniel B., 277, 282, 283
Martin, Sir William Fanshawe, 127
Martin's shells. *See* Shells, molten iron filled, 126
Mason, John Y., 46, 51, 53, 211
Massachusetts, 336
Masts, 37 n., 78, 84, 110, 129, 159, 163, 179, 188, 194, 240, 247, 261, 271, 325, 327
Mathieu, P. L. A., 134
Maximilian towers, 181
Mediterranean, control of, 149–152
Megaera, 36
Melbourne, William Lamb, Viscount, 65
Melville, Robert, 20
Mends, Sir William Robert, 76 n.
Merrick and Sons, 242 n., 269, 367
Merrick, Samuel V., 218
Merrimack. See *Virginia*

INDEX

Metallurgy, 3, 33, 41, 91, 113, 114, 115, 159, 196, 207, 276, 277, 281 n., 331
Meteor, 79, 82, 87, 126, 127
Mexican Navy, 34, 52
Miantonomoh, 304, 305
Michigan (Wolverine), 41, 42
Midship section, 50, 60, 99, 107, 111, 158, 183, 253, 256
Milne, Sir Alexander, 297
Mines, 8, 27
Minnesota, 292, 293, 294, 295, 298, 299
Minor, R. D., 292, 296
Minotaur, 179, 204, 206, 319, 321
Missiessy, Edouard-Thomas Burgues, comte de, 27
Mississippi, 50, 51, 235, 236
Missouri, 50, 51
Mitchell, C., 199
Mogador, 70
Mohawk, 42
Molle, Charles-Henri, 16, 77 n.
Moment of inertia, 93 n., 99
Monadnock, 304, 305
Monarch, 329
Monitor, 79 n., 180, 181, 183, 186, 194, 195, 218, 238, 247, 248, 250, 252, 253–267, 275, 277, 278, 281, 282, 285, 286–290, 293–295, 297–299, 300, 302, 305, 306, 307, 308, 309, 311, 313, 316, 324, 330, 367, 368
Monitor class of vessels, 183, 258, 263, 277, 278, 280, 284, 303, 304–308, 311, 313, 316, 324, 327, 329, 330
Monkey, 11
Montaignac, Louis-Raymond de Chauvance, marquis de, 92
Montauk, 308
Montevideo, 338
Montezuma, 34
Montgéry, P. M. de, 4, 27 and n., 29
Moras, Paul-Marie-Etienne Picot de, 106, 108
Morgan, George D., 279
Morrill, Jonathan, 52
Morris, Charles, 46
Morse, Freeman H., 221 n.
Mortar vessels, 18, 24, 76, 77, 81, 83, 84, 85
Mound City, 244
Murray, E. C., 226, 234
Myers, Myer, 296
Myrmidon, 36

Napier, Sir Charles, 33, 117, 131, 197, 322
Napier and Sons, 36 n., 87, 156, 166, 324
Napoléon, 16, 97, 98, 99, 100, 120, 331, 336
Napoleon I, Emperor of the French, 20
Napoleon III, Emperor of the French, 4, 64, 67, 68, 70, 71, 74 n., 77, 83, 85, 89 n., 92, 95, 101, 104, 105, 112 n., 113, 115, 119, 132, 133, 134, 135, 136, 137, 138, 140, 143, 144, 146, 147, 148, 149, 150, 151, 170, 174, 182, 183, 184, 207, 254, 321, 322, 323, 331, 342, 347
Napoleon, Prince, 151
Naugatuck, 217
Nemesis, 34, 36
Netrone Menia, 199
New Era, 244
New Ironsides, 238, 247, 248, 268, 367
New York Chamber of Commerce, 19, 280
New York *Herald*, 257
Newton, Isaac, 289, 295
Nicolay, John G., and Hay, John, cited, 288
Norcross, J. W., 270
Normandie, 100, 109, 111, 114, 317
North, James H., 225
Northmen, methods of protecting hulls used by the, 4–5
Northumberland, 179, 204, 206, 319, 321
Novelty Iron Works, 266
Numancia, 199

Ocean, 176, 319, 321
Ochoa, Don Juan de, 7, 227
Ogden, Francis B., 13, 34 n.
Olmütz, 30
Onondaga, 305
Opiniâtre, 113
Ordnance
 improvements in, 196, 200, 206, 208
 rifled, 3, 48, 90, 92, 105, 125, 131, 154, 158, 160, 167 n., 177, 179, 180, 191, 192, 194, 196, 197, 204, 205, 206, 207, 209, 210, 217, 230, 232, 271, 323, 364
 See also Guns, breech-loading, Guns, hooped, Shell guns
Ordnance Select Committee, 201
Ordnance tests, 20–26, 28–30. *See also* Armor tests
Orsini, Felice, 119, 134

Paddle wheels, 6, 10, 11, 15, 28, 34, 35, 42, 43, 46, 97, 243, 338
Paget, Lord Clarence, 153, 165 n., 170, 172, 176, 178, 184 n., 186, 192, 194, 206, 313, 322
Paixhans, 103
Paixhans, Henri-Joseph, 4, 17, 18, 21, 23, 24, 25, 26, 28, 45, 49, 70, 219, 330, 331, 364
Pakington, Sir John, 119, 121, 123, 131, 132, 137, 141 n., 153, 155, 176, 323 n.
Palestro, 103
Pallas, 320, 321
Palmer Brothers, 87, 154, 156 n., 157
Palmerston, H. J. Temple, Viscount, 65, 66, 67, 81, 117, 120, 132, 135, 137, 142, 143, 144, 145, 146, 147, 150, 152, 154, 157, 171, 172, 177, 178, 184 n., 191, 312, 315, 321, 322
Palmetto State, 236
Parrott, Robert P., 208
Parseval-Deschênes, Alexandre-Ferdinand, 347
Passaconaway, 305
Passaic, 308
Pastoureau, Jean-Baptiste, 77 n., 90
Patapsco, 308
Patents, 9, 12, 15, 117 n., 162, 180 n., 182, 183, 187, 188, 208, 209, 228, 278, 327, 335
Patrick Henry, 292
Patton, James C., 52, 228
Paulding, Hiram, 214, 240, 247, 248 n., 252, 255, 281, 282, 298 n.
Peel, Sir Robert, 65
Peiho, 103
Pelham, Frederick Thomas, 153 n.
Pélissier, Aimable-Jean-Jacques, duc de Malakoff, 134
Pellion, Odet, 90 n., 93
Pendergrast, Austin, 292
Pensacola, 227
Percy, John, 202 n.
Periscopes, 183
Perry, Matthew Calbraith, 31, 338
Persigny, J.-G.-V. Fialin, duc de, 145-147
Pervenetz, 199
Petin, Gaudet and Company, 73, 78, 94, 102, 105, 283
Peto, Sir Morton, 172, 323 n.
Petropavlosk, 199
Philadelphia Press, 220

Phlegethon, 34
Phoenix, 11
Pigeard, Jean-Charles-Edouard, 114, 323
Pittsburg, 244, 245
Pius IX, 138
Plymouth, 142
Pole, William, 202 n.
Polk, James K., 43
Pollard, Edward A., 223
Pomone, 15
Pontypool Iron Company, 202
Pook, Samuel H., 244 n., 253
Pook, Samuel M., 218, 243, 244
Port shutters, 227, 232, 250, 266, 296, 299, 309
Porter, David D., 239
Porter, John L., 43, 226, 227, 228, 229-230
Ports
  height of, 60, 80, 94, 100, 112, 117, 118, 128, 155, 156, 158, 161, 162, 194 n., 317-318, 319, 364
  size of, 49, 112, 159, 163, 186, 188, 189, 309, 318
Portsmouth, 37, 38, 55 n., 75, 122, 124, 125, 127, 142, 153, 154, 163, 204 n., 325
Powell, Ashmore, 191
Powhatan, 227
Preble, 233
Preston, William Ballard, 47, 211
Prétot, Hippolyte-Louis-Edouard, 101
Prince Albert, 194, 316, 320, 321, 324-325, 326, 327, 366
Prince Consort, 176, 319, 320
Prince George, target ship, 69
Princeton, 13, 14, 16 n., 50, 54
Prinz Eugen, 198
Protectrice, 113
Provence, 113, 320
Prussian Navy, 150, 200 and n.
Puritan, 308

Quinsigamond, 305
Quintard, G. W., 305

Raffin, Ensign de, 84
Rafts, 89, 185-187, 297
Rahmanyeh, 199
Raleigh, 291, 292
Rams, 3, 6, 7, 27, 28, 30, 48, 52, 57, 62, 64, 89, 90 and n., 91, 92, 93, 99, 100, 102, 108, 109, 129, 158, 159,

160, 164 n., 166, 199, 232, 233, 236, 242, 268, 271, 290, 291, 293, 297, 299, 303, 308, 311, 313, 316, 320, 324, 337, 338, 339, 340, 341, 345
Rattler, 13
Razeeing, 26, 27, 98, 117, 175–177, 304, 305, 311, 316, 325
Re d'Italia, 198
Re di Portogallo, 198
Reed, Sir Edward J., 167 n., 179–180
Refuge, 113
Renau d'Eliçagaray, Bernard, 18
Renaud-Ville, ——, 19
Rensselaer Iron Works, 266
Research, 320
Resistance, 157, 159, 160, 161, 317, 318, 366
Revanche, 113
Rhind, A. C., 306
Richmond, 233
Rifled ordnance. *See* Ordnance
Rig, 14, 26, 48, 49, 78, 82 n., 94, 110, 112, 129, 158, 179, 194 n., 247, 258, 261, 269, 327, 329
Rigidity, 94
Rinaldo, 231, 299
Risikoflotte, idea of, 148
Roanoke, 287, 292, 305
Robert F. Stockton, 13
Robertson, James, 52
Robins, Benjamin, 196
Robinson, James, 240 n.
Robinson, Robert Spencer, 169, 173, 174, 193, 315–320, 325
Rochefort, 73, 74, 79, 113
Rodgers, John, 242, 243, 244, 268, 304
Roebuck, John Arthur, 206
Rolf Krake, 324
Rolling, 99, 110 n., 141 n., 164, 253, 306
Romain-Desfossés, Joseph, 90 n.
Roussel, Anselme de, 107
Rowland, Thomas F., 250, 251, 252, 265, 269
Royal Alfred, 176, 319, 321
Royal Oak, 173, 174, 175, 176, 317, 318, 320, 326
Royal Sovereign, 320, 325, 326, 327, 366
Royal United Service Institution, 189
Ruby, target ship, 37, 39
Rudder, protection of, 167 and n., 186, 307, 318, 359
Rush-Bagot agreement of 1817, 42
Russell, John, Earl Russell, 67, 68, 144, 145, 146, 151, 168, 191, 312, 365

Russell, John Scott, viii, 54, 79, 88, 129, 130 n., 188, 190–191, 213
Russian Navy, 70, 81, 89, 96 n., 150, 151, 168, 185 n., 199, 208, 282, 311, 314, 324

Sabatier, Victorin-Gabriel-Justin-Epiphanès, 77 n.
Sabine, 298
Sachem, 266
Saigon, 103
Sails, 16, 26, 60, 79 n., 80 n., 97, 107, 110, 172, 261, 327, 337
St. Lawrence, 287, 292
St. Louis (De Kalb), 244, 245
Salamander, 198
Samuda Brothers, 87, 88 n., 325
Samuda, Joseph D'Aguilar, 203 n.
San Jacinto, 298
Sangamon, 308
Santa Anna, 5
Saroni, Adolph S., 209
Sartorius, Sir George Rose, 341
Sauvage, Frédéric, 15, 336
Savoie, 113
Scharf, J. T., 223
Scharnhorst, Gerhard Johann David von, 21
Schenkl, John P., 209
Schneider and Company, 73, 78, 104 n.
Schuyler, R. and G. L., 45
Scientific American, 285–286
Scofield and Markham, 236
Scorpion, 321, 324, 366
Scott, Winfield, 243
Screw propeller
 introduction of, 3, 9, 11–16, 46, 335–336, 337
 twin, 199, 213, 215, 217, 250
Sebastopol, 83, 92
Sebastopol, 199
Sedgwick, Charles B., 272, 274, 276
Seminole, 227
Senior, Nassau William, 134
Seth Low, 266, 288
Seward, William H., 231, 255
Shackamaxon, 305
Shankland, William F., 368
Sheathing of ships, 4, 5, 110 n., 338
Shell guns, 3, 9, 14, 17–32, 49, 50, 222, 251, 326
Shells
 effect on armor, 85–86

396   INDEX

effect on wooden ships, 4, 17, 25, 69, 292
introduction of, 17–32
molten iron filled, 126, 155 n., 197, 206
Shield ships. *See* Turrets
Shipbuilders
  Arman, Jean-Lucien, 96, 103, 104, 113, 114
  Bergen, A. J., 44
  Fairbairn and Company, 42
  Gouin and Company, 113
  Green, Richard and Henry, 79
  Jackson, Gordon and Company, 33
  Laird, John, and Sons, 179
  Laird, William, and Sons, 33, 40
  Mare and Company, 79, 179
  Merrick and Sons, 242 n., 269, 367
  Napier and Sons, 36 n., 87, 156, 166, 324
  Palmer Brothers, 87, 154, 156 n., 157
  Quintard, G. W., 305
  Samuda Brothers, 87, 88 n., 325
  Schuyler, R. and G. L., 45
  Société des Forges et Chantiers de la Méditerranée, 68 n., 104, 105 n., 199
  Stackhouse and Tomlinson, 42 n.
  Thames Iron Shipbuilding Company, 130, 154, 166, 179, 199, 202
  Tomlinson, Joseph, 43
  Webb, William H., 198
  Westwood, Baillie and Company, 157, 166
  Wilkinson, John, 33
Shirley, John T., 234
Shoeburyness, 178, 191, 201, 204, 205, 313
Shot
  cast-iron, 21, 28, 54, 75, 118, 122, 126, 163, 207, 293, 299
  steel, 97, 126, 131, 205, 206, 207, 299
  wrought-iron, 97, 118, 122, 126, 207, 299
Shrapnel, Henry, 19
Shubrick, W. B., 269
Shuldham, Molyneux, 340
Simoom, 36, 37
Sinnell, Henry P., 240 n.
Sinope, 17, 69, 70 n.
Sirius, 205
Size of ironclads, 94, 99, 101, 103, 113, 128, 129, 131–132, 155–157, 161, 166, 180, 192–193, 220–221, 251–252, 264, 306, 327

Skinner, Charles William, 47, 212
Slater, P., 240 n.
Sleigh, Adderley Willcocks, 162, 215
Slidell, John, 148
Smertch, 324
Smith, Sir Francis Pettit, 12, 13, 15, 60
Smith, Joseph, 46, 247, 250 n., 251, 252, 253, 254, 255, 258, 260, 262, 263, 265, 266, 267, 268, 269, 270, 277, 278, 281, 282, 288, 303, 306, 307, 366, 367, 368
Smith, Joseph B., 292
Smith, Sir Sydney, 21
Sochet, Prix-Charles-Jean-Baptiste, 106, 107
Société des Forges et Chantiers de la Méditerranée, 68 n., 104, 105 n., 199
Solférino, 109, 111, 318, 319, 348
Somerset, Edward Adolphus Seymour, 12th Duke of, 157, 168, 175, 176, 177, 184 n., 190, 191–192, 206, 314, 324, 325, 326
Spanish Navy, 7, 8, 199, 208, 282, 311, 314
Special Committee on Iron, 201–203, 205–206
Special Committee on Iron Plates and Guns, 200–201
Speed, 13, 45, 50, 62, 63, 74, 78, 79 n., 93 n., 94, 97, 99, 101, 103, 105, 106, 108, 110, 111, 118, 123, 128, 129, 155, 156 and n., 158, 159, 160, 162, 166, 167, 170, 173, 192, 193, 239, 240, 250, 251, 256, 257, 259, 261, 269, 271, 306, 307, 317, 318, 319, 325
Spitfire, 84
Spratt, Thomas A. B., 84
Stability, 24, 43, 106, 117, 163, 186, 252, 253, 254, 256, 259, 261, 262, 265, 327, 329
Stackhouse and Tomlinson, 42 n.
Stanton, Edwin M., 297
Stanton, Frederick Perry, 47
Steam
  effect of, on British coast defences, 65
  introduction in warships, 3, 10–16
Steel armor plates, 27, 94, 97, 101, 118, 124, 154, 163, 197, 200, 202, 207, 239 n.
Steel gunboat, Egyptian, 199–200
Steering, 79, 105, 166, 167 n., 266, 287, 289, 293, 299, 306, 318

INDEX

Stem, form of, 159 and n. *See* Rams
Stevens battery, 3, 9, 32, 48–52, 54, 111, 158, 211–219, 246, 254, 368
Stevens "scull," 14, 50, 213, 215, 217
Stevens, Edwin Augustus, 23, 28, 32, 48, 214–219, 228
Stevens, John, 9, 23, 28, 32, 182
Stevens, John C., 48, 215, 228
Stevens, Robert Livingston, 23, 28, 32, 48–52, 54, 211–214, 215, 218, 224, 228
Stevens, T. H., 22 n.
Stevenson, John A., 233
Stewart, Charles, 338
Stimers, Alban C., 216, 263, 288, 289, 293, 295, 367
Stimpson, James, 52
Stockton, Robert F., 13, 14, 16 n., 212
Stonewall, 114 n.
Strasbourg, 29
Stringham, S. H., 216
Stromboli, 11
Submarines, 8, 27, 81, 286
Suez Canal, 152
Sumner, Charles, 274
Sumter, Fort, 222, 223 n., 239, 242
Surveillante, 113, 320
Sveaborg, projected attack upon, 76, 81, 86, 87
Symonds, Sir William, 36

Tactics
  boarding, 26, 112 n., 184, 189, 225, 231, 250, 299
  end-on fighting, 24, 44, 57 n., 268
Targets. *See* Armor tests, Shells
Tattnall, Josiah, 298, 299, 300
Taureau, 311
Taylor, Moses, 218
Taylor, Philip, 68 n. *See also* Société des Forges et Chantiers de la Méditerranée
Teaser, 292
Tennessee, 234
Tennyson, Alfred, 138
Terribile, 198
Terror, 87, 88
Tetuan, 199
Texas, 34 n.
Thames Iron Shipbuilding Company, 130, 154, 166, 179, 199, 202
Thićry, A., 208
Thunder, 79, 82
Thunderbolt, 87, 88

Tift, Nelson and Asa F., 231 n., 235, 236
Timber, supply of, 128, 171–172
Timby, Theodore R., 182, 183, 218
Tocqueville, Alexis-Charles-Henri Clerel de, 133
Tomlinson, Joseph, 43
Tonawanda, 305
Tone, Theobald Wolfe, 21
Tonguing and grooving, 159, 191 n., 203, 205, 268, 351
Tonnage, methods of measuring, 80 n.
Tonnante, 78, 79 n., 80 n., 82, 84, 85, 103
Torch, 36
Torpedoes, 8, 27
Totten, Joseph G., 56, 243
Toucey, Isaac, 221, 239
Toulon, 20, 61, 99, 100, 101, 105, 107, 109, 113, 150
Tousard, Louis de, 22
Tracy, Alexandre-César-Victor-Charles Destutt de, 340
Tramond, Joannès, cited, 24
Treadwell, Daniel, 208
Tredegar Iron Works, 230
Trent affair, 148, 313
Treuille de Beaulieu, Antoine-Hector-Thésèe, baron, 208, 209
Trusty, 79, 82, 131, 154, 155, 156, 191, 192, 205, 327
Turkish Navy, 17, 69–70, 180 n., 200 and n.
Turret tests, 191, 192
Turrets, 45, 88, 181–195, 220, 238, 242, 250, 251, 252, 253, 254, 256, 257, 261, 262, 263, 264, 266, 269, 270, 271, 275, 277, 278, 281, 283, 293, 294, 299, 302, 303, 304, 305, 306, 307, 308, 309, 311, 313, 315, 320, 324–330, 358, 359, 360

Unarmored iron warships, 33–47, 56, 57, 58, 75, 169, 226
Undaunted, 154, 156
Union, 42
United States, diplomatic relations with Great Britain, 42, 43, 48, 52, 176, 283, 317
United States Navy, 3, 8–10, 11, 13–15, 41–47, 53, 65, 211–221, 238–284, 285–301, 302–309, 323–324
Upshur, Abel P., 14, 41, 43, 50

Valeureuse, 113, 320
Valiant, 166, 319, 321

Vanderbilt, 298 n.
Ventilation, 49, 52, 79, 231, 250, 256, 262, 289, 307
Verninac-Saint-Maur, Raymond-Jean-Baptiste, 340
Vesuvius, 11
Victor Emmanuel II, King of Italy, 134
Victoria, Queen of Great Britain, 134, 137, 142, 171
Villafranca, 146, 150, 151
Ville de Paris, 98
Villeroi, Brutus de, 286
Vincennes, 233
Vincennes, experiments at, 71, 75, 94, 95, 96, 97, 101, 103, 106, 109, 113
Virginia, 3, 163, 180, 181, 194, 218, 226, 228, 229, 230, 231, 238, 240, 285, 286, 287, 288, 290–300, 302, 305, 309, 312, 313, 316
Vulcan, 36

Wadsworth, Decius, 23
Walcott, J. E., 341
Walewski, Alexandre - Florian - Joseph Colonna, comte, 151
Walker, Sir Baldwin, 74, 75, 76 n., 77 n., 116, 118, 121, 122, 127, 128, 129, 155, 156, 161, 165, 166
Walter, George, 36
Ward, James H., 251
Warley, A. F., 233, 234
Warren, Charles, 52, 228
Warrington, Lewis, 46
Warrior, 88, 111, 119 n., 131, 154, 155, 156, 157, 158, 159, 164 n., 165, 166, 167, 175, 177, 178, 190, 193, 199, 204, 205, 206, 225, 268, 313, 317, 319, 366
Water ballast, 215, 216, 217 and n., 218, 251
Water Witch, 43, 226, 233
Watts, Isaac, 77 n., 119 n., 157, 161, 163, 186, 189, 192

Webb, William H., 198
Weehawken, 231, 304
Weights of a ship, distribution of, 11, 44, 98, 99, 103, 106, 117, 161, 189, 254, 263, 264
Welles, Gideon, 183, 214, 218, 219, 238, 239, 240, 242, 245, 246, 247, 252, 254, 255, 257, 258, 259, 260, 262, 269, 270, 271, 272, 273, 274, 276, 277, 278, 279, 280, 281, 286, 287, 288, 297, 303, 305, 328, 367
Wellington, Arthur Wellesley, Duke of, 67, 142
Westwood, Baillie and Company, 157, 166
Westwood, John, 242 n.
Whitbread, Samuel, 153 n.
White, Lewis, 269
Whitney, C. W., 250, 251, 252, 269, 277 n., 278 n., 306, 367
Whitworth, Joseph, 119, 125, 197, 205, 206
Wilkinson, John, 33
Willantrois, —— 21
Williamson, William P., 229, 230
Winslow, John Flack, 255 and n., 258, 259, 260, 265, 267, 278, 281, 282, 286
Wise, Henry A., 226 n.
Wivern, 321, 324, 364
Wolverine (Michigan), 41
Wood, Sir Charles, 72 n., 117, 118, 119 n., 122 n.
Wood, W. H., 240 n.
Wool, John E., 231, 288
Woolwich, 28, 36, 118, 122, 191
Worden, John L., 266, 287, 293, 294, 295

Yates, Joseph A., 222

Zealous, 320, 321
Zornlin, John Jacob, Jr., 22